ATLA BIBLIOGRAPHY SERIES
edited by Dr. Kenneth E. Rowe

1. *A Guide to the Study of the Holiness Movement*, by Charles Edwin Jones. 1974.
2. *Thomas Merton: A Bibliography*, by Marquita E. Breit. 1974.
3. *The Sermon on the Mount: A History of Interpretation and Bibliography*, by Warren S. Kissinger. 1975.
4. *The Parables of Jesus: A History of Interpretation and Bibliography*, by Warren S. Kissinger. 1979.
5. *Homosexuality and the Judeo-Christian Tradition: An Annotated Bibliography*, by Thom Horner. 1981.
6. *A Guide to the Study of the Pentecostal Movement*, by Charles Edwin Jones. 1983.
7. *The Genesis of Modern Process Thought: A Historical Outline with Bibliography*, by George R. Lucas, Jr. 1983.
8. *A Presbyterian Bibliography*, by Harold B. Prince. 1983.
9. *Paul Tillich: A Comprehensive Bibliography . . .*, by Richard C. Crossman. 1983.
10. *A Bibliography of the Samaritans*, by Alan David Crown. 1984 (see no. 32).
11. *An Annotated and Classified Bibliography of English Literature Pertaining to the Ethiopian Orthodox Church*, by Jon Bonk. 1984.
12. *International Meditation Bibliography, 1950 to 1982*, by Howard R. Jarrell. 1984.
13. *Rabindranath Tagore: A Bibliography*, by Katherine Henn. 1985.
14. *Research in Ritual Studies: A Programmatic Essay and Bibliography*, by Ronald L. Grimes, 1985.
15. *Protestant Theological Education in America*, by Heather F. Day. 1985.
16. *Unconscious: A Guide to Sources*, by Natalino Caputi. 1985.
17. *The New Testament Apocrypha and Pseudepigrapha*, by James H. Charlesworth. 1987.
18. *Black Holiness*, by Charles Edwin Jones. 1987.
19. *A Bibliography on Ancient Ephesus*, by Richard Oster. 1987.

20. *Jerusalem, the Holy City: A Bibliography,* by James D. Purvis. 1988; Vol. II, 1991.
21. *An Index to English Periodical Literature on the Old Testament and Ancient Near Eastern Studies,* by William G. Hupper. Vol. I, 1987; Vol. II, 1988; Vol. III, 1990; Vol. IV, 1990; Vol. V, 1992.
22. *John and Charles Wesley: A Bibliography,* by Betty M. Jarboe. 1987.
23. *A Scholar's Guide to Academic Journals in Religion,* by James Dawsey. 1988.
24. *The Oxford Movement and Its Leaders: A Bibliography of Secondary and Lesser Primary Sources,* by Lawrence N. Crumb. 1988; Supplement, 1993.
25. *A Bibliography of Christian Worship,* by Bard Thompson. 1989.
26. *The Disciples and American Culture: A Bibliography of Works by Disciples of Christ Members, 1866–1984,* by Leslie R. Galbraith and Heather F. Day. 1990.
27. *The Yogacara School of Buddhism: A Bibliography,* by John Powers. 1991.
28. *The Doctrine of the Holy Spirit: A Bibliography Showing Its Chronological Development* (2 vols.), by Esther Dech Schandorff. 1993.
29. *Rediscovery of Creation: A Bibliographical Study of the Church's Response to the Environmental Crisis,* by Joseph K. Sheldon. 1992.
30. *The Charismatic Movement: A Guide to the Study of Neo- Pentecostalism with Emphasis on Anglo-American Sources,* by Charles Edwin Jones. 1993.
31. *Cities and Churches: An International Bibliography* (3 vols.), by Loyde H. Hartley. 1992.
32. *A Bibliography of the Samaritans,* 2nd ed., by Alan David Crown. 1993.
33. *The Early Church: An Annotated Bibliography of Literature in English,* by Thomas A. Robinson. 1993.

The Early Church

An Annotated Bibliography of Literature in English

by
THOMAS A. ROBINSON

with
Brent D. Shaw
M. James Penton
Terence L. Donaldson
Michael P. DeRoche
ATLA Bibliographies Series No. 33

The American Theological Library Association
and
The Scarecrow Press, Inc.
Metuchen, N.J., & London
1993

British Library Cataloguing-in-Publication data available

Library of Congress Cataloging-in-Publication Data

Robinson, Thomas A. (Thomas Arthur), 1951-
    The early church: an annotated bibliography of literature in
English / by Thomas A. Robinson with Brent D. Shaw...[et al.]
        p. cm. — (ATLA bibliography series; no. 33)
    Includes bibliographical references and indexes.
    ISBN 0-8108-2763-8 (alk. paper)
        1. Church history—Primitive and early church, ca. 30-600—
Abstracts. 2. Church history—Primitive and early church, ca.
30-600—Indexes. 3. Christian literature, Early—Abstracts.
4. Christian literature, Early—Indexes, Topical. 5. Theology—
Early church, ca. 30-600—Abstracts. 6. Theology—Early church,
ca. 30-600—Indexes. I. Title. II. Series
BR162.2.R63 1993
016.23'01—dc20   93-34350

TO:
SHARON
SHAUNA
MARILYN
LOIS
&
TERESA

CONTENTS

TOPICS

INDEXES

EDITOR'S FOREWORD

Since 1974 the American Theological Library Association has been publishing this bibliography series with the Scarecrow Press. Guidelines for projects and selections for publication are made by the ATLA Publications Section in consultation with the editor. Our goal is to stimulate and encourage the preparation and publication of reliable bibliographies and guides to the literature of religious studies in all of its scope and variety. Compilers are free to define their field, to make their own selections, and to work out internal organization as the unique demands of the subject indicate.

We are pleased to publish *The Early Church: An Annotated Bibliography of Literature in English* by Thomas A. Robinson as number 33 in the ATLA Bibliography Series.

Professor Robinson completed an undergraduate program in Greek and Philosophy at the University of New Brunswick (Fredericton, N.B., Canada), studied Biblical Studies at Regent College (Vancouver), and completed the doctorate in New Testament / Early Church History at McMaster University (Hamilton). He has taught at the University of Calgary and is currently Associate Professor of Religious Studies at the University of Lethbridge, in Alberta, Canada.

Professor Robinson has been aided in his work by four colleagues: Professors Brent Shaw, M. James Penton, Terence Donaldson, and Michael DeRoche (see "About the Author and Contributors" p. 495). In particular, the substantial contribution of Professor Brent Shaw of the University of Lethbridge has enriched the volume. Professor Shaw has written widely in the field of Roman history and society, and he has brought a wealth of detail about the scholarship in that field to this volume. He shows the relevance of the wider Roman culture to primary questions confronting those in the field of early Christian studies, encouraging a productive cross fertilization between the two disciplines.

Kenneth E. Rowe
Series Editor

Drew University Library
Madison, NJ 07940 USA

PREFACE

This bibliography grew out of a desire to give students a survey of the rich literature in English on the early church and to provide them with a summary of scholarship on its major topics. The project became more massive and time-consuming than I had initially imagined—hence I owe a debt to various people who gave me encouragement and who contributed sections in their areas of expertise. The first to assist me was Terence Donaldson, professor at the College of Emmanuel & St. Chad in Saskatoon, Saskatchewan. He agreed to compile the chapter on Jewish-Christian relations, and his early interest in the project and his speed in completing his informative entries helped motivate me during long and tiresome stretches of the project.

Later, Brent Shaw, a professor from the Department of History at the University of Lethbridge, became interested in the project, and recognized the mountain of work that still faced me. Volunteering to take time out of an extremely busy schedule to assist me in various areas, Professor Shaw shouldered a massive part of the remaining work. His rich background in the Classics made his contribution an informed and insightful addition to the bibliography for areas in which scholars of the early church often have interest but limited grasp. His input and encouragement, both of which were substantial, were primary factors in bringing the manuscript to completion. Roughly at the same time, Michael DeRoche of the Religious Studies Department at the University of Calgary contributed a chapter on patristic exegesis, adding to the scope of this bibliography. I am thankful to have had colleagues who were real "friends in need" to me, providing significant contributions to the project.

Two graduate students, Kurt Widmer and Daniel Falk, provided several abstracts on fields that they were studying. Brian Smart and Erin Philips of the Religious Studies Department at the University of Lethbridge added a few more near the end of the project. David Plaxton, a student in the Religious Studies Department when I started the project, spent long hours checking to see which volumes were in the holdings of our library. And in the very last weeks of the project, Shauna Shaw spent long hours carefully proofreading much of the manuscript, making numerous suggestions that helped bring clarity to the introductory essays prefaced to each chapter.

Finally, in the tradition of "the last being first," I thank Jim Penton, Professor Emeritus of the University of Lethbridge. He initially suggested the project to me some years ago, and provided a number of abstracts and four of the introductory essays. Although he was interested in sharing more of the load when the project was first conceived, ill health prevented more substantial involvement with the project.

Each of these many people has added to the project; their contributions are appreciated.

I recognize, too, the assistance of the University of Lethbridge Research Fund for early support of the bibliography.

Thomas A. Robinson
Department of Religious Studies
The University of Lethbridge
Summer 1993

INTRODUCTION

The field of *post* New Testament study called Patristics[1] (covering the period from the second to the sixth centuries) is becoming an area of research into which more and more students peer, and then enter. Often those entering come from a prior interest in the New Testament, and sometimes even after long years of study. The boundaries that held students to the New Testament era are dissolving, and the New Testament is, itself, no longer generally seen as a closed, fixed field in which the scholar can raise and expect to answer questions without reference to other fields. An understanding of Graeco-Roman history and culture of the first centuries and of church history *after* the first century are now seen as critical for making sense of early Christian origins and development.

One might try to suggest reasons why the world of English scholarship on the early church seems to be significantly weighted in favor of the first century. The most obvious explanation is that the writings of first-century Christian leaders make up the distinctive Christian canon, and many students interested in the early church have developed that particular interest through their commitment to the Christian faith, in which the New Testament writings naturally dominate. A second factor that may help to explain the focus of scholarship on the first century is the Protestant element, which sometimes has built into it a suspicion of the development that led into Roman Catholicism. This, for many Protestants, was the negative against which they defined themselves. Thus the first century was viewed as pure and undefiled, with the later centuries becoming more and more corrupted as the church experienced success and later favor within the Roman empire. Even a scholar of the stature of Adolf Harnack was unable to distance himself from that kind of understanding of the early church.[2]

But it is not just Protestants who have shown little interest in the centuries immediately following the New Testament era. Catholics, too, have found in other areas a more acceptable focus. In particular, the philosophy of Thomas Aquinas became for many centuries the standard by which Catholic

---

[1]   The word comes from the Greek and Latin root for "father."

[2]   See some of the comments made in this regard by Glenn F. Chesnut, "A Century of Patristic Studies, 1888-1988," in *A Century of Church History: The Legacy of Philip Schaff*, ed. Henry W. Bowden. (Carbondale and Edwardsville, IL: Southern Illinois UP, 1988), pp. 37-41.

scholarship was judged. While the Thomistic world certainly drew its strength from the classical past, it shared little of the perspective of the patristic period, which was largely drawn from different elements in antiquity. Thus, both Catholics and Protestants often found the period of early church history less important or compelling than other periods.

More and more, this lack of attention to the early church is being corrected. Still, there appears to be a particular lack of English scholarship in this field. This is especially the impression left when we consider the quantity of scholarship that has been published in various languages, with French, German, and Italian scholars having provided a wealth of material. That is not to say that English patristic scholars are a new breed: mention of Bishop Lightfoot alone would challenge that. But there has been a sufficient lack of attention to this area to attract notice, and depending on how serious a matter we take this lack of attention to be, we would not be far off the mark to speak of past scholarship as having been unbalanced.

R.P.C. Hanson and Robert M. Grant, both of whom have several works listed in this bibliography, have drawn attention to this imbalance. Hanson said that several dozen research students "could well [dare I say it?] be profitably drafted from pursuing fairly useless researches on the New Testament"[3] for study in other areas of early church history. Robert Grant, noted Hanson's comment, but chose to speak somewhat more cautiously. He said:

> It is time for students of the New Testament and early Christianity to come out of the sacred texts into the world to which and in which the Christian mission was addressed and achieved results. To put it another way, two centuries of work with the microscope have been enough, so that attention can now be directed to other objects in the same field.[4]

Pointing to the same problem, Glenn Chesnut said that "the United States in the late nineteenth century was in great part 'hostile territory' for patristic scholars."[5] But Chesnut thinks that things have substantially changed for the better. In an enlightening and readable survey of the last hundred years of patristic scholarship, Chesnut offers an account of the development of patristic studies within Catholicism and Protestantism—and even outside of confessional commitments altogether, as secular historians also begin to contribute to our understanding of the early church.

---

[3]   R.P.C. Hanson and M. Barley, eds. *Christianity in Britain, 300-700* (New York: Humanities Press, 1968), p. 211; cited by R.M. Grant, "Introduction: Christian and Roman History," in *The Catacombs and the Colosseum,* eds. Stephen Benko and John J. O'Rourke (Valley Forge: Judson Press, 1971), p. 23. Published in England by Oliphants, under the title *Early Church History: The Roman Empire as the Setting of Primitive Christianity.*

[4]   Grant, "Christian and Roman History," p. 23.

[5]   Chesnut, "A Century of Patristic Studies, 1888-1988," p. 41.

But the encouraging interest in the post New Testament era does not necessarily mean that the field is becoming more balanced. One of the reasons why this period has become attractive for students of the early church has been the discovery of numerous Gnostic texts, in what has come to be called the "Nag Hammadi Library." Not to depreciate the valuable contributions from this new sub-field, it must be said that, to some extent, the study of Gnosticism has had a distinctly negative effect for the larger study of the patristic period. The interest in the second and third centuries is often secondary to the interest in Gnosticism, and the broader issues and accomplishments of the majority[6] tradition is thus sometimes not given their due, or they are viewed through the hostile perspective of their Gnostic opponents. In the same way that much of early church scholarship once had been weighted in favor of a canonically-defined first century, so now much of the scholarship on the second century is weighted in favor of an anti-orthodox Gnosticism, or some other option rejected by the early Christian majority. Neither is a particularly healthy or balanced approach to the scholarly discipline of early church history.

Whatever the reasons for the increased interest in the patristic field, when that interest develops, there also develops an increasing awareness that the break made between the first century and second century is somewhat artificial. Or, one might wish simply to say that the break is there, but it is *theological* rather than *historical*. Purely historical scholarship finds it easier to move from the first century into the later centuries than is the case where the move has serious theological implications, as it may well have if one emphasizes the "apostolic" and "normative" character of the first century over against the developments and changes that followed. Often, however, once a scholar moves into the post New Testament era, the significance of the theological and institutional developments are better appreciated, or at least they are not dismissed routinely as misdirections and deformities.

Rarely will one be able to construct a boundary between the first century and the following centuries, and view that boundary as separating alien worlds. The church *after* the apostles is linked in fundamental ways to the church of the first century. Consider, for example, the canon, which has often been the mechanism by which the separation was made or justified.

---

[6] Some will take offense at the use of the word "majority" here. It is popular to try to use terms that are as neutral as possible to describe the various and often diverse Christian movements that were part of the early church. Terms like "orthodoxy" and "heresy," if used at all, are usually placed in quotation marks, for to use them in their full sense would be to identify with a particular party (the winners), and to make some statement about *truth* that would be positively in favor of this group. But there does develop a Great Church tradition, whether we like it or not, and it does no good to deny it the status of "majority." That need not mean that it is "orthodox" from the perspective of some neutral standard—whatever that may be. That is a case for the theologians, and all early Christian groups—both "orthodox" and "heretical"—now have their vigorous advocates.

Although the writings that constitute the canon are largely from the first century, the *collection* of the documents and the concept of a distinct Christian canon are the work of the patristic period. And the church councils, by which orthodoxy came to be defined, belong to this later period too. The two worlds—the New Testament period and the patristic period—belong together.

The neglect of the patristic period and the attention on the New Testament (especially with regard to works in English) have not been without a positive side, however. Often the works intended primarily for students of the New Testament have provided useful information about the later periods of the early church too (showing to some extent how artificial the boundaries between the two fields really are). Admittedly, some of these works, unfortunately, have colored our understanding of the later centuries by an often idealized reconstruction of the first century, in which the church seemed to live in a protective bubble of isolation, going its own way, largely without contact with or influence from the larger society. At one time it was thought that the early Christians did not even speak the same language as the society about them, but rather had their own "biblical Greek," at least for the canonical texts! None would defend such an extreme position now. Scholars of the early church are sensitive to the fact that the early Christians lived, worked, loved, and died like everyone else. Well, almost. For they were *Christians,* and Christians were different. Just ask any Christian or pagan from the period. But Christians were not completely different, like aliens from some strange world. They were Romans and Greeks, or backwoods natives, as fully at home with the everyday activities of the empire as anyone else.

For the purposes of this bibliography, we have not included works specifically on the New Testament, since that would have greatly increased the size of this volume and would have prevented the kind of focus that prompted this project in the first place—a study of the early church without being overwhelmed by the quantity, and shaped by the interests, of New Testament scholarship. That is not to dismiss the usefulness of such works for students of the early church; it is simply to identify the boundaries of this particular project, and to call attention to the growing wealth of scholarship in English on the church from the beginning of the second century to the fifth and sixth centuries.

We have, however, included some materials that are not specifically "early church." In particular, some of the scholarship of historians of the ancient Roman empire has direct relevance to issues in the early church, and we have attempted to include a selection of such works. Scholars of the early church and those of ancient Mediterranean cultures are increasingly recognizing the importance of the contributions being made by each other, and this bibliography is intended to guide the student to some of the more important, and often crucial works from scholars outside the formal "early church" discipline.

INSTRUCTIONS

SELECTION OF LITERATURE

The present work, *The Early Church: An Annotated Bibliography of Literature in English*, is designed as an aid for undergraduates, beginning graduate students, and for interested lay-people. The work is divided into twenty-six distinctive sections representing issues currently of concern to scholars. Each section contains a two to three page introduction, followed by a list of important books and articles on the theme. For each entry, publication information is provided, along with an abstract. The student is thus able to gain a general, introductory knowledge of a particular problem by reading about fifteen pages. From that point, the student can begin to branch out into in-depth study, having a better sense of the primary questions and the solutions already proposed.

Although the bibliography contains abstracts of hundreds of books and articles, this is but a small percentage of the works that have been written about the early church for the period covered by our volume. Selection had to be made from the considerable quantity of useful books and articles that are available, and the task was not without difficulty. Since our main purpose was to provide a general knowledge of the issue, and in doing so, to offer a base for in-depth study, we have given priority to the following in our selection, the first two of which we have marked with symbols to aid the reader.

(1) GENERAL AND INTRODUCTORY WORKS [Symbol ☞]. It is important that the student have a general introduction to the field. For each section we have selected a number of works that provide the reader with a good general introduction to questions, solutions, and technical terminology pertaining to that topic. Often these works will not be significant for some original insight or some new observation, but that is not to depreciate such works. They are probably the best place to start. Various works serve this purpose. Our selection is not meant to suggest that other works do not provide useful introductions; we have simply suggested a few for guidance. The one "ideal" introduction does not exist, since each reader comes to the field of early Christian studies with a different background. What is an adequate introduction for one may be too challenging or too general for another.

(2) SUMMARY ARTICLES [Symbol ◉]. Sometimes there are brief articles that summarize the current state of the debate, or that review recent

major works. We believe that students generally gain a better grasp of the field by having such informed summaries.

(3) READILY AVAILABLE MATERIALS. A further basis for the selection of the works in this bibliography had to do with accessibility. Although major libraries are likely to have most of the works we have listed, some of the smaller libraries (including our own at the University of Lethbridge) cannot offer that kind of selection. Thus we have consciously given priority to books that have recently been published and are likely to be part of the holdings of even smaller libraries, or, if not available there, are nonetheless readily available in bookstores or by special order. All other things being equal, a book still in print was selected over an older out-of-print book. The exception would be to major works that have become classics in the field. Sometimes, but not always, these have been kept in print.

EMPHASIS ON LITERATURE IN ENGLISH

As for our concentration on works in English,[7] we offer the following reasons. First, many of the users of our bibliography will not have useful language skills beyond English. Second, those with adequate language skills to read the vast literature on the early church in German and French (and a few other languages) will find that our entries marked with the enclosed circle ◉ will generally include reference to major foreign language publications. Even those entries marked with the pointing finger ☛ will often have extensive bibliographies that include foreign-language materials, as will other works without any symbol. Further, we have indicated the number of pages of bibliography for each entry. The student interested in works in other languages should refer to a book with an extensive bibliography. Third, the first chapter of our bibliography lists many other bibliographies, and these often include numerous foreign language works. Further, various bibliographies on specific topics are listed at the beginning of the relevant sections in this bibliography. These are marked by the symbol ⊛, and they also often list foreign language works. Fourth, we have included reference to various book reviews. Many of these reviews focus on the place of the reviewed book in the scholarly debate, and reference is sometimes made in such reviews to related foreign language works. Fifth, many of the major works in other languages have been translated into English. Such books are included in this bibliography.

---

[7] A few non-English works have been included in this bibliography. Those included are the type that can be used by the reader of English who has no facility in other languages. For the most part, they are bibliographies (which list English works in English) or indexes to ancient authors, etc., which can be used, sometimes with a little effort, by the English reader without knowledge of other languages.

BIBLIOGRAPHIES

We have supplemented the range of entries in our volume by including other bibliographies in the field. These have been marked by the symbol ⑤, and placed at the beginning of relevant sections or chapters, along with sourcebooks. As well, the first chapter of our volume focuses on works of a bibliographical nature.

SOURCEBOOKS

Another feature of our entries judged to be important for the user is the identification of sourcebooks. Books listed in the bibliography that are primarily collections of passages from ancient authors have been marked by a symbol frequently used on maps to identify the location of ancient sites (🏛). These have been placed at the beginning of the relevant sections along with the bibliographies.

BOOK REVIEWS

Following most of the abstracts of books in our bibliography, a scissors symbol [✂] appears. This symbol introduces references to the book reviews, and the symbol was chosen partly because book reviews sometimes do a "cut-up" job on the works being reviewed.

For the most part, books published within the last two decades are provided with a more extensive list of reviews than are the older works. The main reason for this is that books that are much older and which have been important to the debate are probably already adequately engaged by the present debate in the scholarly literature. Any recently published book in the field ought to have taken account of the significant books from the scholarship of the past, and these newer works probably can evaluate the strengths and weaknesses of the older works better from this advanced point in the debate than could a review of the volume as it comes "hot-off-the-press." Recently published books, themselves, of course, need time to make their own impact, and to provoke published responses or considerations in monographs. The way scholars have of *briefly* engaging new works and placing new theories under more immediate investigation is to respond to new books in book reviews. It is useful for the student to know how scholars in the field are reacting to a new thesis as it hits the scholarly market. The notes on book reviews at the end of most entries in our bibliography direct the user to that kind of reaction.

In this bibliography, we have listed book reviews roughly within the following guidelines. We favored (1) reviews written by noted scholars in the field (thus reviews by Frend, Ferguson, the Chadwicks, R.M. Grant, and a few others appear often); (2) reviews appearing in standard journals, such as *Church History* and the *Journal of Ecclesiastical History*, because these are likely available in most university libraries, though reviews from more obscure journals or journals less directly in the field do appear, especially if they were written by a well-known scholar; (3) reviews of considerable length; and (4) reviews in English, since that is a basic feature of this bibliography. One final point about the book reviews: if a work is particularly significant or controversial, we have listed a rather large number of reviews, hoping to present a fairer picture. Sourcebooks, dictionaries, collections of articles, or bibliographical guides are less likely to have book reviews listed. Our focus for book reviews has been primarily on monographs, though no strict policy on the matter has been followed.

The user should also note that entries for the most recently published books lack references to book reviews. By the time this bibliography is itself on the market, book reviews will have appeared in major journals for the most recent books listed here. Such reviews were, unfortunately, unavailable when our bibliography went to press.

CONTRIBUTORS

Finally, contributors are identified by the following codes, used at the end of each abstract and introduction. Where no code is used, the material is the work of Thomas Robinson. A further note on the contributors is included in the preface.

(DeR)	Michael P. DeRoche
(D)	Terence L. Donaldson
(F)	Dan Falk
(P)	M. James Penton
(Ph)	Erin Philips
(S)	Brent D. Shaw
(Sm)	Brian Smart
(W)	Kurt Widmer

SYMBOLS

[More detailed descriptions of these symbols can be found in the Instructions.]

☞ Indicates an introductory work. Such works will not assume knowledge of the field, and will not be heavily technical.

◉ Indicates a work that reviews or surveys the debate. Often bibliographical in nature.

Ⓑ Indicates an article or book of a bibliographic nature.

🏛 Indicates a book largely made up of passages from ancient authors: a sourcebook.

✂ Indicates the location of a book review for a book listed in our bibliography.

CODES

[Each code is followed by the number of pages of such material; e.g. BI-6 means that there are six pages of bibliography.]

AI	author index
AAI	ancient author index
B	bibliography
B&W	black and white photos and illustrations
BI	Index of biblical citation
C	color photos and illustrations
CT	chronological tables
FT	family tree
G	glossary
GZ	gazetteer
I	index
M	maps
MAI	modern author index
NI	names index
NTI	New Testament index
PI	persons index
SI	subject index
T	tables and charts

ABBREVIATIONS

JOURNALS AND SERIALS

AHR	American Historical Review
AJP	American Journal of Philology
ANRW	Aufstieg und Niedergang der römischen Welt
ATR	Anglican Theological Review
AUSS	Andrews University Seminary Studies
BA	Biblical Archaeology
BAR	Biblical Archaeology Review
BJRL	Bulletin of the John Rylands Library
BR	Bible Review
BS	Bibliotheca Sacra
BT	Bible Translator
CBQ	Catholic Biblical Quarterly
CC	Cross Currents
CCR	Coptic Church Review
CH	Church History
CHR	Catholic Historical Review
CJ	Classical Journal
CP	Classical Philology
CQR	Church Quarterly Review
CR	Classical Review
CRBR	Critical Review of Books in Religion
CSR	Christian Scholar's Review
CT	Christianity Today
CTJ	Calvin Theological Journal
CTQ	Concordia Theological Quarterly
CTSR	Chicago Theology Seminary Register
Currents	Currents in Theology and Mission
DA	Dissertation Abstracts
EHR	English Historical Review
EQ	Evangelical Quarterly
ExT	Expository Times

GOTR	*Greek Orthodox Theological Review*
HibJ	*Hibbert Journal*
HR	*History of Religions*
HTR	*Harvard Theological Review*
JAAR	*Journal of the American Academy of Religion*
JBL	*Journal of Biblical Literature*
JCS	*Journal of Church and State*
JCSD	*Jewish and Christian Self-Definition*
JEH	*Journal of Ecclesiastical History*
JES	*Journal of Ecumenical Studies*
JETS	*Journal of the Evangelical Theological Society*
JHS	*Journal of Hellenic Studies*
JJS	*Journal of Jewish Studies*
JNES	*Journal of Near Eastern Studies*
JQR	*Jewish Quarterly Review*
JR	*Journal of Religion*
JRPR	*Journal of Religion and Psychical Research*
JRS	*Journal of Roman Studies*
JSJ	*Journal for the Study of Judaism in the Persian, Hellenistic, and Roman Period*
JSNT	*Journal for the Study of the New Testament*
JSNTSuppl	*Journal for the Study of the New Testament Supplements*
JSS	*Journal of Semitic Studies*
JTS	*Journal of Theological Studies* new series
KTR	*King's Theological Review*
LondonRB	*London Review of Books*
NIDNTT	*New International Dictionary of New Testament Theology*
NYRB	*New York Review of Books*
NYTBR	*New York Times Book Review*
PBR	*Patristic and Byzantine Review*
PEQ	*Palestinian Exploration Quarterly*
PRS	*Perspectives in Religious Studies*
PSB	*Princeton Seminary Bulletin*
R&E	*Review & Expositor*
RQ	*Restoration Quarterly*
RSR	*Religious Studies Review*
SA	*Sociological Analysis*
SC	*The Second Century*
SCJ	*Sixteenth Century Journal*
SJT	*Scottish Journal of Theology*
SL	*Studia Liturgica*
STFB	*Students Theological Fellowship Bulletin*
StLJT	*Saint Luke's Journal of Theology*
StVTQ	*Saint Vladimir's Theological Quarterly*

SWJT	*Southwestern Journal of Theology*
TDNT	*Theological Dictionary of the New Testament*
TLSuppl	*Times Literary Supplement*
TS	*Theological Studies*
TSFBulletin	*Theological Students' Fellowship Bulletin*
TT	*Theology Today*
USQR	*Union Seminary Quarterly Review*
VC	*Vigiliae Christianae*
VT	*Vetus Testamentum*
W&W	*Word and Work*
WTJ	*Westminster Theological Journal*

OTHER ABBREVIATIONS

ATLA	American Theological Library Association
ET	English Translation
SBL	Society of Biblical Literature
UP	University Press

1
BIBLIOGRAPHIES, INDEXES, JOURNALS, AND SERIALS

Other bibliographies have been published that are relevant to the particular themes and era that we have attempted to cover with the present bibliography. We have included some of these here, largely because our bibliography is not intended to be comprehensive. Rather, we have focused on a few dozen works for each subject, hoping to direct students to useful works that are readily available in even small libraries. We recognized from the start that many works relevant to the early church would not be included in the one-volume work we envisioned. By listing other bibliographies here, we hope to extend the usefulness of our own volume by pointing to sources from which one can gain information about a more complete range of works on the early church.

The bibliographies listed in this section supplement our bibliography in another important way. They often list, as we have not, works in languages other than English. Unfortunately, most of these bibliographies are not annotated; the user will be able, however, at least to find publication information for foreign-language works.

Many of the bibliographies abstracted here list, as we have done, other bibliographies, making it possible for the serious user to gain a working grasp of the literature in the field quite quickly. We have provided only a few of these bibliographies here. We have included those that we judged to be the most useful to the greatest number of students, opening doors to other bibliographic guides. These should be probed by the serious researcher—particularly the various *Religion Indexes* [§1.6; §1.7], and *Religious and Theological Abstracts* [§1.9].

The user should also note that the selection of works for our "Bibliographies" section is consciously more broad than the chronological and thematic limits of other sections of this project. This broader selection was necessary because *peripheral* material in some of these bibliographies is often of critical importance for a study of the early church. Thus, though

1

some bibliographies listed below are largely outside the area of our interest here, particular entries will, nonetheless, be useful.

Besides the bibliographies listed in this section, the student should consult the bibliographies at the end of some recent scholarly volumes listed and abstracted throughout our bibliography. We have indicated the number of pages of bibliography contained in each volume by the letter "B" followed by a hyphen and the number of pages of bibliography (e.g. B-14 indicates that the book being discussed has 14 pages of bibliography). Often these bibliographies are significant works in themselves, providing in some cases almost comprehensive listings. By referring to a major bibliography in a recent book, the student will have at least one author's judgment on the works of note for the topic under discussion. Consider the value to the beginning reader in having perhaps *the* authority in a field sorting through the works available, and compiling a list of books and articles he or she judges to be most useful to the discussion. That is exactly what the student has in the bibliographies provided in books by major scholars.

That is not to say that other bibliographies are to be neglected. Major scholars often have their own considerable biases, and any selected collection for a bibliography will reveal something about the compiler as well as something about the field. That does not devalue the bibliographic collections provided in most major works. Even the most informed librarian cannot provide as useful a bibliography as the substantial ones frequently found in a book by a major scholar in the field. Further, major works in foreign languages will also be listed in such bibliographies. Take advantage of these rich resources, but exercise a little caution—consult the bibliographies of more than one scholar.

The student should also note entries in our bibliography marked with the symbol ◉. This indicates a summary or review article, often of a bibliographic nature. Such works do in more detail what we have attempted to do here. They address a number of key works in the field, and they offer a description of the theses and often an evaluation of the place of these works in the broad scholarship on the topic. (The user should also note that the symbols used in other chapters of our volume to identify works that are bibliographic are *not* used in this chapter, since all the works listed here are largely bibliographical.)

The works in this chapter provide the student with a relatively quick entry into the literature on the various topics relevant to a study of the early church. The entries are grouped into two major sections. The first section deals with serial publications of a bibliographic kind, many of which provide abstracts to articles and books on religious themes. The second section deals with one-time publications with an interest in general themes. Other bibliographies, which are focused more specifically on a topic to which one of our chapters is devoted, will be listed in the relevant chapter. Such bibliographies appear at the beginning of the entries in each section and are marked with the symbol ⑥. All the other entries for each chapter (except for sourcebooks) appear in alphabetical order after that.

With regard to journals and serials, it is not possible to cover all the publications of importance to students of the early church, but we have listed some of the most important ones at the end of this chapter. One is likely to find an occasional article relevant to the early church in hundreds of journals, some of which may appear to be unlikely places from the title of the journal. Since no student has the time to scan all of these publications, various societies and publishers provide periodic indexes and abstracts, listing (sometimes with detailed summaries) recent publications in a specified field. Such indexes must be consulted by students who want to keep abreast of the field.

BIBLIOGRAPHIES IN SERIALS

1.1 *Aufstieg und Niedergang der römischen Welt* (ANRW) (ET: Rise and Decline of the Roman World).

This is a massive project, with the first volume appearing in 1972, published by De Gruyter of Berlin. Although it started out as a mere Festschrift, it now approaches 40 volumes. Some of the finest summaries of the major issues in the study of the classical world are to be found in this series. Many of the articles (often almost book-length themselves) deal with New Testament and early church concerns. Most volumes offer something for the student of the early church; volumes 16-28 deal specifically with religion. This is a "must"; the place to start for any major study. Its solid and informed surveys of both primary and secondary literature will give one a clear grasp of the issues and of the main contributors to the field.

1.2 *Bibliographia patristica: Internationale patristische Bibliographie.*

Berlin/New York: Walter de Gruyter, published annually since 1956. This is the most comprehensive bibliography for our period, with each volume about 300 pages in length. It should be consulted for all in-depth, serious work. The subject sections are well arranged, but the entries are not abstracted. The major disadvantage is that the entries in the bibliography are about five years behind the year of publication, thus the serious researcher must consult other sources for the most recent works on a topic. For the beginning student, this series is most useful in showing dramatically just how much work in the field is not in English—on quick glance it seems that English works account for only about 5% of the entries!

1.3   *Index of Articles on Jewish Studies.*
Published annually since 1966 by the Jewish National and University
Library, each volume contains between 400 and 500 pages. Most
of the articles and books listed will not be relevant to students of
the early church, but three sections could be useful: Post-Biblical
Literature and Early Christianity; Jewish History in the Diaspora;
and various sub-sections of Eretz Israel, dealing with archaeology,
epigraphy, and history. A detailed subject index and author index
are included. Remember: the pages run from back to front, though
the English table of contents is located where the English reader
would expect to find it—at the front.

1.4   *Index to Book Reviews in Religion.*
Begun in 1987, and published quarterly by the American Theological
Library Association, this massive work lists just about every book
review published in the field of religion. Individual volumes cover
the years from 1986 to the present. In 1990 a volume was published,
covering the years from 1949 to 1959 (called volumes 1-4), and in
1992 a volume (called volumes 5-8) was published, covering the
years from 1960 to 1968. The gap from 1969 to 1986 soon will be
filled. Then this series will provide a list of book reviews for all
publications from 1949 to the present. It is well organized under
four headings: Author and Editor Index; Title Index; Series Index;
and Reviewer Index. The user will probably find the title index
most useful. Just look for the book under its title, consulting the
volumes that cover the period one to four years or so after the book
was published. This is a quick way to learn what the immediate
scholarly reaction was to a new thesis.

1.5   *New Testament Abstracts.*
Begun in 1956, this is a collection of abstracts on articles and
books published in the field of New Testament studies, though
some sections deal more specifically with the later period. In
particular, consult the sections on biblical theology and the world
of the New Testament, found in both the section on journal articles
and the section on books. The sections covering articles are further
sub-divided; they deal with such topics as church and ministry,
archaeology, the Jewish world, the Graeco-Roman world, the early
church, and Gnosticism. Very current, with notices and abstracts
appearing generally within a year of publication, and sometimes
within a few months. Abstracts vary in length, from three lines to
the size of the abstracts in our bibliography. About 450 pages each
year, with indexes to scripture, authors, and book reviews. Published

by the Weston School of Theology of Cambridge, MA., with the Catholic Biblical Association.

1.6 *Religion Index One: Periodicals.* Formerly *Index to Religious Periodical Literature.*
Published by the American Theological Library Association of Evanston, IL. Its subtitle explains the arrangement and contents: "A Subject Index to Periodical Literature including an Author/Editor Index and a Scripture Index." Now to volume 24 (1992), consisting of over 650 pages each year, with over 12,000 articles listed. The earliest volume (1955) covers literature from 1949. The entries are remarkably current—often within months of the publication of the work listed. The literature in about 500 periodicals is indexed here. The author/editor index is arranged alphabetically. The subject index is arranged alphabetically by title within each of the thousands (yes, thousands!) of subject headings. The entries are not abstracted (see §1.9 for abstracts), though edited volumes list the titles of the individual articles. This is a major work, and after some use, the student will learn which subject headings yield the most relevant entries for particular topics. Now available on Compact Disc (CD) for fast computer searches. If a library does not have either the hard copy or the CD, on-line searches are available.

1.7 *Religion Index Two: Multi-Author Works.*
Two issues of this work have appeared to date, each with two volumes. The first covers the works from 1970-1975; the second from 1976-1980. It is similar to the other publications under the title of *Religion Index* issued by the American Theological Library Association, differing mainly in that various multi-author volumes, such as Festschriften, are covered in *Religion Index Two.* For such materials prior to 1970, see the O'Brien entry [§1.37].

1.8 *Religious Studies Review.*
Published since 1975 by the Council of the Societies for the Study of Religion, this publication keeps members of religious studies departments informed about what is happening in the academic study of religion. For the student of the early church, there will be occasional extended book review articles and summaries of current scholarship on a variety of topics, numerous book notes, and notices on dissertations in progress. Published quarterly, with about 400 pages each year. An index compiled by Watson E. Mills for all volumes up to 1989 is available.

1.9   *Religious and Theological Abstracts.*
        This massive work was begun in 1958, and is published quarterly,
        with a full annual index in the last issue of each year. About 5000
        articles are indexed and abstracted annually, in one paragraph entries,
        some of which are short, but most of which are close to the length
        of the abstracts in our bibliography. It is divided into four major
        sections, each of which is subdivided. The most useful sections for
        students of the early church are under the main section titled
        "Historical," though other sections should be checked. Subject,
        author, and scripture indexes are provided. These volumes also
        contain up-to-date addresses for journals on religion. The abstracts,
        though short, are particularly useful for determining the content of
        journal articles. The contents of books are more adequately covered
        in the book review sections of various journals. Published by
        Religious and Theological Abstracts of Myerstown, PA.

        NON-SERIAL BIBLIOGRAPHIES
1.10   Alich, Salih H. *International Bibliography of the History of
        Religions.* Leiden: E.J. Brill, 1979. Pp. xxii + 222. I-20.
        This work is divided into eleven sections. Of some use are the
        subsections on Asia Minor, on Greek and Roman Religions, and on
        Hellenistic Religions listed under "Religions of Antiquity" (17
        pages), and the subsections on Origins and on Patristic Literature
        under "Christianity" (33 pages). The limitation of this bibliography
        is that it is not remotely comprehensive, frequently no dates are
        given, and it is more heavily weighted towards French publications.
        On the positive side, many articles are mentioned.

1.11   Bagnall, Roger S. *Research Tools For the Classics.* The Report of
        the A.P.A.'s Ad Hoc Committee on Basic Research Tools. Chico:
        Scholar's Press, 1980. Pp. vi + 61.
        With annotated entries, this work covers 14 topics: Bibliographic
        Works; Greek Language and Literature; Latin Language and
        Literature; Ancient History; Philosophy; Ancient Law; Greek and
        Latin Epigraphy; Papyrology; Antiquity and Christianity; Numis-
        matics; Medieval and Renaissance Latin and Greek; Byzantium;
        Art and Archaeology; and Oriental Languages. About one half of
        the volume deals with works in progress and, though this is not
        complete, it is useful. It also includes discussion of the status and
        needs of research in the field, though this section is now somewhat
        dated. In typescript.

1.12   Baldwin, Barry. "A Bibliographical Survey: The Second Century
        from Secular Sources 1969-1980." *Second Century* 1 (1981): 173-

189.
Baldwin, a professor of Classics, provides a review of current and forthcoming works (monographs, series, and articles) dealing with secular matters in the second century and with editions of the authors from that period. His reviews place each work within the current debate, indicating the strengths and weaknesses. Although the selection of works seems to be largely focused on the period of the second century (rightly so, for an article appearing in the first volume of the journal *The Second Century*), Baldwin's review will nonetheless be of considerable use to most students of the wider early church who do not have a background in the classics.

1.13 Barrow, John G. *A Bibliography of Bibliographies in Religion.* Ann Arbor: Edwards Brothers, 1955. Pp. xi + 489. I-86.
This volume started as a PhD dissertation (1930). Barrow attempted to list and evaluate all published bibliographies in the field of religion. The work has 16 major divisions with numerous subdivisions (annotated and arranged by date of publication). This bibliography is clearly dated, but it has relevance for historical work. Nine pages on the Fathers, but only 2 pages on works published after 1900.

1.14 Blockx, Karel. *Bibliographical introduction to church history.* Uitgererij / Leuven: Acco, 1982. Pp. xii + 98. I-8.
This bibliography was begun for first-year students in the Faculty of Theology at the University of Leuven. Although it covers all of church history, it has adequate emphasis on the early church to make it somewhat useful, though the English user will find that many of the 729 entries are to foreign language works. The entries are not generally annotated, but sometimes a very brief helpful comment is provided. The entries give careful details of the publications, the various reprints, and translations available.

1.15 Brock, S.P., et al. *A Classified Bibliography of the Septuagint.* Leiden: E.J. Brill, 1973. Pp. xviii + 217. I-16.
Divided into 119 sections and well cross-referenced, this select bibliography covers works from 1900-1969, though the emphasis is on the later period. Important sections on the History of the Septuagint; the use of the Septuagint by the Apostolic Fathers, Origen, and Jerome; and sections on the Hexapla and on versions of the Septuagint.

1.16 Case, S.J., et al. *A Bibliographical Guide to the History of*

Christianity. Chicago: University of Chicago Press, 1931. Pp. xi + 265. I-29.

The most important part of this work is the 24-page section on "Christianity in the Roman Empire," which lists 258 books. The chapter on "History of Christianity in General" is useful too. Foreign language works are included, and a rare brief note is given for some of the books. Most works listed in Case's bibliography that have continued to be important to an understanding of the early Church should be found, with annotation, in our own bibliography. Nonetheless, Case's work is valuable for information about numerous once important works, and for older foreign language works.

1.17 Chadwick, Owen. *The History of the Church: A Select Bibliography.* 3d ed. Helps for Students of History 66. London: Historical Association, 1973. (1962^1).

By a leading church historian, this volume provides very brief comment on a number of books, though some books listed lack any comment. Of particular interest are pages 5-18 on general works and on early church history to 461 CE. Entries are arranged by topic. Although brief and becoming dated, it is nonetheless useful to have access to Chadwick's informed judgment on the literature in our field.

1.18 *The Classical World Bibliography of Greek and Roman History.* With a new introduction by Walter Doulan. New York/London: Garland, 1978. Pp. xiii + 234.

This is a reprint of 14 bibliographic surveys that appeared in the journal *The Classical World* from 1954 to 1971. Of particular use to students of the early church are the sections by Louis H. Feldman, "Scholarship on Philo and Josephus (1939-1959)"; and by Walter E. Kaegi, Jr., "Research on Julian the Apostate 1945-1964." Feldmann has continued his bibliographical work on Josephus. See Feldmann, *Josephus and Modern Scholarship (1937-1980)* (Berlin/New York: Walter de Gruyter, 1984), which runs to over a thousand pages; and his supplement, *Josephus, A Supplementary Bibliography.*

1.19 Fitzmyer, Joseph A. *An Introductory Bibliography for the Study of Scripture.* Rev. ed. Subsidia Biblica 3. Rome: Biblical Institute Press, 1981. Pp. xi + 154. MAI-8.

A list of 555 books, with abstracts, some of which are quite extensive. Although most of the works focus on the Bible itself, there are many things here helpful for students of the early church. In

particular, Fitzmyer has a detailed section on other bibliographies and on journals. Much shorter sections of relevance deal with New Testament times, New Testament Apocrypha, Gnosticism, Greek and Roman religious milieu, and Patristic literature. Book reviews are listed for each entry. This is a useful work, even though its main interests lie outside the period of our bibliography.
⊰ Hunt, *CBQ* 44 (1982): 479-480; Moriarty, *TS* 43 (1982): 175.

1.20   Gorman, G.E. and Lyn Gorman. *Theological and Religious Reference Materials. Systematic Theology and Church History.* Bibliographies and Indexes in Religious Studies 2. Westport, CT/London: Greenwood, 1985. Pp. xiv + 402. AI-18; SI-13; Title Index-32.
The most relevant part is the 150-page "Church History" section, divided into subsections of bibliographies, dictionaries, and handbooks. Entries are in alphabetical order of author, and are briefly abstracted. A chronological arrangement may have been better, for the user will need either to scan the pages to find what is relevant, or to use the subject index. This work concentrates on reference materials in its broadest definition. While it covers works in a number of languages, all abstracts are in English. Not the best organized or focused reference work for students of the early church.
⊰ Bradley, *Anglican and Episcopal History* 57 (1988): 119-120; Mazuk, *R&E* 83 (1986): 647-648; Moo, *JETS* 28 (1985): 365-366.

1.21   Griffiths, David B. *A Critical Bibliography of Writings on Judaism.* 2 vols. Lewiston, NY/Queenston, ON/Lampeter, Wales: Edwin Mellen, 1988. Pp. 804.
The larger part of this bibliography deals with Judaism in the medieval and modern periods. Two sections are important to our period: Part 1: Resource Apparatus; and Part 2, Chapter 2: "Judaism in Antiquity, from Late Hellenistic Times to the Closing of the Talmud." Chapter introductions and annotations are intended to "put major works, themes and debated ideas into historical, comparative and critical focus." Not all entries are annotated.

1.22   Halton, Thomas P., and Stella O'Leary. *Classical Scholarship: An Annotated Bibliography.* White Plains, NY: Kraus International Publications, 1986. Pp. xx + 396. AI-18; SI-23.
Annotated with brief but precise and informed comments, and with reference to book reviews, this is an extremely valuable supplement to our own bibliography for those who need access to the classical world. It is based on the earlier work of Martin R.P. McGuire, titled *Introduction to Classical Scholarship: A Syllabus and Biblio-*

graphic Guide (1955,[1] 1961[2]). The present work covers publications to 1980, with some exceptions. Divided into 15 chapters, with sub-topics within these, the student of the early church can quickly find relevant material, though the work is clearly weak on the Christian side of things (to be addressed by Halton's forthcoming *Early Christian Studies: A Bibliographical Guide*). Its principal focus is on texts, language, and writing, and on art and archaeology. The broad new issues brought to importance by sociological concerns are not dealt with in the way that students of the early church would have hoped. Still, a rich resource.
ϑ< Nauert, *SCJ* 18 (1987): 267.

1.23   Halton, Thomas P., and Robert D. Sider. "A Decade of Patristic Scholarship." *Classical World* 76 (Nov-Dec 1982): 65-127; 76 (July-Aug 1983): 313-383. Bound as one volume.
This is perhaps the most valuable tool listed in our bibliography. It is recent enough to provide a survey of modern scholarship, and it is detailed, listing 1545 entries, with paragraph introductions for each of its numerous sections. Although not covering all matters of interest to students of the early church, it is a massive collection of scholarship on patristic *literature* from the second to the fifth century. The work also provides access to foreign language literature.

1.24   Hemer, Colin J. "Bibliographies of Scholars: Resources of Tyndale Library." *Tyndale Bulletin* 33 (1982): 137-164.
A list of bibliographies available in Festschriften and journals, etc. of 237 scholars of biblical studies and related fields. All the materials referred to in this article are in the Tyndale Library, Cambridge, though much of it will be available in any good graduate library. Several important scholars of the early church are included, among whom are Bruce, Case, Cullmann, Goguel, Goodenough, Goodspeed, Jeremias, S.E. Johnson, Jonas, Käsemann, Knox, Kümmel, Moule, Nock, Quasten, W.M. Ramsay, J. Roberts, Sevenster, Simon, Westcott, Wilgren, and Willoughby.

1.25   Hurd, John Coolidge. *A Bibliography of New Testament Bibliographies*. New York: Seabury, 1966. Pp. 75.
Although not specifically focused on our period, some of the sections are of use, such as those dealing with Hellenistic and Roman background, worship and sacraments, early Christian history, Gnosticism, classical antiquity, patristic studies, and Coptic studies. A few of the entries are briefly annotated. The various bibliographies listed provide a good survey of the older works on some topics of relevance

to the study of the early church. Also useful is the longer section regarding bibliographies of the works of specific scholars.

1.26 Judge, Edwin, A. "'Antike and Christentum'. Towards a Definition of the Field: A Bibliographic Survey." *ANRW* 23:1 (1979): 3-58.
Judge's work is valuable as a research tool, covering the period from the Julio-Claudians to the collapse of Roman power in the west (476 CE). After brief reflections on the discipline itself, Judge lists hundreds of articles on early Christian history and the church's relation to the larger culture, with special emphasis on literary styles, poetry, and education; intellectual and ethical ideas; and social structures and issues. Judge also lists major biographies on the church fathers and on some of the Roman Emperors, and on major religious innovators such as Marcion, Mani, and Celsus. The bibliographies provide access to much of the foreign language literature, as well as to the literature in English, though Judge makes little attempt to evaluate the works, or to describe them in more than a line or two, at most. (W)

1.27 Kepple, Robert J. *Reference Works for Theological Research: An Annotated Selective Bibliographical Guide.* 2d ed. Washington, DC: University Press of America, 1981. Pp. xiv + 283. I-33.
Covering a wide field, but with a clear concentration on Christianity, this book is a rich resource. Hundreds of works are listed, with a emphasis on *reference* works, from bibliographies to indexes, directories, encyclopedias, dissertations, book reviews, and periodicals. Such entries make up roughly the first half of the work. The second half deals with particular subject areas. For our interest, the following are most relevant: ch. 26 "Church History: General Coverage" and ch. 27 "Ancient Church History & Patristics." Other sections may be of some use too. The annotations vary from a sentence to a detailed paragraph. This bibliography differs from ours by concentrating on reference works, for which we have dedicated only a few introductory chapters. An important guide.

1.28 Krüger, Gustav. *History of Early Christian Literature in the First Three Centuries.* Translated by Charles R. Gillett. New York: Burt Franklin, 1965. Originally published in 1875. Pp. xxiii + 409. I-17.
This work, though recently reprinted, is useful mainly for those interested in the history of various debates, rather than in the current issues, for it covers works only up to the end of the 1800s. It was designed as a handbook primarily for students, and is divided into 106 sections, many of which are themselves subdivided. Although

the modern student will find it largely of historical interest, the notes on patristic authors are often informative, and useful if checked with modern scholarship on the subject.

1.29   Krüger, Gustav. "A Decade of Research in Early Christian Literature, 1921-1930." *Harvard Theological Review* 26 (1933): 173-321.
A detailed review of research in the 1920s. Although it deals with scholarship that is decades old, the bibliographies are extensive and still useful, and many of the works discussed in some detail have become standard works in the field, still to be consulted for the soundness of judgment or the novelty of their insights. The work is divided according to ancient author, for the most part. Shorter sections deal with general works on a variety of topics.

1.30   Langevin, Paul-Émile. *Bibliographie Biblique* (ET: Biblical Bibliography). 3 vols. Quebec: Les Presses de l'Université Laval, 1972-1985. Vol. 1: 1930-1970 (1972). Pp. xxviii + 941. AI-54; SI-9. Vol. 2: 1930-1975 (1978). Pp. lxv + 1591. AI-118; SI-21. Vol. 3: 1930-1983 (1985). Pp. liii + 1901. AI-149; SI-39.
The three volumes cover the literature from 1930 to 1983 inclusive. Although the work concentrates on the Bible, there is considerable overlap with areas of our interest. The divisions and sub-divisions are numerous, as one can see from the "Table of Headings" index (in English). Many articles from Festschriften, collected works, and journals are listed. This should be checked by the student of the early church; some entries are likely to be relevant, and the arrangement makes access to a specific topic very easy. The subject index in volume 3 (called "Table of Headings") covers all three volumes.
⊱ Epp. *JBL* 106 (1987): 562-563; Fitzmyer, *TS* 40 (1979): 345-347; Fitzmyer, *TS* 47 (1986): 301-303; Torrance, *SJT* 41 (1988): 284-285.

1.31   Lyons, William Nelson, and Merrill M. Parvis. *New Testament Literature: An Annotated Bibliography.* Chicago: University of Chicago Press, 1948. Pp. xiv + 392. AI-22; BI-5; Greek Index-2.
An older work that focuses on the New Testament, yet with about a third of the pages devoted to early church history, theology, literature, and biography. Many of the entries are briefly annotated, often largely in the form of a list of book reviews, which sometimes is quite extensive. Topics of relevance are: ancient interpretation, canon, texts and versions, art and archaeology, Judaism and Hellenism, Church History, including sections on all the leading figures (orthodox or otherwise), creeds, martyrdom, etc. This work

is probably now most useful to researchers who are interested in turning up an older relevant article that may have become overlooked in the more recent discussion.

1.32 McCabe, James P. *Critical Guide to Catholic Reference Books.* Research Studies in Library Science 2. Littleton, CO: Libraries Unlimited, 1971. Pp. 287. I-39.
An annotated bibliography (from a two-line comment to an extended paragraph on each entry). Although the bibliography covers numerous areas beyond the scope of our interests, many of the entries are relevant to the early church, such as the sections on the liturgy, papacy, councils, general church history, and ancient church history. In particular, note pp. 92-98, listing 31 entries on Patrology.

1.33 Metzger, Bruce M. *Index of Articles on the New Testament and the Early Church Published in Festschriften.* Philadelphia: Society of Biblical Literature, 1951. Pp. xv + 182. I-10. Supplement (1955). Pp. viii + 20. I-2.
In typescript. The main index lists 2150 entries (to 1949). It is extensively subdivided and offers much that is useful to our period: Graeco-Roman Backgrounds; Transmission and Canon of the New Testament; Textual Criticism; Councils and Synods; Church and State; Art and Architecture; Rites and Worship, as well as more general topics. The supplement lists another 200 articles, with both volumes covering 640 Festschriften. Good indexes. An important guide for any comprehensive treatment of a subject related to the early church, though it is dated.

1.34 Mitros, Joseph M. Religions: *A Select Classified Bibliography.* Philosophical Questions 8. New York: Learned Publications, 1973. Pp. xix + 435. I-35.
Pages 199-399 deal with various aspects of Christianity, and pages 281-326 deal specifically with the patristic period, though many entries from other sections are relevant to the patristic period. The occasional brief annotation is usually in English (some in German and French). Relatively up-to-date and fairly comprehensive; good for publication details.

1.35 Morris, Raymond P. *A Theological Book List.* Oxford: Blackwell/ Napperville, IL: Allenson's, 1960. Pp. xiv + 242. I-14.
Produced by the Theological Educational Fund of the International Missionary Council for Theological Seminaries and Colleges in Africa, Asia, Latin America, and the Southwest Pacific. The book

lists about 5400 books that are judged essential for a solid seminary library. For most books, only the publication information is given, but for a few, a note about the contents is provided. Most of the works are in English or in English translation. Only a few pages are focused on our period, though reference to other important works will be found scattered throughout the volume. Other bibliographies are likely to be more useful to the student of the early church.

1.36   North, Robert. "Bibliography of Works in Theology and History." *History and Theory: Studies in the Philosophy of History* 12 (1973): 55-140.
       Arranged by topic, and then by year, with an emphasis on later works, though a number of works from the earlier part of the twentieth century are listed too. The most useful section is the fifth: "Post-New-Testament: Apologetic, Patristic, Sectarian," but only some of these entries are relevant. Most of the entries are to German works, but French and English works are cited too. Clearly a highly specialized bibliography. Don't start here!

1.37   O'Brien, Betty A., and Elmer J. O'Brien, eds. *Religion Index Two: Festschriften 1960-1969*. Evanston, IL: American Theological Library Association, 1980. Pp. xxx + 741.
       Very similar to *Religion Index One* [§1.6] and *Religion Index Two* [§1.7] described above in the section on serials, this volume is different only in that it is a one-time effort. It deals specifically with articles in Festschriften, and it does not include a scripture index. Festschriften (singular: Festschrift) are volumes celebrating the accomplishments of a noted scholar by his friends and colleagues, and the O'Brien volume provides a few general comments about such volumes. The 13,000 entries listed from almost 800 volumes will indicate just how massive the religious literature is in Festschriften *alone* for one decade. And this does not include those articles on religious themes that have appeared in more general type Festschriften during this time. Not all the entries in the O'Brien volume deal with the early church, but many do. The few Festschriften listed in our own bibliography are just "a drop in the bucket," as the O'Brien demonstrates well. The O'Brien volume mentions a few other similar volumes focused on works in Festschriften. Current Festschriften are now listed in *Religion Index Two: Multi-Author Works* [§1.7], also published by the American Theological Library Association.

1.38 Sayre, John L., and Roberta Hamburger. *Tools for Theological Research.* Enid, OK: Seminary Press, 1976. Pp. v + 85. I–7.
This guide was designed as a introductory research tool for students at Phillips University Graduate Seminary. It has no distinct section on church history, but major works in our field are mentioned. On average, the description of each entry is between 1/3 and 1/2 page. Some students may find the section on bibliographies helpful, though for major works on the early church, the entries in the Sayer/ Hamburger volume are likely to be found in our own bibliography.

1.39 Scholer, David M. *A Basic Bibliographic Guide for New Testament Exegesis.* 2d ed. Grand Rapids: Eerdmans, 1973. Pp. 94. AI-6.
This work is broader than its title would suggest. In particular, the following sections may be helpful: "Other Bibliographical Surveys"; "Bibliographic Tools"; "Literature, History and Religion of the New Testament World" with subsections on "General and Pagan," "Jewish," and "Early Christian." A few entries are briefly annotated.

1.40 Sieben, Hermann Josef. *Voces. Eine Bibliographie zu Wörtern und Begriffen aus der Patristik* (1918-1978). Bibliographia Patristica Supplementum 1. Berlin/New York: de Gruyter, 1980. Pp. v + 461.
An attempt to produce something like Kittel's *Theological Dictionary of the New Testament* for the patristic literature. A massive review of works published from 1918-1978, arranged by words and concepts used in the patristic period. Half the book is devoted to Greek terms; the other half to Latin. It covers journal articles, books, and theological dictionaries.
✂ McDermott, *TS* 42 (1981): 176.

1.41 Stewardson, Jerry L. *A Bibliography of Bibliographies on Patristics.* Evanston, IL: Garrett Theological Seminary Library, 1967. Pp. v + 52.
Divided into 14 sections, this volume lists 195 bibliographies, and provides comment for most—sometimes extensive, sometimes a sentence or two. By referring to the various bibliographies cited (in German, French and English), the serious student will have access to the wealth of literature in the field of patristics up to 1967 (though some of the bibliographies are specifically limited to the New Testament). The bibliographies cited cover books, journal articles and Festschriften. An important resource that will guide the student to some comprehensive bibliographies, often compiled by top scholars in the field. In typescript.

1.42   Tobey, Jeremy L. *The History of Ideas: A Bibliographical Intro-
        duction.* Volume One: *Classical Antiquity.* Santa Barbara: American
        Bibliographical Center / Oxford: Clio Press, 1975.
        The most useful part of this guide is its material on general
        bibliographical guides in various languages and specific guides to
        ancient history and classical culture and to the wide area of religion
        (with fairly detailed entries). Its survey of material on Christianity
        is helpful too, except for the fact that the author seems to think that
        the only writers whose *biases* affect their work are those who are
        sympathetic to the Christian cause.

1.43   Walsh, Michael J., et al. *Religious bibliographies in serial literature:
        a guide.* London: Mansell Publishing, 1981. Pp. xxiv + 216. SI-5;
        Title Index-7.
        A detailed and highly useful guide to 178 serials that are devoted
        solely to bibliographical material on religious topics, or, as is more
        often the case, that regularly carry articles of a bibliographical
        nature along with more typical journal articles. Each journal is
        described in a page or more, giving publishing detail, arrangement
        (thus showing how easy it should be to access information), the
        coverage, an extended comment on content and usefulness, and the
        address. This is well worth consulting, even though a number of
        the listings there appear in our bibliography as well. But the two
        bibliographies are quite different. Walsh concentrates solely on
        bibliographic materials in serials. A scan of the subject index in
        Walsh's work will determine whether there are relevant serials.
        Almost always, something will be found of use, though Walsh's
        book covers the whole range of religious issues, not just the early
        church.
        ❧ Elliott, *RS* 18 (1982): 552.

1.44   Ward, A. Marcus. *A Theological Book List. English Supplement
        No. 3. 1971.* Bromley, UK: Theological Education Fund, 1971. Pp.
        xxiii + 128. I-22. (With separate sections on works in various
        foreign languages.)
        This book is intended to follow the format of Morris's work [§1.35].
        Some of the works are briefly annotated, and short bibliographic
        essays are included for various issues. The main pages of interest
        to the student of the early church are few: about three on church
        history and patristics, and an occasional relevant reference under
        subjects such as doctrine and liturgy.

JOURNALS

1.45 *Catholic Biblical Quarterly.*
Started in 1939, and published quarterly by the Catholic Biblical Association of America, it is now in its 54th volume (in 1992), and runs to over 800 pages each year. Although its articles are strictly limited to the biblical material, its book reviews, which usually make up one half or more of each issue, cover a wider period. These reviews are usually one to two pages in length, and generally deal with works in English. The journal is usually available even in small libraries, and the book reviews can be of use to those students without more ready access to journals dedicated to the early church, or to journals with more extensive book reviews.

1.46 *Church History.*
Published quarterly by the American Society of Church History since 1932. In recent years, on average, one article per issue deals with a topic related to the first five or six centuries of the church. Usually two or three (sometimes more) one-page book reviews are relevant. But some issues contain nothing relevant to the early church. All articles are in English, though the book reviews do cover foreign language publications. Volumes 1-17 are on microfilm, and available from ATLA Board of Microtext. Volumes 18 to the present are available from University Microfilms.

1.47 *Harvard Theological Review.*
Started in 1908, and now published quarterly and with about 500 pages each year, volume 85 appeared in 1992. Although covering a wide range of religious topics, there is usually something of interest to students of the early church, and sometimes as much as half of an issue with be devoted to this area. It does not carry book reviews, but it has a list of books received. Of some use are the one-page summaries of Harvard doctoral dissertations in the area of religion and Near Eastern languages and civilization. These appear in the last issue of each year.

1.48 *Jahrbuch für Antike und Christentum* (ET: *Yearbook for Antiquity and Christianity*).
Roughly published annually from 1958 to the present, by Aschendorff (Münster). Although most of the articles are in German, these volumes contain a wealth of solid scholarship on a variety of topics, which serves well to illustrate the need for the study of German by serious students of the early church. A few of the articles are in English, with contributions from Frend and Judge, in

particular, and from a few others. Even fewer articles are in French.

1.49   *Journal of Early Christian Studies.*
A new journal, begun in 1993, and published through the Johns Hopkins University Press for the North American Patristic Society. It is intended to be a forum for newer approaches to the study of the early church, using insights from "social history, feminist studies, and literary and philosophical theory," and will deal, too, with the oriental branches of the early church (Syriac, Coptic, Armenian, etc.). Articles representing more traditional approaches will also be included, though there will be less focus of the theology of the period. Plans are to publish the journal quarterly.

1.50   *The Journal of Ecclesiastical History.*
Published quarterly by Cambridge University Press, this journal covers a wide range of topics, from antiquity to the present. Each volume has about twenty articles and 200 book reviews and short notices. Frequently, though not in every year, one of the major articles will be relevant to the early church. Articles and book reviews are now listed in chronological order of topic; the user need only scan the first few entries to determine whether there is material on the early church. Sometimes a substantial review article will appear on recent books in the field of the early church.

1.51   *Restoration Quarterly.*
Published quarterly, this journal reflects the interests of the Churches of Christ, a "denomination" that has a particular theological interest in the primitive church for its own self-understanding as "Disciples." With sound editorial judgments by early church scholars such as Everett Ferguson, the student can expect to find useful articles here from time to time, and several are included in this bibliography. Many of the articles, however, are specifically directed to the interests of the Churches of Christ, and are less relevant to the general reader. Begun in 1957, with about 250 pages each year.

1.52   *The Second Century: A Journal of Early Christian Studies.*
Published quarterly, with a total of about 250 pages. The title is a little misleading, since its articles sometimes range beyond that period, though it does deal mainly with the Christian church in the second century. A few book reviews are usually included. Sometimes an issue will be devoted to a particular theme; other times the articles range widely. The editorial board has many of the leading early church historians (Ferguson, Drijvers, Grant, Koester, Kraft,

Lüdermann, Malherbe, Schoedel, Wilken, and a number of others). Articles by non-English writers are translated into English for the journal. This journal deserves attention by anyone in the field of early Christian history. In 1993, it ceased to exist under this title, merging with the new journal titled *Journal of Early Christian Studies* [§1.49].

1.53 *Vigiliae Christianae. A review of early christian life and language.* An E.J. Brill publication, begun in 1947 and published quarterly, with about 400 pages each year. This journal generally carries one or two major articles in English in each issue (as well as articles in French and German). It is one of the major journals for the study of the early church in the period after the New Testament. About 50 book reviews are published each year, some of considerable length, and often a foreign language work will be reviewed in English. A scan of the table of contents of this journal shows the English student just how much of the scholarly work on the early church is being done in languages other than English.

2

ATLASES, DICTIONARIES, AND ENCYCLOPEDIAS

Some books are not meant to be read from cover to cover. Our bibliography is one such volume, as are the volumes listed in this chapter and in the previous one ("Bibliographies"). These reference works are convenient for the student because they provide, in short, clear, well arranged articles, quick survey of the important core of information on a topic, and they direct the student to the most significant scholarly works. Atlases, too, fit this section. Most atlases in the field of the early church are far from being simply a collection of maps. In many cases, an atlas provides a mini-history of the period, and in some cases, these mini-histories are written by leading experts in the field. Deserving of particular praise here are the various atlases in the "Facts On File" series (see the Chadwick and Evans [§2.2] and the Cornell and Matthews [§2.3] entries below). Somewhat related to this category are the works in our bibliography marked by the symbol ◉. This identifies summary or review articles that provide good introductory surveys of various debates. There is not much more to be said in general terms about such "survey" works, other than that they usually are the best place to start a research project, particularly if the student is beginning from complete ignorance.

The researcher can expect that most review articles and most entries in dictionaries and encyclopedias will be accompanied by at least a short bibliography. These bibliographies generally will list the works that have come to be judged as the standard or significant scholarship on the topic, providing a balanced selection. Thus even though such bibliographical notes are often brief, they are usually particularly helpful at the beginning of one's research. More comprehensive bibliographies will include everything—from standard works to the peripheral and eccentric. The beginning researcher may not have the tools to discriminate.

That is not to say that the short articles in dictionaries and encyclopedias are neutral and bias-free. The bias of the author will often color the writing in some way or another, even in short articles. But there is nothing particularly alarming about this. Of course, one must account for bias. The best way to do that is to see how others perceive the issue at hand. For example, in the short bibliographies that accompany encyclopedia entries, authors writing about the same subject will sometimes list different books that they value as important. Probably the best way to determine what are the *standard* books on a topic is to compare the bibliographies in two or three such articles. Those that are listed by all writers are more likely to be the standard ones.

Being aware of current or past scholarly opinion and being bound by such opinion are quite different things, and even the beginning student need not always take the safe consensus position. The history of scholarly advancement is marked by revolutionary challenges to traditional opinion— even traditional *scholarly* opinion. But there is little that is commendable in being ignorant of the state of contemporary scholarship, or of past contributions, and the most substantial revolutions in perspectives have usually come from individuals who have understood the various opinions and scholarly conclusions, and from that basis of understanding, rejected the consensus position.

There comes a point when even the basic works must be put aside and the original documents considered (what we call the *primary* sources, in contrast to the *secondary* sources, which are the works of authors who write *about* the primary sources). There is some debate regarding when the primary material should be confronted by the student. Some contend that the less a person has been influenced by the opinion of others about a primary document, the more likely one will come to fresh insights in the encounter with the text. Others hold that nothing is to be gained by approaching the primary document with complete ignorance; the more one knows, the better. This bibliography tries to bring to the beginning student some knowledge of the discussion in the secondary literature, so in a way it holds to the latter view.

ATLASES

2.1   Beitzel, Barry J. *The Moody Atlas of Bible Lands.* Chicago: Moody, 1985. Pp. xviii + 234. BI-7; AAI-1; B-2; B&W-4; C-35; CT-4; M-95; GZ-12.

This atlas is focused on the New Testament, with only occasional information on the early church. But the maps (all in color) are very well done—among the clearest I have encountered, with a good selection of photographs, illustrations, and commentary. The atlas concludes with a 10-page discussion of biblical map-making.

୬< Chapman, *PEQ* 119 (1987): 72-73; Davies, *VT* 38 (1988): 488; Drinkard, *R&E* 84 (1987): 125-126; Fleming, *BAR* 12 (1986): 6-10; Rainey, *Trinity Journal* 8 (1987): 101-108; Shea, *AUSS* 24 (1986): 265-267; Thompson, *CBQ* 49 (1987): 296-297.

2.2   Chadwick, Henry, and G.R. Evans, eds. *Atlas of the Christian Church*. New York: Facts on File Publications, 1987. Pp. 240. B-3; I-4; M-42; B&W-63; C-239; CT–1; GZ-5.

Although only the first quarter of this atlas is relevant to the period covered by this bibliography, the book is of such exceptional quality, a student of the early church should not overlook it—it is in many ways the best. Maps are detailed, colorful, and clear; illustrations are well chosen and photographed brilliantly. In addition to the general running commentary, this atlas features many special sections relevant to the early church: Christians and ancient Rome; icons and iconoclasm; the Christian calendar (with chart); monasticism; list of the bishops of Rome; and others. Several other atlases in the "Facts on File" series may be useful too: *Atlas of the Bible* (Rogerson); *Atlas of Medieval Europe* (Matthew); *Atlas of the Roman World* (Cornell and Matthews §2.3); *Atlas of the Jewish World* (de Lange); and *Atlas of the Greek World* (Levi).

⊰ Gaustad, *CH* 58 (1989): 274-275; Hinson, *R&E* 85 (1988): 726; Rajak, *TLSuppl* 4440 (May 6-12, 1988): 510; Rorem, *Currents* 16 (1989): 304.

2.3   Cornell, Tim, and John Matthews. *Atlas of the Roman World.* New York: Facts on File, 1982. Pp. 240. I-4; G-6; AB-3; M-62; C-189; B&W-213; CT-1.

In quality, to be praised as highly as other volumes in this series [§2.2]. The part relevant to this bibliography is written by Matthews, covering basically the same period as our bibliography. The primary Roman provinces are considered separately, and the final chapter deals with the disorder and recovery resulting in Constantine's Christian empire, which itself fell apart about a hundred years later to the barbarians. The text is clear and to the point, featuring special sections useful to the study of the early church: Festivals of the State Religion, Oriental Cults, a chart of the Emperors (Augustus to Justinian), communications, everyday life, Constantinople, Ravenna, and others. Much more than an atlas.

⊰ Currier, *BAR* 9 (Sept-Oct 1983): 84.

2.4   Grant, Michael. *Ancient History Atlas: 1700 BC to AD 565*. 4th ed. Cartography by Arthur Banks. London: Weidenfeld and Nicolson, 1989. NI-7; M-87.

About 30 of the maps cover the period from the first century. Maps are in black and white, and many are over two-page spreads. Although the maps are quite simple, they are generally clear, and offer a wide range of information, from standard sorts of things, like boundaries and Germanic kingdoms to useful but rarer maps of

Roman roads, food supply and trading, homes of the Roman legions, the changing provincial borders under various emperors, places of origin of the Roman emperors, and the spread of Judaism and Christianity. This volume is packed with much useful information for the student of the early church.

2.5   Littell, F.H. *The Macmillan Atlas History of Christianity*. Cartography by Emanuel Hausman. Maps by Carta Ltd. New York: Macmillan/London: Collier Macmillan, 1976. Pp. 176. I-8; B&W-162; T-9; M-197.
Only the first 25 pages are relevant to the early church. Nonetheless, that includes 29 two-color maps, 18 black-and-white illustrations, a dozen striking quotations, and adequate text. Although one can gain a good overview of the expansion of the early church from the first few pages, most readers will find Chadwick's atlas [§2.2] more useful, both because of the extremely well designed maps and the selection of color illustrations in that work. But Littell's work does have one distinct advantage: it provides a map for almost every movement or event, much like its counterpart, *The Macmillan Bible Atlas*.
✄ Elliott, *CBQ* 39 (1977): 594; Thompson, *JES* 14 (1977): 320-323; Shurden, *R&E* 74 (1977): 244-245.

2.6   Talbert, Richard J.A., ed. *Atlas of Classical History*. London and Sydney: Croom Helm, 1985. Pp. vi + 217. B-11; M-135; G-28.
Written by 25 scholars, this work is filled with detailed black and white maps and brief commentary. The atlas ends with Constantine, and well over half deals with the period before the second century. Nonetheless, those sections that are relevant often provide information not likely to be found in an atlas of the early church, such as major road systems, centres of the imperial cult, Roman colonies, trade in the Roman Empire, and for Asia Minor, the tribal areas not attached to cities. A chart of Roman emperors is included, with the names of the dynasties.

2.7   Van der Meer, F., and Christine Mohrmann. *Atlas of the Early Christian World*. Translated and edited by Mary F. Hedlund and H.H. Rowley, London: Nelson, 1958. Pp. 204. M-42.
The grand daddy of all atlases for the early Christian Church and, as yet, trumped by none of the newcomers. The maps are beautiful multi-color productions that illustrate diverse subjects such as "The Earliest Churches"; "The Distribution of Christianity by A.D. 300"; "Churches Founded before the Persecution by Diocletian (304)";

and "Christian Writers." The altas also includes basic political maps for all major regions of the Mediterranean in substantial detail. The *Atlas* consists not just of these cartographic delights, but also a detailed iconographic record of the pictographic and architectural remains of the Christian church from the first to the sixth centuries. All plates are accompanied by detailed descriptions and represent a consistent visual commentary on the history of the Church in the first five or six centuries of its existence. Accompanied by a general geographical index. (S)

DICTIONARIES AND ENCYCLOPEDIAS

2.8   ☛ Aland, Kurt *Saints and Sinners. Men and Ideas in the Early Church.* Translated by W.C. Linss. Philadelphia: Fortress, 1970. Pp. vi + 250.
This is an introductory work, providing 48 brief biographical chapters on key characters (both "heroes" and "heretics") in the early church up to Justinian. While giving a bit more detail than most entries in encyclopedias, it is limited to only the key players. Nonetheless, from these chapters one can gain a sense of the important developments and issues of the growing church. Light, factual, brief, informative, and introductory.

2.9   Blaiklock, Edward M., and R.K. Harrison, eds. *The New International Dictionary of Biblical Archaeology.* Grand Rapids: Zondervan, 1983. Pp. xxvii + 515. C-28; M-23; B&W.
Although focused on the biblical materials, on occasion an article will deal with the period of the early church. Bibliographies are quite short, but sometimes helpful. The scope of the work is larger than the title suggests, and one can find articles on such topics as "Famine," "Marriage," etc. and on key personalities. It includes a 2-page list of archaeology journals in English, with brief comment on their content and usefulness.
✂ Callaway, *BAR* 11 (Nov-Dec 1985): 14; Drinkard, *R&E* 81 (1984): 496-497; Mare, *JETS* 28 (1985): 479-481; Merrill, *BA* 142 (1985): 274-275; Smith, *Currents* 12 (1985): 249; Willis, *RQ* 30 (1988): 257-258.

2.10 Bowder, Diana, ed. *Who Was Who in the Roman World. 753 BC-AD 476.* Oxford: Phaidon Press, 1980. Pp. 256. B-3; G-7; NI-4; B&W– 220; CT-3; FT-7; M-15.
Although this guide covers about a thousand years not related to the time span of our bibliography, most of the material is focused on the period from the first century to the fifth, presented in over 900 brief biographical entries. Thus the volume can serve as a

useful guide for students of the early church. It is extremely well illustrated, especially for busts (many from coins) of the various individuals mentioned. Most useful for the non-Christian Roman world, though the better known Christians are included too. A useful 7-page glossary is provided, dealing with numerous technical terms from the Roman world.

2.11 Briggs, Ward W., and William M. Calder, III. *Classical Scholarship: A Biographical Encyclopedia.* New York/London: Garland, 1990. Pp. xxiv + 534. I-6.
The early church cannot be studied without reference to its Graeco-Roman background. This volume opens up the realm of classical scholarship of the last two centuries (from Wolf to Momigliano), presenting some fifty "bio-bibliographical" entries on the primary scholars, with a discussion of their writings and their place in the developing scholarship. Of particular importance to students of the early church are Momigliano, Mommsen, Rostovtzeff, and others. The volume contains short but useful bibliographies, and a photo or painting of each scholar. The stated aim is to show "how the facts of [these scholars'] lives influenced the way they thought about the ancient world and thus how we think about the ancient world." This volume provides useful insights for understanding many of the debates about the ancient world.

2.12 Cross, F.L., and E.A. Livingstone. *The Oxford Dictionary of the Christian Church.* 2d ed. Oxford: Oxford UP, 1983. Pp. xxxi + 1520.
This is the standard one-volume dictionary on Christianity. Although the entries are often very brief, the bibliographies accompanying the entries are usually detailed, and sometimes even longer than the main text of the entry. For items relevant to the early church, the entries are often between a half to a full two-column page. A 4-page chronological list of popes and anti-popes is included.

2.13 Di Berardino, Angelo, ed. *Encyclopedia of the Early Church.* Translated by Adrian Walford. Foreword and bibliographic amendments by W.H.C. Frend. 2 volumes. Oxford: Oxford UP, 1992. Pp. xxv + 1130. I-34; M-44; C-57; B&W-267; CT-28.
This work covers the first eight centuries of the Christian church. It was originally published in Italian, but its bibliography has been updated, though numerous works cited are Italian, giving the bibliography a distinctive touch. This work is more comprehensive than the *Encyclopedia of Early Christianity* [§2.15], and its

bibliographies are usually more extensive (though geared to foreign-language works). There are, however, puzzling omissions, as, for example, in the variety of topics that could have been addressed in regard to church office. Articles are of similar length to those in the *Encyclopedia of Early Christianity*, but more topics are addressed here. Illustrations are grouped in the latter half of volume two, with reference to these illustrations in the articles. Ancient authors and writings are identified by their numbers in the *Clavis Patrum Latinorum* (CPL), and *Clavis Patrum Graecorum* (CPG). This will be the standard reference work, though the *Encyclopedia of Early Christianity* [§2.15] frequently has the better article and the more useful bibliography.

2.14   Douglas, J.D., ed. *The New International Dictionary of the Christian Church.* Grand Rapids: Zondervan, 1974. Pp. xii + 1074.
Written by a team of almost two hundred scholars, this volume generally will have a brief note on the more important topics of the early church, while people such as Augustine get a page and a half. The bibliographies are short. Students generally will find the volume by Cross and Livingstone [§2.12] the more adequate one-volume dictionary.
&< Porter, *EQ* 52 (1980): 47-48; Wright, *ATR* 58 (1976): 499-500.

2.15   Ferguson, Everett, ed. *Encyclopedia of Early Christianity.* New York/London: Garland, 1990. Pp. xx + 983. I-37; B&W-77; CT-2; M-2.
Almost 1000 entries from 135 scholars of the early Christian period up to 600 CE make this *the* one-volume encyclopedia for our period. The focus of each article is on the developments beyond the New Testament age, since numerous works already available focus on the first century. Each entry is accompanied by a brief bibliography. Ancient authors and their writings are identified by their numbers in the *Clavis Patrum Latinorum* (CPL), *Clavis Patrum Graecorum* (CPG), and *Thesaurus Linguae Graecae* (TLG). Although many entries have but a few lines, generally key people, themes, and terms have much longer entries, sometimes to several pages. The closest comparable work is the two-volume *Encyclopedia of the Early Church* [§2.13], which addresses a wider range of topics.
&< Bonner, *JEH* 43 (1991): 333; Eno, *CHR* 76 (1990): 819-820; Hinson, *R&E* 88 (1991): 464-465; Krentz, *BA* 55 (Mar 1992): 46-47; Malherbe, *RQ* 33 (1991): 106-108.

2.16   ☞ Ferguson, Everett. *Backgrounds of Early Christianity.* Grand

Rapids: Eerdmans, 1987. Pp. xvii + 515. SI-14; BI-2; NTI-4; B&W-101; CT-2.

One of the best organized collections of material reflecting the religious, political, cultural, and literary Mediterranean world in which Christianity took shape. Almost every imaginable aspect is covered, complete with brief bibliographies, and often with notes on recent scholarly discussion. It is divided into six major sections: Political History; Society and Culture; Hellenistic-Roman Religions; Hellenistic-Roman Philosophies; Judaism; and Christianity in the Ancient World. With well over 200 individual topics, this can easily be used as a "dictionary" to almost any subject related to the background of the early church. A table of currency is provided on p. 70.

✄ Brackett, *CH* 58 (1989): 367; Chesnut, *RQ* 31 (1989): 249-251; Finn, *CBQ* 51 (1989): 369-70; Kee, *BR* 5 (1989): 12-3; Shogren, *JETS* 32 (1989): 394-395; Turner, *CRBR* 1 (1989): 290-2.

2.17 ◉ Grant, Michael, and Ruth Kitzinger, eds. *Civilization of the Ancient Mediterranean: Greece and Rome.* 3 vols. New York: Charles Scribner's Sons, 1988. Vol. 1. Pp. xvii + 719. Vol. 2. Pp. xiv + 723-1297. Vol. 3. Pp. xiv + 1301-1980. I; M-11.

Ninety-seven lengthy articles by almost as many modern scholarly experts in their respective fields are at the heart of this massive survey of the state of our knowledge about the Greek and Roman world at the end of the 1980s. The contributions are grouped under headings such as history, population, technology, government and society, economics, religion, private and social life, women and family life, literary and performing arts, philosophy, and the visual arts. Each entry ends with good bibliographic guides to current research on the subject. The quality of the entries vary immensely, with some being rather mundane and uninspired regurgitations of existing received opinions on the subject, while others are almost indispensable guides and new research contributions in their own right. Especially useful are those chapters on subjects where materials are not otherwise available (e.g. book production, Greek and Roman Associations and Clubs), or those which summarize work recently done on new frontiers of the social history of the ancient Mediterranean (notable here are the chapters on women's history, family, and sexuality). Almost any of the chapter entries offers a convenient overview of the subject that is not readily available in any other single work of reference, making this a most useful work, especially if one wishes to direct undergraduate students to competent synopses of large research areas (e.g. the novel). This three-volume set is one of the best current guides to the life and history of the ancient Mediterranean. (S)

2.18   ☛ Grant, Michael. *The Roman Emperors. A Biographical Guide to the Rulers of Imperial Rome 31 BC–AD 476.* New York: Charles Scribner's Sons, 1985. Pp. xiii + 367. AAI-7; FT-7; GZ-15; M-11.
A chronological guide to the Roman emperors. Most of the emperors have one or two pages, sketching the main features of their rule. Major figures have more space dedicated to them (e.g. 7 pages for Constantine). For each emperor, an illustration of a coin or a bust (in black and white) is provided. With a 9-page "key to Latin Terms" and a 7-page index of Latin and Greek authors.

2.19   Grant, Michael. *A Guide to the Ancient World: A Dictionary of Classical Place Names.* New York: H.W. Wilson, 1986. Pp. xxi + 728. B-18; M-15.
Most standard dictionaries or encyclopedias of the early church will have entries on major sites, and even a number of entries on minor ones. Grant's work is worth consulting if nothing can be found in the usual sources, or if the entry there is too brief. Grant's entries run from a quarter page to over two full pages. Of use, too, is the bibliography, which more effectively serves as a mini biographical guide, listing ancient authors and anonymous documents, and providing in one line the place of birth, dates of birth and death, key occupation, and major writings of ancient authors referred to in the text.

2.20   Howatson. M.C., ed. *The Oxford Companion to Classical Literature.* 2d ed. Oxford: Oxford UP, 1989. Pp. ix + 627. CT-9; M-6.
This is a useful work for many students of the early church, in that it does not assume a knowledge of classical literature. Extensively revised from the original edition of fifty years ago, it addresses numerous topics beyond the strictly "literature" focus of the title, covering religious, political, social, and historical matters as well. In addition, it is well cross-referenced and all Latin and Greek terms are translated. But only the most major Christian figures (like Augustine and Jerome) are mentioned here.

2.21   Kelly, J.N.D. *The Oxford Dictionary of Popes.* Oxford: Oxford UP, 1986. Pp. xiv + 347. I-17
This volume provides condensed accounts for all popes and anti-popes of the church, giving (where available) information about each pope's family, social background, and pre-papal career, as

well as details about accomplishments in office. Since it is arranged chronologically, the student of the early church can gain a connected account of this office over the first five centuries by reading the first 50 pages. Each entry has a separate bibliography, with attention to primary sources.

✂ H. Chadwick, *Theology* 90 (1987): 320-321; O. Chadwick, *TLSuppl* 4336 (May 9 1986): 494; Rorem, *Currents* 14 (1987): 453.

2.22   Walker, William O., Jr. gen. ed. *Harper's Bible Pronunciation Guide*. San Francisco: Harper & Row, 1989. Pp. xiii + 170.

Although this book is directed towards students of the biblical materials, 45 pages cover non-biblical terms. Not all are relevant to the early church, but one can learn how to pronounce words like Cerinthus, Chenoboskion, Diatessaron, Didache, docetic, Docetism, Dura-Europos, Ebionite, Encratitic, Fruehkatholizismus, Gemara, geschichtlich, Hermeticum, Irenaeus, Manichaeism, Marcionite, Muratorian, Papias, Tacitus, Theodotion, Valentinus, and others. Given that most works assume (wrongly) that students (and professors) already know how to pronounce the range of foreign terms they encounter in the discipline, any help with pronunciation is to be appreciated.

✂ Brisco, *SWJT* 34 (1991): 72-73; Snyder, *CTSR* 80 (1990): 60; Phelps, *BA* 53 (1990): 176-177.

3
PATRISTIC TEXTS
AND MAJOR WRITERS

The word "patristic" comes from the Greek and Latin root for "father" (*patr-*), and it is used in English—with similar words in other languages—to identify those early writers who are called the church "Fathers," or leaders. The formal study of their writings is called "Patrology."

The student of early Christian literature will find that one of the major problems for the study of the patristic period is that many of the documents of the early church have yet to be translated into English, and that much of the work being done by patristic scholars is being carried out in languages other than English. In fact, we could say that *most* of the work has been carried out in other languages. Although that is changing, it is changing only slowly, and there likely never will be a time when the field will be dominated by English-speaking scholars.

One can see just how much work there is to be done in the field for the English-speaking community by noting how dated many of our translations of patristic texts are. Although there are a number of good and recent English translations of the Apostolic Fathers (a small number of writers from the late-first or early-second century), many of the other patristic writers are available to English readers only in translations that are over a hundred years old. Almost every library will have the thirty-eight volume set of the Ante-Nicene, Nicene, and Post-Nicene Fathers, and this, despite its age, remains the standard reference set in the field for English translations. There are more recent series, with more current critical notes, which are beginning to make their mark, but nothing yet is as extensive as the old standard.

The situation is not uniformly bleak, however. Some writings have attracted the attention of large numbers of scholars, and as a result of that interest, are available now in recent and readable English translations—often several different English translations for a particularly popular writing, just as there are many English translations of the New Testament. For example, several of the works of Augustine, in particular the *Confessions* and *The City of God,* are available in various English translations, as is

30

Eusebius' *Church History.* In some cases, however, there will be only one new translation, and very often none.

Of course, this less-than-desirable state of affairs does not carry over into editions in the original languages. Much work is being done in that field. A halfway point is the Greek-English and Latin-English Loeb Classical Library series, but this series is weak in that it deals with only a very few of the most popular writings of the church Fathers, and though some of these translations remain the standard reference, they are becoming dated. A new series, similar to the Loeb volumes but more extensive, is the Oxford Early Christian Texts, which will become the standard critical edition in English. A massive project in French is the *Sources chrétiennes* series. But this series is for the more serious or advanced scholar, with the necessary language tools, though students without Greek or Latin may find that the French translations can provide access to writings of the Fathers which are yet unavailable in English. Three other series are worthy of note (but all require ancient languages): *Corpus Scriptorum Ecclesiasticorum Latinorum; Griechischen Christlichen Schriftsteller,* and *Corpus Christianorum.* These will replace the old standards, *Patrologia Graeca* and *Patrologia Latina.*

If one wishes to get a better sense of the vast array of the literature available from the first few centuries of the church, simply scan Berkowitz and Squitier's *Canon of Greek Authors and Works,* in the Thesaurus Linguae Graecae project. There one finds entry after entry of works of Christian and non-Christian authors. This is only the *Greek* side of that massive project. There is a huge parallel Latin side too. Again, this is a tool for the scholar with ancient language facility, and it is possibly the most useful tool for the scholar of the early church because it is now available on compact disc (CD) for computers, enabling the researcher to do comprehensive word searches by typing only a few words. A surprisingly vast number of these ancient documents are not yet in English translation. In this bibliography, we have focused on works available in English, and that limitation shows most starkly when we consider the many writings of the Fathers not yet translated.

It is not possible in this section to do justice to all the individuals who made significant contributions to the thought and practice of early Christianity. From all areas of the empire even as early as the second century, numerous people had made their mark on the developing Christian church, leaving their name honored or detested, depending on whether the orthodox church judged them to be saints or heretics. On one side stand individuals such as Ignatius of Antioch, Polycarp of Smyrna, and Justin (associated with Samaria, Ephesus, and Rome), three of the better known among the scores of Christians martyred and remembered, along with numerous theologians and church leaders such as Melito of Sardis, Clement of Alexandria, Irenaeus of Asia Minor and later of Lyons. Against these stand a mixed company, judged by the orthodox to have done damage to the Christian cause by their theology or their practices. The various Gnostic leaders are placed here, with Valentinus of Alexandria high on the list, along with other innovative theologians such as Marcion of Pontus and Rome, and Montanus of Phrygia, and numerous lesser-knowns, named and censured, but without anything more known than a few polemical charges. In the middle stand more ambiguous characters, sometimes condemned and sometimes lauded, such as Origen of Alexandria and later of Palestine, Tertullian of North Africa, and Tatian, proudly denying that he belonged to the empire at all.

Such a list is only a start even for the second and early third centuries. And with each new century, the list of important individuals grows. Cyprian of North Africa, Eusebius of Caesarea, Augustine of Hippo, Jerome of Rome and Palestine, Chrysostom of Antioch and Constantinople, and the scores of names made famous or brought into ill repute by the various councils. At the end of this chapter, we have listed a very limited number of biographies; these are restricted to the *very* most important individuals for whom useful biographies exist.

Many of these biographies are not strictly *bio*graphies; they are biographies structured around theological ideas. This should not be surprising, since the majority of Christian leaders are remembered because of their theological contributions. One need think only of individuals such as Irenaeus, Tertullian, Clement of Alexandria, Origen, Valentinus, and Marcion, and later, Cyprian, Jerome, Basil, and Augustine. Often chapters in the biographies of these individuals serve as solid introductions to the theological disputes and developments in the early church.

The student will notice that the modern evaluation of an early Christian leader of note sometimes will differ from the opinion of that individual expressed by many of his or her contemporaries. In particular, the variety of Gnostics fare better in the modern period, largely because of the change that has taken place in the last half century regarding the definition of orthodoxy and heresy. Modern scholars recognize that the bad press the "heretics" received from their "orthodox" contemporaries often reflected more the general venom of polemics than accurate portrayals of life-styles and character. There is really nothing surprising in this; we all are familiar with the same thing in modern political debate: mud-slinging and slander. The historian must try to strip away the undeserved attacks by opponents of these individuals—as well as the undeserved praise by those who have blindly followed their heroes. But the fault does not always lie with the ancients. Sometimes modern historians cross the line of fair judgment to advocacy, praising the ancient "heretics" with unreserved imbalance that equals in every way the undeserved and unbalanced criticism that the "orthodox" had earlier heaped on these "heretics." A detailed discussion of the problem is provided in chapter 18, "Orthodoxy and Heresy."

Our choice of material to be discussed here is based on the better known works of the Fathers. This is but a small part of the full corpus of early Christian writings. Generally newer translations have been chosen, and usually we have chosen those with a good introduction and critical notes over those that have none. Two kinds of entries are provided below. The first section deals with reference books on the *writings* of the Fathers, covering the standard critical questions of date, authorship, locale, purpose, etc. This section will at least provide a sketch of the patristic literature, even though some of the writings mentioned will not be available to the student limited to English translation. The second section deals mainly with English translations of the writings of church Fathers and with biographies. Some summary articles on research on a particular early Christian writer have been included here as well.

GENERAL INTRODUCTIONS

3.1 Altaner, Berthold. *Patrology.* 2d ed. Translated by Hilda C. Graef. Edited by Alfred Stuiber. New York: Herder and Herder, 1961. Based on the fifth German edition of *Patrologie.* Pp. xxiv + 660. I-14.

As with any work that attempts to cover this vast period, each church Father is addressed only briefly, though the major authors have more extensive coverage (e.g., 5 pages on Ignatius; 9 on Irenaeus; 14 on Jerome; 47 on Augustine). A huge 33-page bibliography offers some brief notes regarding literature on over 28 themes. The remainder of the book deals with particular documents or people (over one hundred sections), and a short bibliography for each is given. The main bibliography, though dated, is still useful, especially as a supplement to Quasten, since Altaner covers the 1950s.

< Hughes, *Churchman* 74 (1960): 123; Metzger, *PSB* 55 (1962): 66.

3.2 ☛ Campenhausen, Hans von. *The Fathers of the Greek Church.* Translated by L.A. Garrard. London: Adam & Charles Black, 1963. Pp. vii + 190. NI-2; B-9; CT-2.

A clear introduction to twelve major Greek Fathers: Justin, Irenaeus, Clement of Alexandria, Origen, Eusebius, Athanasius, Basil the Great, Gregory of Nazianzus, Gregory of Nyssa, Synesius of Cyrene, Chrysostom, and Cyril of Alexandria. The author is mainly interested in providing an account of leading personalities, with a particular emphasis on their theological contributions. A brief 4-page introduction discusses the nature of the field of "patristics" or "patrology," and a 6-page conclusion deals with the end of the age of the Fathers, which Campenhausen connects in some way to the increasing standardization of church dogma in the Constantinian and post-Constantinian period.

ᴈ< Baepler, *CH* 29 (1960): 210-211.

3.3   ☞ Campenhausen, Hans von. *The Fathers of the Early Church.* Translated by Manfred Hoffman. London: Adam and Charles Black, 1964. Pp. vii + 328. NI-3; AB-9; CT-2.

This volume is a collection of biographical sketches of seven of the early Latin Fathers of the church. Although no notes are included, Campenhausen offers a solid introduction to Tertullian, Cyprian, Lactantius, Ambrose, Jerome, Augustine, and Boethius. Each chapter is roughly thirty pages long, though Jerome gets over fifty and Augustine almost one hundred pages.

ᴈ< Evans, *TT* 23 (1967): 578-580; Wilken, *CH* 34 (1965): 457-458.

3.4   ☞ Cross, F.L. *The Early Christian Fathers.* London: Duckworth, 1960. Pp. 218. B-7; CT-2; AAI-5; MAI-4.

A brief informed overview of the patristic writers, from the Apostolic Fathers to Hippolytus (though some later authors are mentioned), with a concluding chapter on hymns, the Acts of the martyrs, and inscriptions. The chapter divisions are largely geographical. Each document or major movement is briefly summarized, and notes on the manuscripts and brief discussions of the scholarly debate are sometimes included. This is a useful guide if one is interested particularly in brief summaries of the main literature of the patristic period.

3.5   ☞ Goodspeed, Edgar J. *A History of Early Christian Literature.* Revised and expanded by Robert M. Grant. Chicago: University of Chicago Press, 1966. Pp. ix + 214. AAI-2; MAI-1; B-8.

Although first published in 1942, and last revised in 1966, this remains a sound introduction to the literature of the early church. Of particular interest is a list of 179 ancient Christian writings known to have existed, but for which we have either no text or no complete text in the original. Grant updates the bibliography in the revised edition, and adds a chapter on libraries and book collections of ancient Christians, and on Eusebius' use of such material. Grant contrasts Eusebius' use of these materials in the *Ecclesiastical History* and the *Preparation of the Gospel.*

ᴈ< Shepherd, *CH* 36 (1967): 64.

3.6 ☞ Grant, Robert M. *The Apostolic Fathers: A New Translation and Commentary*. Volume 1: *An Introduction*. New York: Thomas Nelson & Sons, 1964. Pp. xi + 193. B-3.
This is the introductory volume of the 6-volume work on the Apostolic Fathers, which consists of translations and commentaries by various scholars [§3.27]. In volume one, Grant discusses the general questions of background, such as the use of the Bible, historical circumstances, the theology of the Apostolic Fathers and the nature of the church reflected in these writings. The Fathers are considered, for the most part, individually for each of these issues.
★ Hardy, *CH* 34 (1965): 97; Hinson, *R&E* 62 (1965): 105-106; Jones, *ATR* 49 (1967): 222-225; Malherbe, *JBL* 85 (1966): 266.

3.7 Quasten, Johannes. *Patrology*. 4 vols. Utrecht: Spectrum, 1950. Reprint. Westminster, MD: Christian Classics, 1983. Volume I: *The Beginnings of Patristic Literature*. Pp. 349. I-16; MAI-13; BI-1; PI-4; Greek Words Index-1. Volume II: *The Ante Nicene Literature After Irenaeus*. Pp. 450. I-13; MAI-14; BI-2; PI-6; Greek Words Index-1. Volume III: *The Golden Age of Greek Patristic Literature From the Council of Nicaea to the Council of Chalcedon*. Pp. 605. I-24; MAI-18; BI-2; PI-8; Greek Words Index-3. Volume IV: *The Golden Age of Latin Patristic Literature From the Council of Nicea to the Council of Chalcedon*. Pp. xxviii + 667.
The standard reference work on the Fathers up to the Council of Chalcedon. Especially useful for the extensive bibliographies, though the earlier volumes are beginning to become dated. The discussion of most of the literature is brief (e.g. 14 pages on Ignatius; 7 on Barnabas), but an attempt is made to touch on major points like biography, theology, authenticity, date, and textual matters. More extensive treatment is given to some church leaders: Origen (75 pp.); Hippolytus (46 pp.); Tertullian (95 pp.); Cyprian (43 pp.); Athanasius (60 pp.); Basil (32 pp.); Gregory of Nyssa (42 pp.); Eusebius (35 pp.); and Chrysostom (59 pp.). Indexes are extensive and useful.
★ R.M. Grant, *ATR* 43 (1961): 438; Hardy, *CH* 30 (1961): 233-234; Patrick, *JR* 41 (1961): 308.

3.8 ☞ Ramsey, Boniface. "A Patristic Reading Program." In *Beginning to Read the Fathers*. New York/Mahwah: Paulist, 1985. Pp. 229-237.
For the beginner, Ramsey provides a brief but extremely helpful guide to the literature of the patristic period. Each document is dealt with in one short paragraph, giving author, location, date, situation, and the reasons for its importance. Ramsey even tells the

beginner where the various English translations can be found. In fact, the whole book [§3.9] is skillfully designed as a clear introductory guide to the patristic period.

3.9 ☛ Ramsey, Boniface. *Beginning to Read the Fathers.* New York/Mahwah: Paulist, 1985. Pp. iii + 280. B-9; PI-3; CT-8.
Intended as a non-technical and sympathetic introduction to the patristic literature prior to the Council of Chalcedon, the work is divided, after a general introduction, into eleven themes. These are: Scripture; God; Human Condition; Christ; Church and Ministry; Martyrdom and Virginity; Monasticism; Prayer; Poverty and Wealth; Christian in the World; and Death and Resurrection. An 8-page "Patristic Reading Program" lists 41 patristic works (see description above [§3.8].
✀ Lienhard, *TS* 47 (1986): 319-320; Norris, *Themelios* 13.1 (1987): 30; TeSelle, *CH* 55 (1986): 507-508; Wright, *SJT* 41 (1988): 427-428.

PATRISTIC TEXTS IN ENGLISH: SERIES
3.10 🏛 Ancient Christian Writers Series.
This series, though not as complete as the *Ante-Nicene and Nicene Fathers* series described below [§3.11], will be more useful. The type is much larger and clearer; the translations are fresher. With clear and detailed introductions, very extensive critical notes, fairly detailed indexes, and an occasional bibliography. Published by Paulist Press, (New York and Mahwah), the series now has over fifty volumes, with the first volume published in 1945 under the editorial direction of Johannes Quasten and J.C. Plumpe. These volumes are much smaller than the packed volumes of the *Ante-Nicene* series, and usually are dedicated to one author or to one major work of an author. Compares to the *Fathers of the Church* series below [§3.12]

3.11 🏛 The Ante-Nicene Fathers (10 volumes); The Nicene and Post-Nicene Fathers (in two parts of 14 volumes each).
This is really one set, with each of the three sections distinguished from the others by a band of color on the spine. This series introduced the English world to the vast wealth of the writings of the patristic authors, and the series has been reprinted (though it is a century old) and appears now in most libraries. The main problem is that some of the English translations are dated, and the work cannot be used for serious scholarly study without at least reference to a critical edition. Yet, many of the excursus are still of use, sometimes dealing with subjects that have been forgotten by the paths that

scholarship has taken. The indexes are extensive and offer quick access to most topics; the tables of contents are detailed, and provide almost a summary of the text itself. These features help to keep the series useful.

3.12 🏛 The Fathers of the Church.
More and more, this is becoming the series to turn to for English translations of the writings of the Fathers. Fast approaching 100 volumes, the translations are fresh, and the introductions brief but useful. The length of the notes vary, but they provide adequate information about textual problems, parallels found in other literature of the time (both Christian and non-Christian), and general information about characters and places in the text. The modern debates are generally not addressed, however. Adequate indexes are provided. Published by The Catholic University of America Press, Washington, DC.

3.13 🏛 Library of Christian Classics.
This series was started in 1953, and will be found in many libraries. The documents have brief critical introductions, with bibliographic information (now somewhat dated). The critical notes are sometimes quite extensive, though the indexes tend to be more brief than those in similar series. Only the first eight volumes are relevant to the early church; three of these volumes are dedicated to the writings of Augustine; the other five to a few of the other major writers. Published by SCM (London). The Ancient Christian Writers series [§3.10] generally will be of more use to the student than this series.

3.14 ☞ 🏛 Message of the Fathers of the Church.
This series, now published by The Liturgical Press, offers a selection of the important passages from the ancient authors on a variety of themes. Each volume has a general introduction, with introductory and explanatory notes for the individual passages. Primarily useful for an introduction and overview of a range of opinion in the early church, this series can be compared to the "Sources of Early Christian Thought" series [§3.17]. The primary difference is that the latter uses new translations; this series uses translations already available (some of which are quite old). Both series provide useful introductory collections of the primary materials, and both are reasonably priced.

3.15 🏛 Loeb Classical Library.
The standard series offering Greek or Latin text, along with English translation. The notes and introductions, however, are brief. The

indexes are useful and generally adequate, though the indexes in the Ante-Nicene Fathers and the Nicene Fathers series are better for detail. One disadvantage to the Loeb series is that only a few of the Christian authors are included in this vast series on ancient Greek and Latin texts. The expensive "Oxford Early Christian Texts" [§3.16] series offers the most up-to-date technical editions in English of the patristic writers, though more libraries will have the less expensive Loeb editions and almost all libraries will have the "Ante-Nicene and the Nicene series" [§3.11].

3.16   🏛 Oxford Early Christian Texts.
This is the series to consult for the latest translations and most extensive critical notes. Introductions are detailed, providing information on the major critical problems of date, authorship, manuscripts, content, editions, and translations. Various indexes are included. Like the Loeb editions [§3.15], the Greek or Latin text is provided on the left page, with the English translation on the right. But the notes are considerably more extensive that the Loeb series, and the number of authors included in the continuing series is more extensive than the Loeb series, which does not focus on Christian authors.

3.17   ☞ 🏛 Sources of Early Christian Thought.
A Fortress Press project, edited by William G. Rusch. The series consists of short new English translations of early Christian texts. Volumes are arranged around a particular topic, with the varying points of view presented, thus one can gain a sense of the range of opinions on an issue in the early church. One should note that the volumes do not provide a comprehensive collection of ancient texts on the topic. General introductions averaging about 25 pages provide a clear overview for the average reader, and introduce the passages. The translations are not provided with critical notes, and there is no index, though a 1-2 page bibliography is supplied. These books are useful guides to a survey of the opinion of the early church on a variety of issues. Some of these volumes are listed in more detail elsewhere in our bibliography.

PATRISTIC TEXTS IN ENGLISH: GENERAL
3.18   🏛 Arnold, Eberhard. *The Early Christians: A Sourcebook on the Witness of the Early Church.* Translated and edited by the Society of Brothers at Rifton, NY. Rifton, NY: Plough Publishing House, 1972. Reprint. Grand Rapids: Baker, 1979. Pp. xii + 469. B-15; SI-19; Names and Writings Index-20.

This collection of primary sources is distinctive in that it deals more with Christian life and ethics than with the theological disputes and councils. Further, the aspect of Christian life most clearly of interest to Arnold is that of resistance to the secular powers, and the Christians' separation from the world around them by their radical lifestyle, as is clear from the 55-page introduction. Chapters deal with the state, society, and martyrdom; conduct and practice; the role of Jesus in the early church; meetings and worship; and preaching and prophecy—each with notes. A good collection (though not particularly a balanced one), illustrating how an Anabaptist perspective might develop from reflection on early Christian life.

3.19 🏛 Bettenson, Henry, ed. and trans. *The Early Christian Fathers. A Selection from the Writings of the Fathers From St. Clement of Rome to St. Athanasius.* London: Oxford UP, 1969. Pp. vii + 310. I-6.

A 27-page introduction provides roughly two or three pages on each major author or movement included in the collection. Each selection is arranged by theme within separate chapters for individual authors (Clement of Rome, Ignatius, the *Didache*, the Epistle to Diognetus, Justin Martyr, Irenaeus, Tertullian, Clement of Alexandria, Origen, Cyprian, and Athanasius). Though notes are kept to a minimum, they are well chosen. An appendix gives Latin titles with the common English title by which these works are often better known.

3.20 🏛 Bettenson, Henry, ed. and trans. *The Later Christian Fathers. A Selection from the Writings of the Fathers From St. Cyril of Jerusalem to St. Leo the Great.* London: Oxford UP, 1970. Pp. vii + 294. I-4.

Following the structure of the his earlier collection [§3.19], this volume includes selections from the following authors: Cyril of Jerusalem, Hilary of Poitiers, Basil of Caesarea, Gregory of Nazianzus, Gregory of Nyssa, Theodore of Mopsuestia, John Chrysostom, Ambrose, Jerome, Augustine, Cyril of Alexandria, and Theodoret of Cyrrus. A 33-page introduction provides mini-biographies of these authors, and an appendix gives English and Latin titles of the works represented in this collection.

3.21 🏛 Grant, Robert M. *Second-Century Christianity. A Collection of Fragments.* Translations of Christian Literature 6. London: SPCK, 1957. Pp. 143; B-2.

A collection of second-century fragments, with a brief introduction to each writer, and a relevant comment from Eusebius (when available). If the writer is regarded as a heretic, comments from Pseudo-Tertullian are included (pp. 123-141). After the introduction, three chapters are divided geographically: Egyptian Christianity, Syrian Christianity, and Asiatic Christianity. Then follow chapters on Marcionites and Anti-Marcionites, Montanists and Anti-Montanists, and Romans and their "friends" (that is, people associated with Rome).

3.22 🏛 Placher, William C. *Readings in the History of Christian Theology. Volume 1. From Its Beginnings to the Eve of the Reformation.* Philadelphia: Westminster, 1988. Pp. 204. B-5; I-2.
Most of this volume consists of sources from the period of our bibliography. Each chapter has roughly a one-page introduction, and each source a brief paragraph description. The relevant chapters deal with Gnosticism, the Apologists, the School of Alexandria, and Tertullian; the Trinitarian and Christological controversies; eastern theology after Chalcedon; and Augustine. A few selections from the chapter on the Early Middle Ages are relevant. Many of the translations are from the old "Nicene and Post-Nicene Fathers" series. A good introductory sourcebook.

3.23 🏛 Stevenson, J., ed. *A New Eusebius: Documents illustrating the history of the Church to AD 337.* Revised by W.H.C. Frend. London: SPCK, 1987. Pp. xxii + 404. I-10; B-2; CT-7; G-11.
A collection of 307 important documents and excerpts from the beginning of the church to the death of Constantine. This is the standard one-volume collection of sources, and its usefulness has been recognized since it was first issued in 1957. Frend improves the organization, making it more chronological. Brief notes introduce each selection. The bibliography is very limited—the emphasis is on the *primary* sources.

3.24 🏛 Stevenson, J., ed. *Creeds, Councils and Controversies: Documents illustrating the history of the Church AD 337-461.* Revised with additional documents by W.H.C. Frend, London: SPCK, 1989. Pp. xxii + 410. B-2; CT-8; I-7; Notes on Sources-9.
This volume is a collection of 264 carefully selected documents. These demonstrate the extreme complexity of the post-Constantine early Christian experience. Virtually every major topic important to the church history of the time is covered by the documents. Hence it becomes impossible to list them, even under broad headings. Since neither Stevenson nor Frend have attempted to comment on them, but leave them to speak for themselves, they serve as useful

data for the student who is attempting to form an independent analysis of the range of options during a very complex period in the formation of the Christian tradition. Brief explanatory introductions are sometimes provided. (P)

THE APOCRYPHA

3.25 🏛 Hennecke, Edgar. *New Testament Apocrypha.* Translated and edited by R. McL. Wilson. Philadelphia: Westminster Press, 1963. Volume I: *Gospels and Related Writing.* Pp. 531. Volume II: *Writings Related to the Apostles; Apocalypses and Related Subjects.* Pp. 852. BI-5; SI-36. [A new 1992 edition has recently appeared; the publication data above is to the 1963 edition.]

The Christian movement produced numerous and various kinds of literature from its beginning. The second century was a particularly rich period, with many of the works being attributed to heroes from the Old Testament or from the apostolic period. These writings are often referred to as the "New Testament Apocrypha." The two volumes cover this literature (and some others), providing solid introductions to the critical issues for each document, along with translations, and brief textual notes. This is an important collection for any student who wishes to gain a sense of issues and perspectives of the broad Christian community, both from its centre and from the periphery, including some of the Gnostic material.

✂ Daniels, *JBL* 85 (1966): 524-525; Hull, *R&E* 65 (1968): 374-375; Turner, *ExT* 77 (1966): 333-334; reviews of the German edition: Fitzmyer, *TS* 26 (1965): 116-118; Nock, *JTS* 11 (1960): 63-70; Stead, *JTS* 16 (1965): 171-175; Winter, *PEQ* 92 (1960): 79-81.

THE APOSTOLIC FATHERS

3.26 🏛 *The Apostolic Fathers.* Translated by J.B. Lightfoot and J.R. Harmer. 2d ed. Edited by Michael W. Holmes. Grand Rapids: Baker Book House, 1989. Pp. xvi + 347. SAI-8; BI-6; PI-3; M-2.

This revised volume will probably become the standard text of the Apostolic Fathers in English. The original translation was done primarily by the renowned patristic scholar, J.B. Lightfoot, and the fresh revision of the translation shows respect for Lightfoot's stature. Holmes provides a 27-page general introduction and on average a three or four page introduction for each document. The notes are up-to-date. All the documents generally grouped as of the "Apostolic Fathers" are included, along with 26 fragments of Papias and 5 fragments called "Traditions of the Elders." These fragments are missing from Kirsopp Lake's Loeb edition of the Apostolic Fathers.

3.27   🏛 Grant, Robert M. *The Apostolic Fathers: A New Translation and Commentary.* 6 volumes. New York: Thomas Nelson & Sons, 1964. Translations and commentaries by the following scholars: 1 and 2 Clement (Grant); Didache and Barnabas (Kraft); Ignatius (Grant); Polycarp to the Philippians, Martyrdom of Polycarp, and Fragments of Papias (Schoedel); and Hermas (Snyder). (Note: some of these translators replaced ones originally named in the preface of volume 1.) This set remains useful both for its translations and its detailed notes and introductory material.
✂ Betz, *JBL* 83 (1964): 433-436.

3.28   🏛 Lightfoot, Joseph Barber. *The Apostolic Fathers.* 5 vols. 2d ed. London: Macmillan, 1889-90. 5 vols. Reprint. Grand Rapids: Baker, 1981. Vol. 1: Pp. xii + 496. I-20; B&W-50. Vol. 2: Pp. vii + 532. I-15; BI-3; T-4. Vol. 3: Pp. xxii + 767. I-37; M-1. Vol. 4: Pp. vi + 619. I-19. Vol. 5: Pp. vii + 526. I-11; BI-7.
A massive work on 1 Clement, the letters of Ignatius, and the Martyrdom of Polycarp by the leading nineteenth-century authority on the subject, it remains a standard reference. Lightfoot addressed almost every conceivable question, from biographical detail, to historical context, to manuscript authenticity. The Greek text is provided, along with Lightfoot's own translation and extensive notes. Where manuscripts exist in other languages, the original is given for these too. Includes monograph length chapters on episcopal succession in Rome; Hippolytus; the Acts of Martyrdom; and the Empire under Hadrian, Pius, and Marcus.

AUGUSTINE:
3.29   ⑤ "Bulletin augustinien." In *Revue des Études Augustiniennes.*
An annual bibliography of works on Augustine. Many of the entries are annotated, and all annotations and headings are in French, though the English reader will have no difficulty in using this as a comprehensive bibliographical guide. Most of the entries are to French and German works, but the works in English on Augustine with be listed here too. The bibliography in the 1989 issues runs to over one hundred pages. The serious student of Augustine should be acquainted with the journal too. The *Revue des Etudes Augustiniennes,* in which this bibliography appears, is published quarterly, concentrating on the life and theology of St. Augustine.

3.30   ⑤ Mayer, Cornelius, ed. *Augustinus-Lexikon.* 3 sections in 2 vols. Basel/Stuttgart: Schwabe, 1986-1988. Pp. li + 480.
A massive encyclopedia on all aspects of Augustine's life, work,

writings, and associates, begun in 1976, with volume 1 published ten years later. The work consists of approximately 1200 articles, in German, French, or English, listed in alphabetical order by Latin subject title. Volume 1 contains a useful overview of the history of the collection and of the publication of Augustine's works since the fifth century, along with a 16-page chart of Augustine's writings. Useful bibliographies.

✄ H. Chadwick, *JEH* 40 (1989): 451; Foster, *Downside Review* 107 (1989): 69-71;

3.31   🏛 *The Confessions*. Translated with introduction and notes by Henry Chadwick. Oxford: Oxford UP, 1991. Pp. xxvix + 311. I-5; B-1.
Chadwick offers an 18-page introduction, with generally brief notes. This work is more than Augustine's spiritual autobiography, though it does trace Augustine's early life through childhood and student days, into Manicheanism and Neoplatonism, hounded by mother, sex, and an adequate sense of guilt. At mid-point in the *Confessions,* we learn of Augustine's conversion, the death of his mother, and his reflections on a number of issues related to his past and to the church of which he has become an important part. Chadwick discusses why the *Confessions* might have been written—thirteen years or more after Augustine's conversion and now in his mid-forties, during the last years of the 300s.
✄ Bonner, *JEH* 43 (1992): 459-462.

3.32   Brown, Peter. *Augustine of Hippo, A Biography*. Berkeley / Los Angeles: University of California Press, 1967. Pp. 463. I-11; B-18; CT-15.
When this work first appeared on booksellers' shelves in 1967 it was instantly recognized as a work of genius. And so it remains. No brief excerption of contents can do justice to the subtlety of its interpretation, or its impact on subsequent scholarship. Suffice it to say that Peter Brown managed to interweave, in an effortless and exciting fashion, the often disparate strands of social history, cultural background, belief and conceptions of self, political history, and theological perspectives (often massively contradictory) and to combine them evocatively into a wholly re-lived life. In the first part of the book, Brown lays the foundations of Augustine's life. He provides a wonderful evocation of late antique North Africa, and the circle of family and friends that formed the secular background to Augustine's first belief, his Manichaeism. In the second part, the reader is moved along, following the public career of a successful young rhetor, through conversion, to his return to

Africa and his confessional reflection on his own life. The third part concentrates on the mature Augustine: the bishop of Hippo Regius, and his theology and ecclesiology. Finally, Brown catches the "late" Augustine and his enmeshing with an empire in profound change, all set in the context of a shift from the City of Man to the City of God. No brief recapitulation of contexts, however, can alert the potential reader to the fluid mastery of both the subject and the times—a work in which the modern author is so well attuned to, and indeed, equal to, his ancient precursor. A peerless achievement that is likely to stand alone in that rank for a long time to come. (S)

✂ Bonner, *JEH* 20 (1969): 120-121; Cameron, *NYRB* 11.2 (1968): 28-31; Fortin, *TS* 29 (1968): 328-331; Frend, *JTS* 19 (1968): 654-656.

3.33   ☛ Chadwick, Henry. *Augustine.* Mast Masters Series. Oxford/New York: Oxford UP, 1986. Pp. vi + 122. B-1; I-2; AB-12.

Part of a series designed to introduce important thinkers to the general reader, the volume on Augustine fits well that purpose. The author is a leading modern church historian, and writes with sympathy about the leading theologian of early Christianity. Far more than a biography, Chadwick clarifies Augustine's theology, making sense of it in terms of Augustine's experiences and in terms of the issues in the society in which he lived. A fine place to start, or to review the career and thought of Augustine.

✂ Allard, *Speculum* 62 (1987); 1020-1021; Babcock, *CH* 56 (1987): 108-109; Berthold, *Thomist* 52 (1988): 347-350; Bonner, *JEH* 38 (1987): 627-628; Louth, *Theology* 90 (1987): 70-71; Marceau, *TS* 48 (1987): 587-588; Miles, *ATR* 69 (1987): 91-93; Swift, *CHR* 74 (1988): 343; Wright, *SJT* 41 (1988): 290-291.

3.34   Evans, Gillian. R. *Augustine on Evil.* Cambridge: Cambridge UP, 1983. Pp. xiv + 198. B-5; I-4.

The problem of evil is a central one in Augustine's thought. Evans traces the coherent development of Augustine's views on this subject, and shows how both Manichaeism and Pelagianism helped to focus Augustine's thinking. Markus, in the review mentioned below, thinks that Evans does not give enough attention to the dark side of evil that remained a part of Augustine's thought.

✂ Babcock, *SC* 5 (1985-1986): 52-54; Bonner, *JEH* 35 (1984): 296; Marceau, *TS* 45 (1984): 207-208; Markus, *JTS* 34 (1983): 643-645; Penaskovic, *JAAR* 53 (1985): 146-148; Russell, *CH* 53 (1984): 234; Stead, *ExT* 94 (1983): 376; Williams, *RS* 21 (1985): 95-97; Wright, *SJT* 37 (1984): 407-408;

3.35   ◉ Lawless, George. "On Understanding Augustine of Hippo." *Downside Review* 100 (1982): 31-46.

Lawless provides an introduction to Augustine's thought, largely by attention to the primary sources, with brief reference to some of the works of modern scholars. Lawless dismisses those who see significant Neoplatonic influences in Augustine's thought, and he challenges those who argue that Augustine was a "Crypto-Manichaean" long after leaving this sect. Numerous other issues are briefly touched on. A useful introduction to the thought of Augustine from one scholar's perspective, though it does not engage all recent writing on Augustine.

3.36   Meer, Frederic van der. *Augustine the Bishop: the Life and Work of a Father of the Church*. Translated by B. Battershaw and G.R. Lamb. London: Sheed and Ward, 1961. Pp. xxiii + 679. I-19
Originally published in Dutch in 1949 and then revised in a large-scale French translation in 1959, this grand view of Augustine as bishop was, before the appearance of Peter Brown's biography [§3.32], the finest introduction to the man and the social history of the period. The utility of Van der Meer's work for historians of the period is that it concentrates on the social networks, behaviors and values of north African society of the period and has commensurately less to say about Augustine's theological or ecclesiastical views. In his study of the church in the region of Hippo Regius (Augustine's diocese), the author systematically considers the local economy, the "pagan" background, and the day-to-day pastoral work of the bishop. The remainder of the work is an intensive investigation and wonderful documentation of the actual liturgical practices of the bishop (his involvement in conversion, in preaching, in teaching) and the countervailing world of popular piety (the cult of the martyrs, festivals of the dead, beliefs in magic and miracles). Far from being simply the study of one bishop and his parishioners' lives, this work is one of the finer social histories of a given social and cultural milieu of the world of Late Antiquity. (S)
✂ Beck, *AHR* 68 (1962-63): 92-93; H. Chadwick, *JTS* 13 (1962): 514; O'Connell, *TS* 23 (1962): 475-479; Willis, *JEH* 14 (1963): 86.

3.37   ☛ Smith, Warren Thomas. *Augustine: His Life and Thought*. Atlanta: John Knox Press, 1980. Pp. xiv + 190. I-2; B-4; M-1.
A basic introduction to Augustine. The first third provides a background for his conversion; the remainder is a mixture of insights into Augustine as writer and church leader. As with any brief work with this wide scope of topics, nothing is covered in detail. The *Confessions* merit 4 pages; the Pelagian controversy 8 pages; the *City of God* a chapter (14 pages). Nonetheless, a good starting

point for a study of Augustine.
ᔆ< Rorem, *PSB* 3 (1982): 334-335; Smits, *W&W* 2 (1982): 192-194.

BASIL THE GREAT
3.38   🏛 Barrois, Georges, ed. and trans. *The Father Speak. St. Basil the Great, St. Gregory of Nazianzus, St. Gregory of Nyssa.* Crestwood, NY: St. Vladimir's Seminary, 1986. Pp. 225. AAI-3; M-1.
A fresh translation of 153 passages largely from the letters of these friends and leading churchmen. The volume is particularly well designed. Introductory and explanatory notes are adequate for the beginner, and each letter is clearly titled and dated, where that is possible. The selections are divided among eleven topical chapters, dealing with the following: solitude in Pontus; biographicals; quest for wisdom; monastic ideal; glimpses of daily life; and ailments and deaths. In the middle are five chapters dealing with various aspects of the ordained clergy, from their calling, their duties, the Arian controversy, and some of the clerical frustrations. This collection provides a delightful and insightful glimpse of the more personal side of some early Christian churchmen.

3.39   Fedwick, Paul Jonathon, ed. *Basil of Caesarea: Christian, Humanist, Ascetic. A Sixteen-Hundredth Anniversary Symposium.* 2 vols. Toronto: Pontifical Institute of Medieval Studies, 1981. Pp. xliv + 716. B-74; I-36; AAI-10; BI-3; Basil Index-13; Manuscript Index-7; Greek Index-2.
This is a collection of eighteen papers presented at a symposium in Toronto in 1979, covering the range of topics in contemporary scholarship on Basil. Eleven of the articles are in English: chronological questions (Fedwick); manuscripts and editions (Rudberg): Κατα Ευνομιου (Anastos); Neoplatonism (Rist); the rhetorical tradition (Kustas); exegetical basis for Basil's doctrine of the Holy Spirit (Pelikan); social activity (Karayannopoulos); letters of recommendation (Treucker); translations of Basil's works before 1400 (Fedwick); early medieval Latin canonical collections (Reynolds); and iconography (Fitzgerald). A solid overview of the issues, with a massive bibliography.
ᔆ< Louth, *JTS* 34 (1983): 635-636.

CLEMENT OF ALEXANDRIA
3.40   ◉ Osborn, Eric. "Clement of Alexandria: A Review of Research, 1958-1982." *Second Century* 3 (1983): 219-244.
Osborn breaks his review in several thematic categories: Text; Literary Problems; Clement and the New Testament; Style and the

Man; Pious Forgery (about the Secret Gospel of Mark); Historical Setting (cultural and philosophical background); Development of Doctrine; General Problems; Problems of Ethics; Problems of Theology; Problems of Philosophy. Osborn focuses largely on one key book for each area. This issue of *The Second Century* includes two other articles on Clement: Halton, "Clement's Lyre: A Broken String, a New Song" (pp. 177-199); and Davison, "Structural Similarities and Dissimilarities in the Thought of Clement of Alexandria and the Valentinians" (pp. 201-217).

CYPRIAN

3.41 ⊕ "Chronica Tertullianea et Cyprianea." *Revue des Études Augustiniennes.*

An annual bibliographical review, since 1976, of books and articles on Tertullian and Cyprian. All entries are annotated (in French), and sometimes the annotation is extensive. Headings are in French. Nonetheless, a useful and up-to-date guide, especially since some of the titles are broader, and could be passed over by a student merely scanning the titles of articles and books, looking for the names of Tertullian or Cyprian. In the 1989 issue, 62 entries are cited.

3.42 Sage, Michael M. *Cyprian.* Patristic Monograph Series 1. Cambridge, MA: Philadelphia Patristic Foundation, 1975. Pp. vi + 439. I-9; B-21.

Derived from a doctoral dissertation written under T.D. Barnes at the University of Toronto, this monograph shows all the signs of the incisiveness and attention to detail characteristic of his teacher. It remains, more than a decade an a half after its publication, the best modern-day introduction to Cyprian in English (Benson being entirely outmoded, and Hinchliff somewhat jejune). Sage begins by placing Cyprian in his mid-third century African social context, and in the moral and literary tradition that was dominated by Minucius Felix and Tertullian. He then traces Cyprian's career from professional rhetor to that of bishop, and his rôle in the Decian persecution. Not only does Sage analyze the principal theological disputes of Cyprian's episcopate (the "rebaptism" controversy, the place of martyrdom), but he offers, in appendixes to the main text, a series of thorough and telling analyses of cruces in the texts themselves (especially problems with the dating of the letters and of the treatises). In sum, Sage's book should be more readily available than it is, since it is the best comprehensive overview of one of the most important Christian leaders of the third-century in the West.

In some details, however, his work should be supplemented by the valuable commentaries on the letters of Cyprian by Graeme Clarke in the Ancient Christian Writers series [§3.10]. (S)

✂< Clarke, *Phoenix* 31 (1977): 82-86; Fahey, *TS* 38 (1977): 171-172; Frend, *Latomus* 37 (1978): 213-214; Hardy, *CH* 46 (1977): 101-102; Markus, *CR* 28 (1978): 354.

EUSEBIUS
(also see chapter 11: "Constantine and the Christian Empire")

3.43   Grant, Robert M. *Eusebius as Church Historian.* Oxford: Clarendon, 1980. Pp. viii + 184. AAI-2; MAI-3; SI-2; B-10.

Grant examines the process by which the *Ecclesiastical History* was produced, concluding that it went through three "versions" in times of significant pressures and forces (the final persecution, the conversion of Constantine, and finally during the impact on the church by the confessors). Grant thinks that Eusebius discards Papias and a millennialist eschatology between the first two editions, and comes to depend more heavily on Hegesippus. Solid discussion of Eusebius and his use of his varied sources.

✂< *JTS* 32: 511-514; *JEH* 33: 646-47; *CH* 51: 437; Chesnut, *RSR* 9 (1983): 118-123.

GREGORY THE GREAT

3.44   Straw, Carol. *Gregory the Great: Perfection in Imperfection.* Berkeley/Los Angeles: The University of California Press, 1988. Pp. xiv + 295. I-30; B&W-4.

This book had its origins as a doctoral dissertation done under the aegis of Peter Brown, and published in his "Transformation of the Classical Heritage" series. By working with schemata that harken back to those provided by structural anthropology, Straw is able to polarize the antinomies that characterized the theology of Gregory: with a mind/body duality at its heart, it was marked by other distinctions (interiority/exteriority, love/fear and nature/culture dialectics) for which his core conceptions of redemption and reconciliation functioned. Straw concedes that Gregory's ideas are not all that original, with heavy doses of stoicism, neo-platonism, Ambrose, and Augustine forming the basis of this thinking, but that his great achievement was to provide a convincing and workable synthesis. He firmly fixed an "anthropology" of humans as imperfect persons who had constantly to strive for greater perfection in which their own struggle and prayers, and the role of penitence, were to be central to their improvement. Located at the watershed between the ancient and medieval worlds, Gregory was a complex person whose theology mirrored those difficulties. The clarity of Straw's

exposition guides the reader wonderfully well through this minefield of potential contradictions, and provides us with a standard work on the most important western Father after Augustine. (S)
᠅ Bartelink, *VC* 43 (1989): 298-300; Evans, *JTS* 40 (1989): 261; Richards, *CHR* 75 (1989): 128-129; Sullivan, *AHR* 95 (1990): 147.

IGNATIUS

3.45 ◉ Bammel, C.P. Hammond. "Ignatian Problems." *Journal of Theological Studies* n.s. 33 (1982): 62-97.

The first half of this article provides a detailed review of two books that challenged the "Middle Recension" of the Ignatian letters: J. Rius-Camps, *The Four Authentic Letters of Ignatius, the Martyr* [§3.47]; and Robert Joly, *Le Dossier d'Ignace d'Antioche* (Éditions de l'Université de Brussels, 1979). Also considered is J. Donahue's "Jewish Christianity in Ignatius' Letters." Both Donahue and Ruis-Camps believe that there are two problem groups (Gnostics and Judaizers) confronted by Ignatius. Bammel offers some qualifications. Bammel also considers whether the letters of Ignatius are evidence for the church situation in Antioch or Asia Minor, and then pays considerable attention to the role of the Johannine community and the development of office.

3.46 Lightfoot, J.B. *The Apostolic Fathers.* Part 2. *Ignatius, and Polycarp.* 3 vols. 2d ed. London: Macmillan, 1889-1890. Vol. 1. xxii + 767. I-37; M-1. Vol. 2. Pp. vi + 619. I-19; CT-7. Vol. 3. Pp. vii + 526. I-11; BI-7.

Although over a hundred years old, this is a masterpiece of exacting scholarship on Ignatius and Polycarp. Every topic is considered, with numerous side issues addressed in detail, including a translation and discussion of various of the Acts of Martyrs. No serious scholarship on Ignatius can disregard this classic work.

3.47 Rius-Camps, J. *The Four Authentic Letters of Ignatius, the Martyr.* Christianismos 2. Rome: Pontificium Institutum Orientalium Studiorum, 1979. Pp. 413.

Two things disturb Rius-Camps about the 7-letter corpus of Ignatius' writings. Sometimes Ignatius spoke of his church position involving Syria; sometimes involving Antioch. Sometimes he described himself as bishop; sometimes as deacon. This leads Rius-Camps into a intricate reconstruction of the "original" Ignatian correspondence. He believes only the letters from Smyrna are authentic (Romans, Magnesians, Trallians, and Ephesians). The other three letters (Philadelphians, Smyrneans, and Polycarp), though forgeries, do contain much authentic material cut from the original four letters. The forged letters were from a bishop of Philadelphia, attempting to strengthen his authority.

3.48   Schoedel, William R. *Ignatius of Antioch: A Commentary on the Letters of Ignatius of Antioch.* Hermeneia. Philadelphia: Fortress, 1985. Pp. 305. MAI-2; CAI-3; BI-2; NTI-11; SI-2; PI-3; B-4; Greek Index-2.
Schoedel is a prolific writer on Ignatius and has produced the most recent critical commentary. In this commentary, standard introductory notes are brief, and the translation is the author's own. Schoedel is generally more sympathetic to Ignatius than Walter Bauer was [§18.2], though his analysis of the situation in Asia Minor and Antioch is shaped much by Bauer and P.N. Harrison. Unlike Bauer, however, Schoedel thinks that the three-fold ministry was in place. Further, he places considerable weight on Ignatius' loss of self esteem (due to some failure in Antioch) to explain Ignatius' behaviour and concerns. With Lightfoot, the important commentary in English.
✂ Ettlinger, *TS* 47 (1986): 715-716; Hemer, *Themelios* 12 (1987): 62-63; Holmes, *JETS* 30 (1987): 243-244; Norris, *RSR* 15 (1989): 128-130; Quinn, *CBQ* 49 (1987): 159-161.

IRENAEUS
3.49   ◉ Donovan, Mary Ann. "Irenaeus in Recent Scholarship." *Second Century* 4 (1984): 219-241.
Donovan reviews works that were published on Irenaeus primarily from 1970 to 1982. She gives a careful review of various debates regarding Irenaeus, describing and often evaluating the past and present works. The article is divided into 5 sections: Instruments of Research, Editions and Translations, Irenaeus's Methodology, Irenaeus and the Bible, and Theology of Irenaeus. Some of the issues discussed are the integrity of Irenaeus' reports about the Gnostics, the authority and status of the church at Rome, the unity of book IV of *Adversus haereses,* and Irenaeus' view of the New Testament. The most extensive discussion is on the theology of Irenaeus.

JEROME
3.50   Kelly, J.N.D. *Jerome: His Life, Writings, and Controversies* London: Gerald Duckworth, 1975. Pp. 353. I-13; B&W-1; C-1.
The major biography in English, Kelly's work is useful to both the general reader and the more specialized scholar. Jerome comes to

life as a person filled with contradiction, complexity, and controversy. He is too suspicious of novelty and of heresy to be a creative
theologian. Although prolific in his commentaries, his insights are
"largely derivative." Although a vocal defender of asceticism, he is
criticized for the quality of his own asceticism and is critical of the
quality of the asceticism of others. Kelly sets Jerome and his
voluminous writings in context, revealing him as the best equipped
scholar of his day, but one often vain and petty. Kelly's work also
provides a good review of early monasticism.

JOHN CHRYSOSTOM

3.51 Baur, Chrysostomus. *John Chrysostom and His Time.* 4 vols.
Translated by Sister M. Gonzaga. Büchervertriebsanstalt, 1988. I-6;
B-36.
This is the most detailed work in English translation on John
Chrysostom. The work first appeared in 1929, with a second edition
in 1958. Baur divided his work into 4 volumes, the first two volumes
on John's career in Antioch; the second two of John in Constantinople. Baur, who has been criticized for being a little too sympathetic to his subject, covered almost every topic possible.

3.52 ◉ Carter, R.E. "The Future of Chrysostom Studies." *Studia Patristica*
X. Berlin: Akademie-Verlag, 1970. Pp. 14-21.
A short note, indicating what needs to be done and how resources
could best be used in the study of John Chrysostom. The key for
progress is the provision of a "definitive critical edition of the
entire corpus of Chrysostom's work," a considerable task since
Chrysostom was the most prolific writer of the early church—by
far. Carter thinks the questions of language and style, and biographical details are either settled, or are matters unsettled but
already well enough debated.

JUSTIN MARTYR

3.53 Barnard, Leslie W. *Justin Martyr. His Life and Thought.* Cambridge:
Cambridge UP, 1967. Pp. viii + 194. I-5; B-4; Index to Justin's
works-5.
This focuses on Justin as an apologist and churchman, showing his
theological position and its background in Greek philosophy and in
Judaism. Justin made significant contributions in his interpretation
of the *logos* and in his understanding of the universalistic element
in Christianity. Four appendices: (1) works attributed to Justin; (2)
Hadrian's letter to Minucius Fundanus; (3) Justin's Old Testament
text; and (4) Harnack on the eucharistic elements (use of wine or

water).
ℛ Barnard, *ATR* 50 (1968): 179-182.

ORIGEN

3.54 ◉ Crouzel, Henri. "The Literature on Origen 1970-1988." *Theological Studies* 49 (1988): 499-516.

By a leading scholar of Origen, this review surveys English and foreign language publications on Origen, including publications of various conferences, new editions and translations (some of which are in English), and works on the thought and theology of Origen. Trigg's work [§3.57] is criticized quite severely, and deserves to be replaced by Crouzel's own work on Origen, now translated into English [§3.55].

3.55 Crouzel, Henri. *Origen: The Life and Thought of the First Great Theologian.* Translated by A.S. Worrall. San Francisco: Harper & Row, 1989. Pp. xvi + 278. B-4; MAI-1; AAI-4; BI-3.

A translation from the French of a major work by a leading Origen scholar. The first quarter deals with biographical matters; the final three parts with Origen's thought. A brief part two deals with Origen's exegesis; a larger part three with "Spirituality," which covers topics like the nature of man, concept of knowledge, virginity, martyrdom, marriage, and various mystical themes. Part four is the largest and deals with "Theology," a field in which Origen had a number of critics. Crouzel is sympathetic to Origen, and attempts to make sense of Origen's thoughts on pre-existence of the soul, the reconciliation of all things, and various items related to trinitarian/christological matters. Also addressed are church hierarchy, baptism, the Eucharist, penance, and Origen's attack on heresies.
ℛ Bostock, *ExT* 101 (1990): 216; Clark, *CC* 107 (1990): 372-373; Osborn, *Encounter* 51 (1990): 415-417; Snyder, *CTSR* 80 (1990): 42-43; Trigg, *ATR* 72 (1990): 340-342.

3.56 Kannengiesser, Charles, and William L. Petersen, eds. *Origen of Alexandria: His World and Legacy.* Notre Dame: University of Notre Dame Press, 1988. Pp. viii + 373.

A collection of nineteen articles, from the Origen Colloquy at Notre Dame in 1986. The articles relate to scripture or to theological issues. Under the issue of scripture are chapters on exegetical method (by Scalise, Nodes, Trigg, Cox Miller); Jewish influence (Brooks, Blowers); and textual matters (Ulrich, Petersen, Wright). The other section deals with martyrdom (Bright); prayer (Sheerin); Imagery of Light (Dillon); Trinity (Kannengiesser); sacrifice (LaPorte);

ecclesiology (Verbrugge); saint and sinners after death (Hennessey); ethics (Gorday); pluralism (Dechow); and fourth-century Origenism (O'Laughlin).

&< Berthold, *SC* 8 (1991): 252-253.

3.57   Trigg, Joseph Wilson. *Origen: The Bible and Philosophy in the Third-Century Church.* Atlanta: John Knox, 1983. Pp. ix + 300. I-16; M-1.

The first comprehensive study in English of Origen in the context of his times and theological setting, this book is written for easy comprehension. The author demonstrates Origen's "astonishing coherence and integrity in his work that brings together categories of thought we moderns take for granted as disparate: textual study and allegory, scholarship and piety, Greek philosophy and the biblical tradition." Although Nautin's chronology of Origen's life is used, no discussion of problems relating to it are given. (P)

&< Bussanich, *JAAR* 53 (1985): 145-146; Clark, *CH* 54 (1985): 90-91; Darling, *ATR* 67 (1985): 186-187; de Lange, *JEH* 37 (1986): 141-142; Kelly, *TS* 46 (1985): 174-175; Stead, *Theology* 89 (1986): 161-163; Young, *JTS* 37 (1986): 217-220; White, *BTB* 16 (1986): 159-160.

PELAGIUS

3.58   Rees, B.R. *Pelagius. A Reluctant Heretic.* Woodbridge, Suffolk: Boydell and Brewer, 1988. Pp. xv + 176. I-4; AAI-4; MAI-3; B-19; CT-3.

Pelagius, like most of the "heretics" of the early Christian church, is gaining more fair consideration from modern scholars than from opponents such as Augustine and Jerome. Rees provides a useful historical survey, both of Pelagius and the controversy that he provoked, along with a 2-page appendix of works attributed to Pelagius, and a 5-page account of charges and replies from the Synod of Diospolis. This is a good starting point, though rich resources for the study of Pelagius will be found in most of the substantial works on Augustine, since it is mainly in that light that Pelagius found a space in the history of early Christianity. Rees has also produced a 362-page collection of documents for the study of Pelagius, titled, *Letters of Pelagius and his Followers.*

&< Eno, *CHR* 76 (1990): 101-102; Evans, *New Blackfriars* 70 (1989): 52; Frend, *Theology* 92 (1989): 407-408; Markus, *JTS* 40 (1989): 623-624; Ramsey, *TS* 50 (1989): 398-399; TeSelle, *CH* 59 (1990): 223-224; Wright, *ExT* 100 (1989): 352.

TERTULLIAN

3.59   ⓔ "Chronica Tertullianea et Cyprianea." *Revue des Études Augustiniennes.* See §3.41 above.

3.60   Barnes, Timothy D. *Tertullian: A Historical and Literary Study.*
        Rev. ed. Oxford: Clarendon Press, 1985. (1971[1]). Pp. 320. AAI-2;
        SI/NI-10; B-22; CT-1.
        In this work Barnes provides the fundamental revisionist study of
        Tertullian in English. Iconoclastic on many of the received views
        on Tertullian's upbringing and background (e.g., that he was the
        son of a centurion, jurist, priest, etc.), it must be read in the reprint
        edition (1985) which contains the author's valuable "Tertullian
        Revisited: A Postscript" (pp. 321-35, with "Supplementary Biblio-
        graphy," pp. 336-39) that is characterized by disarmingly honest
        mea culpas on his original version. The text is basically split into
        two parts: the first is the "clearing operation" in which Barnes
        debunked most of the then-current orthodoxies on Tertullian's
        education and family origins, and in which he attempts to bring a
        more systematic and rigorous method to the dating of Tertullian's
        works (see his 1985 "Postscript" on many of these). The second
        half of the work, less successful by Barnes's own admission (with
        chs. 9-10 the "weakest" of these), deals primarily with the content
        of Tertullian's works, his theology, and the location of his rhetoric
        within the so-called Second Sophistic. (S)
        ✄ Frend, *CR* 24 (1974): 72-76; Matthews, *JTS* 24 (1973): 243-245; Sider,
        AJP 95 (1974): 302-303.

3.61   ◉ Sider, Robert D. "Approaches to Tertullian: A Study of Recent
        Scholarship." *Second Century* 2 (1982): 228-260.
        Sider provides a detailed and well organized review of English and
        foreign language works on Tertullian (mainly from the 1970s).
        Seven specific topics are analyzed: (1) Tools for Research and
        Scholarship; (2) Editions; (3) Life and Times of Tertullian; (4)
        Language and Style; (5) Tertullian and the Bible; (6) Tertullian and
        Philosophy; and (7) Tertullian and Theology. The last section is
        further broken down into (a) Tertullian as Theologian; (b) a Question
        of Method; and (c) Aspects of Theology, in which works on
        Tertullian's views of the Trinity, the Church, and ethics are discussed.
        Sider points out that of the Latin Fathers, Tertullian stands third
        after Augustine and Ambrose in terms of attention in the scholarly
        literature. This issue of *The Second Century* also contains two
        other articles on Tertullian: Jansen, "Tertullian and the New
        Testament" (pp. 191-207) and Countryman, "Tertullian and the
        Regula Fidei" (pp. 208-227).

4

GENERAL COLLECTIONS

Many works on the early Church attempt to cover a variety of issues, and thus they cannot easily be placed in one of the more specific categories in this bibliography. Such works have been placed in this chapter. Some of the works included here are single-author collections of quite diverse articles; others are multi-author works with no specific focus. For the books that are primarily collections of diverse articles, we have merely listed relevant chapter titles and the name of each author. If an article in such a collection has had particular impact on its field or summarizes the debate clearly, we have attempted to list these articles separately in the appropriate chapter and have included an abstract there.

The most profitable way to use this chapter is to refer to the main index at the back of this volume. This index will direct one quickly to any entries listed here that are relevant to a particular topic. A search by author may also be fruitful. Collections of the works of individual authors are listed below in alphabetical order in the first section of this chapter, making it easier to locate the occasional writings of an author. As well, the author index (at the back of this volume) will indicate articles published in multi-author collections; a particular author's article might be missed were one to search only by the main title of the volume or by the name of the volume's editor.

We have listed only a few general collections here, out of the numerous ones that are published each year. Often these collections are in honor of a particular scholar—volumes called "Festschriften." Many of these that are primarily focused on a biblical theme will have articles of relevance to a study of the early church. One good way to locate such articles is to check a detailed bibliography in a recent monograph on the topic. Another way to locate articles in multi-author works is to consult periodic indexes designed to find and describe the contents of such volumes. The "Religion Indexes" of the American Theological Library Association are the primary volumes for this kind of information, providing notices of such material within months of the publication date. See *Religion Index Two: Multi-Author Works* [§1.7] and *Religion Index Two: Festschriften 1960-1969* [§1.37].

SINGLE-AUTHOR WORKS

4.1   Barnard, Leslie W. *Studies in the Apostolic Fathers and Their
      Background.* Oxford: Basil Blackwell, 1966. Pp. ix + 177. I-3.
      A collection (and expansion) of eleven essays, all but one of which
      had been previously published as journal articles. Various aspects
      of the Apostolic Fathers are covered, with the Epistle of Barnabas
      considered most often. Besides articles on Barnabas, Barnard
      provides articles on Clement of Rome and Domitian's persecution
      (arguing that there was such a persecution); Background of Ignatius
      (arguing for one heresy among the opponents); Problem of Polycarp's
      letter to the Philippians (dated c. 120); Judaism in Egypt (A.D.
      70-135); Early Alexandrian Christianity; Hadrian and Christianity;
      Hermas and Judaism; and the Enigma of the Epistle to Diognetus.

4.2   Barnes, Timothy D. *Early Christianity and the Roman Empire.*
      London: Variorum, 1984. Pp. x + 314. I-5. CT-3; FT-2; T-12.
      A collection of twenty previously published articles that are,
      according to the author, "used in but not superseded by" his four
      books. The articles cover a 15-year period, and focus on two themes:
      Christianity in the Roman Empire and the history and culture of
      the Roman Empire from Trajan to Constantine. Briefly, the articles
      cover the following topics: martyrdom and persecution; historical
      writing in antiquity (Victor, Eutropius, Eusebius, Tacitus); bio-
      graphical information on Antonius, Methodius, Maximus, Valen-
      tinus, Plotinus, Porphyrius, Tertullian, and Iamblichus; Constan-
      tine's relations with Lactantius, the senate, and Christian bishops;
      rise of Donatism; Roman nobility; and military campaigns.

4.3   Baynes, Norman H. *Byzantine Studies and Other Essays.* London:
      Athlone Press, 1955. Pp. xi + 392. I-4; B&W-1.
      A collection of lectures, articles, and book reviews—most from the
      1920s and 1930s—by a leading scholar in the field. Baynes deals
      with a range of topics: Hellenistic and Byzantine culture, the decline
      of Rome in the west, relations between Alexandria and Constan-
      tinople, idolatry, icons, political ideas of Augustine, the death of
      Julian, the Goths, Armenia, the reforms of Diocletian and Con-
      stantine, Isocrates, Eusebius, Justinian and Amalasuntha, and others.

4.4   Brown, Peter. *Religion and Society in the Age of Saint Augustine,*
      London: Faber & Faber, 1972. Pp. 352. I-14.
      The first collection of papers (to 1969) of the leading interpreter of
      the world of Late Antiquity. Many of these papers were written in
      conjunction with concerns stemming out of Brown's classic bio-

graphy of Augustine [§3.32]. They are grouped under three broad headings: "Religion and Society," "Rome," and "Africa." Of the five papers and three reviews in the first section, perhaps the most influential is his paper on sorcery and witchcraft [12.19]. Those in the second section are devoted to the Christianization of the Roman aristocracy and the social background to Pelagius and the Pelagian schism. Those under "Africa" deal with problems entailed in the interpretation of the "Donatist" schism. Three of these are classic papers concerned with the nature of religious coercion used by the Catholic Church and the Roman State in the face of local dissent, including the critical attitude of Augustine to the use of such force to constrain belief. The other item of note under this rubric is a landmark paper on Christianity and local culture in north Africa that opened up new avenues by which such a cultural transformation could be viewed in other provinces of the empire. (S)

4.5   Brown, Peter. *Society and the Holy in Late Antiquity*. Berkeley: University of California Press, 1982. Pp. viii + 347. I-15.
The second collection of magnificent papers (to 1977) by the greatest modern interpreter of Christianity and the Late Antique world. The first part, entitled "Approaches," is a collection of essays on the modern historiography of the period. It includes two on Gibbon and one on Pirenne. The second part of the book, "Society and the Holy," includes a number of scintillating book reviews, and two classic papers on the role and function of the "holy man" in Late Antique society. The first of these was his more general interpretative piece [§17.8] which used functionalist anthropological models to explain the peculiar place and power such men had in that world; the second (from a conference presentation in 1976) applied this general model to the specific case of Syria. (S)

4.6   Campenhausen, Hans von. *Tradition and Life in the Church. Essays and Lectures in Church History*. Translated by A.V. Littledale. London: Collins, 1968. Pp. 254.
Translated from the 1960 German *Tradition und Leben-Kräfte der Kirchengeschichte*. (The English translation omits five of the chapters in the German volume.) Three chapters in the translation deal with New Testament; the other eight with the early Church: "Tradition and Spirit in Early Christianity"; "Early Christian Asceticism"; "The Problem of Order in Early Christianity and the Ancient Church"; "Christians and Military Service in the Early Church"; "The Theological Problem of Images in the Early Church"; "Augustine and the Fall of Rome"; "The Origins of the Idea of

Priesthood in the Early Church"; and "The Ascetic Ideal of Exile in Ancient and Early Medieval Monasticism."

4.7   Chadwick, Henry. *History and Thought of the Early Church*. London: Variorum, 1982. Pp. v + 344. I-6; B&W-1.

A collection of 18 previously published articles, most of which attempt to relate Christianity to its social and intellectual environment. The main themes are: Roman (and papal) authority; influence of Philo and the Greek synagogue; Christian apologetic (Justin Martyr); and the great debates over Arianism, Christology (in particular, Nestorianism), and Monasticism. Topics not clearly reflected in these subdivisions are: Silence of Bishops in Ignatius; biographical notes on Ossius of Cordova, Eustathius of Antioch, Mark the Monk, John Moschus, Rufinus; Melito's *Pascal Homily;* and the origin of the title "Oecumenical Council."

4.8   Chadwick, Henry. *Heresy and Orthodoxy in the Early Church*. London: Variorum, 1991. Pp. xii + 322. I-6.

A collection of 23 previously published articles by Chadwick, all of which are relevant, though two are in French. Various themes are covered: several on Christianity and paganism and on Augustine; others on the role of Christian bishops; some dealing with aspects of particular individuals, such as Mani, Peter of Alexandria, Philoponus, Boethius (2 articles), and Origen (2 articles); with a range of other topics: asceticism, moral codes, hospitality, Gnosticism, conversion of Constantine, the Chalcedonian Definition, and the church of the third century in the west. As with other volumes in the Variorum reprints, a few brief comments are made by the author on specific articles in the collection in light of recent research.

4.9   Frend, W.H.C. *Religion Popular and Unpopular in the Early Christian Centuries*. London: Variorum, 1976. Pp. ii + 396. I-11; B&W-1.

A collection of 25 previously published articles from a 35-year period in Frend's career. Although the range of topics is broad, most address Christianity's relationship with non-Christian groups or societies and its struggles with internal diversity and schism. Other essays reflect Frend's interest in archaeology. Briefly, the topics are: heresies (Gnosticism, Manichaeism, Monophysitism, and christological conflicts); persecutions; missions; the church in North Africa, Egypt, and India; monasticism; attitude towards pagan Rome and Christian Rome; notes of Augustine, Paulinus of Nola, Athanasius, Tertullian, and the Apologists and the Old Testament.

4.10   Frend, W.H.C. *Town and Country in the Early Christian Centuries.*
       London: Variorum, 1980. Pp. ii + 372. I-11; B&W-9; M-2.
       A collection of 25 previously published articles, divided into 5
       sections: History and Archaeology; Church and the Roman Empire;
       The West; North Africa; and Nubia. Many of the articles relate to
       conversion, missions, and persecution, some to archeology, some
       are book reviews—the range of topics is broad—not all of which
       are reflected in the volume's title, which is merely taken from the
       title of the first article. Other topics concern the Gospel of Thomas;
       theological diversity; the church in the Christian Empire; east-west
       relationships; asceticism; Jews and Christians in Carthage; and
       Berber art.

4.11   Frend, W.H.C. *Archaeology and History in the Study of Early
       Christianity.* London: Variorum, 1988. Pp. x + 308. I-7; B&W-39;
       M-1.
       This is the third Variorum collection of essays previously published
       by Frend. Most of the 21 articles are relevant to our bibliography,
       some of which are themselves abstracted in this bibliography. Topics
       are wide-ranging, but many focus clearly on particular geographical
       areas, and on specific problems in those areas: see articles on the
       Donatists, Montanists, Monophysites, Anti-Chalcedonian Egypt, as
       well as articles on Britain, Syria, Augustine, and several on North
       Africa. Only a few are specifically on archaeology.

4.12   Grant, Robert M. *After the New Testament.* Philadelphia: Fortress,
       1967.
       A diverse collection of fifteen chapters on the early church by one
       of its leading scholars. Section 1: The Study of the Early Fathers
       ("The Study of the Early Fathers in Modern Times"; "The Use of
       the Early Fathers, from Irenaeus to John of Damascus"). Section 2:
       Early Christian Tradition ("Scripture and Tradition in Ignatius of
       Antioch"; "Pliny and the Christians"; "Scripture, Rhetoric, and Theo-
       logy in Theophilus"; "The Book of Wisdom at Alexandria" [impor-
       tant for Egyptian Christianity]). Section 3: Early Christianity and
       Greco-Roman Culture ("Early Christianity and Pre-Socratic Philos-
       ophy"; "Causation and Generation in Early Christian Literature";
       "Aristotle and the Conversion of Justin"; "Theophilus of Antioch
       to Autolycus"; "Irenaeus and Hellenistic Culture"). Section 4:
       Aspects of Christian Gnosis ("Gnostic and Christian Worship";
       "The Mystery of Marriage in the Gospel of Philip"; "Gnosticism
       and the Problem of Methodology"; and "Tatian and the Gnostics").

4.13   Grant, Robert M. *Christian Beginnings: Apocalypse to History.*
        London: Variorum, 1983. Pp. 336. I-3.
        A collection of 27 of Grant's articles (from 1947-1981), most of
        which have some relevance to this bibliography. Six are on Theo-
        philus, a second-century bishop of Antioch; two are on Christianity
        in Egypt (Origen); others deal with Quadratus, Papias, Eusebius,
        Gnosticism, Holy War, Council of Nicea, dietary laws, charges of
        immorality against Christians, sacrifices and oaths, and development
        in early Christian doctrine. This volume provides a convenient
        collection of Grant's wide-ranging articles on the early church,
        about half of which are from journals found in most libraries.

4.14   Hanson, Richard P.C. *Studies in Christian Antiquity.* Edinburgh:
        T&T Clark, 1985. Pp. xi + 394. Ancient Names Index-13; MAI-5.
        A collection of seventeen articles by Hanson; nine on the first three
        centuries, eight on the fourth and fifth centuries. Of relevance is
        the discussion of Origen's use of *homoousios*; eucharistic offering
        in the pre-Nicene Fathers; liberty of the bishop to improvise in the
        liturgy; concept of office [§9.19]; Christian attitude towards pagan
        religion [§12.9]; doctrine of Trinity achieved by 381; transformation
        of images; *filioque*; dogma and formula; the Rule of Faith of Victor-
        inus and Patrick; the church in 5th century Gaul; transformation of
        pagan temples to Christian churches [§6.20]; and the collapse of
        the western empire.
        ✎ Bobertz, *SC* 8 (1991): 51-55.

4.15   Hanson, Richard P.C. *Tradition in the Early Church.* London: SCM
        Press, 1962. Pp. 288. B-8; NI-3; BI-2; AAI-8.
        Although this book is not a collection of scattered essays by Hanson,
        but a focused work on tradition, its chapters fit different chapters
        of our bibliography, thus we have listed it here. The six chapters
        cover oral tradition, the creed, the rule of faith, custom and rite, the
        canon, and an essay on tradition as interpretation, along with three
        short appendices of technical notes. Particularly useful are the
        summaries of various "rules of faith," or creedal statements found
        in various writings of the early church fathers; these summaries
        have been arranged for fairly easy comparison. This is a detailed,
        thorough, and informed work, which is characteristic of Hanson.

4.16   Markus, R.A. *From Augustine to Gregory the Great. History and
        Christianity in Late Antiquity.* London: Variorum, 1983. Pp. ii +
        318. I-5; B&W-1.
        A collection of 17 previously published articles, mainly written

after Markus's *Saeculum: History and society in the theology of Saint Augustine,* and relating primary to Christian self-definition. The book is divided into 4 parts: Historiography; North Africa; Gregory I and His World; and the Papacy (a section not relevant to this bibliography). Topics not identified clearly by these section titles are: Christian attitude to pagan literature; Donatism (character of dissent, and its last phase); North African church structure; Justinian church structure; Gregory and missions; Ravenna and Rome; and Gregory the Great's Europe.

4.17   Momigliano, Arnaldo. *On Pagans Jews and Christians.* Middleton, CT: Wesleyan UP, 1987. Pp. xii + 343; I-19.
A collection and translation of 19 of Momigliano's articles from his *Contributi alla storia degli studi classici e del mondo antico.* The articles are wide-ranging, but several are of interest to students of early Christianity: "How Roman Emperors Became Gods"; "Some Preliminary Remarks on the 'Religious Opposition' to the Roman Empire"; "Roman Religion: The Imperial Period"; "The Life of St. Macrina by Gregory of Nyssa," as well as sections of other articles.

4.18   Stead, G. Christopher. *Substance and Illusion in the Christian Fathers.* London: Variorum, 1985. Pp. 330. I-5.
A collection of the following articles by Stead: "The Significance of the *Homoousios*"; "Divine Substance in Tertullian"; "Platonism of Arius"; "Valentinian Myth of Sophia"; "'Eusebius' and the Council of Nicea"; "Origins of the Doctrine of the Trinity"; "Concept of Divine Substance"; "Rhetorical Method in Athanasius"; "Ontology and Terminology in Gregory of Nyssa"; "The *Thalia* of Arius and the Testimony of Athanasius"; "Athanasius' *De Incarnatione*"; "In Search of Valentinus"; "Individual Personality in Origen and the Cappadocian Fathers"; "Concept of Mind and the Concept of God in the Christian Fathers"; "Motives of Christian Confession"; and "Freedom of the Will and the Arian Controversy."

MULTI-AUTHOR COLLECTIONS
4.19   Balch, David L., Everett Ferguson, and Wayne A. Meeks, ed. *Greeks, Romans, and Christians: essays in Honor of Abraham J. Malherbe.* Minneapolis: Fortress, 1990. Pp. xvii + 404.
A collection of 22 articles by many leading church historians, divided into four major sections: "Schools of Hellenistic Philosophy"; "Hellenistic Literature and Rhetoric"; "Hellenistic Anthropology"; "Hellenistic Social Behavior"; and a one-chapter section on "Archaeology." Many of the articles are tied to specific New Testament

passages, showing Hellenistic parallels. Nonetheless, it is a useful collection for gaining some sense of the Hellenistic world of which both the New Testament and patristic authors were a part. Some of the authors are: Aune, Holladay, Klauck, L.M. White, Olbricht, Stowers, L.T. Johnson, and Koester.

4.20   Benko, Stephen, and John J. O'Rourke. *The Catacombs and the Colosseum*. Valley Forge: Judson Press, 1971. Pp. 318. SI-6; NI-2; AAI-7; BI-2; CT-7; T-2; B&W-1; M-1. Published in Great Britain as *Early Church History: The Roman Empire as the Setting of Primitive Christianity*. London: Oliphants, 1972.
A collection of 12 articles by 11 scholars, with an insightful appeal for work on the early church by R.M. Grant. The articles are (some with shortened titles): "The Sources of Roman History Between 31 B.C.–A.D. 138" and "The History of the Early Roman Empire," (both by Benko); "Judaism on the World Scene" (Kraft); "Religion and Social Class" (Gager); "Social Unrest and Primitive Christianity" (Lee); "Ancient Education" (Townsend); "Roman Law and the Early Church" (O'Rourke); "The Roman Army" (Jones); "Finances" (White); "Religion and the Early Empire" (Winslow); "Persecution and Toleration of Christianity Until Hadrian" (Krodel); and "Collegia, Philosophical Schools, and Theology" (Wilken). With 3-page vocabulary of Latin terms.

4.21   Benoit, André; Marc Philonenko, and Cyrille Vogel, eds. *Paganisme, Judaïsme, Christianisme. Influences et affrontements dans le monde antique*. Mélanges offerts à Marcel Simon. Paris: Éditions E. de Boccard, 1978.
A collection of 28 essays, eleven of which are in English. Under the theme of Paganism and Judaism: "The Romans Through Jewish Eyes" (Bruce); "Paganism and Judaism: The Sardis Evidence" (Kraabel); "Greek Wisdom and Proficiency in Greek" (Werblowsky); and "Jewish Literary Propaganda" (Wilson). Under the theme of Judaism and Christianity: "Romans 11:13-24" (Davies); "Jewish and Christian Benedictions" (Dugmore); "An Early Jewish-Christian Document in the Sibyl" (Flusser); "Jews and Christians in Third Century Carthage" (Frend); "Eusebius and Gnostic Origins" (Grant); and "Christian Transmission of Greek Jewish Scriptures" (Kraft). Under Christianity and Paganism: "On the History of the 'Divine Man'" (Smith).

4.22   Ferguson, Everett, ed. With David Scholer and Paul Corby Finney. *Studies in Early Christianity*. New York: Garland, 1993.

This is a massive 18-volume work, consisting of over 325 articles on the range of issues scholars deal with in a study of early Christianity. The articles have all appeared previously, for the most part in journals. Many of the articles have been included in our own bibliography, and are key contributions to the debate. Each volume provides a useful collection, and the student can quickly gain a sense of the field from reading the full volume. This would be a good collection for libraries which do not have a solid journal collection for the field of the early church.

4.23   March, Eugene. *Texts and Testaments. Critical Essays on the Bible and Early Church Fathers. A Volume in Honor of Stuart Dickson Currie.* San Antonio: Trinity UP, 1980. Pp. xiii + 321. AAI-7; MAI-2; B&W-1; BI-7.
About half of the chapters are relevant. "Marcion Revisited: A 'Post-Harnack' Perspective" (Balás); "'Prophets and Apostles': The Conjunction of the Two Terms before Irenaeus" (Farkasfalvy); "The Covenant Idea in the Second Century" (Ferguson); "Peter and Paul: A Constitutive Relationship for Catholic Christianity" (Farmer); "Understanding the Church of the Second Century: American Research and Teaching 1890-1940" (Olbricht); and "The 'Logic' of Canon-making and the Tasks of Canon-criticism (Outler)."

4.24   McGinn, B., and J. Meyendorff, with J. Leclercq, eds. *Christian Spirituality. Origins to the Twelfth Century.* New York: Crossroad Press, 1986. Pp. xxv + 502. NI-3; B&W-33; SI-5; B-1.
A collection of 19 essays, most of which at least touch on aspects of the early church. A few of the more relevant for the purposes of this bibliography are: "Gnostic Spirituality" (R.M. Grant); "Spiritual Message of the Great Fathers" (Kannengiesser); "Monasticism and Asceticism" (Gribomont and Leclercq); "Pseudo-Dionysius" (Rorem); "Gregorian Reform" (Morrison); "The Trinity" (Hopko and Clark); "Liturgy and Spirituality" (Meyendorff and Gy); "Icon and Art" (Ouspemsky); "Virginity" (P. Brown); and "Birth of the Laity" (Fontaine). Other chapters deal with theological issues or cultural diversity.
✄ Eire, *RSR* 14 (1988): 25-27; Hinson, *R&E* 83 (1986): 640; Kaufmann, *JR* 67 (1987): 547-549; Louth, *JTS* 38 (1987): 217-218; Nineham, *Theology* 93 (1990): 165-166; Norris, *CH* 57 (1988): 528-530; Norris, *Parabola* 12 (1987): 104-108.

4.25   Neiman, David, and Margaret Schatkin, eds. *The Heritage of the Early Church. Essays in Honor of The Very Reverend Georges Vasilievich Florovsky.* Orientalia Christiana Analecta 195. Rome:

Pont. Institutum Studiorum Orientalium, 1973. Pp. 473. I-12; BI-5.
A collection of 24 articles, plus a bibliography of the writings of
Florovsky, and brief notes on the contributors. Florovsky was
Professor of Eastern Church History at Harvard, and about one-third
of the articles deal with aspects that are distinctly eastern. Most of
the articles deal with larger issues, such as early "heretical" movements like Gnosticism, Montanism, and Monophysitism. Others
deal with aspects of the thought of Augustine, Origen, Chrysostom,
Gregory of Nyssa, and some deal with themes like the *lapsi* and
eschatology. Pelikan, Froehlich, Lampe, Daniélou, Frend, and Bruce
are some of the contributors.

4.26   Pearson, Birger A., ed. *The Future of Early Christianity. Essays in
       Honor of Helmut Koester.* Minneapolis: Fortress, 1991. Pp. xx +
       509. AAI-17; MAI-5; Bibliography of Koester-11.
       An important collection of 37 essays, with a 10-page reflection by
       Koester himself on "Current Issues in New Testament Scholarship."
       Five articles deal with Early Christian Literature (*Gospel of Thomas,
       Protevangelium Jacobi, Acts of Thomas,* Ignatius) and three with
       Gnosticism (by Perkins, Pagels, and Pearson). Other useful articles
       are Epp on New Testament manuscripts and letter carrying, Cohen
       on Harnack's view of Christianity's success over Judaism, as well
       as many of the articles that deal more directly with the New
       Testament.

4.27   Schoedel, William R., and Robert L. Wilken, eds. *Early Christian
       Literature and the Classical Intellectual Tradition. In honorem
       Robert M. Grant.* Theologie historique 53. Paris: Beauchesne, 1979.
       Pp. 205. B&W-1.
       About half of this collection of articles is relevant. "Tertullian's
       Principles and Methods of Exegesis" (Waszink); "The Transcen-
       dence and Freedom of God: Irenaeus, the Greek Tradition and
       Gnosticism" (Norris); "From Greek Hairesis to Christian Heresy"
       (Simon); "Pagan Criticism of Christianity: Greek Religion and
       Christian Faith" (Wilken); "The Relativity of Moral Codes: Rome
       and Persia in Late Antiquity" (Chadwick); "God is Eros" (Quispel).
       These essays challenge the long-standing belief of a "sharp dicho-
       tomy between Christian and Graeco-Roman culture." Christian
       authors, even Irenaeus and Tertullian, shared largely the intellectual
       background of the non-Christian thinkers.

4.28   Wikgren, Allen, ed. *Early Christian Origins. Studies in Honor of
       R. Willoughby.* Chicago: Quadrangle Press, 1961. Pp. ix + 160.

B&W-1.

With fourteen chapters, seven of which are relevant for this bibliography. "Resurrection in the Early Church" (Branton); "Social Factors in Early Christian Eschatology" (Wilder); "Christianity in Sardis" (S.E. Johnson); "Early Christian Asceticism" (Deems); "The Sins of Hermas" (Clark); "The Origin of Texttypes of New Testament Manuscripts" (Colwell); and "History and Scripture" (Wikgren). With a 10-page biography/bibliography of Willoughby.

5
GENERAL HISTORIES

The works included in this chapter were intended by the authors to be general surveys or introductions, though the detail and the technical character of the presentations vary substantially from one author to another. For the works listed here, we have attempted to indicate what parts of the book apply specifically to the period covered by this bibliography, and to indicate in what way each work makes a contribution. Most of the general histories listed below cover the major questions, and though each author has a particular perspective and emphasizes different kinds of materials and evidence, few of the works are so shaped by ideological concerns or theological interests to affect their usefulness as general introductions. But one must be cautious—historians can be controlled by particular ideological or apologetic interests, as in Eusebius' *Ecclesiastical History*, written in the interests of the new Christian empire, or Gibbon's *Decline and Fall of the Roman Empire*, written with little of that kind of sympathy.

One trait that has tainted many of the earlier histories of the early church was a commitment by the authors to the defence of "orthodoxy" and a dismissal of "heretics" (or at least to a less-than-complimentary portrayal of persons so labelled). The reader often is able to identify the theological commitments of the author merely by observing who bore the "good guys" and the "bad guys" labels in the author's writing of the history. But historians did not always identify with the winners or the so-called "orthodox." Some historians, with deep theological commitments and sympathies, favored various "heretics" and sometimes even tried to rehabilitate one or another of the notorious heretics of the early church. Whatever the case, whether in defence of orthodoxy or with sympathies for certain "heretical" causes, these historians often themselves entered into the frays of the past, tipping the scales in favor of one side over the other in their presentations.

With developments in the writing of critical histories, the reader is generally less able to detect the theological commitments of those who write histories of the early church. Often historians of the early church have no particular theological commitments, or none that relate much to anything relevant to the centuries that they are studying. Most of the works listed in this bibliography are of that sort. This is especially the case for the more recent ones, though it is still possible to detect the older Catholic/ Protestant tensions or "sympathies" in some of these. Where one is most likely to see this is in the discussions of the development of church hierarchy (see chapter 9) or of the "conversion" of Constantine and the Roman Empire to Christianity (see chapter 11). Sometimes, too, a historian will offer an account of the development of the canon or of the attitudes to martyrs or a number of other issues that reveals the author's own attractions or repulsions. We should note such things, but we need not think that such perspectives and judgments necessarily corrupt what the historian has to say. No one is completely neutral, not even the most conscientious of historians, and we are no worse off knowing where an author stands on particular issues than we are not knowing.

To some degree, the historian's analysis of past events is conditioned by what fits into his or her intelligible world, and this becomes especially important when the historian is examining the intention of one of the ancient players. Sometimes the gulf is so great that the historian's world provides no meaningful way to explain a particular past action than to appeal to the irrational nature of the act. For example, some historians have found Ignatius' passion for martyrdom unexplainable, and have resorted to a diagnosis of the "mental imbalance" of Ignatius (or something of the sort). Here the historian's world seems to clash with the world of the person being analyzed. Another example is the conversion of Constantine, where proponents of the "political" explanation of the conversion often seem unable to understand or allow for genuine religious conversion. In such cases, historians might better serve the reader by simply admitting the unintelligibility of the act, rather than specifying that the intelligibility lies with the ancient period. It could lie with the modern period, of which the historian is part, and for which he or she generally has the greater capacity to understand and to identify with its structures of rationality. Regardless of the historian's genuine sympathies with the cultures of antiquity, if there is a clash between ancient and modern structures of rationality, the modern will generally (and hardly surprisingly) win. Again the historian must be asked to what degree his or her own world is unable (or unwilling) to count as meaningful particular kinds of claimed experiences. That is not to say that the ancients never acted irrationally, but we probably would not be too generous to them to say that they acted rationally *generally*. In fact, the assumption of the *general* rationality of past action is a fundamental starting point for the historian.

Finally, the writing of history is much more than arranging the events of the past in a coherent chronological order. Historians are scholars whose main materials are not the events of the past, but accounts of the events of the past. Here we get at the core of history writing. Historians must make judgments about the authenticity and date of documents; they must determine the worth of particular documents (which are mainly literary, and perhaps elitist) to an understanding of the wider culture, which was more generally illiterate and "popular," and they must take into account the character of the documents: whether propaganda, polemics, apologetics, or exhortation, none of which simply "describe things as they are." Finally they must arrange these diverse pieces to illuminate each other and to make a connected, reasonable, and probable account of the past. The books listed below make that effort.

5.1   🏛 MacMullen, Ramsay, and Eugene N. Lane, eds. *Paganism and Christianity. 100-425 C.E. A Sourcebook.* Minneapolis: Fortress, 1992. Pp. xiv + 296. I-2.
This volume will become a standard sourcebook for students of the early church. Divided into 22 chapters, with numerous passages of various lengths from ancient authors, both Christian and non-Christian. Each passage has a brief introductory note. Chapters cover the following topics: magic, dreams, astrology, superstition, healing, temples, hymns, imperial cult, holy men and women, missions, apologists, Hermetism, Gnosticism, conversion, persecution, and perceptions of Judaism and Christianity. There are separate chapters on Marcus Aurelius, Constantine, and Julian.

5.2   ☞ Aland, Kurt. *A History of Christianity.* Vol. 1. *From the Beginnings to the Threshold of the Reformation.* Translated by James L. Schaaf. Philadelphia: Fortress, 1985. Pp. xiv + 474. CT-33; I-26.
Only the first 212 pages are relevant in this two-volume work, which begins unexpectedly with an analysis of the Christian argument with Paganism, rather than with the more common analysis of the relationship of Christianity with Judaism. Although there is no bibliography or footnotes, the content is clearly informed by recent developments in research, and some of the topics reflect new focuses for scholarship (social structures of the early church; role of women). Many of the topics in Aland's work relate to separate sections in this bibliography (persecution; conversion and missions; "victory" of Christianity over paganism; organization of the early catholic church and development of the monarchical episcopate; development of canon; conversion of Constantine, and the numerous conflicts over doctrine and practice).
⤳ Egan, *Horizons* 14 (1987): 148-149; Frend, *JEH* 37 (1986): 349-350;

McLaughlin, *TT* 43 (1986): 112-114; Monti, *CHR* 73 (1987): 91-92; Moody, *TS* 47 (1986): 189; Renna, *CH* 55 (1986): 82.

5.3   Bainton, Roland H. *Christendom: A Short History of Christianity and Its Impact on Western Civilization.* Vol. 1. *From the Birth of Christ to the Reformation.* Harper Torchbooks. New York: Harper & Row, 1966. Pp. viii + 274. I-9; B-4; B&W-76.
About one hundred pages are relevant (some of ch. 2; all of chs. 3-5). Bainton is an entertaining writer, with bits of wit and memorable detail. The text is aided by numerous photographs and illustrations, each with an extensive explanation. Although most of the issues in the study of the early church are dealt with by Bainton, on average only one to two pages is given to each issue. Further, Bainton is primarily a scholar of the Reformation period. Nonetheless, his work can serve as an informative introduction, which, though short, nonetheless has a surprising wealth of detail.

5.4   Baus, Karl. *From the Apostolic Community to Constantine.* Volume 1 of *Handbook of Church History.* Edited by Hubert Jedin and John Dolan. Freiburg: Herder / London: Burns & Oates, 1965. Pp. xxiii + 523. B-71; I-17.
One of the standard church histories in German, now translated into English. Volume one contains a 56-page introduction to the study of church history, with emphasis on the period from the Reformation and Enlightenment on, where an attempt is made to indicate the theological nature of the discipline. The volume covers all the major topics, in a partly chronological and partly thematic arrangement, down to the impact of Constantine' conversion. The bibliography is massive, and arranged clearly and conveniently, perhaps better than any other bibliography. Most of the works listed here are in German, though there is an adequate selection of works in English.
❧ Review of the German edition: McGuire, *TS* 24 (1963): 695-697.

5.5   Brown, Peter. *The World of Late Antiquity: From Marcus Aurelius to Muhammad.* London: Thames and Hudson, 1971. Pp. 216. I-3; B-4; CT-4; M-1. C-16; B&W-114.
This is a well-illustrated introductory work by one of the better known scholars in the area. Brown is concerned with the changes that are part of the collapse of empires and classical institutions, and with the recovery. He examines three new societies that arose out of the dying empire: the Catholic West, the Byzantium East, and Islam. Religion is, therefore, an important element in this book.

He shows an appreciation of the *achievements* of the new order
(rather than a "decline and fall"), and he shows an awareness of the
differences between East and West.
✂ Frend, *JTS* 23 (1972): 231-233; Murphy, *Downside Review* 89 (1971):
336-337.

5.6   Carrington, Philip. *The Early Christian Church.* Cambridge: Cam-
      bridge UP, 1957. Volume I: Pp. 520. I-13; B&W-31; B-5; CT-4;
      FT-2; M-7. Volume II: Pp. 519. I-26; B&W-32; B-3; CT-8; FT-1;
      M-5.
      These two volumes offer a detailed survey of the major individuals,
      movements, documents, and issues of the church's first three hundred
      years. Only the latter part of volume 1 is relevant to our bibliography,
      but all of volume two is relevant, and the last chapter ends with
      Constantine and Eusebius. Chapters are clearly arranged, with some
      emphasis on geographical divisions, and each chapter is itself
      subdivided into roughly one-page sections. Two appendixes provide
      the text of the "Anti-Marcionite" gospel prologues and the Mura-
      torian fragment. The index to both volumes is found in volume 2.
      These volumes can serve almost as an encyclopedia of the early
      church from its beginnings to Constantine. Its approach is "con-
      servative," as the author, the former Archbishop of Quebec, himself
      admits.
      ✂ Graham, *ATR* 40 (1958): 326-329; Lillie, *SJT* 11 (1958): 430-433;
      Stendahl, *Harvard Divinity Bulletin* 23 (1957-8): 139-141; Stevenson, *JEH*
      10 (1959): 91-92; Turner, *CQR* 159 (1958): 298-301.

5.7   ☞ Chadwick, Henry. *The Early Church.* The Pelican History of
      the Church 1. Harmondsworth: Penguin Books, 1967. Pp. 304.
      B-6; I-9.
      Of the many general introductions to the history of the early church,
      this book most closely covers the period of interest to this
      bibliography. Chadwick is one of the leading historians of the early
      church, and many of his more technical works and articles are
      listed in this bibliography. His volume in the Pelican series is an
      informed and readable account, and has served widely as an
      introductory textbook for college and university classes.

5.8   Chesnut, Glenn F. *The First Christian Histories: Eusebius, Socrates,
      Sozomen, Theodoret, and Evagrius.* 2d ed. Macon, GA: Mercer
      UP, 1986. (1977[1]). Pp. 296. MAI-2; B-30; Greek Index-2.
      Chesnut considers the early historians of Christianity, who are
      basically optimistic compared to Augustine, for example. The main

historians considered are Eusebius, Socrates Scholasticus, Sozomen, and Evagrius, all from the 300s or 400s, with Augustine in the middle period. Chesnut emphasizes the themes of fate and fortune in both pagan and Christian historians. Christians alter the standard line to take account of free will, while recognizing the "fortuitous nature of life." The student of the early church ought to be aware that there was no "standard" interpretation of history even among those sharing common orthodox beliefs.

✂ Benko, *AHR* 85 (1980): 608-609; Burns, *TS* 40 (1979): 185-187; Hinson, *CH* 49 (1980): 205-206; Hinson, *CH* 56 (1987): 549; Markus, *JEH* 32 (1981): 113-114; Norris, *CRBR* 1 (1988): 308-310; Pleket, *VC* 36 (1982): 193-197.

5.9 ◉ Chesnut, Glenn F. "A Century of Patristic Studies, 1888-1988." In *A Century of Church History: The Legacy of Philip Schaff.* Edited by Henry W. Bowden. Carbonville and Edwardsville, IL: Southern Illinois UP, 1988. Pp. 36-73.
Chesnut's article supplies a clear overview of the fortunes and failures of patristic scholarship over the last century. Patristic scholarship had suffered, according to Chesnut, largely because of the Catholic emphasis on Aquinas rather than the Fathers and the Protestant dismissal of Hellenistic influences on Christian development (e.g. Harnack's perspective). Then Chesnut comments on numerous key works that helped to bring the patristic field into the world of sensitive and critical scholarship. This is a highly useful summary of many of the major issues that still concern scholars of early Christianity.

5.10 ☛ Comby, Jean. *How to Understand Church History: From the Beginning to the Fifteenth Century.* Translated by John Bowden and Margaret Lydamore. New York: Crossroad, 1985. Pp. 195. CT-3; M-7; B&W-78.
About one half of this book is relevant to the period of our bibliography. It is as simple and as clear an introduction as can be found, filled with 142 passages from ancient literature, illustrations, and charts. Although the most likely audience will be the general reader rather than university student, even the beginning university student may find the brief, extremely clear, and solid summaries of numerous important issues beneficial. The illustrations and maps are generally crude; use other works for these matters. (R)
✂ Lieu, *ExT* 97 (1986): 312.

5.11 ☛ Daniélou, Jean. *The Christian Centuries.* Vol. 1. *The First Six*

Hundred Years. With Henri Marrou. Translated by Vincent Cronin. London: Darton, Longman and Todd, 1964. Pp. xxix + 525. I-9; B&W-48; BI-3; SI-10; PI-4; B-31; CT-8; FT-1; M-16; T-1.

This is a clearly written work, covering all the topics of interest to students of the early church. Divided into 39 short chapters (and these clearly divided into sections), and filled with helpful maps, photographs, and tables, this is one of the best places for the serious student to gain a solid overview of the period.

5.12 ☛ Davies, J.G. *The Early Christian Church: A History of Its First Five Centuries.* London: Weidenfeld & Nicolson, 1965. Reprint. Grand Rapids: Baker, 1980. Pp. xiii + 314. B&W-31; Floor Plans-22.

Covering roughly the same period and material as Chadwick [§5.7], Davies provides a sound introduction to the period of interest to this bibliography. He has divided his work by centuries (a chapter on each of the first five), and each chapter is further divided into clear sections: Background; Sources; Expansion and Development; Beliefs; Worship; and Social Life. Davies emphasizes worship and architecture (22 church floor plans) more than other introductions do. Clearly written; generally a solid introduction.

✂ R.M. Grant, *VC* 22 (1968): 141-142; Milburn, *JEH* 17 (1966): 244-245; Telfer, *JTS* 17 (1966): 158-160.

5.13 Dowley, Tim, ed. *Eerdmans Handbook to the History of Christianity.* Grand Rapids: Eerdmans, 1977. Pp. xxiv + 656. I-5; PI-7; BI-1; Place Index-3; hundreds of B&W and colour illustrations.

About 200 pages of this work are relevant. Filled with color and black and white photographs and maps, this work attempts to make the history of the Christian church interesting to the general reader. Key chapters are written by W. Ward Gasque, David F. Wright, Richard Todd, and Harry Rosenberg. Brief summaries of key people, events, texts, issues, and movements are provided by experts in the field, such as Everett Ferguson, F.F. Bruce, Edwin Yamauchi, Colin J. Hemer, and H. Dermot McDonald. For the coffee table and a few minutes of relaxation from time to time.

5.14 ◉ Drewery, B. "History and Doctrine: Heresy and Schism." *Journal of Ecclesiastical History* 23 (1972): 251-66.

This is a review article of ten books published in 1970 and 1971. The following seven English works are relevant: J.H. Smith, *Constantine the Great*; W.H.C. Frend, *The Donatist Church: a Movement of Protest in Roman North Africa* [§21.21]; D. Ayerst and A.S.T. Fisher, *Records of Christianity,* I: *In the Roman Empire*;

P. Brown, *The World of Late Antiquity: from Marcus Aurelius to Muhammad* [§5.5]; J.L. González, *A History of Christian Thought, I: From the Beginnings to the Council of Chalcedon* [§5.18]; and W. Bauer, *Orthodoxy and Heresy in Earliest Christianity* [§18.2]. The reviews reflect Drewery's grasp of the extensive debate about orthodoxy and heresy, and many older books are mentioned in his discussion.

5.15 ☛ Frend, W.H.C. *The Early Church.* Philadelphia: Fortress, 1982. (1965[1]). Pp. xi + 273. I-8; B-2; CT-5.
Originally published in 1965 by Hodder & Stoughton, the Fortress Press edition differs from the first printing by revision of bibliography; the text is unchanged. This is a good introduction for the period up to 451 CE. Frend's understanding of archaeology, politics, and society gives this work its distinctive features as an introductory text. The 22 chapters are short, with several of them focusing on a particular individual (Marcion, Origen, Julian, Ambrose, Augustine, and Leo), or a particular event (the Great Persecution, the Arian Controversy, asceticism, development of the papacy). Frend's strength is on the social and political dimensions of the development of the church, rather than on the development of dogma itself. For a more substantial work by Frend on the early church, see the entry following.
✀ R.M. Grant, *CH* 36 (1967): 85.

5.16 Frend, W.H.C. *The Rise of Christianity.* Philadelphia: Fortress, 1984. Pp. xvii + 1022. SI-10; NI-22; B&W-31; B-3; M-7; CT-74.
One of the most massive one-volume works on the period covered by this bibliography, ending with the year 604 CE. The work is divided into four major sections: "Jews and Christians"; "Christianity and the Roman Empire"; "From Constantine to Chalcedon"; ending with a hundred-page discussion of the break between the eastern and the western church. The characteristic strengths of Frend are here: attention to political, economic, and social issues, and suggestive ideas about Judaism's influence.
✀ Babcock, *SC* 5 (1985-86): 250-252; Chappin, *Gregorianum* 68 (1987): 761-763; Clark, *CH* 54 (1985): 380-382; Ferguson, *RQ* 29 (1987): 121-123; Grant, *BAR* 12 (1986): 14-16; Griffith, *JR* 66 (1986): 431-436; Hinson, *R&E* 83 (1986): 126-127; Louth, *Downside Review* 104 (1986): 44-46; Moody, *JAAR* 54 (1986): 337-342; Quispel, *VC* 39 (1985): 82-86; Richardson, *Theology* 90 (1987): 398-400; Saint-Laurent, *Interpretation* 40 (1986): 104; Siddals, *ExT* 97 (1986): 200-202; Yamauchi, *CSR* 16 (1986): 66-70.

5.17 Goguel, Maurice. *The Primitive Church.* Translated by H.C. Snape. New York: George Allen & Unwin, 1953. Pp. 610. B-4; I-4; AAI-12; MAI-4.

This is the third volume of a trilogy, the others being *The Life of Jesus,* 1933 (2d ed. *Jesus,* 1958), and *The Birth of Christianity,* 1953. Goguel, a liberal Protestant, was one of the leading scholars on the primitive church, and an authority (recognized by Catholic and Protestant alike) on the Christian church up to the middle of the second century. He taught at the Faculté de Théologie of Paris, where he was followed by Oscar Cullmann. Goguel saw and appreciated the diversity in the early church, and in his understanding of orthodoxy and heresy he shows the imprint of Walter Bauer. His *Birth of Christianity* is divided into four major sections: "Doctrine," "Organization," "Worship," and "Christian Life."

5.18 ☞ González, Justo L. *The Story of Christianity.* Vol. 1. *The Early Church to the Dawn of the Reformation.* San Francisco: Harper & Row, 1984. Pp. 426. I-12; B&W-89; M-10; CT-15.

About two-thirds of this volume is relevant to the period of our bibliography. González has written one of the clearest introductions to the history of the church, providing an ideal first-year college textbook or an elementary reference work. Each chapter is short (about 11 pages) and each section within is clearly divided. Photographs and maps are numerous, clear, and relevant. Each major division (four in the first volume) is introduced with an extensive chronological table (ranging from 1-9 pages). A two-page appendix on the church councils is included.

❧ Anderson, *JETS* 28 (1985): 467-468; Connelly, *CHR* 73 (1987): 90-91; Gallagher, *Horizons* 13 (1986): 162-164; Leonard, *R&E* 82 (1985): 611-612; Pointer, *CSR* 15 (1986): 205-206.

5.19 ☞ Grant, Robert M. *Augustus to Constantine: The Rise and Triumph of Christianity in the Roman World.* (1970). Reprint: New York: Harper & Row, 1990. Pp. xiv + 334. B-9; I-8; CT-3.

Grant deals with the first three centuries of the church, setting both Judaism and Christianity in the context of the Roman world. The introductory chapter (18 pp.) provides a useful summary of primary features of the Roman world (army, cities, and religion). Grant considers the second century largely on the basis of crises or issues (Apologists, Gnostics, Montanists) and the third century largely on the basis of geographical areas (Rome, Africa, Alexandria, Antioch). The final chapters are reserved for a discussion of the conversion of the empire, followed by brief summaries of the Christian attitude to worship, slavery, ethics, property, sexuality, discipline, creeds, war, the Christian calendar, baptism, Eucharist (with a detailed discussion of the developing sacramental system in the first three centuries), and various others themes.

5.20   ☛ Hazlett, Ian, ed. *Early Christianity: Origins and Evolution to AD 600.* London: SPCK, 1991. Pp. xvi + 335. B-5; G-5; CT-6; BI-1; AAI-3; NI-4; SI-3; M-2; C-2.

This is an unusual book, in that it is a Festschrift-kind of effort for Frend, and thus written by a variety of authors, but it is organized in such a way that all the major topics on the early church are covered, and thus the volume provides a comprehensive and informed discussion of our period by leading scholars in the field. The following are some of the topics discussed: Bible (Rowan Williams); Pagan Background (Luther Martin); Asceticism and Monasticism (Rousseau); the Greek Fathers (Frances Young); Greek Influence (Stead); Gnosticism (Rudolph); Mysticism (Louth); Pagan Perceptions of Christianity (Barnes); Christian Attitudes to poverty and wealth (Boniface Ramsey); and the list goes on. This could serve as an introductory textbook, and its chapters easily supplement the brief discussions we have offered at the beginning of each chapter of this bibliography. A 2-page select bibliography of Frend's works is included.

5.21   Herrin, Judith. *The Formation of Christendom.* Princeton: Princeton UP, 1987. Pp. x + 533. I-30; CT-2; B&W-16; M-3.

Covering the latter period of our bibliography and beyond (from the barbarians to the iconoclastic controversy), Herrin's history often reaches back into the earlier periods and forward into later. There is a heavy emphasis on some of the theological divisions and disputes, including the new problems that came with the rise of Islam. Various other topics will interest the student of the early church: the contribution of Gregory the Great; the church in city and countryside; monasticism, celibacy, east/west differences, and the church's relationship with paganism. Herrin sees two distinct features of her history: (1) the emphasis on the transitional period between Late Antiquity and the Middle Ages, and (2) the emphasis on Byzantium and the east in the development of both the West and Islam.

5.22   Latourette, Kenneth S. *A History of Christianity. Volume I: to A.D. 1500.* Rev. ed. New York: Harper and Row, 1975. Pp. xxvi + 724. I-38; M-19.

Latourette begins with an examination of the overall historical setting of Christianity, and analyzes Judaism and the Graeco-Roman world which provided the immediate background of the church. Only about one-half of this volume is relevant. Latourette emphasizes the expansion of Christianity, the development in organization and doctrine, admission, and discipline, monasticism, and Christian attitudes towards a variety of issues: war, amusements, slavery, property, family, art, etc. Latourette, unlike most modern historians, at times passes judgments on various tendencies and developments, but that does not negate the value of the work. Each chapter has a detailed bibliography, and many entries have a brief comment. A 3-page supplementary bibliography by Ralph Winter updates the bibliographies with entries from 1950 to about 1975. (Sm)

5.23 ☛ Markus, R.A. *Christianity in the Roman World.* London: Thames and Hudson, 1974. Pp. 192; B-3; I-3; B&W-74; M-1.
A brief and readable introduction, covering roughly the period of our bibliography. Markus deals with most of the large issues related to Christianity's struggle and success in the Roman world, and the church's response to the collapse of the Roman world to the barbarians. The illustrations are well chosen, and printed on glossy paper, which make them especially clear. There is a particular interest in the political questions: monasticism gets only brief mention, for example, and Arianism, though mentioned often, is usually discussed in terms of its political character (e.g. as the religion of the barbarians) rather than in terms of the theological. Nonetheless, a good survey for the beginning student.

5.24 ☛ McGonigle, Thomas D., and James F. Quigley. *A History of the Christian Tradition. From Its Jewish Origins to the Reformation.* New York and Mahwah: Paulist, 1988. Pp. vi + 218. I-11.
Only one-third of this book is relevant to our period. It provides a clear introduction to the main issues and people, with an occasional illustration, map, or chart, and a frequent quote when dealing with individuals. The authors have used no technical terminology and at times their Roman Catholic sympathies show, especially in their treatment of the status of the early Roman church. The book is useful primarily for the beginning student of the early church, who wishes to gain a quick 2-hour overview of key issues and people.

5.25 ☛ McManners, John, ed. *The Oxford Illustrated History of Christianity.* Oxford/New York: Oxford UP, 1990. Pp. xi + 724. Slightly over 10% of this massive work deals with the period of this bibliography; its focus is modern Christianity, with half of the work dealing with Christianity from 1800 to the present. But the two chapters dealing with the early church are important in that they were written by leading historians of the period: Henry Chadwick provides the chapter "The Early Christian Community," and Robert Markus provides the chapter "From Rome to the Barbarian Kingdoms (330-700). With the illustrations, maps, neatly sub-divided chapters, and awareness of the current issues and interests, this provides a learned and accessible step into the study of the early church for even the beginner.

5.26   Schaff, Philip. *History of the Christian Church: Ante-Nicene Christianity, A.D. 100-325.* Grand Rapids: Eerdmans, 1980. Pp. xiv + 877. I-18.
        As Volume II of Schaff's *History of the Christian Church,* this is still an important source of information. A reprint of the 1889 fifth edition of that multi-volume work, it is surprising that so much of it has stood the test of time. Beginning with the general literature on the ante-Nicene age, it covers the spread of Christianity, persecution and martyrdom, the contest with Judaism and "heathenism," the organization of the church, Christian worship, the development of doctrine, and a host of other topics. Although more recent scholarship has changed our view of the early church significantly, Schaff gives a fine, generally accurate and detailed overview of its history. (P)

5.27   Schaff, Philip. *History of the Christian Church: Nicene and Post-Nicene Christianity, A.D. 311-600.* Grand Rapids: Eerdmans, 1980. Pp. xvii + 1049. A-12; I-9.
        Volume III of Schaff's *History of the Christian Church,* this is an almost encyclopedic examination of the Church "in union with the Roman Empire." It covers a broad series of topics such as church-state relations, the development of the church in a changed political atmosphere, the doctrinal controversies that rocked the church during this period, and many other matters. Like the other volumes of Schaff's monumental work, it remains useful. However, since much has been researched and written since Schaff's day, particularly on the doctrinal controversies, many of his interpretations are outdated. (P)

5.28   Sheldon, Henry C. *History of the Christian Church.* Vol. 1. *The Early Church.* New York: Thomas Y. Crowell, 1895. Reprint. Peabody, MA: Hendrickson, 1988. Pp. x + 619. I-7; T-4.

Part of a 5-volume work. Although somewhat dated, Sheldon did write at a time when much attention was beginning to be paid to the developing early church, as is indicated by a 5-page appendix on Harnack and Hatch's views on early church organization. Almost every aspect is covered up to 590 CE, from the traditional topics (heresy, struggle with and victory over paganism, church structure) to some topics less adequately covered in other histories, especially regarding matters of worship and religious life (rituals, catacombs, veneration of saints and relics, hymns and liturgies, architecture, and painting).

5.29   ☛ Smith, M. A. *From Christ to Constantine*. London: Inter-Varsity, 1971. Pp. 208. I-4; CT-4; M-3; B&W-49.
Intended as an introduction to the church before Constantine, this book serves the general reader well who has no background in the early church, but is familiar with the New Testament period. The illustrations are well chosen and the text is readable and non-technical, with brief sub-sections in each chapter, and a few notes. The 26-page glossary covers major individuals, movements, disputes, and terms.

5.30   Walker, Wiliston. *A History of the Christian Church*. 4th ed. New York: Charles Scribner's Sons, 1985. (1918[1]). Pp. 756. I-23; B-20; M-9.
This has been a standard one-volume history of the Christian church for much of this century. It has an adequate focus on the early church (about one-third) to make it a useful and informed source on the leading persons and issues. Chapters are usually short and focused on one point, making it almost like an encyclopedia or dictionary, except that it is arranged in chronological rather than alphabetical order. Notes have been kept to the barest minimum, usually consisting to a cross reference or to a reference to a primary source or collection.

5.31   ☛ Walsh, Michael. *The Triumph of the Meek. Why Early Christianity Succeeded*. London: Roxby Reference Books/San Francisco: Harper & Row, 1986. Pp. 256. B-3; I-3; B&W-69; C-55; M-6; CT-5.
Although the title suggests a book about conversion and missions, it really does not fit that section of our bibliography. This book is more a general introduction to the early church, from its beginnings to the conversion of Constantine, and only the second half deals with the second and third centuries. Yet the book is highly recommended for its clear writing, awareness of recent developments

in the field, attractive charts and maps, and for its brilliant collection of photographs (probably as good as is to be found in any introduction). Three chapters are divided geographically: the east, North Africa, the west; three by theme: Ritual/Worship; Attitudes; Persecution.

✄ Clark, *CHR* 74 (1988): 315-316; Hinson, *R&E* 84 (1987): 547-548; Ramsay, *Worship* 61 (1987): 369; Trigg, *CH* 57 (1988): 214-215; Weinrich, *CTQ* 51 (1987): 314-315.

6
ART AND ARCHITECTURE

In the second Council of Nicea in 787 CE (the seventh of the ecumenical councils) a decision was made against a group called the "iconoclasts." The term is a Greek one, meaning an icon-breaker or an image-smasher, and it was largely in the Greek east where the battles were fought over the use of religious art. For some time previous, there had been a significant and violent dispute over the issue, and much of the art in Christian churches was destroyed, sometimes with clear imperial support. The council, however, resolved the matter in favour of the "iconodules" (or image-worshippers).

Although the iconoclasts lost, their perspective has surfaced from time to time throughout Christian history, and even today some Christian denominations are clearly on the side of those who happened to have lost at the council. The iconoclastic position was not without compelling arguments. Images looked too pagan-like, and Christians had made their mark in the empire by their caustic criticism of the pagan gods and their artistic representations—"idols" as they called them. To accept such things now was to pollute the church by approving the sensibilities of a supposedly conquered paganism. Further, the Christian scriptures themselves prohibited such representations, according to the iconoclasts, and they could easily point to the stark command at the very beginning of the "Ten Commandments": "You shall not make for yourself an idol...you shall not bow down to them or worship them..." (Exodus 20:4-5 NRSV).

Various counter-arguments were put forward, and with the monks on side, the iconodules won their case. One supporter of images even argued that the apostles themselves had compellingly approved of Christian art by their example: the apostles had, it was claimed, painted their churches with pictures of religious stories even *before* they wrote the Gospels!

No one accepts that argument now—in fact, not only is there no evidence of Christian art that early, there is not even evidence of distinctive church buildings in which such art could have been displayed. In fact, most scholars note the stark lack of Christian art in the first and second centuries. This lack is recognized in the titles or divisions of many of the works on the topic. For example, in Paul Finney's review, "Early Christian Art and Archaeology I (200-500)" [§6.2], it appears that there is no Christian art before the year 200 CE. Similarly, in Pierre du Bourquet's *Early Christian Art* [§6.7], the first major section begins at the year 200, and the same is true for A. Grabar's *The Beginnings of Christian Art, 200-395* (not abstracted in our volume). This absence, so widely recognized, seems to be true for both Christian art and Christian architecture.

A recent attempt to explain the absence of Christian art in the first two centuries of the church is Graydon Snyder's *Ante Pacem. Archaeological Evidence of Church Life before Constantine* [§6.5]. Snyder basically makes a distinction between "Christian art" and the "art of Christians." That is to say that, though there was little distinctive Christian art in the first two centuries, Christians nonetheless had art—it was simply not distinguishable from the art of the pagan and Jewish society around them until 180 CE. Snyder's thesis, if sound, is useful in calling attention to the possibility that the line between the early Christians and the world they lived in was not always clearly drawn, nor did every aspect of life necessarily become fundamentally different as a result of conversion to Christianity. Snyder further argues that there was considerable conflict within the Christian church over the use of art, and he draws a line between the elite hierarchy, which generally rejected it, and the popular and lower-level members, led by cemetery leaders, who promoted it.

There are several matters to be considered. First, we must be certain that what we identify as a pagan theme or symbol would have been considered by the early Christians in the same way. And that depends on how much of the general cultural life of the world of the Mediterranean would have been considered distinctly pagan (in a religious way) by the early Christians. It is easy to draw the lines too starkly at this point. Art can be primarily decorative, or neutral, and we should allow for this dimension in the use of art—at least, there would seem to be no clear reason to disallow this.

But that does not remove all the problems by any means. Christians did use art. Even though much of the earliest art is from the catacombs and sarcophagi (largely Constantinian or later), even earlier examples exist. Perhaps against a popular use of art by Christians—but not necessarily so—is the polemic against pagan art in many of the early Christian writers. The images of the gods are mocked, as are the stories of the gods, which provided the themes of most of pagan art.

One may attempt to dismiss the significance of this literary evidence, as Snyder has done, restricting the literary evidence to the Christian elites' attitude to art, and contrasting that to the attitude of the average believer. This is an argument based on a recognition of high and low culture, of elite and popular culture—a two-tier system. While there is merit in recognizing that distinction at times, it may have less application to the ancient world than to the modern, as Simon Price has argued in another context (*Rituals and Power: The Roman Imperial Cult in Asia Minor*, pp. 107-109 [§20.37]). Perhaps more recognition needs to be given to the power and popularity that the so-called elite leaders possessed among the common people. Further, the zeal of "converts" much be taken into account. Although no convert can reject every element in his or her past, often conversion involves radical changes—so much so that the world is "turned upside down." Turning from art to architecture: the situation is much the same. There is no evidence in the earliest period for any distinctive Christian architecture. The main reason for this seems to be that Christians simply used their homes for meeting places, sometimes turning the whole house over for that purpose, with slight modifications to the interior. This method of assembly is referred to as a "house church." By the third century, identifiable Christian buildings could be found throughout the empire—even within view of the imperial palace.

After the conversion of Constantine, as paganism receded, closed and deserted temples often were given to the Christian church. The structure of most temples did not serve the Christian needs well. Pagan temples were primarily a place where the individual met his or her god or goddess. But Christians had a clearly communal sense of their assemblying before their god, and required a different kind of sacred space. Further, as R.P.C. Hanson has argued [§6.20], even were the pagan temples fully suitable for Christian corporate worship, the stark sense in the Christian mind that such locales were the habitation of demons would have prevented immediate Christian use of these buildings. Christians had their own needs, and this, under imperial sponsorship, flowered into architectural accomplishments which stand to this day, particularly in some of the churches in Istanbul, such as the Hagia Sophia, built during the reign of Justinian.

GENERAL
6.1   ⑧ Coulson, William D.E., and Patricia W. Freiert. *Greek and Roman Art, Architecture, and Archaeology; An Annotated Bibliography.* Rev. ed. New York/London: Garland, 1987. (1975[1]). Pp. viii + 204. I-32.
This bibliography emphasizes new books and books in print, providing a substantial revision of the first edition done twelve years previously. There are 349 entries, some of which are cross-listed. Annotations are sometimes quite extensive. The most useful are the chapters focusing of Greek and Roman materials, though the "Additional Resources" chapter should be consulted too, where listed general works, museum collections, publications, and additional bibliographies are listed.

6.2 ⑧ Finney, Paul Corby. "Early Christian Art and Archaeology I (200-500): A Selected Bibliography 1945-1985." *Second Century* 6 (1987-88): 21-42; and "Early Christian Art and Archaeology II (200-500): A Selected Bibliography 1945-1985." *Second Century* 6 (1987-88): 203-238. I-7.

This bibliography was prepared as an introduction to the much larger project for *ANRW*. It deals with non-literary and non-documentary sources under the following twelve headings: (1) Archaeological Handbooks and Art Historical Surveys, (2) Exhibition Catalogues, (3) Festschriften, (4) Regions, Sites, Excavations, (5) Architecture, (6) Sculpture, (7) Painting, (8) Mosaics, (9) Small finds, (10) Iconography, (11) Documentary and Literary Sources, and (12) Jewish Antecedents and Parallels. There are 724 entries, a few of which are annotated. Where possible, individual sections are subdivided, sometimes in terms of geography or theme. The index is largely focused on authors.

6.3 🏛 Mango, Cyril. *The Art of the Byzantine Empire 312-1453*. Sources and Documents in the History of Art. Prentice-Hall, 1972. Reprint. Medieval Academy Reprints for Teaching 16. Toronto/Buffalo/London: University of Toronto Press, 1986, in association with the Medieval Academy of America. Pp. xvi + 272. I-6; AAI-6; B-1. M-1. B&W-1.

A collection of primary texts, translated by the author from Greek, Latin, and Slavic sources. The short introduction and the first three chapters (one half of the book) are relevant to this bibliography. Chapter 1 deals with Constantine; chapter 2 with the period from Constantine to Justinian; and chapter 3 with Justinian. Each chapter is introduced by a two to three page discussion. The bulk of each chapter is divided into clear sections (e.g. "Constantine's Coins and Effigies;" "Heterodox Painting;" "Opposition to Religious Art;" "Ravenna"). Each selection includes helpful notes. A map of Constantinople and a floor plan of St. Sophia are included. A useful introduction and reference.

✂ Wortley, *SR* 3 (1974): 292-294.

6.4 ☛ Milburn, Robert. *Early Christian Art and Architecture*. Aldershoot, England: Scholar Press, 1988. Pp. xviii + 318. I-6; B&W-195; AB-7; M-4.

This volume, covering the beginning of the church up to Justinian, is an excellent introduction to a vast number of topics, and provides clearly written and detailed chapters, each illustrated with a collection of fine black and white reproductions and line drawings. One can gain a quick but informed view of house churches, catacombs, church architecture, geographical differences, fonts and baptistries, mosaics, carved ivories, crafts, gems, coins, textiles, books, and writing. Special attention is given to Ravenna and to Justinian. The carefully selected general bibliography will lead the serious student to more detailed bibliographies.

℘< Ferguson, *RQ* 32 (1990): 235-236; Henig, *TLSuppl* 4473 (Dec 23-29 1988): 1416; Krentz, *Currents* 16 (1989): 471; Ramsey, *TS* 50 (1989): 821; Smith, *BAR* 15 (1989): 8.

6.5 ☞ Snyder, Graydon F. *Ante Pacem. Archaeological Evidence of Church Life before Constantine.* Macon, GA: Mercer University Press, 1985. Pp. xiv + 173. I-3; B&W-90; BI-1; CT-2; M-7.

After a review of the discipline, Snyder considers a variety of early Christian symbols, frescoes, mosaics, sarcophagi, various story themes from the Old and New Testament, church buildings, inscriptions and graffiti, and papyrus documents. Brief bibliographies accompany many of the sections. Snyder argues that the reason archaeological evidence for Christianity seems so rare in the early period is that, until 180 CE, Christian art simply used the elements common in the society—that despite the Christian literary (and "elitist") polemic against the culture of the day. In fact, Snyder sees the church's attitudes divided between an urban group (led by bishops) and an "extra-urban" group (led by cemetery leaders). For Snyder, the crucial point is around 180, when Christianity began to differ visibly in cultural expression; it is then that Christians encountered their most bitter opposition. The most serious objection to Snyder's methodology is whether one can understand archaeological material without reference to the literature of the early Christians.

℘< Finney, *CH* 56 (1987): 375-377; Hinson, *R&E* 84 (1987): 148-149; Krentz, *Currents* 13 (1986): 181-183; Pearson, *BAR* 13.1 (1987): 10-13; Ramsey, *CHR* 73 (1987): 128-129; Scroggs, *CTSR* 75 (1985): 25-27; Seasoltz, *Worship* 61 (1987): 550-551; Strange, *BA* 49 (1986): 249-251; Talbert, *PRS* 13 (1986): 175-176; White, *JBL* 106 (1987): 560-562; Whitehurst, *Dialogue* 21 (1988): 163-165.

ART

6.6 Barnard, Leslie W. "The 'Cross of Herculaneum' Reconsidered." In *The New Testament Age: Essays in Honor of Bo Reicke.* Vol. 1. Edited by William C. Weinrich. Macon, GA: Mercer UP, 1984. Pp. 14-27.

Barnard reviews the debate about a mark that has come to be considered the first known use of the cross symbol in Christianity, pointing out other possible interpretations (Jewish use, or the markings left by a wall bracket for a shelf). Barnard opts for the possibility that even *first*-century Christians used the cross symbol. There is also a brief general discussion of the cross in early Christian art and literature, and of the possibility that the cross symbol appears in Pompeii too.

6.7 Bourquet, Pierre du. *Early Christian Art*. Translated by Thomas Burton. Forms and Colors Series Books. New York: Reynal & Co. in cooperation with William Morrow & Co., 1971. Pp. 220. B-2; B&W-126; C-60; M-2.

This work is divided into three major sections, offering beautiful reproductions of early Christian art from roughly the third century into the Constantinian period. The sections are "Semiclandestinity" (200-260); "Period of Emergence" (260-312); and the Constantinian period. The 7-page introduction summarizes the main changes in art and architecture under Christian influence, with new church buildings shaped to serve the needs of Christian worship, a switch from statues to paintings, and major developments in book illustration.

6.8 ☛ Daniélou, Jean. *Primitive Christian Symbols*. Translated by Donald Attwater. London: Burns & Oates, 1964. Pp. xvi + 151. I-5; B&W-15.

A collection of articles on early Christian art by Daniélou, who argues for the Jewish roots to many of the symbols that become common in Christianity. Individual chapters deal with the palm and the crown, the vine and the tree of life, living water and the fish, the ship, Elijah's chariot, the plough and the axe, the star of Jacob, the twelve Apostles and the zodiac, and the *taw* (or cross) sign. Daniélou bases his work primarily on early Christian literature. This makes the work a useful supplement to more recent works that emphasize the archaeological remains.
✂ R.M. Grant, *JES* 2 (1965): 124-125.

6.9 Finegan, Jack. *The Archaeology of the New Testament: The Life of Jesus and the Beginning of the Early Church*. Princeton: Princeton UP, 1969. Pp. xxiv + 273. I-11; BI-2; B&W-296.

Much of this covers the period of the New Testament, with an emphasis on Palestine. Each photo or illustration is accompanied by a description, sometimes brief but often quite long. Of particular interest to students of the early church will be the notes on tombs and burial practices, and the extensive 40-page discussion on the

use of the cross in Judaism and early Christianity, in which Finegan
suggests that the Christian use of the cross may stem from Jewish
use of the *taw*-mark as a symbol of salvation, though the case is
not generally considered a convincing one. Also, Finegan discusses
ancient sources, ancient measures of length, and statements about
direction in ancient literature.

ᖾ Fitzmyer, *CH* 39 (1970): 391-392; Kane, *Religion* 2 (1972): 57-75;
Karris, *CBQ* 32 (1970): 604-606; Kraabel, *JBL* 89 (1970): 363-366; Marshall,
SJT 24 (1971): 113-114.

6.10   Fishwick, Duncan. "On the Origin of the Rotas-Sator Square."
       Harvard Theological Review 57 (1964): 39-53.
       Fishwick attempts to determine the origin of the ROTAS-SATOR
       "magic square" found at Pompeii. The letters can be arranged into
       various patterns, one being a cross shape forming the words PATER
       NOSTER ("Our Father"), with the letters alpha and omega at the
       end of the lines. This has led some scholars to speak of the square
       as a Christian sign. Fishwick considers various options and problems,
       concluding that it more likely is of Jewish origin, which could
       explain its use by Christians too. Various others problems are
       considered.

6.11   Henig, Martin, ed. *A Handbook of Roman Art: A Survey of the
       Visual Arts of the Roman World.* Oxford: Phaidon, 1983. Pp. 288.
       B-10; I-8; C-35; B&W-210; M-1; G-4.
       This is a delightful and informative guide into the field of art in the
       Mediterranean world (not just Rome). Eleven authors contribute
       twelve chapters on all aspects of the field: early Roman art; archi-
       tecture; sculpture; wall painting and stucco; mosaics; the luxury
       arts (metalwork, gems and jewelry); coins and medals; pottery;
       terracotta works; glass; epigraphy; and art in late antiquity. Chapters
       are clearly divided, the illustrations are well chosen, and even the
       black and white illustrations have been very carefully photographed
       and reproduced. A fine introduction to the field, and serves well as
       a background for a study of Christian art.

6.12   Hutter, Irmgard. *Early Christian and Byzantine Art.* Translated by
       Alistair Laing. London: Weidenfeld and Nicolson, 1971. Pp. 192.
       I-4; B&W-140; C-49; B-2.
       Only the first half is relevant to our period. This volume serves as a
       fine introduction to the range of art and architecture of the early
       church, including some floor plans of churches, and examples of
       manuscript art. The first quarter deals with the period before

Justinian; the second relevant part is from Justinian to the iconoclastic controversy. The illustrations are numerous and striking, with detailed description of each. Even the black and white illustrations serve the reader well.

6.13 ☛ Meer, F. van der. *Early Christian Art.* Translated by Peter and Friedl Brown. London: Faber and Faber, 1967. Pp. 149. I-3; B&W-48.

A good introduction to Christian art, with a sketch of the history of interest in such remains, and a review of some of the misconceptions about early Christian life read from the materials (especially in regard to the catacombs). A summary of the location of the preserved art is included, along with chapters on the basilica, the "memoria" for the martyrs, baptisteries, cemeteries, the basilica wall paintings, portraits, holy books, and a discussion of the continuity and discontinuity of Christian art with the art of the pagan past. The plates (all black and white) are clearly produced, and detailed description of each is provided. A clear introduction.

6.14 Metzger, Bruce M. "A Lexicon of Christian Iconography." *Church History* 45 (1976): 5-15.

Although intended as a review of Herder's multi-volume *Lexikon der christlichen Ikonographie,* it is much more. Besides comparing that work favorably to other works available, Metzger offers frequent insights into many areas as he points to some weaknesses in this major work. Of interest is the artistic representations of Jesus (ugly or handsome; bareheaded, as is represented, or covered, as would have been more likely); the method of crucifixion (particularly the nailing of the feet and the crotch-support on which the victim sat, rather than the footrest that has become popular in Christian art, though it is based on no ancient authority). Also a few comments about Mary, the use of Alpha and Omega, and a number of other ideas.

6.15 Murray, Sr. C. *Rebirth and Afterlife. A study of the transmutation of some pagan imagery in early Christian funerary art.* Oxford: B.A.R., 1981. BAR International Series 100. Pp. vii + 223. B&W-39.

Murray challenges the widely held view that early Christian art stemmed from laypeople, and was generally disapproved by the clergy. He attempts to make a case for a more positive view of art in the early Christian church. But note the rather sharp criticism by Breckenridge in the short *JTS* review.

✂ Breckinridge, *JTS* 34 (1983): 630.

6.16   Schreckenberg, Heinz, and Kurt Schubert. *Jewish Historiography and Iconography in Early and Medieval Christianity*. With an Introduction by David Flusser. Assen/Maastricht: Van Gorcum / Minneapolis: Fortress, 1992. Pp. xviii + 307. B-13; AAI-14; NI-7; MAI-7; B&W-67.
Divided into two parts, the first part, by Schreckenberg, deals with Josephus and is the less relevant. The second part, by Schubert, is titled "Jewish Pictorial Traditions in Early Christian Art." The most striking thing one notices about Christian art (even Constantinian and post-Constantinian art) is how deeply indebted Christian art is to Jewish art. Schubert looks in detail at the synagogue, with special emphasis on the one at Dura Europos. Also, he considers the art in the Via Latina Catacomb, and in a sixth-century manuscript. A brief discussion of Jewish attitudes to art is provided.

6.17   Smith, Robert Houston. "The Cross Marks on Jewish Ossuaries." *Palestine Exploration Quarterly* 106 (1974): 53-66.
Smith considers various cross-like marks found on many of the Jewish ossuaries discovered in the vicinity of Jerusalem, and reviews some of the debate. (Ossuaries were the limestone containers, two to three feet in length, into which bones were placed to make room available in tombs for new corpses.) Smith argues that in most cases the cross marks were crude means of identifying matching lids and containers, and of indicating in which way the ill-fitting lids should be placed. In a few other cases, the marks may have been guides used by the mason. None has religious significance, according to Smith, though he seems to be forcing the issue at times, especially with what appears to be a clear chi-rho symbol.

ARCHITECTURE

6.18   ☛ Davies, J.G. *The Origin and Development of Early Christian Church Architecture*. London: SCM, 1952. Pp. xvi + 152. I-4; B-5; G-3; M-1; B&W-60.
Davies offers a review of church architecture which is still useful though forty years old. He emphasizes the considerable diversity in form, imposed by the local culture and materials, though there is an overall similarity imposed by the common liturgical function which the church building served in all areas. Forty-five floor plans are provided, along with chapters on the basic structure of the basilica, furniture, adjoining buildings (with some attention to martyrias), and with separate consideration of a number of different geographical areas.
☛ Milburn, *JTS* 4 (1953): 269-271; Rice, *JEH* 4 (1953): 218-219.

6.19   ◉ Finney, Paul Corby. "Early Christian Architecture: The Beginnings (A Review Article)." *Harvard Theological Review* 81 (1988): 319-339. B-2.
Finney reviews six major writers on early Christian places of worship. The theses of the former three (Deichmann; Süssenbach; and H.W. Turner) are criticized for the heavy theological assumptions about the nature of the "church" (whether "building" or "people"). The latter three (Krautheimer; Rordorf, and L.M. White) work from more clearly historical grounds, and are more favorably reviewed by Finney. Moving from house church to Constantinian basilicas, the overall impression is that (1) structures and locations were largely chosen for practical reasons; (2) there was no uniform or approved form; and (3) a significant amount of wealth seems to have been at the disposal of Christians.

6.20   Hanson, Richard P.C. "The Transformation of Pagan Temples into Churches in the Early Christian Centuries." In *Studies in Christian Antiquity.* Edinburgh: T&T Clark, 1985. Pp. 347-358.
Some scholars have argued for a transformation of pagan temples into Christian churches as early as the reign of Constantine or only slightly later (Jones, Cochrane, Avi-Jonah). Hanson argues against this, claiming that the first reaction of Christians after Constantine's conversion was to tear temples down, even against the wishes of the emperor. Furthermore, secular buildings were more suitable for adaptation as churches than were pagan temples. Finally, Hanson considers the evidence that the temples were dedicated to Christian heroes in such a way as to correspond to the former pagan deity. Not until 435 (after legislation) did Christians normally preserve and adapt the old temples.

6.21   Krautheimer, R. *Early Christian and Byzantine Architecture.* 2d ed. Baltimore: Penguin, 1975. Pp. 575. B-3; I-23; B&W-406; M-2; G-5.
This is the most detailed work on the subject, covering roughly the period of our bibliography for the west and a much longer period for the east. It is a standard reference work on early Christian architecture, dealing with everything from the major and well known buildings to some quite minor. Divided into nineteen chapters, it has only one chapter on the period prior to Constantine, since Christian architecture does not make its mark in earnest until the state started supporting it. Major sections are divided chronologically, and chapters within these are grouped by geographical area.
⤛ A few of the criticisms of the first edition are considered in the preface

of the second edition.

6.22   White, L. Michael. *Domus Ecclesiae — Domus Dei. Adaptation
        and Development in the Setting for Early Christian Assembly*, PhD
        Dissertation, Yale University, 1983. Pp. 693. [DA 44 (1983) 197A].
        White's research is now available in *The Social Origins of Christian
        Architecture*. Volume I: *Architectural Adaption among Pagans,
        Jews, and Christians*. Volume II: *Texts and Monuments*. Harvard
        Theological Studies. Minneapolis: Fortress, 1993. Vol. I: Pp. 232.
        Vol. II: Pp. 336.
        White studies the shift in the normal locations for meetings of
        Christian congregations in urban settings—from the private home
        in the first century to the church and basilica in the fourth. White
        argues that the church/basilica as an architectural form did not
        evolve out of the large house, but rather was a conscious introduction
        by the emperor Constantine. As for the previous "house-church"
        (*domus ecclesiae*), a wide variety of structures are found which
        therefore permitted and encouraged adaptation to local needs and
        conditions. In his survey of the pre-Christian use of houses as
        meeting places (e.g., in Judaism, Mithraism) White outlines the
        main archaeological, epigraphical, papyrological, and literary
        evidence in some detail. He then outlines the stages in the
        development of the house-church meeting place. (See, too, White's
        work titled *Building God's House in the Roman World: Architectural
        Adaptation among Pagans, Jews, and Christians*. Baltimore/London:
        John Hopkins UP, 1990. Pp. xv + 211. I-5; B&W-27. (S)
        ✄ Smith, *SC* 8 (1991): 253-255.

7
THE CANON
AND TEXTUAL CRITICISM

Early Christians used the Bible of the Jews as their canon. By the second century, Christians began to emphasize, in addition to this, a new body of documents (what comes to be called the "New Testament") as their canon. This new collection was not even in existence in the earliest years of the church. The process by which this change and development took place has been one of the primary discussions attracting the interests of scholars of the early church.

The Jewish Bible, or Old Testament, was hardly an "old" Testament for its first Christian users. The scriptures of the Jews served the early Christian communities well, and with a focus on the prophets, bore witness for them to the authenticity of Jesus as God's agent. Those parts of the Hebrew Bible that did not speak so directly to the concerns of the early church were frequently allegorized into usefulness and relevance. Although that interpretative method may leave something to be desired in the eyes of most modern critical interpreters, it was one already used by the Hellenistic Jewish community, which was seeking to render the Hebrew Bible meaningful to diaspora Jews and interested Greeks. Christian theologians like Clement of Alexandria and Origen gained much from the Jewish philosopher Philo. (See chapter 19 for a discussion of the practice of interpretation—called "exegesis"—among the early church theologians.)

But not every kind of interpretation was accepted as valid. Gnostic interpretation, for example, was judged by many leading churchmen to have gone beyond the acceptable. Not only did the Gnostics use a fairly free-wheeling interpretation of the canonical texts, they challenged the church by introducing new "apostolic" and "primitive" documents. They were not alone in this productive literary effort; a variety of Christian groups produced literature, using an apostolic label to give authority to the writing. Various first-century individuals were credited with new works written in the second century, and on occasion, individuals from the beginnings of the biblical story were tagged as the author—even Adam. This explosion of literature forced Christians to wrestle with the problems of what literature was authori-

91

tative and what was not; what literature was useful and what was, in the language of some church leaders, deadly poison.

The process of approving or banning literature is one aspect of the task of creating a "canon"—an authoritative collection of documents for religious use. This process marks one of the primary activities by which orthodoxy received its definitive character. But not all the efforts to discriminate between acceptable and unacceptable literature were themselves approved. One notable case was the effort made by Marcion. He rejected the Hebrew Bible in any of its interpreted forms; it was, he judged, the work of a foreign God of the Jews and had no connection to the God revealed by Jesus, and it could not be rescued by allegory, or by anything else. It was not only the borrowed material from Judaism that was discarded by Marcion; much of the early church's own novel literary production was discarded too. Marcion rejected all the Gospels except that of Luke, and all the letters, except those from Paul. Even these were thought by Marcion to be tainted by their creation and preservation in a Jewish context, and he cut away all material that did not fit with his radical rejection of Judaism.

For this reason, Marcion has become a key figure in the scholarly debate regarding the development of the canon. The question is one of credit. Was the church consciously responding to Marcion's offensive, restrictive, and excised collection of authoritative writings when it created its own broader list? This would make Marcion a considerable innovator and genius. Or was Marcion merely offering a different selection of documents from one that already operated at some level (conscious or otherwise) in the Christian community of which he was a part? This would make Marcion's contribution somewhat less significant—or at least less novel. In other words, was Marcion presenting to the Christian church a new concept (a *Christian* canon) or a new list (a *de-Judaized* canon)?

Another individual has gained a place of prominence in the discussion of the forces that gave rise to the Christian canon. He is Montanus, the founder of a charismatic and apocalyptic protest movement in Phrygia in west-central Asia Minor (Turkey). Montanus and his followers seem to have promoted various kinds of "inspired speech" through which a "living" and current word of God could be made available to the church. Any such claim went against one of the emphases that was developing within the second-century church: that is, the giving of pride-of-place to the "apostolic traditions" of the first century and to the idea of "antiquity" in general, against the new voices of the second century. In support of this emphasis on the apostolic past was the developing hierarchical structure of the church, in which bishops, as leaders, became more the conservative preservers and interpreters of the apostolic tradition than radical and independent innovators.

Much of the debate over canon depends on judgments about "why" and "when" the early documents came to be collected. The question of "where" the documents came to be collected may be important too, for there seems to be, for whatever reason, a particularly active interest in such collections in western Asia Minor. It might even be argued that this was the area that gave birth to the canon, in terms of both its production of early Christian literature and its collection of these writings into mini-canons or proto-canons, apparently quite early. For example, the Pauline letters are thought to have been collected by the turn of the first century, and perhaps even earlier, and the most likely place for that effort is western Asia Minor. A corpus of Johannine material may have been taking shape in the early part of the second century in the same area. The *Diatessaron* of Tatian (c. 150 CE) would seem to suggest that the gospels appeared as a collection or unit before the middle of the second century. And this effort, too, may have had a western Asia Minor connection, since Justin was the teacher of Tatian, and Justin had lived in Ephesus (but the point should not be pressed). All of these collections basically predate Marcion (though there are questions about the adequacy of the accepted chronology of Marcion). That being said, there may have been a significant trend towards "canon" within the Christian community to which Marcion could himself have been responding.

Collecting documents is only one part of the process of canonization. The collected documents must be granted authoritative status. Two questions are important here. One is: What allowed a document into the collection? The second: What kept a document out? These questions raise the issue of apostolicity and pseudonymity. Such questions occupied the church for some time, and it is not until the fourth century that we find "canonical lists" that correspond to what came to be accepted as the canon. Eusebius, writing around the time of the conversion of Constantine, pointed out the still unsettled status of particular writings. But for the larger number of documents that were to form the final Christian canon, their status was recognized relatively early and widely. Frequently scholars speak of a "Muratorian Canon" in this regard. That canon is a list of New Testament books, discovered by Ludovici Antonio Muratori (1672-1750), and the list generally has been dated to the late second century, though questions have been raised about that date.

Another broad field of study related to the canon is what is called "textual criticism." This deals with the *transmission* of documents through the years of scribal copying. Unlike printed books, where there is an established text, with each copy identical in every way, early "publication" of documents required that a scribe copy each word by hand for hundreds and hundreds of pages, referring to an earlier copy, which itself had been copied in the same way. This, of course, introduced errors (both intentional and unintentional), and no two texts were identical. When texts differed at particular points, scholars were required to decide which reading (or variant) was true to the original copy (or autograph).

Initially, the study of the text was affected by the fact that most of the surviving manuscripts were based on one "text type" or "family." In other words, the surviving manuscripts represented less diversity than what actually had existed in the manuscript tradition in the early period. Of course, scholars were not aware of this quirk in the manuscript holdings, all of which were relatively recent copies in the 1500s, when Erasmus initiated the effort to establish a reliable text. But by the 1800s, many very old manuscripts had been found, and some of these offered readings more diverse than what was offered in the more recent manuscripts. Over a hundred years ago, Westcott and Hort, founders of a rigorous methodology for establishing a critical edition of the Greek New Testament, concluded that there were three text types: the western (which was represented in the recent manuscripts and in many of the older ones); the Byzantine; and the neutral, which was judged to be the most reliable. Besides this, efforts were made to establish a sound methodology of textual criticism, by which decisions about variant readings could be made. The debate continues.

CANON

7.1   Ackroyd, P.R., and C.F. Evans. *From the Beginnings to Jerome.* Vol. 1 of *The Cambridge History of the Bible.* Cambridge: Cambridge UP, 1970. Pp. 649. I-17; B&W-25; BI-7; NTI-7; B-12; AAI-11.
A collection of 28 articles, most of which are relevant to this bibliography, dealing with issues such as biblical languages, books in the ancient world, all the general issues of text and canon, and specific articles on Origen, Theodore of Mopsuestia, Jerome, Augustine, the place of the Bible in the liturgy, and biblical exegesis in the early church. Of general interest are the articles by C.F. Evans, "The New Testament in the Making"; R.M. Grant, "The New Testament Canon"; and J.N. Birdsall, "The New Testament Text." Various plates of manuscripts and fragments are provided.

7.2   *Biblia Patristica: Index des Citations et Allusions Bibliques dans la Littérature Patristique.* Edited by Equipe de Recherche Associée of the Centre d'Analyse et de Documentation Patristique. 5 volumes. Paris: Centre National de la Recherche Scientifique. Vol. 1: Pp. 546; Vol. 2: Pp. 468; Vol. 3: Pp. 472; Vol. 4: Pp. 330; Vol. 5: Pp. 412. AAI-2.
Volume 1 (1975) covers the period from the beginnings to Clement of Alexandria and Tertullian; volume 2 (1977): the third century, excluding Origen; volume 3 (1980): Origen; volume 4 (1987): Eusebius of Caesarea, Cyril of Jerusalem, Epiphanius of Salamis;

volume 5 (1991): Basil of Caesarea, Gregory of Nazianzus, Gregory of Nyssa, Amphilochius of Iconium. Based on the resources at the University of Strasbourg, these volumes make available a comprehensive collection of citations of, and allusions to, the Old and New Testament, and Jewish noncanonical materials which are found in the patristic literature. This is a massive work, and is easily enough used by the English reader. The arrangement is simple and clear: scripture references, verse-by-verse (including the Apocrypha) are placed in order (of the LXX), and the reference to patristic writers follows on the same line.

7.3   Blackman, E.C. *Marcion and his Influence*. London: SPCK, 1948. Pp. x + 181. AI-2; BI-3; SI-2; B-3.
In chapters two and three, Blackman considers the impact of Marcion on the idea, content, and text of the Christian canon. He opposes or modifies Adolf Harnack's position at many points, primarily by requiring a distinction between the *idea* of a canon and the *fixation* of a canon. Marcion's influence is certainly provocative, but the church, itself, always had a canonical sense, according to Blackman. Rather than seeing the orthodox canon as a process of *collection*, he sees it as one of *selection*. Further, Blackman wants more attention focused on Montanism for the concept of a closed, apostolic canon. He thus reduces Marcion's impact.
⋊ Knox. *CH* 19 (1950): 295.

7.4   ☛ Bruce, F.F. *The Canon of Scripture*. Downers Grove, Ill: InterVarsity, 1988. Pp. 349. B-4; I-11.
Bruce's book deals with the canon (both Old Testament and New Testament) in the Christian church up to the Reformation, though primarily the book deals with the earlier period. All the major issues are covered briefly and clearly, and English translations are given for important canonical lists and for patristic passages such as the Marcionite prologues, the Muratorian Canon, decisions of councils, and comments by the fathers. Bruce thus provides a wealth of information about primary sources, in addition to important historical and biographical details. As is typical of Bruce, he shows critical trust rather than the more common critical scepticism regarding his sources. Also included is an 18-page appendix on the "Secret" Gospel of Mark.
⋊ Beckwith, *EQ* 62 (1990): 180-181; Beckwith, *JTS* 41 (1990): 207-208; Geer, *RQ* 32 (1990): 231-234; Green, *PRS* 17 (1990): 267-269; Miller, *JETS* 33 (1990): 119-120; Smith, *Faith and Mission* 7 (1990): 78-80.

7.5 Campenhausen, Hans von. *The Formation of the Christian Bible.*
Translated by John Austin Baker. London: Adam and Charles Black,
1972. Pp. 342. AAI-3; MAI-5.
A thorough treatment, dealing with the church's acceptance of the
Jewish canon (chs. 1-3); the development of the New Testament
(chs. 4-6); and theological reflection on the two-part canon (ch. 7).
Campenhausen emphasizes the original and unique contribution of
Marcion, and argues that no four-fold Gospel existed prior to
Marcion. As for the closing of the canon, Campenhausen emphasizes
the importance of Montanism in the process. Also discussed is the
importance of the New Testament as a means of safeguarding the
original traditions about Jesus, and the relative *unimportance* of
apostolic authorship as a criterion for accepting a document into
the canon.
⊰< Achtemier, *JES* 11 (1974): 128-130; Bruce, *CT* 18 (Feb 1974): 31-34;
R.M. Grant, *ATR* 55 (1973): 359-361; Groh, *Interpretation* 28 (1974):
331-343; Hanson, *JTS* 24 (1973): 570-572; Marshall, *ExT* 84 (1973): 247-
248; McArthur, *CBQ* 35 (1973): 520-521; Metzger, *PSB* 66 (1973): 131-132.

7.6 ◉ Carroll, Kenneth L. "Toward a Commonly Received New Testament." *Bulletin of the John Rylands University Library* 44 (1962):
327-349.
Carroll, unlike many scholars, does not look to Marcionism or
Montanism to explain the development of the catholic canon. Rather
he sees the significant increase in pseudepigraphy in the last two-
thirds of the second century forcing the Roman church to specify
the writings which were to be approved. Carroll is influenced, in
part, by the belief that the Muratorian Fragment is second century,
a point that is disputed. In spite of that, Carroll does offer a fine
review of the use of the "New Testament" writings by various
churchmen in the second century and by various centres. The article
concludes with ten canonical lists: Muratorian, Clement of Alexandria, Origen, Hippolytus, Clermont, Eusebius, Cheltenham (Mom-
msenian), Athanasius (Festal Letter), Jerome, and Augustine.

7.7 Childs, Brevard S. *The New Testament As Canon: An Introduction.*
Philadelphia: Fortress, 1985. Pp. xxv + 572. B-16.
While this volume will be of primary interest to students of the
New Testament, a good review of the debate regarding the validity
of the canon is provided in Part One, especially in Ch. 1: "The
Role of the Canon within New Testament Introduction" and Ch. 2:
"The Canon as an Historical and Theological Problem." Childs is
more interested in the theological aspects of the canon than in the

historical aspects, as can be seen from the sketchy outline of the latter.

&< Davies, *JTS* 37 (1986): 161-164; Drury, *Theology* 89 (1986): 60-62; Gamble, *JBL* 106 (1987): 330-333; McKnight, *TSF Bulletin* 10.5 (1987): 22-24; with reply to McKnight from Childs, in *TSF Bulletin* 10.5 (1987): 24-25; Rodd, *ExT* 97 (1986): 97-100; Smith, *Interpretation* 40 (1986): 407-411; Wenthe, *CTQ* 50 (1986): 301-303; Williams, *CRBR* (1988): 19-41.

7.8   Dahl, Nils A. "The Origin of the Earliest Prologues to the Pauline Letters." *Semeia* 12 (1978): 233-277. B-6.
Dahl challenges the widely held view that the prologues to the Pauline letters originated in a Marcionite setting (as put forward by de Bruyne, Corssen, and Schäfer). He believes that it is just as probable that the Marcionite prologues were copied from ones already existing. In part, Dahl's hypothesis depends on the existence of two quite different collections of the Pauline letters: one with a 7-part focus (in supposed chronological order, like Marcion's collection), the other with a 13- or 14-letter focus, thus providing an alternative to theories by Mitton and Kümmel. Dahl thinks the prologues probably originated in Antioch, though Ephesus is a possible locale.

7.9   ● Dungan, D.L. "The New Testament Canon in Recent Study." *Interpretation* 29 (1975): 339-51.
This article is useful primarily for its list of literature from 1960 to 1975. Although the author does evaluate this material, many of the comments are flawed by the author's love for novelty—his tendency is to short-change traditional views and approaches. Dungan concludes with a list of questions for further reflection. These are of value, but the solid answers to these questions may come more often from works that Dungan dismisses than from his own reflections.

7.10   Farmer, William. *Jesus and the Gospel: Scripture, Tradition and Canon.* Philadelphia: Fortress, 1982.
Farmer argues backwards, from the closing of the canon (the lists of Athanasius and Amphilochius), to the Alexandrian School, to Irenaeus, to the beginning of the canonical process in the second century. He pays particular attention to Origen's role in bringing the more narrow, 22-book, western canon into the East, and finds a clue to Origen's sense of "apostolic" from Origen's insistence that the Epistle to the Hebrews be retained. "Martyrdom" becomes the specific criterion of "apostolicity." In regard to Marcion's canon,

Farmer believes it is dependent on a primitive canon in Rome.
Good general, and sometimes quite original, discussion of most of
the issues.

✂ Barta, *CBQ* 47 (1985): 352-353; Collins, *TT* 40 (1983): 233-235;
Gruenler, *JBL* 104 (1985): 141-143; Harrington; *Horizons* 11 (1984): 427-
428; Hoffmann, *PBR* 2 (1983): 114-118; Kalin, *Interpretation* 39 (1985):
88-90; Meyer, *SC* 5 (1985-86): 165-171; Thompson, *RQ* 27 (1984): 235-237;
Trafton, *CSR* 15 (1986): 57-59.

7.11   Farmer, William R., and Denis M. Farkasfalvy. *The Formation of
the New Testament Canon. An Ecumenical Approach.* Theological
Inquiries: Studies in Contemporary Biblical and Theological
Problems. Introduction by Albert C. Outler. Edited by Harold W.
Attridge. New York: Paulist, 1983. Pp. ix + 182. CAI-4.

Farmer's half of this work ("A Study of the Development of the
New Testament Canon" is substantially a reprint of his thesis
presented in [§7.10]). Farkasfalvy (pp. 97-178) is primarily interested
in the principle of "apostolicity." He argues that the authority granted
to the apostles was transferred to the writings of the apostles, and
these, being understood as sources of revelation, were naturally set
along side the Jewish scriptures. Early Christian pseudepigrapha
and patristic writings (ending with Irenaeus) are examined. Marcion's
role is made less significant; the closing of the canon stands in a
consistent line of development from the earliest period, in which
the apostolic witness had a definitive character.

✂ Dunbar, *Trinity Journal* 5 (1984): 217-219; Fee, *Interpretation* 39
(1985): 328; Gamble, *JBL* 105 (1986): 168-169; Harrington, *CBQ* 47 (1985):
163-165; Meade, *TSF Bulletin* 9 (1985): 29.

7.12   Ferguson, Everett. "Canon Muratori: Date and Provenance." *Studia
Patristica* 17.2 (1982): 677-683.

Ferguson argues specifically against Sundberg's 1973 article [§7.25],
responding point-by-point, rejecting or heavily qualifying each
argument. He contends that the traditional date and locale (late
second century and western) is unshaken by Sundberg's article,
and that Sundberg puts too much significance on the list itself.
According to Ferguson, the list is unique *as a list,* not in what the
list specifies as authoritative early Christian writings. That kind of
decision had been largely made by the end of the second century,
and a number of church writers from that period reflect this.

7.13   ☛ Gamble, Harry Y. *The New Testament Canon: Its Making and
Meaning.* Guides to Biblical Scholarship. Philadelphia: Fortress,
1985. Pp. 95.

A good introduction to the range of questions arising from discussions about the canon. After detailed definition of the words "canon," "scripture," and "New Testament," Gamble looks at the second century, dealing first with the Gospels and then with Paul's letters. Briefer comments are provided on the other writings of the canon and on the third and fourth centuries. Then Gamble considers each of the many factors in the formation of the canon, and the specific criteria of canonicity, concluding with a discussion of the New Testament as canon. The appendix gives in English the full text of the Muratorian Canon list, which Gamble holds to be late-second/early-third century (*contra* Sundberg [§7.25]). Another introductory discussion of the canon is provided by Gamble's "The Canon of the New Testament, in *The New Testament and Its Modern Interpreters*, edited by E.J. Epp and G.W. MacRae, pp. 201-243. This contains a 14-page bibliography up to the early 1980s.
" Marrow, *CBQ* 48 (1986): 746-447; Omanson, *R&E* 83 (1986): 298-299; Wicks, *Gregorianum* 67 (1986): 368-370.

7.14 * Grant, Robert M. "The New Testament Canon." In *From the Beginnings to Jerome*. Vol. 1. *The Cambridge History of the Bible*. Edited by P.R. Ackroyd and C.F. Evans. Cambridge: Cambridge UP, 1970. Pp. 284-308.
Grant reviews a few of the main issues in brief but straight-forward language. Topics cover the early use of some of the first-century documents, some apocryphal documents, the Old Testament canon, the Muratorian list, the Alexandrian use of early Christian literature, and the complications and ambiguities arising from that. Further, Eusebius' contribution to our understanding of the development of the canon is considered, as are the various attitudes in the early church towards particular documents.

7.15 Groh, Dennis E. "Hans von Campenhausen on Canon." *Interpretation* 28 (1974): 331-343.
Although Groh is sympathetic to Campenhausen's work, he thinks it is complicated by a "somewhat Protestant way of defining canon" (i.e., Gospels and Paul) and by a wide range of specific meanings in Campenhausen's use the term "canon." Groh compares Campenhausen's work to the various works of Sundberg, whose definition is more closely tied to canonical *lists* and whose date for the closing of the canon is later than Campenhausen. Included, too, are a few comments about a "canon within a canon" and about the trend toward codification in the general culture about the year 200.

7.16   Hahneman, Geoffrey Mark. *The Muratorian Fragment and the Development of the Canon.* Oxford Theological Monographs. Oxford: Clarendon, 1991. Pp. xi + 237. B-16; I-3; T-7.
Building on Sundberg's work, Hahneman argues for a fourth-century date of the Muratorian Fragment. This, he contends, makes it fit with other canonical catalogues of the period; were it from the second century, it would be an anomaly. One full chapter is given to the *Shepherd of Hermas,* since a passage in this document is crucial to the early dating of the fragment. Another chapter discusses the general issues in the debate over the formation of the canon, and this is followed by examination of various fourth-century catalogues or canonical lists. Hahneman then considers what is taken to be peculiarities in the texts, contending that these can be explained by a late date for the fragment. Only the four gospels have become a fixed collection in the second century, according to Hahneman.

7.17   ☛ Hanson, R.P.C. "The Canon of the New Testament." In *Tradition in the Early Church.* London: SCM Press, 1962. Pp. 187-236.
Hanson considers the early evidence for the existence of a Christian canon, looking in particular at second-century evidence. He challenges the widespread conclusion that Marcion compiled the first canon, against which the main church compiled its own; rather, Marcion selected from an already existing collection, according to Hanson. Further, Paul's letters were in an authoritative collection before the four Gospels. Hanson considers the four-gospel collection a late development, largely because of questions surrounding the Gospel of John, which arose because of John's use in Gnostic circles. Gnostics, generally, accepted the developing canon; their extra writings were not intended to replace it. Hanson then offers an extended discussion on the use of the word "scripture" for these writings, and what force that term might have had. (It may have been quite qualified.) Then follows a section on "Norms of Canonicity" and "Uncanonical Tradition." This article is more detailed than most works we have indicated as "introductory," nonetheless, it is one of the better places to start.

7.18   ☛ Harrop, Clayton. *History of the New Testament in Plain Language.* Waco, TX: Word Books, 1984. Pp. 158. I-2.
Clearly written, thus true to its title, this book serves as an elementary introduction to most of the questions that arise in a discussion of the canon. Six of the eight chapters are relevant to the early church, dealing with the papyri, uncial and minuscule manuscripts, lection-

aries and versions; scribal practice; the practice and history of textual criticism; and the process of the development of the canon. Although much of this is best suited for the average layperson, chapter five provides examples of variant readings, which could be of use to a more serious beginning student.

⚻ Omanson, *R&E* 82 (1985): 446-447.

7.19   Lemcio, E.E. "Ephesus and the New Testament Canon." *Bulletin of the John Rylands University Library* 69 (1986): 210-234.
Lemcio puts forward a strong case for the significant role that Ephesus played in shaping the canon. The tendency in scholarship has been to overlook this important centre and to give pride-of-place to Rome. But Lemcio's collection of evidence for the importance of Ephesus, which had a concentration of vast and varied canonical materials and credible leaders, should cause some rethinking of the issue.

7.20   Meade, David G. *Pseudonymity and Canon. An Investigation into the Relationship of Authorship and Authority in Jewish and Earliest Christian Tradition.* WUNT 39. Tübingen: Mohr (Paul Siebeck), 1986 / Grand Rapids: Eerdmans, 1987. Pp. vii + 257. B-10; BI-16; PI-2; AI-5; SI-2.
In what is the first English monograph on the topic, Meade considers the possibility for and implications of the inclusion of pseudonymous documents in the Christian canon. After a brief discussion of the debate, Meade focuses on Jewish literary practice of authorship and attribution. From his examination of Jewish prophetical, wisdom, and apocalyptic literature, he concludes that authorship claims are more an assertion about authoritative tradition than about authorship *per se.* He finds a similar mind set in the New Testament literature, and argues that this in no way need taint our ideas of canon or inspiration.

⚻ Campbell, *EQ* 61 (1989): 269-271; Gallagher, *CBQ* 50 (1988): 143-144; Gamble, *JBL* 107 (1988): 560-562; Grech, *Biblica* 68 (1987): 286-289; McCartney, *WTJ* 51 (1989): 167-171; Rowland, *JTS* 40 (1989): 588-590.

7.21   ☛ Metzger, Bruce M. *The Canon of the New Testament. Its Origin Development and Significance.* Oxford: Clarendon Press, 1987. Pp. x + 326. I-11.
The heart of this book (Part II) deals with the development of the canon until its close in the East and the West. Although dealing with a fairly technical topic, with frequent reference to various names and documents, Metzger provides adequate historical and

biographical detail to keep even the beginner with him. Part I deals with the literature on the canon from the 1600s to the modern period. Part III focuses briefly on the matters related to the criteria for canonicity, the plurality of the gospels, the concept of a canon within a canon, the question of "open" or "closed" canon, and inspiration. Valuable appendices on the word "canon," and the sequence, titles, and early lists of books that came to comprise the canon. Also see Metzger's *The Early Versions of the New Testament* (Nashville: Abingdon, 1981).

ঌ Beckwith, *Churchman* 103 (1989): 262-263; Bruce, *Eternity* 39 (1988): 35-36; Dillon, *Biblica* 70 (1989): 133-137; Elliott, *JTS* 39 (1988): 585-588; Fee, *Interpretation* 43 (1989): 410-412; Gamble, *JBL* 108 (1989): 551-552; Geer, *RQ* 32 (1990): 231-234; Grant, *CH* 57 (1988): 522-523; Greer, *TS* 49 (1988): 734-735; Hall, *JEH* 40 (1989): 253-261; Henderson, *JETS* 33 (1990): 117-119; Hughes, *ATR* 70 (1988): 357-360; Marshall, *EQ* 61 (1989): 274-275; Perkins, *CBQ* 51 (1989): 161-162.

7.22   ☛ Moule, C.F.D. "Collecting and Sifting the Documents." In *The Birth of the New Testament*. 3d ed. San Francisco: Harper & Row, 1982. Pp. 235-269.

It is unwise to disregard the cautious and balanced observations of this respected scholar. Moule, unlike many, is sympathetic to the idea of a canon. He deals mainly with the Gospels, the Pauline letters, and the Johannine (or Ephesian) material, thus his discussion is not comprehensive. Yet he does provide a solid review of scholarly opinion on the major topics concerning the canon (with particular emphasis on English scholarship). Moule also gives considerable place to the question of authority and the shift from oral testimony to written documents.

7.23   Roberts, C.H., and T.C. Skeat. *The Birth of the Codex*. Oxford: Oxford UP, 1983. Pp. 76. B&W-6.

While not specifically on the development of the canon, this brief volume is important to the subject because the codex ("book" as opposed to "scroll") was the primary form that Christians used in publishing their texts, seemingly against the common practice of the society. (It was not until the fourth century that the codex became a more popular format.) The authors also deal with the locale of origin of the codex, and the reasons why Christians adopted the format.

ঌ Bammel, *JTS* 38 (1987): 516-519; Birdsall, *Theology* 92 (1989): 56-58; Grant, *CH* 54 (1985): 438-439; Hall, *JEH* 40 (1989): 253-261; Kilpatrick, *VC* 38 (1984): 409-412; Lloyd-Jones, *JEH* 35 (1984): 499; Parsons, *CR* 37 (1987): 82-84; Wilson, *TLSuppl* 4226 (Mar 30 1984): 355.

7.24 ☛ Schneemelcher, W. "The History of the New Testament Canon." In *New Testament Apocrypha*. Edited by E. Hennecke and W. Schneemelcher. Philadelphia: Westminster, 1963. 1:21-68.
This chapter serves as the introduction to the two-volume Hennecke/ Schneemelcher *New Testament Apocrypha*. It was originally published in German, and its secondary literature is primarily German. In addition to a solid review of the usual questions about the canon, this chapter discusses the distinction between "canonical" and "apocryphal." Translations of various canon lists are provided: (Muratori; Codex Claromontanus; so-called Decretum Gelasianum; Stichometry of Nicephorus; and Catalogue of the 60 Canonical Books). As well, relevant passages are included from Origen, Eusebius, and Athanasius.

7.25 Sundberg, Albert C. "Canon Muratori: A Fourth-Century List." *Harvard Theological Review* 66 (1973): 1-41.
The Canon Muratori is a list of New Testament books discovered by Ludovici Antonio Muratori (1672-1750). It was widely thought that the list came from Rome, and was to be dated to the late second century. Sundberg challenges this, arguing that it is an eastern, not western, list (Palestinian or Syrian), and that it dates from the fourth century. He calls attention to three features: (1) the status of the *Shepherd of Hermas;* (2) the inclusion of the Wisdom of Solomon; and (3) the uncertain status of the apocalypses of John and Peter. Sundberg finds in Eusebius' approach to the canon the closest parallels to the Muratori list. But see Ferguson [§7.12].

7.26 Westcott, Brooke Foss. *A General Survey of the History of the Canon of the New Testament*. 6th ed. Macmillan, 1899. Reprint. Grand Rapids: Baker Book House, 1980. Pp. 593. AAI-3; SI-6.
This is the classic work by one of the pioneers in modern textual criticism. Westcott covers the history of the canon in detail up to the councils (Chapter 3 deals with the Reformation period, and thus is not relevant to this bibliography). The treatment is divided into geographical areas or key individuals or movements, and written with a good sense of what kinds of issues played a role in the development of the canon. Although old, this is still a valuable resource.

7.27 Williams, C.S.C. "The History of the Text and Canon of the New Testament to Jerome." In *Cambridge History of the Bible*. Vol. 2. *The West from the Fathers to the Reformation*. Edited by G.W.H. Lampe. Cambridge: Cambridge UP, 1969. Pp. 27-53.

As the title suggests, this article has two main parts. In the first part Williams describes the manuscript traditions of the New Testament that emerged during the first 450 years of Christianity. As expected, the large variety of Greek manuscripts dominate the discussion, but Williams also discusses the Syriac, Old Latin, Coptic, and Bohairic versions. In the second part, Williams discusses the canonization of the New Testament writings. He identifies three stages through which New Testament writings passed on route to being recognized as canon. In the first stage a writing would be found to be helpful and/or inspiring to specific Christians. In the second stage a writing would be used in a specific locale as a source of Christian teaching. And finally, in the third stage a writing would acquire "apostolic" status. Of course, not all Christian writings passed through this three-staged system at the same rate. The gospels appear to have acquired canonical status first, followed by the bulk of Paul's letters. The remainder of the New Testament writings took a longer period of time to pass through the three stages. Williams also notes that there were many disputed writings; some finally acquiring canonical status (eg. Hebrews), and others not (eg. 1 Clement). Williams also discusses major figures who contributed to the sense and development of the canon, including Polycarp, Marcion, Justin, Clement, Origen, Irenaeus, Hippolytus, Tertullian, and Eusebius. (DeR)

TEXTUAL CRITICISM
7.28   ⑲ Elliott, J.K. *A Bibliography of Greek New Testament Manuscripts.* Society for New Testament Studies Monographs 62. Cambridge, Cambridge UP, 1989. Pp. xxi + 210.
Elliott provides a good resource for students of the Greek New Testament manuscript tradition. Manuscripts are divided into papyri, uncials, cursives, and lectionaries, and Elliott indicates whether the manuscript has been published (in facsimile, for example), where it has been published, and whether a major textual work has been written on it. Elliott also explains the value of other works on manuscripts (Aland, Gregory, von Soden, von Dobschütz, Metzger, and numerous others). With a 10-page introduction.
✄ Birdsall, *JTS* 41 (1990): 209-212; Muddiman, *ExT* 101 (1989): 29-30.

7.29   Aland, Kurt, and Barbara Aland. *The Text of the New Testament: An Introduction to the Critical Editions and to the Theory and Practice of Modern Textual Criticism.* 2d ed. Translated by Erroll F. Rhodes. Leiden: E.J. Brill/Grand Rapids: Eerdmans, 1989. Pp. xviii + 366. I-12; B&W-65; BI-7; T-14. Manuscripts Index-8.
About 170 pages deal with the early church period, covering primarily

the manuscripts and versions of the New Testament. One short chapter covers the collection of New Testament documents, the development of the canon, origin, and spread of different text types, and the centers of manuscript production. In addition, there is a 36-page section of actual passages on which the methodology of textual criticism is demonstrated, and a 12-page evaluation of tools available to the textual critic. Included is a 17"x17" chart of the textual contents of New Testament uncial manuscripts and New Testament papyri.

☞ Birdsall, *BT* 39 (1988): 338-342; Elliott, *ExT* 99 (1988): 183; Epp, *Interpretation* 44 (1990): 71-75; Fee, *Crux* 24 (1988): 33-34; Holmes, *JBL* 108 (1989): 139-144; Hurtado, *CBQ* 50 (1988): 313-315; Kilpatrick, *NovT* 30 (1988): 380-383; Parker, *SJT* 42 (1989): 418-420; Silva, *WTJ* 50 (1988): 195-200.

7.30 ☞ Birdsall, J.N. "The New Testament Text." In *From the Beginnings to Jerome.* Vol. 1. *The Cambridge History of the Bible. Edited* by P.R. Ackroyd and C.F. Evans. Cambridge: Cambridge UP, 1970. Pp. 308-377.
A solid review of the issues, with a brief discussion of the earlier approaches. Birdsall is careful to point out the contribution made by significant scholars throughout the history of the debate. A wide range of topics is covered, including the weakness of rating the value of "text-types" and the importance of the various versions. He then considers the value of the Diatessaron, and the evidence that some textual variations stem from doctrinal interests as early as the second century, or from a desire merely to simplify the text for its audience or to keep up with the changing Greek language. Of particular value is the use of examples.

7.31 ◉ Epp. Eldon Jay. "Textual criticism." In *The New Testament and Its Modern Interpreters.* Edited by E.J. Epp and G.W. MacRae. Atlanta: Scholars, 1989. Pp. 75-126. B-21.
This is a solid review of the issues and the history of textual criticism by one of the leading scholars in the field. Critical editions are discussed, as are various versions and manuscripts. The section on methodology provides deals with the two opposing approaches to establishing an acceptable text (the historical-documentary method and the rigorous eclectic method). Reflections on the present and future issues are provided, as well as an extensive bibliography.

7.32 ☞ Lohse, Eduard. "The Text of the New Testament." In *The Formation of the New Testament.* Translated by M. Eugene Boring.

Nashville: Abingdon, 1981. Pp. 233-248.
A very brief but nonetheless useful introduction to the field of
textual criticism and the New Testament manuscript tradition. The
chapter is divided into four sections: "The Task of New Testament
Text Criticism"; "The Manuscripts of the New Testament"; "The
History of the Printed New Testament Text"; and "The Present
State of New Testament Text Criticism."

7.33   Metzger, Bruce M. *The Text of the New Testament. Its Transmission,
       Corruption, and Restoration.* New York/Oxford: Oxford UP, 1968.
       (1964[1]). Pp. xii + 284. I-7; B&W-21; NTI-2.
       Metzger, whose impressive work in the field of New Testament
       textual criticism (serving as an editor of the standard version of the
       Greek New Testament) provides a clearly written introduction to
       the field. After discussing the practice of writing in the ancient
       world, Metzger discusses the features of critical editions of the
       New Testament designed to aid the reader. Various witnesses to
       the text are discussed (manuscripts, versions, patristic quotations of
       the New Testament), and a survey of the history of textual criticism.
       The second half of the book discusses the actual practice of textual
       criticism (that is, the restoring of a reliable text). A solid introduction
       and survey, serving various levels of readers.
       ✄ Brock, *JTS* 16 (1965): 484-487; Epp, *JBL* 86 (1967): 339-341; Fitzmyer,
       TT 21 (1964): 386-388; S. Johnson, *PSB* 58 (1964): 62-63; Reese, *CBQ* 26
       (1964): 492-493; Taylor, *ExT* 75 (1964): 299; Van Elderen, *WTJ* 28 (1965):
       53-57; R.M. Wilson, *SJT* 19 (1966): 491-492.

7.34   Metzger, Bruce M. *The Early Versions of the New Testament:
       Their Origin, Transmission, and Limitations.* Oxford: Clarendon,
       1977. Pp. xix + 498. I-20; NTI-7; Manuscripts Index-7.
       This is a highly technical book for the most part, dealing with early
       versions (translations) of the New Testament. The various Syriac
       versions are examined, then Coptic, Armenian, Georgian, Ethiopic,
       and the minor eastern versions. In regard to the west, these are
       largely Latin, but the Gothic and Slavonic versions, and minor
       versions are discussed too. Metzger is the primary author, with a
       few other experts providing sections on highly specialized areas.
       ✄ Barr, *JTS* 30 (1979): 290-303; Beardslee, *Interpretation* 33 (1979): 94;
       Bruce, *Churchman* 92 (1978): 157-159; Kilpatrick, *ExT* 89 (1978): 185;
       Kubo, *AUSS* 17 (19790: 126-127; Meyer, *CTJ* 13 (1978): 226-228; Millard,
       EQ 51 (1979): 47-49; Omanson, *BT* 30 (1979): 144-145; Wikgren, *CBQ*
       40 (1978): 641-643.

7.35   ◉ Pack, Frank. "One Hundred Years Since Westcott and Hort:

1881-1981." *Restoration Quarterly* 26 (1983): 65-79.

Pack reviews the significant contribution made by Westcott and Hort for a critical edition of the text of the New Testament, especially in their revolutionary departure from the Textus Receptus (the Greek "Received Text," going back to Erasmus). The various criticisms of Westcott and Hort are considered (including the alternative "eclectic" approach of Colwell, Elliott, and Kilpatrick), which Pack rejects in favor of the soundness of the judgments of Westcott and Hort. Further, Pack discusses various editions of the Greek Testament, and briefly mentions the sources used by scholars in reconstructing the text of the New Testament: early versions (Syriac, Latin, Egyptian); lectionaries, and quotations in the church fathers.

7.36 Petersen, William L., ed. *Gospel Traditions in the Second Century: Origins, Recensions, Text, and Transmission.* Christianity and Judaism in Antiquity 3. Notre Dame/London: University of Notre Dame Press, 1989. Pp. xi + 174.

A collection of eight articles, all but one in English, dealing with various technical matters of the text of the gospels; "Western Text (Birdsall); "Text of Synoptic Gospels" (Koester); "Nature and Purpose of Redactional Changes" (Wisse); "Significance of Papyri (Epp); "Extra-Canonical Sayings (Delobel); "Lost Old Syriac" (Brock); "Factors in the Harmonization of the Gospels, Especially in the Diatessaron of Tatian" (Baarda). This collection provides students with a sense of how scholars tackle various problems with the transmission of the gospels (and of early Christian materials generally).

⊰ Kee, *CBQ* 54 (1992): 396-397.

8
CHRISTOLOGY

There is an abundant literature in the field of christology. The person of Christ and doctrines relating to him over the ages continue to excite the world of modern scholarship as well as ordinary Christians. Yet the field seems to produce as much heat as it does light. Theologians, church historians, and lay persons of various persuasions often come to very different conclusions on what the New Testament teaches about Jesus, a fact that is attested to by the many differing New Testament christologies that have been produced since the Second World War.

Christology is a very difficult subject of study. Its primary problem lies with the fact that there is no systematic christology as such in the New Testament. While the four gospel writers give us partial and not always consistent pictures of the life of the man Jesus of Nazareth, only the Gospel of John deals with his preexistence. Other possible references to that preexistence occur at such places as Philippians 2:5-11, Colossians 1:15-20, and Hebrews 1:10-12, but these passages—all of which are poetic in nature— are open to various interpretations. They are therefore often hotly disputed. Equally significant, it is difficult to determine from the Scriptures what the relationship of the Christ—the Son of God—is to God the Father or to the Holy Spirit. These matters do not seem to have concerned the first Christians as they have their spiritual descendants in later centuries.

It is possible to determine that by the end of the first century Christians were intent on defending the idea that Jesus had truly come in the flesh—not as a phantom as certain Gnostics or proto-Gnostics were asserting. That can be seen from 2 John 7-11 and the writings of Ignatius of Antioch. Nonetheless, this was only a first step towards far more elaborate definitions of christological doctrine that were to occur over the ages. Thus James D.G. Dunn, in his book *Unity and Diversity in the New Testament: An Inquiry Into the Character of Earliest Christianity* (1977), may be right in asserting that the first Christians had no orthodox christology, at least in the sense that later Christians were to have. The relatively recent important, often controversial works that are abstracted below—along with works in other languages—tend to demonstrate that that was the case.

Although fundamentally conservative in outlook, George L. Prestige made a major contribution to early church scholarship in 1930 with his *God in Patristic Thought* [§8.19]. In it Prestige defined much of the theological-philosophical language that was used in early church debates over the nature of God and the nature of Christ. Hence he gave to English-speaking scholars the necessary tools to examine early church teachings and controversies.

More recently Harry A. Wolfson [§8.23] has made a similar contribution by putting early Christian doctrine into a philosophical context. As will be seen below, Wolfson attempts to show the intellectual relationship of Philo of Alexandria to the early Christian fathers. While some of Wolfson's ideas are contested, they have served as a firm basis for other studies.

Perhaps the most significant recent advances in christological studies have been those produced about the so-called Arian controversy of the fourth century. Until recently, scholars regarded Arius as an arch-heretic whose ideas were at best quasi-Christian. Influenced by the long-standing tradition of the great churches, east and west, such scholars dismissed Arius and any who took positions close to his. As many of the works listed below attest, however, Arius and his supporters are now much better understood than in the past. They are now seen more objectively, if not necessarily always more favorably. This has come about through a more careful examination of the possible antecedents of Arius and the realization that in many ways his position at Nicaea in 325 CE was more conservative than that of his major adversaries.

Martin Werner's *The Formation of Christian Doctrine* [§8.20] published originally in German, did much to set the stage for this new scholarship, for it developed what was to become known as "angel christology." Despite severe criticism of Werner's work, a number of scholars have followed in his footsteps, at least in part, by producing a number of works on early Jewish Christianity. These studies show the tremendous diversity of early Christian Christology, much of which was closely linked to late Jewish angelology.

In more recent years, a number of Anglican academics and clerics in Great Britain have challenged traditional christology by questioning the orthodox doctrine of the incarnation and by producing highly controversial studies of early church christology. Of these Anglicans, two in particular—Maurice Wiles [§8.21] and Frances Young [§8.24]—have added substantially to our knowledge of christology.

In the United States, Robert C. Gregg and Dennis E. Groh have also made a major contribution with the publication of their *Early Arianism: A View of Salvation* [§8.10]. Although their basic thesis that Arius and the "Arians" were more concerned with soteriological concerns than with theological or christological ones has been criticized, it raises questions which have generally been ignored in the past. Perhaps, however, their examination of Arius' thinking throws as much light on that of his primary adversary, Athanasius, as it does on his. It makes the reasons behind the development of orthodox Trinitarian and incarnational doctrine far more understandable.

Of course, christological studies have not been confined to the questions raised by the Arian controversy. The discovery of both the Dead Sea scrolls and the Nag Hammadi corpus of Gnostic works has greatly broadened our knowledge of the religious context in which early Christianity developed. So, too, have other studies in the fields of early Judaism and Graeco-Roman paganism. It is therefore important to note the significance of Robert M. Grant's contributions, for he gives the interested student and the intelligent lay reader a general overview of the complexity of the religion and, specifically, the christology of the first Christian centuries.

Although less well cultivated, the field of post-Nicene, christological studies is now beginning to receive more attention as well. There are a few works on various councils and theological debates which were so important in defining medieval orthodoxy, but in most cases anyone wanting to understand their significance must take time to read some of the general studies of the development of doctrine during the era. (P)

8.1   🏛 Norris, Richard A., trans. and ed. *The Christological Controversy.* Philadelphia: Fortress, 1980. Pp. 162; B-2.
A thirty-one page introduction gives a synopsis of christological problems from New Testament times to the Council of Chalcedon. The translated documents which form the body of this volume are from Melito of Sardis, Irenaeus, Tertullian, Origen, Athanasius, Apollinaris of Laodicea, Theodore of Mopsuestia, Nestorius, Cyril of Alexandria, Pope Leo I, and the Council of Chalcedon. Carefully translated into readable English, these documents serve the student well. Weaknesses are that the writings of earlier Christian Fathers are ignored and, except for those by Apollinaris and Nestorius, all the primary works published are from within the orthodox tradition. (P)

8.2   🏛 Rusch, William G. *The Trinitarian Controversy.* Sources of Early Christian Thought. Philadelphia: Fortress, 1980. Pp. viii + 182. B-2.
A collection of thirteen important texts from the main players in the trinitarian disputes, such as Arius, Alexander, Eusebius, Athana-

sius, Gregory of Nazianzus, Gregory of Nyssa, and Augustine. Decisions of the Councils of Antioch and Nicea are included as well, and this focuses most of the material on the Nicene period and the immediate reactions and modifications. Rusch's 27-page introduction ranges more widely, however, providing some review of the biblical and second and third century background to the Nicene crisis. As with other volumes in this series, the introduction discusses the key players, issues, and documents, and by so doing provides the beginning student a solid foundation. The texts are quoted in full, where possible.

⊱⊰ Aune, *CSR* 11 (1982): 377-378; Balas, *SC* 1 (1981): 191-192; Lienhard, *RSR* 8 (1982): 330-337; Weinrich, *CTQ* 45 (1981): 327-328.

8.3 ⑧ Schadel, Erwin. *Bibliotheca Trinitariorum. International Bibliography of Trinitarian Literature.* Paris: K.G. Saur, 1984. Volume I. Pp. cxi + 624. Volume II. Pp. xxxvii + 594.
This massive project lists the works of 4712 authors. Some entries are accompanied by brief annotations. Volume 2, basically an index volume, includes 47 review articles of volume 1 (mainly in German); this takes up 112 pages! A 15-page introduction explains the reasons for the project, and reviews the philosophical climate over the past 200 years, during which the doctrine of the Trinity is seen to have been neglected. A comprehensive resource tool, but certainly not the place to start.

⊱⊰ Bracken, *TS* 46 (1985): 753; Panikkar, *CC* 38 (1988): 119-120.

8.4 Barnard, L.W. "The Antecedents of Arius." *Vigiliae Christianae* 24 (1970): 172-186.
An examination of the possible Alexandrian antecedents of Arius, this article gives a brief overview of the theology of such Alexandrians (either known or supposed) as Athenagoras, Origen, Dionysius of Alexandria, Theognostus, Pierius, and Peter the Martyr. From his survey, Barnard states that while all these men held certain ideas similar to those of Arius, they did not produce an Alexandrian "theological tradition" as such out of which Arius derived his thinking. Rather, Arius was an eclectic who "took what he wanted from earlier thinkers." Barnard denies T.E. Pollard's contention that Arius drew his theological system primarily from Antiochene influences as exemplified by Lucian. (P)

8.5 Chesnut, Roberta C. *Three Monophysite Christologies: Severus of Antioch, Philoxenus of Mabbug, and Jacob of Sarug.* Oxford Theological Monographs. London: Oxford UP, 1976. Pp. viii + 158. B-11; I-4.

By studying the abundant original documents that have come down to us from the three Monophysites examined here, Chesnut attempts first to show that christological disputes continued well past Chalcedon and that Monophysitism had different aspects to it. Severus explained Christ as "three hierarchically arranged levels of being." Philoxenus held that there was no natural humanity in Christ and no natural participation of humankind in God. Jacob felt that Christ's reality lay in the hidden and secret presence of the Word in Christ. Chesnut gives a fine introduction to an area of Christian doctrine seldom studied. The bibliography is most useful. (P)

ᢞ< Frend, *JEH* 28 (1977): 319-320; Norris, *AHR* 83 (1978): 411-412; Rusch, *Currents* 5 (1978): 62; Torrance, *SJT* 32 (1979): 183-185; Wickham, *JTS* 28 (1977): 567-571.

8.6   Grant, Robert M. *Gods and the One God.* Library of Early Christianity. Philadelphia: Westminster, 1986. Pp. 211; I-5; AB-5.

Grant sets the development of the Christian doctrine of God in the context of the various religious and philosophical options of the day, making suggestive comments about the points of contrast and similarity, often using specific examples from the religions of the Mediterranean. The book is divided into 3 sections and 13 chapters: the first section deals with general comments on religion in the area; the second on "praise and denunciation of the Gods," and the third and longest on "Basic Doctrines." The last section is particularly important for understanding the development of the Christian doctrine of God, up to the conclusions of the creeds. Although the chapters do not always appear connected, the book as a whole helps to clarify the Christian development by attention to the pagan options.

ᢞ< Cameron, *Theology* 90 (1987): 318-320; Chadwick, *CH* 57 (1988): 519-520; Gallagher, *CBQ* 49 (1987): 340-341; Marshall, *EQ* 60 (1988): 77-78; Perkins, *CC* 36 (1986): 230-233; Placher, *Thomist* 51 (1987): 542-545; Slusser, *TS* 48 (1987): 173-175; Stacey, *JTS* 39 (1988): 214-215.

8.7   Grant, Robert M. *Jesus After the Gospels: The Christ of the Second Century.* The Hale Memorial Lectures of Seabury-Western Theological Seminary 1989. Louisville: Westminster/John Knox, 1990. Pp. 134. I-3; B-5.

Grant offers seven short lectures on christological issues related to the second century, though the first two are more strictly concerned with the first century (issues of "humanity" and "divinity" of Christ).

Then follow chapters on Gnostic Christologies; the Apostolic Fathers and Justin; the Jewish-Christian Christology of Theophilus; Heresy and Christology; Irenaeus' Theology and Christology, and a 4-page appendix on Irenaeus' use of Middle Platonic thought against the Gnostics. This can serve as a useful survey of the diversity of opinion on a matter that receives considerably more focused attention in the centuries following, and Grant, as usual, offers many suggestive comments.

⇥ Black, *Perkins Journal* 43 (1990): 31-32; Hurtado, *CRBR* (1991): 306-308; Perkins, *CBQ* 54 (1992): 153-154; Winslow, *CH* 60 (1991): 372-373.

8.8   Gray, Patrick T.R. *The Defense of Chalcedon in the East (451-553)*. Studies in the History of Christian Thought 20. Leiden: E.J. Brill, 1979. Pp. ix + 189. I-2; PI-3; B-6.

This is a highly technical study of a very difficult subject. Its primary thesis is that the majority of Eastern Chalcedonian Christians were intent on maintaining the basic christology of Cyril of Alexandria against Leonitus of Byzantium and Eutychianism. In the end, the majority's claim to interpret Chalcedon was affirmed by Constantinople II. In rejecting the idea of a simple Chalcedonian orthodoxy, and in proposing that the controversies within the pro-Chalcedonian party be understood as part of earlier struggles, Gray has opened a new understanding of a generally neglected period of christological controversy. Important in this study are the examination of the role of the Emperor Justinian I and the condemnation of Origen. (P)

⇥ Meyendroff, *StVTQ* 25 (1981): 284; Price, *Sobornost* 3 (1981): 112-114; Wickham, *JTS* 35 (1984): 252-253.

8.9   Gregg, Robert C., ed. *Arianism. Historical and Theological Reassessments*. Papers From the Ninth International Conference on Patristic Studies. September 5-10, 1983. Patristic Monograph Series 11. *Oxford England*. Philadelphia: Philadelphia Patristic Foundation, 1985. Pp. vi + 380. B-10.

This volume contains twenty-two papers by some of the most outstanding English-speaking scholars of Arianism. The papers are broken down into three sections: (1) Arius and Arianism: Sources and Distinctions; (2) Arian Faith and Worship; and (3) Arians and Nicenes: Background, Issues and Episodes. Because of the scarcity of Arian sources and their often possible misquotation in Nicene documents, many of the papers show the difficult, tentative nature of present Arian studies. Certain papers emphasize, however, that important strides have been made in the understanding of Arianism.

For example, R.P.C. Hanson's "The Arian Doctrine of the Incarnation" shows that Arians did not believe that Jesus had a human soul. The papers in the third section clarify more about the Nicene tradition than Arianism. (P)

❧ Groh, *ATR* 68 (1986): 347-355; Stead, *JTS* 38 (1987): 199-205.

8.10   Gregg, Robert C. and Dennis E. Groh. *Early Arianism: A View of Salvation*. London: SCM, 1981. Pp. xiv + 209. AAI-3; I-12.

Gregg and Groh hold that Arianism is "most intelligible" as a "scheme of salvation." Christ is "the Son: one of the many brothers" who pre-existed in heaven as the Logos, God's first creation. As the human Son of God, he served as a moral example for Christians in gaining salvation through acts of freedom of the will. By denying that Christ was *homoousios* with the Father, the early Arians rejected the "essentialist" christology of Athanasius, which held that Christ, as the second person of the Trinity, had to be joined to human nature to save humanity. The last chapter in *Early Arianism* deals with "Claims on the Life of St. Anthony." (P)

❧ Ferguson, *CH* 52 (1983): 201; Frend, *SJT* 36 (1983): 116-118; Hanson, *JEH* 33 (1982): 431-437; Lienhard, *RSR* 8 (1982): 330-337; Louth, *Theology* 85 (1982): 139-141; McIntyre, *ExT* 93 (1981): 88-89; Meijering, *VC* 36 (1982): 67-68; Patterson, *Historical Magazine of the Protestant Episcopal Church* 52 (1983): 69-72; Pervo, *ATR* 66 (1984): 103-104; Slusser, *TS* 42 (1981): 684-685; Stead, *JTS* 33 (1982): 285-289; Volz, *W&W* 2 (1982): 291-293; Winslow, *SC* 2 (1982): 51-52.

8.11   Grillmeier, Aloys, S.J. *Christ in Christian Tradition*. Vol. 1. *From the Apostolic Age to Chalcedon*. Translated by John Bowden. Atlanta: John Knox, 1975. Pp. xxii + 599. B-11; SI-5; AAI-4; SI-2; MAI-7.

A conservative, Roman Catholic study, volume I gives an amazing amount of information about christological doctrine from New Testament times to the Council of Chalcedon. Its major strength is that it is based on much of the vast body of scholarship in English, French, and German which was produced up to 1975. Its primary weaknesses are that it is too doctrinaire and often ignores those aspects of patristic thought which do not fit Catholic dogma. By the omission of data, some patristic writers are made to appear more orthodox than they were. Conversely, heretics such as Arius are explained in terms of Platonic philosophy rather than Christian, biblical theology. The bibliography is excellent. (P)

❧ Henry, *CH* 47 (1978): 216-217; Hinson, *R&E* 74 (1977): 431-432; Newlands, *SJT* 29 (1976): 482-484; Wiles, *JEH* 27 (1976): 307-308.

8.12 Grillmeier, Aloys, S.J. *Christ in Christian Tradition.* Vol. 2. Part One. *From Chalcedon to Justinian I.* Translated by Pauline Allen and John Cawte. Atlanta: John Knox, 1987. Pp. xxi + 340 B-3.
This volume begins with the Council of Chalcedon. Grillmeier asserts that that council served as a theological "stumbling-block." It caused schisms from which Christendom still suffers. He does not simply recount the history of Chalcedon and subsequent events, however; he discusses the present state of research on them and includes translations of numerous primary documents from the schismatic, eastern, and western churches of the period. In this way he makes Volume II more valuable to the scholar than Volume I. The bibliography—largely of works in French and German—is rather short and not very useful to persons who do not know those languages. (P)
❧ Louth, *JTS* 39 (1988): 618-619; Urban, *ATR* 70 (1988): 367-369; Wickham, *SJT* 41 (1988): 557-558.

8.13 Hanson, R.P.C. *The Search for the Christian Doctrine of God.* Edinburgh: T&T Clark, 1988. Pp. xxi + 931. B-23; I-21; MAI-5; BI-5.
The crowning achievement of the late Bishop Hanson, this is a well-written, thoroughly documented account of the Arian Controversy. Part I discusses Arius's teachings, supporters, antecedents, and rationale, plus events leading to the Council of Nicaea and Nicaea itself. Part II covers the "period of [christological] confusion" between the Councils of Nicaea and Constantinople I. Part III describes the emergence of "rival answers," including those of Athanasius and other pro-Nicenes. Part IV gives a clear assessment of the orthodox settlement that was brought to completion at Constantinople in 381. No student of christology can afford to overlook this work; it is outstanding. (P)
❧ Bray, *Churchman,* 103 (1989): 178-179; Frend, *ExT* 100 (1989): 419-421; Hall, *KTR* 13 (1990): 23-26; Kannengiesser, *CHR* 76 (1990): 579-583; Lienhard, *TS* 51 (1990): 334-337; Louth, *Theology* 92 (1989): 405-407; Stead, *JTS* 41 (1990): 668-673.

8:14 Hurtado, Larry W. *One God, One Lord: Early Christian Devotion and Ancient Jewish Monotheism.* Philadelphia: Fortress, 1988. Pp. xiv + 178. AAI-6; MAI-4.
This fine study discusses the nature of Jewish and earliest Christian concepts of monotheism and divine agency out of which later theological problems grew. It begins by holding that the primary problem for Christians was and is to be found in Paul's words at 1

Corinthians 8:6 out of which the title is taken. Hurtado examines
many aspects of divine agency in ancient Judaism as a prelude to
understanding the early Christian view of Jesus as a divine being.
These include angels, divine attributes, ancient patriarchs, Wisdom
and Logos. In a final chapter Hurtado shows how Christians
"mutated" these concepts and applied them to their Lord. (P)
⊱< Elliott, *SC* 8 (1991): 56-57; Polish, *JES* 28 (1991): 158-159.

8.15 Kannengiesser, Charles. *Arius and Athanasius: Two Alexandrian
      Theologians.* London: Variorum, 1991. Pp. xiv + 330. BI-2; Index
      Athanasianum-3.

      This is a collection of 15 previously published essays by Kannen-
      giesser: four on Arius; the remainder on Athanasius, though of
      course many articles relate to both. All but four of the articles are
      in English. A 5-page preface reviews some of the more recent
      debate about Arius, which tends now to place Arius in the
      Alexandrian tradition, rather than a supposed "school" of Antioch.
      Kannengiesser is sympathetic to both men, and he recognizes that
      it is crucial to evaluate the two as men of distinctively different
      generations and centuries: Arius, a pre-Constantinian theoretician;
      Athanasius, a pastor and participant in the Constantinian world.

8.16 Lonergan, Bernard. *The Way to Nicea: The Dialectical Development
      of Trinitarian Theology.* Translated by A. O'Donovan. Pp. xxix +
      143. NI-3; SI-2.

      Although written from an orthodox Roman Catholic stance which
      tries to explain the development of trinitarian doctrine dialectically,
      The Way to Nicea contains much useful information for anyone
      interested in the pre-Nicene intellectual world of Christianity. It
      gives a good account of Christian and Gnostic teachings prior to
      the fourth century, and it is particularly useful in its description of
      Judeo-Christian beliefs and various "heretical" movements such as
      Adoptionism, Patripassianism, Sabellianism, and Subordinationism.
      Section X deals with "The Structure of the Ante-Nicene Movement."
      (P)
      ⊱< Hanson, *JEH* 33 (1982): 431-437; Lienhard, *RSR* 8 (1982): 330-337;
      O'Donovan, *TS* 38 (1977): 782-783; Sherrard, *JEH* 28 (1977): 234; Turner,
      Churchman 91 (1977): 189-191; Wickham, *JTS* 33 (1982): 571-573.

8.17 Meyendorff, John. *Christ in Eastern Thought.* 2d ed. Translated by
      Yves Dubois. Crestwood: St. Vladimir's Seminary, 1975. Pp. 248.
      I-6.

Written by one of the leading historians of eastern orthodoxy, Meyendorff traces the Christological debates in the east from the Council of Chalcedon (451 CE). He deals with the Monophysite controversy (fifth and sixth centuries), the "Origenist Crisis" (sixth century), in which he challenges some of the recent attempts to rehabilitate Origen, and takes exception to Harnack's description of Byzantine Christianity as "hellenized." The contributions of other persons, such as Cyril of Alexandria, Pseudo-Dionysius, and St. John of Damascus, are presented. Meyendorff demonstrates the importance of the soteriological dimension in the development of Christological doctrine, making an informed case for the balanced Byzantine contribution to the debate.

8.18 Norris, R.A. Jr., *Manhood and Christ: A Study in the Christology of Theodore of Mopsuestia*. London: Oxford UP, 1963. Pp. xv + 274. B-7; NI-2; SI-2.
Norris attempts to uncover the roots of Antiochene christology by studying Theodore of Mopsuestia. Theodore was primarily a biblical theologian who developed and systematized the outlook of the Antiochene School of Theology. Later Antiochenes such as Nestorius drew on his thinking. Norris reviews the philosophical context of the fourth and fifth centuries and discusses the then current anthropology (doctrine of the nature of humanity) in broad terms. He deals with anthropological issues in the christology of Apollinaris of Laodicea and then analyses Theodore's anthropology and its bearing on his christology. In two appendixes Norris evaluates discussions of Theodore from both his own and our times. (P)
>< Hinson, *R&E* 61 (1964): 227-228; Jenson, *Dialog* 3 (1964): 306-308; Lampe, *Churchman* 77 (1963): 130-131; Musurillo, *TS* 24 (1963): 680-682; H.E.W. Turner, *JTS* 15 (1964): 168-170.

8.19 Prestige, George L. *God in Patristic Thought*. London: SPCK, 1952. Pp. xxxiv + 318. I-4; AAI-12.
Although published originally in 1936, this is still a very important work. It is the first and only major study in English which attempts to define the philosophical–theological language used by both the Greek and Latin Fathers of the church in carrying on discourse, polemicizing, and in defining doctrine. Because of his approach to his subject, Prestige deals with it topically rather than chronologically. For anyone wishing to study traditional Christian theology, *God in Patristic Thought* is a must. Care should be taken in using it, however, as many of its definitions have been revised or superseded

by more recent scholarship. (P)

8.20   Werner, Martin. *The Formation of Christian Dogma: An Historical Study of Its Problem*. Translated with an introduction by S.F.G. Brandon. San Francisco: Harper and Brothers, 1957. Reprint. Boston: Beacon Press, 1965. Pp. xvi + 352. AI-15.
        Werner holds that a shift from an early Christian unitarian theology occurred as a result of the delay of the parousia. He argues that such unitarianism was based on what he calls "angel christology." Unitarianism and angel christology were gradually eroded, however, as a consequence of the church's conflict with Gnosticism, Irenaeus's acceptance of Johannine Logos christology, the conflict with modalism, and the ultimate victory of trinitarianism. According to Werner, Arius and his colleagues were the last major representatives of angel christology. Although severely criticized by more orthodox scholars, *The Formation of Christian Dogma* has had an important effect on more recent studies of early Jewish Christianity. (P)
        ❧ Hardy, *ATR* 40 (1958): 329-331; Mascull, *JEH* 9 (1958): 261-263; Richardson, *TT* 15 (1958): 410-412; Robinson, *WTJ* 21 (1958): 88-90; Schmidt, *Interpretation* 14 (1960): 102-104; Smith, *JBL* 77 (1958): 288; H.E.W. Turner, *CQR* 159 (1958): 442-445.

8.21   Wiles, Maurice. *The Making of Christian Doctrine: A Study in the Principles of Early Doctrinal Development*. Cambridge: Cambridge UP, 1967. Pp vii + 184. I-3.
        Wiles asks and attempts to answer why certain doctrines developed, how we can determine whether their development was logical or not, and how the results of doctrinal deliberations such as those of Nicaea and Chalcedon do or do not remain valid today. He examines a number of orthodox doctrines and finds them wanting. This is particularly true of the Trinity and Incarnation. He concludes: "The true test of the development of doctrine is not whether it preserves all distinctions of the old in their old form; it is whether it continues the objectives of the Church..." This is an important study because of its analytical nature. (P)
        ❧ Holland, *CH* 37 (1968): 110-111; Mascall, *JTS* 19 (1968): 399-340; H.E.W. Turner, *Theology* 71 (1968): 30-32.

8.22   Williams, Rowan. *Arius. Heresy and Tradition*. London: Darton, Longman, and Todd, 1987. Pp. xi + 348. AAI-4; MAI-3; B-14.
        An important study, this is definitely a book written for specialists. Because of its dense nature, many will find it hard reading. None-

theless, it covers important new ground. Like a number of recent scholars, Williams argues that Arius was a "dedicated theological conservative" who wanted to defend the oneness and freedom of God. His "heresy" developed out of his attempt to wed Christian doctrine with Hellenistic philosophical ideas and techniques. In discussing these matters, Williams gives much attention to the political and intellectual world in which Arius and his contemporaries lived. No one should attempt to understand the Trinitarian controversy without reading this book. (P)

✂ Bray, *Churchman* 103 (1989): 362-363; Gregg, *JTS* 40 (1989): 247-254; Minns, *New Blackfriars* 69 (1988): 199-200; Patterson, *ATR* 71 (1989): 201-206; Young, *SJT* 42 (1989): 263-267.

8.23   Wolfson, Harry A. *The Philosophy of the Church Fathers,* Volume I: *Faith, Trinity, Incarnation.* Cambridge, MA: Harvard UP, 1964. (1956¹). Pp. xxviii + 635. SI-9; AAI-14.

This study demonstrates how Philo's thought—which united Jewish tradition with Greek philosophy—became basic to the christology and pneumatology of the early Christian Fathers. Wolfson argues that Philo, and from him most of the Fathers to Origen, held that God always had logos (*reason*) within him, but at a certain instant *before time* he issued forth the Logos (*Word*) who became a separate being—a second divine being. Additional topics discussed are early explanations of the Trinity, the Incarnation, Gnosticism, and various heretical movements. An important work, *The Philosophy of the Church Fathers* deals with aspects of early christology long ignored in standard, orthodox works. (P)

✂ Cotton, *Interpretation* 11 (1957): 477-479; Fehl, *ATR* 39 (1957): 88-89; Markus, *Judaism* 5 (1956): 375-379; Musurillo, *TS* 32 (1971): 138-139; Oulton, *JTS* 8 (1957): 333-335; Williams, *Harvard Divinity Bulletin* 21 (1956): 81-91.

8.24   ☛ Young, Frances M. *From Nicaea to Chalcedon: A Guide to the Literature and Its Background.* Philadelphia: Fortress, 1983. Pp. ix + 406. B-64. SI-6; Greek Index-2.

In this detailed handbook, Young brings together a vast amount of information on one of the most important periods for the development of doctrine in Christian history. She gives careful sketches of the men and movements of that era that were to influence subsequent church history in so many ways. She often presents strikingly fresh, but carefully documented, appraisals based on the most recent research. For example, she asserts that it seems probable that "Arius had fundamentally conservative intentions." This book is valuable not only for the information it presents but for the clear way in which it is written. Young's bibliography is an excellent supplement to standard patrologies. (P)

✂ Chadwick, *ExT* 96 (1984): 93-94; Dewart, *Horizons* 12 (1985): 378-379; Hall, *KTR* 7 (1984): 29-30; Henry, *SC* 4 (1985): 187-189; Rusch, *Dialog* 24 (1985): 156-157; Santer, *Theology* 87 (1984): 144-145; Stead, *JEH* 35 (1984): 147-149; TeSelle, *CH* 53 (1984): 381-382; Volz, *W&W* 5 (1985): 112-113; Winslow, *ATR* 66 (1984): 446-448.

9
CHURCH OFFICE
AND HIERARCHY

The principal issue in a discussion of church order is the development of church offices, in particular the rise of the monarchical office, or "bishop." Questions regarding the models that influenced early Christian organization (from the synagogue or from Graeco-Roman society) drove much of the debate. Of the earliest primary source materials, the Pastoral Letters (1 Timothy, 2 Timothy, and Titus), 1 Clement, the Didache, and the letters of Ignatius offer the most explicit information.

Many questions are yet unanswered about early church order and structure. In fact, most of the questions are yet unanswered. One reason for this is that the literature of the early church did not always address the issue of structure, and it is only by reading between the lines that information about church order can be gleaned. Another cause of difficulty is the possibility that when church order was addressed as a key theme in a document, it spoke of the ideal rather than the reality—an exhortation to a desired order rather than a description of an established order. And a third problem is the likelihood that development of church order and structure was not uniform throughout all areas of the early church's expansion, thus the structure of the church expressed in one document may have little application to other communities.

This leaves us often largely in a state of ignorance, but at least the questions are clear. Were there various forms of church structure? Did the early church copy structures from contemporary groups or did it strike out for a novel organization? How did development occur that led from apostolic authority to the authority of the bishop as early as the beginning of the second century in some areas? Were various structures in competition or did each dominate and control particular geographical areas?

---

* Parts of this introduction appeared earlier in Robinson, "From the Apostolate to the Episcopate: Reflections on Development," in *Self-Definition and Self-Discovery in Early Christianity: A Study in Changing Horizons.* Essays in appreciation of Ben F. Meyer, edited by David J. Hawkin and Tom Robinson (Lewiston, NY: Mellen, 1990), pp. 233-236.

In spite of these recognized uncertainties about fundamental issues, there are certain points of general agreement among schools of scholarship. (1) The office of elder seems to have been rooted in the synagogue, thus probably it was an early term used by Christians. (2) Christian vocabulary generally was not based on the Israelite priesthood for the technical terminology for church office; for whatever reason, it turned elsewhere, even taking up terms that were neither particularly Jewish or religious (e.g. bishop). (3) The term "bishop" and "elder" were used as synonyms in the first-century literature by a diverse group of authors. (4) A clear three-part structure of office (bishop, elder, deacon) appears first in western Asia Minor (present-day western Turkey), though that statement is to some extent based on our lack of information about church office in other areas, rather than on a wide and rich knowledge of church organization in the early period. (5) A matter more disputed than the previous four points of general agreement: it is held that the monarchical office (i.e. bishop) was established by the early second century in places; the reasons for the rise and the reception of the novel office are, however, matters far from any consensus.

We have already noted some of the problems in dealing with this literature. Even when the literature is unambiguous, there are problems. For one thing, the key body in the early church, called "The Twelve," was not perpetuated; this body of the inner circle of Jesus' disciples was not apparently seen as replaceable, thus it cannot be considered permanent, or even important beyond the first generation of the Christian community. Further, there is some inconsistency in the use of the term "apostle" in the first-century literature. That office, too, is not perpetuated; it is used in much of the early writings largely as a synonym for "The Twelve." By the time the office of bishop is clearly distinguishable from the office of the presbytery (in the early second century in some areas), that office has somewhat the appearance of the Apostolic office. At least, the authority of the bishop is similar to the authority of the earlier apostles. By the end of the second century, theologians were putting forward the concept of apostolic succession, arguing that bishops held the apostolic office.

But the idea of bishops holding the apostolic office seems to have been proposed or at least emphasized in order to secure the authority of the bishop against schismatic groups in the church. Good grounds exist for arguing that the link between the office of bishop and the office of apostle was not part of the church's perspective in its first century and a half. For one thing, as was pointed out well over a century ago, the very fact that a new term was used for the office suggests that the office of bishop was not merely a continuation of the office of apostle. If the same office, why not the same name? Further, the term "bishop" was used in the early period, at the same time that the term "apostle" was being used. Yet there appears to be no evidence of confusion or interchange of these two terms, as one would have expected if they referred roughly to the same office. There is, however, interchange of the terms "bishop" and "presbyter." In the first clear use of the term "bishop" where it is distinguished from the term presbyter, it is the term "presbyter," not "bishop," that is associated with the office of apostle. This being the case, the use of the term "bishop" in a more refined way suggests a change within the structure of the presbytery, rather than any continuation of the office of apostle.

There is, then, considerable obscurity regarding the development of the office of bishop, though we can say with a degree of certainty that this office was not merely an extension of the office of apostle. Even leading churchmen from the fourth century recognized that the term "bishop" was more closely related to the term "presbyter" than to the term "apostle."

Several other offices developed during the first three centuries. Besides the offices of bishop, presbyter, and deacon, there are scattered references to several other church positions. Unfortunately, often the references are too oblique to read much from them, and certainly too oblique to reconstruct the development of these offices. There were exorcists, readers, grave-diggers, watchmen of the cemeteries, and doorkeepers, whose general duties are revealed by the terms themselves. There were sub-deacons, and country bishops, and psalmists, and acolytes. From the evidence we have, there appears to have been little tension among these groups. Further, considerable work is now being done on the role of women in the early church, especially in regard to the category of "deaconess" and of "widow" (see chapter 25 for specific entries).

More tension may be found among the higher offices. Deacons often pressed their rights against the rights of the presbytery, and sometimes the presbytery pressed theirs against the rights of the bishop, and the metropolitans and the bishops against each other. Much has been made, too, of the tensions between some of the more charismatic offices (apostle, prophet, teacher) and the more institutionalized ones (bishop, presbyter, deacon). Perhaps some of this tension is reflected in the dispute about the role of "prophet" that arose between the Montanists and the larger church.

The more serious evidence of tension in the higher leadership is visible in the relationship between the bishop of Rome and other bishops in the west, and between competing bishops at various times in Rome, and between bishops in North Africa, particularly with the Donatist schism. In an earlier period of scholarship, the discussion about the position of the bishop of Rome produced much that bore the marks of polemics or apology, as Catholics emphasized the superior position of the bishop of Rome over other bishops, against the challenge of Protestant scholars. But much of that kind of scholarship has largely disappeared. That does not mean, however, that the issue is a clear one, or that consensus has been reached. It simply means that the sides in the continuing debate are less likely to reflect a clear

Catholic/Protestant division of some of the earlier debates.

Although entries in this bibliography are largely restricted to the period after the first-century, some works in this chapter deal with the first century. This is necessary to give a coherent account of the issues and the debate, since much is rooted in the tensions of the first century, especially with regard to Paul and the apostolic office, and with regard to the relationship between a charismatic and a hierarchical ministry.

Some of the works listed below seem a little removed from present discussions. Authors from a few decades ago often were writing with firm personal commitments to particular kinds of order—or personal hostility to certain hierarchical structures. Apostolic succession was a hot issue. But not everyone was out to justify a present structure on the basis of the primitive past. Lightfoot, an Anglican bishop (and thus episcopal), found that the presbytery was the more primitive office, and that the office of bishop (*episkopos*) developed, not from the apostolic office, but from the body of presbyters. Ferguson's article below [§9.16] reviews much of the older debate.

9.1 🏛 Cunningham, A. *The Bishop in the Church: Patristic Texts on the Role of the Episkopos.* Message of the Fathers of the Church 14. Wilmington: Glazier, 1985.
   Another in the "Message of the Fathers" series [§3.14], providing a selection of texts illustrate the position and function of the bishop in the early church.
   ≏ Grimes, *TS* 47 (1986): 310-311.

9.2 🏛 Eno, Robert B. *Teaching Authority in the Early Church.* Message of the Fathers of the Church 14. Wilmington: Michael Glazier, 1984. Pp. 168. B-1.
   After a brief introduction, in which he discusses the Rule of Faith, the role of bishops in guaranteeing the tradition, the authority of scripture against competing claims, and finally the use of councils to solve disputes about doctrine and practice, Eno supplies a multitude of original comments from early church writers on a variety of matters related to authority. Figuring prominently are quotes from Tertullian, Cyprian, and various councils, with particular emphasis on Augustine, though a number of other persons are quoted too. The passages are then grouped by theme, and a final chapter brings together passages on the authority of the Roman church. Brief introductions to most of the authors or issues are provided. A useful sourcebook.
   ≏ Grimes, *TS* 46 (1985): 583-584; Volz, *CH* 56 (1987): 519-520.

9.3   🏛 Hinson, E. Glenn., trans. and ed. *Understandings of the Church.* Sources of Early Christian Thought. Philadelphia: Fortress, 1986. Pp. x + 116. B-2.

A volume in the "Sources of Early Christian Thought" series, with an 18-page introduction and 24 selections, from one paragraph to over 20 pages. The introduction basically provides a brief description of the context of each of the selections. Not all passages are related specifically to church office; most deal more with how the church understood itself and how it was understood by others.

✂ Davis, *R&E* 85 (1988): 713-714; Ferguson, *CH* 57 (1988): 220; Gordy, *JES* 24 (1987): 666; Tripp *SC* 7 (1989-90): 113-115.

9.4   🏛 Lienhard, Joseph T. *Ministry.* Message of the Fathers of the Church 8. Wilmington, DE: Michael Glazier, 1987. Pp. 183. B-3.

Part of an inexpensive series of selected texts from the fathers. Eighteen different authors or documents are considered. Each text is introduced by a half-page discussion of its date, author, and context. An 11-page introduction sketches the debate, addressing matters like apostolic succession and the various offices. The authors are all well-known early Christian leaders, and the selections are of the most important passages. This is a good place to gain a sense of the range of opinions and concerns on this topic. All books in this "Message of the Fathers of the Church" series are useful at the introductory level.

9.5   ◉ Agnew, Francis H. "The Origin of the New Testament Apostle-Concept: A Review of Research." *Journal of Biblical Literature* 105 (1986): 75-96.

It is difficult to gain an understanding of the development of church office without attention to the first century. There the term "apostle" is a key one. Agnew divides his detailed survey into three main chronological/thematic periods: (1) from Lightfoot (1865) to Rengstorf, focusing on roots in the Jewish concept of designated agent (or "sent-one"); (2) from about 1949, when the "apostle" concept came to be viewed as a Christian innovation or a borrowing from Gnosticism (Schmithals); to (3) a return to the idea of Jewish roots, since the Old Testament is filled with ideas of such commissioned "sending." Discussion is clear; reference to current literature extensive.

9.6   Barnett, James Monroe. *The Diaconate: A Full and Equal Order.* Minneapolis: Seabury, 1981. Pp. xvi + 230. B-14; I-8.

This book was written by a zealot for the diaconate. Barnett wants the office restored to its full responsibilities in the modern church. The latter half of his book makes that case. The first half suits our purposes more, where Barnett traces the evidence for the role of the deacon from the first century to the fourth. He notes some of the considerable responsibility that deacons could assume, even rising from that office to that of bishop, without advancing through the presbytery. The profound shift and restriction on the diaconate came with the conversion of Constantine and the influx of people into the church, with an increasing liturgical role for presbyters, and a greater degree of presbyterial control over the appointment of the bishop. A more secular idea of office was put in place, reflecting a vertical or hierarchical structure.

⸕ Bonner, *JEH* 33 (1982): 645; Booty, *ATR* 64 (1982): 432-433; De Ridder, *CTJ* 18 (1983): 63-66; Ferguson, *CH* 52 (1983): 350-351; Jay, *SC* 3 (1983): 171-173; Kent, *ExT* 97 (1986): 217; Porter, *Worship* 57 (1983): 185-186; Wright, *SJT* 39 (1986): 269-270.

9.7   Barrett, C.K. *The Signs of an Apostle.* Cato Lecture 1969. London: Epworth, 1970 / Philadelphia: Fortress, 1972. Pp. xvi + 144. B-4.
The American edition has a helpful 14-page review of the debate by John Reumann, with primary attention to Barrett's significant and various contributions. The key points of Barrett's contribution are in the section titled "The Apostles in the New Testament" (pp. 23-81). He argues that the concept of "the Twelve" is likely pre-Easter. It is Luke that makes the Twelve into missionaries (apostles), and this rises out of Paul's shaping of the term "apostle" as one focused on mission. The term itself may have been used originally for the Twelve (as agents—not missionaries), but because of Paul's use of the term, it did not become the term of preference for the Twelve until Luke's writings.

⸕ Agnew, *CBQ* 35 (1973): 219-221; A. Hanson, *ATR* 55 (1973): 362-364; Moule, *Church Quarterly* 3 (1971): 331.

9.8   ☛ Brown, Raymond E. *Priest and Bishop: Biblical Reflections.* Paramus, NJ: Paulist, 1970. Pp. vii + 86.
An understanding of developing church office cannot be gained without careful consideration of the New Testament evidence. The question is the degree of continuity or discontinuity that marks the shift from first-century or apostolic office to second-century or monarchical office. Brown offers a clear, balanced, and suggestive review of the evidence for the early development of office.

9.9 ⊛ Burtchaell, James Tunstead. *From Synagogue to Church: Public services and offices in the earliest Christian communities.* Cambridge: Cambridge UP, 1992. Pp. xviii + 375. AI-4; BI-7; AAI-7.
Burtchaell reviews the debate regarding church office since the Reformation, with particular emphasis on the last two centuries. The Protestant and Catholic interests in the debate are clear, and the work of various scholars is discussed briefly in individual sections of about 5 pages each: Baur, Ritschl, Lightfoot, Hatch, Harnack, Sohm, Weizsäcker, Sabatier, Holtzmann, Lietzmann, Swete, Holl, Götz, Streeter, Linton, Kirk, Manson, Davies, Reid, Weber, Bultmann, Campenhausen, Schweitzer, Goppelt, Theissen, Gager, Holmberg, Verner, Meeks, Küng, Schillebeeckx, and Fiorenza. Burtchaell himself emphasizes the difference between charismatic and presiding officers, and sees roots of these latter officers in the synagogue, arguing that such officers existed in the first century, though they are not heavily emphasized in the literature of that period.

9.10 Campenhausen, Hans von. *Ecclesiastical Authority and Spiritual Power in the Church of the First Three Centuries.* Translated by J.A. Baker. Stanford, CA: Stanford U.P., 1969. Pp. vii + 308. AAI-2; MAI-4.
Campenhausen contends that the early church was not dominated by either authoritarian order or chaotic freedom. It is not tradition over spirit or spirit over tradition. Both tendencies are there: Paul representing the freedom; those churches with presbyters, the order. The two features are held together in the apostles. Once the apostles passed from the scene, office tended to dominate over charisma, as there was a need to preserve the tradition or the preaching. Although Campenhausen has distanced himself from the clear-cut way some Germans saw the tension between office and charisma, Ferguson [§9.16] thinks he is still too bound by that paradigm.
✂ Frend, *JEH* 22 (1971): 126-127; Graham, *ExT* 81 (1969): 78; R.M. Grant, *CH* 38 (1969): 525-526; Strand, *AUSS* 10 (1972): 204-206; D.F. Wright, *SJT* 24 (1971): 346-347.

9.11 Chadwick, Henry. *The Role of the Christian Bishop in Ancient Society.* Colloquy 35. Berkeley: Center for Hermeneutical Studies in Hellenistic and Modern Culture, 1979. Pp. 47.
This is the record of a lecture and resulting debate on the role of the bishop. Chadwick reflects on the evidence for the development of the office of bishop, paying particular attention to the mechanism for election, the various duties of the office (especially those related to the poor and the widows), and the relationship between that

office and the developing offices of metropolitans and patriarchs. As well, Chadwick deals with some of the early criticisms of the bishops. This is followed by extended responses from Peter Brown, Ramsay MacMullen, and Massey Shepherd, and a summary of the discussion that resulted.

9.12   ⊛ Crocker, John. "The Apostolic Succession in the Light of the History of the Primitive Church." *Anglican Theological Review* 18 (1936): 1-21.
While this article is weaker than most included in this chapter, it is useful for its review of the debate over apostolic succession in the earlier part of this century. Crocker emphasizes the Jewish roots of the Christian presbyterate, and the double stream of Christian ministry (both charismatic and settled) from the beginning.

9.13   Ehrhardt, A.A.T. *The Apostolic Succession in the First Two Centuries of the Church.* London: Lutterworth, 1953. Pp.168. I-5; BI-1; AAI-3.
Ehrhardt considers the evidence for the doctrine of apostolic succession in the early church. The roots are Jewish, he argues, and connected with succession in the priesthood. Further, there is evidence of some conflict over the issue: some put James first and some put Peter first. In the second century, the idea of succession was tied to apostolic tradition, against the claims of the heretics. Irenaeus was the key individual in the development of the theme, and his ideas were developed by Hippolytus and Tertullian. There were other ideas of succession, too, in the early church: Ehrhardt mentions prophets and teachers.

9.14   Eno, Robert B. "Authority and Conflict in the Early Church." *Église et Théologie* 7 (1976): 41-60.
Eno reviews the extensive evidence for conflict over authority in the early church, showing that it appears early and is recognized by all parties involved (even by non-Christians). Special attention is paid to corruption within the office of bishop itself, with evidence from Cyprian and Origen, and the supporting evidence of the rise and attractiveness of monasticism. Eno then addresses the conflict caused by the rise of theologians, but he points out that in the early period this conflict was usually between theologians and the populous or popular leaders rather than between theologians and bishops. Finally Eno looks at the rise of powerful cities as centres of authority and the role of councils against the authority of such cities.

9.15   Faivre, Alexandre. *The Emergence of the Laity in the Early Church.*

Translated by David Smith. New York/Mahwah: Paulist, 1990. Pp. iii + 242. AB-4; B&W-12; M-1.

Faivre divides his work into three sections: (1) first and second centuries; (2) third century; and (3) fourth to sixth century. It is his contention that the concept of laity did not exist before the end of the second century. Even then, before the term "laity" came to mean believers in general apart from the clergy, it was used (for about 50 years) to specify baptized, monogamous male believers. Not until the fourth century was the term applied also to women, at which time it started to be used for the non-clergy. This division was shifted within a century to allow for a third group, the monks.

⊰ Dupuis, *Gregorianum* 68 (1987): 348-352; Granfield, *CHR* 78 (1992): 433-434; Hinson, *PRS* 18 (1991): 201-203; Loewe, *TS* 51 (1990): 781-782; Anonymous, *CCR* 11 (1990): 92-94.

9.16 ◉ Ferguson, Everett. "Church Order in the Sub-Apostolic Period: A Survey of Interpretations." *Restoration Quarterly* 11 (1968): 225-248.

Ferguson does exactly what he sets out to do, providing an excellent survey of major views, clearly written and with an element of evaluation of the theories. Mainly emphasizing English scholarship (but not exclusively), Ferguson considers Lightfoot's "Essay of the Christian Ministry" [§9.26]; Telfer's *The Office of a Bishop* [§9.40]; Gore's *The Church and the Ministry;* Kirk's *The Apostolic Ministry* [§9.25]; Hatch's *The Organization of the Early Christian Churches* [§9.21]; Harnack's *The Constitution and Law of the Church in the First Two Centuries;* von Campenhausen's *Ecclesiastical Authority and Spiritual Power in the Church of the First Three Centuries* [§9.10] (in its German original); and two works in French by Colson. Ferguson provides a brief, clear, and informed starting place for the student.

9.17 ◉ Fuellenbach, John. *Ecclesiastical Office and the Primacy of Rome. An Evaluation of Recent Theological Discussion of First Clement.* The Catholic University of America Studies in Christian Antiquity 20. Washington: Catholic University of America Press, 1980. Pp. ix+ 278. B-18.

Catholic and Protestant understandings of church office starkly differ, and scholars on both sides of the debate claim to be able to support their position by appeal to antiquity. Fuellenbach surveys the views of fifteen Protestant and eighteen Catholic scholars (most of them German). This provides a useful review of the modern debate regarding the development of church office, as well as a useful introduction to the related discussion of *1 Clement.* The scholars considered are: Harnack, Sohm, Knopf, Seeberg, Lietzmann, Holl, Gerke, Bauer, Meinhold, Eggenberger, Campenhausen, Käsemann, Schweizer, Opitz, Goppelt, Beyschlag (all Protestant); and for the Catholic side: Scherer, Altaner, Lösch, Clarke, Sanders, Peterson, Quasten, Fischer, Stuiber, Ziegler, Knoch, McCue, Milat, Brunner, Weiss, Hassenhüttl, Martin, and Zollitsch.

9.18   Hanson, Richard. *Christian Priesthood Examined.* Guildford/ London: Lutterworth Press, 1979. Pp. 128. B-1; BI-2; SI-2; NI-4.

Though Hanson has particular interests that are more theological than historical, and though he may restrict the practical definition of "priest" unnecessarily, he does offer a good review of the use of the term "priest" and related sacerdotal language for the Christian ministry. He looks at the meaning attached to the eucharistic *sacrifice,* and argues for the important role of Cyprian in the development of a Christian "priesthood," largely focused on the bishop. He also discusses various functions of the bishop, and the bishop's relationship with other church officers.

⊱ Dowell, *Theology* 83 (1980): 62-63; Rodd, *ExT* 90 (1979): 322-324.

9.19   ◉ Hanson, Richard. "Office and the Concept of Office in the Early Church." In *Studies in Christian Antiquity.* Edinburgh: T&T Clark, 1985. Pp. 117-143.

Hanson, an Anglican, is more sympathetic to developments in church structure than are some scholars. In this article, he both reviews and analyzes all the major contributions in the debate. More important, he offers fresh insights on a variety of issues regarding pre-Constantinian ecclesiastical offices. (Unlike Hanson, many scholars concentrate only on the New Testament period.) Further, Hanson often focuses on the key problems of the debate, providing the critical observation or question that identifies a crucial flaw in a hypothesis or that indicates the reason for the importance of a piece of data in the debate.

9.20   Hardy, E.R. "The Decline and Fall of the Confessor-Presbyter." In *Studia Patristica* XV. Edited by Elizabeth A. Livingstone. Berlin: Akademie-Verlag, 1984. Pp. 221-225.

Many Christians were imprisoned or otherwise punished, perhaps by being sent to the mines, for their confession (or witness). Those who were released without denying Christ seem to have been considered living martyrs, or "confessors." As such, they had considerable status, and in some ways acted as presbyters, forgiving sins and admitting the lapsed back into communion. Hardy shows the attempts by the church hierarchy to limit the influence of the confessors, sometimes by ordaining them to *lower* orders, thus demonstrating that they were not equal to the presbyters. There were a few survivors from the Great Persecution, and a few under Julian the Apostate, who could claim the status. Later, a few monks earned the title.

9.21   Hatch, Edwin. *The Organization of the Early Christian Churches.* Bampton Lectures 1880. London: Rivingtons, 1881. Pp. xxviii + 216.
The 20-page table of contents offers a detailed synopsis of this work. Hatch lays out his methodology carefully. Although the work is well over 100 years old, many issues of contemporary interest are addressed: churches as associations; philanthropic focus of the churches, and the possibility that the Christian office of bishop was copied from secular organizations. Hatch deals, too, with the change in status of the deacons, to the advantage of the presbytery, and with the close association between bishops and deacons. The origins of presbyters is sought within Judaism. Hatch also attempts to explain the supremacy of the bishop in this organization, and addresses the issues of the distinction between clergy and laity, and the importance of monasticism, among other topics. Hatch's work shows how little some of the questions have changed in a hundred years of debate.

9.22   Jalland, T.G. *The Origin and Evolution of the Christian Church.* London/New York: Hutchinson, 1950. Pp. 200. I-5; BI-3.
This work concentrates on the origin and growth of Christian ministry and worship. Although Jalland's work is frequently referred to, Greenslade, in the review listed below, is particularly critical of the book, charging that it is little more than an uncritical summary of the article by Gregory Dix in Kirk's collection [§9.25]. Jalland looks to Judaism and the synagogue for parallels to Christian church offices, rather than to the Hellenistic environment. In this he reflects part of a trend to recognize the Jewish background of Christianity. See Chapter 26 on "Worship and the Liturgy" in this bibliography for similar trends in that field.
⊰ Greenslade, *JEH* 2 (1951): 102-103; Parker, *CQR* 151 (1950): 97-99.

9.23   ◉ Jay, E.G. "From Presbyter-Bishops to Bishops and Presbyters. Christian Ministry in the Second Century: a Survey." *Second Century* 1 (1981): 125-162.

Jay surveys the evidence for a distinction between the offices of presbyters and bishops, looking at the *Didache,* Clement of Rome, Ignatius, Polycarp, Hermas, Justin, Hegesippus, Irenaeus, Tertullian, Hippolytus, and the situation in mid-second-century Rome. To a lesser degree, Jay engages in dialogue with the works of a few modern authors, Dix, in particular. Jay thinks that the monepiscopate arose out of a naturally formed "president" of the presbytery, for which there were examples in the larger society. Too, the idea of apostolic succession did not arise until Hegesippus, and was developed by Irenaeus and Tertullian, largely in a fight with the Gnostics. Finally, apostolic tradition was not made the monopoly of a self-supporting group of bishops until the time of Hippolytus, when bishops had special consecration, and were ordained by other bishops. Jay's concentration on the second century is important, for that is the period of the fundamental shift.

9.24 ◉ Kirk, J.A. "Apostleship since Rengstorf: Towards a Synthesis." *New Testament Studies* 21 (1974/5): 249-64.
This is a solid review of the debate since Rengstorf. Kirk points out the necessary qualifications to Rengstorf's well known parallel between the Christian apostle and the Jewish *shaliah.* He then takes issue with both sides of the debate—those who think the idea of apostle originated with Paul, and those who make it pre-Pauline, but deny that it goes back to the circle in Jesus' ministry. With balance and daring, Kirk argues for several not widely accepted points: (1) the roots of the idea of apostle lie in Jesus' own ministry; (2) there is no fundamental clash between the Pauline and Lukan idea of apostle; (3) the terms "Twelve" and the "apostles" refer to the same company, though there is a wider meaning for "apostle"; and (4) the writers of the New Testament share a common view on the question of apostleship, in spite of the disparate material.

9.25 Kirk, Kenneth E., ed. *The Apostolic Ministry: Essays on the History and the Doctrine of Epicopacy.* London, Hodder & Stoughton, 1946. Pp. xiv + 573. BI-7; NI-7; SI-7.
A collection of 10 essays, which became a hot volume for some time. The subtitle reveals the general stance—episcopacy and the ministry of the apostles are profoundly linked. Only two essays deal directly with our period. But these two are important. In "The Ministry in the Early Church," Dom Gregory Dix argued for the independence of origin of the offices of bishop and presbyter, both of which were rooted in Judaism (the *shaliah* and the synagogue elders), and he made a case for the an implicit "apostolic succession"

quite early. In "The Doctrine of the Parity of Ministers," T.G. Jalland discussed the evidence for the important role of the presbyters in the western church, taking over liturgical functions from the bishops. Dix noted a similar change.

9.26 Lightfoot, J.B. *The Christian Ministry*. Edited with an Introduction by Philip Edgcumbe Hughes. Wilton, CT: Morehouse-Barlow, 1983. Pp. 115. Originally part of Lightfoot's commentary on Philippians (1868), and reissued as a separate work in 1901 by Macmillan. Reprint: Peabody, MA: Hendrickson, 1981, pp. 181-269.
Lightfoot's ideas have had tremendous impact on the way scholars have come to view the development of the Christian ministry. Two points were put forward: first, the mon-episcopacy evolved out of a presbytery, which was itself rooted in the synagogue; and second, the sacerdotal understanding of Christian ministry was foreign to the New Testament and early patristic writers. Although Lightfoot admits the obscurity of the period in which the office of bishop (as distinct from the presbytery) developed, he places that development in Asia Minor, and grants to John considerable responsibility for the development.

9.27 Manson, T.W. *The Church's Ministry*. London: Hodder and Stoughton, 1948. Pp. 112. AAI-3; I-5.
This little book was provoked by the publication of the collection of essays edited by Kirk under the title, *The Apostolic Ministry* [§9.25], and by the conviction of the authors in that volume that the last word had somehow been said. Against this, Manson attempted to qualify the importance of the position of the "apostle" (which means, for all practical purposes, "bishop" on Kirk's view) by emphasizing in more abstract ways the centrality of the church, of which the apostle is but one of many working parts. There is an ecumenical interest in Manson's position, and that theme comes often enough to the fore. Nonetheless, Manson knows his topic, and offers useful insights.
❯ Burleigh, *SJT* 2 (1949): 83-85; Gilmour, *JBL* 69 (1950): 294-295; Shepherd, *ATR* 32 (1950): 165-166.

9.28 McCue, James F. "The Roman Primacy in the Second Century and the Problem of Development of Dogma." *Theological Studies* 25 (1964): 161-196.
A survey of the second-century evidence used in reconstructions of early church office, especially the evidence used to argue that the primacy of the bishop of Rome was recognized early. After a

consideration of *I Clement,* Ignatius, Irenaeus, and of the Quartodeciman controversy, McCue dismisses the theory. There follows a
brief discussion of the role of Peter portrayed in the New Testament,
along with some reflection on the implications of certain assumptions
in the debate.

9.29 ◉ Müller, Dietrich. "apostle." In *NIDNTT* I:126-135.
Müller offers an up-to-date, clear and brief review of the debate
about the title "apostle." He raises a number of key questions and
points out where various positions are weak or strong. A note by
Colin Brown follows (pp. 135-136), in which he points out—and
argues against—the tendency of German scholars (contra English-
speaking scholars) to see a sharp difference between the Luke/Acts
picture and the Pauline picture of apostle. A bibliography is included
(pp. 136-137).

9.30 Munck, Johannes. "Paul, the Apostles, and the Twelve." *Studia
Theologia* 3 (1950-51): 96-110.
Munck's main contribution to the debate is to make Paul crucial to
the development of the concept of apostle. He argues for three
different uses: a pre-Pauline, a Pauline, and a post-Pauline. It is
Paul's view of himself as *the* apostle of Christ or as *the* apostle to
the Gentiles that links the pre-Pauline view (apostle as any messenger
or a missionary specifically appointed by Christ) to the post-Pauline
view of the *twelve* apostles. The idea of the Twelve as "tireless
missionaries" is, according to Munck, the result of a "later transfer-
ence of Paul's apostolate to the twelve disciples."

9.31 Osborne, Kenan B. *Priesthood: A History of the Ordained Ministry
in the Roman Catholic Church.* New York/Mahwah: Paulist, 1988.
Pp. vii + 388. AI-8; M-1.
Only about a third of this book is relevant to the period of the early
church. Of primary importance are parts 3 to 5; Ministry: 27 to 110
A.D.; Ministry in the Second Christian Century: 90-210 A.D.; and
Ministry in the High Patristic Church: 210 to 600 A.D. Although
Osborne does not offer much that is original for our period, he is
familiar with contemporary scholarship, and he does provide a
suitable overview of the general discussion, and offers an extensive
discussion of apostolic succession.
⊱< Chirico, *Horizons* 17 (1990): 154-155; Huels, *Worship* 64 (1990): 92-94;
Orsy, *TS* 51 (1990): 378; Power, *CHR* 76 (1990): 318-319.

9.32 Rengstorf, K.H. "Apostolos." *TDNT* 1: 398-447.

As is standard in this 10-volume dictionary of the vocabulary of the New Testament, this article traces in detail the use of the word "apostle" (and its various cognates) in pre-Christian and Christian literature. Rengstorf argues that the closest parallel to the Christian apostle is the Rabbinic *shaliah*, an official agent of sorts. Although the article is now sixty years old, it remains a significant discussion about the use of the term. It should, however, be read with a modern reflection on the topic, such as J.A. Kirk's "Apostleship since Rengstorf: Towards a Synthesis" [§9.24].

9.33   Robeck, Cecil M. *Prophesy in Carthage: Perpetua, Tertullian, and Cyprian*.Cleveland, OH: Pilgrim, 1992. Pp. xii + 329. B-15; SI-7; AAI-9; MAI-4.

By concentrating on a closely concatenated series of North African Christian texts: the Passion of Perpetua, the writings of Tertullian, and those of Cyprian, Robeck seeks to elucidate charismata, in particular the gift of prophesy, as exemplified in dream messages. The different texts give Roebeck the opportunity to study the role and function of dreaming in an actually reported case, that of Perpetua; in interpretations of the cause and meaning of dreams, and of their control in the context of a church fraught with formal and ecstatic (Montanist?) elements in the writings of Tertullian; and, finally, the (perhaps cynical?) deployment of dream messages in order to stabilize an ecclesiastical hierarchy in a period of great stress (the dreams of Cyprian in the Decian persecution). Although Robeck's treatment is rather plodding, and his conclusions equally prosaic, his account is a good survey of the principal ancient evidence and of a wide range of modern scholarly opinion. In addition, the author provides ten "appendixes" which are in fact graphic outlines of the dreams, their contents, and their basic structure. Not without its faults, especially in its coverage of non-English language scholarship on the problems, this survey is recommended both for the convenience of its coverage and as a synoptic review of this important aspect of early Christian life. (S)

9.34   ◉ Sabourin, Leopold. *Early Catholicism and Ministries: Bibliographical Commentary*. Burlington, Ontario: Trinity, 1989. Pp. 126. B-10.

This book provides a detailed review of a few key books and articles on the theme of "early catholicism," focusing especially on the development of church office and canon, and in particular on arguments put forward by Siegfried Schulz and responses to Schulz, and to books by H.-J. Schmitz and Bartsch. Briefer mention is made of numerous other articles and books, providing an indispensable introduction to this topic. Sabourin is a Catholic scholar and has more sympathy for developing catholicism than do many of the authors he reviews.

9.35   Schmithals, Walter. *The Office of Apostle in the Early Church.* Translated by John E. Steely. Nashville/New York: Abingdon, 1969. Pp. 288. B-5.

Schmithals' thesis is that the office of apostle was native to Jewish or Jewish-Christian Gnosticism, and that it was borrowed by the Pauline tradition and the catholic church. The thesis is probably too dependent on the hypothesis of a fully developed and defined pre-Christian Gnosticism. In spite of that, Schmithals' work provides a solid collection and review of the wide-ranging references to an office of apostle. Further, Schmithals deals with all the main questions regarding the apostles and the "Twelve," as well as commenting on the formation of the canon and on apostolic succession.

✂ Furnish, *Perkins Journal* 24 (1970): 56; R.M. Grant, *JES* 8 (1971): 161-162; Hooker, *Theology* 74 (1971): 372-374; Horbury, *JTS* 23 (1972): 216-219; Karris, *CBQ* 33 (1971): 297-299; Polhill, *R&E* 67 (1970): 501-502; Snyder, *JBL* 89 (1970): 253-255.

9.36   ◉ Schnackenburg, R. "Apostolicity—the Present Position of Studies." *One in Christ* 6 (1970): 243-73.

This brief article provides a good review of the debate concerning Paul's concept of apostleship and the impact of earlier ideas on Paul's thought and the impact of Paul's own idea on the later developments. Schnackenburg's main points are: (1) there was a pre-Pauline concept of apostleship; (2) the apostolic office was primarily that of the itinerant missionary; (3) there was no uniform concept or clear-cut criteria; and following from this, (4) in Jerusalem, an apostle needed an experience of the risen Lord, but in the Hellenistic mission, successful missionary activity was the certifying mark of an apostle.

9.37   Schneemelcher, Wilhelm. "Writings Relating to the Apostles: Non-biblical Material about the Apostles: Introduction." Translated by George Ogg. In *New Testament Apocrypha.* Vol. 2. Edited by Edgar Hennecke. Translated and edited by R. McL. Wilson, pp. 25-87. Philadelphia: Westminster Press, 1963.

Schneemelcher provides a brief review of the debate about the office of the apostle in the first 7 pages, and in the final 4 pages deals with the origin of the pseudo-apostolic literature. He rejects

Rengstorf [§9.32], and is sympathetic to theories that contend that neither "the Twelve" nor the "apostles" were rooted in the historical Jesus. "Apostle" is a Hellenistic category; "the Twelve" is a post-Easter apocalyptic category. Following Schneemelcher's section is a section titled: "The Picture of the Apostle in Early Christian Tradition," written by Walter Bauer and M. Hornschuh.

9.38   Streeter, Burnett Hillman. *The Primitive Church, Studied with Special Reference to the Origins of the Christian Ministry.* London: Macmillan, 1929. Pp. xiv + 323. I-13; NI-4; CT-3; M-1; T-1.
For a long time, Streeter's work was a standard one on the issue. It closely follows Lightfoot's reconstruction on many issues. An important role is given to the Johannine contribution to church office. Separate chapters on Asia, Syria, Rome, and Alexandria. With several appendices: Pionius' *Life of Polycarp*, The Date of The Letters of Ignatius and Polycarp; Origin and Date of the *Didache*; Irenaeus and the Early Popes. Streeter contends that various types of ministry existed in the second century, after which the episcopal office won out.

9.39   Swete H.B., ed. *Essays on the Early History of the Church and the Ministry.* 2d ed. London: Macmillan, 1921. Pp. xxxvi + 446. BI-3; AAI-10; MAI-4; NI-7; SI-11; Greek and Latin Index-2.
A collection of six articles, most of which have left their imprint in the continuing debate: "Conceptions of the Church in early times" (A.J. Mason); "The Christian Ministry in the Apostolic and sub-Apostolic periods" (J.A. Robinson); "Apostolic Succession" (C.H. Turner); "The Cyprianic Doctrine of the Ministry" (J.H. Bernard); "Early Forms of Ordination" (W.H. Frere); and "Terms of Communion, and the Ministration of the Sacraments, in early times" (F.E. Brightman). Swete's preface sets the articles within the scholarly debate, and in the second edition, released after Swete's death, Turner answers some of the reviewers' criticism, and defends the essays and supplements his own.

9.40   Telfer, W. *The Office of a Bishop.* London: Darton, Longman & Todd, 1962. Pp. xvii + 214. I-3.
Telfer argues that the office of bishop was rooted in the specific role that James played in the mother church at Jerusalem, rather than in an "apostolic" role played by the Twelve. Further, he argues that the institution spread rapidly throughout Asia Minor and Syria because of the crisis the resulted from the fall of Jerusalem, with the loss of the mother church. Each church needed to become

autocephalous (i.e. having its own head). Telfer then discusses the
evidence for monarchical bishops in the east (from Ignatius on);
the issue of apostolic succession; some of the criticism of bishops;
their various roles, in particular, as magistrates, as judges over
theologians, and as trustees of church property and charity. Finally
he discusses the ordination of bishops. The work is still a good
review of the role of the bishop in the early church, in spite of
Telfer's thesis concerning the origin of the office not being compelling.
⊰ Blake, *TT* 20 (1963): 442-443; Wand, *CQR* 164 (1963): 379-380.

9.41   Turner, C.H. "The Organization of the Church." In *The Cambridge
       Medieval History.* Vol. 1. *The Christian Roman Empire and the
       Foundation of the Teutonic Kingdoms.* Cambridge: Cambridge UP,
       1911. Pp. 143-182.
       Turner briefly traces the development of the main church offices,
       but turns in detail to some of the matters not often addressed in
       works on church office, such as the minor orders and the changes
       in duties of the major orders. Turner emphasizes how the growth of
       the church made it necessary to shift some of the duties of the
       presbyters, in particular, and of others. He points to the problematic
       position of the deacons, and their success in promotion of their
       office often against the presbytery, and he discusses in detail the
       position of bishop, as well as the office of reader, country bishop,
       archdeacon, and others, and the development of the position of the
       metropolitan. Discussions of promotion from one rank to another
       (and exceptions to the normal practice), the increasing distance
       between the bishop and the laity, and the role of councils and
       development of creeds make this a dense and valuable discussion
       of church office.

10
CHURCH AND STATE

From persecuting monster of the Apocalypse to chosen agent of God—
that is the change in perception that the early Christians went through in
their view of the emperor of Rome in little more than two centuries. That is
not too say that there was a uniform Christian opinion on the matter. Some
Christians seemed considerably more prepared to see the emperor, even
prior to Constantine, as a divine tool and a force of good and stability.
Others, even after Constantine's conversion and his clear actions in favor of
the church, continued to view him with suspicion, and at times hostility.

Many of the issues that touch on the relations between the church and
the state in the early period have been dealt with in special chapters in this
bibliography. For example, chapter 11 deals with Constantine, whose
conversion led to dramatic shifts in church/state relations. Chapter 20, on
persecution and martyrdom, covers a much darker period in the relationship,
when Christians were subject to death from imperial authorities. Another
chapter deals with the church and society, and many of the issues addressed
there touch on the political aspect of things.

One thing is clear from the primary documents. Christians held various
views about the relationship. But, generally, it might be said that in so far as
Christians were not the objects of attack from the authorities, they went
about their business, rarely acting as revolutionaries against the state. Indeed,
some scholars have accused the early Christians of not being revolutionary
enough, faulting them for allowing the status quo to remain much as it was
(with slavery put forward as the starkest and most troubling example). The
revolutionary fringe, perhaps with apocalyptic longings, were largely simply
that—a fringe; not representing the heart of the Christian perspective about
the state, however ambiguous and troubling the church's relation with the
state was at times.

It was not only Christians who had reason to reflect on the relationship
between the church and the state. The larger society also had reason to
reflect on the relationship, and to feel concerned. For one thing, a certain
amount of civic responsibility is required of the members of any society,
and this was as true in the ancient world as it is in our own. And politics and

religion were often intertwined, whether in the form of the imperial cult in the provinces, in the religious character of the military, or in the threat of the barbarians, which would not be repelled if the gods of Rome were not "on side."

Putting aside the religious element in the relationship, which was serious enough, and which was frequently the stated point of the pagans' concerns, there was the practical reality that the state could not function without considerable contributions from it citizens, especially from the more wealthy. As the burden of the empire became greater, the responsibilities and the expenses of holding office made such appointments less and less desirable. That is not to say that Christians never served—there is evidence to suggest that by the time of Constantine, Christians had come to occupy numerous positions in the civil service, from low to high office. Yet, there was enough Christian "non-participation" in such matters for Christians to be considered by many as nothing more than parasites on the society—a charge that some Christians took seriously enough to respond.

One of the more visible places where Christian loyalty to the state could be displayed was in service in the army. One section of this chapter deals with the recent debate between vigorous proponents of a near normative early Christian "pacifism" and proponents of a newer perspective, who emphasize the broad and diverse opinions on the matter. We certainly know that Christians did serve in the army prior to Constantine, but such service could not have been without its difficulties, given the religious character of the army and the frequent admonitions against violence and killing from within the church. That changed, of course, when Constantine became master of the army and the empire, and made his military victory the act of the Christian God.

GENERAL

10.1   🏛 Coleman-Norton, P.R. ed., *Roman State and Christian Church: A Collection of Legal Documents to A.D. 535*, London, SPCK, 1966; Vol. 1: Pp. lxvii + 1-370; Vol. 2: Pp. 371-844; Vol. 3: Pp. 845-1358. I-93; BI-4; AAI-10.

All significant laws (mandata, constitutiones, senatus consulta, and similar laws) governing relationships between the Roman state and the Christian church are presented in this essential collection of texts in English translation. Each selection is prefaced with a brief introduction and significant problems and cruxes in each text are explained in the footnotes. Volume One which contains documents numbered 1-177 (113-381 CE), also has a valuable preface to the history of the Roman legislation, a general table of all the documents, and a chronological table for the main emperors. Volume Two contains documents numbered 178-486 (178-453 CE). Volume Three contains documents numbered 487-652 (453-534 CE), and an appendix providing full legal documentation on the persecutions; a table of titles of address in Church and state; a glossary of the main legal and cultural terms; and indexes of sources, persons, places, and subjects. An invaluable work of reference for the period. (S)

10.2 🏛 Cunningham, Agnes, ed. *The Early Church and the State.* Translated by Agnes Cunningham and Michael di Maio. Sources of Early Christian Thought. Philadelphia: Fortress, 1982. Pp. viii + 117. B-3.

The introduction to this volume of primary sources gives a short but excellent history of the tension that existed in Christian relations with the Roman state. Although Christians prayed for their secular rulers, they also felt it wrong to obey men rather than God in matters of principle. This led to their persecution, because often secular and religious practices were linked in the Roman world. Thus, when Christians refused to obey the commands of Caesar and his officials, they suffered, sometimes even to death. The documents show changes in Christian attitudes in the Constantinian and post Constantinian eras. Documents included are: Pliny and Trajan's correspondence; Tertullian; Edict of Galerius; Edict of Milan; Eusebius' Oration on the 13th anniversary of Constantine's reign; three letters of Eusebius of Vercelli; three letters and a sermon of Ambrose. (P)

✄ Barkley, *SC* 4 (1984): 248-249; McNicol, *RQ* 27 (1984): 244; Summerlin, *JCS* 26 (1984): 143.

10.3 🏛 Whittaker, Molly. *Jews and Christians: Graeco-Roman Views.* Cambridge Commentaries on the Writings of the Jewish and Christian World, 200 B.C.–A.D. 200. Cambridge: Cambridge UP, 1984. Pp. ix + 286. I-12; B-2; CT-4; M-3.

The sixth volume in the Cambridge series on original documents in translation relating to the early Jewish and Christian communities in the Mediterranean, Whittaker's text is divided into three major headings: Judaism, Christianity, and the Pagan Background. Within each section she provides a general background to the translated texts (usually arranged in coherent subsections: e.g., subsections on Moses, Sabbath, Food Laws, Circumcision, Government Attitudes, in the section on "Judaism"). Each of the sets of translated texts in each subsection is accompanied by explanatory notes. All

translations were done afresh by the editor. (S)
>< Goodman, *JJS* 37 (1986): 120; Grant, *CH* 55 (1986): 508-510; Kingsbury, *Interpretation* 42 (1988): 105-106; Rodd, *ExT* 96 (1985): 163-164; Rowland, *JTS* 37 (1986): 491-492; Whitarce, *CSR* 15 (1986): 197-198.

10.4   ◉ Aland, Kurt. "The Relation between Church and State in Early Times: A Reinterpretation." *Journal of Theological Studies,* ns 19 (1968): 115-127.
Aland's article was read as a paper at the 5th International Conference on Patristic Studies at Oxford, September, 1967. He examines statements in the writings of such Christian apologists as Latantius, Melito, and Tertullian which describe most Roman emperors as benign towards Christians despite those same writers' accounts of severe persecutions by numerous emperors. He explains that this curious perspective was the result of the Christians' basic doctrine of the nature of the state based on Romans 13 and 1 Peter 2:13-17. Aland dismisses the contention that Christian writers were simply trying to ingratiate their community with the state or that persecutions were not severe. He argues that the Church's later positive attitude toward Constantine and his successors was an outgrowth of what was, essentially, a generally positive sentiment towards the Roman imperial state. (P)

10.5   Barnard, Leslie W. "Church and State Relations A.D. 313-337." *Journal of Church and State* 24 (1982): 337-355.
A survey of the reign of Constantine, Barnard's article argues that church-state relations during the period present a checkered picture. Eusebius regarded Constantine as the spokesman of the Logos, but there is no evidence that Constantine saw himself in that light. His religion was a strange mixture of pagan and Christian. Constantine had no fixed program for the church, and the church was unprepared for the problems and dangers arising from Christianity becoming a legal religion. In the East, Eusebius opposed Athanasius more on political and personal grounds than on doctrinal. Only some time later did doctrinal issues become central to relations between the East and the West and in relation to the Roman state. This article is an excellent, short survey. (P)

10.6   Celsus. *On the True Doctrine: A Discourse Against the Christians.* Translated by R. Joseph Hoffmann, New York/Oxford: Oxford UP, 1987. Pp. xiii +145. B-2.
Hoffmann's translation of *On the True Doctrine* is a useful document in itself. Taken from Origen's *Against Celsus,* it is the best extant

ancient critique of Christianity available to the modern world by a believer in traditional Roman values. Significantly, it uses many of the same arguments against early Christianity that are used by secularists against certain modern-day peace churches and sects. Hoffmann's general introduction is a most valuable statement on early Christian and anti-Christian polemicism up to and including Celsus. It also deals with the questions of who Celsus was and when he lived. (P)

⊰ Hall, *JEH* 40 (1989): 253-261; Krupp, *JETS* 32 (1989): 399; McVey, *ATR* 71 (1989): 214-215; Quentin, *Concordia Journal* 14 (1988): 443-444; Trigg, *CH* 57 (1988): 353-354; Weinrich, *CTQ* 51 (1987): 296-297.

10.7 ⦿ Frend, W.H.C. "Church and State: Perspective and Problems in the Patristic Era." In *Studia Patristica*. Vol. 17.1. Edited by Elizabeth A. Livingstone. Oxford: Pergamon Press, 1982. Pp. 38-54.
Frend discusses the various Christian attitudes toward the state. He finds, in particular, a difference between the eastern and western attitudes. In the east, there was a clearer sense that the Christian empire was part of a longer history, with the past being part of the divine order of things, whereas in the west there was a greater sense of the discontinuity between the pagan past and the Christian present, and a clearer sense of distance between church and state (the two-swords idea). This latter view could lead, it seems, to a third, more revolutionary view, as demonstrated in North Africa. Frend looks for Jewish influences behind these attitudes.

10.8 Gregory, Timothy E. *Vox Populi: Popular Opinion and Violence in the Religious Controversies of the Fifth Century A.D.* Columbus: Ohio State UP, 1979. Pp. xii + 245. I-3; B-12.
Theological controversies in the early church were not the sole domain of the theologians and church hierarchy. Lay people of quite a mixed bag discussed the issues, and sometimes became violently involved. Gregory attempts to explain this phenomenon by examining four incidents: Synod of the Oak (403); Council of Ephesus (431); Robber Synod (449); and Council of Chalcedon (451). He does not find explanations primarily in secular terms convincing; the religious and the secular were interwoven, and the genuine religious concerns of the lay people must be recognized.

⊰ Baldwin, *AHR* 85 (1980): 866-867; Kruf, *CH* 50 (1981): 466; Thiel, *JAAR* 49 (1981): 690-691.

10.9 Hardy, E.G. *Christianity and the Roman Government: A Study in Imperial Administration.* London: George Allen and Unwin / New

York: Macmillan, 1894. Pp. xiv + 161.
Although rather dated, Hardy's study is still useful. It is not a
history of Christianity or the early Church, nor is it concerned
primarily with the nature of Roman state religion. Rather, it is an
examination of Roman administration's dealings with foreign cults,
and it is an attempt to find a common administrative policy which
may explain the "diversified facts on record." In his study, Hardy
surveys the attitude of Rome to foreign cults, the treatment of
Judaism, the early appearance of Christianity, Christianity under
later emperors, persecution for the name "Christian," and Christianity
in its relation to "collegia." The final chapter contains two "acta
martyrum." (P)

10.10   Ramsay, W.M. *The Church in the Roman Empire: Before A.D.
170.* Mansfield College Lectures. New York and London: G.P.
Putnam's Sons, 1912. Pp. 494. I-14; B&W-3; M-2.
Only Part II of this book deals with post-apostolic, Roman and
Christian history. In it, Ramsay develops what may be described as
a social rather than a doctrinal history. This is based on secular,
Roman data as well as on Christian accounts. Much of what he
discusses is therefore written from the standpoint of Roman emperors
and the Roman imperial government rather than that of the Christians.
Yet he also gives thorough attention to Christian beliefs and attitudes.
He attributes the persecution of Christians to the fact that they
were regarded as inimical to Roman imperial unity. (P)

10.11   Sordi, Marta. *The Christians and the Roman Empire.* Translated by
Annabel Bedini. London: Croom Helm, 1986. Pp. 215. I-11.
Sordi's thesis is that Christian conflict with the state, and the
persecutions that resulted from this conflict, rarely had a political
flavor. The one exception may be the Montanist movement.
Generally Christians were loyal (in political terms), and conflict
was largely of a religious nature. Persecutions were usually the
result of mob pressures. The first nine chapters deal with the church
under various emperors; the latter four chapters with general
questions about church/state relations.
⊱ Benko, *AHR* 93 (1988): 130; Benko, *JR* 68 (1988): 96-97; Bryant,
Review of Religious Research 30 (1988): 87-89; Crook, *JEH* 38 (1987):
625-626; Gustafson, *Dialog* 26 (1987): 320.

WAR AND THE MILITARY
10.12   🏛 Swift, Louis J., ed. *The Early Fathers on War & Military
Service.* Messages of the Fathers of the Church 19. Wilmington,

Delaware: Michael Glazier, 1983. Pp. 164. B-4.

This volume is a gold mine of readily available primitive Christian source materials from the fathers of the church on the subject of war. It contains writings from the Apostolic Fathers through the apologists to figures in the post-Constantinian era such as Augustine, Sulpicius Severus, Paulinus of Nola, and Prudentius. Also important is Swift's excellent "Introduction" which shows that while most Christians during the first three centuries were opposed to war, there were always problems—both practical and traditional—with their stance. In particular, the Old Testament countenanced war, the New Testament used military terminology, and the Revelation spoke of Christ coming again as a warrior king. Although short, the bibliography is most informative. (P)

✂ Cunningham, *TS* 45 (1984): 771-772; Dekar, *Theodolite* 7 (1986): 14-18; Elliott, *PSB* 5 (1984): 263-266; Hunter, *RSR* 18 (1992): 87-94; Webster, *CSR* 15 (1986): 86-88.

10.13 ◉ Bainton, Roland H. "The Early Church and War." *Harvard Theological Review* 39 (1946): 189-212. Reprinted in *The Church, the Gospel, and War.* Edited by Rufus M. Jones. New York: 1948. Pp. 75-92.

Bainton reviews scholarly studies on early Christian attitudes towards war. He cites Harnack, Moffatt, Cadoux, and Leclercq to show that the early Christians were pacifists. He also surveys modern interpretations of data from pre-Constantinian times and discusses modern debates over the proper Christian attitude towards war. He then gives a more extended review and analysis of early Christian statements on the issue and shows the complexity of the problem of Christian pacifism, particularly in the light of the Old Testament sanction of theocratic warfare. Bainton also discusses briefly the incorporation of pagan concepts of peace and war into Christian thinking. (P)

10.14 Cadoux, C. John. *The Early Christian Attitude to War: A Contribution to the History of Christian Ethics.* With a Foreword by Rev. W.E. Orchard, D.D. London: George Allen & Urwin Ltd., 1940. Reprint: Seabury, 1982.

Published originally in 1919, this book has become a classical evaluation of the early Christian attitude to war. In the Foreword, Orchard describes the volume as the English language equivalent to Harnack's *Militia Christi,* which it is. Although Cadoux admits writing as a pacifist, he attempts to give an objective historical account of the early Christian attitudes to war and military service

embedded in Christian ethics in general. Although somewhat dated and superseded by later authors such as Roland Bainton [§10.13] and Jean Hornus, *The Early Christian Attitude to War* remains an important study, especially from an historical perspective. (P)
⊰ Hunter, *RSR* 18 (1992): 87-94.

10.15   Campenhausen, Hans von. "Christians and Military Service in the Early Church." In *Tradition and Life in the Church: Essays and Lectures in Church History.* Translated by A.V. Littledale. London: Collins, 1968. Pp. 160-170.
Campenhausen argues that while the New Testament says nothing about military service, until 175 CE there were no Christians known to be soldiers in Roman armies. He holds that this was because Christians were "strangers in the world" who wanted to heal it rather than destroy it. After 175, however, a new attitude began to develop which caused some Christians to perform military service—Christians were coming to be criticized as parasites on the society, drawing from it but not giving to it, so Celsus charged, and this became all the more obvious as the empire found itself threatened by forces on its borders. The empire needed the support of *all* its citizens, and Christian participation in the army increased. Many, however, including Tertullian, Origen, and even a number of people after the legalization of the church by Constantine, continued to believe that military service was wrong. (P)

10.16   Driver, John. *How Christians Made Peace with War: Early Christian Understandings of War.* Peace and Justice Series 2. Scottdale/Waterloo: Herald Press, 1988. Pp. 96.
This is a popular treatment (from the perspective of a pacifist) of what has come to be called the "Constantinian shift" in Christian attitudes to war. Driver attempts to show a gradual change in thought as some Christians became involved in the military. He closes with Augustine, who argued for a supportive relationship between the church and the structures by which the state preserved itself.
⊰ Brubacher, *Conrad Grebel Review* 8 (1990): 98-101; Williams, *RQ* 32 (1990): 247-248.

10.17   Harnack, Adolf. *Militia Christi: The Christian Religion and the Military in the First Three Centuries.* Translated by David McInnes Gracie. Philadelphia: Fortress, 1981. Pp. 112. AAI-5.
A translation of Harnack's work of 1905 which remains the fundamental point of departure on the debate, part one of which deals with the simple factual background of the actual service of

Christians as soldiers in the Roman army. The second parts covers the thornier and more disputed problem (as in modern times) of under what conditions a Christian was able to accept service in the army or whether such service should be refused altogether, even to the point of martyrdom. The translators' introduction (pp. 9-22) sets Harnack's monograph in context, and outlines some of the subsequent and sometimes harsh criticisms it received (e.g. by John Cadoux §10.14). This work needs to be supplemented by John Helgeland's work [§10.18]. (S)

⊱< Daly, *Horizons* 10 (1983): 374-375; Hunter, *RSR* 18 (1992): 87-94; Swift, *ATR* 65 (1983): 99-101; Volz, *Dialog* 22 (1983): 312-324; CH 53: 127.

10.18 ☛ Helgeland, John, Robert J. Daly, and J. Patout Burns. *Christians and the Military: the Early Experience.* Philadelphia, Fortress, 1985, Pp. ix + 101. B-3; I-5.

A most valuable complement first to Harnack's classic foundational account [§10.17] and Hegleland's survey article in *ANRW*. The authors move, successively, through the pre-Christian evidence on attitudes to military service and thence to the basic New Testament texts on the subject. They emphasize the specific minor treatises of Tertullian on the subject (ch. 3) as establishing a classic Christian response. In surveying the second and third century materials they discuss the role of ritual and belief as it was knit into the basic requirements of service in the Roman army ("Roman Army Religion") and on the record of those Christians who were willing to suffer martyrdom rather than accede to these sorts of demands (chs. 8-9). The book ends with the formal resolution of these conflicts under Constantine (the evidence of Eusebius) and the fourth century Fathers (Ambrose and Augustine). The main primary texts are cited in translation. (S)

⊱< Grau, *Horizons* 14 (1987): 153-154; Hinson, *CH* 55 (1986): 251-252; Hunter, *RSR* 18 (1992): 87-94; Louth, *Theology* 91 (1988): 148-149; Swift, *CHR* 73 (1987): 147-148; Thompson, *PBR* 5 (1986): 237-239.

10.19 Hornus, Jean-Michel. *It Is Not Lawful for Me to Fight.* Scottdale /Waterloo: Herald Press, 1980. Pp. 384.

Arguing from a pacifist position, Hornus surveys the early Christian writings for comments about war, violence, and the state. He contends that the church in its first three centuries was solidly opposed to Christian participation in the military, and he tries to explain the change to a less disapproving attitude in the fourth century. Hornus is clearly unsympathetic towards this shift.

❧ Bonner, *JEH* 33 (1982): 277-278; Bray, *Churchman* 95 (1981): 371;
Deats, *JCS* 25 (1983): 168-169; Friessen, *Mennonite Quarterly Review* 57
(1983): 78-79; Goetz, *TT* 38 (1981): 431-434; Hunter, *RSR* 18 (1992):
87-94; Price, *Sobornost* 3 (1981): 232-233; Weed, *SC* 2 (1982): 188-190;
Winters, *TS* 43 (1982): 145-146; Young, *ExT* 92 (1981): 248-249

10.20 ◉ Hunter, David G. "A Decade of Research on Early Christians
and Military Service." *Religious Studies Review* 18 (1992): 87-94.
Hunter reviews the recent contributions to the debate, discussing
both the "pacifist consensus" and the challenges to that. John
Helgeland [§10.18] and James Turner Johnson (in various writings)
represent the new voice; Harnack (with qualification) [§10.17],
Cadoux [§10.14], and Hornus [§10.19] represent the traditional, in
which Christians were thought to resist military service because
they were "forbidden to kill"—a straight-forward pacifist approach.
But there may have been other reasons for Christian reservations
about the military: the army was "religious," and this could have
conflicted with the commitments of the Christian recruit. Johnson
points to the increasing number of Christians found in the army in
the early period, arguing that there was a range of opinions on the
subject. Swift's collection of sources [§10.12] is also reviewed.
The bibliography is up to date.

10.21 Liebeschuetz, J.H.W.G. *Barbarians and Bishops: Army, Church,
and State in the Age of Arcadius and Chrysostom.* Oxford: Clarendon,
1990. Pp. 320. B&W-7.
Liebeschuetz discusses the change in the character of the Roman
army as it became increasingly made up of members of the barbarian
tribes. The political maneuverings in Constantinople, by which the
non-Roman army was controlled by the civil authorities, are
discussed, as well as Chrysostom's conflict with these powers.

11
CONSTANTINE
AND THE CHRISTIAN EMPIRE

The conversion of Constantine came at a moment when the Christian church was enduring its greatest trial. The conversion immediately reversed the fortunes of the church and forever changed its character, taking it almost overnight from threatened extinction to favored status. According to Eusebius, the famous Christian historian and bishop who wrote during this time, Constantine was nothing less than God's chosen agent, who convincingly engaged the forces of paganism and vanquished them. But the matter was not nearly so clear cut. Socrates, a Christian historian of a century later, was more sharply critical of Constantine and the conversion of the empire, and even some Christian groups within the empire were opposed to the so-called "Christianizing" of the empire under Constantine. They felt that rather than "Christianizing" the empire, Constantine's "conversion" brought about the paganizing of the church. No longer did converts display the rigor gained from profound conversion in the midst of adversity, as had been the case when the sides were more clearly drawn. The state then had been a threat, not only to the existence of the church, but to the life of individual members whose loyalty to Christ set them apart as a foreign and dangerous element in the state. But once Constantine converted to Christianity, the once despised religion became an easy option for those who wanted to align themselves with the "proper" people. Many who protested this dilution of Christian rigor and piety made their way to the deserts and became the founders of Christian monasticism. Opposition also arose because Constantine's goal of Christian unity and uniformity alienated dissident Christian groups (such as the Donatists of North Africa), and these came to view themselves not simply as different Christians, but as the only true ones.

Scholars recognize that the period and issues are maddeningly complex. They have repeatedly been drawn into a seemingly bottomless vortex of unanswerable questions. One of these is whether the conversion of the empire to Christianity was inevitable. The answer to this involves resolution of the question of the strength of paganism. Some argue that paganism was bankrupt, offering nothing to those caught in the web of anxiety in a decaying empire. Others argue that this is a false perception of Graeco-Roman religion, for paganism continued as a viable force long after the conversion of Constantine (see chapter 12 "Conversion, Missions, and the Early Christian Apologetic").

Another much debated question is the depth of the conversion of the empire and of Constantine himself. Prior to Constantine, the emperor had been viewed by many Christians as the head of the forces of evil that brutally persecuted the Christian community. Although many of the Roman emperors were disinterested in this new and, in their eyes, insignificant, religious movement, making life relatively peaceful for the average Christian, Christians nonetheless normally saw themselves as a distinctive group, set apart from the larger society, and frequently disadvantaged by that. They even sensed themselves to be a "third race" within the empire. Although Christians settled into society, there was always the sense of distance from the society, as Christian exclusivity prevented members from participation in many of the social and civic activities of the local communities, especially in a society where a sense of community was often expressed in devotion to the gods of the empire and of the local area.

It was not easy for every Christian to step from this minority (and sometimes persecuted) position to that of imperial favorite. Many Christians long retained their suspicions about the emperor, but most, like Eusebius, had little but praise for the change. The benefits of Constantine were seen to be concrete and massive.

But was Constantine's conversion really a conversion in significant religious terms, or was he primarily an astute politician, playing numerous forces against each other until he had control of the empire? Scholars have yet to come to a consensus. W.H.C. Frend, for example, in his book, *The Rise of Christianity* [§5.16], is suspicious about the slowness of Constantine's conversion and the continuing attachment of Constantine to pagan elements, as is A.H.M. Jones in *Constantine and the Conversion of Europe* [§11.12] and Ramsay MacMullen in the final chapter of his *Christianizing the Roman Empire* [§12.33]. Other scholars are more sympathetic, such as A. Alföldi in *The Conversion of Constantine and Pagan Rome* [§11.6], and Norman H. Baynes in *Constantine the Great and the Christian Church* [§11.9]. Most recently, Robin Lane Fox, in his *Pagans and Christians* [§12.2], offers a particularly sympathetic account of Constantine's conversion and his abilities. But whatever the conclusion about the depth of Constantine's conversion, and despite the need to admit that he was not the first emperor to halt the persecution of Christians, Constantine must be credited for raising Christians above a merely tolerated group to the imperial favorite, and this was the most profound change the church had to deal with since its establishment.

Prior to Constantine's rise to power, the empire had experienced massive economic and political instability. Diocletian, whose name is somewhat unfairly listed with the most violent persecutors of Christians, made a series of reforms to revitalize and stabilize the empire, and his actions against Christians were brief compared to what happened in the eastern half of the empire. Constantine, while reversing some of the structural changes brought about by Diocletian, no doubt benefited from other of the recent reforms. But the empire, at its heart, was not healthy. Supported by either the pagans gods or by the Christian God, it was dying. Within a hundred years of the conversion of Constantine, the capital city, Rome, would be sacked by a "barbarian" tribe, and though the western empire would live on in name until 476 CE, its disintegration was increasingly likely. Both pagan and Christian loyalists to the empire struggled with this loss. Pagans blamed the collapse on the offence to the pagan gods brought on by Constantine's conversion; Christians saw it as judgment by God for the shortcomings of the church. Some distanced themselves from the fortunes of the Roman empire altogether, shaping their history to make the collapse of the empire an insignificant matter in terms of the grand-scale divine purpose, as Augustine did, for example, in *The City of God*.

The "barbarian conquest" of the western part of the empire is a crucial juncture in a number of developments. It sharpens the differences between the eastern and the western church, and though those differences were more linguistic and cultural than theological, the tension was real enough, and finally led to a formal separation in 1054 CE. Another important development stemming from the collapse of the west was the increasing political importance of the Bishop of Rome. Even before the deposing of the emperor in the west by the Germanic invader-allies, the Bishop of Rome was seen as a unifying force, and his importance to the west was made even more central as the church took over many of the functions of the imperial government, such as treaty negotiations with the barbarians and economic relief in times of famine and other hardships. Some tension developed between the Bishop of Rome and the eastern emperor, who saw himself as the sole emperor of the Roman empire after the removal of the western emperor by the "barbarians."

But even when the relations between west and east were good, the eastern empire was simply too weak and hampered by its own problems to assist the west. Only briefly in the 500s under the Emperor Justinian was there a revival in the fortunes of the empire, and even at that, it was the east that gained most clearly from it. That, too, was temporary. In the 600s and 700s, large parts of both the eastern and the western empires were lost to the rapid advance of Islam. That advance was halted, in part due to the growing strength of the Christian Franks in the west and in part to the breakdown of the Muslim Ummayad empire centred in Damascus, and the shift of one of the centres of the divided Muslim empire farther east to Baghdad. But that's another story—beyond the scope of this bibliography.

GENERAL
11.1   Baus, Karl, et al. *The Imperial Church from Constantine to the Early Middle Ages.* History of the Church 2. New York: Seabury, 1980. Pp. xvii + 846.
This is one of the standard church histories in German, and now has been translated into English. See §5.4 for a full description of the two-volume work. The bibliography is massive, and arranged clearly and conveniently, perhaps better than any other bibliography. Most of the works listed here are in German, though there is an adequately rich selection of works in English.

11.2   Bowder Diana. *The Age of Constantine and Julian.* London: Paul Elek, 1978. Pp. xv + 230. I-13; B&W-51; CT-4; FT-1; M-1.
A study of religious life in the Roman empire in the fourth century, with a sympathetic treatment of Constantine's conversion, even though Bowder admits that Constantine did not initially see the boundaries of Christian belief clearly in the early years. She provides a sympathetic treatment of the Christian success against paganism, explaining the similarities between Constantinian Christianity and paganism by the influence of a common background rather than significant Christian borrowing from paganism. She also considers the success of the pagan emperor Julian, especially in the cities, and supports her views by frequent appeal to art and architecture. A 64-page chapter deals with Christian and pagan life and art. (S)
✄ Hunt, *CR* 30 (1980): 100-102; Hunt, *JRS* 71 (1981): 193-197; Rexine, *GOTR* 25 (1980): 206-209.

11.3   Brown, Peter. *Power and Persuasion in Late Antiquity: Towards a Christian Empire.* Madison, WI: University of Wisconsin Press, 1992. Pp. x + 182. I-24.
In these four studies, originally delivered as the Curti Lectures at the University of Wisconsin in 1988, Brown turns away from the "micro" concern of the individual (see *The Body and Society* §14.4) to the problems of the collective power of the élites of the ancient Mediterranean. In his introductory chapter, he outlines the nature of the structure of the secular power held by the traditional élite at the center—in the large towns and cities of the empire. In his successive analytical attacks on how this power was at once maintained and transformed, Brown concentrates first on how bishops were able to co-opt and transmute the traditional *paideia* or cultural élite of the empire—so forging a new empire-wide "habitus" for the élite. He further demonstrates the novel empowerment of the Church and its leaders through its organization and

mobilization of the large urban poor masses. Finally, he studies the challenge of Christianity and its "wise men" in their affronts, which were sometimes violent, to the traditional classes of secular philosophers. Along with Cameron's study of the new rhetoric of Christianity [§25.10], this work will transform our thinking about the material/moral matrix that defined late antique society. (S)

11.4   Markus, R.A. *The End of Ancient Christianity.* Cambridge: Cambridge UP, 1990. Pp. xvii + 258. B-21; I-8.
Markus deals with the shifts that take place in Christianity in the period from the post-Constantinian era to Gregory the Great (ca. 400-600), or from "ancient" to "medieval" Christianity. A number of topics are considered: conversion, martyrs, festivals, monasticism, and community, with particular emphasis on the broad concepts of sacred time and space. Markus sees a shift that increasingly reduces the secular realm until, by the time of Gregory, it has almost ceased to exist. Special attention is given to Augustine, whose assumptions and attitudes are contrasted to those reflected in Gregory.
✂ Bonner, *JTS* 43 (1992): 705-712; Foster, *Downside Review* 110 (1992): 69-77; Frend, *ExT* 102 (1991): 318-319; Hill, *New Blackfriars* 72 (1991): 248-249; Kaufmann, *TS* 52 (1991): 742-744; O'Donnell, *CHR* 77 (1991): 494-495; Wilken, *First Things* 20 (1992): 54-57.

11.5   Meyendorff, John. *Imperial Unity and Christian Divisions: The Church 450-680 A.D.* Volume 2 of *The Church in History.* Crestwood, NY: St. Vladimir's Seminary, 1989. Pp. xv + 402. I-22; B&W-30.
This is one of the rare histories in English by an eastern orthodox scholar. Six of the ten chapters are relevant to our bibliography. In Chapter 1 there is a discussion of the situation in the empire after the conversion of the emperor, the impact of that conversion on legislation, and the problem of cultural pluralism. Chapter 2 deals with church structure (bishops, celibacy, primacy of regions and of Rome, etc.); Chapter 3 with liturgy, monasticism, relics, saints, etc.; Chapter 4 with diverse eastern areas of missionary activity and indigenous churches (Syria, Armenia, Georgia, Arabia, Egypt, Ethiopia, Nubia); Chapter 5 with western areas (Danube, Gaul, British Isles, Spain and Africa); and Chapter 6 with the Council of Chalcedon and its aftermath.

CONSTANTINE
11.6   Alföldi, A. *The Conversion of Constantine and Pagan Rome.* Translated by Harold Mattingly. Oxford: Clarendon, 1948. Pp. xi + 140. B-4.

Alföldi argues that the move of the capital from Rome to Constantinople did not make Rome into a back-water. Rather, it became a powerful voice of moral paganism against the newly approved Christianity. Alföldi provides a sympathetic account of Constantine's conversion, while admitting the uncritical and sometimes superstitious elements in his Christianity. Further, he sees Constantine's "revolution" primarily as a necessary development, given the problems of the day, though Constantine's policy was motivated more by religious omen than by political calculation.

᠈< Downey, *AJP* (1950): 100-104; Every, *HibJ* 47 (1948-49): 306-308; Moss, *JRS* 39 (1949): 167-169; Sutherland, *CR* (1950): 140-142

11.7   Barnes, Timothy D. *Constantine and Eusebius*. Cambridge, MA: Harvard UP, 1981. Pp. vi + 458. I-14; B-39; CT-3; M-1; Index of Eusebius-2.

In his usual iconoclastic style Barnes tackles one of the most difficult and ideologically misconstrued central periods of western history and historiography. Marked, as is his companion volume *The New Empire of Diocletian and Constantine* [§11.8], by what Peter Brown has rightly called "Barnes' magnificent obsession with getting the record straight," Barnes demonstrates, that Constantine's attachment to Christianity was genuine, and, was also something that he skillfully exploited to further his own power. On the other side, Barnes devotes much critical acumen to the analysis of the great Christian chronicler of the period, Eusebius of Caesarea, to demonstrate how many of the features usually labelled as characteristic of "Constantinian" Christianity were in fact well entrenched in the last decades of the third century. The chapters that will be of special interest to the student of Christianity are those on the great persecution (ch. 9), Eusebius as apologist (ch. 10), and on the Council of Nicaea and "ecclesiastical politics" (chs. 11-12). (S)

᠈< Ashanin, *CH* 52 (1983): 352; Cameron, *JRS* 73 (1983): 184-190; Chesnut, *RSR* 9 (1983): 118-123; Drake, *AJP* 103 (1982): 462-466; Frend, *JEH* 33 (1982): 590-595; Miles, *SC* 4 (1984): 37-40; Kaegi, *AHR* 87 (1982): 1372; Rougé, *Phoenix* 37 (1983): 75-78; Vinra, *ATR* 65 (1983): 224-226; Warmington, *CR* 33 (1983): 278-284; Williams, *GOTR* 30 (1985): 381-383.

11.8   Barnes, Timothy D. *The New Empire of Diocletian and Constantine*. Cambridge, MA / London: Harvard UP, 1982. Pp. 305. NI-11; B-25; FT-3; T-13; AAI-3.

This series of technical studies forms the pendant to Barnes's *Constantine and Eusebius* [§11.7]. In his usual manner Barnes lays great stress on "getting the facts right"—and therefore especially on establishing the chronology of events, the precise location of places, the exact identity of persons, and the place, powers, and duration of state offices, especially in the massively confusing and complicated period between about 280 CE and the consolidation of Constantine's uncontested rule over a re-unified Mediterranean empire. Almost an indispensable reference work for the period since it lays out, in impeccable and exacting detail, the primary evidence behind modern assumptions on these basic "facts" of the period (many of them which are shown to be nothing more than unsubstantiated modern myths). There are many chronologies throughout the book. (S)

&< Cameron, *JRS* 73 (1983): 184-190; Ladouceur, *CH* 53 (1984): 80-81; Vinra, *ATR* 65 (1983): 224-226; Rougé, *Phoenix* 37 (1983): 75-78; Warmington, *CR* 33 (1983): 278-284.

11.9   Baynes, Norman H. *Constantine the Great and the Christian Church.* The Raleigh Lecture on History 1929. In *Proceedings of the British Academy* 15 (1931): 341-442. 2d ed. With preface by Henry Chadwick. London: Oxford UP, 1977. (1972[1]). Pp. viii + 107. I-3.
A short work, in which Baynes, accepting the accounts of Eusebius regarding Constantine, argues for the authenticity of Constantine's conversion to Christianity. Constantine was, for Baynes, not merely a "philosophical monotheist with a faith derived from religious syncretism." Constantine's identity was clearly with the Christian church, and he had a sense of divine mission clearly within that church. Baynes' work engages a host of works prior to 1930 dealing with Constantine's edicts, letters, and the Council of Nicaea. The notes are extensive. Chadwick's preface surveys the period to 1972, noting the criticisms of Baynes' view and the recent defenses.
&< Millar, *JTS* 24 (1973): 345-346.

11.10 Chadwick, Henry. "Conversion in Constantine the Great." In *Religious Motivation: Biographical and Sociological Problems for the Church Historian.* Papers read at the sixteenth summer and seventeenth winter meeting of the Ecclesiastical History Society. Studies in Church History. Edited by Derek Baker. Oxford: Blackwell, 1978. Pp. 10-13.
Chadwick points out how little in the empire changed with the conversion of Constantine. Chadwick attempts to demonstrate this by showing how alike are Constantine (the first Christian emperor) and Diocletian (the last pagan emperor in the west). Constantine is seen as basically a conservative. Chadwick takes a middle ground with regard to the conversion of Constantine. He rejects Burckhardt's view, which made Constantine's decision politically motivated, but qualifies Constantine's conversion more than Baynes has done

[§11.9]. Chadwick thinks that Constantine's conversion in 312 was not one that made Christianity Constantine's only religion; he continued to appreciate monotheistic tendencies within paganism.

11.11 Dörries, Hermann. *Constantine the Great.* Translated by Roland H. Bainton. New York: Harper & Row, 1972. Pp. xi + 250. B-11; I-4; CT-2.

A sympathetic account of Constantine's conversion and a positive evaluation of Constantine's contribution to the church. Dörries does not deny the political element in Constantine's conversion, but it is not so much the favor of the Christians that Constantine sought (which would be purely political) but the favor of the Christian's God (which makes the conversion genuinely religious). Constantine's relationship with the church and with the continuing paganism is treated, as well as the efforts of Constantine's sons as Christian emperors. Dörries concludes with a brief review of scholarship on Constantine over the centuries.

✂< Markus, *History* 58 (1973): 250-251.

11.12 Jones, A.H.M. *Constantine and the Conversion of Europe.* Toronto /Buffalo: University of Toronto Press in association with The Medieval Academy of America, 1978. Originally published as part of the "Teach Yourself History Library" series, edited by A.L. Rowse, 1948. Pp. 223. I-7; AB-2; CT-2; FT-1.

A strongly unsympathetic analysis of Constantine's place in history, denying that Constantine deserves either the title of "Great" or "Saint." In all but the military policy, Constantine was a failure, due to both "temper and general weakness of resolve," according to Jones. All this, in spite of good intentions and a rigorous morality, at least in sexual areas. Jones' judgment is that the conversion was "mainly bad" for the church, and he has little sympathy for "caesaropapism." Constantine's conversion to Christianity is seen to have many points of ambiguity.

11.13 ☛ MacMullen, Ramsay. *Constantine.* New York: Dial Press, 1969. Reprint. New York: Harper & Row, 1971. Pp. 263. AB-3; I-14; B&W-35; M-1.

An early work of MacMullen's that is already characterized by his typically pragmatic approach to understanding difficult problems in the history of the Roman social order—ones sometimes needlessly convoluted by modern-day pedantry (compare his *Christianizing the Roman Empire* §12.33). His survey of Constantine's reign and the political history of the Constantinian age is a merciful relief from the overly-done scholarly *Wissenschaft* that often marks studies of this particularly heavily-fraught area of the interface between classical Roman political history and the "great transformation" to the Christianization of the Roman state. As such, MacMullen's book, though perhaps too superficial on some of the knotty problems, remains one of the simplest and most readable surveys of this critical period. Although it is quite dependable and accurate in terms of its narrative of the events, the prospective reader must be warned that it is shorn of the normal apparatus of scholarship (e.g. detailed footnoting). The account proceeds chronologically from a survey of the status of the eastern and western empires before Constantine's rise to power down to the Council of Nicaea; the final three chapters evaluate the nature of Constantine's government and court politics, and offer a general assessment of his "historical significance." (S)

❧ Armstrong, *JAAR* 39 (1971): 237-238; Clover, *CJ* 67 (1971-72): 179-181.

JULIAN

11.14   Athanassiadi-Fowden, Polymnia. *Julian and Hellenism: an Intellectual Biography.* Oxford: Clarendon, 1981. Reprint: London/New York: Routledge, 1992. Pp. vii + 245. B-6; I-7.

Along with the works by Browning [§11.16] and, especially, Bowersock [§11.15], that of Athanassiadi-Fowden, completed a revitalized and revisionist evaluation of the emperor Julian by English scholarship in the 1970s. By concentrating on Julian's perceptions of, and relationship to, classic Greek *paideia*, Athanassiadi-Fowden manages to place Julian's paganism is a more specific context. She does this by situating Julian's interest in the context of a revitalization of the mainstream "secular" culture of his time, linkages to the revival of the second Sophistic, a minor revival in Greek letters that was taking place in Athenian society of the period, and the philosophical antecedents of neo-Platonism. Finally, she emphasizes connections with potential "competitors" allied to this tradition that might have been more malleable than Christianity and which might have offered a *modus vivendi* for both a vibrant "mystery" religion and traditional Graeco-Roman culture (she considers Mithraism in particular). A rich study whose complex arguments cannot be adequately summarized in a brief notice such as this, and which is a "must" for a better understanding of what it was that Julian thought were realistic alternatives to the great threat he was attempting to meet. (S)

❧ Armstrong, *JTS* 34 (1983): 297-299; Bowersock, *AHR* 88 (1983): 90-91; Bowersock, *CR* 33 (1983): 81-83; Cameron, *TLSuppl* 81 (1982): 206;

Nicholson, *Theology* 87 (1984): 377-378; Armstrong, *JTS* 34 (1983): 297-299.

11.15   Bowersock, Glen W. *Julian the Apostate*, Cambridge, MA: Harvard UP, 1978. Pp. xii + 135. B-4; T-5; M-1; CT-1; B&W-9.
Unlike Robert Browning's *The Emperor Julian* [§11.16], Bowersock's treatment is brief almost to the point of abruptness. The succinct approach is justified on two grounds: the life and reign of the emperor were both short (he died in his thirties and reigned for just over two years). Secondly, there is the fact that the hard evidentiary basis relating to what can be known about the man and his actions, though apparently bulky (e.g., the emperor's writings about himself) is small when compared to a mountain of distorted modern interpretation (much of it a form of unseemly speculation). Bowersock's book, therefore, has the great merit of being a sharp and incisive treatment of a subject hitherto obscured by over treatment. Bowersock's command of matters such as the Roman provincial administration in the East, the epigraphy of the region, and of numismatics, permits him to place Julian in a better context than any competing modern interpretation. His work is therefore, as Sir Ronald Syme justly remarked, "indispensable for any serious study of the fourth century." (S)
❊< Athanassiadi-Fowden, *JTS* 30 (1979): 331-335; Frend, *NYRB* 35.17 (1978): 28-29; Rexine, *GOTR* 25 (1980): 206-209; Tomlin, *Phoenix* 34 (1980): 266-270; Woloch, *CJ* 75 (1980): 366-368.

11.16   Browning, Robert. *The Emperor Julian*. London: Weidenfeld & Nicolson / Berkeley: University of California Press, 1976. Pp. xii + 256. I-8; B&W-12; AB-3; CT 2; FT-1; M-3.
Appearing slightly before Bowersock's *Julian the Apostate* [§11.15], this somewhat more prolix treatment has become the conventional narrative in English of this emperor's reign. In a sense, it is the English language counterpart of Bidez's classic narrative in French. It retells the story of the "last pagan" emperor of Rome. As Peter Brown noted in a perceptive review, Browning's work recapitulated existing trends in interpretation of Julian, and marked out the limits beyond which the then-existing modern scholarship on Julian (and pagan tradition) was not yet prepared to go. That is to say, it is a very well written *bilan* of research on the subject to the mid 1970s. As such, Brown was able to note many contradictions which seemed apparent to Browning, and which have been better confronted by succeeding treatments of the apostate emperor (see Athanassiadi-Fowden §11.14 and Bowder §11.2). (S)
❊< P. Brown, *TLSuppl* 76 (1977): 425-426; Cameron, *JHS* 97 (1977): 234-

235; Frend, *JEH* 27 (1976): 414-415; Grant, *CH* 45 (1976): 524; Rexine, *JAAR* 45 (1977): 237-238; Van Halsema, *ATR* 59 (1977): 450-453.

THEODOSIUS

11.17   🏛 Pharr, Clyde ed. *The Theodosian Code.* The Corpus of Roman Law (*Corpus Juris Romani*). Princeton, Princeton UP, 1952. Reprint. Westport, CN: Greenwood, 1969. Pp. xxvi + 643. I-37; B-4; M-1.

One of the basic reference works for one of the major Roman law codes, assembled under the aegis of the Roman emperor Theodosius II in 438 CE. It included legal decisions (*constitutiones*) issued by Roman emperors between Constantine in 313 and the date of issuance of the Code in 438. All the laws, together with the preambles and subscripts, are translated and accompanied with useful footnotes on technical points of law. With a glossary of legal terms. (S)

✄ Metzger, *PSB* 46 (1953): 42-43; Zeitlin, *JQR* 43 (1953): 392-394.

11.18   King, N.Q. *The Emperor Theodosius and the Establishment of Christianity.* Philadelphia: Westminster, 1960 / London: SCM, 1961. Pp. 135. NI-6; SI-2; B-4; M-1.

A study of the general religious policy of Theodosius, with a focus on the positive and negative sides of close church/state relations. The establishment of Christianity was a slow process (because of the continuing strength of paganism and heresies). Even after a policy of coercion that provided an influx of pagans into the Church, "paganism" continued to survive within Christianity itself, so much so for King that he is able to say that "western man remains very much of a pagan." With five appendices (Council of 381; Patmian canons; chronology; types of legislation; coins).

✄ A.H.M. Jones, *JTS* 13 (1962): 433; Ehrhardt, *JEH* 14 (1963): 215; Lessly, *JR* 43 (1963): 82.

THE END OF THE WESTERN EMPIRE
AND THE RISE OF "BARBARIAN" KINGDOMS

11.19   🏛 Gordon, C.D. *The Age of Attila: Fifth Century Byzantium and the Barbarians.* Foreword by Arthur E.R. Boak. Ann Arbor: University of Michigan Press, 1960. Pp. xx + 228. B-4; I-8; CT-1; FT-1; Geographical Index-6.

As one reviewer noted, the scope of this volume is somewhat broader than its title might otherwise indicate. It is, in fact, a fine political narrative of the history of the eastern Roman empire from the beginning of the fifth century to 491 CE—it therefore covers the critical years of the "collapse" of the eastern empire, as told in the words of Priscus, Malchus, Olympiodorus, Joannes Antiochenes, and Candidus—the major historians of the time. It is a major primary source collection which gives access in English translation to the major surviving "fragments" of these historians (each fragment is numbered and keyed to the standard editions in the original Greek). "Appendix A" gives dates and sources of the translated fragments; "Appendix B" is a guide to the historians themselves. Extensive endnotes add modern commentary. (S)

๛ Downey, *AJP* 83 (1962): 223; Maenchen-Helfen, *Speculum* 36 (1961): 657; Thompson, *Phoenix* 16 (1962): 289-290.

11.20   Burns, Thomas. *A History of the Ostrogoths.* Bloomington, IN: Indiana UP, 1984. Pp. xvii + 299. B-31; I-9; B&W-22; M-4; FT-1.
Following the final collapse of the Roman state in the west, the Ostrogoths were the main successor kingdom in Italy from 554 CE. Burns begins his account of their place in late Antique / early Medieval development by placing them in the context of the Roman state's general history of relationships with the northern "barbarians." Following this introduction, Burns outlines what can be known about Ostrogothic society, and the main reasons for its expansion beyond their original homeland east of the Dniester River. Burns concentrates on the history of the great Ostrogothic king Theodoric, the Ostrogothic kingdom and its institutions, and local Roman traditions during his reign. This is one of the more detailed synthetic pictures of one of the major "post-Roman" peoples, and is characterized by a fine admixture of literary and archaeological evidence. (S)

๛ Liebeschuetz, *CR* 36 (1986): 158-159; Markus, *History* 70 (1985): 275-276.

11.21   Gibbon, Edward. *History of the Decline and Fall of the Roman Empire.* Edited by J.B. Bury. 7 Volumes. London, 1896-1900.
This is by far the oldest work of a "modern" author listed in this bibliography. The original edition was published between 1776 and 1788, and became the primary analysis around which the debate was to continue. Gibbon's description of the new order as the "Triumph of Barbarism and Religion" reveals his negative evaluation of the change to a Christian empire. Merely contrast those historians who speak favorably of the same events as the "Social Triumph of the Church." Pelikan's *The Excellent Empire: The Fall of Rome and the Triumph of the Church* [§11.29] engages much of Gibbon's work.

11.22   Goffart, Walter. *Barbarians and Romans, AD 418-584: The Techniques of Accommodation.* Princeton: Princeton UP, 1980. Pp. xv +

278. I-12; MAI-7.

Goffart asks the important questions. Although battles and specific violent encounters did mark the Roman empire in the west, much of the occupation of northern Europe by so-called "barbarian" peoples was a lengthy, peaceful, and orderly process. So, how did it happen? Although some of his interpretations are characteristically extravagant and forced, there is a great deal of value in this, the most convincing of Goffart's iconoclastic works intended to reshape our thinking on the great transitions that marked late Roman antiquity. Part of his argument is that the legal and customary institutions of guest-friendships and clientage offered a firm transitional bridge for both local Roman lords and barbarian chieftains. Provocative. (S)

✃ Christiansen, *EHR* 98 (1983): 841-842; Thompson, *TLSuppl* 80 (1981): 414.

11.23   Hanson, R.P.C. "The Reaction of the Church to the Collapse of the Western Roman Empire in the Fifth Century." *Vigiliae Christianae* 26 (1972): 272-287.

Hanson examines the various early Christian attitudes to the sack of Rome and the collapse of the western empire. Christian historians from antiquity had to make sense of the collapse against the charges of pagans. Hanson considers four historians: Paulus Orosius, Augustine, Salvian, and Sidonius Apollinaris. These historians reflect a range of opinions, from optimism that the barbarians could now more easily be brought into the Christian fold, to detachment, to hopeless pessimism. Hanson then shows various effects of the fall: well trained civil servants taking leadership roles in the church; a boom in western monasticism as a result of the chaos; an increased role for the bishop in dealing with the concerns of the poor, the sick, and the captured prisoners in need of ransoming. Further, as education declined, the only educated people were in the service of the church, and that made the barbarians quite dependent on the church.

11.24   James, Edward. *The Franks.* Oxford/New York: Blackwell, 1988. Pp. xii + 265. B-7; I-15; B&W-47; T/M-15.

One of the books in a new series on "The Peoples of Europe," edited by Barry Cunliffe, James' book-length study of the Franks is the first modern treatment in English. His work is one of a series of "new generation" of synoptic studies of the so-called "barbarian" peoples of western Europe who succeeded to the Roman Empire. The first two chapters lay out the sources (historical, archaeological,

linguistic) and the "Roman" period history of the Franks down to
Childeric. These chapters are followed by a history of their expansion
and conquest of Gaul. The chronological survey is then supplemented
by a series of thematic surveys of Frankish religion (the process of
their conversion to Christianity), their political structure (mainly
the kings and followers), and economy. James' approach, with its
systematic integration of new archaeology (e.g. settlement surveys)
exemplifies the best in new "barbarian" studies. (S)
৯< Ward-Perkins, *JRS* 80 (1990): 263-264.

11.25   King, P.O. *Law and Society in the Visigothic Kingdom.* Cambridge:
Cambridge UP, 1972. Pp. xiv + 318. B-21; I-9; Index of Laws-9.
The Visigoths came to control the whole region of what was later
Portugal, southern France, and almost all of modern-day Spain.
The Visigothic kingdom was one of the most stable of the "barbarian"
successor states of the Roman empire. By using the extensive
Romano-barbaric law codes of the Visigoths, King gives a detailed
outline of the government, society, and economy of the area. The
principal interest for the historian of the early church is King's
study of the development of the Christian church and the development
of moral codes, especially those centered on family and sexuality
(Chs. 5 and 8). Finally, he sheds light on the treatment of outcast
and heretical groups, principally the Jews. (S)
৯< Chaney, *CH* 42 (1973): 422-423; Hillgarth, *JTS* 24 (1973): 602-604;
Wallace-Hadrill, *EHR* 88 (1973): 873-874.

11.26   Maenchen-Helfen, Otto J. *The World of the Huns: Studies in their
History and Culture.* Berkeley/Los Angeles: University of California
Press, 1973. Pp. xxix + 602. B-93; I-24; B&W-75.
Otto Maenchen-Helfen, one of a host of emigré scholars from Nazi
Germany, was also one of the great scholars of his age, having
done archaeological field work in central Russia, Siberia, and
Mongolia in the 1920s. His raw materials for this synthesis of a
lifetime's work was left in rather chaotic form on his death in
1969. It took the devotion of a team of editors headed by Max
Knight to save the best for the scholarly world. Maenchen-Helfen,
who was armed with a unique knowledge of the primary languages
and sources, from Greek to Chinese, offers a near-comprehensive
survey of the evidence, the history of the Huns and their "invasions"
(centred on the figure of Attila), the economy, religion, art, and
language. Five appendixes are devoted to special chronological
and prosopographical problems. A great work of traditional scholarship—different in tone, however, from more recent approaches to

western "barbaric" peoples (see, e.g., Burns §11.20 and Edward James §11.24). (S)

11.27   ◉ Momigliano, Arnaldo. "Christianity and the Decline of the Roman Empire." In *The Conflict between Paganism and Christianity in the Fourth Century.* Edited by A. Momigliano. Oxford: Clarendon, 1963. Pp. 1-16.
Momigliano reviews the various theories, from ancient to modern, about the collapse of the Roman empire and the shift from pagan to Christian. He deals with a range of issues, from the contentious debate over when the Roman empire fell to why it fell, and the evidence for its decay in the third and fourth centuries. The relationship of church to state is also discussed, both in the east and the west, as well as the role of monasticism and the ability of the Christians to deal with the barbarians more effectively than the pagans could. Several other chapters in this volume are worth attention.

11.28   ◉ Musset, Lucien. *The Germanic Invasions: The Making of Europe, AD 400-600.* Translated by Edward and Columba James. University Park, PA: Pennsylvania State UP / London: Elek, 1975. Pp. xiii + 287. B-29; I-3.
Originally part of a standard French series on the history of the world, each volume of which was intended to give a synopsis of current academic literature on the "main problems," plus generous bibliographic guidance to that literature, this book was one of the best in that series and received a knowledgeable and accurate translation by two experts in the field. Musset not only gives a coherent overview of the process of the disintegration of the Roman Empire in the west, but also encapsulates what is known about the history and society of each of the successor "barbarian" peoples and states. The book is perhaps most valuable for its bibliographic guide—which has a special updated section for English-speakers added by the translators . (S)
⊰ Markus, *History* 62 (1977): 94; Oost, *AHR* 81 (1976): 1085-1086.

11.29   Pelikan, Jaroslav. *The Excellent Empire: The Fall of Rome and the Triumph of the Church.* Rauschenbusch Lectures, n.s. 1. San Francisco: Harper & Row, 1987. Pp. xv + 133. NI-3; C-9; B&W-3.
Responding to the impact of Gibbon's analysis of the collapse of the Roman Empire and western thought, Pelikan focuses on the social triumph of the church as understood by churchmen involved first-hand in the ferment of those times. The responses were varied.

Jerome's sympathies were with the Christian empire, though he was too rooted in Christian apocalyptic to identify with "Rome" entirely. Augustine, in *The City of God,* was able to see the fall as part of the divine plan, without linking the success of Christianity to the success of a Christian empire. Various other views are considered, though Gibbon's perspective is engaged most often.

❥ Snyder, *CTSR* 80 (1990): 59-60; Barnes, *Speculum* 65 (1990): 218-219; Lindsey, *CRBR* 1 (1989): 334-336; Grant, *CH* 58 (1989): 503-504; Wilken, *TS* 50 (1989): 204-205; Kaegi, *CHR* 75 (1989): 127; Hinson, *R&E* 86 (1989): 123.

11.30   Thompson, E.A. *The Visigoths in the Time of Ulfila.* Oxford: Clarendon, 1966. Pp. xxiii + 174. I-8; M-1.
One of two early classic "small" works by the doyen of Northern "barbarian" studies from Nottingham. The Visigoths, who by the late fourth century came to dominate roughly the modern-day state of Romania, are one of the few Germanic successor people of whom we have detailed knowledge. In part because of the work of Ulfila, who translated the Bible into Gothic, they were one of the first of the Germanic peoples to be converted to Christianity. After an outline of the political, social, and economic history, Thompson turns in detail to the story of the process of conversion. This analysis contains a wonderfully evocative chapter on the "Passion of St. Saba" and how this martyr act illuminates our understanding of village life amongst the Visigoths. (S)

❥ P. Brown, *History* 54 (1969): 79-80; Browning, *CR* 17 (1967): 354-356; Greenslade, *JEH* 19 (1968): 235-236; Wallace-Hadrill, *EHR* 83 (1968): 146-147.

11.31   Thompson, E.A. *The Goths in Spain.* Oxford: Clarendon, 1969. Pp. xi + 358. IA.
The last great work by the leading authority on the subject at the time, on one of the most important successor states at the end of the Roman empire—the northern "barbarian" peoples called the Goths. They were the successors to the Romans as rulers in Spain in the sixth and seventh centuries CE. As outsiders and converts to "Arian" Christianity, the Goths represent one of the best documented and interesting studies in a potential clash of cultures in late Roman antiquity. Although Thompson devotes several chapters of his book to studies of the political administration, history, economy, and social structure of the Goths in Spain, the parts of the book that are most relevant to readers of this bibliography are those devoted to the "religious policy" of the Gothic kings, the great church councils at Toledo, and the ecclesiastical structure of the church in Spain.

CONSTANTINE AND THE CHRISTIAN EMPIRE / 165   §11

(S)
✂ P. Brown, *TLSuppl* 68 (1969): 635; Frend, *JEH* 21 (1970): 206-208; Lourie, *JEH* (1969): 635; Walsh, *CR* 21 (1971): 300-301.

11.32   Wolfram, Herwig. *History of the Goths*. Translated by Thomas J. Dunlap. Berkeley/Los Angeles/London: University of California Press, 1988. Pp. xii + 625. B-37; I-39; M-9. CT-7.
This book attempts to remove the historically unreliable elements (both attractive and unattractive) that are part of the Gothic myth. It examines the diverse groups that come to bear the name "Goth," the development of the Gothic kingdoms, and the relationship of the Goths to the Roman Empire and to various groups within the empire. It is a detailed investigation, not only of the history of the Goths, but of the history of scholarship on the Goths.
✂ Fanning, *CHR* 76 (1990): 104-106; Rosenberg, *CH* 59 (1990): 225.

THE BYZANTINE EMPIRE AND JUSTINIAN
11.33   🏛 Watson, Alan, ed. *The Digest of Justinian*. Text of Theodor Mommsen and Paul Kreuger. 4 volumes. Philadelphia: University of Pennsylvania Press, 1985. Pp. lxix + 969. G-13.
Probably the fundamental new work of basic sources in translation to appear in the last couple of decades. An immense project of scholarship under the general editorship of Alan Watson (who assigned segments of the original text to different translators), this work deals with the great early sixth-century codification of the Roman law—the "Digest" of the opinions of all major Roman jurisprudents between the late Republic and the Severan age—made by the jurist Tribonian at the behest of the emperor Justinian. This large four-volume set offers not only the original Latin text, but also a complete English translation of the whole (on facing pages) [Volume 1 = Books, 1-5; 2 = 16-29; 3 = 30-40; 4 = 41-50]. This is certainly an indispensable work of scholarship for anyone interested in the state and social relationships in the Roman Empire and, needless to say, the manner in which its legal norms impinged on the emerging Christian Church. This translation does not just supersede earlier attempts (such as S.P. Scott's antiquated effort)—it represents a major work of interpretation in its own right, being an accurate and up-to-date reflection of the way in which contemporary Romanist scholarship currently understands the various parts of this great legal text—along with the Bible, one of the two fundamental literary pillars of Western Civilization. (S)

11.34   Browning, Robert. *Justinian and Theodora*. Rev. ed. London:

Thames and Hudson, 1987. (1971[1]). Pp. 189. I-5; B&W-29; B-2; CT-5; FT-2; M-7.
This is the standard biography on Justinian and his powerful prostitute / actress wife. An 8-pp. introduction sketches the division between the eastern and western empires; the remainder focuses on Justinian's time. Besides the normal biographical and political details one would expect to find, there are rich little additions, such as a description of everyday life in Constantinople, the treatment of "deviant" religious groups within the empire, the expenses of running an empire, building projects, and the relations between the emperor and the pope as the eastern empire regained the west from the Germanic tribes.
✂ Arnheim, *JRS* 72 (1972): 186-187; Barker, *Speculum* 47 (1972): 748-750; Nicol, *JEH* 23 (1972): 180-181.

11.35 Downey, Glanville. *Constantinople in the Age of Justinian.* The Centers of Civilization Series 3. Norman, OK: University of Oklahoma Press, 1960. Pp. xiii + 181.
An introduction to Justinian and the beginnings of Byzantine culture. Chapter 1 provides a "tour" of the city of Constantinople at its glorious best under Justinian. Then follows extensive discussion of Justinian and his contribution to law, architecture, and theology, and his political and military skills in bringing about a restored and stable empire after its fifth-century problems.
✂ Rexine, *StVSQ* 7 (1963): 94.

11.36 Mango, Cyril. *Byzantium: The Empire of New Rome.* London: Weidenfeld and Nicolson; New York, Scribner's, 1980. Pp. xiii + 334. B; I; B&W-24; M-3.
The standard current one-volume survey of classic Byzantine civilization. Mango's text is divided into three parts, the first of which deals with the synchronous survey of various social and economic aspects of Byzantium—demography, language, economy, cities, and education. Also included in the first section are matters relevant to Christianity that have a strong social aspect (e.g., dissent, monasticism). The second part is devoted to the conceptual life of Byzantine civilization—its art, theology, and philosophy. The final, and briefest, part of the book deals with the subsequent influences of Byzantium on European culture. The text is a model of clear writing, and is admirably illustrated. An appendix provides a chronological list of Byzantine emperors. (S)
✂ Angold, *CR* 31 (1981): 278-280; Browning, *TLSuppl* 79 (1986): 1061; Hitchner, *BA* 45 (1982): 249-250; Rexine, *PBR* 1 (1982): 252-253.

12
CONVERSION, MISSIONS, AND THE EARLY CHRISTIAN APOLOGETIC

The Christian movement was born into a strange and diverse religious world. The traditional religions of Greece and Rome appeared in some ways to be crumbling (the extent and reasons for which have been debated by modern scholars), but a general religious sensitivity had not suffered much from decline. Judaism was vigorous, and even after various military defeats at the hands of the Romans, it still had considerable presence throughout the Mediterranean, especially in the religious marketplace where the new Christian movement made its way. Later, Judaism became more isolated and inward, somewhat due to the Christian missionary success, but even then it offered Christianity a serious challenge. In addition to Judaism, "eastern" religions—esoteric and foreign, and sometimes outlawed—were still growing, often with considerable success, filling a void by promising and providing security. Greek philosophy stirred this religious mixture by providing polemical fodder and an intellectual context for at least the beginnings of robust, and sometimes even respectful, dialogue.

It was into such a market that the early Christians made the first presentations of their religious wares. The Christian view of the world did not appear fully tailored to win the day. Its connections to Judaism had both positive and negative sides—positive by giving it antiquity (an important element in the Graeco-Roman sense of worth), but negative, in that the majority of Jews had rejected it, thus giving Greeks and Romans good reason to dismiss it too. Further, its borrowed Jewish view of the physical resurrection of the dead, and its apocalyptic tone made it poor company in the philosophical circles of the day (which were critical enough of even Greek religion) or in the political circles (which generally had deep appreciation for the Mediterranean peace won and maintained by the Roman military).

Insofar as it could be clearly distinguished from Judaism, Christianity did not fare much better. Its worship of an executed apostate Jew and the various misunderstandings that Christianity endured (everything from charges of atheism, baby-eating, and incest) should have made this new religion a slow mover on the religious "stock exchange." Yet within three centuries, the Emperor had become a Christian and the church had gained protected and favored status in the state.

The primary question about the transformation of the Christian church from its apocalyptic Palestinian roots to its status as the respected religion of the Empire is how did it happen at all—what conditions made Christianity attractive enough to win the day? This question has created a more refined secondary question. What was the nature of the conversion? Was it deep or surface, or were there varieties of conversion experiences?

This leads, in turn, to the question of the character of the religion which Christianity replaced. Did Christianity take on a dying, unsatisfying, failed religion—already void of vigor, or did it take on a vital, dynamic religion, and in armed philosophical and spiritual combat, sap it of its strength? In either case, why was it Christianity that accomplished this feat when various other new religious options failed, being themselves defeated by Christianity?

Then there is the issue of the response to the Christian success. Not every Christian was happy with the "Christian victory." In the chapters on Constantine and the Christian Empire (Ch. 11) and Monasticism (Ch. 17), various entries deal with Christian concerns about the new relationship between the church and the state. Monasticism itself, and various nationalist movements (in particular, the Donatists in North Africa) found that the conversion of the emperor and empire was at best ambiguous in terms of the benefits to Christianity, and often, it was starkly negative. The beastly persecutors of the Apocalypse merely changed persecuting hats for groups such as the Donatists, and this sometimes led to blanket condemnation of the *Christian* Roman state by Christians! That attitude has left a deep imprint. Even in the twentieth century, some Christian groups date the *fall* of the church to the conversion of Constantine. In fact, any Christian tradition with a "restorationist" mentality, by idealizing either the New Testament period or pre-Constantinian Christianity, reveals a certain difficulty in accepting as positive those changes and developments that occurred within the structures of the church as it moved from a persecuted and powerless minority (shaped by a sense of the church against the world) to become the imperial favourite— almost overnight.

There are three centuries to account for from the birth of the church to its conquest of the emperor, if not yet the whole empire. The first century was one of self-definition against the parent structures of Judaism. Once Christians had adequately distinguished themselves in their own minds from Judaism, they could more easily be seen as something distinctive in the larger religious world of the Mediterranean. To some extent, the second century was one of misunderstandings and adjustments to which the Apologists bear clear witness. In the third century, Christianity had become a serious enough competitor on the religious market not just to cause accusing fingers to be pointed in its direction but to prompt hostile organized action against itself. According to Tertullian, who lived around the beginning of the third century, Christians were blamed for every disaster that fell upon the state, and there were plenty of disasters to be blamed for. The third century was particularly chaotic for the empire, given the stability of the previous two hundred and fifty years. Inflation, famine, decreases in population, political instability, and threats along the border now became features of everyday life.

E.R. Dodds, in his influential work, *Pagan and Christian in an Age of Anxiety: Some Aspects of Religious Experience from Marcus Aurelius to Constantine* [§12.26], argued that Graeco-Roman religion was too bankrupt to provide the security people sought in this age of chaos. Although this thesis has had considerable influence on the way that Graeco-Roman religion in its last days has been viewed, many recent scholars have tried to challenge that evaluation. Paganism does seem to have remained a vital force for some time *after* the imperial favor had turned towards the Christians, and the upper classes of Rome claimed that the city should remain pagan, regardless of what happened elsewhere in the empire. In addition to evidence for the continuation of paganism in urban areas, it has been widely argued that the rural parts of the empire also remained pagan for centuries after the conversion of Constantine.

Further, some of the conversions seem to have had very little Christian content, initially at least. Consider the incident in which soldiers who had asked for baptism were given brief, on-the-spot instruction in elementary Christian belief. When the preacher came to the story of the crucifixion of Jesus, the soldiers shouted out: "That wouldn't have happened had we been there!" This is a considerable misunderstanding of the Christian message. Little surprise, then, that the church considered it necessary to make the act of conversion part of a long period of instruction, or catechism, which lasted for about three years.

Another major question in this debate is the nature of conversion itself. A.D. Nock [§12.35] dealt in detail with conversion, and noted the difference between cultic observances that were at the heart of Greek religion, and philosophic commitment, which involved several features that were to be found in Christian conversion (e.g. moral structure, scheme of life, and dogmatic doctrine). Nock's analysis is called into question by Ramsay MacMullen [§12.31–12.34], who thinks that Nock dealt too much with the "high-brow," or intellectual, conversions. MacMullen argues that most conversions were "low-brow" and as such, were motivated more by the miraculous than the intellectual, and allowed for the continuation of previous religious practice in a way that contrasted with the renunciation that philosophic or intellectual conversion required. In response to MacMullen's recent work, scholars are becoming more conscious of the complexities of this issue, and tend to admit that Christian conversion probably reflected a mixture of intellectual and miraculous elements.

One further issue that still needs attention is the conversion of the countryside, or the contrasting success of the church in urban areas compared to rural settings. It has become commonplace now in scholarship to assume a more staunch commitment to paganism in the rural or less Hellenized areas, which tended to be more traditional. But there are problems for those working with such themes. The most serious one is that the rural areas were rarely literate enough to have produced lasting documentary evidence of their existence or strength; most of the literature that has been preserved (whether it is pagan or Christian) is from the perspective of the cities. Second, a few pieces of evidence lead one to suspect that, at least in particular areas, the countryside had its own considerable positive response to Christianity. Perhaps scholars need to pay more attention to the rural societies, though the study of ancient rural societies is often neglected simply because of the difficulty or the impossibility of finding adequate documentary or archaeological remains that could serve as evidence.

Some related material on the theme of conversions and missions can be found in chapter 11 ("Constantine and the Christian Empire"), chapter 17 ("Monasticism"), and chapter 23 ("Society and Social Issues").

GENERAL
12.1   Baker, Derek, ed. *The Church in Town and Countryside*. Papers read at the seventeenth summer meeting and the eighteenth winter meeting of the Ecclesiastical Historical Society. Oxford: Basil Blackwell, 1979. Pp. xvi + 486.
Only the first five essays (about one-sixth of the book) deal with our period. The volume is important, nonetheless, because it addresses directly the issue of the conversion of the countryside in a way that receives often only passing attention in other works. The articles are: "Country bishops in Byzantine Africa" (Markus); "Problems arising from the conversion of Syria" (Liebeschuetz); "Town and countryside in early Christianity" (Frend); "From town to country: the Christianization of the Touraine 370-600" (Stancliffe); and "Early Merovingian devotion in town and country" (Wood). These articles and the whole discussion should be read along with the W.H.C. Frend's article [§20.10], titled "The Failure of the Persecutions in the Roman Empire," which provides (perhaps even

unintentionally) evidence for significant success of Christianity in the countryside by the third century.

⊰ Briggs, *JEH* 32 (1981): 513-14; Hinchliff, *JTS* 32 (1981): 308-10; McGaffrey, *SJT* 33 (1980): 494-5.

12.2 Fox, Robin Lane. *Pagans and Christians*. New York: Alfred A. Knopf, 1987 Pp. 799. I-13; M-5

Fox's book opens a door on the world of antiquity, presenting with clarity and sympathy the religious world of pagans and Christians and the shift within that world to Christianity, in spite of the vitality of paganism. The topics range from general discussions of the role of religion and the understanding of the divine, to detailed discussions of persecution and martyrdom, bishops and authority, the spread of Christianity, the importance of visions and prophecy, the beginnings of monasticism, and Constantine's role in the changes. Besides providing a solid survey of the issues, at times Fox engages in exacting and original analyses of specific scholarly problems, as in the case of the martyrdom of Pionius, Constantine's Good Friday Sermon of 325, and pagan oracles.

⊰ Brown, *NYRB* 34.4 (March 12 1987): 24-27; Clark, *Commonweal* 114 (June 19 1987): 388-390; Grant, *CH* 56 (1987): 379-381; Greer, *This World* 19 (Fall 1987): 127-131; Hinson, *R&E* 86 (1989): 633-634; Louth, *Theology* 90 (1987): 317-318; Roberts, *LondonRB* 9 (Feb 5 1987): 20-21; Snyder, *CTSR* 80 (1990): 40-41; Wilken, *Commonweal* 115 (March 11 1988): 154; Wilken, *NYRB* 92 (Feb 1 1987): 26.

12.3 Harnack, Adolf. *The Mission and Expansion of Christianity in the First Three Centuries*. Translated and edited by James Moffatt. London: Williams & Norgate, 1908. Reprint. With introduction by Jaroslav Pelikan. New York: Harper & Brothers, 1962. Pp. 527. I-5; NTI-3; B-2; GI-1.

Harnack is perhaps the foremost church historian of the last two centuries. His work is filled with insights that still are worthy of attention after almost a century. Although much of the book relates to the New Testament, Harnack does treat questions related to Christian missions, church structure, and church development in confrontation with various external and internal forces. Many recent histories of early Christianity are still heavily influenced by Harnack, especially in regard to church office and the use of the *Didache* to explain that development. The work also includes several short essays, from travel and exchange of letters to the names of Christians, syncretism, and the primacy of Rome.

12.4 Momigliano, Arnaldo, ed. *The Conflict between Paganism and*

Christianity in the Fourth Century. Oxford: Clarendon, 1963. Pp.
222. I-4; B&W-16; FT-1; CT-1.
A collection of eight lectures delivered in the academic year 1958-59
at London's Wartburg Institute. Momigliano supplies a general
introduction: "Christianity and the Decline of the Roman Empire,"
and a chapter on pagan and Christian historiography. Momigliano's
first chapter gives a good review of the theories regarding the
collapse of the Roman empire. Other chapters are: A.H.M. Jones
(social background of the conflict); J. Vogt (pagans and Christians
in Constantine's family); E.A. Thompson (Christianity and the
northern barbarians); A.A. Barb (survival of magical arts); H.I.
Marrou (Synesius of Cyrene and Alexandrian Neoplatonism); P.
Courcelle (anti-Christian arguments and Christian Platonism); and
H. Bloch on (pagan revival in the west).

PERCEPTIONS AND POLEMICS
12.5   ☛ Barnes, Timothy. "Pagan Perceptions of Christianity." In *Early
Christianity: Origins and Evolution to AD 600.* Edited by Ian Hazlett.
London: SPCK, 1991. Pp. 231-243.
Barnes surveys the comments made about Christians in the pagan
literature of the first four centuries. Comments from the first and
second century are rare, misinformed, and contemptuous. The most
sympathetic view would be that the Christians were stupid. By the
late-second century, Christians were becoming more accepted into
the society at all levels, and though Christians came to be persecuted
in a decaying Roman empire, the pagan "mob" was a less obvious
player than at earlier times. Barnes briefly discusses the more
sustained attacks on Christianity by Celsus, Porphyry, and Julian.

12.6   Benko, Stephen. "Pagan Criticism of Christianity During the First
Two Centuries A.D." *ANRW* II.23.2 (1980): 1055-1118
A rather mechanical recapitulation of the principal pagan authors
who commented on Christians, from Suetonius, Tacitus and the
Younger Pliny to Galen and Celsus, arranged by author. Most of
the basic passages are quoted in translation. Mostly reportative,
and rather weak on analysis. The material is replayed in his book
on the same theme [§12.7] (S)

12.7   Benko, Stephen. *Pagan Rome and the Early Christians.* Bloomington, IN: Indiana UP, 1984. Pp. xi + 180. I-4; B-13.
Against the general tendency in scholarship to dismiss some of the
more offensive charges against Christians as merely ignorant or
vicious polemics of pagans, Benko tries to make the case that

many of these charges were on the mark. The bibliography is broken in several sections: General; Pliny and Trajan; Tacitus; Suetonius; Peregrinus Proteus; Cynicism; Marcus Aurelius; Epictetus; Charges of Immorality and Cannibalism; Holy Kiss; Lucius Apuleius; Alexander of Abonuteichus; Magic; Galen; and Celsus. Each of these topics are covered by specific chapters in Benko's work. Chapter 1 deals with the name "Christian."

✂ Grant, *CH* 54 (1985): 382; Keresztes, *CHR* 73 (1987): 126-127; Nash, *CC* 102 (June 5-12 1985): 593; with reply from Benko (Oct 16 1985): 933; White, *JBL* 105 (1986): 743-745; Wilken, *TS* 47 (1986): 189-190;

12.8   Conteras, Carlos A. "Christian Views of Paganism." *ANRW* 23.2: 974-1022.

Conteras points out that the Apostolic Fathers were largely interested in propagating their own view of the world, much less in developing detailed critiques of non-Christians. It is in the succeeding generations between the writer of the *Epistle to Diognetus* and the great African Latin Fathers such as Tertullian that there developed two distinct Christian responses to paganism. The first, especially evident in the latter authors, is very hostile and centers on a critique of idolatry, culminating in the complex attacks of Tertullian that link the illegitimacy of pagan idols and divinities with the actual immoral actions and behavior of the pagans themselves. The other stream, marked at its inception by Justin Martyr and Clement of Alexandria, through the second century, tended to preserve the validity of pagan élite culture and viewed its ideas, mainly its philosophies (and, here, especially that of Plato and his successors), as something worth merging with Christian ideology. Conteras argues that the distinction in attitudes is largely cut along lines of class, education and personal temperament, with élite derived Christians seeking to salvage what was "of worth" from pagan culture, while others, such as Tatian, were content to indulge in outright condemnation of pagan idolatry and immorality as part of a seamless web of a past that had to be rejected. (S)

12.9   Hanson, R.P.C. "The Christian Attitude to Paganism up to the Time of Constantine." *ANRW* II.23.2 (1980): 910-973. Reprinted in Hanson, *Studies in Christian Antiquity*. Edinburgh: T&T Clark, 1985. Pp. 144-229.

A survey from the perspectives of Christian polemics against pagan religions, through the development of a consistent Christian view of what religion should be like. The polemical side concentrates on the Christian rejection of animal sacrifice, iconographic representations of deities (statues), and criticism of the mythical elements in pagan cults. Hanson notes that the Christians gradually developed a "radical destructive" critique of all pagan beliefs and practices, culminating in the rejection of the cult of the emperor, that exposed them to charges of atheism. Christians tended to deny the existence of pagan gods altogether or to attribute their existence to demonic forces (Nock). Hanson notes the remaining areas of strong overlap between pagan and Christian belief (e.g., belief in the efficacy of oracles and dreams), and concludes by investigating the debates over where the first Christian emperor, Constantine, stood with respect to these two worlds. (S)

12.10   Henrichs, Albert. "Pagan Ritual and the Alleged Crimes of the Early Christians." In *Kyriakon: Festschrift Johannes Quasten*. Edited by Patrick Granfield and Josef A. Jungmann. Vol. 1. Münster: Verlag Aschendorff, 1970. Pp. 18-35.
Henrichs tries to account for the shocking charges that were laid against Christians in the second century, from incest, to ritual murder and cannibalism. After examining the literary evidence, both Christian and pagan, which even when taken together is scanty enough, Henrichs makes several suggestions about the charges. (1) The initial accusations could have come from Roman Jews who wished themselves to escape such charges. (2) The Roman government at its various levels, rather than the general population, kept the charges alive. (3) Certain Gnostic sects seem to have incorporated such practices into their ritual. (4) The activities were, themselves, not foreign to pagan life in the empire. Here Henrichs follows Dölger. He then considers a Greek romance, known only from some fragments in the collection at the University of Cologne, which recounts similar activities among a pagan group, and Henrichs argues that these kinds of stories provided a framework for the charges against the Christians.

12.11   Walsh, Joseph J. "On Christian Atheism." *Vigiliae Christianae* 45 (1991): 255-277.
Walsh argues that the charge of atheism (a serious enough one when brought against the Christians) was a late charge, after numerous other things about Christians had disqualified them in the eyes of the society. After reviewing the evidence for the charge in the second century, Walsh, following Bowersock, contends that the earthquakes in Asia in 160/161 CE and various other calamities caused the society to appeal in the emergency to the gods, at which time the refusal of the Christians to participate became an issue and the size of the movement a matter of concern. This happened

in the reign of Marcus Aurelius, and in the late years of his reign, the charge of atheism became the dominant one, and one of considerable seriousness.

THE APOLOGISTS

12.12   Grant, Robert M. *Greek Apologists of the Second Century*. Philadelphia: Westminster, 1988. Pp. 254. B-10; I-4; B&W-8.
Grant provides a clear introduction to the major issues and individuals at the heart of the early disputes between Christian intellectuals and the pagan world about them. The apologists are placed, as much as possible, in the context of specific historical events. All Apologists are considered, but the emphasis is on Justin and Theophilus. Grant goes beyond the chronological limits suggested by the title, considering the New Testament period and the third century, as well as the use of the Apologists in the Middle Ages and later. Chapters are clearly subdivided.
✂ Barnard, *JTS* 40 (1989): 612-613; Hinson, *R&E* 86 (1989): 448; Louth, *New Blackfriars* 71 (1990): 314-316.

12.13   ◉ Malherbe, Abraham J. "Towards Understanding the Apologists: A Review Article. *Restoration Quarterly* 11 (1968): 215-224.
Malherbe concentrates on Justin, for in him "Christian apologetic comes of age." He contends that Justin and the other apologists fare better when they are judged against the standards of their age, rather than against Plato himself. He then reviews several works: *The Cambridge History of Later Greek and Early Medieval Philosophy;* Henry Chadwick's *Early Christian Thought and the Classical Tradition* [§24.9]; L.W. Barnard's *Justin Martyr* [§3.53]; R.M. Grant's *The Early Christian Doctrine of God;* and E.R. Dodds' *Pagan and Christian in an Age of Anxiety* [§12.26].

APPROPRIATION OF PAGAN CULTURE

12.14   Laistner, M.L.W. *Christianity and Pagan Culture*. Ithaca: Cornell UP, 1951. Pp. 145.
Laistner concentrates on the process of education in pagan and Christian culture. His description of classical learning in the later empire is largely negative: it was in decline and offered little that was original, primarily serving for a career in the civil service. He then deals with the Christian attempts at instruction, showing that Christians were both hesitant about using pagan literature and yet prepared to employ it in the service of the church (e.g. the Apologists). Laistner includes his own translation of Chrysostom's *Address on Vainglory* and *the Right Way for Parents to Bring Up Their Children*.

12.15   Leare, G. "Mithraism and Christianity Borrowings and Transforma-
        tions." *ANRW* II.23:2. Pp. 1306-1332.
        Since the second century, the similarities between Christianity and
        Mithraism have often been noted. The central point of discussion is
        which movement borrowed from the other. Leare's article deals
        with both Christian and Mithraic origins and connections, accounting
        for the similarities by positing that both had origins in the same
        milieu. He dismisses direct theological borrowing, while admitting
        Christian borrowing of art motifs from Mithraism. Leare focuses
        on three points of similarities and distinctions: (1) cosmogony, (2)
        redeeming mediator, and (3) eschatology. He emphasizes the *dis-
        tinctiveness* of the two movements; the similarities are minute and
        can be found in many other religious traditions as well. (W)

12.16   Weltin, E.G. *Athens and Jerusalem: An Interpretative Essay on
        Christianity and Classical Culture.* AAR Studies in Religion 49.
        Atlanta: Scholar's Press, 1987. Pp. 257. I-12; B-9.
        Weltin's work reflects a positive appreciation for Christianity's
        incorporation of various strands of Greek and Roman culture (contra
        Harnack's *What is Christianity*, for example). Although selective
        in regard to the elements it incorporates, the church was clearly
        informed by much of classical culture, according to Weltin. This
        occurs in spite of the roots of early Christianity originating in
        Judaism and in spite of the presence of elements in the church that
        resisted such incorporation. Weltin considers several issues: totali-
        tarianism, rationalism, legalism, aristocraticism, and humanism.
        ✂ Kopecek, *JAAR* 57 (1989): 677-80; Norris, *ATR* 70 (1988): 365-7;
        Wilken, *JR* 69 (1989): 604.

        THE USE OF MAGIC AND MIRACLE
12.17   ◉ Aune, David E. "Magic in Early Christianity." *ANRW* II.23.2
        (1980): 1507-1557.
        Aune notes that through the 1960s there developed a more impartial,
        view of the rôle of magic in the society and social environment of
        New Testament times, but that this new approach met with a
        "backlash" from "theologically" oriented scholars in the following
        decade. Both the availability of new documentation (e.g., the
        preparation of revised editions of the Egyptian papyrological texts
        on magic in the mid-1970s), and a host of new scholarship (Brown,
        [§12.19], J.M. Hull and Morton Smith), have assured the validity
        of the new approach. Aune surveys the comparative methodologies
        developed by Evans-Pritchard, Mauss, Durkheim, and then advances
        to a study of the rôle of magic in the New Testament texts, especially

in the miracles of Jesus (e.g., as set against the background of the
wonderworkers attested in Josephus). By the use of comparative
materials, and by setting these works in a wider Mediterranean
context of the time (e.g., the evidence of magical terms and gestures
attested in the Greek magical texts in papyri), Aune seeks to explain
the significance of the deployment of magic as something that was
successful because of its location in a context of "social deviance."
Both his claims about the nature of magic and of its context (e.g.,
that it was specific and irregular in application, that it was far more
popular amongst the "lower" and "less educated" classes) are certainly open to question—but the survey and analysis remains perhaps
one the best short entrées to the subject. (S)

12.18   Barb, A., "The Survival of Magic Arts." In *The Conflict Between
Paganism and Christianity in the Fourth Century*. Edited by A.
Momigliano. Oxford: Clarendon, 1963. Pp. 100-125.
The problem of the continued strength of magic and the evil arts in
the last centuries of the empire in the West, long after the adoption
of Christianity as the official religion of the state, poses a problem
of interpretation. In his survey, primarily of the literary and legal
sources on the problem, Barb attempted to resolve the apparent
contradiction by seeing the effusion of magical arts in the fourth
and fifth centuries as a "degraded" form of the "decaying" and
"decomposition" of the old pagan cults that had been "normal" and
"central" to the pre-Christian world. Some interesting observations
and interpretations, but the tendency has been to seek answers
more along the lines suggested by Peter Brown [§12.19] (under the
influence of Mary Douglas). (S)

12.19   Brown, Peter. "Sorcery, Demons and the Rise of Christianity: from
Late Antiquity into the Middle Ages." In *Witchcraft, Confessions
and Accusations*. Edited by M. Douglas. London: ASA Monographs
9 (1970): 17-45. = *Religion and Society in the Age of Saint Augustine*.
Faber and Faber: London, 1972. Pp. 119-46
A pathbreaking article that permitted the succeeding generation of
young scholars working with subjects such as magic and heresy in
the early Christian Church to take an entirely new, and it must be
said, far more impartial and productive, view of the subject. Located,
quite appropriately, in a volume edited by Mary Douglas, Brown
used her insights into the "definitional" properties of a cultural
artifact and practice (such as sorcery) in order to reveal this
"functional" aspect of "disorder," worked within the context of
early Christianity to sharpen its definitions (very much reflecting

Douglas' "grid-group" analysis). Still retains all its innovative force, and will remain one of the fundamental turning points of modern scholarship in this most important aspect of early Christianity. (S)

12.20   Remus, Harold. *Pagan-Christian Conflict over Miracle in the Second Century.* Patristic Monograph Series 10. Cambridge, MA: Philadelphia Patristic Foundation, 1983. Pp. xiii + 371.
Some scholars have begun to emphasize the importance of miracle in early Christian successes at conversion. Remus surveys the second-century evidence from a sociological perspective, showing in many cases the remarkable similarity of sensibilities between pagan and Christian on the topic of miracles, and the use of such appeal in polemics. Various individuals are considered: Justin, Celsus, Aelius Aristides, Alexander of Abonuteichus, Lucian, as well as groups such as the Montanists and the devotees of Asclepius. With six appendixes.
⊱ Cameron, *JEH* 36 (1985): 670-671; Hinson, *CH* 54 (1985): 89; Kee, *SC* 5 (1985-6): 57-58; Kee, *JEH* 36: 670-671; Kee, *JBL* 104 (1985): 371-373; Malina, *RSR* 12 (1986): 35-39; Meredith, *JTS* 36 (1985): 465-467; Schoedel, *RSR* 12 (1986): 31-35; Siddals, *Theology* 88 (1985): 61-63.

12.21   Smith, Jonathan Z. "Towards Interpreting Demonic Powers in Hellenistic and Roman Antiquity. *ANRW* II.16.1 (1978): 425-439.
In this dense interpretive essay, Smith surveys the main elements in "Devil Worship" as his point of departure in which he first redefines such demonic activity as a "locative category" of human behavior, and then, by the excellent use of diagrammatic presentation, offers a critique of the traditional ways (Tylor, Otto, Nilsson, and their modern progeny) have misinterpreted the role and meaning of demons in ancient societies. Noting the heavy propensity of people in such societies to map and define their world, he appeals especially to the work of Peter Brown as a model of the way in which such "out of place" forces can be interpreted by modern-day historians. (S)

CONVERSION AND THE DECLINE OF PAGANISM
12.22   🏛 Croke, B., and J. Harris. *Religious Conflict in Fourth-Century Rome. A Documentary Study.* Sources in Ancient History. Edited by E.A. Judge. Sydney: Sydney UP, 1982. Pp. xvi + 139. I-5; AB-3; T-2; Glossary of Deities and Rites at Rome-6.
A collection of 94 documents (or selections) with brief annotations and notes. The material is from the Latin west, in particular, from Rome. It reflects the debate between Christian and pagan aristocrats in the late fourth century. The focus of the collection is on two

events: (1) the petition to restore the altar of victory to the senate–house in 384, and (2) the public revival of pagan ceremonies during the reign of the usurper Eugenius in 394. Includes a 6-page glossary of deities and rites at Rome.

12.23 🏛 Hilgarth, J.N., ed. *Christianity and Paganism, 350-750: The Conversion of Western Europe.* Philadelphia: University of Pennsylvania Press, 1986. Pp. xvii + 213. I-7; I-2; M-1.
This is largely a collection of the documentary evidence for the long process of the conversion of Europe after Constantine. One section deals with the Mediterranean area, the other with the North and West (or the non-Roman world). An eight-page introduction highlights the shift from pagan to Christian, and each of the fourteen sections has a 2-4 page introduction. The first half is most relevant to our period, covering various topics: (baptism, martyrs, relics, monasticism, laws of the Christian empire, attempts to convert the countryside, and the church's mission to the barbarians. The date of the document is provided, wherever possible, and the selections provide a good sense of the religious consciousness of the period. Some important documents, such as the Rule of St. Benedict, have been omitted since they are readily available elsewhere.
↜ Carpe, *CH* 56 (1987): 268-269.

12.24 Bonner, Gerald. "The Extinction of Paganism and the Church Historian." *Journal of Ecclesiastical History* 35 (1984): 339-357.
Why did pagans become Christians? And just how Christian did they become? And how quickly? Bonner discusses these questions, arguing that full-fledged paganism had already lost some of its appeal before Constantine, yet unless Christianity directed itself to those needs that pagans had as *pagans,* Christianity would not have appeared as a valid option. He discusses the common attitude between paganism and philosophy; and the attempts by some individuals to revive paganism, and by others to destroy it. He then presents the "semi-Christians" and the "paganized Christians" as the means by which elements of paganism were brought into the church and remained there. His thesis is that the monastic movement seemed to offer the place where salvation was to be found, as the *evolution* of paganism to Christianity allowed elements of paganism to remain in society.

12.25 Brown, Peter. *The Making of Late Antiquity.* Cambridge, MA: Harvard UP, 1978. Pp. 129. I-5.
Brown departs from the usual description of the difficult centuries

immediately before the conversion of Constantine as the "Age of Anxiety" (contra Dodds §12.26), describing it rather as the "Age of Ambition." From a religious view, Brown sees a shift away from the idea that each individual has access to the divine to the idea of mediation by "holy men," whose access to the divine seemed more certain. The final chapter deals with Anthony and Pachomius. This brief work is a solid examination of some of the differences between pagan and Christian core religious perceptions from one of the leading scholars in the field. Any of Brown's many works serve the student of the early church well.

✂ Cox, *CH* 49 (1980): 206-207; Douglas, *RSR* 6 (1980): 96-99; Gallagher, *TS* 40 (1979): 546-548.

12.26 Dodds, E.R. *Pagan and Christian in an Age of Anxiety: Some Aspects of Religious Experience from Marcus Aurelius to Constantine.* Cambridge: Cambridge UP, 1965. Pp. 144. I-6.
A short work that has left its imprint widely. Dodds dealt with the third century, when Christianity seems to have made significant inroads into the fabric of the Graeco-Roman world. Dodds believed that the failure of paganism in the time of cultural, economic, political, and religious insecurities could account for the openness of society to religious novelty and, in turn, for the success of Christianity. Although the trend of present scholarship is to view the general pagan character of the third century as more vital than that, Dodds' work still provides useful comment on a number of issues, in particular, on religious experience, both pagan and Christian—in contrast to the usual treatments of Christianity that focus on dogma.

12.27 Fowden, Garth. "Bishops and Temples in the East Roman Empire. *Journal of Theological Studies* n.s. 29 (1978): 53-78.
Fowden discusses the sensitivity required by the Roman government after the conversion of Constantine. With bishops and monks anxious to eliminate paganism, yet with paganism still strong, the emperors, (who were themselves desirous to eliminate paganism) had to entrust that task to government officials rather than to the bishops. Bishops and monks from time to time enraged the pagan population by their extreme actions against pagan temples. It was a hundred years after the church gained legal status in the empire before it was given legal authority over paganism (407/408), and it was not until 435 when a general decree was issued for the destruction of pagan temples. Fowden's article shows the continuing strength of paganism for decades after Constantine's conversion.

12.28 Geffcken, Johannes. *The Last Days of Greco-Roman Paganism.* Translated by Sabine MacCormack. Europe in the Middle Ages. Selected Studies 8. Amsterdam / New York / Oxford: North-Holland Publishing Co., 1978. Originally published in 1920. The English translation is from the 1929 revised edition. Pp. xii + 343. I-16.
This is an attempt to account for the decline of paganism, while doing justice to the continuing vitality of paganism well into the era of the Christian empire. Dealing with the period roughly between the third and fifth centuries, Geffcken dismisses the theory of a significant moral decline in pagan religion. He is skeptical of easy explanations for the success of Christianity, especially those that dismiss the inner strength of paganism, and that fail to recognize the shifting religious loyalty of the masses. An important role is given to the monks, which Geffcken calls the "shock troops," in the process of conversion.

12.29 Jones, A.H.M. "The Social Background of the Struggle between Paganism and Christianity." In *The Conflict between Paganism and Christianity in the Fourth Century.* Edited by Arnaldo Momigiano. Oxford: Oxford UP, 1963. Pp. 17-37.
Jones lines up the evidence for the continuing strength of paganism, particularly in the west, after the conversion of Constantine. Christianity was, according to Jones, still largely *urban* and *Greek,* though there were exceptions in Asia Minor, North Africa, and Egypt. Among the educated, the aristocracy (Roman senate), the military, and the peasantry, paganism held. Jones examines the relationship between Constantine and the senate, and points to differences between the Roman senate (largely pagan and somewhat insignificant after the Diocletian changes and the move of the capital to Constantinople) and the newly established senate in Constantinople, which was made up of persons not necessarily from one of the "ancient families." This wider mix brought more Christians into the structures of power.

12.30 Liebeschuetz, J.H.W.G. *Continuity and Change in Roman Religion.* Oxford: Clarendon, 1979. Pp. xv + 359. I-17; B-33.
This study focuses on the religion of the upper class Romans, thus giving a perspective that is restricted by being only Latin and only literary. He starts with the late Republic and ends with the consequences of Constantine's conversion. Distancing himself from views that Christianity was successful because of the supposed "inadequacies" of paganism, Liebeschuetz believes the success was tied primarily to the political instability of the third century, which

left the impression that traditional religion had failed. Only with Constantine and the political adequacy of Christianity does Christianity take over the empire.

⸕ Crook, *JEH* 31 (1980): 489-91; Millar, *EHR* 95 (1980): 840-1; Palmer, *AHR* 85 (1980): 865-6.

12.31   MacMullen, Ramsay. *Paganism in the Roman Empire*. New Haven/London: Yale UP, 1981. Pp. xv + 241. I-7; B-28; B&W-5; T-2; M-1.
MacMullen objects to two features of the modern understanding of Graeco-Roman paganism. It was neither dehabilitated and dying in the two centuries before Constantine, nor did it die a sudden death with Constantine's conversion. MacMullen argues for the continued vitality of paganism, examining the character of paganism, its chief religious cults, its rituals, and the needs it met. He strives for a balanced understanding of paganism by recognizing that the surviving materials usually reflect an upper class perspective. Further, he warns that one cannot judge the vitality of paganism in terms of a decrease in religious inscriptions or the loss of the more visible elements.

⸕ Grant, *JR* 65 (1985): 448; Krentz, *Currents in Theology and Mission* 11 (1984): 119-120; Millar, *AHR* 87 (1982): 756.

12.32   MacMullen, Ramsay. "Two Types of Conversion to Early Christianity." *Vigiliae Christianae* 37 (1983): 174-192.
First, MacMullen discusses the world-view of Christians and pagans, arguing that something of substance must have been shared by these groups before conversion would have been possible. At the same time, MacMullen recognizes that large elements of the respective world-views were *not* shared: the attitude toward other people's gods, eternal punishment for evil and eternal life for good, and dualism that demanded choice for good or evil. Then MacMullen looks briefly at the literate elite (10% of the population), granting that argument and scripture could have played a role in conversion at that level. But for the vast majority of the population, the "wonderful works" and displays of power, either attributed to Jesus or present in the Christian community, played the key role in conversion.

12.33   MacMullen, Ramsay. *Christianizing the Roman Empire (A.D. 100-400)*. New Haven, CT: Yale UP, 1984. Pp. 185. I-3; B-13.
MacMullen begins his book: "My object is history. It might be, but it isn't, theology." Which firmly sets the tone for an investigation

of the old problem of conversation the rather unremittingly harsh light of the secular factors involved in why individuals and communities decided to accept the new faith. While it has received much criticism for ignoring the moral and psychological dimensions of that process, it is a much needed antidote to the usual approach to the subject (from Adolf Harnack and Arthur Darby Nock to present). MacMullen considers the earlier, pre-Constantinian phase of conversion where Christianity spread through "small-scale" networks (e.g., personal contacts, the household) and depended on spectacular performance for its proof and persuasion (e.g., miracles, revelation, prediction)—as opposed to the post-Constantinian phase when the weight of official patronage, both imperial and local, could offer substantial benefactions (promotion to higher office, material rewards, higher social status and prestige) to the potential convert. Finally, the imperial government could add the sheer power of violent coercion to the list. MacMullen also questions the simplicity of the term "conversion" by attempting to be more specific about different types and degrees of adherence to Christianity. Though somewhat controversial, and perhaps too schematic, in some of its claims, MacMullen's works is a much needed antidote to the more strictly theological and church oriented approaches of previous scholars, and has had a commensurate impact on recent surveys (see, e.g., Fox, *Pagans and Christians* §12.2). (S)

୬< Frend, *Downside Review* 105 (1987): 60-61; Mueller, *SA* 47 (1986): 267-270; Groh, *JAAR* 54 (1986): 596-598; Williams, *CH* 55 (1986): 84-85; Wild, *BAR* 11 (Sept-Oct 1985): 18-19; Hinson, 102 (May 15 1985): 504-506.

12.34   ☛ MacMullen, Ramsay. "Conversion: A Historian's View." *Second Century* 5 (1985-1986): 67-81.
This brief article is useful for three reasons. (1) There are numerous suggestive insights. (2) There is a summary of MacMullen's key points, in particular, about the different understanding of "religion" between the Graeco-Roman world and Jews and Christians, and the role of miracle over doctrine in the usual conversion. (3) There is a critique of Nock [§12.35], who earlier brought the theme of conversion to scholarly attention. This critique is particularly valuable because MacMullen is now the leading scholar in the discussion of this theme.

12.35   Nock, A.D. *Conversion: The Old and the New in Religion from Alexander the Great to Augustine of Hippo.* Oxford: Oxford UP, 1933. Pp. xii + 309. I-7.
A classic work discussing the phenomenon of conversion in the

Graeco-Roman world. About sixty percent the book deals with conversion generally and with eastern cults in the west; the remainder deals specifically with Christianity. Nock tries to account for the success of Christianity, discussing in particular the impact of martyrdom, the ability of Christianity to satisfy human needs, and the attractiveness and intelligibility of various aspects of the Christian proclamation (God as Father, reasonable ethical system, appeal to prophecy and miracles). Even the idea of the birth and death of the Son of God is judged by Nock to have been intelligible, though the incarnation and resurrection of the body would have struck pagans as strange in this period.

12.36 ◉ Rambo, L.R. "Current research on religious conversion." *Religious Studies Review* 8 (1982): 146-159.
Although this article deals with conversion generally, and is most focused on new religious movements, its bibliography includes many entries of importance to students of early Christian conversion. The reader will need to scan each of the seven sections for relevant entries, though one section is dedicated exclusively to Augustine's conversion (6.2) and one to Paul's conversion (7.1). This is a bibliographical survey, and the notes on particular books or general issues are short and not particularly useful for our purposes.

12.37 *The Second Century* 5 (1985-86): 67-96.
This entire issue is dedicated to the theme of conversion. Three of the articles deal with MacMullen's recent views, one deals with Harnack's. MacMullen presents his views briefly in "Conversion: A Historian's View," followed by two responses: William S. Babcock, "MacMullen on Conversion: A Response," and Mark D. Jordan, "Philosophic 'Conversion' and Christian Conversion: A Gloss on Professor MacMullen." MacMullen argues for two types of conversion [§12.31–12.33], against which Babcock argues that the distinction is far more fluid between so-called "hi-brow" and "low-brow" types, and Jordan argues that the type of conversion encouraged by the Graeco-Roman philosophers is different from conversion in the Christian sense, and that some of the confusion in the debate results from "equivocations in all the central terms" such as "conversion" and "religion."

12.38 Smith, Robert C., and John Lounibos, eds. *Pagan and Christian Anxiety: A Response to E.R. Dodds.* Lanhan/New York/London: University Press of America, 1963. Pp. viii + 239. I-7.
Reproduced from typescript, this volume is a collection of revised

papers which grew out of a 1979 summer seminar at Princeton University. Each article focuses on one aspect of E.R. Dodds' *Pagan and Christian in an Age of Anxiety* [§12.26], and includes a short bibliography. John Gager provides an 11-page introduction, dealing mainly with Peter Brown's challenge to Dodds' thesis. Chapters deal with the following topics: "Ascetic Madness" (S. Davies); "Problems of Definition and Interpretation" (B. Barrett); "Talking Like Gods: New Voices of Authority" (J. Soldati); "*Logismos* and *Pistis*" (J. Bregman); and with the following people: Aelius Aristides (R. Smith); Perpetua (M. Rossi); Plotinus (J. Lounibos); and Origen and Celsus (C. Hovland).

12.39   Trombley, Frank R. "Paganism in the Greek World at the End of Antiquity: The Case of Rural Anatolia and Greece." *Harvard Theological Review* 78 (1985): 327-352.
Trombley reviews the substantial evidence for the survival of paganism, especially in the countryside of Asia Minor and Greece, well into the post-Constantinian era. He works particularly with evidence from John of Ephesus in the 500s. John claims to have baptized 80,000 pagans, built 98 churches and 12 monasteries. Trombley, against the judgment of some scholars, thinks the tradition is reliable, and he gives some interesting statistical details about the size of villages. It is clear, and Trombley provides extensive evidence, that pagan practices continued in these areas, especially in rural parts, and that the countryside was often not christianized until the closed pagan temples were razed and monasteries established in the areas. Often, monks took on some of the roles of the replaced pagan holy men. Though Trombley's evidence is important, it should be remembered that 80,000 converts is less than a third the population of the city of Ephesus alone.

MISSIONS AND EXPANSION
12.40   ☛ Bruce, F.F. *The Spreading Flame. The Rise and Progress of Christianity from its First Beginnings to the Conversion of the English.* Grand Rapids: Eerdmans, 1979. Pp. 432. I-12. Originally published in three volumes between 1950-52.
Part 2 deals with Christianity from the fall of Jerusalem to Constantine (here Bruce is heavily dependent on Eusebius). Part 3 deals with the period from Constantine to 800 CE. This book offers a clear introduction to the church in its formative period. The added value of this book is that it provides six chapters (66 pp.) on early Christianity in Britain and Ireland, an area not usually covered in general introductions. Also, the occasional quote (sometimes exten-

sive) of ancient and modern authors adds to this readable work.

12.41   Cameron, Averil. *Christianity and the Rhetoric of Empire: the Development of Christian Discourse*. Berkeley / Los Angeles, University of California Press, 1991. Pp. xiv + 261. B; I; SI.
The twin ideologies of deconstruction and post-modernist literary criticism has drawn considerable attention to the significance of rhetorical construction in the making of everyday life. Cameron uses the best impulses in this linguistic and literary research as a platform for an historical analysis of the forging of a peculiar Christian rhetoric in this world. Beginning with the debate over types of rhetorical exposition existing in the non-Christian world and their appropriation by Christians (e.g., by embedding them in preaching and sermons), she advances to a treatment of the spectacular (visual signs) in reconfiguring rhetorical presentation in the late antique world, and the relationship of this "high art" to the more ordinary discourse of "stories" and "novels." Her study concludes with an analysis of "The Power of the Past: Accommodation and Appropriation," that is the gradual move of Christian discourse into more public and political realms with the advance of the fourth century. No simple synopsis like this can do justice to what is likely to be a fundamental and thought-provoking work over the next decade. (S)

12.42   Green, Michael. *Evangelism in the Early Church*. Grand Rapids, MI: Eerdmans, 1970. Pp. 349. AI-3; SI-3; B&W-14.
Much of this work deals with the New Testament period, though Green has carried his investigation to the middle of the third century. Green focuses specifically on evangelism, with little on the social and political aspects. Methods and motives of evangelism, the importance of the household, processes of conversion, and the missionaries themselves are all dealt with in some detail. Green's own concerns as an evangelist himself sets the tone for much of this work.

12.43   Hinson, E.G. *The Evangelization of the Roman Empire. Identity and Adaptability*. Macon, GA: Mercer U.P., 1981. Pp. x + 332.
Contra Latourette (*A History of the Expansion of Christianity*) but following Nock [§12.35], Hinson emphasizes the *institutional life* of the church as an explanation for its success (catechumenate, baptism, discipline, Eucharist, scripture and creeds, and apostolic ministry), relegating its asceticism and its adaptation to Greek models and methods to a minor role. In part one, Hinson discusses the role

of sacraments, apologetics, morality, and the promise of immortality; in part two, missionary zeal and exclusivistic outlook; in part three, controlled accommodation and adaptation; and in part four, "Enlistment": baptism, Eucharist, discipline, and scripture.

✄ Gros, *JES* 20 (1983): 140; Martinez, *Worship* 57 (1983): 553-554; Rosenberg, *JCS* 25 (1983): 151-152; Rusch, *CH* 52 (1983): 349-350.; Wiles, *R&E* 80 (1983): 136-137.

12.44 ☛ Schäferdiek, Knut. "Christian Mission and Expansion." In *Early Christianity: Origins and Evolution to AD 600*. Edited by Ian Hazlett. London: SPCK, 1991. Pp. 65-77.
This brief article offers an adequate survey of the expansion of early Christianity (from Ireland to Sri Lanka, though the focus is on the Roman world). Key individuals in the missions are mentioned, and attention is paid, in particular, to the rise of national churches, and some of the religious and political factors in their formation. This is more a review of what happened, not a discussion of why and how it happened.

13
DEVELOPMENT OF THE CREEDS

Developed over the centuries following the Nicene Council of 325 CE, the ecumenical creeds of the early church give us an outline of doctrinal development within both eastern and western churches from the first years of the fourth century to the early middle ages. They also tell us what Christendom came to regard as "orthodox" during that period. But in discussing these creeds, it is important to note, first, that the history of Christian creeds as such reaches back into the New Testament period and beyond, and, second, that Nicaea and the post-Nicene creeds represent only the positions of what were the winning sides in bitter doctrinal disputes.

It is generally accepted that written early creedal statements appear in the New Testament and also during the period immediately following. As Oscar Cullmann [§13.7] rightly points out, those from the early post-apostolic era were all christological in nature. It is notable, however, that such early statements stand in some contrast to later ecumenical creeds produced by church councils. They were far more simple. Many of the questions of faith that the ecumenical creeds attempted to answer had not yet arisen and, therefore, what was "right doctrine" was not so narrowly defined as it was to be after Nicaea.

Until recently, most scholars who studied and wrote on the creeds took the rather simplistic tack that what happened in adopting them was what should have happened. These scholars paid little attention to many early church movements. They labelled various forms of Monarchianism, Arianism, Apollinarianism, Nestorianism, and a number of other doctrinal positions as "heresies," though the adherents of those movements often considered themselves to be within the mainstream of Christian thought during their times. For example, even following Nicaea for some decades, probably a majority of eastern Christians were more in harmony with Arius, or at least his supporters, than they were with the position enunciated by the Nicene fathers.

Of course, it is not strange that until recently most of those who produced works on the creeds took the positions that they did. Roman Catholic, Eastern Orthodox, Anglican, Lutheran, and Reformed scholars were, by the nature of their own traditions, bound to regard the seven great ecumenical creeds of the early church as normative statements of faith and hence true. In consequence, they could do nothing other than dismiss the doctrinal positions that the creeds rejected as heresies. It is equally unsurprising that post-Reformation, non-creedal Christians spent little time challenging such scholars in their assertions about the creeds. While many of them regarded the creeds as non-binding on Christians, they often accepted the doctrines enunciated by them, or, if they did not, they disregarded the creeds completely and turned, supposedly exclusively, to the Scriptures as a source of spiritual authority.

Recently, however, certain scholars—largely within the great churches—have begun to examine the creeds anew and have taken more neutral stands towards both them and the issues that they originally responded to. Some of the more conservative scholars continue the older tradition of defending the creeds as binding, orthodox statements of faith, but it is those who are willing to reexamine them from a more neutral position who are using a study of the creeds and the events surrounding their formulation to add most significantly to our knowledge of the development of doctrine within the early church.

While the works listed below include a number of older studies that give the texts of the creeds and traditional attitudes towards them, most of the entries are to more recent publications and are generally of greater value to the contemporary student. Among the latter, Oscar Cullmann's *The Earliest Christian Confessions* [§13.7] sets the stage for understanding what early confessions of faith were all about. Leo Donald Davis [§13.8] and J.N.D. Kelly [§13.13] put the development of the later ecumenical creeds into the intellectual context of the times out of which they developed. Importantly, they and others clearly demonstrate that to understand the creeds, one must have some grasp of Graeco-Roman philosophy, Judaism, and Gnosticism. Otherwise, when the creeds are read, too often they make little sense to the ordinary twentieth-century reader. Significant, too, is the fact that scholars like Kelly and Charles Kannengiesser have begun to look more closely at the figures and events that were connected to the formulation of specific creeds. Thus a sort of historical demythologization has begun to take place that gives a far different picture of what happened than has been promoted by the great churches throughout the ages. Persons such as Athanasius are coming to be seen more as clerical politicians than as saintly defenders of the faith. Yet they are not being discounted for this reason. Their lives, thoughts, and actions have been of profound importance to Christian history, and they therefore receive careful analysis. This is sepecially true of Athanasius.

It must be emphasized, however, that although recent works on the creeds are significant, much more time and energy need to be given to them.

While it is to be expected that a number of conservative works like Gerald
L. Bray's *Creeds, Councils and Christ* [§13.5] will continue to be produced
as apologies for traditional orthodoxy, it is far more likely that future studies
will examine the creeds from the standpoint of relevance to modern
Christianity. This is the fruitful approach which Alan Richardson takes in
his *Creeds in the Making: A Short Introduction to the History of Christian
Doctrine* [§13.16]. (P)

13.1   🏛 Schaff, Philip. *The Creeds of Christendom.* 3 vols. Grand Rapids:
       Baker, 1977. (1877¹). Reprint from the 1931 edition.
       This set is a useful, general overview of the creeds of Christendom
       and their textual history. In many cases Schaff has printed the
       creeds in English along with the original text or texts in whatever
       languages they were first written. Unfortunately, the organization
       of documents is not chronological as one might expect; rather, it is
       strange by almost any standard. In Volume I only the first 82 pages
       of out of a total of 947 are devoted to the creeds of the early
       church. In Volume II only 73 pages out of 634 are given to those
       creeds. Volume III has no information on them. (P)

13.2   🏛 Tanner, Norman P. *Decrees of the Ecumenical Councils.* Vol. 1.
       Nicaea I to Lateran V. London: Sheed & Ward / Washington, DC:
       Georgetown UP, 1990. Pp. xxv + 655.
       Based on the work of G. Alberigo and others, under the title *Concili-
       iorum Oecumenicorum Decreta.* Only the first 120 pages are relevant
       to our period. Each council is provided with a brief introduction
       and bibliography of 2 or 3 pages; then follows the text of the
       councils, in Greek, Latin, and English. Notes are brief. The indexes,
       which are found in volume 2, are highly useful and extensive. This
       will establish itself as the standard reference work in English on
       the councils.
       ✄ Cunningham, *Commonweal* 117 (1990): 590-591.

13.3   Babcock, F.J. *The History of the Creeds.* New York: Macmillan,
       1938. Pp. xiv + 249. M-1.
       Written as a text to assist theological students, this volume is a
       fairly simple but reasonably complete reproduction of the creeds of
       the early Church. The creeds included are the Apostles' Creed,
       Eastern baptismal creeds of the fourth century, Antiochene creeds,
       Western European creeds, the Creed of Rome from the fourth century,
       the Creed of Marcellus of Ancyra, the Nicene Creed and the Quicun-

que Vult. In addition to the creeds themselves, Babcock gives much information on their development over time and modern scholarly studies of them. (P)

13.4 Bindley, T.H. *The Oecumenical Documents of the Faith.* 4th ed. Introduction and notes by F.W. Green. London: Methuen, 1950 (1899[1]). Pp. 246. I-5; BI-3; PI-2.
Bindley assumes that orthodox creeds from Nicaea to Chalcedon were based on the implicit teachings of Christ and the apostles. He dismisses Monarchianism, Arianism, and the ideas of Apollinaris, Nestorius, and Eutyches as heresies whose only positive contributions were to help clarify traditional doctrines regarding the nature of God and Christ. He covers the creeds immediately prior to Nicaea, the Epistles of Cyril, the Tome of Leo, the Chalcedonian definition of faith, and provides translations of certain primary documents. (P)
⊰< Chadwick, *JTS* 3 (1952): 119-120; Kelly, *JEH* 2 (1951): 224-225.

13.5 Bray, Gerald L. *Creeds, Councils and Christ.* Leicester, UK/ Downers Grove, IL: Inter-Varsity, 1984. Pp. 224. I-3; AB-5; CT-4.
This is a conservative approach to early Christian understanding of Jesus, the creedal developments stemming from that, and a number of other questions in early church history (canon, expansion, and a polemic against some of the tendencies in modern theology). Bray writes clearly, attempting to make sense of the various issues, even though not every reader will identify with Bray's sympathies. One appendix gives modern translations of the Apostles,' Nicene, and Athanasian creeds; the second appendix supplies Greek or Latin texts of various creedal statements (Apostles' Creed, the Niceno-Constantinopolitan Creed, The Chalcedonian Definition, and the Athanasian Creed).
⊰< Bayer, *EQ* 58 (1986): 180-181; Hall, *SJT* 39 (1986): 287-288; Kelly, *TS* 46 (1985): 388-389; Klooster, *CTJ* 20 (1985): 128-132; Weinrich, *CTQ* 49 (1985): 234-236.

13.6 Burn, A.E. *An Introduction to the Creeds and to the Te Deum.* London: Methuen, 1899. Pp. xiv + 323. I-5.
Although rather dated, Burn's work is a sensitive approach to the history of creedal development. Burns respects the need to base beliefs on solid historical data. Thus he introduces his ultimate examinations of the Nicene Creed, the Athanasian Creed (Quicunque Vult) and the Apostles' Creed with background studies of the New Testament and the second, third, and fourth centuries. He also

discusses what was known about the creeds academically at the
end of the nineteenth century. Still somewhat useful. (P)

13.7   Cullmann, Oscar. *The Earliest Christian Confessions*. Translated
by J.K.S. Reid. London: Lutterworth, 1949. Pp. 64.
In this short study, Cullmann asks a number of questions respecting
the origins of confessions of faith in the post-apostolic church. He
then suggests that there were five sets of causes for their development:
(1) those surrounding baptism and catechumenism, (2) those related
to liturgy and preaching, (3) those involved with exorcism, (4)
those concerned with persecution, and finally, (5) those associated
with polemic against heretics. Cullmann argues that the confessions
were all Christological in nature and were, therefore, of the greatest
significance. The creeds relate to the divine plan of salvation and
thus put the Christian in touch with the past, present and future. (P)
ἐ× Torrance, *SJT* 5 (1952): 85-87.

13.8   Davis, Leo Donald. *The First Seven Ecumenical Councils (325-787):
Their History and Theology*. Wilmington: Michael Glazier, 1987.
Pp. 342. I-9; G-5.
Partially based on lectures, Davis' work includes an excellent chapter
on the Roman world of the third century and the Christian role in it
is an introduction to a study of the first seven ecumenical councils.
The short chapters that follow give a clear picture of the issues
dealt with by each of the councils studied. Chronologies are appended
to each chapter, plus excellent select bibliographies. The glossary
of theological terms is most useful. (P)
ἐ× Bruce, *AUSS* 26 (1988): 186-187; Kelly, *CH* 58 (1989): 218-219;
Rorem, *Currents* 16 (1989): 464-465; Slusser, *TS* 50 (1989): 202-203;
Weinrich, *CTQ* 53 (1989): 309-310; Wesche, *StVTQ* 33 (1989): 413-415;
Young, *CHR* 76 (1990): 100-101.

13.9   Dvornik, Francis. *The Ecumenical Councils*. Twentieth Century
Encyclopedia of Catholicism 82. New York: Hawthorn Books, 1961.
Pp. 112. B-2.
Written at the time of the summoning of Vatican II, Dvornik's
purpose in producing this short study was, in part, to show the
bond that exists between Rome and the Eastern churches because
of their common participation in the first seven ecumenical councils
and the development of the creeds which grew out of those councils.
Only the first 40 pages relate to the history of the early church.
Although of some use to persons wanting a basic knowledge of the
councils, it can be ignored by more serious students. (P)

>< Rexine, *StVSQ* 7 (1963): 95.

13.10   Hanson, R.P.C. "The Creed." In *Tradition in the Early Church.* London: SCM Press, 1962. Pp. 52-74.
Hanson examines the development of the creed, beginning with passages in the New Testament and in Aristides and Justin. But Hanson finds too little there to suggest a fixed kind of creedal statement. In fact, there seems to be a number of creedal statements used in baptisms in the second and third century, and these, being *interrogative,* do not seem to be rooted in the earlier creedal-like statements, which were *affirmative.* In addition, the baptismal creed was too bare to safeguard against heresy, as a formal creed would have needed to do. Hanson then considers the possibility of other forms of the creed, but basically cannot find the affirmative creed (which could be used in tests for orthodoxy) before the middle of the third century. Hanson also considers the "rule of faith" briefly, and in pp. 75-129 of the same book, discusses the "rule" in detail.

13.11   Hughes, Philip. *The Church in Crisis: A History of the Twenty Great Councils.* London: Burns and Oates, 1961. Pp. 342. I-12.
Written under the imprimatur of Francis Cardinal Spellman, this is a Catholic history. Only its first 140 pages are relevant to the history of the early church, covering, as they do, the story of the first seven ecumenical councils. Although the running accounts of the events surrounding the councils are generally accurate, Hughes' study is biased by the fact that he holds that the Roman Catholic Church has the right to state with finality what should be believed as Christ's teachings. Hence, the councils are seen as pronouncements of divine truth rather than dialectical compromises often influenced by secular political considerations. (P)

13.12   Kelly, J.N.D. The Athanasian Creed. New York: Harper & Row, 1964. Pp. xi + 140. I-4.
Delivered originally as the Paddock Lectures for 1963 at The General Theological Seminary, New York, this is the first scientific study of the Athanasian Creed (or Quicunque Vult) since 1909. Kelly surveys the known history of it, plus scholarly studies of it up to the present. He discusses its text, translations, parallels, and its early use. He then evaluates its rhythm, style and vocabulary. He claims the creed dates from the 5th or early 6th century and is not the work of either Ambrose or Vincent of Lerins. Finally, Kelly considers it in the light of two primary doctrines: the Trinity and the Incarnation. (P)

⤝ Crehan, *JTS* 16 (1965): 510-511; Henry, *CT* 9 (Apr 23, 1965): 36;
Holland, *CH* 35 (1966): 107-109; Klooster, *WTJ* 28 (1966): 190-198;
Woollcombe, *SJT* 20 (1967): 472-474.

13.13   Kelly, J.N.D. *Early Christian Creeds*. 3d ed. London: Longman /
San Francisco: Harper and Row, 1978. Pp. xii + 511. I-11.
The most recent overall study of the creeds in English, this is by
far the best. It covers the period from the beginnings of the Christian
church to Medieval times. Part I includes background studies of
the patristic era, Judaism, Graeco-Roman religion, Graeco-Roman
philosophy, and Gnosticism. In addition, it contains discussions of
the Old and New Testaments and their interpretations. Part II deals
with pre-Nicene theology, the development of trinitarianism, the
beginnings of christology, soteriology, and ecclesiology. Part III
covers the Nicene crisis and the history of post-Nicene christology,
Christian controversies over the nature of humanity, Nicene and
post-Nicene soteriology, ecclesiology, and sacramental doctrine.
An epilogue evaluates the subjects of eschatology, the development
of dogma, the resurrection, Christ's second coming, life everlasting,
and Mary and the saints. Sources are carefully footnoted. (P)
⤝ Carpenter, *JTS* 2 (1951): 100-102; Fulton, *ExT* 62 (1952): 127-128;
Metzger, *TT* 9 (1952): 127-128; Stephenson, *Theology* 76 (1973): 604-606;
Telfer, *JEH* 2 (1951): 103-105; H.E.W. Turner, *CQR* 151 (1950): 92-97.

13.14   Kelly, J.N.D. "The Nicene Creed: A Turning Point." *Scottish Journal
of Theology* 36 (1983): 23-39.
What is called the Nicene Creed is, in reality, the Niceno-
Constantinopolitan Creed. Scholars long argued that there was no
proof that it had really been produced at Constantinople in 381.
Kelly holds, however, that there is now good evidence to show that
it was. He also asserts that the Nicene Creed and the Niceno-
Constantinopolitan Creed brought about a "revolution" in Christian
theology. Prior to Nicaea, Christians, following Origen, generally
posited "an ineffable Godhead with two subordinate and...disparate
hypostases." After Constantinople, the Son and Holy Spirit were
asserted to be co-equal and co-eternal with the Father. (P)

13.15   Margull, Hans Jochen, ed. *The Councils of The Church: History
and Analysis*. Philadelphia: Fortress, 1966. Pp. xvi + 528. I-18.
Developed as a response by Protestant, Anglican, and Orthodox
Christians to the calling of Vatican II as a Roman Catholic "ecumenical council," this volume of articles is nonetheless of prime
importance to an understanding of the first Christian ecumenical
councils. Among those articles, Georg Ketschar's "The Councils of

the Ancient Church" is particularly relevant. So, too, is Emilianos of Meloa's "The Nature and Character of Ecumenical Councils" and Edmund Schlink's "Ecumenical Councils Past and Present." Unlike most histories of the councils, this work does not assume the validity of the conciliar tradition as such, but seeks, rather, to examine the theory behind it. (P)

13.16 Richardson, Alan. *Creeds in the Making: A Short Introduction to the History of Christian Doctrine.* London: SCM, 1941. Pp. 132. I-2.

Richardson presents a historical analysis of the development of the creeds. He asserts that Christianity, being a belief in a person, not in a doctrinal system, must make afresh its interpretation of the Christ event in every age. Hence, the creeds, as they developed over time, were the attempts of Christians to come to grips with problems that arose out of their understanding of that event and their relation to it. In his study, Richardson gives a short but useful résumé of the development of trinitarian and anti-trinitarian doctrines, christological doctrines, and doctrines of the atonement. He is refreshingly non-doctrinaire. (P)

13.17 Sellers, R.V. *The Council of Chalcedon: A Historical and Doctrinal Survey.* London: SPCK, 1953. Pp. xviii + 361. I-11.

Sellers begins with an examination of the events that led to Chalcedon, giving an overview of earlier christological concepts. He nolds that Chalcedon brought together Alexandrian, Antiochene, and Western traditions, and approved of what was "orthodox" in all three, irrespective of their origins. He provides a detailed account of the council itself and, in the second part of his study, makes a careful examination of the Creed of Chalcedon. After mentioning briefly a later controversy with Monophysitism and the gradual clarification of Chalcedonian doctrine, he asserts that it possesses a "treasure of faith" for the church. (P)

⊰ Foster, *ExT* 65 (1954): 106-107; Grillmeier, *JEH* 6 (1955): 91-93; Hendry, *TT* 11 (1955): 568-570; Telfer, *JTS* 5 (1954): 109-111; H.E.W. Turner, *CQR* 155 (1954): 71-73.

14
ETHICS AND SEXUALITY

The subjects of ethics and sexuality were as important in the age of the first Christians as they are today. But the society of imperial Rome was very different from our own, and Christians living in that world were influenced by traditions and situations that were often quite different from those that affect modern men and women. Although we have only a partial understanding of that world, the great body of data from it in the form of both written documents and archaeological evidence indicates that the issues were very complex. Nowhere was this more true than in the areas of ethics and human sexuality. After all, the Roman Empire was a vast state that included within it many diverse peoples, religions, and social classes.

In contrasting the early Christian ethical values with those of their "pagan" neighbors, many modern scholars have assumed that those of the former were far more "elevated" than those of the latter. Even if one believes this assumption to be true from an ideal standpoint, however, certain caveats need to be raised respecting it. First, while early Christians did have highly developed ethical standards, they did not always live up to them. For example, it is well known that the church took a strong stand against induced abortion, but that did not always mean that Christian women forewent obtaining abortions. Also, despite the strong admonition of churchmen such as Tertullian in support of Christian pacifism, by the last years of the second century many Christian men were serving in the Roman army. Second, while it is true that Christian ethics did differ in a few outstanding ways from pagan ethics, it is important to note that pagan ethics greatly influenced both Judaism and Christianity. Stoicism in particular made a lasting impact on those faiths, and it is impossible to understand the development of Christian ethical and sexual values apart from Stoicism and other philosophical movements that were current in the first several centuries of our era. Finally, when Christians tried to differentiate their ethics from those of their polytheist contemporaries, they were challenged by the latter. Pagans, for example, contended that the idea that love was central to ethics was as much theirs as it was Christian.

Ethical questions included, of course, far more than a concern with human sexual relations. Relations with the Roman state, Jews, pagans, and the practices of all three were matters of great concern. As the New Testament and post-apostolic Christian history show, a major desire of early Christians was to keep themselves "unspotted from the world" which, in their view, lay in the power of Satan. Hence questions involving participation in public office, patriotic exercises (such as burning incense to the emperor's genius), participation in the military, dietary issues (involving the eating of blood), capital punishment, abortion, and a host of sexual matters were of great and special importance to them. So too were issues involving business transactions, the charging of interest, the treatment of slaves and many other matters that involved their relations both with other Christians and with their non-Christian neighbors.

Although many of the fathers of the early church gave attention to some of these issues, Tertullian probably discussed more of them than any other early Christian writer, at least before the fourth and fifth centuries. Tertullian has had a bad press in the twentieth century, however, for what is regarded as his extremely rigorous and "narrow" stands on many issues. He has been criticized as an anti-intellectual and a male chauvinist. Feminist writers have censured him for his famous or infamous remark that woman—Eve and, through her, her female descendants—"is the devil's gateway." But Forrester F. Church [§14.6], for one, feels capable of asserting that a broader analysis of Tertullian's writings gives a very different picture of what he believed.

Of greater importance to the history of western Christian ethical thought have been the works of another North African, Augustine. Augustine has had a profound impact on both Catholics and Protestants in so far as their views of the nature of the body, sin, and relations between the sexes are concerned. Margaret Ruth Miles' *Augustine on the Body* [§14.14] and Elaine Pagels' *Adam, Eve, and the Serpent* [§14.17] are major contributions to the understanding of his thought. Both should be consulted in any attempt to evaluate the ethics and the impact of that great saint's thought.

The study of early Christian sexual ethics is understandably important to contemporaries. Since the sexual revolution of the last several decades and the legalization of abortion in most western, nominally Christian lands, there has been a strong desire to examine the history of Christian values either to give support to the radical changes that have taken place in our day or to buttress more traditional values. Here again, Elaine Pagels has made valuable contributions, as have authors such as W. den Boer [§14.3] and Michael Gorman [§14.8]. Gorman's work is most interesting because, not only is he one of the few scholars who deals with the issue of abortion among early Christians, but he discusses the whole matter of violence and the taking of human life as an aspect of early Christian thought.

Surprisingly, the number of studies in the area of early Christian ethics is relatively small, and much more needs to be researched and written on the subject. Nevertheless, in two areas there is a good deal of literature. These are, first, those works which relate to military service and Christian pacifism and, second, those which discuss the roles of women in the first several centuries of our era. But both of these areas are so important in themselves that they appear under separate chapter headings in this bibliography. Therefore, anyone wishing to study early Christian attitudes towards the issues of war and peace and ethical matters involving early Christian women will find helpful entries in sections §10.12 - 10.21 and in chapter 25. (P)

14.1 🏛 Malherbe, Abraham J. *Moral Exhortation, A Greco-Roman Sourcebook*. Library of Early Christianity. Philadelphia: Westminster, 1986. Pp. 178. B-5; NI-3; SI-7; NTI-3; AAI-1.

A collection of seventy-one passages from primary sources, covering a wide range of topics. Not only are "conventional subjects" covered (anger, slavery, sexual conduct, civic responsibility, retirement, etc.), but, as well, the setting of moral teaching, the aims and character of the teacher, methods and means of instruction (e.g. speeches, letters, epitomes, protrepsis, paraenesis, diatribe), compilations of moral teaching, and various moral "lists." With a 6-page introduction, and a 5-page description of sources. Each section has a brief introductory note.

✂ Danker, *Currents* 16 (1989): 135; Elliott *SC7* (1989-90): 182-184; Hinson, *CH* 57 (1988): 73-74; Martin, *CRBR* 1 (1988): 304-307; Mitchell, *TS* 48 (1987): 737-739; Snyder, *CTSR* 78 (1988): 54; Stowers, *JBL* 108 (1989): 259-360; Talbert, *Interpretation* 42 (1988): 206.

14.2 🏛 Womer, Jan L., trans. and ed. *Morality and Ethics in Early Christianity*. Sources of Early Christian Thought. Philadelphia: Fortress, 1987. Pp. viii + 135. B-2.

Another in a useful introductory collection of primary sources. A 29-page introduction explains the issues, and comments briefly on the sources used. The ten chapters that follow are divided mainly in terms of authors, though one deals with the *Didache* and one with the Council of Elvira. The authors are important churchmen who have commented on some aspect of Christian behavior. They are: Aristides, Clement of Alexandria, Tertullian, Cyprian, Basil the Great, Ambrose, Augustine, and Theodoret of Cyrrus. The passages are sufficiently long to give a balanced view of each author's thought.

✂ Hall, *JEH* 40 (1989): 253-261; Hinson, *R&E* 85 (1988): 382-383; Monti, *CH* 58 (1989): 138; Rorem, *Currents* 15 (1988): 372; Rowold, *International Review of Mission* 78 (1989): 226-228; Slater, *Perkins Journal*

42 (1989): 31.

14.3   Boer, W. den. *Private Morality in Greece and Rome. Some Historical Aspects.* Leiden: E.J. Brill, 1979. Pp. xii + 305. I-4; AAI-5; MAI-2; BI-1; NTI-1; B-6.
Although only peripherally concerned with personal morality in a Christian context, Boer's study is highly useful for an examination of the moral values and practices of the world in which the first Christians lived. While Boer indicates clearly that the picture of private morality in the ancient world is and must remain hazy, he gives a wealth of information on it in many areas. Besides discussing the various punishments, the treatment of orphans, widows, and the deformed, he deals with the rich and the poor, citizenship, slavery, women in religion and morality, and abortion and family planning. Although condemned by the church, abortion continued in Christian times. (P)

14.4   Brown, Peter. *The Body and Society: Men, Women, and Sexual Renunciation in Early Christianity,* New York, Columbia UP, 1988. Pp. xx + 504. B-45; I-10; CT-2; M-1.
Very few academic works merit exclamations of "wonderful" and "majestic," but this is surely one of them. In this large and expansive work, Brown with his usual sensitivity to, and delicate interplay with, the words and actions of his antique actors, weaves his way carefully through the creation of a new and complex mode of thinking about sex and sexuality in the ancient Mediterranean. After briefly outlining the significance of the body and sexuality in terms of the reproduction required by the classical city state, Brown launches into a massively detailed study of how this ideology, so central to the existence of all pre-Christian Mediterranean societies, came to be challenged by what were previously marginal ideas restricted to small numbers of persons—either a philosophical élite or unusual fringe religious cults. Brown traces the encratitic urge from these peripheral sources, including Jewish sects, to a first stage of integration in Alexandrian Christian thought onwards to Tertullian's initial summation in the West. On this foundation, Brown builds an elaborate analysis, first of the ascetic movement in the eastern Mediterranean, anchored in multitudinous desert communities and wandering saints, to culminate in the ideas of John Chrysostom in the Greek city. Set against this is the Latin tradition from Tertullian to Jerome—an ideology increasingly hostile to the body and sexuality, which was tamed and reshaped into the classic definition of western sexuality by the genius of Augustine. Brown's work

will become the classic guide through a minefield of texts of bewildering complexity through which a new inner-identification of sexuality, its threats and its modes of control, came to be placed at the heart of the conception of the personal self in the West. (S)
๛ Bossy, *Past and Present* 124 (1989): 180-187; Brundage, *JEH* 41 (1990): 76-77; H. Chadwick, *TLSuppl* 4473 (Dec 23-29 1988): 1411; Clark, *JR* 70 (1990): 432-436; Egan, *Horizons* 17 (1990): 152-153; Frend, *NYRB* 36 (Feb 2 1989(: 39-41; Hunter, *TS* 50 (1989): 361-365; Lawrence, *StLJT* 32 (1989): 283-287; Leithart, *WTJ* 52 (1990): 163-165; Louth, *JTS* 41 (1990): 231-235; Meeks, *Commonweal* 116 (1989): 246-247; Sanders, *NYRB* 93 (Dec 25 1988): 1, 20-21; Stroumsa, *HR* 30 (1990): 100-102; Williams, *Theology* 92 (1989): 338-341.

14.5   Cameron, Averil. "Virginity as Metaphor: Women and the Rhetoric of Early Christianity." In *History as Text: The Writing of Ancient History*. London: Duckworth, 1989. Pp. 181-205.
Beginning with the lead sentence: "The rhetoric of the early church was a male rhetoric," Cameron advances without any fanciful asides directly to her purpose: "to show how the misogynistic rhetoric of the early Christian texts became established." She rightly and forcefully draws attention to the fundamentals: that "the debate was conducted...by men about women and in the context of unquestioned assumptions about the nature of women." Part of her argument is that the powerful rhetorical vehicle of "woman as metaphor" was already well developed by pre-Christian writers, and was a reservoir of verbal power that was pre-eminently exploitable and well suited to the development of a peculiar Christian rhetoric that presented its message in terms of one "needing to be uncovered from layers of symbol, allegory, and metaphor." The study of cases of women like Thekla and Perpetua, and the history of the emergence of significant numbers of women into the center stage of Christian writing in the fourth century (principally because of their high social status), is used to illustrate the connection between this repressive rhetoric and the male domination of the new ecclesiastical power. (S)

14.6   Church, F. Forrester. "Sex and Salvation in Tertullian." *Harvard Theological Review* 68 (1975): 83-101.
Two phrases of Tertullian have given him an undeserved, negative reputation. These are: "What have Athens and Jerusalem to do with one another?" and "You [woman] are the devil's gateway." Church focuses on the latter statement because of the rise of feminism and a number of scholarly works which accuse Tertullian of misogynism and a low estimate of the flesh. A broader evaluation of his

writings shows, however, that Tertullian should not be judged on the basis of this comment. He regarded Adam, not Eve, as responsible for original sin and its transmission to humankind. In other instances, he speaks highly of women who, in marriage, have no "difference of spirit or of flesh" from men. (P)

14.7   Forrell, George Wolfgang. *History of Christian Ethics: From the New Testament to Augustine.* Minneapolis: Augsburg Publishing House, 1979. Pp. 247. B-7; BI-3; NI-6; SI-14; Index of Greek and Latin Terms-1.

Volume I of a three-volume set, Forrell's study emphasizes the praxis of Christianity rather than an examination of ethical propositions as such. After discussing New Testament ethics from that standpoint, he deals with ethics in the early Christian fathers and then moves on to examine the viewpoints of Tertullian, Clement of Alexandria, Origen, some Christians during the fourth century, Basil, John Chrysostom, and Augustine. While Forrell's insights are often extremely valuable, his work is a history of Christian ethics in only a very limited sense. (P)

⤢ Beach, *JAAR* 49 (1981): 342-343; Countryman, *CH* 51 (1982): 86-87; Gessell, *StLJT* 24 (1981): 300-302; Hastings, *SJT* 36 (1983): 427-428; Keane, *TS* 41 (1980): 612-613; May, *Horizons* 8 (1981): 408-409; Reid, *AUSS* 19 (1981): 80-81; Stout, *Ethics* 91 (1981): 328-329; Weinrich, *CTQ* 46 (1982): 345-346.

14.8   Gorman, Michael J. *Abortion & the Early Church. Christian, Jewish & Pagan Attitudes in the Greco-Roman World.* Downers Grove, Ill: InterVarsity, 1982. Pp. 120. B-2; I-2.

A brief survey of the frequency and methods of abortion in the ancient world, followed by a more detailed examination of scores of texts from pagan, Jewish, and Christian sources, in which the practice comes under criticism. Gorman attempts to identify the different reasons for opposition to abortion (rights of state, husband, etc.). Further, the status of the fetus is often a matter of concern (whether "formed" or "unformed"). Gorman's conclusion is that Christian opposition to the practice is motivated from a general opposition to violence.

⤢ Aden, *Journal of Psychology and Christianity* 3 (1984): 80-81; Gamble, *WTJ* 45 (1983): 199-200; Hann, *JES* 20 (1983): 470-471; Schatkin, *TT* 40 (1983): 249; Yanney, *CCR* 4 (1983): 38-39.

14.9   Hunter, David G. "Resistance to the Virginal Ideal in Late Fourth Century Rome: The Case of Jovinian." *Theological Studies* 48 (1987): 45-64.

Condemned by a synod at Rome under Pope Siricius, by Ambrose at Milan, and by both Jerome and Augustine, Jovinian represented a reaction against the ascetic enthusiasm which spread throughout the Western Church in the fourth century. Although there was opposition to the emphasis on virginity and asceticism during the period, Jovinian was unique in expressing theological criticisms. Hunter evaluates his thinking and concludes that he was probably orthodox, with a desire to condemn the extreme asceticism of the Manichees and the Priscillianists. Nonetheless, he was condemned by the church of his day, perhaps because Siricius was the first pope to insist on the celibacy of the higher clergy. (P)
⤸ Clark, *CH* 56 (1987): 257-258.

14.10   Hunter, David G. "The Paradise of Patriarchy: Ambrosiaster on Woman as (Not) God's Image" *Journal of Theological Studies* 43 (1992): 447-469.
An article that forms a wonderful "other half" of the diptych of his fundamental study of the emergence of the ideal of Mary figure in the 380s CE [§14.11]. In this study, Hunt examines the writings of Jerome's contemporary, Ambrosiaster, who took an "anti-ascetic" line that was very much in favor of the existing powers of the formal hierarchy of the church, of traditional Roman social values, and hence mainstream moral, sexual, and marital practices and values. In doing so, he was led away from the concentration on the virginal body of woman as the model of social understanding, and to a repeated insistence on the idea (first espoused in the west by Tertullian—but with no systematic followers until Ambrosiaster) of the intrinsically imperfect nature of woman and her body, which he come gradually to entrench in the fundamental justification of the "woman as Eve" theme. Interestingly, this alternative, and just as highly polarized model of women, emerges as part of the self-same series of debates amongst men that simultaneously produced the prefect model of woman in the virgin Mary. Both were then to become established as central ideal-figures at the core of western theology for the next one and half thousand years. (S)

14.11   Hunter, David G. "Helvidius, Jovinian, and the Virginity of Mary in Late Fourth-Century Rome." *Journal of Early Christianity Studies* 1 (1993) : 47-71.
Hunter offers a very clear exposition of one of the most significant and yet complicated problems of western theology and church politics: the emergence of the doctrine of the perpetual virginity of Mary. He begins by tracing the fierce polemical struggle in the

early 380s CE which pitted Jerome against two earlier proponents
of the "humanness" of Mary: Helvidius who rejected the doctrine
of Mary's continuing virginity after she had given birth to Jesus;
and Jovinian, who even rejected the idea that she had remained a
virgin in the process of giving birth to Christ. Ambrose and Jerome
virulently contested these views and managed to entrench the idea
of the perpetual virginity of Mary as doctrine in Catholic theology
down to the twentieth century. Hunter demonstrates that this was
an unusual development insofar as this doctrine (in either form)
had almost no place in western theology until the end of the fourth
century. Its origins can be traced to certain writings of Origen and
the so-called *Protevangelium of James* (end of the second century
CE)—but their views remained marginal, even in their eastern
context. It was the acerbic quarrels over the role of the body,
sexuality, and asceticism in the power struggles of the late fourth
century in the West that in effect created a new ideology. (S)

14.12   Leuchli, Samuel. *Power and Sexuality: The Emergence of Canon
        Law at the Synod of Elvira*. Philadelphia: Temple UP, 1972. Pp. ix
        + 143. I-7.
        The Synod of Elvira, at modern-day Granada in Spain (309 CE),
        one of the most formative of the early Church Councils, passed
        eighty-one canonic decisions that were to have a considerable impact
        on subsequent ecclesiastical legislation in the West. Leuchli notes
        that a substantial proportion of the canons have to do with problems
        of sexuality or, at least, of regulating the status, position, and behavior
        of women. He traces this to the problem of defining the position of
        women within a church that was rapidly formalizing its ecclesiastical
        hierarchy, and so had to define the precise powers of men and
        women, especially with regard to their access to formal positions
        of power in the church itself. The second crisis facing the rapidly
        emerging power of the church was another aspect of self-definition:
        that of Christians versus other social groups (non-Christian
        polytheists, Jews, so-called heretical sects, Manichaeans, and others).
        In this confrontation, the position and status of Christian women,
        and their sexual purity, came to be central to Christian ideology. A
        study of these canons, therefore, reveals much not only about
        formalized Christian canonical norms regarding female sexual
        behavior, but also about the more general history of men's attempts
        to constrain women's behavior by legislative means. In an appendix
        (pp. 126-135), Leuchli offers his own translation of the original
        text of the eighty-one canons. (S)

14.13   McNamara, Jo Ann. "Sexual Equality and the Cult of Virginity in
        Early Christian Thought." *Feminist Studies* 3 (1976): 145-158.
        Beginning with the Pauline dictum that "in God there is neither
        male nor female," McNamara argues that the Church Fathers recog-
        nized the capacity of women to perform well in a wide range of
        social roles. Even in their attempts to regulate what women "should
        do," they tried, if somewhat imperfectly, to impose ideological
        constraints of relatively egalitarian expectations concerning proper
        sexual behavior on both men and women. Some (like Caesarius of
        Arles) even railed against the double-standard accepted by men in
        such matters. The Fathers, however, were limited to a great extent
        by the dominant vocabularies of their time. They tended to express
        the achievements and powers of the best of Christian women
        (including consecrated virgins and female martyrs) as "virile" and
        "man-like" in nature. McNamara contends that, since "social reform
        was not their object," they were attempting to formulate a tran-
        scendent ideology, a celestial condition in which there would be
        genuine equality between women and men "before God." (S)

14.14   Miles, Margaret Ruth. *Augustine on the Body*. American Academy
        of Religion, Dissertation Series 31. Missoula, MT: Scholars Press,
        1979. Pp. vi +184. B; I; Augustine Index.
        Acknowledging Augustine to be one of the primary theorists in the
        body/mind problematic in western culture, and that such theoretical
        disposition lies at the very heart of who we conceive ourselves to
        be, Miles begins with a consideration of Augustine's "theory of
        sensation" from its earliest recorded development (Cassiacum) to
        the *Civitas Dei* (*The City of God*. She advances to the problem of
        asceticism and traces its development to the point of Augustine's
        engagement in the debates with Pelagius. She shows how this
        development is linked to the problem of incarnation, and finally to
        that of resurrection of the body. The premise of incarnation finally
        settles the question of the value of the body for Christians against
        "pagans," but it did not resolve the problem of "how." Much of
        Augustine's actual doctrine on the body, she claims, is misunderstood
        precisely because he was the first to bring "to conscious realization
        and painstaking systematic articulation the task of reuniting soul
        and body." (S)
        ✄ Wright, *JTS* 32 (1981): 524-526.

14.15   Miller, Patricia Cox. "The Blazing Body: Ascetic Desire in Jerome's
        Letter to Eustochium." *Journal of Early Christian Studies* 1 (1993):
        21-45.

Contributing to an increasing literature that focuses on the subject of the physical body and its sexuality (see Brown, *Body and Society*, §14.4), Miller concentrates on one of the more lurid, if not near hysterical, praises of virginity from the world of late antiquity: Jerome's letter to Eustochium (*Letter*, 22). She demonstrates how Jerome's discourse, by concentrating so heavily on the body, ends in a "paradox wherein erotic sensibilities are both denied and intensified." Jerome attempts to resolve the problem of the body by virtually effacing its corporeal reality and by replacing it with a body "rewritten" as a series of scriptural tropes. Miller shows how this strategy finally fails. In her words, he is left with no metaphor for his own body, is compelled to collapse all distinctions between male and female bodies, and so destroys the interstitial middle ground in which a true love or *eros* could exist. Jerome's strategy, therefore, only increased the very "burning desire" of the body which he so futilely tried to erase with his hard-line asceticism. (S)

14.16   Pagels, Elaine H. "Adam and Eve, Christ and the Church: A Survey of Second Century Controversies Concerning Marriage." In *The New Testament and Gnosis: Essays in Honour of Robert McL. Wilson.* Edited by A.H.B. Logan and A.J.M. Wedderburn. Edinburgh, 1983. Pp. 146-175.

In this finely detailed analysis of the debates over the status of marriage and sexual intercourse amongst the Church Fathers, Pagels begins with the basic *loci classici* from the New Testament, both the sayings attributed to Jesus, and the Pauline and deutero-Pauline writings. She points out how Jesus radically altered traditional Jewish thinking on marriage, which was principally directed towards reproduction and therefore accepting of polygamy and divorce in favor of hypervaluing the marriage of the couple by making the marriage bond indissoluble and by setting marital obligations of the individuals above the social obligations to procreate. Pagels also demonstrates how Paul set celibacy in precedence over marriage itself, and then she details the reaction of the deutero-Pauline writings that attempted to soften considerably Paul's hard-line anti-marriage arguments. The Apostolic Fathers seized upon the latter "tamed and domesticated" version of Paul to combat the "ascetic extremists." Pagels then notes the development of extremist camps: the ascetics who wished to abolish marital intercourse, and their opposites (e.g., Valentinian) who wanted to make it the primary symbol of sanctification. Clement and orthodox thinkers, in reaction, relied on the Hebrew Bible and the deutero-Pauline materials to reject the revolutionary and sometimes more egalitarian tendencies of either

camp to affirm traditional marriage, and with it, the husband's
position of domination over his wife as something consonant with
nature. (S)

14.17   Pagels, Elaine. *Adam, Eve, and the Serpent.* New York: Random
House, 1988. Pp. xxviii + 190. I-13.
Pagels' main thesis is that the stories of creation in Genesis 1-3 are
basic to values associated with the Christian tradition. She also
holds that specific attitudes towards human sexuality evolved during
the first four centuries of the Christian era within the church itself.
Most significant was the revolution in thinking that occurred with
Augustine of Hippo. Prior to Augustine, Christians had emphasized
freedom of the will and freedom from domination by both ecclesiastical and secular authority. Augustine's new interpretation of Romans
5:12 posited that sin was passed from father to child in the father's
semen. Hence, he laid the basis for the idea that all humans are
born in sin, are essentially depraved, and must be subjected to
outward coercion. (P)
✂ Cavadini, *Thomist* 53 (1989): 509-512; Fox, *NYTBR* 93 (Aug 21 1988):
15-16; Frend, *NYRB* 35 (June 30 1988): 27-31; Groh, *ATR* 72 (1990):
221-223; Jacobs, *Reformed Journal* 39 (Feb 1989): 21-25; Klinghoffer,
Commentary 86 (1988): 77-79; Lawrence, *StLJT* 32 (1988): 56-58; Leithart,
WTJ 51 (1989): 183-187; Miles, *Christianity and Crisis* 48 (1988): 347-349;
O'Connell, *TS* 50 (1989): 201-202; Perkins, *CBQ* 52 (1990): 168-169;
Peters, *Dialog* 29 (1990): 48-49; Remus, *Consensus* 16 (1990): 137-139;
Trevett, *JEH* 42 (1991): 294-295; Trumbower, *JR* 70 (1990): 80-81; Weaver,
Interpretation 44 (1990): 105-106; Williams, *Theology* 92 (1989): 338-341.

14.18   Rousselle, Aline. *Porneia: On Desire and the Body in Antiquity.*
Translated by Felicia Pheasant. Oxford: Blackwell, 1988. Pp. x +
213. B-13; I-2
Very much under the influence of the structuralist and post-
structuralist Parisian thinkers (above all Foucault), Rousselle offers
a body-oriented evaluation of the moral codes of pagan society in
the ancient Mediterranean. She traces metachanges in its dominant
ideologies from ones of "openness" and "flow" to an increasing
dominance of paradigms of "control and continence" that produced
a new view of body relationships that came to value abstinence and
virginity, and hence the new moral milieu in which Christianity
found its place. As elements in this transition, Rousselle devotes
specific chapters to illicit love, divorce, prostitution, and even child
sacrifice. This work should be read along with the formative volumes
in Foucault's *History of Sexuality* that provoked it, and with Peter
Brown's *Body and Society* [§14.4] as a control over its excessive

claims (e.g., "castration complexes," and infant murder and sacrifice). (S)

✂ Gardner, *CR* 39 (1989): 329-330; Hunter, *TS* 50 (1989): 361-365; King, *History* 74 (1989): 476; Lefkowitz, *TLSuppl* 4455 (Aug 19-25 1988): 912.

14.19   Ruether, Rosemary Radford. "Misogynism and Virginal Feminism in the Fathers of the Church." In *Religion and Sexism: Images of Women in the Jewish and Christian Traditions*. Edited by Rosemary Radford Ruether. New York: Simon and Schuster, 1974. Pp. 150-183.
Beginning with the origins and developments of the peculiar mind-body dualism in Eastern and Western Christianity (the East preferring a sexless monism as the original state and nature of divinity; the West an original male state), Ruether advances to consider the implications of this dualism for views of women as body and as inferior. She is particularly trenchant and incisive on Augustine's view of the origins of humans as sexed but as lacking libido or the drive of desire which, after the Fall, induces in men an uncontrollable and irrational urge that overpowers both rationality and good in them. In this scheme, women become a bodily appendage to men, who can only be persons through them, but whose bodies and visual image constantly threaten men's salvation. This leads to a severe polarization of women as whores, wives and virgins, which finds its final and perhaps most pathological expression in Jerome. Ruether's fine piece should also perhaps be supplemented by a reading of Averil Cameron [§25.10]. (S)

14.20   Whittaker, John. "Christianity and Morality in the Roman Empire." *Vigiliae Christianae* 33 (1979): 209-225.
In seeking to specify the possible ethical originality of Christianity, Whittaker hones in on the distinguishing claim—going back to Matthew 5:44f and Luke 6:27f and emphasized by the early church Fathers like Tertullian (*Ad Scap*. 1)—that Christians, unlike non-Christians, not only loved their friends, but even their enemies. By a systematic examination of the original source materials, Whittaker demonstrates that Tertullian's claim is, in effect, a type of "oratorical excess," and that the idea that one should even "love one's enemies" was a commonplace of "Hellenistic ethical systems." Whittaker further shows that neither most Christians nor their "pagan" detractors saw Christian ethics as unusual in this respect. Whittaker's examination is most thorough. To his credit, though to the disadvantage of the Greekless and Latinless reader, most of the primary texts (cited *in extenso*) are left in their original languages. (S)

15
GNOSTICISM
AND RELATED MOVEMENTS

Interest in Gnosticism exploded in the 1950s as a result of the discovery in 1945 of a collection of thirteen Coptic books containing some fifty-two documents. The find was made in the Upper Nile region of Egypt, near the town of Nag Hammadi, thus the name "The Nag Hammadi Library" is widely used for this collection. Many of these "Nag Hammadi" documents reflect developed Gnostic systems. These documents had been buried, apparently in an attempt to hide and protect them, possibly sometime in the latter fourth century. That date is determined by palaeographic analysis, by which the age of the handwriting can be determined. For the Nag Hammadi materials such analysis indicates that some of the manuscripts could not have been copied before the middle of the 300s. The date of the *composition* of the writings, as opposed to the *copying*, is less clear. We know from the evidence of the church fathers that Gnosticism was perceived to be a serious problem in the second century, and it is thought that many of these documents are as old as that.

The attention directed to these writings (as the documents slowly made their way to the scholarly market) has resulted in a whole new field of study, similar in many ways to the field of the "New Testament" and "Patristics." Whether such attention is out of proportion to the significance of these writings for a balanced understanding of early Christianity is a matter of dispute. The fact that we have a separate section in this bibliography for Gnosticism is an indication of the importance we place on Gnosticism as a key for understanding early Christianity. The fact that we have one section on Gnosticism, and not many, is also an indication.

The primary question over which long and inconclusive battles have been waged is whether Gnosticism was pre-Christian (and thus "non-Christian") or whether it was Christian. In order words, the primary question is one of origins: did Gnosticism need an ingredient found only in Christianity for it to develop into the coherent, complex religious systems we find in the second century? Or did its origins lie outside the Christian movement, finding in a Jewish or a pagan religious milieu all the elements that it needed to become what it became? Of course, if Gnosticism could be understood as non-Christian in origin, that would not necessarily imply that it was pre-Christian. The various theories that Gnosticism developed out of a failed apocalyptic Judaism would make Gnosticism "post-Christian" in strict terms of origin, without making it dependent on Christianity.

Some of the attention given to Gnosticism results directly from the kind of studies done by Bauer [§18.2] and Koester [§18.19], which attribute considerable strength to Gnosticism in the earliest period of Christianity. Bauer's thesis was that Gnosticism was often the dominant (and frequently the original) form of Christianity in many areas. The question of the strength of Gnosticism is a difficult one, muddled by a number of factors. For one thing, it is not certain to what extent the Gnostics wished to be a majority; perhaps an elitism was built into the Gnostic perspective, and a good case can be made for Gnosticism's attempt to be included within the fabric of the larger church, perhaps making it difficult to distinguish between Gnostic members of the church and the non-Gnostic members. Further, it is notoriously difficult to measure the strength of a movement on the basis of the decibel of the polemic directed against it, and largely that is what we have in the literature about Gnosticism. The polemics often reflect more the personality of the heresiologist. The more mild the writer, the less polemical the writing; the more high-strung, the more polemical. Then, too, the decibel of the polemic often depends on the *perceived* threat—not the *real* threat. While it is possible that the heresiologist correctly perceived the seriousness of the threat from Gnosticism, it is often likely that the perception was more in terms of what the threat could become than what it was when it was attacked in the polemical literature. The heresiologists may have overestimated the threat, as polemical literature often does. Whatever the case, Gnosticism was perceived as a serious threat only in the second century, and this should caution us against measuring the strength of Gnosticism from the threat of Gnosticism as perceived by the early orthodox leaders. Finally, there were bright lights and original thinkers in Gnosticism, and these often had high visibility. But, again, the high visibility of a Gnostic teacher is not necessarily a good indicator of the strength of the movement that stems from him. All this leaves us in a state of uncertainty about the strength of Gnosticism.

Whatever the difficulty of measuring the strength of Gnosticism or even of distinguishing between Gnostic and non-Gnostic in the somewhat amorphous church of the early period, the case for Marcionism is different. This movement was somewhat like Gnosticism, though the parallels have been debated. Marcionism was attacked by a whole range of persons from varying theological perspectives. Further, the evidence for Marcionism's considerable success in the late second century is difficult to discount, but the evidence is more ambiguous for the lasting impact of Marcionism on the developing Christian church. In the late 1800s, Adolf Harnack did much to rehabilitate Marcionism, making it the qualified preserver of Paulinism in the second century and granting it the status of innovator in shaping a distinctive Christian canon. That particular issue remains unsettled to this day: many scholars see the orthodox canon as a response to the novelty of Marcion's canon; others see Marcion producing a revision to a common Christian sense of authority, which included within its compass the writings of the early Christian leaders. (Refer to chapter 7 on the "Canon" for further discussion.)

Several other issues are debated by scholars of Gnosticism. One is the ethical stance of the Gnostic groups. From the polemical writings of the orthodox leaders, almost every nasty thing that could be said about Gnosticism was said. But there is some question just how accurate those descriptions were; they may have come simply from a basic stock of polemical terms that opponents were accustomed to hurling at one another. If Marcionism is taken as an example, it is likely that, in any comparison of an ethical rigor of members of the catholic community and of the Marcionite, the Marcionite would more often be judged the more rigorous. But Marcionism was not the only representative of the diverse Gnostic movement. There is enough evidence to make a case for the conduct of at least some Gnostic groups going beyond even the periphery of acceptable behavior (even allowing for the polemical nature of these charges).

Books on Gnosticism now flood the market. Publishers in the business seem to be marketing "more than their share." New fields tend to be like that, and it will take a few more decades for the dust to settle enough before a balanced judgment can be made about the degree of significance that should be assigned to Gnosticism for an understanding of the development of catholic Christianity, and of the various other streams of the early church. We list below a few of the standard or summary volumes and collections. Attention should also be called to E.J. Brill's on-going and massive project under the title "Nag Hammadi Studies." This is a technical series, offering detailed examination of a range of relevant topics. This series will need to be consulted for any serious study of Gnosticism.

Separate subdivisions at the end of this chapter deal with three areas of study related to Gnosticism. One is Simon Magus, the proposed, and perhaps mythical, founder of Gnosticism, though the matter is much debated. Another is Marcionism, a movement with Gnostic-like traits, and a history roughly contemporary with Gnosticism. It, too, is a matter of considerable debate. A third area of study is Manichaeanism, which became a serious competitor to Christianity after Gnosticism itself had lost its strength.

GNOSTICISM

15.1 ⒷScholer, David M. *Nag Hammadi Bibliography 1948-1969.* Nag Hammadi Studies 1. Leiden: E.J. Brill, 1971. Pp. xvi + 201. MAI-11.

This volume lists over 2400 articles on Gnosticism (thus covering more than its title suggests). Many of these entries are to book reviews. The bibliography is divided into six chapters: general; previously known Gnostic texts; Gnostic schools and leaders (with 29 sub-divisions); the New Testament and Gnosticism; Qumran and Gnosticism; and the various texts from the Nag Hammadi library itself. In the introduction, Scholer refers to previous bibliographic articles and books which had, in some way or another, dealt with Gnosticism. The entries are not annotated, but detailed publication information is provided. Scholer has kept the bibliography up-to-date by annual supplemental bibliographies published in article form in the journal *Novum Testamentum*, beginning with Issue 13 (1971). These supplements, which are published in the fourth quarter of each year, are titled "Bibliographia Gnostica."

15.2 ⒷTardieu, Michel, and Jean-Daniel DuBois. *Introduction à la Littérature Gnostique: I. Collections Retrouvées Avant 1945.* Initiations au christianisme ancien. Paris: Éditions du CERF / Éditions du C.N.R.S., 1986. Pp. 152.

Although this work is in French, it is largely bibliographical, and the student should be able to gain useful information about sources, both in English and other languages, with a bit of effort. The work is divided into 140 sections, and the French headings should not be that much of a puzzle to block the non-French reader. The sections cover topics such as the history of the word "Gnostic"; and the various scholarly aids available for the study of Gnosticism (with two pages on bibliographies). The major part of the book deals with the manuscript discoveries since 1945, with special attention the various collections.

15.3 🏛Foerster, Werner, et al. *Gnosis: A Selection of Gnostic Texts.* Translated and edited by R. McL. Wilson, et al. Oxford: Clarendon, 1972. Volume I: *Patristic Evidence:* Pp. viii + 367. AAI-2; BI-7; B-3. Volume II: *Coptic and Mandean Sources:* Pp. vii + 360. B-2; Index of Gnostic Concepts-27; Index of Mandean Sources-2.

These volumes introduce the world of Gnosticism from two perspectives: (1): passages from the patristic writers who dealt with Gnosticism (vol. 1), and (2): passages from Gnostic writers themselves, especially from the Nag Hammadi and Mandean materials.

There are useful surveys and introductions to the Nag Hammadi
discovery itself, and to each of the documents, and to various themes
within the Gnostic writings. The Mandean material is largely grouped
by theme; the Nag Hammadi by document; the patristic references
by school. Foerster was aided on this project by Ernst Haenchen,
Martin Krause, and Kurt Rudolph, which makes the volumes valuable
for that reason alone. Not as comprehensive for the Nag Hammadi
materials as is Robinson [§15.5], but it covers a far broader field.

⸂< Vol. 1: J.G. Davies, *ExT* 84 (1973): 216-217; R.M. Grant, *VC* 28
(1974): 153-156; Higgins, *SJT* 27 (1974): 494; Pagels, *TS* 34 (1973):
497-498; Santer, *TT* 77 (1974): 39-40; Steely, *CH* 42 (1973): 420; Vol. 2:
J.G. Davies, *ExT* 86 (1974): 25; H.E.W. Turner, *Churchman* 88 (1974):
210-211.

15.4   ☛ 🏛 Layton, B. *The Gnostic Scriptures: A New Translation.* New
York: Doubleday, 1987. Pp. xiii + 526. BI-6; NTI-6; SI-46; B-4;
M-6; T-6.
A discussion and translation of a selective collection of Gnostic
and related writings. Useful for the beginner, in that terms are
always explained, general information about Christian scriptures is
provided, and various selections have brief historical introductions
and bibliographies. The five sections are: Classical Gnostic Scripture;
The Writings of Valentinus; The School of Valentinus; The School
of St. Thomas; and Other Early Currents." But the volume is useful
for the more advanced too, in that Layton provides fresh insights
and reconstructions. The texts are from Gnostic documents themselves and from comments made by the orthodox critics. A well-
organized collection, for beginner or established researcher.

⸂< Attridge, *CRBR* 1 (1988): 301-304; Grant, *CH* 57 (1988): 215-216;
Hall, *JEH* 40 (1989): 617-618; Johnson, *CBQ* 51 (1989): 746-747; Logan,
JTS 40 (1989): 349; Mirecki, *BA* 52 (1989): 49-50; Quispel, *VC* 42 (1988):
199-201 Wilson, *ExT* 99 (1988): 214-215.

15.5   🏛 Robinson, James M., gen. ed. *The Nag Hammadi Library in
English.* 3d ed. Leiden: E.J. Brill/San Francisco: Harper, 1988.
(1977[1]). Pp. xv + 549.
This is the standard English translation of the Nag Hammadi texts,
done by 39 members of the Coptic Gnostic Library Project at Clare-
mont. The 47 tractates are each introduced by a brief analysis of
key questions (averaging 1-3 pp.). A review of the publishing history
of these documents is provided in the preface, and Robinson's
26-page introduction deals with the basic questions, such as the
stance of the texts (non-Christian, for some); the physical condition
of the manuscripts; the connection of the library to Pachomian

monasticism and the possible conflicts of Gnostic-influenced monks with the orthodox church; and the discovery and final purchases of the manuscripts themselves. Also included is an 18-page afterword by Richard Smith on "The Modern Relevance of Gnosticism."

&< Boring, *Encounter* 50 (1989): 386-388; Elliott, *NovT* 33 (1991): 285-287; Grant, *CH* 59 (1990): 389-391; Matthews, *BTB* 19 (1989): 154-155; Snyder, *CTSR* 79 (1989): 66; Wilson, *JTS* 41 (1990): 217-218; reviews of earlier editions: Fiorenza, *Horizons* 6 (1979): 128-129; Grant, *JR* 59 (1979): 105-106; Green, *Numen* 26 (1979): 111-112; Kraft, *RSR* 8 (1982): 32-52; MacRae, *JAAR* 47 (1979): 666-667; Pagels, *BA* 42 (1979): 250-251; Perkins, *CBQ* 41 (1979): 167-170; Williams, *JBL* 97 (1978): 610-612; Yamauchi, *CT* 23 (Oct 6 1978): 36.

15.6 Barc, Bernard, ed. *Colloque international sur les textes de Nag Hammadi.* Bibliothèque Copte de Nag Hammadi, Études 1. Quebec: Les Presses de L'Université Laval, 1981 Pp. xii + 462. AAI-11; MAI-5; NI-2; B&W-4; BI-1; NTI-2; T-5; Nag Hammadi Index-7.
A collection of papers given at the International Colloquium on Nag Hammadi Texts at Quebec City (August 22-25, 1978). Though most of the articles are in French, seven English ones are included. They are: "From the Cliff to Cairo. The Story of the Discoverers and the Middlemen of the Nag Hammadi Codices" (J.M. Robinson); "Twenty Years After" (Wilson); "The Pagan Elements in Early Christianity and Gnosticism" (Säve-Söderberg); "The Attitude of the Gnostic Religion Towards Judaism" (Tröger); "The "Opponents" in the New Testament in Light of the Nag Hammadi Writings" (Wisse); "Vision and Revision: a Gnostic View of Resurrection" (Layton); "*The Gospel of Thomas* Revisited" (Quispel). A fuller list and discussion of contents is found in van den Broek [§15.9].
&< Epp, *JBL* 103 (1984): 499-500.

15.7 Bianchi, Ugo, et al. *Gnosis.* Festschrift für Hans Jonas. Göttingen: Vandenhoeck & Ruprecht, 1978.
In celebration of one of the leading scholars of Gnosticism, this collection has eight articles in English: "Gnosis and Greek Philosophy" (Armstrong); "Gnosticism and the New Testament (Robinson); "Nag Hammadi and the New Testament" (MacRae); "The Tractate Marsanes (NHC X) and the Platonic Tradition" (Pearson); "Visions, Appearances, and Apostolic Authority: Gnostic and Orthodox Traditions" (Pagels); "Gnosticism and Early Monasticism in Egypt" (Wisse); "One Text, Four Translations: Some Reflections of the Nag Hammadi Gospel of the Egyptians" (Wilson); "The *pihta* and *mambuha* Prayers. To the Question of the Liturgical Development among the Mandaeans" (Segelberg). A bibliography

of Jonas is included. A fuller list and discussion of contents is found in van den Broek [§15.9].

15.8   Broek, R. van den, and M.J. Vermaseren, eds. *Studies in Gnosticism and Hellenistic Religions Presented to Gilles Quispel on the Occasion of His Sixty-Fifth Birthday.* Études préliminaires aux religions orientales dans l'Empire Romain 91. Leiden: E.J. Brill, 1981. Pp. xiv + 622. I-6; AAI-27; B&W-2; BI-4; NTI-3.

A collection of 27 articles (17 in English) from leading scholars on Gnosticism. The English articles (with abbreviated titles) are: "Alexandrian Orphic Theogony" (Amersfoort); "Relevance of Lk 20:34-36" (Bianchi); "Adam's Psychic Body" (van den Broek); "Origins of Gnostic Dualism" (Culianu); "Christians and Manichaeans in third-century Syria" (Drijvers); "Dove Cult of the Samaritans" (Fossum); "Charges of 'Immorality' against Various Religious Groups in Antiquity" (Grant); "Anti-Gnostic Polemic in Rabbinic Literature" (Gruenwald); "Flood Story in the Apocalypse of Adam" (Klijn); "Bad World and Demiurge" (Mansfeld); "Catalogues of Sins and Virtues Personified" (Mussies); "Jewish Elements in Corpus Hermeticum" (Pearson); "Hellenistic Magic" (Segal); "Gnosis and the Mysteries" (Wilson); "Translation of Gen 1:2a" (van Winden); "Jewish Gnosticism?" (Yamauchi); "'Teachings of Silvanus' and Jewish Christianity" (Zandee). A fuller list with a discussion of contents is found in van den Broek [§15.9].

⊰ Louth, *JTS* 34 (1983): 283-284; Turner, *JAAR* 50 (1982): 623-624.

15.9   ◉ Broek, R. van den. "The Present State of Gnostic Studies." *Vigiliae Christianae* 37 (1983): 41-71.

Van den Broek provides a clear and insightful summary of the state of Gnostic research, under five headings: "The purpose and character of the Nag Hammadi Collection" (a diverse, not solely Gnostic collection, for edification of Pachomian monks); "Gnosticism and the Church Fathers" (i.e., how accurate they were in their description of Gnosticism in light of the evidence we have from the Nag Hammadi collection); "Gnosticism and Judaism" (where he finds the roots of Gnosticism); "Gnosticism and Philosophy" (Greek philosophy is fundamentally more positive about the world, but some of its ideas could be appropriated, in altered form, by Gnostics); and "Gnosticism and Christianity" (question of Gnostic influence in the New Testament is unclear; the relationship of Gnostics to the orthodox closer than the orthodox wanted to admit). This review focused primarily on four collections of essays on Gnosticism published between 1978 and 1981, listed in this chapter

[§15.6; §15.7; §15.8; §15.20].

15.10 ☞ Dart, John. *The Jesus of Heresy and History. The Discovery and Meaning of the Gnostic Nag Hammadi Library.* San Francisco: Harper & Row, 1988. Pp. xvii + 204. B-5; I-6; M-2; B&W-9.

An extensively revised edition of a work originally published in 1976, titled *The Laughing Saviour: The Discovery and Significance of the Nag Hammadi Gnostic Library.* This is an informed, journalistic introduction to the Nag Hammadi codices by a reporter for the *Los Angeles Times.* The first quarter deals with the discovery and release of the codices; the remainder is divided into three sections: "The Jewish Connection"; "The Jesus of Heresy" (Gnostic views about Jesus); and "The Jesus of History" (focusing on Koester and the *Gospel of Thomas*). A 17-page translation of the *Gospel of Thomas* (Lambdin's translation) is included.

❧ Grant, *CH* 59 (1990): 389-391; Matthews, *BTB* 19 (1989): 154-155; Snyder, *CTSR* 80 (1990): 60.

15.11 Desjardins, Michel R. *Sin in Valentinianism.* SBL Dissertation Series 108. Atlanta: Scholars Press, 1990. Pp. ix + 157. AAI-3; B-17; MAI-2.

Desjardins is mainly interested in doing three things. (1) To show that at least some branches of Gnosticism had as rigorous ethical concerns as any other group in early Christianity (contrary to the impression left by their victorious opponents). (2) In light of that, to raise questions about the reasons the church fathers represented Gnosticism in the way they did. (3) To suggest, in the footsteps of Walter Bauer [§18.2] that the character of primitive Christianity was diverse and that "heretical" expressions of the Christian message were as "authentic" as the so-called more "orthodox" expressions. Putting these aside, Desjardins does provide a solid overview of the ethical dimension of one Gnostic group and of its treatment in the hands of orthodox writers.

❧ King, *JAAR* 59 (1991): 162-164; Vallée, *SR* 20 (1991): 361-362.

15.12 ◉ Drijvers, Han J.W. "The Origins of Gnosticism as a Religious and Historical Problem." *Nederlands Theologisch Tijdschrift* 22 (1968): 321-351.

This is a good review of the scholarship (up to the late 1960s) on the puzzling origins of Gnosticism, covering the discussions of the Colloquium in Messina, where an attempt was made to work out some common terminology and definitions for a discussion of Gnosticism. The views of numerous scholars are considered in detail, making this a good place to get a sense of the key issues and players at a crucial point in the history of Gnostic studies.

15.13   Filoramo, Giovanni. *A History of Gnosticism.* Translated by Anthony Alcock. Cambridge, MA/Oxford: Blackwell, 1990. Pp. xx + 268. B-13; I-10.
Besides being a useful survey of the various issues of importance in Gnostic studies (dualism, the demiurge, creation, Simon Magus, key Gnostic teachers, ascetic and libertine tendencies), all of which are dealt with at length, Filoramo has attempted to offer a convincing account for the rise of Gnosticism, and its mentality. Rather than merely specifying parallel elements in other systems in an attempt to locate "origins," Filoramo looks broadly at the age itself. Here the old religious structures were being replaced by new religious horizons. The ways by which the older systems had broken down the barriers between humans and the divine lost their effectiveness when "replaced by a God transcendent and unknowable, at least by the normal methods of reason." This situation called for new ways of knowing, of which Gnosticism was but one example.

15.14   Goehring, James E., et al. *Gnosticism & the Early Christian World.* Sonoma, CA: Polebridge Press, 1990. Pp. xxiv + 200. B-23; AAI-7; MAI-4; SI-5.
A collection of essays in honor of James M. Robinson, with a 4-page biography of Robinson. The eleven articles are (with abbreviated titles): "Hypostasis of the Archons" (K. King); "Genealogy and Sociology in the Apocalypse of Adam" (L. Martin); "Trimorphic Protennoia and the Prologue of the Fourth Gospel" (G. Robinson); "Nag Hammadi, Odes of Solomon, and New Testament Christological Hymns" (J. Sanders); "Apocalypse of Peter and 2 Peter" (Pearson); "Proverbs and Social Control" (A. Jacobson); "Greco-Roman Origins of a Type of Ascetic Behavior" (V. Wimbush); "Reconsideration of an Early Christian Myth" (Attridge); "Chrysostom and Porphyry" (K. Wicker); "The Social and Economic World of Early Egyptian Monasticism" (Goehring); and "Reconstructing a Dismembered Coptic Library" (S. Emmel).
✂ Collins, *CBQ* 54 (1992): 392-393.

15.15   Grant, Robert M. *Gnosticism and Early Christianity.* 2d ed. New York and London: Columbia UP, 1966. Pp. ix + 227. B-6; I-9.
A collection of six lectures delivered in 1957-1958, with the addition of a chapter on the gospels of Thomas, Philip, and Mary. Grant's distinctive understanding is that Gnosticism arose out of failed

Jewish apocalyptic hopes stemming from the fall of Jerusalem. To show this link with apocalyptic thought, Grant discusses the calendar and the dualistic language. Simon Magus and Simonian Gnosticism are separated, with the latter stemming from failed apocalyptic. Extensive discussion on Saturninus, Marcion, Valentinus, and Basilides, and on the Gnostic reading of apocalyptic (and non-apocalyptic) passages from the New Testament. Grant later reflects on this work, and judges it to be perhaps too interested in history and chronology (see *Jesus after the Gospels: The Christ of the Second Century* [Louisville, KY: Westminster/John Knox, 1990], p. 10). He may have been too severe on himself.

ᢀ< Farmer, *Perkins Journal* 14 (1961): 42-43; Fitzmyer, *TS* 21 (1960): 294-297; Frend, *JTS* 12 (1961): 90-91; Kelly, *JEH* 12 (1961): 91-92; H.E.W. Turner, *CQR* 162 (1961): 105-107; R.M. Wilson, *ExT* 72 (1960): 74; R.M. Wilson, *TT* 17 (1960): 116-118.

15.16   Green, Henry A. *The Economic and Social Origins of Gnosticism.* SBL Dissertation Series 77. Atlanta: Scholars Press, 1985. Pp. xv + 304 . T-7; M-1.

This book is Green's 1982 PhD dissertation done under R. McL. Wilson at St. Andrew's University, with the chapter on methodology omitted. Green works as a trained sociologist (mainly influenced by Weber), focusing on the economic and social dimensions of Gnostic origins. Green thinks two features could account for the origins of Gnosticism: (1) the impact of the change from Ptolemaic to Roman economic policy, and (2) the closure of avenues of upward mobility to educated Jews, who had been open to Hellenism as a means for social advancement. Unfortunately, Green fails to engage Roberts' [§18.26] analysis of Gnosticism in Egypt.

ᢀ< Adler, *Journal for the Study of the Pseudepigrapha* 1 (1987): 116-119; Desjardins, *SR* 18 (1989): 111; Lieu, *SJT* 41 (1988): 555-556; Segal, *JQR* 77 (1986): 244-246; Turner, *JBL* 107 (1988): 156-158; Williams *SC* 7 (1989-90): 104-106.

15.17   Hedrick, Charles W., and Robert Hodgson, Jr., eds. *Nag Hammadi, Gnosticism, and Early Christianity.* Peabody, MA: Hendrickson, 1986. Pp. 332. MAI-4; B-29; B&W-14; BI-1; NTI-5; T-2.

A collection of 13 papers discussed at the 1983 Springfield, Missouri Working Seminar on Gnosticism and Early Christianity, with contributions from better known scholars of Gnosticism: Koester, Layton, MacRae, Pagels, Pearson, Perkins, Robinson, Schenke, Wisse, Gero, Attridge, Parrott, Turner, and Hedrick. The articles are grouped under three headings: "Non-Christian Gnosticism"; "Gnosticism, New Testament, and Early Christian Literature"; and "Gnosticism and the Early Church." Though many of the articles are technical, the book is introduced by an 11-page "Beginner's Guide" to Nag Hammadi, Gnosticism, and Early Christianity. Contains many fresh ideas.

୫< Gorday, *CH* 57 (1988): 352.-353; Hinson, *R&E* 87 (1990): 505; Johnson, *TS* 49 (1988): 576; Tuckett, *ExT* 99 (1987): 91; Painter, *Pacifica* 3 (1990): 226-229; Quispel, *VC* 42 (1988): 198-199; Timbie, *CBQ* 50 (1988): 156-157.

15.18   ☞ Hedrick, Charles W. "Nag Hammadi, Gnosticism, and Early Christianity—A Beginner's Guide." In *Nag Hammadi, Gnosticism, and Early Christianity*. Edited by C.W. Hedrick and R. Hodgson, Jr. Peabody, MA: Hendrickson, 1986. Pp. 1-11.

Divided into seven short sections, with suggested further reading for each section, this is a solid introduction to the various issues in current discussions of Gnosticism. Various problems are considered: terms, sources, and origins. The Nag Hammadi Library is described, and the Gnostic influence on the New Testament is discussed. The final page provides a brief note on the other articles included in the volume, which is abstracted at §15.17.

15.19   Jonas, Hans. *The Gnostic Religion: The Message of the Alien God and the Beginnings of Christianity*. Boston: Beacon Press, 1963. (1958[1]). Pp. 358. NI-14; AB-3.

Jonas provided one of the first comprehensive treatments of Gnosticism produced after the discovery of the Nag Hammadi documents. He emphasized the radical anti-cosmic dualism of the period, and he has been criticized for not being discriminating enough in his use of this category for his analysis of quite diverse individuals, and for the age in general. Nonetheless, this is one of a few of the major works on Gnosticism, ranking with that of Rudolph [§15.30] for its comprehensive discussion, though Rudolph's work is now the more up-to-date.

୫< R.M. Grant, *CH* 27 (1958): 77; R.M. Grant, *JR* 36 (1956): 56-57; Markus, *Downside Review* 74 (1956): 167-168.

15.20   Layton, B. ed. *The Rediscovery of Gnosticism*. Volume 1: *The School of Valentinus*. Volume 2: *Sethian Gnosticism*. Studies in the History of Religions (Supplements to *Numen*) 41/42. Leiden: E.J. Brill, 1981. Pp. xvi + 427.

About the same time as the publication of the Nag Hammadi Library, the International Conference on Gnosticism was held at Yale University, March 28-31, 1978. The two volumes are from that conference, which featured major scholars in the field. Volume 1 has four general articles and eight shorter papers on Valentinianism, Platonism, and Iconography. The contributors to Volume 2 reach no consensus regarding the so-called "Sethian Gnosticism." Some deny its existence (Wisse, Rudolph); others see it as a self-conscious movement, complete with a system of belief and practice. Most of the general questions of origins and methodology are also addressed. A fuller list and discussion of contents is found in van den Broek [§15.9].

⊱< Klijn, *NovT* 25 (1983): 90-94; Drewery *JTS* 34 (1983): 277-279; Epp, *JBL* 102 (1983): 165-167.

15.21 Logan, A.H.B. and A.J.M. Wedderburn, eds. *The New Testament and Gnosis: Essays in Honour of Robert McL. Wilson.* Edinburgh: T&T Clark, 1983. Pp. xiv + 258. B&W-1
This book contains seventeen articles divided into three sections: I: Gnosis, Gnosticism and the New Testament: Definition and Nature; II: Gnosis, Gnosticism and Christian Origins; and III: Nag Hammadi Texts and the New Testament. J.M. Robinson provides an introductory article. Others, with shortened titles, are "Definition" (Rudolph); "Greek Origins of Gnostic Ontology" (Bianchi); "Judaism" (Quispel); "Etymology for Jaldabaoth?" (Black); "Philo" (Pearson); "Manichean Myth" (Böhlig); "Corpus Paulinum" (Schmithals); "Apocalypse of John" (Barret); "Prolegomena" (Wisse); "Marriage" (Pagels); "Graeco-Roman Society" (Grant); "Christianization of Gnostic Texts" (Krause); "Thomas Parables" (Koester); "Gospel of Philip" (Segelberg); "Book of Thomas" (Schenke); and "Trimorphic Protennoia" (Janssens). Includes a 14-page bibliography of Wilson's works to 1981.

⊱< Frend, *ExT* 95 (1984): 374-375; Hall, *JEH* 36 (1985): 103-108; Lindars; *SJT* 38 (1985): 263-264; Meyer, *JR* 67 (1987): 91-92; Rowland, *JTS* 36 (1985): 457-458.

15.22 MacRae, George W. *Studies in the New Testament and Gnosticism.* Selected and edited by Daniel J. Harrington and Stanley B. Marrow. Good News Studies 26. Wilmington, DE: Michael Glazier, 1987. Pp. 277. I-3.
A selection of articles by MacRae, well-known New Testament scholar and Harvard professor, published two years after his death. Part Three (about 100 pages) contains seven articles on Gnosticism, and the 9-page bibliography lists almost forty more articles relevant to Gnosticism. MacRae argues for a Gnosticism that is in origin non-Christian, and which is at least contemporaneous with Christianity. He emphasizes the Jewish character of Gnosticism, and its

similarities to apocalyptic, and argues that the orthodox rejected Gnosticism on three grounds: ethics, salvation-history, and incarnation.
⊰ Attridge, *CBQ* 50 (1988): 746-747; Krentz, *Currents* 16 (1989): 230.

15.23   Pagels, Elaine. *The Gnostic Gospels*. New York: Random House, 1979. Pp. xxxvi + 182. I-8.
Pagels offers a sympathetic approach to Gnosticism in this somewhat diverse collection of six articles. A helpful 23-page general introduction concerning the discovery of Gnostic documents and the scholarly debate it engendered begins the work, followed by chapters on the resurrection of Jesus, the dispute about the role of the bishop, the feminine in Gnosticism, the passion of Jesus and its connection to persecution, conflict with the "orthodox" over what constituted the true church, and self-knowledge as knowledge of God. Although Pagels uses Valentinian texts primarily, most of the issues are central to any consideration of Gnosticism, and Pagels reflections are not to be disregarded.
⊰ Arthur, *JES* 17 (1980): 676-678; Efroymson, *TS* 42 (1981): 136-138; Flory, *JETS* 24 (1981): 251-264; Frend, *JEH* 32 (1981): 337-342; Gannon, *SA* 41 (1980): 399-401; McVey, *TT* 37 (1981): 498-501; Pearson, *RSR* 13 (1987): 1-3; Pervo, *ATR* 63 (1981): 331-332; Quispel, *VC* 34 (1980): 99-101; Segal, *JAOS* 102 (1982): 202-204; Strousma, *Numen* 27 (1980): 278-286; Wilson, *ExT* 91 (1980): 343-344; Wisse, *Interpretation* 35 (1981): 206-207.

15.24   ◉ Pearson, Birger A. "Early Christianity and Gnosticism: A Review Essay." *Religious Studies Review* 13 (1987): I-8. B-1.
Pearson looks at five books on Gnosticism, and offers insightful analysis of the value and weaknesses of each. The reviewed books are: Elaine Pagels, *The Gnostic Gospels* [§15.23]; Pheme Perkins, *The Gnostic Dialogue* [§15.26]; Simon Pétrement, *Le Dieu séparé* (now in English translation [§15.27]); Gedaliahu Stroumsa, *Another Seed*; and Kurt Rudolph, *Gnosis* [§15.30]. Each review takes about a two-column page of *Religious Studies Review*, though the analysis of Pétrement's work is twice that length, providing a fair survey of Pétrement's ideas. Pétrement believes that Gnosticism is a Christian creation, thus she opposes the dominant view that Gnosticism is pre-Christian, for which she is criticized by Pearson. Pearson offers a particularly useful summary of Pétrement's thirty hypotheses.

15.25   Pearson, Birger A. *Gnosticism, Judaism, and Egyptian Christianity.* Studies in Antiquity and Christianity. Minneapolis: Fortress, 1990. Pp. xx + 228. AAI-10; MAI-4.

Thirteen articles by Pearson, ten of which had been published previously, appearing here with revision. Pearson, a leading scholar of Gnosticism, emphasizes the "Jewish" and "Egyptian" character of Gnosticism, or Gnostic *origins*, and he examines exegetical traditions and etymologies. The final article, "Gnosticism in Early Egyptian Christianity" is a good survey of the evidence. Pearson disagrees with Bauer [§18.2] about the origins of Christianity in Egypt and the numerical strength of the Gnostics, though he finds much of worth in Bauer's classic work.

✂ Little, *CBQ* 54 (1992): 197-199; Perkins, *SC* 9 (1992): 120-121; Tuckett, *ExT* 102 (1991): 247-248.

15.26   Perkins, Pheme. *The Gnostic Dialogue. The Early Church and the Crisis of Gnosticism.* Theological Inquiries. New York/Ramsey /Toronto: Paulist, 1980. Pp. xi + 239. T-6; B-4; MAI-2; NTI-2; SI-4; PI-2; Index of Nag Hammadi Citations-7.

Perkins attempts to understand Gnosticism in the context of forces at play in the second and third centuries. After treating the techniques, narrative setting, and the content of the Gnostic revelation "dialogues," Perkins gives attention to the missionary, ascetic, and polemical character of these writings. She is especially critical of Pagels' exaggerated praise for the ancient Gnostics, which she believes stems from a misunderstanding of ancient Gnosticism. The Gnostics, Perkins claims, "lagged behind their orthodox counterparts in adapting to the larger cultural changes in the third and the following centuries..." Too, Perkins considers the benefits gained by the orthodox community from the development of the canon.

✂ Meyer, *SC* 1 (1981): 251-253; Pearson, *RSR* 13 (1987): 3-4; Yamauchi, *CSR* 11 (1982): 171.

15.27   Pétrement, Simone. *A Separate God: The Christian Origins of Gnosticism.* Translated by Carol Harrison. San Francisco: Harper, 1990. Pp. viii + 542. AI-5; SI-8.

This huge work challenges the widespread opinion that Gnosticism was pre-Christian. In clearly divided chapters, Pétrement examines the nature of Gnosticism in detail, finding the most plausible source for the ideas in a second-century interpretation of the Pauline and Johannine material. Then the importance of various individuals linked to Gnosticism is discussed (from Simon, the anonymous "Gnostics" at Corinth, and Apollos, to Cerinthus, Menander, Saturnilus, Basilides, Carpocrates, Valentinus, the "Apocryphon of John," the "So-Called Non-Christian Works Found at Nag Hammadi," and various pagan "Gnoses." Whatever one thinks of the conclusions of this work, it is solidly argued, and shows how weak some of the popular views of Gnosticism are, and how ancient texts must be read with caution.

⊱< Duchesne-Guillemin, *HR* 25 (1986): 282-284; Ellis, *SWJT* 35 (1992): 56-57; R.M. Grant, *Encounter* 52 (1991): 320-321; Hall, *Theology* 95 (1992): 57-58; Logan, *JTS* 43 (1992): 657-661; Pearson, *RSR* 13 (1987): 4-6; Tuckett, *ExT* 102 (1991): 380; Yarnold, *New Blackfriars* 73 (1992): 625-626.

15.28   Quispel, Gilles. *Gnostic Studies I.* Istanbul: Nederlands Historisch-Archaeologisch Instituut, 1974. Pp. xiv + 239. *Gnostic Studies II.* Istanbul: Nederlands Historisch-Archaeologisch Instituut, 1975. Pp. vi + 307.
A collection of papers from one of the leading researchers in Gnosticism. Eighteen of the thirty-two articles are in English, dealing with a wide range of topics. There are four main sections. In volume one: "Valentinian Gnosis and the Jung Codex" and "The Jewish Origins of Gnosticism"; in volume two: "The Gospel of Thomas and Jewish Christianity" and "Gnosis and Modern Times."

15.29   ⊛ Robinson, James M. "The Nag Hammadi Library and the Study of the New Testament." In *The New Testament and Gnosis Essays in Honour of Robert McL. Wilson.* Edited by A.H.B Logan and A.J.M. Wedderburn. Edinburgh: T&T Clark, 1983. Pp. 1-18.
Robinson discusses the treatment of Gnosticism and, in particular, the Nag Hammadi materials, in four major introductions to the New Testament: W.G. Kümmel, *Introduction to the New Testament;* P. Vielhauer, *Geschichte der urchristlichen Literatur: Einleitung in das Neue Testament, die Apokryphen und die Apostolischen Väter;* H.-M. Schenke and K.M. Fischer, *Einleitung in die Scfriften des Neuen Testaments;* Helmut Koester, *Introduction to the New Testament.*

15.30   Rudolph, Kurt. *Gnosis: The Nature and History of Gnosticism.* Translated and edited by Robert MacLachlan Wilson. San Francisco: Harper and Row, 1983. Pp. xii + 411. I-8; B&W-58; C-4; B-14; CT-3
Rudolph has provided what has become a standard work on Gnosticism, covering the history and beliefs of a wide-ranging collection of diverse Gnostic groups. He concludes that Gnosticism was pre-Christian, that it was rooted in Jewish scepticism, and that substantial evidence for Gnostic influence on Christianity can be found within the New Testament itself. He emphasizes that not all Gnostics

were docetic, nor did all deny the reality of Jesus' death, and he examines Gnostic worship and sacraments in some detail. Rudolph also provides a 24-page section on the Mandaeans. Rowan Williams, in the *JTS* book review listed below, provides some crucial criticisms. ⊱ Culianu, *JR* 70 (1990): 303-304; *JTS* 37: 202-206; 7-8; Drane, *EQ* 59 (1987): 178-181; Hall, *JEH* 36 (1985): 103-108; Lieu, *SJT* 38 (1985): 265-266; McGuire, *SC* 5 (1985-86): 47-49; Pearson, *RSR* 13 (1987): Perkins, *Parabola* 9 (1984): 118-122; Williams, *JTS* 37 (1986): 202-206.

15.31 ☛ Rudolph, Kurt. "Gnosticism." Translated by Gregory D. Alles. In *Early Christianity: Origins and Evolution to AD 600.* Edited by Ian Hazlett. London: SPCK, 1991. Pp. 186-197.
Rudolph is one of the leading authorities on Gnosticism, and he provides here a concise and informative introduction to Gnosticism, including a review of the documentary sources and their worth, with a description of the Nag Hammadi corpus, and the Gnostic texts available before that discovery. The main characteristics of Gnosticism are specified, along with comments on where such traits have shown up in religious traditions (especially in some branches of Islam). A brief account of the history of the debate is also provided.

15.32 Sanders, E.P., ed. *Jewish and Christian Self-Definition.* Vol. 1. *The Shaping of Christianity in the Second and Third Centuries.* Philadelphia: Fortress, 1980. Pp. 314. B-19; NI-8; CAI-3; BI-2; Jewish Author Index-1; Nag Hammadi Codices Index-4.
A collection of papers from the McMaster University project on Jewish and Christian self-definition in the Graeco-Roman period. Four chapters are of particular relevance to Gnosticism: "Why the Church Rejected Gnosticism" (MacRae); "Normative Self-Definition in Gnosticism" (Ménard); "Jewish Elements in Gnosticism and the Development of Gnostic Self-Definition" (Pearson); and "Theological and Non-Theological Motives in Irenaeus's Refutation of the Gnostics" (Vallée).

15.33 *The Second Century* 7 (1989-90): 1-56.
All three articles in this issue of *The Second Century* deal with the Gospel of Thomas. Kenneth V. Neller ("Diversity in the Gospel of Thomas: Clues for a New Direction?" pp. 1-18), questions whether studies on the origin and environment of the Gospel of Thomas have assumed a relatively undeveloped tradition (from origin to its burial at Nag Hammadi) when a better assumption would be to admit the diversity and complexity of the tradition. Klyne R.

Snodgrass ("The Gospel of Thomas: A Secondary Gospel" pp. 19-38), argues against theories of the independence for the Gospel of Thomas tradition, contending that the bulk of its material is, in indirect ways, dependent upon the canonical gospels. Charles W. Hedrick ("Thomas and the Synoptics: Aiming at a Consensus" pp. 39-56), contends that individual *logia* in the Gospel of Thomas are independent enough of the synoptic tradition as to demand equal billing in terms of authenticity and antiquity.

15.34   Vallée, Gérard. *A Study in Anti-Gnostic Polemics. Irenaeus, Hippolytus, and Epiphanius.* Studies in Christianity and Judaism 1. Waterloo, ON: Wilfrid Laurier UP, 1981. Pp. xi + 114. B-10; T-3.
Vallée presents a study of three heresiologists, covering a two hundred-year period from the late second century to the late fourth. In addition to providing an analysis of the writings of three leading voices against heresy, Vallée offers some thoughts on heresiology as a literary genre. Further, Vallée attempts to rehabilitate the orthodox heresiologists, who have been pushed aside by the recent fixation of scholars on Gnosticism and Nag Hammadi. Fully aware that orthodox writers did not offer an unbiased account of heresy, Vallée recognizes, nonetheless, the usefulness of these writings in showing what orthodox Christians judged pivotal to Christianity and what they found lacking in heresy.
&< Grant, *JR* 65 (1985): 143; Hanson, *JEH* 33 (1982): 645-646; Stead, *JTS* 34 (1983): 285-286; *CH* 52: 527; Corbett, *SR* 12 (1983): 100-101.

15.35   Wilson, Robert McL. *Gnosis and the New Testament.* Oxford: Basil Blackwell, 1968. Pp. viii + 149. I-3.
In Chapter one, Wilson gives a good overview of the discussion regarding Gnosticism in the twentieth century debate. He then raises the question of "Gnosticism in the New Testament," finding convincing examples of Gnosis-like elements only in John and the Pastorals. Chapter three is a less than sympathetic (though accurate) treatment of Gnostic use of the New Testament. Chapters four and five deal with various Gnostic documents (mainly from Nag Hammadi), in dialogue with the position of other scholars on these documents. The final chapter discusses Schenke's positive treatment of Gnosticism. Wilson's work is still valuable for its common sense.
&< Anderson, *SJT* 23 (1970): 365-367; Evans, *Theology* 72 (1969): 84-85; MacRae, *Biblica* 50 (1969): 133-135; Stead, *JTS* 20 (1969): 626-627.

15.36   Wisse, Frederik. "The Nag Hammadi Library and the Heresiologists." *Vigiliae Christianae* 25 (1971): 205-223.

Wisse notes the changes in scholarly opinion regarding the reliability of the descriptions of Gnosticism found in the writings of the early heresiologists (i.e., orthodox heresy-fighters). Wisse points to: (1) the significant lack of overlap in Gnostic material cited by the fathers and that found at Nag Hammadi; (2) the failure of the Nag Hammadi literature to fit neatly into the categories of Gnostic schools mentioned by the heresiologists, so much so that we may be unable to tie particular Gnostic literature to specific schools. Wisse is suspicious of the source of the labelling used by the Fathers. Then Wisse gives an in-depth review of the sources used by anti-Gnostic writers, focusing particularly on Irenaeus. Part of the difficulty in labelling and grouping the Gnostics is that "the more Gnostic a tractate is, the more heterogeneous its teachings." Gnostics saw themselves, not so much as members of a particular school, but as *pneumatikoi* (spiritual), in contrast to everyone else.

15.37   Wisse, Frederik. "Prolegomena to the Study of the New Testament and Gnosis." In *The New Testament and Gnosis: Essays in Honour of Robert McL. Wilson.* Edited by A. Logan and A. Wedderburn. Edinburgh: T&T Clark, 1983. Pp. 138-145.
A short but important article calling for balance in the treatment of Gnostic questions. In particular, Wisse emphasizes the lack of developed and coherent *systems* of Gnostic thought—such systemizing is more characteristic of tendencies within orthodoxy. Further, Wisse challenges the identification of the Nag Hammadi library with Gnosticism, and he calls for more careful definition of what precisely is Gnostic literature, and raises questions about what we mean when we speak of Gnosticism in the Pauline and Johannine literature. As well, Wisse suggests a closer relationship between Gnostic teachers and the orthodox church. An overall useful word of caution for all students of Gnosticism.

15.38   ◉ Yamauchi, Edwin. *Pre-Christian Gnosticism: A Survey of the Proposed Evidences.* 2d ed. Grand Rapids: Baker, 1983. (1973[1]). Pp. xvi + 278. MAI-7; SI-5; BI-2; B-11.
Yamauchi is the leader of a minority school in Gnostic studies that argues that Gnosticism was not pre-Christian. Two lines of attack are used. (1) Yamauchi attempts to demonstrate that works that are clearly Gnostic are not early. (2) He attempts to show that works that are clearly early are not Gnostic. The result is a good general survey of the position of various writers on Gnosticism, as well as a good exercise in methodology. The second edition differs from the first by the addition of a new chapter, "A Decade Later." The

11-page bibliography is also updated. The result is a useful reference work and solid statement of the anti-"Bultmannian" position.

⊱ Dombrowski, *SR* 4 (1974-75): 89-90; Drane, *EQ* 46 (1974): 54-55; Hendricks, *SWJT* 16 (1973): 99; Hurley, *WTJ* 36 (1974): 242-244; MacRae, *CBQ* 36 (1974): 296-297; Painter, *Churchman* 87 (1973): 221-222; Scholer, *CT* 18 (May 10, 1974): 46-47; Steely, *Rel Life* 43 (1974): 121-122; J. Turner, *JBL* 93 (1974): 482-484.

MANICHAEISM

15.39   Lieu, Samuel N.C. *Manicheism in the Later Roman Empire and Medieval China.* Wissenschaftliche Untersuchungen zum Neuen Testament 63. Tübingen: J.C.B. Mohr (Paul Siebeck), 1992. Pp. xxii + 370. I-16; B-30; M-3.

The first edition was published in 1985 by the Manchester University Press, based on a 1981 Oxford dissertation. This is a substantial revision of that work. Although the book goes beyond the scope of our bibliography, about two-thirds of the material relates to the period of the early church. The work is the most substantial treatment of the topic, dealing with Mani's life; the background, especially Manicheism's relationship to Judeo-Christian groups; its mission, with attention both to the reception and the opposition Manicheism faced in the Roman empire, and its harsh treatment under the church. One 40-page chapter treats Augustine's relationship to Manicheism, the most famous of its adherents—and critics.

⊱ Bonner, *Speculum* 63 (1988): 431-432; Fox, *JTS* 38 (1987): 524-526; Frend, *JEH* 37 (1986): 622-623; Gardner, *KTR* 9 (1986): 69-71; Stroumsa, *CR* 37 (1987): 95-97; Werblowski, *Numen* 33 (1986): 241-269.

15.40   Widengren, Geo. *Mani and Manichaeism.* History of Religion Series. Revised by the author and translated by Charles Kessler. London: Weidenfeld and Nicolson, 1965. Pp. v + 168. I-8; B&W-12; AB-14; T-1.

An introduction to Manichaeism, detailing the political, cultural, and religious situation in Persia at the time of Mani. A chapter on the life of Mani is followed by two chapters on Mani's teaching; one on the literary character of the movement; one on ecclesiastical organization and ritual; one on Manichaean art; one on the spread of Manichaeism in the east and the west (and the resulting clash with Christians); and a final chapter on Mani as a personality. Widengren praises Mani's energies and organizational skills, but dismisses his system as one which was quite flawed (as did most of Mani's contemporaries).

⊱ R.M. Grant, *CH* 35 (1966): 363-364; Kleinz, *TS* 27 (1966): 458-460.

MARCIONISM

15.41   ⊙ Balás, David L. "Marcion Revisited: A 'Post-Harnack' Per-
        spective." In *Texts and Testaments: Critical Essays on the Bible
        and Early Christian Fathers.* Edited by W.E. March. San Antonio:
        Trinity UP, 1980. Pp. 95-108.
        Balás thinks that a new study of Marcion is in order, and he believes
        that Harnack's picture of Marcion will be substantially altered as a
        result. Harnack makes the Gnostic Marcion less Gnostic and more
        Pauline and biblical than he really was, claims Balás. Further,
        Marcion's innovative role in the formation of the canon is exagger-
        ated. And Harnack's view of the second century as being theolog-
        ically impoverished—except for Marcion—is not a balanced view.
        Balás mentions a few of the scholars who have engaged in debate
        with Harnack's views.

15.42   Blackman, E.C. *Marcion and his Influence.* London: SPCK, 1948.
        Pp. x + 181. AI-2; BI-3; SI-2; B-3.
        Intended to demonstrate the effect of Marcion on the developing
        catholic church, Blackman, not without some sympathy for Marcion,
        nonetheless disputes Harnack's high estimate of Marcion's signifi-
        cance. All features of Marcionite thought are discussed. Blackman
        agrees with the orthodox rejection of Marcion and appreciates the
        middle road of orthodoxy in regard to theology and tradition.
        Marcionism is judged more as an exaggeration of Christian truths
        than an introduction of alien ideas. Seven appendices are included:
        one 41 pages in length; another, a technical appendix on the influence
        of Marcion's text on the old Latin text (which Blackman judges to
        have been limited).

15.43   Hoffmann, R. Joseph. *Marcion: On the Restitution of Christianity.
        An Essay on the Development of Radical Paulinist Theology in the
        Second Century.* American Academy of Religion Academy 46.
        Chico, CA.: Scholars Press, 1984. Pp. xxv + 329. B-19; T-1.
        Hoffmann attempts to put forward a new portrait of Marcion, with
        a reevaluation of his impact on the larger church. The key to
        Hoffmann's reconstruction is a redating of the beginning of Mar-
        cion's activity to 110 or 120 CE. Hoffmann attempts to present
        Marcion not as one who took away the Jewish part of the Christian
        heritage but as one who guaranteed the inclusion of the Pauline
        part. He contends that Marcion was close to the Judaism of the
        diaspora in terms of exegesis, ethics, and philosophical innocence,
        and that Marcion was not anti-semitic. See, too, Hoffmann's article
        "How Then Know This Troublous Teacher? Further Reflections on

Marcion and his Church" in *The Second Century* 6 (1987-88): 173-191.
୬< Bammel, *JTS* 39 (1988): 227-232; Bray, *Themelios* 11 (1986): 67-68; Eno, *TS* 46 (1985): 173-174; Farmer, *Perkins Journal* 40 (1987): 52-53; Gamble, *SC* 4 (1984): 245-247; Houlden, *ExT* 95 (1984): 345; Lewis, *CH* 54 (1985): 230; *SBL* 105: 343-346; Saint-Laurent, *JAAR* 54 (1986): 176-177.

15.44 ◉ May, Gerhard. "Marcion in Contemporary Views: Results and Open Questions." *Second Century* 6 (1987): 129-151.
May provides an excellent review of the problems and questions surrounding the debate about Marcion. He distinguishes between two different traditions about Marcion, evaluates the various sources, and shows the advances in the debate since Harnack's foundational work. Of particular importance is May's discussion of the nature of Marcion's theology, especially as it relates either to Gnosticism or Platonism. May distances Marcion from Gnosticism, though he admits that the movement soon went in that direction (under Apelles). This is the place to begin a study of Marcion. Note: this issue of *The Second Century* is dedicated to Marcionism, with articles by Drijvers ("Marcionism in Syria") and Hoffmann [§15.43].

SIMON MAGUS
15.45 ◉ Meeks, Wayne A. "Simon Magus in Recent Research." *Religious Studies Review* 3 (1977): 137-142.
Taking Ernst Haenchen's 1952 article, in which he argued that Simon Magus was the prime example of pre-Christian Gnosticism, Meeks considers a number of books and articles (mainly from the decade ending in 1976). Special attention is given to the works of Frickel, Salles-Dabadie, Beyschlag, and Lüdermann. Meeks concludes that Haenchen has been refuted—reports about Simon Magus do not provide evidence for a pre-Christian Gnosticism. Further, the development of Simonianism is still obscure (e.g. its connections to Samaritanism, or to Valentinianism). Even the terminology is obscure. A bibliography of 32 entries (not all of which deal exclusively with Simon) is included.

16
JEWISH/CHRISTIAN RELATIONS

Until comparatively recently, church historians have been characterized by what Marcel Simon has called a "determined indifference" to Judaism and its significance for the development of Christianity in the patristic period. This indifference stands in striking contrast, however, to the apparent interest in Judaism taken by the patristic writers themselves. As can be seen from the catalog of works provided by A. Lukyn Williams [§16.37] or Robert Wilde [§16.32], virtually every Christian writer of the period under consideration in this bibliography engaged in extensive argument *adversus Judaeos* (against the Jews)—in full tractates devoted to the topic, in significant portions of other writings, or, often, in both.

History is written by the winners, it is often observed; and the shape of the victory determines the way in which the history is written. It is now apparent to scholars that the reason the church expended so much energy defending its position (social and theological) over against that of Judaism was not merely that its relationship with Judaism was a well-known feature of its origins in the past; but that even well into the fourth century, Judaism continued as an active and vigorous participant in Graeco-Roman society, attractive to many pagans (and even Christians), and thus representing a significant rival. Indeed, to many intelligent Roman observers, Judaism appeared to be preferable to its upstart offspring: while its customs were considered strange, at least they were dictated by ancestral tradition; and by attempting to live according to the prescriptions of the Law, Jews seemed to have a more legitimate claim to the Old Testament than did the Christians, who disregarded large parts of it simply on the authority of a Messiah whose messianic credentials had not impressed the Jews. Caught between Roman valuation of antiquity and of divine immutability, from the outside, and the internal threat of Marcion's attempt to jettison the Old Testament link entirely, the church, if it was going to win a hearing at all, had to claim the Old Testament for itself and deny it to the Jews. Hence the substance and harsh tenor of its anti-Judaic rhetoric.

Somewhat surprisingly from the standpoint of historical probabilities, this struggle between Judaism and Christianity for the sympathies, or at least the tolerance, of the Graeco-Roman world came to an end with the conversion of an emperor and, consequently, of the Roman empire. So complete was the Christian triumph that the nature and critical significance of the Christian struggle with Judaism became obscured.

Harnack's approach may be taken as typical. In his standard work *The Mission and Expansion of Christianity in the First Three Centuries* [§12.3], he assumes that after the two disastrous wars with Rome (66-70, and 132-135 CE), Judaism retreated from active participation in the wider Graeco-Roman world into an insulated and inward-looking subculture. Correlated with this is the assumption that the major apologetic challenge faced by the church, and thus the major influence in the development of Christian thought, came from Hellenism. The *adversus Judaeos* tradition was therefore a marginal thing—an idle construct patched together by Christian apologists after hours as a means of resting from their debates with the Greeks (as Wilken describes it in the article cited below! [§16.33]), or at best the residue of a lingering evangelistic interest in the Jews. As for the harsh anti-Judaism of much of this literature, it was assumed that Christians shared with wider Graeco-Roman society an antipathy towards Jews and Judaism, couching it in their own terms without adding anything essentially new.

From the perspective of more recent studies, however, it is apparent that this construal of the tri-cornered relationship among Hellenism, Judaism, and Christianity represents not so much an accurate historical portrayal as a retrojection into the pre-Constantinian period of the shape of the Christian victory: Hellenistic society capitulating to Christianity, and Judaism continuing in a ghetto existence on the margins. The extent to which Judaism's marginalized existence was determined by the Christian victory itself—as the church was able to use its newly-acquired political power to shunt its former rival to the periphery—was lost in the process.

This paradigm enjoyed a long reign. Even as late as 1967 Wilken could complain that Marcel Simon's *Verus Israel* [§16.29], which clearly demonstrated the centrality of the "Israel question" for Christian self-definition vis-a-vis the Graeco-Roman world, was largely ignored by church historians, the major reviews appearing elsewhere and by others. Since then, however, a significant shift has taken place, with Wilken's own work representative of—and, in no small measure, contributing to—a new approach among church historians.

Several factors can be identified as precipitating this shift. First, the early years of this century saw the beginning of a new spirit of scholarly dialogue between Jews and Christians. Jewish scholars such as C.G. Montefiore and S. Schechter labored to make Jewish sources and Jewish self-understanding accessible to Christians; Christians such as G.F. Moore, H.L. Strack and R.T. Herford [§16.13] responded with sympathetic portrayals of Judaism. Next, and building on this general scholarly base, were pioneering works devoted to the more specific topic of Christian-Jewish relations in the first few centuries of the common era. Of most significance here are the books by James Parkes (*The Conflict of the Church and the Synagogue* [§16.20]) and Marcel Simon (*Verus Israel* [§16.29]). But more than anything else, it was the awful impact of the Holocaust that forced the necessary re-evaluation of church-synagogue relationships.

In the painful search for answers to the question of how such a thing could have happened in the heart of Christian Europe, it became apparent to many that, while Naziism was not Christian, it could not have borne such bitter fruit if the soil had not been cultivated by centuries of Christian preaching against the Jews. Jules Isaac's *Jesus and Israel* (1948) was an impassioned book written while its author was in hiding and on the run from the Nazis. Its theme that Christian interpreters from the patristics to the present were consistently more anti-Jewish than the New Testament texts that they were interpreting did much to unsettle Christian consciences in this regard. Indeed, it became apparent that a straight line could be drawn back to the *adversus Judaeos* tradition of the earliest centuries, in which the Gentile church's basic stance against the synagogue was first developed. When the *adversus Judaeos* tradition was thus thrust into the center of scholarly attention, the significance of the work of Parkes and Simon began to be recognized. By the time Rosemary Ruether published her influential and controversial *Faith and Fratricide* in 1974 [16.25], the importance of Judaism for early church history and the development of Christian self-understanding was fully established.

This is not to suggest that Ruether has had the last word. Indeed, scholarly response has made it clear that, by overstating the case, her work runs the risk of a new retrojection in which the full responsibility for later Christian anti-Semitism is laid at the door of a Justin Martyr or John Chrysostom, without due sensitivity to the socio-religious situations in which these early Christians found themselves. Robert Wilken's sensitive treatment of John Chrysostom [§16.35] is a healthy corrective, and an example of the sociologically informed work that needs to be done. The bibliography below contains other examples of fruitful areas of research: the debates with Judaism in literature other than the *adversus Judaeos* tradition (e.g. Efroymsen on Tertullian §16.9); the influence of the debate with Judaism on the development of patristic theology (e.g. Wilken on Cyril §16.34); the social history of the wider Roman milieu (e.g. Meeks and Wilken on Antioch §16.16); the variety and nuance within the *adversus Judaeos* tradition itself (e.g. Neusner on Aphrahat §16.18); influence of the Christian-Jewish debate on the normative self-definition of Judaism (e.g. Sanders §16.26, Segal §16.27–16.28, Wilson §16.38). (D)

16.1   ⑨ Manns, Frederic. *Bibliographie du Judéo-Christianisme*. Preface
        by P.B. Bagatti. Studium Biblicum Franciscanum Analecta 13.
        Jerusalem: Francisan Printing Press, 1979. Pp. 265. MAI-13; B&W-
        11; BI-2; PI-1; M-1
        A French work that lists almost 2000 publications on Jewish Chris-
        tianity (up to the year 1978). It is divided into 6 sections: General
        Works on Jewish Christianity; Theology; Jewish-Christian Exegesis;
        Archaeology of Jewish Christianity; and Ambience of the Jewish
        Christians. The indexes are well conceived (Scripture; Patristic
        Citations; Geographical Terms; Symbols; Biblical Personalities; and
        Modern Authors). Even though section titles and the introduction
        are in French, many English works are listed, and most of the
        section titles can be read by an English reader without any French
        because the technical vocabularies of the two languages are so
        similar.
        ℈⊰ Vermes, *JJS* 31 (1980): 135; *RSR* 7 (1981): 73.

16.2   🏛 Conzelmann, Hans. *Gentiles/Jews/Christians: Polemics and
        Apologetics in the Graeco-Roman Era*. Translated by M. Eugene
        Boring. Minneapolis: Fortress, 1992. Pp. xxxvii + 390. B-36; SI-4;
        AAI:2; MAI:6.
        This is a substantial consideration of the primary literature on the
        place of Jews in the Graeco-Roman world, and the self-understanding
        of the various groups involved in the process of defining the rela-
        tionships with each other. Although Greek, Hebrew, and Latin are
        used, English translations are provided. Various critical questions,
        such as authenticity, date, chronology, sources, etc., are addressed,
        and the views of modern scholars are considered. Conzelmann
        divides his work into four major sections: "The Political Back-
        ground"; "The Evaluation of Judaism in Graeco-Roman Literature";
        "The Debate of Hellenistic Judaism with the Hellenistic-Roman
        World"; and "Christians and Jews from the Beginning of Christianity
        until the Time of Origen." The book is worth consideration for the
        collection of sources and the associated technical literature alone.

16.3   🏛 Stern, Menahem. *Greek and Latin Authors on Jews and Judaism*.
        Vol. 2: *From Tacitus to Simplicius*. Jerusalem: Israel Academy of
        Sciences and Humanities, 1980. Vol. 3: *Appendixes and Indexes*.
        Together with Volume 1, treating the earlier period, this represents
        the standard collection of ancient Graeco-Roman references to Jews
        and Judaism. Each entry contains a brief introduction to the ancient
        author, a bibliography of secondary literature, the texts themselves
        in Latin or Greek, and translations into English. The relevance of

the book for present purposes is not restricted to instances where authors (e.g. Celsus, Julian) also touch on Christianity. Studies of early Jewish-Christian relations need to take into account Graeco-Roman attitudes to Judaism itself, as evidenced in these texts. A complete index, together with fragments and some less certain texts, are contained in a third volume. (D)

❧ Brooke, *JSS* 31 (1987): 92-96; Efroymson, *JES* 19 (1982): 824; Kamesar, *JJS* 37 (1986): 251-252; McKleney, *CBQ* 50 (1988): 311; Runia, *VC* 39 (1985): 409-411.

16.4   Barrett, C.K. "Jews and Judaizers in the Epistles of Ignatius." In *Jews, Greeks and Christians: Essays in Honor of W.D. Davies.* Edited by R. Hamerton-Kelly and R. Scroggs. Leiden: Brill, 1976. Pp. 220-224.

The letters of Ignatius to churches in Asia, written while he was in transit to Rome to face martyrdom, offer one of the earliest, albeit obscure, post-New Testament glimpses of Christian-Jewish relationships. Barrett surveys scholarly opinion on two of the questions raised by the epistles: (1) In his denunciations of Judaizers and of Docetists, was Ignatius attacking one group, or two? (2) Do the statements of Ignatius reflect the situation in Antioch, in Asia, or both? Barrett concludes that Ignatius was addressing a single group of opponents in Asia, a strand of Hellenizing Judaism that had adopted some aspects of Christianity that they found useful. (D)

16.5   ◉ Bokser, Baruch M. "Recent Developments in the Study of Judaism. 70-200 C.E." *Second Century* 3 (1983): 1-68. B-28.

This entire issue of *The Second Century* is given to Bokser's review, and about one-half of that review is given to a detailed bibliography. Almost all of the works cited are from the 1970s or the early 1980s. Bokser provides a paragraph on other reviews of scholarship; he then divides his review into the following sections: Archaeological and Epigraphic Sources; Non-Jewish Literary Sources; Gnostic Literature; Pseudepigrapha; Josephus; the Chronicles; Mishnah and Tosefta; Midrash; Targum; Impact of the Two Revolts and of the Temple's Destruction: the Formation of Rabbinic Judaism; Composition of Early Rabbinic Judaism; Judaism, Christianity and other Graeco-Roman Cults; Charisma, Wonderworking, and Piety; Mystical and Esoteric Tradition; Political and Social History; and Comprehensive Studies of Judaism.

16.6   ☛ Callan, Terrance. *Forgetting the Root: The Emergence of Christianity from Judaism.* New York/Mahwah: Paulist, 1986. Pp. vii

+131. B-10; AAI-ll; MAI-l .

Responding to Ruether's *Faith and Fratricide* [§16.25], Callan argues that the separation of Christianity from Judaism was a gradual process, resulting not from the essential anti-Jewishness of its christology, but from the more contingent process of the "gentilization" of the Church. This process involved the decision by most of the early Jewish Church that Gentiles did not need to keep the law, the growing preponderance of such Gentiles in the Church, and the gradual disappearance of what he calls the "liberal Jewish Christians." To develop the thesis, Callan provides the reader with a helpful survey of the major streams of Christianity (Jewish and Gentile) from New Testament times through to the fourth century. (D)

✄ Rosenbaum, *JES* 25 (1988): 107; Harrington, *TS* 48 (1987): 580-581; Blasi, *RRR* 29 (1987): 78.

16.7   DeLange, N.R.M. *Origen and the Jews: Studies in Jewish-Christian Relations in Third-Century Palestine*. Cambridge: Cambridge UP, 1976. Pp. x + 240. B-7; AAI-19; I-6.

Since Origen was the first church father to devote himself to Biblical study, and since in order to place Christian study of the Bible on a firm footing he became conversant with Jews and Jewish exegetical traditions, the question of Origen's relationship with Judaism, De Lange argues, should have received more scholarly attention than it has. To make up for this neglect, De Lange subjects Origen's Caesarea period to three lines of investigation: (1) the light shed on third century Palestinian Judaism, since Origen represents virtually the only Greek source; (2) the extent to which Origen was influenced by Jewish thought and exegetical techniques; (3) the nature of the debate between Jews, Christians and pagans. (D)

16.8   ☞ Efroymson, David P. "The Patristic Connection." In *Antisemitism and the Foundations of Christianity*. Edited by Alan T. Davies. New York/Toronto: Paulist Press, 1979. Pp. 98-117.

Efroymson's article is part of an important collection of essays responding to Rosemary Ruether's *Faith and Fratricide* [§16.25]. He argues that her treatment of the *adversus Judaeos* tradition, convincing though it is, needs to be set in a wider context. His point is that patristic thinking about Judaism, which comes to concentrated expression in tractates "Against the Jews," was motivated and shaped by factors in which Judaism was involved only indirectly. He develops his point with reference to the internal threat of Marcionism and the external challenge of the Roman valuation of antiquity. (D)

16.9   Efroymson, David P. "Tertullian's Anti-Jewish Rhetoric: Guilt by
        Association," *Union Seminary Quarterly Review* 36 (1980-81): 25-
        37.
        Efroymson believes that the thesis of Simon, Ruether and others—
        that early Christianity was preoccupied with the need to define
        itself over against Judaism—has been convincingly demonstrated,
        at least with respect to the *adversus Judaeos* literature on which
        these studies have tended to concentrate. In this paper he asks
        whether it also holds true outside this narrow range of literature,
        using Tertullian as a test case. His findings are clearly affirmative:
        in two-thirds of his writings, throughout his career, and against
        every major opponent (even Marcion), Tertullian uses a rhetorical
        device in which the opposing position is shown to be in some way
        "Jewish" and therefore (this is usually taken for granted) wrong.
        (D)

16.10   Feldman, Louis H., and Gohei Hata, eds. *Josephus, Judaism, and
        Christianity.* Detroit: Wayne State UP, 1987. Pp. 448. I-11; Josephus
        Index-11.
        The survival of the writings of Josephus is due in large measure to
        the high esteem in which he was held by the church in both patristic
        and medieval periods. He was valued, by writers such as Origen,
        Eusebius, and Jerome, as much for apologetic as for historical
        reasons: his treatment of the Jewish war with Rome provided a
        historical buttress for Christian arguments concerning God's
        rejection of the Jews, especially since his friendliness to Rome and
        animosity towards the Jewish rebels was easily transposed, post-
        Constantine, into a Christian-Jewish register. For this reason, the
        third section ("Christianity") of this notable collection of scholarly
        essays on Josephus deserves mention here. (D)
        ✄ Vermes, *JJS* 41 (1990): 130-131.

16.11   Frend, W.H.C. "Early Christianity and Society: A Jewish Legacy
        in the Pre-Constantinian Era." *Harvard Theological Review* 76
        (1983): 53-71.
        A broad survey of Christian social and political attitudes from New
        Testament times through to the end of the third century. Frend
        observes that, except for a few marginal (the book of Revelation)
        or heterodox (Montanists, Donatists) cases, the church took a quietist
        stance, accepting and even sanctifying the status quo. Noting the
        continuing influence of the synagogue on the church (the separation

of the two took longer than was previously supposed), he argues
that the church in large measure took its cues on this issue from
Judaism, which exhibited a parallel range of attitudes towards the
state. (D)

16.12   Gager, John G. *The Origins of Anti-Semitism: Attitudes Towards
        Judaism in Pagan and Christian Antiquity*. New York/London:
        Oxford UP, 1983.
        Gager argues against two common assumptions concerning early
        Christian-Jewish relations: (1) that Christian anti-Judaism was
        simply a carry-over from Graeco-Roman attitudes; and (2) that
        post-70 CE Christianity was predominantly hostile to Judaism. He
        argues against (1) that through to the fourth century pagans were
        generally sympathetic, and even attracted to Judaism; and against
        (2) that early Christianity contained a much wider range of attitudes
        towards Judaism than those eventually recognized as orthodox. A
        disproportionate part of the book is given over to an elaboration of
        Gaston's "two covenant" reading of Paul. (D)
        ✂ Darling, *RSR* 11 (1985): 341-347; De Lange, *JEH* 36 (1985): 111-114;
        Droge, *JR* 66 (1986): 99-101; Everett, *JCS* 27 (1985): 525-527; Goldenberg,
        RSR 11 (1985): 335-337; Marsh, *TT* 41 (1984): 275-279; Rodd, *ExT* 95
        (1984): 225-227; Siker, *USQR* 41 (1986): 60-65; Stroumsa, *Numen* 32
        (1985): 287-289; Townsend, *ATR* 67 (1985): 183-186; Zaas, *RSR* 11 (1985):
        337-341.

16.13   Herford, R. Travers. *Christianity in Talmud and Midrash*. Clifton,
        NJ: Reference Book Publishers, 1966. (1903[1]). Pp. xvi + 449. I-6;
        BI-9; Rabbinic Index-4.
        While understandably dated, Herford's attempt to identify and
        discuss all Rabbinic references to Jesus and Christianity has not yet
        been supplanted. He begins with an introductory survey of the
        shape and spirit of Rabbinic literature, displaying a sympathetic
        attitude unusual for a Christian writer of the period. The bulk of
        the book is given over to the texts themselves, topically arranged
        under two broad headings —Jesus, and "minim" ("heretics," whom
        he identifies as Jewish Christians). In each case, he provides the
        texts in English translation (the Hebrew and Aramaic originals are
        included in an appendix), followed by his own commentary. He
        summarizes his findings in two concluding chapters. (D)

16.14   Hulen, Amos B. "The 'Dialogues with the Jews' as Sources for
        Early Jewish Arguments against Christianity." *Journal of Biblical
        Literature* 51 (1932): 58-70.
        Hulen begins by observing that the "astounding abundance" of

Christian treatises "against the Jews" is not matched by Jewish treatises "against the Christians." Nevertheless, he believes that Jews did develop coherent and cogent arguments against the Christian claims, and that the Christian "dialogues with the Jews," despite their artificiality, can still provide evidence for the Jewish counter-position. While dated (he does not recognize the extent to which the *adversus Judaeos* tradition was directed at a Roman audience), his treatment of the dialogues (Justin–Trypho, Jason–Papiscus, Gregentius–Herbanus) is sensitive and still of value. (D)

16.15   Lieu, Judith, et al. *The Jews Among Pagans and Christians in the Roman Empire*. London and New York: Routledge, 1992. Pp. xvii + 198. I-5; B&W-1; M-2; CT-2; G-1.

These eight essays come from a series of Ancient History seminars at the Institute of Classical Studies in London. The intent was to show the significant role of Judaism in the empire during the rise of the Christian movement, which is usually the focus of attention for this period. The chapters are by some of the leading scholars in the field: Rajak, "The Jewish community and its boundaries"; Hengel, "The pre-Christian Paul"; Goodman, "Jewish proselytizing in the first century"; Lieu, "History and theology in Christian views of Judaism"; Millar, "The Jews of the Graeco-Roman Diaspora between paganism and Christianity, AD 312-438"; Drijvers, "Syrian Christianity and Judaism"; Weitzman, "From Judaism to Christianity: The Syriac version of the Hebrew Bible"; North, "The development of religious pluralism."

16.16   Meeks, Wayne A.. and Robert L. Wilken. *Jews and Christians in Antioch in the First Four Centuries of the Common Era*. SBL Sources for Biblical Study 13. Missoula, MT. Scholars Press, 1978. Pp. x + 127.

The result of a fruitful collaboration between a New Testament scholar with an interest in social description (Meeks) and a historian specializing in Christian-Jewish relationships in the first Christian centuries (Wilken), interests which converge naturally in Antioch. While the book begins with a stimulating social history of Jewish and Christian existence in Antioch from Paul to John Chrysostom, its primary purpose is to provide resources for further study. The major portion of the book, then, is given over to fresh translations of such resource material: inscriptions; nine letters of the fourth century rhetorician Libanius, together with his oration on patronage; and Chrysostom's homilies against the Jews. (D)

ℬ Aune, *CBQ* 42 (1980): 276; Barrett, *ExT* 91 (1979): 25; Darling, *CH*

49 (1980): 204-205; Greenwood, *TS* 40 (1979): 743-744; Osiek, *JES* 17 (1980): 690-691.

16.17   Meyers, Eric M., and James F. Strange. *Archaeology, the Rabbis and Early Christianity*. Nashville: Abingdon, 1981. Pp. 207. I-7; B-1; B&W-13; CT-l; M-l. G-4.

A translation and study of those sections of the demonstrations of Although this volume contains a chart of Palestinian history from 523 BCE to 400 CE, it primarily discusses Palestinian archaeology as a supplement to literary sources in the first Christian centuries. Besides dealing with the cultural setting of Judaism in Galilee and the broader context of Christianity throughout Palestine, the authors give important information about such matters as the languages of Roman Palestine, Jewish burial practices and view of the afterlife, and evidences of early Christian churches and Jewish synagogues. Maps and illustrations are included to aid the reader. (D)

✃ Bruce, *ExT* 93 (1982)): 122; Collins, *CBQ* 45 (1983): 663-664; De Lange, *JT* 34 (1983): 621-622; Groh, *ATR* 64 (1982): 393-399; Mare, *JETS* 25 (1982): 114-115; Sigel, *JBL* 102 (1983): 482-483; Silberman, *BA* 46 (1983): 125-126; Storvick, *Interpretation* 37 (1983): 314; Wiseman, *Churchman* 96 (1982): 57-58.

16.18   Neusner, Jacob. *Aphrahat and Judaism, The Christian-Jewish Argument in Fourth Century Iran*. Leiden: E. J. Brill, 1971. Pp. xiii + 265. I-12; Bible and Talmud Index- 9.

A translation and study of those sections of the demonstrations of Aphrahat (Aphraates) dealing with Judaism. Neusner demonstrates the striking contrast between the Greek and Latin *adversus Judaeos* tradition, and the style of argumentation used by Aphrahat: viz. serious attention to the opinions of actual Jewish interlocutors; arguments based on texts and methods of interpretation accepted by both parties; reliance on the literal sense of the scriptures and not on typological and allegorical readings convincing only to Christians. Consequently, he judges this Persian monk to be "the worthiest participant in the Jewish-Christian dialogue put forth in antiquity by either side" (p. 244). (D)

✃ Stott, *Churchman* 86 (1972): 136.

16.19   Neusner, Jacob. *Judaism and Christianity in the Age of Constantine: History, Messiah, Israel and the Initial Confrontation*. Chicago/ London: University of Chicago Press, 1987. Pp. xv + 246; B-5; AAI-6; I-4.

Neusner argues that with the conversion of Constantine, Judaism found it necessary for the first time to reply seriously to the Christian claim. The fourth century, then, represents a unique moment in the

Christian-Jewish relationship, in that both sides engaged for the first time in a serious intellectual confrontation, whose outcome shaped the relationship between the two in the West up to the present. Neusner thus argues against those who interpret Judaism in this period as largely unconcerned with and unaffected by the claims and success of the church. The three main sections of the book take up the three central issues in the debate as Neusner sees them: (1) the meaning of Israel's history; (2) the Messiah; (3) the identification of Israel. (D)

✴ Armstrong, *CH* 57 (1988): 520-522; Baskin, *TT* 45 (1989): 494-495; Bonner, *Theology* 92 (1989): 54-56; H. Chadwick, *TLSuppl* 4453 (Aug 5-11 1988): 866; Hinson, *R&E* 87 (1990): 349-350; Lange, *JEH* 40 (1989): 617; Livermore, *CSR* 19 (1990): 303-304; McCullough, *JAAR* 56 (1988): 810-812; Siker, *Horizons* 15 (1988): 388-389; Stemberger, *JSJ* 19 (1988): 252-253; Wild, *TS* 49 (1988): 576-577.

16.20   Parkes, James. *The Conflict of the Church and the Synagogue: A Study in the Origins of Antisemitism.* New York: Atheneum, 1985. (1934[1]). Pp. xviii + 430; BI-2; AAI-11; I-11.
Prompted by the author's experience of European antisemitism as a relief worker after World War I, this study represents the first detailed scholarly recognition that the roots of modern antisemitism are to be found not in the medieval period, nor in a generic reaction to Jewish "clannishness," but in the attitudes towards Judaism developed within the church as it separated from the synagogue and attempted to make its way in the Roman world. The book documents the social situation of Jews and Judaism from the Roman period to Visigothic Spain, making its major contribution in its ground-breaking treatment of the patristic period. (D)

16.21   ☛ Parkes, James. "Jews and Christians in the Constantinian Empire." In *Studies in Church History.* Vol. 1. Edited by C.W. Dugmore and C. Duggan. London: Thomas Nelson, 1964. Pp. 69-79.
Those who have read Parkes' longer work [§16.20] will find nothing new here. For those who have not read it, though, this article serves as a useful summary of some of its main themes: (1) the unique nature of Christian anti-Judaism; (2) the origin in the earliest centuries of the attitudes that shaped Christian anti-Judaism up until the twentieth century; (3) the conflict over the possession of the Old Testament as the source and occasion of these attitudes; (4) the decisive significance of the fourth century Christianization of the Empire, resulting in the gradual reshaping of social legislation in conformity with these attitudes. (D)

16.22   Pritz, Ray A. *Nazarene Jewish Christianity, From the End of the
         New Testament Period until its Disappearance in the Fourth Century.*
         Leiden: E.J. Brill/ Jerusalem: Magnes Press (Hebrew University),
         1988. Pp. 153; AAI-7; MAI-3; BI-2; SI-4; B-6.
         A collection and analysis of the evidence for the Nazarenes, with
         particular emphasis on the writings of Epiphanius and Jerome, and
         on the Gospel according to the Hebrews. Pritz also discusses the
         name of the group, and provides three appendixes—one on the
         historicity of the Pella tradition.

16.23   Rokeah, David. *Jews, Pagans and Christians in Conflict.* Studia
         Post-Biblica 33; Jerusalem Magnes Press/Leiden: Brill, 1982. Pp.
         232.
         A study of debates among Jews, pagans and Christians, as reflected
         in representative pieces of literature. Rokeah's thesis is that until
         mid-2nd century CE, Jews were actively engaged in disputes,
         attempting to win others to their point of view; after, their direct
         involvement diminishes, and they appear more as grist for pagan
         and Christian mills. This is an older position, one seriously called
         into question by Simon [§16.29] and others. The value of the book
         is also limited by a tendency to blend disparate literature into an
         artificial homogenization. Nevertheless, it provides a useful intro-
         duction to a wide range of literature. (D)
         ℁ Attridge, *CBQ* 46 (1984): 362-363; Eron, *JES* 24 (1987): 308-309;
         Neusner, *JQR* 74 (1984): 313-320.

16.24   Ruether, Rosemary Radford. "Judaism and Christianity: Two Fourth
         Century Religions." *Studies in Religion / Sciences Religieuses* 2
         (1972): 1-10 .
         While the self-identifying story of Christianity begins with Jesus,
         and that of Judaism with Moses, Ruether argues that the classical
         form of both religions did not emerge until the fourth century. The
         bulk of the article, though, is devoted to a presentation of the
         contrasts between the two: in social structure (Christianity: cen-
         tralized, hierarchical, cultic; Judaism: decentralized, democratic,
         non- sacerdotal); ideals of holiness (withdrawal from the world;
         sanctification of all of life); boundary maintenance (state-enforced
         orthodoxy; communal solidarity in orthopraxis), and so on. The
         irony, she asserts, is that Christianity continues to assert its superiority
         over Judaism, even as it struggles to reform itself in directions that
         have characterized Judaism all along. (D)

16.25   Ruether, Rosemary Radford. *Faith and Fratricide: The Theological*

Roots of Anti-Semitism. Minneapolis: Seabury, 1974. Pp. ix + 294. BI-5; AI -3.

An epoch-making book, forcing the topic of Christianity and anti-Semitism onto the agenda of Biblical and theological scholarship. Her thesis is that, since Christianity's assertions about Christ are necessarily paired with negations about Judaism, Christianity is anti-Judaic at its center, inevitably becoming anti-Semitic whenever the Church has social and political power. While she covers a broader area than is of interest here (Graeco-Roman world, New Testament, medieval Christendom), her treatment of the *adversus Judaeos* material from the patristic period constitutes the longest, and most convincing, portion of the book. (D)

>< Armentrout, *StLJT* 20 (1977): 233-235; De Ridder, *CTJ* 11 (1976): 102-105; Hare, *RSR* 2 (1976): 19-21; Miller, *JCS* 18 (1976): 355-358; Ryan, *JES* 12 (1975): 603; Wilken, *ATR* 59 (1977): 354-356.

16.26   Sanders, E.P. et al., eds. *Jewish and Christian Self-Definition.* Philadelphia: Fortress. Volume One: *The Shaping of Christianity in the Second and Third Centuries* (1980); Pp. 314; B-19; AI-8; API-14. Volume Two: *Aspects of Judaism in the Greco-Roman Period* (1981); Pp. 485; B-30; AI-13; AAI-23. Volume Three: *Self-Definition in the Greco-Roman World* (1982); Pp. 295; B-22; MAI-10; AAI-21.

These volumes contain papers presented by an international array of scholars at symposia sponsored by McMaster University (Hamilton, Ontario), as part of a five-year research project dealing with the emergence of Christianity and Rabbinic Judaism. In particular, the project concerned itself with the process by which both groups developed from a situation of flux and diversity in the first century to a more narrowly defined self-understanding by the early third. While not all of the articles deal directly with topics relevant to the concerns of this bibliography, the project as a whole is based on the assumption that in its process of "normative self-definition," each group was affected by the other. The bibliographies alone render this work highly valuable. (D)

>< Armstrong, *JTS* 36 (1985): 470-471; Clark, *RSR* 11 (1985): 129-133; Countryman, *SC* 1 (1981): 113-115; De Lange, *JEH* 33 (1982): 111-114; 449-451; Efroymson, *Horizons* 8 (1981): 378-380; Finn, *JR* 64 (1984): 111-114; Goulder, *JSNT* 18 (1983): 123-126; Grant, *JR* 65 (1985): 274-275; Halperin, *RSR* 11 (1985): 133-136; Hayman, *SJT* 35 (1982): 377-379; Hoffmann, *JES* 21 (1984): 501-502; Horbury, *JTS* 33 (1982): 273-275; Horbury, *JTS* 34 (1983): 581-584; Kraabel, *Interpretation* 36 (1982): 68-71; Kraabel, *Dialog* 23 (1984): 76-77; Lienhard, *TS* 45 (1984): 174-175; Neusner, *SC* 1 (1981): 245-247; O'Neil, *SC* 4 (1984): 117-118; Richardson, *SR* 12 (1983): 98-100; Saldarini, *Interpretation* 37 (1983): 310-312; Yamauchi, *JETS* 26 (1983): 229-231.

16.27   Segal, Alan F. *Two Powers in Heaven: Early Rabbinic Reports about Christianity and Gnosticism.* Leiden: Brill, 1977. Pp. xxiv + 313. BI-5; I-12.
A detailed investigation of rabbinic polemic against belief in "two powers in heaven," and of the groups that may have been the targets of such polemic. Segal demonstrates that before such language was used with reference to the *opposing* divine entities of the Gnostics, it was applied to *complementary* divine roles assigned to Christ by the church, and (earlier still) to principal angels or hypostatic manifestations of one sort or another, within marginal Jewish circles. For present purposes the book is of interest for the light it sheds on rabbinic perceptions of Christianity, and of the role played by christology in Jewish opposition to the Christian movement. (D)
✂ Fallon, *JAAR* 49 (1981): 142; Gaylord, *JSJ* 10 (1979): 234-235; Hedrick, *JBL* 99 (1980): 638-639; Lightstone, *SR* 10 (1981): 494; Quispel, *VC* 33 (1979): 86-87.

16.28   ☛ Segal, Alan F. *Rebecca's Children: Judaism and Christianity in the Roman World.* Cambridge, MA/London: Harvard UP, 1986. Pp. viii + 207. BI-2; I-9.
While its scope (200 BCE–200 CE) overlaps only partially with the period of the early church, this stimulating and readable book deserves to be included here. Combining current sociological and anthropological insights with sensitive readings of the primary material, Segal traces the parallel emergence of the "twin brothers" of Christianity and Rabbinic Judaism. He emphasizes their common parentage in the sectarianism of the later Second Temple period; the mutually formative influence of their fraternal dispute over the family birthright; and their distinctive ways of appropriating the family heritage as they each developed a view of their place in the wider world. (D)
✂ Alder, *JES* 25 (1988): 293-294; Cohen, *AHR* 93 (1988): 129-130; Eisen, *CRBR* 1 (1988): 43-60; Kee, *JBL* 107 (1988): 317-319; O'Toole, *TS* 48 (1987): 347-348; Overman, *TT* 45 (1989): 512-513; Fernandes, *JSJ* 18 (1987): 252-254; Quispel, *VC* 42 (1988): 100-101; Richardson, *RS* 16 (1987): 498; Sanders, *JTS* 39 (1988): 581-584; Schwartz, *BA* 52 (1988): 43-45; Sherman, *JR* 67 (1987): 369-370; Visotzky, *USQR* 42 (1988): 64-67.

16.29   Simon, Marcel. *Verus Israel: A Study of the Relations between Christians and Jews in the Roman Empire.* Edited by H. McKeating. Oxford: Oxford UP, 1986. (1948[1]). Pp. xviii + 533. B-14; I-7.
First published (in French) in 1948, and reissued in 1969 (with a 32 page postscript), this masterful survey has not yet been surpassed in English. Simon studies the developing Christian attitude toward

Judaism in the period between the defeat of Bar Cochba, which coincides with the emergence of Church and Synagogue as separate entities, and the Theodosian Code, which crystallized the Church's triumph over Judaism in legislative form. His basic assumption, widely accepted now but unusual in 1948, is that far from retreating from active participation in the Hellenistic world after 70 CE, Judaism continued to represent an active, and attractive, rival to Christianity. It is in this context, Simon contends, that the *adversus Judaeos* tradition needs to be understood. (D)

⊱ Horbury, *Theology* 90 (1987): 142-143; Krentz, *Currents* 15 (1988): 209-210; Werblowski, *Numen* 35 (1988): 142.

16.30   Smallwood, E. Mary. *The Jews under Roman Rule: From Pompey to Diocletian.* Leiden: Brill, 1976. Pp. xviii + 595. I-21; M-3; FT-1.

The standard treatment of Jewish political history within the Roman empire in the pre-Constantinian period. Her choice of a *terminus ad quem*—the first Christian emperor, whose conversion ensured that "the official attitude of the Roman government towards Judaism was bound to shift eventually from one of benevolence to one of repression" (p. 543)—indicates the extent to which her study of the Jews in the Roman empire is shaped by the growing importance of a third party in the relationship, i.e. the Christians. Significant aspects of this tri-partite relationship are treated authoritatively as they come up. (D)

⊱ Rajak, *JJS* 28 (1977): 207-208; Saldarini, *CBQ* 40 (1978): 283-284.

16.31   Walzer, R. *Galen on Jews and Christians.* London: Oxford UP, 1949. Pp. 101. I-3.

In contrast to the ridicule and hostility common in early Roman references to Christianity, Galen (c. 129-199 CE) is notable for the fairness and irenic spirit of his comments; even his criticisms reflect a desire to understand the other, and to give credit where it is due. The fact that he also mentions Judaism, sometimes in connection with Christianity, means that he provides an important window into the climate of opinion in which Christianity attempted to frame its apologetic *adversus Judaeos*. In this book, Walzer discusses all Galen's references to Jews and Christians, including those preserved only in Arabic sources. Despite its date, it is still a valuable study. (D)

⊱ R.M. Grant, *ATR* 32 (1950): 163-164; Kilpatrick, *JTS* 1 (1950): 189-190.

16.32   Wilde, Robert. *The Treatment of the Jews in the Greek Christian*

Writers of the First Three Centuries. Washington, DC: Catholic University of America Press, 1949. Pp. xviii + 239. I-7; B-5.

Originally a doctoral dissertation, this book is largely a detailed *ad seriatum* description of the discussion of Judaism in the writings delimited in the title. While not without critical perspective and analytical insight, the book is representative of an older, apologetic approach: the Graeco-Roman world was largely hostile to the Jews; Christians shared in the "general hostility toward the Jews" (p. 231), differing from their pagan neighbors only in the (theological) content of their anti-Judaism; the Christian critique of Judaism was largely correct. Still, a handy introduction to the literature surveyed. (D)

16.33 ☛ Wilken, Robert L. "Judaism in Roman and Christian Society." *Journal of Religion* 47 (1967): 313-330.

In his various writings (see also the following entries), Wilken has sought to demonstrate that church historians have failed to recognize the importance of Judaism for the development of Christian thought. The patristic writers produced literature "against the Jews" not only because they inherited a debate with the synagogue from the early church; and not only because the Romans raised questions about their relationship with Judaism; but also (he argues) because Judaism continued to be a vital force and an attractive alternative in the Roman world. But history is written by the winners, and the church's victory over Judaism was so complete that the crucial nature of the church's relationship with the synagogue has become obscured. This early article sets the stage for Wilken's later work by first sketching this thesis, and then showing how the differing anti-Judaism of the Christians (thoroughgoing, theologically based), as compared to that of the Romans (ad hoc, socially based), produced a progressive deterioration of the social status of the Jews in the post-Constantine period. (D)

16.34 Wilken, Robert L. *Judaism and the Early Christian Mind: A Study of Cyril of Alexandria's Exegesis and Theology.* New Haven/London: Yale UP, 1971. Pp. xiv + 257. B-17; I-6; BI-2; Greek Index-1.

The first of two studies of representative figures in the leading centres of eastern Christianity (for Antioch, see next entry). Previous assessments of Cyril's importance have tended to focus on the christological debates with Nestorius, dismissing his extensive exegetical writings, with their harsh denunciations of Judaism, as insignificant. Wilken argues that this results from an over-estimation of the influence of Hellenism on patristic thought, and an underestimation of that of Judaism. Wilken argues that Judaism was still an attractive option in fifth century Alexandria, that this socio-historical situation influenced Cyril's exegesis, and that both factors influenced his christology. (D)

❧ Edwards, *ATR* 54 (1972): 42-43; Eno, *CBQ* 33 (1971): 623-624.

16.35 Wilken, Robert L. *John Chrysostom and the Jews: Rhetoric and Reality in the Late Fourth Century.* Berkeley/Los Angeles/London: University of California Press, 1983. Pp. xvii + 190; MAI-2; SI-4; B-19.

A study of a series of sermons preached by John Chrysostom over a two year period in late fourth century Antioch. Drawing on a wide array of evidence, Wilken argues that the harsh polemic of these sermons is understandable (though not defensible) given the context: the continuing vitality and appeal of Judaism in the Roman world, with even a troubling number of Christians participating in Jewish ritual and community. While acknowledging Chrysostom's influence on later Christian anti-Judaism, he maintains that "too much of the later unhappy history of Jewish-Christian relations has been projected...onto John Chrysostom" (p. xvi). (D)

❧ Clark, *CH* 53 (1984): 527-528; Cohn-Sherbok, *JAAR* 54 (1986): 200; Darling, *RSR* 11 (1985): 341-347; De Lang, *JEH* 36 (1985): 140; Droge, *JR* 67 (1987): 541-542; Efroymson, *JES* 22 (1985): 796-797; Geller-Nathanson, *JQR* 75 (1985) 408-410; Kelly, *JTS* 36 (1985): 483-484; Papademetriou, *GOTR* 31 (1986): 437-440; Seaver, *AHR* 89 (1984): 1059-1060; Sigal, *Judaism* 35 (1986): 243-247; Stroumsa, *Numen* 32 (1985): 287-289; Zaas, *RSR* 11 (1985): 337-341.

16.36 Wilken, Robert L. *The Christians as the Romans Saw Them.* New Haven/ London: Yale UP, 1984. Pp. xix + 214. B-3; I-9.

The scope of this book is much broader than Christian-Jewish relations. But given the increasing recognition that Christian attitudes towards Judaism were in significant measure formed in response to Graeco-Roman criticism, a study such as this one is of intrinsic importance. The fact that Wilken has also made important contributions to the narrower topic of Christian-Jewish relations (see other entries) makes this book especially significant. His treatments of Galen, Celsus, Porphyry and Julian are of particular value. (D)

❧ Achtemeier, *Interpretation* 40 (1986): 219-220; Boer, *VC* 39 (1985): 86-90; Bruce, *CSR* 15 (1986): 196-197; Clark, *TT* 41 (1984): 342-346; Crook, *JEH* 37 (1986): 140; Ferngren, *Fides et Historia* 18 (1986): 65-71; Finn, *SC* 4 (1984): 243-245; Frend, *CR* 37 (1987): 124; Garnsey, *JTS* 36 (1985): 481-483; Groh, *ATR* 67 (1985): 187-190; Hall, *Theology* 88 (1985): 240-242; Martin, *JAAR* 53 (1985): 319-320; Mueller, *SA* 47 (1986): 267-270; Wild, *BAR* 11.5 (1985): 18-19; Williams, *CH* 53 (1984): 526-527.

16.37   Williams, A. Lukyn. *Adversus Judaeos: A Bird's-Eye View of Christian Apologiae until the Renaissance.* Cambridge: Cambridge UP, 1935. Pp. xvii + 428. I-8; A-1; BI-3.

An oft-cited descriptive survey of (extant and non-extant) treatises devoted to a discussion of Judaism. While mildly critical in places— Williams recognizes the lack of probative value in typological exegesis, for example—the book bears the marks of its origin in classes training men [sic] for Christian missionary work among Jews: a tone bordering on hagiography; an acceptance of the basic validity of the Christian assessment of Judaism; despite an awareness of James Parkes' work, an assumption that the primary motivation behind this literature was the conversion of Jews. Still valuable as a catalogue of relevant literature. (D)

16.38   Wilson, Stephen G., ed. *Anti-Judaism in Early Christianity. Vol. 2: Separation and Polemic.* Studies in Christianity and Judaism 2. Waterloo: Wilfrid Laurier UP, 1986. Pp. xi + 185. NI-5; BI-2; NTI-2; PI-3.

A selection of papers from the last two years of a five-year seminar held annually (ending in 1982) at the meetings of the Canadian Society of Biblical Studies. The collection covers the period from 70–200 CE. The general sense left by the articles is that Christian attitudes to Jews were complex and diverse, leaving no simple explanation. Barnabas, Ignatius, Marcion, Justin, and Melito are considered from the Christian side. Two chapters deal with the Jewish side. The summary article by Lloyd Gaston focuses the primary issues for the continuing discussion. (D)

᠅ Campbell, *Christian Jewish Relations* 20 (1987): 61-64; Desjardins, *SR* 16 (1987): 364-366; Kraabel, *CBQ* 50 (1988): 351-353; Kraemer, *JES* 25 (1988): 628-629; Thrall, *ExT* 98 (1987): 350.

17
MONASTICISM AND ASCETICISM

The deserts of Egypt and Syria provided a refuge for some Christians who found life intolerable or life-threatening in the cities. At first, Christians discovered in these isolated areas a place of security from the brutal persecutions of the anti-Christian emperors and from the general decay of the cities and their infrastructures as the third century was coming to a close. These secluded people were to become one of the important sources for Christian monasticism. Indeed, the word "monk" is related to the Greek word "monos," meaning "only." Thus it is an ideal word to describe people who had isolated themselves from society and lived alone in the desert.

But the move to the desert was only a trickle during the final years of the anti-Christian Roman empire compared to the flow that was to occur *after* the conversion of Constantine and the establishment of imperial patronage for the church. This needs explanation. The church was now at peace; Christians were safe—and not only safe, but favored. Why would any Christian want to flee those conditions after having endured the disadvantages and threats that Christians often experienced in a hostile and consciously anti-Christian empire? The answer to that question may get at the heart of the monastic motivation and mentality.

Not every Christian was happy with the changes in the church that had occurred with the conversion of Constantine. Some Christians found it impossible to reconcile the disadvantaged, persecuted, minority status of the church in its first three centuries with its new status as the privileged and pampered imperial religion. Thus it was possible, depending on what one chose to focus on in the conversion of the empire, to speak of a "fall" of the church at the very point that it had been made the favorite of the emperor.

Sometimes the disappointment with the new Christian empire was so great that whole areas opted out of the imperial church, as in North Africa with the Donatists (though there was a complex of factors involved in that decision). The problem of schism became more serious as the eastern and western churches went their separate ways, and the Eastern church became more Greek and Byzantine, sometimes suppressing diverse forms of Christianity within its sphere. Many of the theologically distinctive movements in the east "opted out" of the imperial church, creating national or indigenous churches, which were viewed as schismatic by the imperial authorities, and as a result of that judgment, were often the object of persecution.

But there was another way to "opt out" of the imperial church. An individual, uncomfortable with some aspect of the new church-state alliance, could separate himself or herself from the regular routine of society and church, and move to the deserts (or often, to the periphery of towns) to engage in more fulltime and rigorous spiritual exercises. In other words, the discontented could become monks. This "opting out" did not necessarily imply a rejection of the imperial church. A whole range of relationships with the organized church existed for such people in the early years of the rather amorphous and varied monastic movement. Monasticism offered a means to put some distance between society (now "Christian" at least in name) and those who believed that the new alliance had harmful and polluting consequences.

For such discontented or spiritually-motivated people, several things in the Christian empire caused concern. For one thing, the change from persecuted to favored status was a difficult one for a movement that had, to some extent, defined itself positively in terms of persecution and disadvantage. The "world" and the "church" had been two clearly distinct entities, more often than not in some sort of tension. We might say that the church had a clear vision of the "them" and the "us," and the "them" was the empire. But that distinction was considerably weakened when the empire became Christian. The "world" had eradicated the formal boundaries of separation between themselves and the Christians, allowing Christians to become regular members of their society. It was expected that the church would return the favor by allowing the "world" (i.e. the society) into the church. That is not to say that the normal mechanisms by which a person became a member of the church had to be discarded; clearly, however, the church was under new pressures as more and more people wanted to follow the emperor into the church, having found that the church no longer represented "disadvantage" but "advantage." There was some question in the minds of the older Christians who had suffered for the "Name"—what was it that was actually attracting some of these new converts into the church? Was it merely the thing to do in an empire now sympathetic to the Christian cause? Those who perceived that there was a decline in rigor in the church by the influx of pagans often sought some structure where the old rigor would be the norm.

Histories of early monasticism focus on Egypt and usually give a prominence to Anthony and Pachomius. According to this widely accepted view of the development of monasticism, Anthony provided the initial form: that of the hermit, who was separated from society (holy or otherwise) except for brief contacts with groups of disciples. This form of monasticism is called "anchorite," meaning to withdraw or retire. It was followed by a communal form of monasticism, called "coenobitic" or "cenobitic," that emphasized the "common" life. From these sources come both the rich Syrian monasticism and the Eastern form, structured by Basil, and the western form, contributed to by people like Augustine and structured finally by Benedict, whose rule still holds a prominent place in monasteries in the west.

Philip Rousseau [§17.18] reminds us that such a history may be more orderly than the forces at work in the period could ever allow. For one thing, the roots of monasticism did not start with Anthony and Pachomius; the roots were older and drawn from a variety of pagan and Jewish sources, as well as from reflection on the Bible itself. Further, tidy lines of development fail to show that the primary alternative views were, in fact, contemporary in the earlier period—they are competing views, not successive parts of some linear development. Further, the sources that we have for the history of early monasticism are problematic, and they may reflect more what monasticism came to be than what it was in its earliest days. Possibly, too, they offer an idealized view, unconsciously perhaps, due to the nature of some of the literature, such as biography and monastic rules.

Whatever the real history of the development of monasticism and whatever the most accurate way to account for its influence, once monasticism developed, the church had a new set of problems. The first issue to be settled was the relationship between the monastics of the desert and the clergy of the churches of the cities, towns, and countryside. The monastics were isolated; the clergy were not. Yet the sacramental character of the church and the indispensable role of an *ordained* clergy seem to have already reached a fairly developed stage by this time (as is made clear by a document such as *The Apostolic Tradition* of St. Hippolytus of Rome). Did the monks need the clergy? Should they themselves seek ordination? From their perspective, the clergy might wonder what role the monastics could play, since the clergy themselves were supposedly meeting the spiritual and often the material needs of the people.

The clergy had reason to be concerned. They knew from past experience that the laity could easily hold unordained members in special awe, as was the case with the martyrs and the confessors. But since martyrdom was no longer a possibility in a Christian empire, some monastics counted their asceticism as a "living martyrdom," and a few of the monks attracted huge followings of religious expectants, who apparently were not turning to their bishops and priests, for whatever reason.

But rather than becoming competing forces of religious authority, the two groups frequently pooled their resources, with monks becoming bishops (often against their wishes) and with the bishops looking for monastic support in some of the heated theological debates or in the suppression of paganism. The latter is perhaps the monks' most colorful and violent role, though they were to play a crucial part in the expansion and preservation of the church throughout its history.

17.1 ⋔ Chadwick, Owen, ed. *Western Asceticism.* The Library of Christian Classics 12. London: SCM, 1958. Pp. 368. B-2; I-3; BI-3.

Chadwick provides a 20-page general introduction to the roots of asceticism and monasticism in the early church, after which he gives translations of *The Sayings of the Fathers, The Conferences of Cassian,* and *The Rule of Saint Benedict.* All three texts help to show the nature of the discipline of monastic life and the various motivations that drove people to these kinds of solitudes. Brief introductions are offered to these texts. Notes are kept to a bare minimum, and generally consist of references to a scriptural parallel. A 23-page appendix on *The Sayings of the Fathers* provides textual notes, usually commenting on the Latin used in the original.

✂ Cameron, *ExT* 71 (1960): 168-169; Routley, *SJT* 12 (1959): 443-444.

17.2 ⋔ Russell, Norman, trans. *The Lives of the Desert Fathers.* Introduction by Benedicta Ward. The Historia Monachorum in Aegypto. London: A.R. Mowbray/ Kalamazoo: Cistercian, 1980. Pp. x + 181. SI-8; NPI-7; T-2; M-1; B-3; CT-2.

Ward's 46-page introduction to the *Historia Monarchorum,* an account of a trip in 394 CE into the deserts of Egypt by seven monks from Palestine, is very useful, and adds much to this volume of primary texts. Besides addressing textual questions, Ward discusses almost every aspect of monastic life in Egypt. Included are 15 pages of notes on the text, 16 pages showing the differences between the Latin text (Rufinus) and the Greek text, and 4 pages on the Syriac version.

✂ Chrysostomos, *GOTR* 26 (1981): 361-362; Doran, *Speculum* 57 (1982): 655-656; Hanson, *CH* 52 (1983): 202; Sherrard, *JEH* 33 (1982): 646; Ware, *Sobornost* 6 (1984): 100-102;

17.3 ⋔ Van Bavel, Tarsicus J. *The Rule of Saint Augustine: Masculine and Feminine Versions.* Translated by Raymond Canning. London: Darton, Longman & Todd, 1984. Pp. v + 120.

Augustine composed a rule for communal religious life about the year 397 CE. This Rule is important because, though there were earlier rules in the east (e.g. Pachomius, Basil, and others), Augustine was the first to produce a Rule for the west. Benedict's famous Rule is well over a century later. Van Bavel has supplied a 6-page

introduction, and two-thirds of the book consists of his commentary
on the rule itself. The text of the rule takes up only 28 pages in the
versions for men and for women combined. Canning offers a fresh
English translation of the rule from the Latin.

17.4 🏛 Veilleux, Armand, trans. *Pachomian Koinonia.* Forward by
Aldabert de Vogüé. Introduction by Veilleux. Kalamazoo: Cistercian
Publications. Cisterian Studies 45-47 Volume I: *The Life of St.
Pachomius and his Disciples.* (1980). Pp. xxx + 493. I-5; NI-5;
BI-30; NTI-31; CT-8; T-1; M-1. Volume II: *Pachomian Chronicles
and Rules* (1981). Pp. iii + 239. B-12. Volume III: *Pachomian
Koinonia. Instructions, Letters, and Other Writings of Saint Pachomius and his Disciples.* (1982). Pp. ix + 313. B-13.
Pachomius played a critical role in harnessing monastic life in such
a way that this new institution, though seemingly peripheral and
isolated, became at times the instrument by which the church was
able to survive grave crises. This he did by gathering the monastic
zeal into a communal structure. Out of this community, a rule for
monastic living was established, providing a template for other
rules that would follow. Veilleux provides a wealth of primary
materials, ranging widely, from biographical writing about the
founder of the movement to the regulations of the society he created,
to personal correspondence.
✄ Yanney, *CCR* 5 (1984): 34-35; Peifer, *Worship* 57 (1983): 164-166;
Schatkin, *Speculum* 57 (1982): 948-949; Schatkin, *Speculum* 59 (1984):
990-991; Brother Syavos, *StVTQ* 27 (1983): 61-64

17.5 🏛 Ward, Benedicta, trans. *The Sayings of the Desert Fathers. The
Alphabetical Collection.* Foreword by Metropolitan Anthony.
London: A.R. Mowbray / Kalamazoo: Cistercian, 1975. Pp. xviii +
228. I-6; B-3; NPI-3; CT-2.
A translation of the *Apophthegmata Patrum,* arranged about the
end of the sixth century, and preserving saying of monks over a
300-year period. Each saying usually has a brief biographical note.
With a 2-page glossary and a 7-page cross referenced index to
volumes V and VI of *Vitae Patrum* (Rosweyde), this serves as a
useful sourcebook for English readers.
✄ Slade, *Theology* 79 (1976): 116-117.

17.6 🏛 Ward, Benedicta. *Harlots of the Desert: A Study of Repentance
in Early Monastic Sources.* Kalamazoo, MI: Cistercian Publications,
1987. Pp. ix + 113. I-3.

Largely a selection of primary texts, with detailed introductory
discussions, of five prostitutes who became Christian converts, and
whose lives were the subject of popular accounts read by monks.
The women considered are: Mary Magdalene, Mary of Egypt,
Pelagia, Thaïs, and Maria the niece of Abraham. Augustine's account
of his conversion is used as an introductory model. Ward sympa-
thetically explains why this literature was popular with the monks,
and offers a sketch of attitudes to prostitution, though much of this
discussion deals with a period beyond the scope of our bibliography.
>< Brock, *New Blackfriars* 69 (1988): 303; Cameron, *JEH* 40 (1989):
586-589; Johnson, *CHR* 75 (1989): 471-472; Watson, *CCR* 9 (1988): 57-60;
Wemple, *Speculum* 65 (1990): 777-778.

17.7 🏛 Wimbush, Vincent L., ed. *Ascetic Behavior in Greco-Roman
Antiquity: A Sourcebook.* Minneapolis: Studies in Antiquity &
Christianity. Fortress, 1990. Pp. xxviii + 514. I-5; AAI-9; B&W-7;
BI-9; B-4; CT-19; M-7; Foreign Words Index-2.
This is a collection of 28 chapters, by different authors, with each
chapter dealing with a passage or document. Largely, it provides in
English translation a wide range of primary literature, most of it
Christian. Brief introductions (1-3 pages) are given for each chapter;
a few notes also are provided but these are generally brief, though
some authors have provided quite detailed comments. Each chapter
has roughly a half-page bibliography. An 11-page introduction to
the volume highlights some of the major issues. A useful collection
of texts in English.

17.8 Brown, Peter. "The Rise and the Function of the Holy Man in Late
Antiquity." *Journal of Roman Studies* 61 (1971): 80-101. *Society
and the Holy in Late Antiquity.* London: Faber & Faber, 1982. Pp.
103-152
One of the fundamental modern articles on the religious landscape
of the late Antique world—a miniature *tour de force* which single-
handedly provoked a rush of interest in, and work on, apparently
marginal figures such as the holy man. Brown's approach, which
focused renewed interest in these penumbral figures of the late
Antique world, was based on functionalist explanations derived
from anthropological models (Mary Douglas, yet again). As Brown
points out, the hagiographical accounts of these figures provide the
social historian with most of what they know of the life of average
persons in the eastern empire. What Brown wished to do was to
explain why the figure of the "holy man" came to have such an
important functional role. In attempting to answer this question, he

eschewed the easy and convenient form of crude functional explanation (e.g., the holy man as one who was able to perform spectacular feats of political intervention), choosing instead to try to explain why it was at this time (the fifth and sixth centuries) and in this place (Syria—the province of "ascetic stars") that holy men became so prominent. Brown ends his study on the concentration of forces on these men as "allayers of anxiety" with a demonstration of how their efflorescence "marked out Late Antiquity as a distinct phase of religious history." To understand the peculiar presence of "the holy man" in this place and time, therefore, becomes a key to understanding one of the great transformations of the ancient world. (S)

17.9   Chitty, Derwas J. *The Desert a City: An Introduction to the Study of Egyptian and Palestinian Monasticism Under the Christian Empire.* Oxford: Blackwell, 1966. Reprint. Oxford: Mowbrays, 1977. Pp. xvi + 222. AB-8; B&W-17; PI-12; SI-17; CT-8; M-3; Place Index-7.

Chitty's classic study traces the origins of the eastern monastic movement, beginning with its founding figures, Anast, Anastasius, Anthony and Pachomius, and moves forward to a history of the institution in its "golden age" in the fourth and fifth centuries. His narrative is mainly a continuous story of the principal figures and historical events, and the controversies between the orthodox Church and the "extremist" monks, to Justinian and the end of Roman rule in the east. Chitty's work has been superseded by some specialist studies in English (see e.g., Rousseau on Pachomius §17.17) but it remains, and is likely to remain, the standard narrative history of the movement. (S)

⮾ H. Chadwick, *JTS* 18 (1967): 494-496; Frend, *JEH* 19 (1968): 275-276; Markus, *History* 52 (1967): 304-305; Yanney, *CCR* 1 (1980): 183-184; Gero, *GOTR* 24 (1979): 83-84; *JEH* 19: 275-76.

17.10 Cox, Patricia. *Biography in Late Antiquity: A Quest for the Holy Man.* Berkekey/Los Angeles: University of California Press, 1983. Pp. xvi + 166. B-14; I-3.

Part of Peter Brown's "Transformation of the Classical Heritage" series, this work is written in the recondite style of the master— though sometimes with an allusiveness and opaqueness that obscures and baffles rather than enlightens. Originally from a doctoral dissertation under Robert Grant at the Divinity School of the University of Chicago, the first half of Cox's book is devoted to a synopsis of the form and function of biographical writing in the

Graeco-Roman tradition, especially with regard to the biographies of philosophers, wise men, and "sages" (e.g. Pythagoras, Apollonius of Tyana). In her analysis of the literary type of biography, Cox comes to reject convenient structural claims about uniform types of ancient biographies, noting that almost all such attempts to provide a coherent unity account of biography as a form have failed. The second part of her book then focuses on two type cases, Eusebius' *Life of Origen* and Porphyry's *Life of Plotinus* as modes of investigating the relationship between accounts of the individual, the role of myth and the narrative form of history. Instead of attempting to use biography as a literary category into which to "slot" these lives, Cox tends to interpret the writing of "lives" as a literary strategy that permitted the author to use tropes to evoke the manner in which the heroic individual or the holy man could be seen as simultaneously transcending and linking the chasm between the holy and the secular, the human and the divine, fact and fantasy, earth and heaven. As with most of Cox's work, it is both a risky experiment and a boldly suggestive new way of looking at old problems. (S)

ℬ< Barnes, *CR* 35 (1985): 197-198; Chadwick, *TLSuppl* 83 (1984): 272; Clark, *JAAR* 52 (1984): 604-605; Gallagher, *JBL* 104 (1985): 373-375; O'Brien, *Worship* 59 (1985): 184-185; Sage, *AHR* 90 (1985): 394-395; Tripolitis, *CH* 53 (1984): 522.

17.11   Harvey, Susan Ashbrook. *Asceticism and Society in Crisis: John of Ephesus and The Lives of the Eastern Saints.* The Transformation of the Classical Heritage 18. Berkeley, CA: University of California Press, 1990. Pp. xvii + 226. B-20; I-8; M-1.
A study of John of Ephesus, the sixth-century ascetic monk of the monastery of Mar John Urtaya. He is a bilingual source of unusually good location for observing the everyday life of his time. A friend of the empress Theodora, John was commissioned by Justinian to convert the remnant pagan elements in the heart of Asia Minor, a mission he carried out with some success. He composed his *Ecclesiastical History* in prison in the 580s CE in the midst of a final repression of Monophysite Christians. Harvey uses John's "History" as a sociological document, especially for the small, but important number of female ascetics on whom he reports. Two sisters, Mary and Euphemia, represent two types of Monophysite saints— anchorites and low-key ascetics. Harvey offers a valuable counterpoint to the court-ecclesiastical perspective of Procopius, and a wonderful insight into the alien, sometimes downright bizarre, world of monks and female ascetics in the sixth century east. (S)

&< Chadwick, *TLSuppl* (1990); 737; Frazee, *CH* 61 (1992): 395-396; Morales, *Theology* 23 (1991): 1052-1053.

17.12 Kirschner, Robert. "The Vocation of Holiness in Late Antiquity." *Vigiliae Christianae* 38 (1984): 105-124.
Kirschner discusses the role of pagan sage, Christian monk, and Jewish rabbi as "holy men." Two common features were: (1) the degree of power attributed to these individuals and (2) the dedicated attachment of disciples. The most extreme behavior *in every way imaginable* is found in the Christian monks, and this resulted in a special sense of power. Kirschner provides many illustrations both of the extreme asceticism (e.g. touching one's toes 1244 times!) and of remarkable power (e.g. breaking glass with the sign of the cross to entertain beggars). Normally the monks avoided formal office within the church (unless compelled to take it). Nonetheless, because of the impression that these were persons of rare holiness, they often had considerable influence in the society.

17.13 Lawless, George P. *Augustine of Hippo and his Monastic Rule.* Oxford: Clarendon Press, 1987. Pp. xx + 185. I-5; B-9; CT-1; T-3.
Lawless specifies five original features of this discussion: (1) the development of Augustine's monasticism from 386-396, and its indebtedness to the best of the Graeco-Roman intellectual traditions; (2) the importance of the three-fold renunciation of sexuality, property, and power; (3) the existence of a *bona fide* monastery at Thagaste during 388-391; (4) for the first time in English in a single volume, the text of the *Ordo Monasterii*, the *Praeceptum*, and the *Obiurgatio* (= *Epistula* 211.1-4), including facing Latin pages; (5) again for the first time in English, a study of disputed authorship, dates of composition, and original audience for the three works above. With two appendices: one on the later version of the rules; one on the current state of research on *Ordo Monasterii*.
&<Bonner, *JEH* 39 (1988): 457-459; Burns, *JR* 69 (1989): 551-552; Gavigon, *Aug. Stud.* 19 (1988): 199-201; Leinhard, *TS* 50 (1989): 202; Markus, *TLSuppl* 87 (1988): 257; O'Donnell, *CHR* 75 (1989): 126; TeSelle, *CH* 59 (1990): 73-74; Tugwell, *JTS* 40 (1989): 625-627.

17.14 Meredith, Anthony. "Asceticism—Christian and Greek." *Journal of Theological Studies* ns 27 (1976): 313-332.
Meredith examines the varied fourth-century Christian and pagan ascetic practices to determine the relationship between the two. Anthony, Basil, and Gregory of Nyssa are compared with each other and with various pagan ascetic trends. Although there are similarities between the pagan and the Christian, the *differences*

are considered to be more profound and significant. In particular, Meredith points to the role of prayer, the sense of the encounter with demons, and the solid grounding in scripture that distinguishes Christian practice from pagan. Some of the *similarities* are little more than borrowing from the popular morality, rather than from specifically ascetic groups of pagans, such as the Pythagoreans, to which comparison has sometimes been made.

17.15   Pearson, Birger A. and James E. Goehring, eds. *The Roots of Egyptian Christianity*. Studies in Antiquity and Christianity. Philadelphia: Fortress, 1986. Pp. 319. B&W-1; T-2.
        The first volume of a series, intended to offer a comprehensive history of Christianity in Egypt from its beginnings to the Arab invasions. The last four chapters deal with monasticism, and are intended to summarize the current state of scholarship. J.E. Goehring writes on "New Frontiers in Pachomian Studies"; J. Timbie on "Career of Shenoute of Atripe"; A. Veilleux on "Monasticism and Gnosis"; and G.G. Stroumsa on "Manichaean Challenge to Egyptian Christianity." The articles are also significant for the question of the borders between orthodoxy and heresy. See §21.16 for an abstract of the full book and for book review notes.

17.16   Rousseau, Philip. *Ascetics, Authority, and the Church in the Age of Jerome and Cassian*. Oxford: Oxford UP, 1978. Pp. x + 277. B.
        A doctoral dissertation completed under the guidance of Peter Brown, Rousseau's work seeks to explicate the great transformations in the work of monasticism, from lonely figures in the eastern deserts to the formal institutions of the Roman west. Rousseau begins by studying the transformation of the behavior of the individual hermit into the institution of the monastic community, principally in Egypt. The figure that is seen as critical to the transition of this ideal to the west is that of Jerome. Through his writings on asceticism the ideal and modes of organizing it passed to Hilary of Poitiers and Gregory of Tours. Rousseau stresses how written texts such as the "sayings" of the Desert Fathers, Sulpicius Severus' *Life of Martin,* and the works of John Cassian, were the critical bridgework by which the power of the individual holy man, his charisma, was transformed into the institutionalized monastic community of the western empire. Whereas the eastern world never moved decisively away from the personal power of the individual monk (consider Pachomius' defense of his personally bestowed charisma to a council of bishops in 345), John Cassian, and his imitators, forged a coenobitic model of institutional monasticism that was more appropriated to the social

structures dominant in the western Roman empire. (S)

< Constable, *Speculum* 54 (1979): 625-626; Darling, *CH* 49 (1980): 207-208; Frend, *JTS* 30 (1979): 564-567; Hunt, *JRS* 71 (1981): 193-197; Markus, *History* 64 (1979): 259-260; O'Donnell, *CW* 73 (1979-1980): 253-254.

17.17 Rousseau, Philip. *Pachomius: The Making of a Community in Fourth Century Egypt.* The Transformation of the Classical Heritage. Berkeley/Los Angeles/London: University of California Press, 1985. Pp. xvi + 217. I-5; B-20; M-2; T-1.

Rousseau's book is an extension of existing work on the emergence of the ascetic and monastic movement in Egypt that was so influential in the development of western Christendom (see Chitty, §17.9). It contains valuable introductory chapters on Egypt and Egyptian Christianity up to the time of Pachomius, and on the source materials for this history. Rousseau's book is, however, much more than a good supplement to existing works on early monasticism. He builds on the fundamental insights of Peter Brown to make linkages between the experiences of one young man, Pachomius, on the formation of the monastic community and its ideals (compare the way in which his work is re-integrated by Peter Brown into his own work in the eleventh and twelfth chapters of his *Body and Society*, §14.4). (S)

< Abrahamse, *Speculum* 62 (1987): 469-471; Bonner, *JEH* 39 (1988): 108-112; Carpe, *CH* 56 (1987): 268; H. Chadwick, *TLSuppl* 4363 (Nov 14 1986): 1288; Johnson, *CHR* 73 (1987): 130-131; S. Lieu, *JRS* 77 (1987): 216-218; Pagels, *CPh* 83 (1988): 377-379; Ware, *JTS* 39 (1988): 604-606.

17.18 ☛ Rousseau, Philip. "Christian Asceticism and the Early Monks." In *Early Christianity. Origins and Evolution to AD 600.* Edited by Ian Hazlett. London: SPCK, 1991. Pp. 112-122.

This is a short but insightful overview of the matters widely accepted in the history of early monasticism—matters which, according to Rousseau (a leading scholar in the field) must be reconsidered. In particular, Rousseau calls for more caution with the use of relevant texts, for they are often tendentious, and can obscure the diversity of early monastic consciousness. In fact, the texts tend to provide a too linear view of the development of monasticism. Further, the sources of monasticism must be reconsidered, giving attention to the varied pagan and Jewish influences. A solid overview with probing questions.

17.19 Shiels, W.J., ed. *Monks, Hermits, and the Ascetic.* Papers read at the 1984 summer meeting and 1985 winter meeting of the Ecclesiastical Historical Society. Studies in Church History. Oxford:

Basil Blackwell, 1985.
Three articles are of importance: "The Ascetic Ideal in the History
of the Church" (H. Chadwick); "Christian Asceticism and the Early
School of Alexandria" (J.A. McGuckin); and "The Death of Ascetics:
Sickness and Monasticism in the Early Byzantine Middle East" (P.
Horden). According to Chadwick, Augustine believed that authentic
Christianity had a serious and ascetic side, against the shallow
commitment to Christianity that Augustine witnessed in many of
his contemporaries; yet Augustine's monasticism was largely mod-
erate and communal. McGuckin looks for the roots of Christian
monasticism in Judaism and in Jesus' own behavior. Horden looks
at monastic responses to pain and dying, and notes the monks'
favorable attitude to medicine.

18
ORTHODOXY AND HERESY

The issue of orthodoxy and heresy is part of a larger issue, for which the technical term "self-definition" is frequently used. Self-definition is the process by which a community consciously defines and understands itself. Part of this process involves specifying which beliefs and practices are to be approved and promoted and which are to be condemned and eradicated. The terms "orthodoxy" and "heresy" are labels that conveniently specify these kinds of decisions made by a community as it comes to self-consciousness. As the terms have been applied throughout the history of the church, it is the perspective of the *majority* group, which became the religion of the empire, that is represented.

There have been complaints about the adequacy of the labels "orthodoxy" and "heresy." The terms are loaded, for they specify the "true" and the "false" from the perspective of a *particular* group. They work, in other words, from an "insider's" position. Further, they are born in the heat of polemics, and function as weapons, to strengthen or to destroy particular positions. Should the modern historian be bound by these judgments of the past? Were there not other *distinctly Christian* options during the early period, which would have viewed the application of the labels much differently, reversing the parties commended and condemned by the labels? Are the terms *merely* a way of identifying what one group liked and disliked, rather than identifying what is "true" at some ultimate or cosmic level?

Historians are generally cautious about describing particular beliefs as "true" or "false," and they are often uncomfortable in using terms that are so biased in favor of one group over another. It is commonplace now for early church historians to dismiss "orthodoxy" as merely *the heresy that won out.* Nonetheless, the labels have generally stuck, largely because no others seemed any better. The only real change in the use of the terms is that they are stripped of their original meanings. "Orthodoxy" now refers to the imperial church, including its pre-Constantinian roots. "Heresy" refers to all the groups outside what constitutes "orthodoxy." There is no sense of "truth" and "error" associated with the use by most modern scholars.

259

For much of the history of the Christian church, orthodoxy was assumed to be the uniform belief system held by the apostolic, or first-century, church, and passed on faithfully from one generation to the next. Alternative theological views were thus judged to be non-apostolic, and therefore unacceptable (i.e., heretical). From this perspective, it could be argued that the true church should have a uniform belief and practice at all times, and that any deviation from what is judged to be "apostolic" should be declared unacceptable. This view received its classic exposition in *The Ecclesiastical History,* a work of Eusebius, a bishop of Caesarea and friend of the new Christian emperor, Constantine the Great.

Eusebius' history is a perspective from one of the pivotal points in the early church's development. Constantine had identified himself with the church, and expressed concern about disunity in the church. Some historians have pointed to Constantine's efforts to create theological uniformity throughout the Christian churches of his empire, calling attention to his actions with regard to the Donatist controversy of North Africa in the first decade of his reign and to the Arian controversy in the second decade.

But it would be misleading to think that Constantine initiated this drive towards uniformity, or that Eusebius was merely following the imperial will. The concern with and the drive towards an "apostolic orthodoxy" is found early and often in the literature of the early church, and many of the novel elements introduced by church leaders seem to have been created specifically to serve the interests of uniformity and orthodoxy. Such things as the canon and the hierarchical church offices, particularly the office of bishop, demonstrate this concern. More directly, there are the clear and abundant statements from pre-Constantinian theologians who have a sense of orthodoxy. Thus, though this particular view of orthodoxy and heresy has come to be known as the "Eusebian" view, Eusebius was dependent for this perspective on a number of older orthodox writers; he was no mere parrot of the new imperial will. The Constantinian concerns for uniformity and orthodoxy have deep roots in the pre-Constantinian period.

Those judged as heretics by the larger church never had much sympathy for the perspective of Eusebius, for he had dismissed their views as novel, non-apostolic, and errant. It was not until the twentieth century that a voice from within orthodoxy successfully challenged the Eusebian view. In 1934, Walter Bauer, known mainly for his lexicography of the New Testament and other early Christian literature, wrote his *Rechtgläubigkeit und Ketzerei im ältesten Christentum.* Although it made little impact when it was first published (perhaps due to the coming war and the tensions between England and Germany), a considerably more positive reception was given to the second German edition in 1964 and the English translation (*Orthodoxy and Heresy in Earliest Christianity*) in 1971 [§18.2].

Bauer argued that the various forms of Christianity that came to be dismissed as "heresy" had as much claim to antiquity and apostolicity as the form that came to be called "orthodoxy." Such a view posits a diverse Christianity in the early period, with various competing groups. Bauer then accounted for the drive towards uniformity by pointing to the Roman church, and charging that church with political ambitions as it tried to extend its influence throughout the empire. Although a large number of scholars follow Bauer, most have qualified his theory in certain areas, and some have recognized the Protestant/Catholic tension in Bauer's position. He was a Protestant, and often a Protestant perspective had less sympathy for development than a Catholic perspective had, simply because Catholicism linked itself consciously with a past chain of tradition whereas Protestantism emphasized misdirection in the history of the church, and emphasized a "biblical" or "apostolic" purity.

Two scholars in particular reflect the influence of Bauer, though no historian of the early church has been left unaffected by him. Helmut Koester [§18.19] is the closest follower of Bauer, and along with James Robinson [§18.27], he offered the paradigm of "trajectory" to account for early Christian development and diversity. This has been a widely used tool in reconstructions of the early church. The image is that of the arc of a projectile, and the assumption is that one can plot the development of stages of an idea on such a trajectory. This has allowed scholars to place otherwise undatable documents in a scheme of development and to make suggestions about the roots of particular ideas and the connections between groups and concepts. But this principle is perhaps too artificial and inflexible. The human element in the development of ideas may make the idea of "explosion" rather than that of "trajectory" the better paradigm for development. Such a paradigm more comfortably allows for the irregular, the unexpected, and the uncontrolled. In spite of these inadequacies, many of the recent reconstructions of the early church have worked with the ideas of a trajectory and of relatively consistent and stable development.

The other scholar who has done much to lend credibility to Bauer's work has been James Dunn. Dunn noted that Bauer had dealt mainly with the second and third centuries; he believed that the same approach could be applied to the first century. In his book *Unity and Diversity in Early Christianity,* Dunn attempted to demonstrate that the first-century church was theologically diverse, and that such diversity was a matter of little concern to those in the church. This would support Bauer's findings that the second-century church was diverse, and support, too, his contention that such diversity was rooted in the first century and that the interest of the "orthodox" in uniformity was a novel second-century idea. But some scholars have protested that Dunn has not given sufficient attention to the presence of a sense of "orthodoxy" in the first century.

There have been both benefits and losses in our understanding of the early church as a result of Bauer's study. On the positive side, positions dismissed as "heresy"—and for that reason, previously disregarded—are now receiving fresh and more fair attention. The substantial contributions of such groups to the early church are being recognized, and there has come about greater understanding and sympathy for these positions. Some positions are found to have been more at the center than the developing church had been prepared to recognize. But there has been a negative side to Bauer's work too. The increasing sympathy for the "heretical" positions has often led to an inability to appreciate the "orthodox" side. In many circles, the orthodox position is given little attention, and dismissed with off-handed comments about its political agenda. This imbalance is seen in the incredible interest in Gnosticism, often at the expense of the orthodox.

18.1   Baker, Derek, ed. *Schism, Heresy and Religious Protest*. Studies in Church History 9. Papers read at the tenth summer meeting and the eleventh winter meeting of the Ecclesiastical History Society. Cambridge: Cambridge UP, 1972. Pp. xv + 404.
Only the first 4 essays (63 pages) relate to our period. They are: "Heresy and schism in the later Roman empire" (Greenslade); "Christianity and dissent in Roman North Africa: changing perspectives in recent work" (Markus); "Heresy and schism as social and national movements" (Frend); and "Attitudes to schism at the Council of Nicaea" (Ferguson). Ferguson discusses the status of reconciled clergy from various schisms. The first three discuss the Donatists at some length, though Greenslade's article is considerably more broad than that, looking mainly at heresy as a phenomenon rather than focusing on any particular heresy.
⊰ Bainton, *CH* 42 (1973): 275-276; Hendrix, *JAAR* 41 (1973): 636-637; Shriver, *ATR* 55 (1973): 246-248; Simon, *JEH* 25 (1974): 89-90.

18.2   Bauer, Walter. *Orthodoxy and Heresy in Earliest Christianity*. Translated by a team from the Philadelphia Seminar on Christian Origins. Edited by Robert A. Kraft and Gerhard Krodel. Philadelphia: Fortress, 1971. Pp. 326. I-10. Originally published as *Rechtgläubigkeit und Ketzerei im ältesten Christentum*. Beitrage zur historischen Theologie 10. Tübingen: Mohr/ Siebeck, 1934. Reprinted with two supplementary essays by Georg Strecker in 1964.
This work has provoked new reconstructions of early Christian history. Focusing on the diversity of forms of Christianity in distinctive geographical areas, Bauer contended that the dominant and

earliest forms of Christianity in areas like Egypt and Edessa were heretical by the standards of Roman Christianity. Bauer contended that the case was not much different for Syria, Asia Minor, and Greece. But "heresy" was the wrong term for these alternative theological positions, according to Bauer. The term was polemical, not descriptive, and functioned as part of the tactic by the Roman church to discredit and overpower views just as ancient and apostolic as their own.

✂ The English translation includes a 30-page appendix on the reception of Bauer's German work. Many of the book reviews discussed there are in English.

18.3 ◉ Betz, Hans Dieter. "Orthodoxy and Heresy in Primitive Christianity: Some critical remarks on Georg Strecker's republication of Walter Bauer's *Rechtgläubigkeit und Ketzerei im ältesten Christentum.*" *Interpretation* 19 (1965): 299-311.

After brief summaries of the positions of Bauer and Strecker (who wrote an appendix on Jewish Christianity for the second edition), Betz argues that the field has changed so much since Bauer's 1934 book as to prevent a mere application or confirmation of Bauer's thesis. Betz reviews some of Bauer's works before 1934 to show that, early in his writings, Bauer had a view of a fluid primitive Christianity. He criticizes Bauer for not taking seriously enough the evidence for a sense of orthodoxy in the New Testament. Betz points out the relevance of the "historical Jesus" question, and argues for a theological side to the historical quest for the "authentically Christian" view of Jesus.

18.4 Brown, Harold O.J. *Heresies: The Image of Christ in the Mirror of Heresy and Orthodoxy from the Apostles to the Present.* Garden City, N.Y.: Doubleday & Company, 1984. Pp. xxvi + 477. I-9.

The first half (about 200 pages) is relevant to this bibliography. Brown attempts to account for the phenomenon of heresy in various Christologies through the centuries. The work is detailed and clear, and generally shows what is at the heart of the issue for all sides in the debates. Also, Brown does a good job in relating each issue to the past debate, and placing each in a stream of development. Primarily Brown sees heresy as a concentration on one aspect of Christology, to the exclusion or depreciation of the range of other aspects. His sympathies are clearly with the orthodox positions. Brief bibliographies follow most chapters.

✂ Butterworth, *ExT* 100 (1989): 271-272; Galvin, *TS* 46 (1985): 141-142; Hanson, *R&E* 86 (1989): 631-632; James, *JETS* 28 (1985): 361-362.

18.5   Burke, G.T. "Walter Bauer and Celsus: The Shape of Late Second-Century Christianity." *Second Century* 4 (1984): 1-7.

Burke provides a fresh attack on Bauer's thesis [§18.2]. He is interested in examining Bauer's thesis from an outside perspective (neither heretical nor orthodox), and he finds this in Celsus' *On the True Doctrine* (preserved in Origen's *Against Celsus*). From this perspective, Burke criticizes three of Bauer's main points: (1) the chronological priority of heresy over orthodoxy at a number of locations, (2) the numerical superiority of the heretical over the orthodox in the broad Christian population, and (3) the victory for the orthodox stemming from Rome's assistance. Although the article is short, it represents one more angle from which the Bauer thesis is being examined and found wanting.

18.6   ◉ Chapman, G. Clarke, Jr. "Some Theological Reflections on Walter Bauer's *Rechtgläubigkeit und Ketzerei im ältesten Christentum*. A Review Article." *Journal of Ecumenical Studies* 7 (1970): 564-74.

As the title indicates, Chapman is primarily interested in the theological questions raised by Bauer's work [§18.2]. After a brief review of Bauer's thesis and a summary of four responses (Koester [§18.19], Ehrhardt [§18.8], Turner [§18.31], and Dibelius), Chapman asks the theological questions: What does theological adequacy mean? How is historical inquiry different from theological inquiry? Is orthodoxy a developing concept? Is theology merely "an ideological tool, and expression of corporate self-interest"? Although many historians will not be convinced by Chapman's defence of the theological endeavor, Chapman does raise some interesting points about the reasons why Bauer's thesis is attractive to so many.

18.7   ◉ Desjardins, Michel. "Bauer and Beyond: On Recent Scholarly Discussions of Αἱρεσις in the Early Christian Era. *Second Century* 8 (1991): 65-82.

Desjardins provides a review of the debate provoked by Bauer [§18.2], paying particular attention to the responses of Turner [§18.31] and Robinson [§18.28]. He then reviews the use of the term αἱρεσις (commonly translated "heresy") in Graeco-Roman, early Christian, and Rabbinic literature, here paying particular attention to Le Boulluec's work. Desjardins appeals for caution in the debate and encourages a middle ground.

18.8   Ehrhardt, Arnold. "Christianity Before the Apostles' Creed." *Harvard Theological Review* 55 (1962): 73-119.

Ehrhardt attempts to show not only the diversity of belief in the early Church but the acceptable character of that diversity. Not only was there no uniformity in the early period, there was not even a credible attempt to achieve it—at least not by excommunication. His review of Bauer's reconstruction of various geographical areas is sympathetic, but reserved for Antioch and Asia Minor, and for the role of Rome, he disagrees strongly. His final point is that the "creed" did not serve as a touchstone for orthodoxy in the first or second centuries. Also, he offers interesting views on Samaritan Christianity and Gnosticism, and heresy as "excess" rather than "error."

18.9   Flora, Jerry R. "A Critical Analysis of Walter Bauer's Theory of Early Christian Orthodoxy and Heresy." Th.D. diss., Southern Baptist Theological Seminary, 1972. Pp. xii + 248. B-24.
Flora divides his work into four parts: "Bauer's Theory in the Context of his Career"; "Bauer's Theory in the Evolution of Scholarship"; "Bauer's Theory as Historical Explanation"; and "Bauer's Theory in Later Research." Parts 1 and 4 provide the most useful and, in English, otherwise unavailable material. Part 4 discusses the response of Goguel, Bultmann, Conzelmann, Käsemann, Koester, Colwell, Turner, Altendorf, Moffatt, Ehrhardt, Goppelt, and R.M. Grant. This review, along with Appendix 2 in Bauer's book [§18.2] provides a considerable overview of issues and positions concerning orthodoxy and heresy in primitive Christianity.

18.10 Frend, W.H.C. *The Rise of the Monophysite Movement. Chapters in the History of the Church in the Fifth and Sixth Centuries.* Cambridge: Cambridge UP, 1972. Pp. xxi + 405. I-13; B-24; CT-4; M-2.
A sympathetic history of the Monophysite movement, from the Council of Ephesus (431) to the Arab invasions. Frend tries to account for the failure of the Eastern Empire against the Arabs by granting to the Monophysites a status as the third Christian force. Though initially driven by religious concerns, the oppression of the Monophysites by the Emperor caused the Monophysite movement to become identified with regional separation in Syria, Egypt, and Armenia, and even led to a preference for Arab rule. Chalcedon is viewed as an alliance of Rome and Constantinople against the eastern patriarchs. Appendices provide English translations of the *Henotikon* (482); *Petition of the Monophysites to Justinian* (532); and the *Second Henotikon* (571). But note the treatment of Frend's work in the reviews, such as that by Barnard.

❯< Atiya, *JEH* 25 (1974): 200-201; Barnard, *JRS* 63 (1973): 275-276;
Bird, *WTJ* 36 (1974): 240-242; Jorgenson, *StVTQ* 17 (1973): 297-299;
Lampe, *ExT* 84 (1973): 280; Meyendorff, *TS* 34 (1973): 719-722; Wickham,
JTS 24 (1973): 591-599.

18.11   Frend, W.H.C. *Saints and Sinners in the Early Church: Differing
and Conflicting Traditions in the First Six Centuries.* Walter and
Mary Tuohy Lectures 1981. London: Darton, Longman and Todd,
1985. Pp. 183. I-7.
For the general reader, this collection (patterned on Prestige's work
§18.25) provides a sympathetic account of some of the individuals
of the early church who followed diverse options of belief and
practice (in more traditional terms: "heretics"). There are separate
chapters on Origen, Donatus, Pelagius, Nestorius, and Severus of
Antioch, and more general chapters on the development of orthodoxy
and heresy, Gnosticism, and various other movements rejected by
the early church. Frend tends to emphasize the Jewish dimension
wherever possible.
❯< Bebawi, *SJT* 40 (1987): 319-320; Hinson, *R&E* 83 (1986): 129; Stead,
JEH 37 (1986): 484; Tsirpanlis, *PBR* 5 (1986): 67-69; Webber, *TSFB* 10
(1987): 47; Young, *ExT* 97 (1986): 312-313.

18.12   ⊛ Frend, W.H.C. "Montanism: Research and Problems." *Rivista di
Storia a litteratura Religiose* (Turin) 20 (1984): 521-537. B-2.
The first half of this article provides a summary of the history of
the Montanist movement and of related questions. The latter half
provides a summary of the modern debate about Montanism (from
the middle of the 19th century). Particular attention is paid to works
by Pierre de Labriolle, W.M. Ramsay, W.M. Calder, Wilhelm Sche-
pelern, Kurt Aland, and Massingberd Ford. The "Christians for
Christians" inscriptions are discussed, along with the question of
the rural/urban character of early Christianity, and the continuing
interest in prophecy after the first century. In the final paragraph,
Frend identifies significant questions which remain unanswered.

18.13   Greenslade, S.L. *Schism in the Early Church.* 2d ed. London: SCM,
1964. (1953[1]). Pp. xxii + 253. NI-7; SI-3; B-9.
This book, stemming from the Edward Cadbury Lectures of 1949-
1950, is about schisms rather than heresies. Greenslade focuses on
ecclesiastical causes of schism (differences in liturgy; problems of
discipline and purity) and secular causes (personal rivalry, rational-
ism, social and economic influences, rivalry between chief churches).
Then he discusses ways the church dealt with schism, disagreeing
at points with the views of Augustine and Cyprian. Though the

subject is schism in the early church, the author's real concern is with schism in the modern church. A nine-page synopsis of the major schisms is included.

⊰ Bruce, *EQ* 25 (1953): 185-186; Burleigh, *SJT* 7 (1954): 304-306; R.M. Grant, *ATR* 36 (1954): 154-155; Hope, *Interpretation* 8 (1954): 356-357; Telfer, *JEH* 4 (1953): 220-221; H.E.W. Turner, *CQR* 154 (1953): 241-244.

18.14 ◉ Harrington, Daniel J. "The Reception of Walter Bauer's Orthodoxy and Heresy in Earliest Christianity During the Last Decade." *HTR* 73 (1980): 289-98.

This is a good, brief review of the debate about Bauer's work [§18.2] after its publication in English. Numerous book reviews are mentioned, and major responses are considered, with some interesting suggestions. Harrington is particularly concerned that Bauer has not adequately accounted for the eventual triumph of orthodoxy.

18.15 Hawkin, David J. "A Reflective Look at the Recent Debate on Orthodoxy and Heresy in Earliest Christianity." *Eglise et Theologie* 7 (1976): 367-78.

Hawkin charges that Bauer "lacked the conceptual tools to deal with orthodoxy as a development incorporating the past, accommodating to the present, and anticipating the future. Hawkin is more comfortable than many with the work of Turner [§18.31], who has a sense of the *fixed* and the *flexible* elements in the Christian tradition—a sense that Bauer did not seem to have. This article is sensitive to the phenomenon of development in a way that neither Bauer nor many of his followers are.

18.16 Henry, Patrick. "Why Is Contemporary Scholarship So Enamored of Ancient Heresies?" In the *Proceedings of the 8th International Conference on Patristic Studies*. Edited by E.A. Livingstone. Oxford: Pergamon Press, 1980. Pp. 123-126.

A brief article but important for Henry's sharp and insightful polemic. Henry charges that "in much current writing about Christian origins, the Fathers are no longer put on a par with the heretics; they are put on the defensive, and it is assumed that the heretics are the true religious geniuses..." He traces the development in historical criticism from support of orthodoxy, to an evenhandedness, to "historical advocacy," attempting to explain the development. See, too, Henry, *New Directions in New Testament Studies* (Philadelphia: Westminster, 1979), pp. 107-119 and 180-202, for further balanced observations.

18.17   Heron, A.I.C. "The Interpretation of I Clement in Walter Bauer's
        'Rechtglaubigkeit und Ketzerei im ältesten Christentum." *Ekklesias-*
        tikos Pharos 55 (1973): 517-545.
        Heron offers the most detailed analysis of Bauer's reconstruction
        of the situation in Corinth at the time of the writing of *1 Clement*.
        After some general comments on Bauer's lack of caution in his
        reconstructions, Heron focuses on the Corinthian and Roman
        situation at the end of the first century. Heron challenges Bauer at
        three points: (1) Rome's motivation, (2) the use of earlier literature
        (Paul's letters) and later literature (*Acts of Paul*) to explain the
        situation at the end of the first century, and (3) the description of
        the problem—judged by Heron to be considerably less important
        in terms of orthodoxy than Bauer made it.

18.18   Käsemann, Ernst. "The Canon of the New Testament and the Unity
        of the Church." In *Essays on New Testament Themes*. Translated
        by W.J. Montague. Studies in Biblical Theology 41. London: SCM,
        1964. Pp. 95-107.
        This article is important as one that helped to cause a shift to a
        general recognition of diversity, not just in the church of the second
        century (as even the church fathers admitted and fought), but within
        the New Testament itself. The New Testament witnesses to a wealth
        of theological positions which, in many cases, are incompatible
        with each other, according to Käsemann. His position argues against
        granting much respect to the canon that came to be the authoritative
        collection of Christian writings. This opens the door for a greater
        appreciation of the vast quantity of censured literature in the post-
        New Testament period.

18.19   Koester, Helmut. "GNOMAI DIAPHOROI: The Origin and Nature
        of Diversification in the History of Early Christianity." *Harvard*
        Theological Review 58 (1965): 279-318.
        This widely-quoted article represents a clear development of and
        support for Bauer's thesis. Koester, the most influential of Bauer's
        disciples, tries to draw lines from the first century into the later
        centuries, something Bauer did not bother to do. He takes a close
        look at three areas: Palestine and western Syria; Edessa and the
        Osrhoëne (with particular attention to the Thomas tradition); and
        the countries around the Aegean. In the introduction, he challenges
        the notions of canon and of orthodoxy and heresy. Although he
        follows Bauer a little too faithfully, his observations are such to
        require attention by those who wish to deal seriously with the
        questions arising from definitions of orthodoxy and heresy, if these

terms are to be used at all.

18.20 Kraft, Robert A. "The Development of the Concept of 'Orthodoxy' in Early Christianity." In *Current Issues in Biblical and Patristic Interpretation*. Studies in Honor of Merril C. Tenney. Edited by Gerald F. Hawthorne. Grand Rapids: Eerdmans, 1975. Pp. 47-59.
Kraft was one of the editors of the English translation of Bauer's work. In this article, he provides a review of major issues (use of terms, evidence of a sense of orthodoxy in the New Testament, evidence for theological diversity in the first century, and the reasons for claiming apostolicity for a document). Kraft argues that Paul took an untraditional attitude towards "orthodoxy," and he refers to the Gnostic links to Paul. Finally, he deals with the influence of Montanism and of persecution in giving shape to orthodoxy and the canon.

18.21 Marshall, I. Howard. "Orthodoxy and heresy in earlier Christianity." *Themelios* 2 (1976): 5-14.
Marshall challenges the view of Bauer [§18.2] and his disciples that the first-century church was marked by diversity of belief, without any controlling sense of orthodoxy. Marshall argues that there is plenty of evidence within the New Testament that early Christian leaders were prepared to pronounce particular beliefs false, and to act against these. Further, Marshall raises a number of issues for further exploration (some with distinctly theological interests). The article is a useful balance to Bauer's view of the first century, and raises questions about the way in which deviation was handled in the first-century church.

18.22 Martin, Brice L. "Some reflections of the unity of the New Testament." *Studies in Religion* 8 (1979): 143-52.
Martin reviews the debate engendered by Bauer's work, and he is especially critical of what he contends is the German failure to grasp the middle position in a discussion of diversity. Between positions which are complementary (i.e. harmonizable) and positions which are incompatible (i.e. contradictory), there are those positions which are noncomplementary *but* compatible. Martin is influenced by Bernard Lonergan, whose writings generally are sensitive to diversity and development in a way that those who study the issue of orthodoxy and heresy could learn much.

18.23 Norris, Frederick W. "Ignatius, Polycarp, and I Clement: Walter Bauer Reconsidered." *Vigiliae Christianae* 30 (1976): 23-44.

Norris hits hard at Bauer, challenging his reconstruction of the dominance of heresy in Asia Minor and Antioch, criticizing his understanding of Rome's leadership in orthodoxy, asserting a clear sense of orthodox boundaries in Ignatius' thinking, and pointing to problems in Bauer's use of terms. In particular, Norris points to centers of orthodoxy, such as Asia Minor, which puts Roman orthodoxy to shame. Of particular importance and insight is Norris' list of five important contributions to orthodoxy made by Asia Minor and Antioch. Says Norris, in criticism of the scholarly acceptance of Bauer's thesis: "The fallacy of both [of Bauer's] positive theses... has not been properly emphasized."

18.24   Norris, Frederick W. "Asia Minor before Ignatius: Walter Bauer Reconsidered." In *Studia Evangelica*. Vol. 7. Papers presented to the Fifth International Congress on Biblical Studies (1973). Edited by Elizabeth A. Livingstone, 365-77. Texte und Unter-suchungen zur Geschichte der altchristlichen Literatur 126. Berlin: Akademie-Verlag, 1982. Pp. 365-377.
A short but insightful and damaging critique of Bauer's reconstruction of early Christianity in Asia Minor. Norris reviews the situation in Ephesus as reflected in the Pauline circle of New Testament writings; he then considers the Apocalypse, and finally raises questions about Bauer's claim that Christianity was heavily Gnostic in the area. He concludes that orthodoxy was much stronger in Ephesus and Asia Minor that Bauer contended.

18.25   Prestige, G.L. *Fathers and Heretics: Six Studies in Dogmatic Faith with Prologue and Epilogue*. The Bampton Lectures 1940. London: SPCK, 1958. Pp. vii + 211. I-4.
Six of the eight chapters deal with specific individuals in the early church involved in orthodoxy/heresy debates. They are: Callistus, Origen, Athanasius, Apollinaris, Nestorius, and Cyril. The other two chapters are more general. "Tradition: or, The Scriptural Basis of Theology" is a sympathetic presentation of tradition and the creeds, the process of development, and the relation of scripture to tradition. "Eros: or, Devotion to the Sacred Humanity" has five pages that are relevant to the early church, in which Prestige presents a survey of patristic thought on the "creaturely flesh" of Jesus.

18.26   Roberts, Colin H. *Manuscript, Society, and Belief in Early Christian Egypt*. The Schweich Lectures of the British Academy for 1977. London: Oxford UP, 1979. Pp. x + 89.
Roberts argues against Bauer's thesis [§18.2] of the heretical

character of Egyptian Christianity. By looking at the surviving Christian and Jewish literary papyri, and especially at the treatment of the *nomina sacra* (sacred name), Roberts concludes that Christianity was tied closely to Judaism until the time of Trajan. Roberts offers a cautious treatment of the extent of Gnosticism in Egypt, claiming that the evidence for a sharply Gnostic character of Christianity in Egypt is scanty, even in the Coptic literature. With five brief appendices on Jewish theological papyri; date of Chester Beatty 𝔓 vi; "Psalm of the Naassenes"; Christianity and magic in the papyri; and eccentric forms of the *nomina sacra*.

⊰ Cummings, *TS* 41 (1980): 235-236; Frend, *JEH* 31 (1980): 207-208; Kilpatrick, *VC* 36 (1982): 87-94; Price, *Sobornost* 2 (1980): 86-89; Skeat, *JTS* 31 (1980): 193-186; Smith, *JAOS* 102 (1982): 201-202; Smith, *Currents* 10 (1983): 118-119.

18.27   Robinson, James M., and Helmut Koester. *Trajectories through Early Christianity*. Philadelphia: Fortress, 1971. Pp. 297. AI-3; SI-4; AAI-8.

A collection of essays by Robinson and Koester. Each in his own way develops and sharpens the thesis of Bauer, though Robinson less closely follows Bauer. The concept they work with is that of "trajectory," by which they visualize various arcs of development, on which are plotted the wide range of documents from the early period. The assumption is that development has a certain coherence and continuity, allowing for placing documents in a scheme of development based on the evolution of the ideas they contain. A significant work, but the whole concept of trajectory needs more rigorous examination than these authors offer, especially in light of the wide and uncritical popularity it has gained.

⊰ Agnew, *CBQ* 34 (1972): 532-534; Glynn, *TS* 33 (1972): 134-136; Harmerton-Kelly, *TT* 28 (1972): 521-523; Haulotte, *Biblica* 55 (1974): 112-117; Kistemaker, *WTJ* 35 (1973): 338-340; Longenecker, *CT* 16 (Apr 14, 1972): 27-28; Stagg, *R&E* 71 (1974): 395-397; R.M. Wilson, *JTS* 23 (1972): 275-277.

18.28   Robinson, Thomas A. *The Bauer Thesis Examined: The Geography of Heresy in the Early Christian Church*. Studies in the Bible and Early Christianity 11. Lewiston/Queenston: Edwin Mellen, 1988. Pp. xi + 248. B-15; CAI-2; MAI-2; NTI-2; SI-4; PI-3; Walter Bauer Index-2.

Robinson takes issue with Bauer's work [§18.2], claiming that Bauer failed to show that heretical forms of Christianity were both early and strong. Robinson contends that many areas of early Christianity provide too little data for any confident reconstruction, and he dismisses as imaginative and hypothetical the various reconstructions of Bauer and one of Bauer's leading disciples, Koester [§18.19]. Robinson then concentrates on the area where primary literature is extensive (in western Asia Minor), arguing that Bauer's thesis does not bear well for that area. The letters of Ignatius play a crucial role in Robinson's reconstruction.

✄ Boring, *Interpretation* 44 (1990): 104-105; Bruyn, *SR* 18 (1989): 492-493; Desjardins, *SC* 8 (1991): 65-82; Finn, *JECS* 2 (1993): 217-219; Norris, *Themelios* 16.3 (1991): 35; Wild, *CBQ* 52 (1990): 568-569; Wright, *EQ* 62 (1990): 280-282.

18.29   Simon, Marcel. "From Greek Hairesis to Christian Heresy." In *Early Christian Literature and the Classical Intellectual Tradition. In honorem Robert M. Grant.* Edited by William R. Schoedel and Robert L. Wilken. Theologie historique 53. Paris: Beauchesne, 1979. Pp. 101-116.

Simon considers the use of the term *hairesis* (heresy) in the ancient period, and shows how the Christian use of the terms "orthodoxy" and "heresy" have roots in Jewish sectarian and Greek philosophical use. Simon points out the possible positive and negative aspects in the use of the term *hairesis* and *heterodoxia* (heterodoxy), and attempts to show the Christian influence on the terms, making the two to serve as synonyms, and using them as negative opposites to the word *orthodoxia* (orthodoxy).

18.30   Strecker, Georg. "On the Problem of Jewish Christianity." In *Orthodoxy and Heresy in Earliest Christianity*, by Walter Bauer. Philadelphia: Fortress, 1971. Pp. 241-285.

Strecker, the editor of the revised edition of Bauer's *Rechtgläubigkeit und Ketzerei im ältesten Christentum.* [§18.2], felt that Bauer that overlooked the strongest evidence of diversity in early Christianity and the strongest challenge to the claim of "catholic" Christianity that it was the valid representative of apostolic tradition. Strecker considers three witnesses to early Jewish Christianity: (1) the *Didascalia*, (2) *the Kerygmata Petrou* (The Preaching of Peter), and (3) the stereotypical and misinformed reports about the Ebionites by various ecclesiastical authors.

18.31   Turner, H.E.W. *The Pattern of Christian Truth: A Study in the Relations between Orthodoxy and Heresy in the Early Church.* Bampton Lectures 1954. London: A.R. Mowbray & Co., 1954. Pp. xvi + 508. SI-5; PI-5.

Turner offered the first extensive and informed response to Bauer's thesis [§18.2]. An Anglican, Turner had less hesitation than the Lutheran Bauer in seeing positive features in the early church's development towards Catholicism. In addition to confronting Bauer head-on, Turner offers a thoughtful (though often criticized) view of the nature of orthodoxy and heresy in the early period. His most recognized distinctive contribution to the debate is the emphasis on *lex orandi,* a full and fixed *experimental* grasp of Christian faith, apart from and prior to creeds and systematic statements of belief. This book, along with Bauer's, offers the standard detailed treatments on the question.

ঝ< Desjardins, *SC* 8 (1991): 65-82; R.M. Grant, *ATR* 38 (1956): 100-102; Grensted, *CQR* 156 (1955): 198-200; J.N. Sanders, *JTS* 7(1956): 119-123; Editor, *ExT* 66 (1955): 161-162.

18.32   Wilken, Robert L. *The Myth of Christian Beginnings. History's Impact on Belief.* Garden City: Doubleday, 1971. Pp. xi + 218.
About half of this book is relevant. Wilken's work is a popularization of Bauer's thesis, extended throughout all Christian history. Highly skeptical of tradition and of any past that is viewed as authoritative, pure, or perfect, Wilken discusses the use of the past, the appeal of the orthodox to tradition, Eusebius' failings as a historian, and the problems of the councils. Wilken describes his book as "a critical examination of the Christian attitude to change, as reflected in the Christian construction of the past." More sympathetic approaches to tradition are needed to balance Wilken views—see Wilken's own work below.

ঝ< Dulles, *TS* 32 (1971): 510-511; Mitchell, *ATR* 54 (1972): 133-134; Pherigo, *CH* 40 (1971): 476.

18.33   Wilken, Robert L. "Diversity and Unity in Early Christianity." *Second Century* 1 (1981): 101-110.
Wilken discusses the impact of Bauer's work [§18.2] on scholarly debate regarding early Christian development, and reactions stemming from it. Wilken is sympathetic to challenges to Bauer from Moffatt and Turner [§18.31], who have a theological interest in the development and victory of orthodoxy. He further points to the sense of orthodoxy or center that the early church possessed, and shows that the "great church" or the "centrist party" was recognized as the credible representative of the Christian church by informed critics such as Celsus in the second century and Plotinus in the third century.

18.34   Williams, Rowan, ed. *The Making of Orthodoxy. Essays in Honour of Henry Chadwick*. Cambridge: Cambridge UP, 1989. Pp. xxv + 340. AAI-19; NI-7; MAI-6.
Sixteen articles by leading scholars in the field, and an 11-page bibliography of Chadwick's writings. A variety of topics are covered, but all deal with the early church. Some of the articles are (with shortened titles): "Pre-Nicene orthodoxy?" (Williams); "Rule of faith in second century" (Osborn); "Eusebius' *Life of Constantine*" (Barnes); "Eusebius and *lex orandi*" (H.B. Green); "Achievement of orthodoxy in fourth century" (Hanson); "Pelagianism" (Wickham); "The legacy of Pelagius" (Markus); "Augustine and millenarianism" (Bonner); and "Origins of monasticism" (O'Neill).

18.35   Wisse, Frederik. "The Use of Early Christian Literature as Evidence for Inner Diversity and Conflict." In *Nag Hammadi, Gnosticism, and Early Christianity*. Edited by Charles W. Hedrick and Robert Hodgson, Jr. Peabody: Hendrickson, 1986. Pp. 177-190.
Wisse considers the polemical literature of the early church, and after outlining F.C. Baur and Walter Bauer's handling of this matter, presents a few suggestive comments. Wisse thinks that, without some standard regarding what constituted correct belief, writers were more or less forced to make apostolic claims for their writings to get a hearing. He suggests that orthodoxy (or specifically, *orthocracy*) won because of its interest in "coherence." He offers some interesting comments on the idiosyncratic, speculative, and *acceptable* character of much of the literature later labelled "heretical." Finally (and wisely), he cautions against creating hypothetical heretical communities on the basis of the existence of diverse perspectives preserved in the literature.

19
PATRISTIC EXEGESIS

No study of the patristic period would be complete without some discussion of the approach of the fathers to the biblical text. Indeed, it can be argued that no other aspect of the study of the fathers can proceed without an awareness of their attitude to the Bible. Their theology, Christology, ecclesiology, and indeed their entire world view is bound up with this book. To paraphrase one textbook's comment on Clement, "the Bible held the same position in patristic thought that the basic premises of logic held in Greek philosophy."

The primary conviction governing the patristic attitude to the Bible was that it constituted divine revelation. This attitude was not unique to the fathers; rather they inherited it from Judaism, which held that its holy writings, which were to become the Christian Old Testament, were a record of God's revelation to Israel through its many prophets. Whenever Jesus or his early followers refer to the Hebrew scriptures, it is clear that they regard them as God's inspired word. "All Scripture," the author of 2 Timothy 3: 16 writes, "is inspired of God and is useful for teaching, for reproof, correction, and training in holiness so that the man of God may be fully competent and equipped for every good work." The interesting thing about the above citation is its view that scripture has a practical purpose. It is not just a relic of or memorial to an encounter with the divine. The scriptures were thought of as a gift from God for the purpose of guiding the lives of the faithful; they were meant to instruct the Christian in the ways of holiness, enabling one to do the work of the Lord. Of course the "scripture" of which 2 Timothy 3 speaks is the Jewish Bible. Indeed, for the first century or so the only corpus of texts that qualified as scripture would have been the Jewish Bible (see ch. 7 on the canon). Thus from the very beginning a primary issue confronting the followers of Jesus was the relationship between the Jewish scriptures and their own message. While the Christians accepted the Jewish position regarding the inspired status of these writings, they could not accept the Jewish interpretation of them.

The addition of the New Testament to the Jewish Bible constituted a fundamental change. While the Bible was understood as a witness to the divine purpose, as was the case in Judaism, for the Christians the teachings and person of Jesus Christ, as preserved initially in oral teachings of the church and then in the New Testament, gave a new meaning to God's purpose. If the Jewish Bible, as understood by the Jewish religion, recorded God's purpose for Israel, for the Christians the fulfillment of that purpose was to be found in Jesus and the Church, the new Israel. Thus the *real* meaning of the Old Testament was, like the meaning of the New, to be found in the person of Jesus Christ. For Christians, Jesus was the measure of any acceptable reading of the Old Testament.

Such a conclusion was not without its difficulties, the greatest of which is the fact that the Old Testament does not obviously concern itself with Jesus: it does not even mention his name. In the minds of many, there were other obvious difficulties. While Jesus preached of the love of God and humankind, the Old Testament portrayed a jealous God intent, it seemed, on extracting revenge at every turn. While the Old Testament described God as a giver of laws, Jesus spoke of unlimited forgiveness, faith, and divine grace. These differences were brought to the fore by groups like the Marcionites and Gnostics, who decided that the Old Testament was not compatible with the teachings of Jesus Christ. In their view it was not inspired by the transcendent God represented by Christ, but by an evil or lesser being they called the demiurge. For these groups the Old Testament was not to be accepted as scripture (this was Marcion's position), or it was to be substantially rewritten (as some Gnostic groups attempted to do with key stories).

These tendencies, however, represented only a minority view. Most Christians maintained the Old Testament as scripture, and argued for the harmony of its message with that of Jesus Christ and the writings of the New Testament. The relationship between the two was understood in terms of prophecy and fullfillment. The expectations in the Jewish Bible for a people of Israel fully cognizant of God and fully members of his kingdom were understood by the fathers to have been realized with the coming of Jesus Christ according to the tradition taught in the writings of the New Testament. If the Old Testament portrayed God in different terms than the New, it was, Irenaeus states, not without a purpose. Since the Jews of Old Testament times did not know Christ, God could not use the language of the New Testament in his dealings with them. According to Irenaeus, the Old Testament represents the divine message in terms that would have been understandable to the Jews of that time. Thus while it was viewed as containing the truth, it was in a language that concealed it. Moreover, since, as noted above, the fathers understood the Old Testament as prophecy, it could not be expected to speak in plain terms. Prophecy, as it was understood at that time, was by nature cryptic. It would be unfair to judge the words of the Old Testament by the plain meaning of its words. What was needed to properly understand the Old Testament, then, was the key to its special code, and for the church fathers that key was Jesus.

The method typically used by the church fathers to find the Christian message in the Old Testament was not "allegory," as is sometime thought, but, as J.N.D. Kelly observes, "typology." Typology is an interpretive approach based on recognising an underlying pattern in different events. Thus, Moses was understood as a type of Christ. As Moses brought a new covenant to Israel, so Christ brings a new covenant to the new Israel. Certainly the new covenant was understood as a fuller expression of God's will and purpose, but the old initiates or establishes a pattern of divine action and redemption that is continued in the new. For typology to work properly, therefore, it requires that the events involved should be in some sense true.

Allegory was typically used to establish the deeper level of meanings thought to exist in the Bible. In contrast to typology, allegory posits a rift between what a text says and what that text means. In an allegory the words of a text are not taken literally, but as symbols of some deeper truth, usually of a moral or spiritual kind. A well known example is Augustine's analysis of the parable of the Good Samaritan, according to which the traveller is understood not as a traveller, but as a reference to Adam. Jerusalem is not primarily a reference to Jerusalem, but to the city of God. Jericho stands for the moral depravity into which Adam fell, the thieves for Satan, the Samaritan for Christ, the inn for the Church, and so forth.

The grand master of Christian allegory was Origen of Alexandria. Origen was a Platonist at heart, and as such was convinced that the things of this world were only imperfect images of and pointers to things in the spiritual world. For the Bible this meant that the surface or literal meaning of the text was only a pale reflection of a more important, deeper level of meaning. Based on this belief, Origen was the first Christian to formulate a systematic theory of meaning. According to his theory, the Bible has three levels: the literal, the moral, and the spiritual. The literal was the surface meaning of the text. Origen did not completely ignore this meaning, as has sometimes been asserted, but for him it was less important than the other two. Its utility was in its value for instructing the "simple," who did not have the spiritual discipline to explore the deeper meanings of the text. The moral meaning was a higher meaning designed to instruct the Christian in a properly pious life style. The spiritual meaning, containing the deepest Christian truths, informed the student about the most important things: the nature of Christ, his relationship to the Father, the mysteries of the Atonement, the nature and condition of the human soul, and so forth. J.N.D. Kelly points out in *Early Christian Doctrinres* [§24.20], however, that in his actual exegetical practice Origen appears to have followed a somewhat different three-fold system of interpretation, consisting of the plain or literal sense, the typological sense, and the spiritual sense.

Although Origen was the first Christian to employ allegory in a thorough-going manner, he did not originate the method. Allegory had long been in use by Stoic philosophers who had used it as a means of interpreting traditional Greek myths and legends. Origen's most important antecedent was another Alexandrian, a thoroughly Hellenized Jewish philosopher named Philo, who was concerned to demonstrate the compatibility of the Bible with the teachings of Greek philosophy. From this perspective, with its Jealous God who is often more interested in war and vengeance than spiritual truths, the Bible is not very attractive. Philo found in the allegorical method a way of reading these texts in a way more palatable to his Hellenistic sensibilities.

From Origen, allegory made it into the repertoire of most patristic exegesis. Despite its popularity, however, it did not have universal assent. One group that expressed concern about the method was the Antiocene fathers, who, on this issue, are probably best represented by Theodore of Mopsuestia. Theodore and his colleagues did not deny that the Scriptures contained meanings other than the literal, but for them it was unacceptable to divorce the text's spiritual meaning from its literal meaning. For them the primary principle of exegesis was what was called "insight," in which any spiritual meaning must be based on the literal meaning of the text in question. The earlier event may contain within it or refer to a truth greater than itself—this is the "insight." Nonetheless, it would be a mistake to dismiss the original event and its literal meaning. For this reason, Antiocene exegesis usually elaborates the literal meaning of the text more than the Alexandrians did, who wanted quickly to get passed the "simple" meaning to the greater spiritual truths they claimed were to be found there. (DeR)

19.1 🏛 Froehlich, Karlfried., trans. and ed. *Biblical Interpretation in the Early Church.* Sources of Early Christian Thought. Philadelphia: Fortress Press, 1984. Pp. 135; B-3.
A collection of primary texts, in English translation, outlining the principles of biblical interpretation expounded by a number of early Christian thinkers. This book contains excerpts from the writings of Ptolemy, Irenaeus, Origen, Diodore of Tarsus, Theodore of Mopsuestia, and Tyconius. The collection also contains a copy of Papyrus Michigan Inv. 3718. (DeR)

19.2 🏛 Megivern, James J. *Bible Interpretation.* Wilmington, NC: McGrath, 1978. Pp. xxxv + 466.
A collection of primary texts about the principles of Christian biblical interpretation. This work is invaluable for the undergraduate because it brings together in English translation documents that are otherwise difficult to find. Although it covers the entirety of Christian history,

there is a large selection of texts from the patristic age, including writings by Irenaeus, Tertullian, Origen, Eusebius, Cyril, Athanasius. Jerome, Augustine, and Vincent of Lérins. There are also excerpts from the Muratorian Fragment, the Council of Hippo, and a letter from Pope Leo I, all bearing on patristic Bible exegesis. (DeR)

19.3 Balás, David L. "The Use and Interpretation of Paul in Irenaeus's Five Books, *Adversus Haereses*." *Second Century* 9 (1992): 27-39. Irenaeus was the major critic of the Gnostics and their interpretative methods. Balás explores Irenaeus' use of the Pauline epistles in his arguments against Gnostics, examining the effect of two factors on Irenaeus' method: (1) the principle of the unity of Scripture— including both the Old and New Testaments; and (2) the normative role of the apostolic tradition as preserved by the church. (DeR)

19.4 Bethune-Baker, J.F. *An Introduction to the Early History of Christian Doctrine to the Time of the Council of Chalcedon*. London: Methuen, 1958. (1903[1]). Pp. xxvi + 458. I-8 A classic study of all aspects of early Christian doctrine, Bethune-Baker's discussion of Scripture and its interpretation occurs in chapters four through six. In Chapter Four, Bethune-Baker places the early Christian debate over the inspiration of Scripture, and its role in biblical exegesis, in the wider context of Greek culture. Specifically, he places his discussion of the interpretive methods of Irenaeus, Clement, Origen, Tertullian, Augustine, the Cappadocians, and several other Christian groups in the context of the textual theories found in Philo and Homer. Chapter Five is a rare treasure, discussing the interpretive procedures of the Ebionites and other groups of Jewish Christians. Chapter Six is devoted to an examination of the interpretive procedures of the various Gnostic groups, including Marcion, Carpocrates, the school of Basilides, and the Valentinians. (DeR)

19.5 Caspary, Gerard E. *Politics and Exegesis: Origen and the Two Swords*. Berkeley: University of California, 1979. Pp. xv + 215. Using the image of the two swords in the Gospel of Luke as a focal point, this book examines the relationship of Origen's biblical exegesis and his theology of politics. There are comprehensive yet easily understood chapters examining Origen's interpretation of the Old and New Testaments, as well as a chapter devoted to the hermeneutical principles informing his interpretive methods. The latter part of the book is an exploration of the relationship between these principles and Origen's political theory. (DeR)

⧐ Costigan, *TS* 41 (1980): 236.

19.6   Coggins, R.J., and J.L. Houlden, eds. *A Dictionary of Biblical Interpretation*. London: SCM / Philadelphia: Trinity, 1990. Pp. xvi + 751.
A one-volume dictionary focusing on issues pertaining to the interpretation of the Bible. The relevant entries include: John Barton, "Canon," and "Eisegesis"; Anders J. Bjørndalen, "Allegory"; Averil Cameron, "Women in Early Christian Interpretation"; Henry Chadwick, "Augustine"; Stuart G. Hall, "Gnosticism," "Marcion," and "Tertullian"; Andrew Louth, "Allegorical Interpretation"; Brian McNeil, "Typology"; R. A. Norris, "Antiochene Interpretation"; Christine Trevett, "Apostolic Fathers," "Irenaeus," and "Papias"; Francis Young, "Alexandrian Interpretation," "Literal Meaning," "Origen," "Rhetoric," and "Spiritual Meaning." (DeR)

19.7   Cox, Patricia, "Origen and the Witch of Endor: Towards an Iconoclastic Typology." *Anglican Theological Review* 66 (1984): 137-147.
When one thinks of Origen's interpretation of the Old Testament, one thinks immediately of the allegorical and typological methods. But the matter is more complex. Cox provides an assessment of these methods in the light of Origen's "literal" reading of "historical" texts such as 1 Samuel 28:5-14. (DeR)

19.8   ☛ Danker, Frederick W. "Biblical Exegesis: Christian Views." In *The Encyclopedia of Religion*. II: 142-152.
A survey article covering the entire Christian tradition. A useful brief overview of developments within patristic exegesis can be found on pages 143-145. (DeR)

19.9   ☛ Dockery, David S. *Biblical Interpretation Then and Now: Contemporary Hermeneutics in the Light of the Early Church*. Grand Rapids: Baker, 1992. Pp. 247; G-7; B-41; I-13.
An easy read, this book approaches the question of early Christian biblical interpretation from a historical and hermeneutical perspective. Beginning with the interpretive methods Jesus used in his reading of the Hebrew Scriptures, Dockery sketches the development of the principles of Christian biblical interpretation from their beginnings to the Council of Chalcedon (451 CE). By tracing this development within the Jewish and Hellenistic interpretive traditions of the day, Dockery places Christian theories of biblical interpretation within their wider cultural context. Yet he appreciates the unique

contribution Christians themselves have made to later developments in interpretation theory. With a glossary of technical terms and a thorough bibliography, this work is highly recommended to the undergraduate about to embark on a study of patristic hermeneutics. (DeR)

19.10   Edwards, M. J. "Gnostics, Greeks, and Origen: The Interpretation of Interpretation." *Journal of Theological Studies* n.s. 44 (1993): 70-89.

This article compares the use of allegory as a literary technique and as an interpretive method in the writings of non-Christian Greek philosophers, Gnostics, and early Christian thinkers. It is important to understand this matter, especially since the orthodox were sensitive to, and often sharply critical of, the exegetical methods employed by the Gnostics. (DeR)

19.11   Fahey, Michael Andrew. *Cyprian and the Bible: A Study in Third-Century Exegesis.* Tübingen: Mohr, 1971. Pp. 696. B-14.

Originally Fahey's doctoral dissertation, this is a detailed study of the biblical exegesis of Cyprian. After discussing Cyprian's definition of scripture, canon and inspiration, Fahey outlines his exegetical method. He places Cyprian's typological method within the context of his Christology, and his belief in the unity and totality of Scripture. Fahey illustrates these principles with a long and detailed analysis of the many biblical texts interpreted by Cyprian. (DeR)

✂< Bruce, *EQ* 44 (1972): 49-50; Greenslade, *JEH* 23 (1972): 178-180; Norris, *JBL* 92 (1973): 305-306; Hughes, *WTJ* 35 (1973): 355-356; O'Doherty, *CBQ* 34 (1972): 212-213.

19.12   Gorday, Peter. *Principles of Patristic Exegesis: Romans 9-11 in Origen, John Chrysostom, and Augustine.* New York / Toronto: Edwin Mellen, 1983. Pp. xvii + 403; B-29; BI-6; AI-5; AAI-7; SI-3.

Originally the author's dissertation, this is a detailed analysis of the interpretation of Romans 9-11 by three important exegetes of the patristic period. After discussing the character of patristic interpretation in general, and trends in the patristic approach to Romans 9-11 in particular, Gorday offers a detailed examination of the interpretations of this important text by Origen, Chrysostom, and Augustine. (DeR)

✂< Kelly, *JBL* 105 (1986): 166-168; Trigg, *CH* 54 (1985): 91-92; Young, *JTS* 36 (1985): 484-487.

19.13 ☛ Grant, Robert M, and David Tracy. *A Short History of the Interpretation of the Bible*. 2d ed. Philadelphia: Fortress Press, 1984. Pp. 213. I-9; B-5.

Originally titled *The Bible in the Church*, the current volume is the second edition under the title *A Short History of the Interpretation of the Bible*. The fifteen chapters of part one are by Grant. Chapters 5-7 are especially important: "The Bible in the Second Century"; "The School of Alexandria"; and "The School of Antioch." Grant discusses a trend in interpretive theory away from the allegorical methods of the Alexandrian school of Clement and Origen to the more literal methods of interpretation associated with Antioch. Further, unlike some recent works, Grant shows more sympathy for the hermeneutics of the orthodox than of the Gnostics. Part 2, on interpretation theory, was written by Tracy. This is a solid general introduction to the main methods used in the interpretation of scripture.

✀ Bray, *Churchman* 98 (1984): 341; Reese, *BTB* 15 (1985): 158.

19.14 Greer, Rowan A. *The Captain of Our Salvation: A Study in the Patristic Exegesis of Hebrews*. Tübingen: Mohr, 1973. Pp. 371. B-6; BI.

An analysis of the relationship between scripture and theology, this study explores the use made by the third and fourth century church fathers of the Epistle to the Hebrews in the developing Christology of the early church. In order to highlight the particularities of the Antiochene exegetical tradition, which is the book's focus, Greer discusses the way the Alexandrians and Cappadocians used the epistle in their respective Christologies. The book includes detailed studies of Origen, Athanasius and the Cappadocians, Eustace, Diodore, Theodore, Chrysostom, Theodoret, Cyril, and Nestorius. The study is particularly sensitive to the ambiguity of the claim that the Bible is the source of theology while its meaning is in many ways determined precisely by that theology. (DeR)

✀ Hughes, *WTJ* 37 (1974): 123-127; Kelly, *JBL* 93 (1974): 316-319; Schatkin, *TS* 37 (1976): 331-332; Swetnam, *CBQ* 36 (1974): 401-403.

19.15 Hamilton, Gordon J. "Augustine's Methods of Biblical Interpretation." In *Grace, Politics & Desire: Essays on Augustine*. Edited by Hugo A. Meynell. Calgary, AB: University of Calgary Press, 1990. Pp. 103-119.

Hamilton discusses Augustine's eclectic approach to biblical interpretation, including his definitions of literal meaning, allegory, and typology, in the context of his concern for the Christian community and its experience of God. (DeR)

19.16   Hanson, R.P.C. *Allegory and Event: A Study of the Sources and Significance of Origen's Interpretation of Scripture.* Richmond: John Knox, 1959. Pp. 400. B-6; I.
In many ways the classic study in English of Origen's method of biblical interpretation. This work places Origen's allegorical and typological methods in the context of Jewish biblical interpretation, especially that of Philo and Paul. Hanson discusses in detail Origen's theory that scripture has three senses—the literal, the moral, and the spiritual. He offers lengthy discussions of the role of the Bible in Origen's definition of inspiration and history, and in his understanding of the Christian sacraments, the Jewish Law and eschatology. (DeR)
✂ Chadwick, *ExT* 70 (1959): 168-169; Greenslade, *CQR* 160 (1959): 536-537; Turner, *JTS* 10 (1959): 382-384.

19.17   Heine, Ronald E. "Stoic Logic as Handmaid to Exegesis and Theology in Origen's Commentary on the Gospel of John." *Journal of Theological Studies* n.s. 44 (1993): 90-117.
An analysis of Origen's use of Stoic logic in his commentary on the Gospel of John. In particular the article explores Origen's use of Stoic forms of the syllogism and the proposition, focusing his discussion on the relationship between the Father and the Son, and on his refutations of both the Monarchian notion of God and the Heracleon doctrine of Christ's natures. (DeR)

19.18   Horbury, William. "Old Testament Interpretation in the Writings of the Church Fathers." In *Mikra: Text, Translation, Reading and Interpretation of the Hebrew Bible in Ancient Judaism and Early Christianity.* Ed. M. J. Mulder. Assen/Philadelphia: Van Gorcum/Fortress, 1988. Pp. 727-787; B-56; I.
Horbury examines the patristic approach to the Old Testament along two different lines. First, he discusses the different ways the Old Testament was used in various types of Christian literature, including homily, commentary, catechesis, apologetic, ecclesiastical law, liturgy, poetry, and art. This is followed by a description of the different methods used by patristic exegetes, including typology, allegory and the literal sense. The article ends with a useful list of patristic exegetes, organised by the school of interpretation to which they belonged. (DeR)

19.19   Jansen, John F. "Tertullian and the New Testament" *Second Century*

2 (1982): 191-207.

A general discussion of Tertullian's exegesis of the New Testament, with some comments on the shape of the canon at the time of Tertullian, the text of the New Testament used by Tertullian, and the authority of the canon in that period. It is Jansen's contention that Tertullian has no strict method of interpretation—he simply is not an exegete, and his use of the Bible is almost always in the context of polemics. (DeR)

19.20   Kugel, James L., and Rowan A. Greer. *Early Biblical Interpretation.* Library of Early Christianity 3. Philadelphia: Westminster, 1986. Pp. 214. BI-6; B-4.

Only the second part of this book, written by Greer, is of importance here (Part One is Kugel's study of early Jewish Bible interpretation.) Greer's essay is composed of four chapters, each devoted to a different aspect of the issue. In his first chapter he discusses how the growth of the Christian Bible, a process that spans 30-180 CE, can be seen as an expression of the growing sense of unity that developed within the Christian community over this same period. According to Greer, Irenaeus represents the climax of both processes. In Chapter Two Greer explores the place of the Hebrew Scriptures in the early church. Greer sees the methods of interpretation developed by the early church as a reflex of the wider discussion regarding the status of these writings in the early Christian community. The central issue of the debate was their witness to Christ. In the remaining two chapters Greer discusses the role of the Christian Bible, especially the New Testament, in the formation of the church's Rule of Faith. In Chapter Three he explores how it was that the Bible came to be the primary guide in issues of theology, Christology, and Christian life. In the last chapter he discusses the underlying principles of Christian exegesis, including those informing allegory, typology, the discovery of the moral meaning of the text, as well as its literal meaning. (DeR)

⤢ Armstrong, *CH* 56 (1987): 102; Black, *JAAR* 55 (1987): 605-607; Danker, *CBQ* 49 (1987): 508-509; Eisen, *CRBR* (1988): 43-60; Gerstmyer, *CRBR* (1988): 130-132; Metzger, *TT* 43 (1987): 598-601; Murphy, *Interpretation* 41 (1987): 310; Newsom, *JR* 67 (1987): 538-539; Perkins, *Cross Currents* 36 (1986): 230-233; Snyder, *CTSR* 79 (1989): 65; Stacey, *JTS* 39 (1988): 214-215; Wilken, *TS* 48 (1987): 537-538.

19.21   Lampe, G.W.H. and K.J. Woollcombe, *Essays on Typology.* London: SCM, 1957. Pp. 80.

In Chapter Two, the authors discuss the use of typology as a method for exegesis of the Old Testament by the church fathers, paying particular attention to the use of that method in the New Testament, especially in the writings of Paul. (DeR)

>< Brown, *CBQ* 19 (1957): 533-535; Farrer, *TS* 9 (1958): 122-124; Hooke, *CQR* 159 (1958): 291-292; Markus, *SJT* 10 (1957): 416-418.

19.22 O'Malley, T.P. *Tertullian and the Bible: Language—Imagery—Exegesis*. Utrecht: Dekker & van de Vegt, 1967. Pp. xvi + 186. B-6.

O'Malley explains Tertullian's sensitivities to the language and imagery of the Bible in the context of the tension that Tertullian perceived between the classical and biblical worlds. After discussing Tertullian's understanding of the relationship between revelation, the church, and scripture, in the third chapter the author discusses Tertullian's exegetical methods, focusing on his use of the terms, *aenigma, allegoria, figura, portendere,* and *simplicitas*. (DeR)

>< Hammond, *JTS* 20 (1969): 309-311; Hardy, *JBL* 89 (1970): 259.

19.23 Pagels, Elaine. "The Politics of Paradise: Augustine's Exegesis of Genesis 1-3 Versus that of John Chrysostom." *Harvard Theological Review* 78 (1985): 67-95.

Pagels points to the politics of the imperial church to account for the shift from the positive interpretation of Genesis 1-3 in Chrysostom to the negative one proffered by Augustine. A less technical version of this article appears as Chapter Five of Pagels' best-selling *Adam, Eve, and the Serpent* [§14.17]. (DeR)

19.24 Reijners, G.Q. *The Terminology of the Holy Cross in Early Christian Literature*. Nijmegen-Utrecht: Dekker & van de Vegt, 1965. Pp. xxiv + 230. B-7.

The early Christians believed that numerous passages in the Old Testament prophesied clearly of the death of Jesus. Reijners, in this philological study, analyzes the terminology for the cross in Christian literature between the period of the New Testament and the third century. He refers specifically to those Old Testament texts thought by the early Christian authors to prefigure typologically the death of Jesus. The study is comprehensive, touching on most of the extant literature from the period under consideration. A knowledge of Greek and Latin would be a definite asset. (DeR)

>< Yarnold, *JTS* 18 (1967): 483-484.

19.25 Rogers, Jack B., and Donald K. McKim, *The Authority and Interpretation of the Bible: An Historical Approach*. New York: Harper & Row, 1979. Pp. xxiv + 484. NI-4; SI-8.

A survey of the interpretation of the Bible within the history of Christianity. The patristic period is discussed in Chapter One; here the authors trace the shift from allegorical to grammatical interpretation in the context of both the Greek philosophical and the Christian theological traditions. A short "Select Bibliography" is provided at the end of each chapter. (DeR)

⊰ Caemmerer, *CC* 97 (1980): 263; Pinnock, *Sojourners* 9 (1980): 35-36.

19.26   *Studia Patristica* 10 (1970).
The following articles are relevant. G.T. Armstrong ("The Genesis Theophanies of Hilary of Poitiers") explores the role played by Hilary's typological interpretation of the theophanies in Genesis in the context of his disputations with the Arians; S.P. Brock ("Origen's Aim as a Textual Critic of the Old Testament") discusses the relationship between Origen's apologetic concerns and his work on the text of the Old Testament; J. Duncan M. Derrett ("The Parable of the Prodigal Son: Patristic Allegories and Jewish Midrashim") discusses the gulf between the Jewish type of Old Testament exegesis that Jesus assumes in his parables, and the allegorical methods used by the church fathers in their interpretation of Scripture. (DeR)

19.27   *Studia Patristica* 12 (1975).
The following articles are relevant. J.T. Cummings ("St. Jerome as Translator and Exegete") examines how Jerome's theological, philosophical, and rhetorical concerns affected the language of the Vulgate; E. Fasholé-Luke ("Who is the Bridegroom? An Excursion into St. Cyprian's Use of Scripture") explores Cyprian's typological use of the Old Testament to define the Christian priesthood, and to defend the notion that Jesus Christ is the Church's only bridegroom; D.F. Heimann ("The Polemical Application of Scripture in St. Jerome") focuses on Jerome's, *Adversus Jovinianum*, exploring the way in which Jerome used the Bible in his polemical writings. Making a distinction between interpretation and application of scripture, Heimann places polemic in the latter category. (DeR)

19.28   *Studia Patristica* 14 (1976).
Two of the articles in this volume are particularly relevant. N. R. M. de Lange ("Origen and the Rabbis on the Hebrew Bible") focuses on the issue of the authority of the Hebrew Bible, exploring the relationship between Origen's allegorical and the rabbi's midrashic approaches to these scriptures. F. Hockey ("St. Augustine and John I,3-4") examines the relationship between Augustine's Christology and his choice of New Testament versions. (DeR)

19.29 *Studia Patristica* 15 (1984).

A number of articles are relevant in this collection. J. S. Alexander ("Aspects of Donatist Scriptural Interpretation at the Conference of Carthage of 411") examines the Donatist's use of Scripture in the defense of their position on the priesthood and on the proper way of performing the sacraments; G.W. Ashby ("The Hermeneutic Approach of Theodoret of Cyrrhus to the Old Testament") explores the relationship between the historical/literal and typological methods of interpreting the Old Testament in the thought and exegesis of Theodoret of Cyrrus; W.J.P. Boyd "Galilaea—A Difference of Opinion Between Augustine and Jerome's 'Onomastica Sacra'") focuses on the different interpretations of the name "Galilaea" in the biblical exegesis of Augustine and Jerome, this article explores an interesting facet of the Christocentric reading of the Old Testament by the church fathers; K.W. Noakes ("The Metaphrase on Ecclesiastes of Gregory Thaumaturgus") argues that Gregory's rewriting of Ecclesiates is not just a paraphrase, but a description, based on the thought of Origen, of man's real good and how it can be attained. (DeR)

19.30 *Studia Patristica* 16 (1985).

A number of articles are relevant in this collection. A. Meredith, ("Allegory in Porphyry and Gregory of Nyssa") compares the different ways in which Porphyry and Gregory used the allegorical method in their respective interpretations of the Odyssey and the Bible; W.S. Babcock ("Augustine and Paul: The Case of Romans IX") explores of the role played by Romans 9 in the development of Augustine's notion of divine grace; P. Hebblethwaite ("St. Augustine's Interpretation of Matthew 5,17") discusses the role played by Matthew 5:17 in Augustine's dialogue with the Manichees, and the implications this dialog had on Augustine's understanding of the relationship between Christianity and Judaism. (DeR)

19.31 *Studia Patristica* 17 (1982)

A number of articles are relevant in this collection. H.A. Blair, ("Allegory, Typology and Archetypes") discusses the typologies used by the early church to link Jesus Christ to the Old Testament; James Barr ("The Vulgate Genesis and St. Jerome's Attitude to Women") explores Jerome's ambiguous attitude towards women as reflected in the language of the Vulgate; Patout J. Burns ("The Function of Christ in Ambrose of Milan's Interpretation of the Command Given to Adam") examines how Ambrose used the New Testament portrayal of the life of Jesus as a model for interpreting

God's command to Adam not to eat from the tree of the knowledge of good and evil. (DeR)

19.32   Terab, J.M. "The Labourers in the Vineyard: The Exegesis of Matthew 20,1-7 in the Early Church." *Vigiliae Christianae* 46 (1992): 356-380.
An inventory of the different interpretations of the Parable of the Labourers in the Vineyard offered by Christian expositors from the second through sixth centuries. Terab focuses particularly on the way they interpreted the hours of the day mentioned in the parable. Texts and/or interpreters examined include the Valentinian Gnostics, Hippolytus of Rome, Ephrem of Nisibis, Origen, Eusebius of Caesarea, Jerome, Ambrose, Hilary of Poitier, Augustine, John Chrysostom, Basil of Caesarea, and Cyril of Alexandria. (DeR)

19.33   Thiselton, Anthony C. *New Horizons in Hermeneutics: The Theory and Practice of Transforming Biblical Reading.* Grand Rapids: Zondervan, 1992. Pp. xii + 703; B-41.
A thorough-going study of the history of hermeneutics (the principles underlying and informing interpretive methods). In Chapter Four, Thiselton examines the methods employed during the patristic period. After discussing the relationship between pre-modern, modern, and post-modern hermeneutics, he discusses the hermeneutic systems employed by the church fathers in the context of the debate over the status of the Old Testament; and the Gnostic system of interpreting Scripture. There is an analysis of the rise of and debate over the allegorical method of interpretation favored by Origen and the Alexandrian church. (DeR)
✄ Moo, *Trinity Journal* 13 (1992): 250.

19.34   Torjesen, Karen Jo. "'Body,' 'Soul,' and 'Spirit' in Origen's Theory of Exegesis." *Anglican Theological Review* 67 (1985): 17-30.
An interesting exploration of the relationship between Origen's anthropology and his methods of biblical interpretation. Torjesen explains Origen's theory that the Bible has three levels of meaning—literal, mystical, and moral—in terms of his anthropological theory that a human being is composed of three entities—a body, a soul, and a spirit. (DeR)

19.35   Turner, H.E.W. "Orthodoxy and the Bible." In *The Pattern of Christian Truth: A Study in the Relations Between Orthodoxy and Heresy in the Early Church.* Bampton Lectures 1954. London: A.R. Mowbray, 1954, 1978. Pp. 231-306.

These pages comprise Chapter Five of Turner's Bampton Lectures of 1954. Here he explores the principles of biblical exegesis employed by the church fathers in the context of the debate over the definitions of orthodoxy and heresy. After discussing the growth of the Christian canon, Turner examines the methods of patristic exegesis in the context of the principles that nothing in scripture is irrelevant, accidental, unworthy of God, trivial, or absurd. (DeR)

19.36 ☛ Vawter, Bruce. *Biblical Inspiration.* Philadelphia: Westminster, 1972. Pp. xii + 195; B-6.

In Chapter Two of this general introduction to the issue of biblical inspiration, Vawter discusses, in brief, the allegorical method and the tendency towards harmonization in the context of the patristic understanding of the divine authorship of scripture. (DeR)

⊁ Burtchaell, *CBQ* 35 (1973): 560-562; O'Rourke, *TS* 34 (1973): 524-525; Richardson, *JEH* 24 (1973): 322-3236

19.37 Visotzky, Burton L. "Jots and Titles: On Scriptural Interpretation in Rabbinic and Patristic Literatures." *Prooftexts* 8 (1988): 257-269. In the second and third centuries Christian and Jewish exegetes agreed that nothing in their scriptures was superfluous. This article compares the way in which these two interpretive traditions applied this principle to the Bible during these formative centuries. The focus is on Origen for Christianity, and for Judaism on the competitive exegetical systems of Akiba and Yismael. (DeR)

19.38 Wallace-Hadrill, D S. *Christian Antioch: A Study of Early Christian Thought in the East.* Cambridge: Cambridge UP, 1982. Pp. viii + 218. B-8; I.

In Chapter Two of this book on the church at Antioch, a leading scholar of the area discusses the role played by the idea of history in the biblical interpretation of the Antiochene fathers. Frequent and informative contrast is made with the allegorical interpretation of the Alexandrian church. Such differences as those identified by Wallace-Hadrill provide the basis for those who argue that distinct theological "schools" or tendencies existed at Antioch and Alexandria, a view now widely held. (DeR)

19.39 Waszink, J.H. "Tertullian's Principles and Methods of Exegesis." In *Early Christian Literature and the Classical Intellectual Tradition: In Honorem Robert M. Grant.* Edited by W.R. Schoedel and R.L. Wilken. Paris: Beauchesne, 1979. Pp. 17-31.

Tertullian was a complex individual of considerable rhetorical skills

whose solid contributions in the defense of orthodoxy was qualified
by his later sympathies and defense of the Montanists—a movement,
which the orthodox had dismissed as heretical. Waszink analyzes
Tertullian's eclectic use of interpretive methods in the context of
his training in Roman law and the forms of classical legal argumentation, showing, as Young has done more widely [§19.42], the
impact of the culture on aspects of Christian interpretation of Scripture (DeR)

19.40   Weaver, David. "From Paul to Augustine: Romans 5:12 in Early
        Christian Exegesis." *St. Vladimir's Theological Quarterly* 27 (1983):
        187-206.
        Weaver examines the way the different understandings of sinfulness
        in the Greek and Latin churches affected the way they interpreted
        Romans 5:12. The church fathers examined include Irenaeus, Justin
        Martyr, Clement, Origen, Athanasius, Augustine, and Pelagius.
        (DeR)

19.41   Wilken, Robert L. "*In novissimis diebus*: Biblical Promises, Jewish
        Hopes and Early Christian Exegesis." *Journal of Early Christian
        Studies* 1 (1993): 1-19.
        This article explores the early Christian interpretation of the phrase,
        "in the last days," (*novissimis diebus*), found in Isaiah 2 and Micah
        4. Wilken discusses the ways in which major Christian exegetes
        interpreted the prophets, focusing on the "spiritual" or "allegorical"
        method and on the "historical" or "literal." Wilken argues that it is
        too simplistic to say that Christians preferred the allegorical approach
        in their interpretation of the prophets—rather, that approach was
        made necessary by the Christians' messianic claims for Jesus set
        against a rival Jewish *messianic* understanding of these passages.
        (DeR)

19.42   Young, Francis. "The Rhetorical Schools and Their Influence on
        Patristic Exegesis." In *The Making of Orthodoxy: Essays in Honour
        of Henry Chadwick*. Edited by R. Williams. Cambridge: Cambridge
        UP, 1989. Pp. 182-199; AAI; MAI.
        Young explores early Christian exegesis (particularly that in the
        Antiochene tradition) against the background of classical rhetoric.
        She argues against those who see history as the informing principle
        of the Antiochene approach to biblical interpretation. Young's kind
        of analysis helps us realize just how widely Christians were informed
        by the culture around them—even in something as specifically
        Christian as the interpretation of scripture. (DeR)

20
PERSECUTION AND MARTYRDOM

Minorities often experience persecution. It did not take Christians long to become the new visible minority in the Roman Empire. Neither language, nor skin color, nor distinctive dress drew the attention of the larger society. Christians faded into the crowds more easily than the Jews, more easily than the philosophers of various shades, and certainly more easily than some of the visitors and immigrants from the borders of the empire. As a late second-century Christian text put it: "Christians are not distinguished from the rest of humanity by country, language, or custom. For nowhere do they live in cities of their own, nor do they speak some unusual dialect, nor do they practice an eccentric life-style....They live in both Greek and barbarian cities, as each one's lot was cast, and follow the local customs in dress and food and other aspects of life..." *Epistle to Diognetus* 5:1-4.

Christians did, nonetheless, stand out. This was largely because Christians refused to participate in the normal activities that counted as expressions of piety and civic loyalty. Once Christians were viewed with suspicion, further misunderstanding was inevitable. The charges against them came to include everything from atheism to cannibalism and incest. Any of these charges would have made the situation for Christians in the empire a less-than-hospitable one.

But Christians were well prepared for their minority status in the empire. Jesus himself was executed by the Romans, as were some of the early leaders of the church. These early persecutions and martyrdoms would have been sufficient to cause the Christian community to reflect on the theme of martyrdom, and to reconcile the horror of the event with the piety of those who died. The martyrdom that required explanation was that of Jesus himself. Once the death of Jesus was explained within the framework of service to God, other martyrdoms could be made sense of against that exemplary death.

Christians found resources within Judaism to deal with the problem. The prophets of the Hebrew Bible frequently themselves had to deal with persecution and rejection, which caused them to reflect on and reconcile the hostility of society within an understanding of the will of God. That problem was more sharply confronted during the time of the Maccabees (ca. 160s

BCE), when religious piety became the direct cause of persecution, and religious essentials became capital offences. Writings from the Maccabean period were part of the Jewish and Christian "canon," insofar as that term is applicable in the early period. For Jews, these accounts of the pious faithful were heightened in importance during difficult times, as was the case in the first century when Palestine, under the control of the Romans, was pressed by economic crises and taxation. Reflection on such crises often led to an apocalyptic view of the world, in which suffering and martyrdom were very much part of the fabric of life and could be made understandable within the context of piety. Christians did not need to revise the Jewish perspective at all to make it work in their own situation. Add to this that Christian reflection included at its center the image of God's own Son as martyr, and one can see that they had considerable resources for making martyrdom a meaningful act.

While scholars readily admit that a widespread positive Christian attitude towards persecution and martyrdom existed in the early years of the church, they generally have found it more difficult to determine the extent of persecution of Christians in the Roman Empire. Although the Christian writings themselves address the issue, scholars are uncertain about the reliability of the source of the information in them. The problem reduces to this. It would take only one martyr in a community for that community to reflect on the theme of martyrdom, and this focus could be expressed in one way or another in their writings. Thus one martyrdom or one hundred martyrdoms could produce a similar kind of contemplation on suffering and death, and unless the writer chose to give statistical information, the historian would be unable to say much about the *extent* of persecution from an account that indicated that some persecution did occur. The second problem that confronts the historian in determining the extent of the persecution of Christians is that the emperors seem to have taken a fairly distant, or even disinterested, stance to the new religious movement. Scholars must balance the stories about Nero and Domitian as haters and hunters of Christians with the actual legislation of the emperors Trajan and Hadrian. The fact is that Christians did survive in the empire, and in many places they became a significant minority. By the third century, they were secure enough to have their own buildings for assembly, and Christians were engaged in almost all walks of life, even in the military and the government.

That is not to say that Christians were not disadvantaged in the empire. There are too many accounts of local violence against Christians to dismiss, and a growing list of martyrs was one of the sobering features of Christian communities. Further, Christians were, at best, misunderstood by large elements of the population, and at times they were maliciously misrepresented (see chapter 23: "Society and Social Issues" and chapter 12: "Conversion, Missions, and the Early Christian Apologetic").

Scholars have generally recognized two distinct periods in the suppression of Christians. The first started with the persecution stirred up by Jews in Palestinian areas and extended to Jewish agitation against Christians in various areas of the diaspora, and, then, as Christians became a more visible element in the larger society, to outbreaks of hostility prompted by the local inhabitants in various areas of the empire. Included in this era of persecution are the various attacks in which Christians suffered from the action of an emperor, provided that these attacks were (1) localized (as in the case of Nero), or (2) not specifically against Christians, though Christians could have been included (as in the case of Domitian).

The second period of persecution of Christians started with Decius in 250 CE and, in three distinct *general* persecutions, lasted until 311 CE in the western part of the empire and to about 324 in the eastern part. The most serious times were in the years 250-251 (under Decius), 257-259 (under Valerian), and 303-305 (under Diocletian, who gave it all up to grow cabbages). In each of these persecutions, there was a conscious attempt, *on an empire-wide scale*, to cause Christians to apostatize and return to pagan religion.

Several other questions have surfaced about the persecution of Christians. The most pressing one is why were Christians persecuted at all. From this a related question arises: what was the legal status of Christians in the empire? Sherwin-White gives a review of the debate from the former half of this century [§20.26]. He points out three main theories. One theory specifies that some early edict making Christianity illegal remained in effect until the time of Constantine. In other words, Christianity, in and of itself, was illegal. The second is the *coercitio* (coercion) theory. It contends that the Roman emperors did not need specific legislation against Christianity in order to take action against it. Emperors had an obligation to maintain public order. Insofar as Christians jeopardized this order, they could be suppressed. Those who support this theory can point to a number of specific actions of Christians to account for the public perception that Christians were a threat to the public order. The third theory explains the persecution of Christians by reference to already existing laws against certain kinds of behavior judged to be criminal acts (e.g. child-murder, incest, or illegal assembly). Thus Christians were killed, not for being Christians, but for specific offenses regarding which anyone would have been executed. These kinds of issues have been at the heart of much of the scholarly debate.

Two distinctive developments in Christianity can be traced back to the Christian experience of persecution and martyrdom. One is the cult of the saints; the other is monasticism. Martyrs were highly esteemed by the local assemblies of which they had been members, and their martyrdom in some ways was seen as a sign of God's special favor. These individuals entered immediately into God's presence (not unlike the view in present-day fundamentalist Islam, where interest in martyrdom may involve a minor debt to the early Christians). Other Christians who died natural deaths were thought to await the general resurrection at the end of the age. Thus martyrs were close to God in a way that others could not be, and they became links for the living to the very presence of God. Out of this developed an interest in relics of the saints. Even the church calendar began to reflect the elevated status of martyrs, as the day of their death (or the day of their "birth into eternity") became annual celebrations. This heightened importance of martyrs led to serious conflicts with the hierarchy of the church, since persons under the sentence of death or those who had been released from the sentence of death without denying Christ or sacrificing to the gods were given the status of "living martyr" or "confessor." The word "confessor" is simply the Latin word for the Greek word "martyr." The problem was that confessors and martyrs were popularly thought to be able to forgive sins (or, at least, a confessor's request to a priest to restore people to communion carried considerable weight). In that the forgiveness of sins related directly to the issue of membership in the Christian community, the confessors could influence the character of the church. This was a threat to the clergy, because it infringed on their role in, and control of, the local assemblies.

The second development with roots in the Christian experience of martyrdom was monasticism. To a degree, monasticism can be considered to be a continuation of the mentality of martyrdom after martyrdom had ceased to be a possibility for Christians. The turning point was the unexpected conversion of Constantine, which brought to an end the disadvantaged position of Christians in the empire. The rigor shown by the martyrs had now to be displayed in a "bloodless" way, and monasticism, with its radical commitment to the cause of God and its uncompromising opposition to the normal pleasures of life became almost a living death (see chapter 17: "Monasticism and Asceticism"), thus carrying forward an elitist mentality into the consciousness of the Christian church.

20.1 🏛 Canfield, Leon Hardy. *The Early Persecutions of Christians.* Columbia University Studies in the Social Sciences 136. New York: Columbia UP, 1913. Reprint. New York: AMS. 1968.
A collection of primary sources relevant to the persecution of Christians. All selections are provided in English translation, and the Greek and Latin originals are provided for many of the passages.

20.2 🏛 Musurillo, Herbert, ed. and trans. *The Acts of the Christian Martyrs.* Oxford: Clarendon, 1972. Pp. lxxiii + 377. I-4; BI-3; AAI-3; NI-6; Geographical Index-3.

The *Acts* of the martyrs represent not only one of the fundamental "documentary" sources for the history of the early church, but also an extremely valuable, and hence increasingly used, source for the social history of the second to the fourth centuries CE. In what is still the standard work of collected original texts in Greek and Latin, with matching English translation on facing pages, Musurillo selects twenty-eight numbered *acta* extending from the martyrdom of Polycarp and the Scillitan martyrs of the second century down to the last martyrs of the "Great Persecution" under Diocletian and his successors. These are the twenty-eight texts which the editor considers "the most reliable" or, even when somewhat fictional, at least "important and instructive." In an extensive introductory section he offers an outline of what is known about the historical context and the textual history of each of the *acta*. With slight revisions, the texts are those of existing standard editions. Musurillo's translation, though readable, is strewn with technical inaccuracies—as are many of the historical claims made by him. These parts of the text must therefore be used with considerable caution (see Millar's review). (S)

≻< Millar, *JTS* 24 (1973): 239-243.

20.3   Barnes, Timothy D. "The Pre-Decian *Acta Martyrum*." *Journal of Theological Studies* 19 (1968): 509-531.
This is a fundamental hard-line analysis of the probable historical validity of the major "martyr acts" that record events of individual outbreaks of persecution before the mid-third century Decian persecution. In his usual probing, meticulous and highly critical style, Barnes offers what is now the standard source-critical analysis of the genuine nature and historical dependability of the earliest Christian martyr texts. Required reading for anyone making serious use of these documents. (S)

20.4   Bisbee, Gary A. *Pre-Decian Acts of Martyrs and Commentary.* Harvard Dissertations in Religion No. 22. Philadelphia: Fortress, 1988. Pp xv + 187.
Originally a doctoral dissertation at Harvard (1986), this study by Bisbee is a detailed analysis of the literary form of the *commentarius* (a trial transcript), in which early Christian martyr acts were redacted. Bisbee begins by dissecting what is known of previous trial transcripts in the secular context of Roman courts. He then tests this standard form both against the acts of the so-called "pagan martyrs" from Alexandria and against some of the earliest martyr *acta* from the Greek east (those of Justin Martyr, Polycarp, and

Ignatius). Further, Bisbee provides plenty of citations of primary source materials from which the reader can assess the difference between the Roman court documents and the use of this form by the authors of the Christian martyr *acta*. (S)

✂ Frend, *JEH* 41 (1990): 77-78; Hinson, *R&E* 86 (1989): 632-633; Huelin, *ExT* 100 (1989): 392-393; MacDonald, *CRBR* (1991): 281-283.

20.5   Brunt, Peter A. "Marcus Aurelius and the Christians." In *Studies in Latin Literature and Roman History*. Edited by C. Deroux. Brussels: Collection Latomus no. 164, 1 (1979): 483-520.

Beginning with the text of Marcus Aurelius' *Meditations* 11.3, Brunt discusses its import as a possible reference to the behavior of Christians—i.e., that their martyrdoms might be interpreted as a species of voluntary suicide as understood by the primary Stoic thinkers of the second century (especially Epictetus) under whose influence the emperor's thinking worked. Brunt reaches the conclusion that "no covert references to the Christians can be found in Marcus' text, and the one explicit mention of them does not fit the sense of the passage where it occurs." He therefore rejects this explicit notice as a later gloss, probably by a pagan reader who was aware that persecutions of the Christians continued under Marcus' reign. In the second half of the article Brunt then discusses the evidence of the persecutions themselves, arguing that they were mainly under the control of local governors and magistrates who, under popular pressure, even disregarded imperial rulings. Furthermore, though these events might be of great importance to us, there is no evidence that the emperor gave much thought to them. (S)

20.6   ☛ *Christian History* 9:3 (1990).

This volume (no. 27) of *Christian History* has as its theme "Persecution in the Early Church." It provides an attractive, informed, and clear introduction to all the issues, with articles by some leading scholars: "Persecution in the Early Church" (Frend); "The Piety of the Persecutors" (Wilken); "Controversial Constantine" (Wright); "How the Early Church Viewed Martyrs" (Bixler); and "Cowards Among the Christians" (Gooch). Also included are useful biographical sketches and the texts of important documents (Tacitus on Nero's persecution of Christians, Pliny's letter to Trajan, accounts of Perpetua and Polycarp's martyrdom, the "Edict of Milan," and Cyprian's letter to banished Christians). A brief, well illustrated introduction.

20.7   Droge, Arthur J., and James J. Tabor. *A Noble Death: Suicide and*

Martyrdom Among Christians and Jews in Antiquity. San Francisco: Harper, 1992. Pp. Xii + 203. B-7; I-5.

The authors examine the attitudes towards "voluntary death" from Socrates to Augustine. They argue that one of the problems of the scholarly study of this issue is caused by the failure of ancient secular historians to give adequate attention to martyrdom in their extensive discussion of suicide, and of early church historians to do the reverse. It was Augustine, they contend in a sometimes cautious way, who argued effectively against suicide (using Plato more than the Bible), and shortly thereafter (563 CE), Christian funerals were forbidden for those who had died by suicide. The title is somewhat misleading in that pagan views are considered too. Views of prominent patristic thinkers are considered individually, and much attention is given to biblical examples and passages, with the final chapter on "The Augustine Reversal." To some extent, the authors' concerns are shaped by the contemporary discussion of suicide.

20.8 ☛ Fox, Robin Lane. "Persecution and Martyrdom" In Fox, *Pagans and Christians.* New York: Alfred A. Knopf, 1987. Pp. 419-492

Fox provides a solid review of the Christian experience of martyrdom and of a number of related issues. He writes in one of the clearest and most delightful styles, providing clear observations and explanations that help to make the world of antiquity come alive. Included is an extended discussion of the martyrdom of Pionius in Smyrna under Decius in 250 CE. Fox gives a detailed defense of the integrity of the account. His work is further made useful by his frequent reference to primary source material, though this sometimes results in only brief reference to the modern debates. The full book is abstracted at §12.2.

20.9 Frend, W.H.C. *Martyrdom and Persecution in the Early Church: A Study of a Conflict from the Maccabees to Donatus.* Oxford: Basil Blackwell, 1965. Reprint. Grand Rapids: Baker, 1981. Pp. xx + 626. B-33; I-21.

The standard work on the topic. Frend supplies a fifty-page discussion of martyrdom in Judaism, showing that Jewish martyrdom in the Maccabean period set a primary example for later Christian martyrs as much as for Jewish ones. He also demonstrates how Gnostics such as Basilides attacked the tradition of martyrdom and how the Apologists softened and weakened it somewhat by asserting the reasonableness of Christianity. Finally, he indicates how and why the Roman persecution of Christians to the time of Decius ebbed and flowed. Various related topics are addressed, such as Rome and foreign cults (ch. 4); the imperial cult; (ch. 5); and the triumph of the church (ch. 14). Specific persecutions are addressed, ending with the Donatist controversy after the conversion of the emperor to Christianity (ch. 16). Frend supplies a wealth of information on the subject, but Frend's interpretations must now be received with caution, given the challenges raised to them by Barnes [§20.3].

✂ P. Brown, *EHR* 83 (1968): 542-558; Mattingly, *History* 52 (1967): 168-171; Millar, *JRS* 56 (1966): 231-236; *Ste. Croix, JTS* 18 (1967): 217-221.

20.10   Frend, W.H.C. "The Failure of the Persecutions in the Roman Empire" *Past & Present* 8 (1959): 10-27. Reprinted in *Studies in Ancient Society*. Edited by M.I. Finley, London: 1974. Pp. 263-87; and in Frend, *Town and Country in the Early Christian Centuries*. London: Variorum, 1980.

In his analysis of the general problem, Frend concentrates on the so-called "Great Persecution" of 303-312 to try to explain the failure of the Roman state to repress Christianity by state supported persecution of its followers. Firstly, he points out that the persecutions and punishments themselves could never be severe enough. A premodern state simply did not have the resources for a totalitarian proscription of its ideological enemies. Hence martyrs were turned into heroic figures that only further confirmed the strength of the Church; priests and bishops who were exiled spread the message of Christianity further afield. The Christian Church was successfully able to establish a whole alternative system of institutions and rewarding careers and, by the co-optation of some of the "better minds" was able to absorb the best of pagan ideologies (e.g., the fusion with Platonism). By the last decades of the third century these factors, and others, meant that the Christian Church and its attendant ideology was in a position of such strength that mere persecution of it, on the scale that the ruling orders could mount or, indeed, could afford to undertake, was insufficient to destroy it. (S)

20.11   Hopkins, Keith. *Death and Renewal*: Sociological Studies in Roman History 2. Cambridge: Cambridge UP, 1983. Pp. xx + 276. B&W-4; T-29; B-9; SI-5; NI-6.

The second of Hopkins' set of "sociological studies" of Roman society (for the first, see Hopkins, *Conquerors and Slaves*, 1978), this volume has at its core (chs. 2-3) highly detailed statistical studies of continuity and discontinuity in the high office-holding élite that governed Rome and its empire in the late Republic and early Empire. Perhaps of greater interest to the readers of this volume, however, are the studies that preface and follow this core of the book. The first chapter, entitled "Murderous Games," is a wonderfully evocative "thick description" (under the influence of Geertz) of the gladiatorial games that lay at the heart of Roman society and social experience. By drawing on snippets of literary descriptions, and on bits of epigraphical and archaeological evidence, Hopkins succeeds in transporting the reader into "that world"—one whose experience from the spectators' point of view, needless to say, it is necessary to understand if we are to comprehend better the nature of the persecution and punishment of Christians. The final chapter follows much this same method in a discussion of "Death in Rome." In it Hopkins attempts to convey to the reader the sentiments and duties attendant upon death in Roman society, the social arrangements for dealing with the dead, and some of the implications (e.g., legacy hunting) that stemmed from these practices. (S)

✂ Bradley, *CP* 81 (1986): 263-270; Duncan-Jones, *CR* 34 (1984): 270-274; Runcimm, *JRS* 86 (1986): 259-265; Shaw, *EMC* 28 (1984): 453-479; Treggiari, *AJP* 106 (1985): 256-262.

20.12   Hummel, Edelhard L. *The Concept of Martyrdom according to St. Cyprian of Carthage*. Catholic University of America Studies in Christian Antiquity 9. Washington, DC: Catholic University of America Press, 1946. Pp. xviii + 199. B-4; I-6; BI-1; AAI-1; MAI-2; Cyprian Index-3.

The episcopate of Cyprian at Carthage in the mid-250s CE was at a critical juncture where the occasional and localized persecutions of Christians of earlier periods turned, with the emperor Decius, into a more systematic and dangerous thing. Hence the great significance of coming to terms with the fact of martyrdom and its place within the increasingly solid structure of the hierarchy of ecclesiastical organization. The writings of Cyprian are located at this crossroads, in which the bishop himself was martyred. He had to attempt to define who and what martyrs were, and what their rôle within the Church was to be. Hummel's first two chapters are devoted to Cyprian's conception of martyr and confessor. He then advances to Cyprian's basic idea of martyrdom as a form of spiritual warfare. He then studies the basic motivations and justifications for martyrdom: imitation of Christ, a renewed and especially empowering baptism, the social status (*dignitas*) and special rewards bestowed on the martyr and confessor. Hummel's study is then completed with a long analysis of the problems of power posed to the orthodox hierarchy, especially the formal power of bishops, by martyrs and confessors and the specific ways in which Cyprian attempted to confront and contain this threat to order from within the Church. This final part of Hummel's study is, alas, its least satisfactory part. Otherwise, this book remains most useful, as do others in the same series, for its extensive quotation of, and reference to, the primary sources. (S)

20.13 Janssen, L.F. "'Superstitio' and the Persecution of the Christians." *Vigiliae Christianae* 33 (1979): 131-59.
Bypassing much of the recent work on persecution in English-language scholarship (e.g., the critical paper by Barnes [§20.3), Janssen returns to Mommsen's 1890 reply to Neumann's monograph of the same year on *Staat und Kirche* to try to understand what it was that was rooted in the mere *nomen Christianum*—the name "Christian"—that elicited the fury of the Roman magistrates and the hostility of local populations. To this extent he does accept the arguments of Ste. Croix [§20.28; 20.29] against Sherwin-White [§20.26] to the effect that the mere "name" was sufficient proof to have the accused put to death. Relying on an earlier study of his own (*Mnemosyne*, 28 [1975]: 135-88), Janssen offers a detailed explication of what precisely was meant by *superstitio*, the deployment of any means, including illicit magic, to save the individual and assert his/her rights and powers against those of state and community, to give a better understanding of the power of the labelling of Christianity as a detestable "superstition." Valuable in some respects, it is odd that Janssen leaves the matter in the realm of semantic analysis, and does not seem able to tie his observations to Millar's fundamental point [§20.36] that the persecutions cannot be understood in legal/semantic terms, but must be seen in the terms of the local social context, and the motivating "fears of common people." (S)

20.14 Keresztes, Paul. "The Imperial Roman Government and the Christian Church I. From Nero to the Severi." *ANRW* II.23.1 (1979): 247-315. B-7.
Drawing largely from primary source material, Keresztes documents the persecutions of Christianity during the first and second centuries (Nero, Domitian, Pliny and Trajan, Hadrian's Rescript, Antoninus Pius, Marcus Aurelius, and the peace under Commodus). He discusses not only the reasons for persecution but also the forms of punishment carried out by the state. Too, he offers a good discussion of the three current theories regarding the legal grounds for the persecution of Christians. Keresztes finds evidence for substantial

enough persecutions in various parts of the empire, but notices that in the latter part of the second century, Christians were less the object of such actions. Keresztes deals with a range of questions, attempting to account for the occasional actions against Christians by examining the situation of the times (Parthian threat) or by pointing to local characteristics (the Greek attitudes in Asia). (W)

20.15   Keresztes, Paul. "II. From Gallienus to the Great Persecution." *ANRW* II.23.1 (1979): 375-386.

In his second and somewhat shorter article, Keresztes deals with isolated incidents of persecution. He contends that, for the most part, the Roman state was tolerant of Christians and that the incidents of persecution that did occur were the result of criminal offenses rather than a general persecution. He cites the Theban legion, and other "military martyrs," as examples of the exercise of military discipline rather than evidence of general persecution. During the period under review, Christians were generally persecuted for some other offense or irregularity than merely their being Christians. (W)

20.16   Pagels, Elaine H. "Gnostic and Orthodox Views of Christ's Passion: Paradigms for the Christian's Response to Persecution?" In *The Rediscovery of Gnosticism.* Edited by B. Layton. Leiden: E.J. Brill, 1980. Pp. 262-288.

Pagels reviews the patristic attacks on the Gnostic attitude to martyrdom. Although the orthodox uniformly censured the Gnostics, a surprising number of Gnostic texts seem to have given a high value to martyrdom and the sufferings of Jesus, and some even attacked docetic positions! The Gnostic position is then, at best, not uniform on the theme of martyrdom. Pagels attempts to make sense out of the Gnostic comments by noting the distinction that some Gnostics made between the psychic and the spiritual Christ. The last five pages record a discussion that followed Pagels' paper, with comments by Meeks, B. Aland, Quispel, Stead, Koester, Jonas, Attridge, and Mortley. (A less technical version of this paper appears as ch. 4, "The Passion of Christ and the Persecution of Christians," in Pagels, *The Gnostic Gospels,* [New York: Random House, 1979], pp. 70-101.)

20.17   Riddle, D.W. *The Martyrs: A Study in Social Control.* Chicago: University of Chicago, 1931. Pp. xi + 231. I-6; AAI-6.

Donald Riddle was a scholar who wrote widely on subjects not only of religious import, but also on ones as far afield as American history and politics (Abraham Lincoln). An interesting researcher who had strong overlapping interests between history, sociology and religion, he was greatly influenced by the historically-based critical approaches of Shirley Jackson Case and the modern functionalist school of sociology, both then espousing novel approaches to their respective fields at Riddle's own University of Chicago. In his study of the phenomenon of martyrdom, Riddle was particularly interested in it as an example of "social control" or the conflictual means by which the "persecuting group" tried to enforce its norms on the "persecuted group" which had to develop cogent strategies to convince its members of the superior value of resisting. In using this approach, Riddle argued for the great value of working "backwards," from what was better documented: the patristic texts and martyr acts of the mid-second to mid-third century to the earlier materials (e.g., in the New Testament) that are much less well known, rather than the other way around. Especially important here are his second and third chapters in which he attempts to study the "preparation of the martyr" and the "production of attitudes" that encouraged individuals to believe that witnessing to the point of death was a valuable action worthy of emulation. The latter chapters, in which he attempts to retroject this approach to the earlier texts, are far less successful. Although the sociological approach being adopted by Riddle was clearly still in its infancy, this remains a valuable study, with many good insights, some of which foreshadowed later "more scholarly" achievements of half a century later (e.g. Barnes [§20.22] on the early persecutions as sporadic and local, and the distinction between these "persecutions" and the more general ones from Decius onwards). (S)

20.18   Rush, Alfred C. *Death and Burial in Christian Antiquity*. Catholic University of America Studies in Christian Antiquity 1. Washington, DC: Catholic University of America Press, 1941. Pp. xxviii + 282. B-6; I-13; BI-1; B&W-8.

Despite a burgeoning modern scholarly literature on death and dying in the Greek and Roman worlds, it is difficult to find a simple and ready guide to the principal Christian practices in the western Roman empire during the period of the Christian church's initial ascendancy. This old, and unjustly neglected, work of Rush's remains, therefore, a good guide to some of the fundamental aspects of this problem, sharing the considerable merits of the series which it launched, that is, strong attention to citation of the primary sources. The "pagan" contexts within which Rush sets Christian practices are now much better analyzed in more modern works, but parts of his survey of the Christian concept of death (as sleep, as a journey to the Lord, as a day of birth, the birthday of real and eternal life), his study of the actual rituals centred on dealing with the body (its laying out, the celebrations attendant on burial, the funeral procession) and the actual modes of interment, are still very useful. (S)

20.19   Seeley, David. *The Noble Death: Graeco-Roman Martyrology and Paul's Concept of Salvation.* JSNTSuppl 28. Sheffield: JSOT, 1990. Pp. 170. AI-2; BI-2; B-14.
Although Seeley's work on Paul's concept is outside of the period of our bibliography, the wider issues that affected Paul's interpretation of martyrdom were also part of the culture that would have had some impact on the thought of the developing Christian church after Paul. In Ch. 4, Seeley discusses and dismisses influence from the Mystery religions; in Ch. 5, he discusses the views in 4 Maccabees (with criticism of Lohse), and in Ch. 6, he provides a useful collection of primary sources from the Graeco-Roman philosophical literature dealing with suicide (the noble death), and he argues that this context was the most influential on Paul's ideas.
⸕ Gillman, *CBQ* 54 (1992): 172-174.

20.20   Weinrich, W.C. *Spirit and Martyrdom: A Study of the Work of the Holy Spirit in Contexts of Persecution and Martyrdom in the New Testament and Early Christian Literature.* Washington, DC: University Press of America, 1981.
The first two chapters (of what is a revised edition of Weinrich's dissertation) deal with Old Testament, Intertestamental, and New Testament literature relevant to his topic. Chapters three through seven are evaluations of the accounts of the martyrdom of Ignatius of Antioch, Polycarp, the martyrs of Lyons and Vienne, and Perpetua and Felicitas. Chapter seven provides a summary of Tertullian's views on martyrdom. In his conclusion, Weinrich holds that Christian martyrdom differed from Jewish martyrdom—by psychologically participating in the death and resurrection of Christ, Christians experienced a sense of joy in their suffering which Jews did not. (P)
⸕ Arnold, *GOTR* 31 (1986): 442-444; Neyrey, *CBQ* 45 (1983): 334-335; Baumeister, *VC* 37 (1983): 308-310; Ashanin, *CH* 52 (1983): 347-348.

20.21   Workman, Herbert B. *Persecution in the Early Church: A Chapter in the History of Renunciation.* 4th ed. London: Epworth, 1923 (1906[1]). Pp. 382. I-5; CT-5.
This was for many decades the standard critical work in English on

the topic of persecution. Some of the various brief appendixes are still useful, and many of the positions taken by Workman are not much changed almost a century later. In fact, many of his conclusions were themselves based on even earlier ones (Ramsay, Harnack, and in particular T. Mommsen, *Provinces of the Roman Empire*). Christians were persecuted by random police action rather than a universal law. Workman is an interesting writer, and his work can provide a clear and still fairly informed introduction to many of the issues.

LEGAL PROCESS

20.22   Barnes, T.D. "Legislation Against the Christians." *Journal of Roman Studies* 58 (1968): 32-50.
Few scholarly contributions to the much debated subject of the causes of the persecution of the Christians in the Roman Empire can be considered as fundamental as this one. It is now regarded as one of the basic turning points in modern analyses of the question. What Barnes did was a rather simple thing. He made no assumptions about the nature of the persecutions themselves, but rather began with the surviving evidence on the problem, which he then analyzed in his usual exacting manner. What the bare evidence showed beyond any reasonable doubt was a quite different situation than had generally been assumed to be the case. Basically Barnes' revisionist view has at least the following elements to it: (1) there is no evidence for any general law or empire-wide edict against the Christians before the reign of the emperor Decius (in the mid-third century CE), (2) the persecutions were therefore both sporadic and local in nature, (3) their local geographical and cultural context, and time-specific temporal context, means that local forces in particular towns, cities, or regions were the ones that sparked specific incidents of persecution, and (4) the rôle of the Roman governor was critical in his reaction to these local pressures—in some cases he assented to and colluded with local persecuting forces; in others he resisted and denied them. These new elements in our understanding of the nature of the persecutions have radically and permanently altered scholarly analysis of the problem. (S)

20.23   Garnsey, Peter. "Legal Privilege in the Roman Empire." *Past & Present* 41 (1968): 3-24. Reprinted in *Studies in Ancient Society*. Edited by M.I. Finley. London: RKP, 1974. Pp. 141-65.
A synoptic view of his book on the same subject [§20.24]. For those who do not have the time or energy to attend to the fine detail and scholarship of the original, this is a *non pareil* distillation

for non-professional readers. See book description for his main theses. (S)

20.24   Garnsey, Peter. *Social Status and Legal Privilege in the Roman Empire.* Oxford, Clarendon, 1970. Pp. xiii + 320. AAI-21; I-10.
A landmark study that attempted to map the frontiers of accessibility to equal treatment in the law and before the courts in the Roman Empire, both in terms of actual treatment and in terms of legislation that governed differential sentencing of defendants by judges. Given the nature of the Roman judicial system, which relied heavily on plaintiffs bringing and actioning their own charges, the system itself was very heavily weighted in favor of the wealthy and the privileged. The favorable status accorded to more powerful citizens can be traced throughout the first two centuries of the empire. From the early second century CE onwards, however, this differential treatment actually began to be formalized almost in direct relationship to the extent to which Roman citizenship was extended and thus "diluted" in its effects. There emerged a "dual penalty" system in which the harsher penalties and more summary punishments were reserved for so-called *humiliores* ("the humble") of Roman society, whereas lighter penalties and more privileged judicial process was accorded the so-called *honestiores* ("the better sort" of people). Some of the argument, especially in the first two or three chapters is a bit complicated for the non-expert reader, and so recourse to Garnsey's abbreviated article version [§20.243] is recommended. (S)
⊰ Brunt, *IRS* 62 (1972): 166-170; Crook, *CR* 22 (1972): 238-242; Sherwin-White, *Latomus* 31 (1972): 580-585.

20.25   Shaw, Brent D. "The Passion of Perpetua." *Past & Present* 139 (1993): 3-45.
Shaw examines in detail the narrative of the execution of a number of North African Christians in Carthage in 203, describing the imprisonment, the execution, and the nature and expectation of the games in which these Christians were to die. The heart of Shaw's article turns, however, from a mere description of events to an examination of the unusual nature of the document itself. For one thing, the core of the document is an autobiographical account from Perpetua as she reflected on the events (including her dreams) leading up to the day of the execution. This is the only surviving extensive piece of narrative writing by a woman from this period. But more important for Shaw is the way in which Perpetua's account is "framed" by the hand of a male editor, altering the perceptions

of the reader as he or she "enters" and "exits" the document through the added materials. These additions are more heavily theological and tuned to the interests of the official church. Related to this, Shaw shows how the story was retold in the annual celebrations of Perpetua and Felicitas' martyrdom, preached by men who sometimes felt constrained to explain how it was that women (in their "womenly weaknesses") were being remembered as such outstanding martyrs. Particular attention is paid to Augustine.

20.26   ◉ Sherwin-White, A.N. "The Early Persecutions and Roman Law Again." *Journal of Theological Studies* 3 (1952): 199-213. Reprinted with slight additions in *The Letters of Pliny* (1966).

Sherwin-White provides a review of the three major theories regarding the legal grounds upon which Christians were subject to persecution in the Roman Empire (see "Introduction" to this chapter). He then argues his own position, contending that Christians were too insignificant in the early years to have become a focal point of Roman legislation. When Christians were persecuted, the religious aspect of the movement was not the cause for the persecution, and their treatment was little different from that experienced on occasion by other groups that disturbed the public peace by behaviour that was judged as arrogant and stubborn. See the challenge by Ste. Croix [§20.28; 20.29].

20.27   Sherwin-White, A.N. "Why were the Early Christians Persecuted? An Amendment." *Past & Present* 27 (1964): 23-27. Reprinted in *Studies in Ancient Society*. Edited by M.I. Finley. London: RKP, 1974. Pp. 250-55.

A reply to the arguments of Ste. Croix [§20.28; 20.29]. Sherwin-White claims that Ste. Croix's arguments, with their emphasis on popular opinion and attitudes of the government, is highly misleading in interpreting these factors including "godlessness" as the basis for persecution of the Christians because that trend only became clear "much later" when authorities (and, presumably, others) acquired a clear and coherent knowledge of just who the Christians were. For the earliest phases of maltreatment of Christians, there is no such evidence, and so magistrates were dealing with them harshly simply for their *contumacia* ("obstinate refusal to obey duly constituted authority"). Sherwin-White's arguments are not convincing, and the remark in his introduction, that Ste Croix "has given what will for long rank among the most satisfactory treatments of the theme" stands despite his own objections. (S)

20.28   Ste Croix, Geoffrey E.M. de. "Why were the Early Christians Persecuted?" *Past & Present* 26 (1963): 6-38. Reprinted in *Studies in Ancient Society*. Edited by M.I. Finley. London: RKP, 1974. Pp. 210-49.
With characteristic attention to the minutia of the primary evidence relating to the problem (probably reflecting his early training in the law) Ste Croix established certain positions regarding this subject from which there can be no reasonable return. His first was to downplay certain circumstantial parts of the persecutions (e.g., worship or sacrifice to the emperor) as opposed to the fact that "the mere name" of "Christian" was the full and sufficient basis for the prosecution of Christians. He successfully disputes Sherwin-White's [§20.26] contention that *contumacia* or the Christians' immoderately willful refusal to obey reasonable magisterial orders was the basis of their official persecution. (S)

20.29   Ste Croix, Geoffrey E.M. de. "Why Were the Early Christians Persecuted? A Rejoinder." *Past & Present* 27 (1964): 28-33. Reprinted in *Studies in Ancient Society*. Edited by M.I. Finley, 256-262. London: RKP, 1974.
A refutation of Sherwin-White's view that it was the special "crimes" (*flagitia*) and sheer obstinacy (*contumacia*) to accept Roman rule and the orders of its magistrates that lay at the basis of the state's persecution of the Christians and execution of them on such charges. The evidence of the primary texts themselves does not support Sherwin-White's interpretation. Ste Croix is right. (S)

PUNISHMENTS

20.30   Barton, Carlin. "The Scandal of the Arena." *Representations* 27 (Summer 1989): 1-36.
A scintillating "must read" (in addition to Hopkins §20.11 and Coleman §20.31) for anyone wishing to understand the world of the Roman games, and the rôle the arena had in the symbolic power of punishment in the Roman empire. Greatly influenced by the work of Foucault and current post-modern literary theory in its interpretation, Barton's treatment of the significance of gladiatorial contests in the matrix of "Roman morality" is part of a projected larger work (*The Sorrows of the Ancient Romans,* Princeton, 1992) that is sure to be a provocative incentive to new research. (S)

20.31   Coleman, Kate M. "Fatal Charades: Roman Executions Staged as Mythological Enactments." *Journal of Roman Studies* 80 (1990): 44-73.

Along with Hopkins and Barton [§20.30], Coleman's study represents one of the "new wave" of attempts to understand better the significance and modes of punishment in the Roman empire, not as a species of modern moral criticism but as a genuine empathetic study in sociological and psychological "understanding" of the phenomenon. Coleman specifically hones in on the interplay between the spectators' knowledge of common mythical stories in their own culture and the "mocking" of the condemned in the arena. Vital to a better understanding of Christian martyrs and their punishment in the public venues of the empire. (S)

20.32   MacMullen, Ramsay. "Judicial Savagery in the Roman Empire." *Chiron* 16 (1986): 147-66.
This study, along with a number of others of recent vintage on legal punishment in the Roman Empire (Barton §20.30; Brunt §20.5; Coleman §20.31; and Garnsey §20.23; 20.24) is of particular significance to those who wish to gain a better understanding of the deployment of specific types of punishments during the persecutions of the Christians. Taking the joint evidences on torture and on crimes subject to the death penalty, MacMullen traces the growth both in the number of such crimes and the application of violent corporal punishment to an ever-widening circle of persons in the empire, finally to include even privileged upper-class citizens. He points out that the dramatic public staging of such punishments was an increasing part of their execution. As reasons for these harsh developments, MacMullen singles out the increasing power and remoteness of an autocratic government, and the restriction of "real" citizenship to those culturally defined as "acceptable persons." Ste. Croix's [§23.17] views on the social/economic shifts that were responsible for these changes should probably also be taken into account. (S)

20.33   Millar, Fergus, "Condemnation to Hard Labour in the Roman Empire, from the Julio-Claudians to Constantine." *Papers of the British School at Rome* 52 (1984): 124-47
Part of the renewed interest in the subject of punishment in the Roman empire, Miller's paper concentrates less on the symbolic interpretation of the significance of such punishments than on a systematic attempt to sort out the legal and evidentiary basis for a modern interpretation of the meaning and function of hard labor as a form of punishment. In his usual thorough and systematic manner, Miller culls all the literary and legal testimonia relevant to the subject. Evidence drawn from the acts of the Christian martyrs is

central and therefore of interest (e.g., on condemnation "to the mines"). (S)

THE IMPERIAL CULT

20.34 Jones, Donald L. "Christianity and the Roman Imperial Cult." In *ANRW* II.23.2 (1980): 1023-1054.
Jones offers a competent survey of the main work available on the subject through the mid 1970s. He groups the evidence succinctly under successive chronological series of dynasties of Roman emperors from the "Julio-Claudians" through "the Antonines" and "the Severi" down to "Diocletian and Constantine." As such, his work offers a suitable overview of the "state of the question" as it stood at the time, which is as good a measure as any of the revolution in understanding of this subject that took place subsequently (see especially the work of Simon Price, as well as Duncan Fishwick and Stefan Weinstock—none of whom are used by Jones). (S)

20.35 Fishwick, Duncan. *The Imperial Cult in the Latin West.* Vol. 1.1-2. and 2.1-2 *Studies in the Ruler Cult of the Western Provinces of the Roman Empire.* Leiden, E.J. Brill, 1987 & 1991. Pp. 884. B&W-113.
In this multivolume work, Fishwick, arguably the leading expert on the history of the imperial cult, reproduces both his previously published contributions (in updated and corrected versions), along with new articles that make the series into a more coherent whole. Vol. 1.1 (pp. x + 1-194, plates 1-38) is a general introduction to the subject of the ruler cult in the Graeco-Roman world, from Hellenistic background to Augustus, and the beginnings of the extension of the ruler-cult through the Roman empire under Augustus. Vol. 1.2 (pp. 197-371, plates 39-73) and 2.1 (pp. 375-626, plates 74-113) are devoted to studies in the imperial cult in special settings or provincial contexts. Vol. 2.2 (pp. 627-867) includes a select bibliography (pp. 638-676) and a comprehensive set of indexes (pp. 673-867), on coins, inscriptions, places, literary sources, names, and papyri. This will remain a basic reference work on the subject. For a different, more social-scientific interpretation of the significance of the cult see Price [§20.37]. (S)
⊱ Liebeschuetz, *CR* 39 (1989): 321-322; Price, *Phoenix* 42 (1988): 371-374; Smadja, *JRS* 79 (1989): 239-240.

20.36 Millar, Fergus. "The Imperial Cult and the Persecutions." In *Le culte des souverains dans l'empire romain.* Entretiens sur l'Antiquité classique: Fondation Hardt 19. Edited by W. den Boer. Geneva: Vandouevres, 1973. Pp. 145-175.

Directing the observations of Ste. Croix [§20.28; 20.29] against Sherwin-White [§20.26; 20.27] and Barnes [§20.22], Millar argues that the persecutions cannot be understood purely in the "legal" terms in which they have been placed from Mommsen and Neuman onwards, nor in the sphere of some purely ideological conflict between a uniform Christianity on the one side and the "official cult" of the Roman state on the other. Rather, the response to the Christians has to be rooted firmly in local, and therefore popular, responses to the challenges posed by Christians in their communities —local situations that could evoke hostility based on "religious feelings" and on the "fears of the common people." In some ways, this prefigures the work of Simon Price on the significance of the power relationships of the imperial cult in local communities [§20.37]. Although the extent to which Millar wishes to downplay the importance of the imperial cult, as opposed to worship of the traditional gods, in the persecutions might seem to be a distinction that is too finely drawn at times, his insistence on the paucity of surviving evidence to make that connection is a valuable caution against making unquestioned assumptions about the significance of emperor worship in motivating the prosecution of Christians. (S)

20.37   Price, Simon R.F. *Rituals and Power. The Roman Imperial Cult in Asia Minor*. Cambridge: Cambridge UP 1984. Pp. xxvi + 289. I-6; AAI-2; B&W-30; B-8; M-6.

The pathbreaking modern work on this subject in the English language. Whereas the work of Duncan Fishwick on the "imperial cult" represents a near exhaustive survey of all the known evidence, a collation of original sources, and detailed criticism of them in their individuality, Price provided the first modern analysis and interpretation of the phenomenon of worship of the Roman emperor. Using the best documented regional sample—the epigraphical evidence from the Greek cities of Asia Minor)—Price relied on modern anthropological analyses of symbol, cult, and belief (especially work by Pierre Bourdieu, Mary Douglas, and Dan Sperber) to explain the function that worship of the emperor played in the specific context of these cities and their élites. The location of the emperor as an intermediary between "the divine" and "the human" offered a symbolic power, a "cultural capital," that could be exploited by these élites in mediating their power relationships with the conquering Roman state. The significance of this interpretation to the Christians' difficult relationship to the Roman state (specifically a divine emperor) and their inability to exploit this same resource, should be noted. (S)

&< Alles, *History of Religions* 26 (1986): 99; Garnsey, *JTS* 36 (1985): 479-481; King, *Man* 21 (1986): 166-167; Krentz, *Currents* 15 (1988): 208-209; Liebeschuetz, *JRS* 75 (1985): 262-264; Martin, *JAAR* 54 (1986): 189-190; Mellor, *AJP* 107 (1986): 296-298; Sherwin-White, *TLSuppl* 83 (1984): 1332; Yamauchi, *AHR* 90 (1985): 1173.

20.38   Taylor, Lily Ross. *The Divinity of the Roman Emperor*. Middletown, CN: American Philological Association, 1931. Pp. xv + 296. I-12; B&W-47.

Although one of the oldest of "modern" works on the so-called "imperial cult," this work retains much of its usefulness and relevance to the scholarly debate because of the high standards of scholarship set by the author. More recent works on the imperial cult, especially those of Duncan Fishwick and, especially, Simon Price, which pay more attention to the development of the cult in the full period of the Roman empire, should be consulted, but this remains a most useful, even if dated, work. Taylor's book is especially strong on the schematic outlining of precedents, as for example, on the divinity of kings in the Near East (on which there are two valuable appendixes on worship of the monarch in the Persian empire and the practice of *proskynesis* as transferred to Hellenistic monarchs by Alexander the Great), and on the idea of the linkage between "man" and "king" in the earlier Roman Republic. The core of her work, however, centers on Julius Caesar and Octavian/Augustus, and, on the former, her main theses and claims must be supplemented by the more detailed work in Weinstock's *Divus Julius* [§20.39]. (S)

20.39   Weinstock, Stefan. *Divus Iulius*. Oxford: Clarendon, 1971. Pp. xvi + 469. SNI-35; B&W-31; AAAI-15; Greek and Latin Index-3.

A rich, complex, and marvelously positivistic work of nineteenth-century *Wissenschaft* by one of the eminent scholars of a generation of continental erudites, a not inconsiderable number of whom, like Weinstock himself, ended in exile from Italy and Germany after the mid-1930s. In his relentless pursuit of how and why it was that Julius Caesar was the first Roman to attempt to institute himself, and to be instituted, as a divine being, Weinstock sets out an amazing array of evidence: arcane epigraphical texts, numismatic legends and iconography, architectural plans, and archaeological data, in addition to the "normal" literary texts. It is not so much Weinstock's answers or his theories that matter, as it is his deep textual description of the institutions, practices, beliefs, and theologies surrounding divinized humans, especially élite political figures, in the Hellenistic and Roman worlds. Indeed, he offers a near-encyclopedic survey of the evidence relevant to the question. Weinstock's work was, in effect, the final word that "conventional" or "traditional" scholarship had to offer on the subject to the end of the 1960s, after which one moves to the works of scholars such as Simon Price [§20.37] and Richard Gordon [§22.45], who set the understanding and interpretation of emperor worship on a new course. (S)

✂ North, *JRS* 65 (1975): 171-177; Palmer, *Athenaeum* 51 (1973): 201-213; Sumner, *AJP* 95 (1974): 304-308.

21
REGIONAL DISTRIBUTION
OF CHRISTIANITY

The growing strength of orthodoxy, and later the efforts of the Christian emperors to create unity, would help to give an impression of uniformity that had not always been characteristic of the early Christian movement. Even with this conscious effort to present a facade of uniformity, enough diversity shows through to caution against viewing early Christianity as monolithic, and indeed, remnants of some national churches that developed during this time are still with us (e.g., Coptic and Nestorian). Thus the current emphasis on diversity in the primitive church in both practice and belief seems proper.

Christianity spread rapidly, growing from an isolated, esoteric Palestinian subspecies of apocalyptic Judaism to the world-affirming, politically astute state religion of the Roman Empire. In the process of this growth, Christianity was forced to engage a variety of cultural and religious options to which it had to respond and by which its own identity was informed. To what extent local factors played a significant role in shaping the character of geographically distinctive Christian communities is a matter of considerable scholarly debate. Several factors leave the matter unsettled.

Supposing that one could associate distinctive forms of Christianity with particular geographical areas, this should not lead immediately to a conclusion that local religion and culture played a *dominant* role in giving each particular form of Christianity its own distinctive shape. Almost without doubt, that distinctive and geographically-isolated form of Christianity would simply be the particular form of Christianity that won out there. Several forms of Christianity probably existed in many if not most areas: some would have died out, while others would have gone on to considerable success. The immediate conclusion often is that the "winner" was the form of Christianity that allowed itself to be most shaped by the culture around it. Although that seems a reasonable supposition on initial consideration, too many factors play a role in the success of novel religious movements to make that general conclusion certain. Why one form won and another lost may have had little to do with the broad cultural sensitivity of one form over another. Both may have been equally novel and shocking; both may have been equally sympathetic and appealing. Factors such as the charisma of one of the leaders, or the personality of one of the converts, perhaps can account in large measure for the success of a particular form. Also, one must consider the possibility that some wondrous deed was the crucial factor in the conversion of an area, which complicates the picture considerably for the historian. (See chapter 12 for extensive discussion of conversion.)

Whenever we have evidence of a distinctive form of Christianity in an area, we must recognize that the evidence is almost always "literary," and of course, literary material generally will be weighted in favor of the community that became dominant. There need be nothing sinister in this. It is natural enough for a community not to preserve literature that it does not use. Granted, a community may take steps to destroy literature that it finds offensive, but it need not. Even if it takes no steps to suppress certain literature, that literature will pass into oblivion simply through lack of use. The loss could be quite unintentional, or at least quite unconscious. Thus literary sources, when they clearly describe a community (which they do not always do), speak about the "winners" and their favorite literature.

Any reconstruction that emphasizes a geographical distribution of particular forms of Christianity is probably closer to the truth if the distribution is seen as the end of a process—a process that involved considerable diversity within each geographically distinct area. Areas were not isolated units, free from outside influences. In fact, Rome itself became the home of almost everything that called itself Christian. Nonetheless, scholars have tended to see distinctive emphases or traits in particular areas. Syria, for example, appears to have been a more receptive home to extreme asceticism; Asia Minor had its ambiguous attachment to Jewish practices, as is witnessed by the Quartodeciman controversy; Phrygia may have been ripe for apocalyptic and charismatic emphases; and Alexandria had its philosophical and wisdom orientations. But these may be caricatures and exaggerations, and they must be treated with caution.

Diversity may not always be geographical. Within communities, it is possible, *but not necessary,* to have "popular" views in conflict with the views of the elite, or to have clashes between the interests of the urban population and the rural. All such matters must be considered in any serious investigation of diversity within early Christianity.

Other causes of diversity also need to be considered. For one thing, it takes time to develop structures of organization and office (see chapter 9, "Church Office and Hierarchy"). A charismatic leader could have gathered about him a group of followers without the approval of a bishop and without membership in the dominant body. The probability that such communities were formed—and were successful—is suggested by the basic structure for regular corporate worship in the first two centuries of the church. As far as can be determined, Christians worshipped in small house-church units, probably in groups consisting of no more than about thirty people. Even given an accepted monarchical episcopate over the individual house-church units, the primary unit of the house-church offers the potential for control by individuals whose belief and practice may not have been in the mainstream. We know from the letters of Ignatius that such groups did exist, and although they maintained some loose association with the bishop's church, they seem to have gone their own way, holding their own regular gatherings without the bishop's approval.

One further point which has not been addressed in many studies of early Christian diversity is the following. Christians sensed themselves to belong to a universal church in a way that pagans did not seem to, and this idea of union with other believers probably aided the church in maintaining a level of uniformity that was, in spite of admitted diversity, a considerable accomplishment in itself. That success must be given some attention as we trace the development of early Christianity. And as we do that work, we should avoid dismissing uniformity as a political accomplishment. It is perhaps no more a historically accurate view than the opposite view put forward by some of the early church leaders, who dismissed diversity as the product of Satan and his heretical children. The trend has been to identify with one extreme or the other: idealizing diversity or idealizing uniformity. Neither will do credit to the serious historian.

But the question remains whether the diversity has a geographical character. Although one form may have been dominant in a particular area, several factors suggest that considerable diversity of Christianity probably existed in almost every region—providing a full range of trends and options for people to chose from.

In addition to the works listed below, some of the more general introductions have helpful overviews on particular areas. Consult the indexes of works listed in the "General Histories" section of this bibliography.

GENERAL
21.1   Henry, Patrick, ed. *Schools of Thought in the Christian Tradition.* Philadelphia: Fortress, 1984. Pp. xiv + 193. B-12; NI-5.

A collection of 10 chapters, presented to Jaroslav Pelikan on his 60th birthday. The relevant ones are: "The Idea of "Development" in the History of Christian Doctrine" (A.C. Outler); "Alexandria: A School for Training in Virtue" (R.L. Wilken); "Christian Culture and Christian Tradition in Roman North Africa" (W.S. Babcock); "Fourth-Century Jerusalem: Religious Geography and Christian

Tradition" (F. Cardman); and "Byzantium as Center of Theological Thought in the Christian East" (J. Meyendorff). All chapters deal in some way with the preservation and passing on of tradition. Includes a 12-page bibliography of Pelikan's writings.

๛< Meynell, *JES* 23 (1986): 134; LaBarge, *Horizons* 13 (1986): 164-165; TeSelle, *CH* 54 (1985): 548-549; Wells, *TSF Bulletin* 10.4 (1987): 41-42.

ARABIA

21.2   Bowersock, G.W. *Roman Arabia*. Cambridge, MA: Harvard UP, 1983. Pp. xiv + 224. B-19; I-14; B&W-16; C-1; M-8.
Covers the Nabataean area, from the 4th century BCE to Constantine. Although most of the work does not address Christianity, it is a major work on the area. The main focus is a political history, and thus Bowersock deals primarily with the politics of the relationship between Arabia and the Roman empire.

๛< Bowsher, *PEQ* 118 (1986): 158; Parker, *ASOR Bulletin* 258 (1985): 75-78; Rainey, *BAR* 11 (1985): 15-17.

21.3   Trimingham, J. Spencer. *Christianity Among the Arabs in Pre-Islamic Times*. Arab Background Series. London: Longman/ Beirut: Librairie du Luban, 1979. Pp. xiv + 342. B-13; I-13; M-15; FT-3; T-3.
A general history of the Arabs in the early period is provided in the introduction, followed by a discussion of Christian expansion. The sections are largely divided by regions: Syro-Arab; North-Western Bedouins; Mesopotamian-Babylonian; Arabian Peninsula; and Southwest Arabia. Special topics include the influence of monasticism and anchorite traditions, the Monophysite and Nestorian movements, the concept of holy man, the cult of the saints, and the use of relics.

๛< Ayoub, *JAAR* 49 (1981): 688; Fiey, *Theological Review* 2 (1979): 45-48; Shahid, *JJS* 26 (1981): 150-153.

ASIA MINOR

21.4   ⑤ Oster, Richard E. *A Bibliography of Ancient Ephesus*. ATLA Bibliography Series 19. Metuchen, NJ / London: American Theological Library Association and the Scarecrow Press, 1987. Pp. xxiv + 155. SI-17.
It is rare to find such a comprehensive bibliography on one city of early Christianity. Oster, who knows Ephesus and the literature on Ephesus well, provides a valuable research tool, listing 1535 articles and books. Oster's introduction is useful for gaining some sense of important sources of information on Ephesus (inscriptions, numis-

matics, architectural monuments, plastic arts, paintings), and he has an insightful five-page discussion of the neglect of Ephesus in New Testament scholarship. Entries are not abstracted.

21.5 🏛 Heine, Ronald E. *The Montanist Oracles and Testimonia.* Patristic Monograph Series 14. Macon, GA: Mercer UP, 1989. Pp. xiv + 190. BI-3; I-3; B-2. Greek Index-2; Latin Index-2.

The Montanists represent a movement in the Phrygian area of Asia Minor. The movement, though judged as heretical by many of its contemporaries, attracted to it some of the church's brightest minds— Tertullian being the most striking example. Heine collects and translates the vast literature of oracles and testimonia up to the ninth century, though most of these are early. The selections are grouped mainly by geographical area. This is *the* sourcebook for scholars of Montanism.

⧓ Boring, *CBQ* 52 (1990): 562-564; Ferguson, *RQ* 32 (1990): 246-247; Hall, *JTS* 41 (1990): 643-644; Williams *SC* 8 (1991):57-59.

21.6 ◉ Johnson, Sherman E. "Asia Minor and Early Christianity." In *Christianity, Judaism, and other Greco-Roman Cults.* Edited by Jacob Neusner. Studies in Judaism in Late Antiquity 12:2. Leiden: E.J. Brill, 1975. Vol. 2. Pp. 77-145.

Johnson reviews some of the significant contributions to our understanding of Christianity in Asia Minor. Although some of the article deals with the New Testament, Johnson focuses much on the second century, and considers, in briefer subsections, Marcion, Gnosticism, Melito of Sardis, and Montanism. This article can also serve as a solid introduction to the field, as well as a balanced review of scholarship by a seasoned scholar who long understood the importance of Asia Minor, which had been overlooked by much of scholarship.

21.7 ◉ Johnson, Sherman E. "Unsolved Questions About Early Christianity in Anatolia." *Supplements to Novum Testamentum* 23:181-193.

Johnson recognizes the importance of Asia Minor (Anatolia) in the years 50-150 CE. He raises twelve questions that further research should consider. In addition to the standard questions about theological movements in the area are the following: What was it like to be an Anatolian who had absorbed Greek culture? Who were the Judaizers in western Asia Minor? Why do we see in the literature of western Asia Minor so little trace of synoptic materials? What are the origins of Christian prophecy in western Asia Minor? How much anti-imperialism existed in Anatolian Christianity? A good summary of the debates.

21.8   Trebilco, Paul R. *Jewish Communities in Asia Minor*. Society for New Testament Studies Monograph Series 69. Cambridge: Cambridge UP, 1991. Pp. xvi + 330. B-37; AI-8; SI-6; AAI-16; M-1.

Trebilco recognizes the importance of Jewish communities in Asia Minor, neglected in scholarship because of the attention given to Alexandria and Rome. He looks at the literary evidence in Ch. 1, and then deals with Sardis and Priene (Ch. 2), Acmonia (Ch. 3), and Apamea (Ch. 4). Then he turns to particular issues: women (Ch. 5), the evidence for Jewish syncretism (Ch. 6), and the God-fearers (Ch. 7). The final chapter deals with the relationship of the Jewish community to the larger civic order, and the status of Jews within the Greek cities. Trebilco believes that Jewish communities were integrated into the social network of the cities without seriously compromising their Jewish identity and their religious attachments to Jerusalem.

>< Horst, *JSJ* 22 (1991): 292-295; Noy, *JTS* 43 (1992): 564-566.

BRITAIN
21.9   Thomas, Charles. *Christianity in Roman Britain to A.D. 500*. Berkeley: University of California, 1981. Pp. 408. B-2; I-4; B&W-65; NI-8; M-23; Foreign Words Index-4.

This book is valuable for two reasons. One, it is the first "definitive" account on Christianity in Britain since Hugh Williams' 1912 work. Two, it challenges the theory that Christianity was almost wiped out by the Saxon conquests. Emphasizing the continuity of Christianity in Britain up to the arrival of Augustine in Canterbury, Thomas deals extensively with archeological remains, while covering all the other relevant topics, such as persecutions, heresies, literature, languages, and missions.

>< Birley, *AHR* 88 (1983): 967; Grant, *SC* 3 (1983): 69-70; Kelly, *Speculum* 57 (1982): 942-943; Pfaff, *CH* 52 (1983): 493-494; Wright, *ATR* 66 (1984): 200-201.

EASTERN CHRISTIANITY
(also see "Syria and Antioch" and "Egypt")
21.10   Atiya, Aziz S. *A History of Eastern Christianity*. London: Methuen, 1968. Pp. xiv + 486. B-8; I-27; B&W-19; C-1; M-7.

This volume covers the history of various groups of Eastern Christian from their beginnings to the present, with the material divided into six sections: Alexandrine Christianity (i.e. the Copts), Antioch and the Jacobites, Nestorian Church; Armenian Church, St. Thomas and South India, the Marionite Church, with a final chapter on the "vanished" churches, which disappeared under Islam. Each chapter covers the history, religion, and culture, with specific sections on rites and liturgy, the hierarchy, art and architecture, and other topics. ❯< Nicol, *JEH* 20 (1969): 149-150.

21.11   Pelikan, Jaroslav. "The Two Sees of Peter: Reflections on the Pace of Normative Self-Definition East and West." In *Jewish and Christian Self-Definition.* Vol. 1. Philadelphia: Fortress, 1980. Pp. 57-73.
Pelikan addresses the differences between Eastern and Western Christianity in the second and third centuries. In both the capital of the west (Rome) and in the "capital" of the east (Antioch), the churches claimed Peter as their first bishop, as did some other churches. Pelikan considers the differences reflected in the Easter controversy (and later related debates), the obligation of celibacy, the Diatessaron (and other efforts to reduce the gospels to one unit or to provide a gospel harmony). Pelikan contends that *custom* was the key standard used in the East, and he collapses the whole debate between the two groups into an emphasis either on antiquity (custom) or apostolicity.

21.12   Zernov, N. *Eastern Christendom: A Study of the Origin and Development of the Eastern Orthodox Church.* London: Weidenfeld and Nicolson, 1961. Pp. 326. I-8; B&W-71; AB-14; M-2.
Only about the first fifth of this book is relevant. The first chapter deals with the church's break from Judaism and its internal and external struggles until its eventual victory over Roman religion, concluded by a discussion of Eastern writers and teachers. The second chapter deals with Constantine, Arianism, and various other disputes, the councils, the impact of mass conversions on the church, monasticism, Christianity outside of the Byzantine empire, and the formation and separation of the "oriental" churches.
❯< Hussey, *JEH* 15 (1964): 102-103; Mathew, *JTS* 14 (1963): 255-256; Rexine, *GOTR* 9 (1963): 133-135.

EGYPT
21.13   ☛ Bowman, Alan K. *Egypt after the Pharaohs: 332 B.C.-A.D. 642: from Alexander to the Arab Conquest.* Oxford: Oxford UP, 1990. (1986[1]). Pp. 268. B-10; I-6; C-34; B&W-110; M-2; T-2.
This is a thematic, rather than chronological, introduction to life in

Egypt from the conquest of Alexander the Great to the fall of the area to the rapidly expanding Muslim empire. Much of this period involves the growing significance of the Christian church. Bowman considers the politics and economics of Egypt, and deals with the relationship between Greeks and Egyptians. One section deals with religion, with 13 pages specifically on Christianity. The final chapter focuses on Alexandria, the dominant city and center of Greek life. Beautifully illustrated, and with appendices on the Ptolemies; money and measurements; and the archaeological evidence.
⊰ McCleary, *BA* 52 (1988): 52-54.

21.14   Griggs, C. Wilfred. *Early Egyptian Christianity. From its Origins to 451 C.E.* 2d ed. Coptic Studies 2. Leiden: E.J. Brill, 1991. Pp. vii + 276. M-2; B-18; PNI-15; I-8.
The volume is based on Griggs' 1979 PhD dissertation from the University of California Berkeley. Griggs supplies a overview of some of the key issues in Egyptian Christianity, such as the origin of the church, the diversity in form (orthodoxy and heresy), the catechetical and monastic developments and their relationship with the catholic church and the various schisms. Against the background of these general issues, Griggs focuses on what he calls the reluctant establishment of a national (Coptic) church in Egypt, for which the Council of Chalcedon (451) is to take most of the blame. He deals with three factors that helped to isolate the Egyptian church from other churches in the East: the rise of Constantinople, the enduring theological conflicts with Antioch, and the anti-Origenist theology.
⊰ Widdicombe, *JTS* 43 (1992): 229-231.

21.15   McCue, James. "Orthodoxy and Heresy: Walter Bauer and the Valentinians." *VC* 33 (1979): 118-30.
A solid counter to Bauer's argument that Gnosticism was the original and dominant form of Christianity in Egypt. By examining the Valentinian Gnostic group, McCue concludes that Valentinian self-identity was shaped by a revealing relationship with the orthodox group, and that the evidence seems to indicate, even from the Valentinian perspective, that the orthodox was the main body. Further, the *orthodox* New Testament is used by the Valentinians in a way that suggests that "Valentinianism developed within a mid-second century orthodox matrix." McCue's rigorous methodology deserves notice.

21.16   Pearson, Birger A., and James E. Goehring, eds. *The Roots of Egyptian Christianity.* Studies in Antiquity and Christianity.

Philadelphia: Fortress, 1986. Pp. 319. B&W-1; T-2.
The first volume of a series, intended to offer a comprehensive history of Christianity in Egypt from its beginnings (in a Jewish context in Alexandria) to the Arab invasions. The seventeen chapters are revised papers presented in a September 1983 founding conference. The papers were intended to summarize the current state of scholarship on Egyptian Christianity. The book is divided into five parts: Greek, Coptic, and Arabic Sources; Environment of Early Christianity; Emergence of Christianity; Theological Speculation and Debate; and Monasticism. J.M. Robinson, A.F.J. Klijn, R.M. Grant wrote three of the chapters.

&< Finney, *SC* 8 (1991): 62-64; Frend, *JEH* 38 (1987): 327-328; Gruner, *SA* 50 (1989): 95-96; Hinson, *R&E* 84 (1987): 331-332; Ray, *ExT* 98 (1986): 85-86; Rorem, *Currents* 15 (1988): 286-287.

21.17   Vivian, Tim. *Saint Peter of Alexandria. Bishop and Martyr.* Studies in Antiquity and Christianity. Philadelphia: Fortress, 1988. Pp. vxii + 231. I-4 ; B-8; B&W-1; T-3.
Scholars have been content to probe no more deeply about Peter, the last martyr of the Egyptian church, than the few comments made about him by Eusebius. Vivian, by critically examining a wealth of material about Peter from Coptic hagiography, hopes to offer a more comprehensive biography, giving Peter his proper place in church history. He asks for a reappraisal of Peter's theological writings (whether they are really anti-Origen) and of his contribution to the development of the penitential system. New translations are provided for some of Peter's writings, and one-third of Vivian's work focuses on the *Canonical Letter* (306 CE).

&< H. Chadwick, *ExT* 100 (1989): 191; Ettlinger, *TS* 50 (1989): 612-613; Hinson, *R&E* 86 (1989): 283-284; Patterson, *ATR* 71 (1989): 437-441; Slusser *SC* 7 (1989-90): 187-188

ETHIOPIA
21.18   ⑧ Bonk, Jon. *An Annotated and Classified Bibliography of English Literature Pertaining to the Ethiopian Orthodox Church.* ATLA Bibliography Series 11. Metuchen, NJ/London: American Theological Library Association and The Scarecrow Press, 1984. Pp. xi + 116. I-10.
Although much of this bibliography is beyond the chronological scope of our bibliography, the Ethiopian church traces its origin to the early 300s, and is often a neglected part of the study of the early church. Most of the entries are annotated, sometimes only briefly; others are quite detailed.

JERUSALEM AND PALESTINE
(also see ch. 16: "Jewish/Christian Relations")

21.19   ⑤ Purvis, James D. *Jerusalem, the Holy City: A Bibliography.*
ATLA Bibliography Series 20. Metuchen, NJ/London: American
Theological Library Association and The Scarecrow Press, 1988.
Pp. xii + 499. AI-49; SI-19.
The most relevant sections are "Roman Jerusalem" and "Christian
Jerusalem." The latter section deals with the various kinds of
Christian interest in Jerusalem. Of particular importance are the
sections that deal with pilgrimage and the holy sites.

21.20   Lüdermann, Gerd. "The Successors of Pre-70 Jerusalem Christianity:
A Critical Evaluation of the Pella-Tradition." In *Jewish and Christian
Self-Definition* Vol. 1. Philadelphia: Fortress, 1980. Pp. 161-173.
A brief but thorough examination of the evidence for a flight of the
Jewish-Christian community from Jerusalem to Pella during the
Jewish War. Lüdermann shows that neither the literary nor historical
materials support the likelihood of such a flight. For one thing, the
earliest reference of such a flight is from Eusebius, and all other
references seem to depend on that. Lüdermann also considers the
New Testament evidence, as well as various conflicting evidence
regarding the fate of the Jerusalem community.

NORTH AFRICA
21.21   Frend, W.H.C. *The Donatist Church: A Movement of Protest in
Roman North Africa.* Oxford: Clarendon Press, 1952. Pp. xviii +
361. I-9; B-10; AB-5; M-3.
When this work was first published in 1952, it marked a watershed
in the study of a schismatic movement in the early Church—in
fact, one of the most important of those movements—in that it
systematically introduced the North African social background as
an integral understanding to the development of the peculiar brand
of Christianity that came to have such terrible consequences in the
post-Constantinian Church. Frend's systematic exploitation of
archaeological and epigraphical evidence in the whole picture was
novel for the time, especially in the English-speaking world. The
main theses of the work, however, of "Donatism" as a particularly
"Numidian" and "rural" movement, and as one of "protest" have
been severely questioned, if not entirely controverted, by recent
research. (S)
✁ *JEH* 23 (1972): 251-266.

21.22   Frend, W.H.C. "The Early Christian Church in Carthage." In *Excavations at Carthage 1976 Conducted by the University of Michigan.* Edited by J.H. Humphrey. Ann Arbor: University of Michigan, 1978. Vol. 4. Pp. 1-14.

Frend provides a useful survey of the evidence for the church in Carthage, emphasizing the archaeological data, especially with regard to church architecture and locations, and the literary evidence concerning these same questions. Concerning church offices, the important role of the bishop in both Catholic and Donatist churches is emphasized, and various other offices are discussed. Frend points to the rigor and the success of the Christian movement in the area, with North Africa having some 700 bishops at the time of Augustine, and to the initial opposition to monasticism. Left as a puzzle is the dramatic decline of the North African church *before* the conquests of Islam. With charts of basilicas and other archaeological finds.

21.23   Shaw, Brent D. "African Christianity: Disputes, Definitions, and "Donatists."" In *Orthodoxy and Heresy in Religious Movements: Discipline and Dissent.* Edited by Malcolm R. Greenshields and Thomas A. Robinson. Lewiston, NY: Edwin Mellen, 1992. Pp. 5-34.

Shaw presents a sympathetic treatment of the Donatists' claim to represent the authentic Christianity of North Africa. He offers a review of the history of the Donatist movement, its analysis in the modern secondary literature, and the origins of the label "Donatist." He also provides a close analysis of the word-by-word record of the debate in the great Conference between the Donatists and the Catholics, held in Carthage between June 1st and 8th, 411 CE. By analyzing the verbatim transcripts of speeches, he seeks to demonstrate how the behavior of the so-called "Donatist" bishops at the Conference can be reread to highlight the micro-resistances that the "losers" deployed to undermine the legitimacy of the predetermined and pre-authorized decision that was to be issued by the Conference president. He concludes with an analysis of the manner in which the "Donatists" successfully challenged the labelling of themselves by Catholic "orthodoxy."

ROME

21.24   ☛ Brown, Raymond E., and John P. Meier. *Antioch and Rome: New Testament Cradles of Catholic Christianity.* New York and Ramsey: Paulist, 1983. Pp. 242. SI-6; B-15.

Brown writes the half on Rome. He posits a heavily Jewish character for the earliest form of Christianity there, relying on Paul's letter to the Romans, which he finds cautiously written by Paul in order not to offend Jewish sensibilities. 1 Peter and Hebrews provide information for reconstructing the second generation, and *1 Clement* the information for the third generation. Seven other documents (four of which are non-canonical) supplement Brown's reconstruction. His purpose, as is Meier's [§21.30] is to show that Rome and Antioch represent more the mainstream of early Christian thought than does the thought of Paul.

᠄< Balch, *JBL* 104 (1985): 725-728; Ciuba, *CBQ* 45 (1983): 476-478; Drane, *EQ* 58 (1986): 176-177; Duling, *USQR* 39 (1984): 243-250; Dunbar, *WTJ* 46 (1984): 424-426; Hunter, *TS* 45 (1984): 354-356; Marshall, *JSNT* 25 (1985): 125-126; Logan, *SJT* 38 (1985): 266-268.

21.25   Heron, A.I.C. "The Interpretation of I Clement in Walter Bauer's *Rechtgläubigkeit und Ketzerei im ältesten Christentum.*" *Ekklesiasikos Pharos* 55 (1973): 517-45.

Heron challenges Bauer's reconstruction of Christianity in Corinth in the late first century. Bauer thought the epistle of *I Clement* reflected a Gnostic takeover of the leadership there, with the Roman church reacting to reverse this situation. Heron points out how speculative Bauer's reconstruction is—a reconstruction based on scanty and dated literature (1 Corinthians), and worse, one that disregarded the content of *I Clement* itself. The Roman church's involvement is considerably less sinister than Bauer had made it.

21.26   ☛ Jeffers, James S. *Conflict at Rome: Social Order and Hierarchy in Early Christianity.* Minneapolis: Fortress, 1991. Pp. viii + 215. I-4; B-12; B&W-13.

Jeffers examines *1 Clement* (social elite) and *The Shepherd of Hermas* (sectarians), concluding that they represent two approaches to church structure in the Christian community at Rome. Whether one agrees with Jeffers' analysis of the situation, he does offer useful brief introductions to various topics of importance: city life, foreigners, Jews, prominent Roman Christians and their place in society, associations, house churches, catacombs, Roman Christian literature, household rules, hospitality, patronage, citizenship, and discipline. He concludes with a sociological analysis of the Christian community in Rome. Compare Maier's book [§21.27].

᠄< Benko, *JCS* 34 (1992): 267-268; McDonald, *TS* 53 (1992): 181; Osiek, *JBL* 111 (1992): 731-733; Pervo, *SC* 8 (1991): 255-256; Wansink, *TT* 49 (1992): 283.

21.27   Maier, Harry O. *The Social Setting of the Ministry as Reflected in the Writings of Hermas, Clement and Ignatius.* Dissertations SR 1.

Waterloo, ON: Wilfrid Laurier UP, 1991. Pp. viii + 230. B-26.
Using four major data bases—the Pauline letters, the *Shepherd of Hermas*, *I Clement*, and Ignatius' letters—Maier concentrates on the household and family as the focus of "ministry" in the immediate post-Apostolic phase of the expansion of Christianity in the Mediterranean. After laying out his basic methodological premises (in the introduction) Maier uses the first chapter of his work to review the structure and function of "the Graeco-Roman household." Each of the succeeding chapters is then devoted to one of the major sources. Maier is not concerned just with the social structure and importance of households, but also the way in which social structure in general affects the nature of the "message." So, for example, in the case of Ignatius it is the problem of bringing communities under the control of leaders and the need for the legitimation of these leaders' authority that provoked the type of message being produced. Nevertheless, the centrality of powerful household heads is a major theme in Maier's thesis, and so it is weakened to a large extent by the fact that he has incorporated too little of what has been published on precisely that subject (i.e., family and household in Greek and Roman societies) in the last two decades. (S)
⪥ Hollerich, *TS* 53 (1992): 383-384; Sly, *Method and Theology in the Study of Religion* 3 (1991): 279-284.

21.28   ☛ O'Grady, Desmond. *Caesar, Christ, & Constantine: A History of the Early Church in Rome*. Huntington, IN: Our Sunday Visitor, 1991. Pp. 180. I-13; B&W-10.
This is one of the more popular level books included in this bibliography, but it is of value to the beginning student because it is well written and informed. The history of the empire is sketched, largely around the careers of the emperors (who are described in interesting detail). The development of the church in Rome, with its sorrows and successes, is also discussed. O'Grady gives the reader numerous lively descriptions. Although O'Grady is a journalist rather than an academic, he is informed about the scholarly issues, and his work is a reliable introduction to the main features of the Christian church in the world of Rome.

SYRIA AND ANTIOCH
21.29   Brock, Sebastian. *Syriac Perspectives on Late Antiquity*. London: Variorum Reprints, 1984. Pp. 336. I-7.
This is a collection of fifteen articles that appeared between 1973 and 1982. The following articles in the collection are relevant to the period covered by this bibliography: "Early Syrian Asceticism";

"Greek into Syriac and Syriac into Greek"; "Aspects of Translation Technique"; "Some Aspects of Greek Words in Syriac"; "From Antagonism to Assimilation: Syriac Attitudes to Greek Learning"; "A Letter Attributed to Cyril of Jerusalem on the Rebuilding of the Temple under Julian"; "An Early Syriac Life of Maximus the Confessor." Some articles present Syriac sources not before published, and many extend beyond Syria itself to the wider empire.

⨾< Murray, *JTS* 38 (1987): 220-221.

21.30   ☛ Brown, Raymond E., and John P. Meier. *Antioch and Rome: New Testament Cradles of Catholic Christianity.* New York and Ramsey: Paulist, 1983. Pp. xii + 242. B-15; MAI-4; SI-6.

Meier wrote the section on Antioch. Relying heavily on the Gospel of Matthew, Meier reconstructs the history of the church in Antioch. Meier's problem is that Matthew (which, for Meier, is a kind of mid-point between Paul and Ignatius) is considerably more Jewish than either Paul or Ignatius. While not harmonizing the thought of Matthew and Paul, Meier does try to bring them closer together. The task is more difficult for the thought of Matthew and Ignatius. Meier is, however, compelled to made an effort, for the more that Matthew seems an oddity, the less likely that Gospel should be used in a reconstruction of the situation in Antioch. Galatians, Acts, and the *Didache* are also examined.

⨾< See the entries under §21.24 for book reviews.

21.31   Downey, Glanville. *A History of Antioch in Syria: From Seleucus to the Arab Conquest.* Princeton: Princeton UP, 1961. Pp. xix + 767. I-13; B&W-12; B-22; CT-4; M-9.

Able to draw extensively on the archaeological excavations of Princeton University in Antioch and region, Downey was able to write one of the best narrative histories available for a single large city in the Roman empire. He systematically introduces the geographical milieu and evaluates the surviving types of evidence available for its history. He then traces its history and development from Antioch's foundation under Antiochus I, the Seleucid, down to Heraclius, and the seventh-century Arab conquests. Of special interest are his general survey of the Christian community in the city (Ch. 11), on Julian (Ch. 13), and his extensive "Topographical Excursus" (pp. 597-679). Must now be supplemented by Liebeschuetz's book on late imperial Antioch, which is by far the superior in historical analysis [§21.37]. (S)

⨾< R.M. Grant, *CH* 30 (1961): 362-363; Heichelheim, *ATR* 44 (1962): 230-231; A. Jones, *JTS* 13 (1962): 432-433; Smith, *JBL* 80 (1961): 377-379.

21.32 Drijvers, Han J.W. *Cults and Beliefs at Edessa*. Études Preliminaires aux Religions Orientales dans L'Empire Romain. Leiden: E.J. Brill, 1980. Pp. 204. I-4; B&W-34; B-16.

Drijvers points out that the focus of much of the study on Edessa is on the Christian character of the area, this being, according to the Abgar legend, the first Christian kingdom. Although Drijvers himself has written much on the Christian aspect of Edessa [§21.32 – §21.35], he turns here to an extensive treatment of religion more broadly, and examines the shift from pagan to Christian.

✂ Greenfield, *Numen* 28 (1981): 251-255; Marks, *JAOS* 101 (1981): 441-442.

21.33 Drijvers, Han J.W. *East of Antioch: Studies in Early Syriac Christianity*. London: Variorum Reprints, 1984. Pp. 340.

Drijvers is a leading scholar on Syriac Christianity, and this volume is a collection of sixteen articles on the subject written between 1967-1984. Nine articles are in English: (I) East of Antioch. Forces and Structures in the Development of Early Syriac Theology; (IV) Hellenistic and Oriental Origins; (VI) Facts and Problems in Early Syriac-Speaking Christianity; (IX) The 19th Ode of Solomon: Its Interpretation and Place in Syrian Christianity; (X) Odes of Solomon and Psalms of Mani. Christians and Manichaeans in Third-Century Syria; (XI) Bardaisan of Edessa and the Hermetica. The Aramaic Philosopher and the Philosophy of his Time; (XIV) Quq and the Quqites. An Unknown Sect in Edessa in the Second Century A.D.; (XV) The Origins of Gnosticism as a Religious and Historical Problem; and (XVI) The Persistence of Pagan Cults and Practices in Christian Syria.

✂ Abramowski, *JTS* 38 (1987): 218-219.

21.34 ◉ Drijvers, Han J.W. "Facts and Problems in Early Syriac-Speaking Christianity." *Second Century* 2 (1982): 157-175. Reprinted in *East of Antioch: Studies in Early Syriac Christianity*. London: Variorum Reprints, 1984.

This serves as a good review of the scholarship on Edessa, and the disputed conclusions. Drijvers discusses the Abgar story (the alleged correspondence between Jesus and King Abgar), the Thomas tradition, the puzzling apostle Addai, the influence of the Manichaeans, referring frequently to the main literature and players in the history there.

21.35 Drijvers, Han J.W. "Jews and Christians at Edessa." *Journal of Jewish Studies* 36 (1985): 88-102.

Like Alexandria and Rome, Edessa had a significant Jewish population that must be taken into account when the growth of the Christian church is considered. Drijvers reviews the evidence from the first to the fifth century, demonstrating that Jews and Christians, though competitors, were not always locked in hostile combat; in fact, there were a number of common features between the two groups. In particular, Drijvers points to the evidence for substantial Christian borrowing from Judaism, and the continued attraction of Judaism to Christians.

21.36   Gero, Stephen. "With Walter Bauer on the Tigris: Encratite Orthodoxy and Libertine Heresy in Syro-Mesopotamian Christianity." In *Nag Hammadi, Gnosticism, and Early Christianity*. Edited by Charles W. Hedrick and Robert Hodgson, Jr. Peabody: Hendrickson, 1986. Pp. 287-307.

Gero examines the evidence for Christianity in Edessa in the first five centuries. He refutes the general view among scholars (heavily influenced by Bauer) that Syrian/Mesopotamian Christianity (including all of its Gnostic expressions) was uniformly encratite and that libertine Gnosticism was "but an invention of the hostile orthodox heresiographers and apologists." Gero's thorough examination of a widespread Gnostic group called the Borborites is the basis for his reconstruction. He also discusses the late influence of Marcionism in eastern Mesopotamia, the importance of the Thomas tradition, and the political factors that gave longer life to heretical movements in the east.

21.37   Liebeschuetz, J.H.W.G., *Antioch: City and Imperial Administration in the Later Roman Empire*, Oxford, Clarendon Press, 1972. Pp. xiv + 302. M-2. I-12; B-8; Greek Index-1.

One of the finest single studies devoted to a large city in the ancient Mediterranean. It is a necessary supplement to Glanville Downey's study of the same city [§21.31]. Based for the most part on a close reading of the writings of Libanius (outlined in Part One), Liebeschuetz produced a remarkable total portrait of the functioning of a late antique city: its territory, population, and the occupations of its inhabitants (Part Two), its local government (Part Three) and the interrelationships, which were sometimes violent, between the local community and its leadership, and the imperial government in the east (Part Four). In the final section of the book (Part Five) Liebeschuetz then studies the dynamics in the change of these fundamental structures of the city during the course of the fourth century, especially through the functioning of patronage, the impact of new

religions and their organizations, and the reaction of old paganism in its rhetorical schools and higher education. (S)
⊰< Colledge, *CR* 24 (1974): 95-97.

21.38 ⊚ Liebeschuetz, J.H.W.G. "Problems Arising from the Conversion of Syria." In *The Church in Town and Countryside.* Edited by J. Baker. Oxford: E.H.S. and Blackwell, 1979. Pp. 17-24.
A short but insightful article covering the main issues and problems in the study of Christianity in Syria. Liebeschuetz's main concern is with the rural and urban divisions, and the success of the Christian movement against that framework. He examines the inscriptional evidence for a Christian presence (in particular, the "One God" inscriptions), economic factors in the conversion to Christianity, and monasticism. A suggestive review of early Christianity in Syria.

21.39 ☞ McCullough, W. Stewart. *A Short History of Syriac Christianity to the Rise of Islam.* Chico, CA: Scholars Press, 1982. Pp. 197. I-5; B-3; M-1.
All but Chapters 10 and 11 deal with the period of this bibliography. McCullough intends his work as a introductory survey for the general public. The work is divided into western Syria (under Roman and, after that, Byzantine rule) and eastern Syria (under the Parthians). Important movements, people, and events are addressed in brief but useful detail. The greater detail is given to the less familiar church of the east. McCullough offers a more neutral account of the beginnings of the early church in Syria than does Bauer [§18.2], and would be better read first, but note review criticisms. With 4 appendixes.
⊰< Donner, *JNES* 47 (1988): 233-235; McVey, *JAAR* 51 (1983): 695; Segal, *JSS* 28 (1983): 371-373; Tsirpanlis, *PBR* 4 (1985): 64-65.

21.40 Meeks, Wayne A., and Robert L. Wilken. *Jews and Christians in Antioch in the First Four Centuries of the Common Era.* Missoula: Scholars Press, 1978. Pp. x + 127.
An attempt to describe the relationship between the Jewish and Christian communities in Antioch, without subordinating interest in the Jewish community only to those areas where it might enlighten our understanding of the Christian community. Material is scarce, however, for such reconstructions (both Libanius and Chrysostom, on whom Meeks and Wilken depend heavily, are fourth century—and Christian). Inscriptions also are used to help illustrate the situation of Jews in Antioch.
⊰< Aune, *CBQ* 42 (1980): 276; Barrett, *ExT* 91 (1979): 25; Darling, *CH*

49 (1980): 204-205; Greenwood, *TS* 40 (1979): 743-744; Hann, *StLJT* 25 (1981): 75-77; Mayer, *Currents* 8 (1981): 50-51; Osiek, *JES* 17 (1980): 690-691.

21.41   Murray, Robert. *Symbols of Church and Kingdom: A Study in Early Syriac Tradition.* Cambridge: Cambridge UP 1977. (1975[1]). Pp. xv + 394. B-13; I-3; AAI-8; MAI-4; BI-2; NTI-2; T-11.
Murray surveys all the Syriac literature up to the early fifth century, concentrating on the writings of Aphrahat and Ephrem, in order to gain an understanding of perceptions of the church. As important as that discussion is, the 38-page introduction itself provides an adequately detailed general discussion of the early history of the church in Syria, informed by reference to various modern reconstructions of that history. Syriac language is also discussed, making Murray's introduction useful to the beginner and his full work useful to the seasoned scholar.

21.42   Wallace-Hadrill, D.S. *Christian Antioch. A Study of Early Christian Thought in the East.* Cambridge/London/New York: Cambridge UP, 1982. Pp. viii + 218. I-4; B-8; M-1.
After a brief survey of the history of the city of Antioch to the 7th century CE, the author considers various aspects of Antiochene Christianity: religious background (pagan, Jewish, Gnostic); exegesis of Scripture; interpretation of history; doctrine of the nature of God; use of Greek philosophy; humanity of Christ; salvation; theology; and religious life. Included are appendixes on Eastern representation at Nicea and on the feminine element in Syrian Christianity. But note the somewhat severe *JTS* review by Murray.
✎ Grant, *CH* 52 (1983): 494-495; Griffith, *CHR* 75 (1989): 123-124; Hanson, *ExT* 94 (1983): 186-187; Murray, *JTS* 35 (1984): 232-235; Slusser, *TS* 44 (1983): 505-507; Wickham, *SJT* 37 (1984): 255.

SPAIN AND GAUL
21.43   Stancliffe, Clare. *St. Martin and his Hagiographer: History and Miracle in Sulpicius Severus.* Oxford: Clarendon Press, 1983. Pp. xiv + 396. B; I; B&W-3; M.
In the development of Christian institutions, in particular those of the ascetic movement, Martin, bishop of Tours ca. 372-97 CE, was the western European equivalent of Anthony in the eastern Mediterranean. Although each was not the very first monastic of his kind, they were the men who set the principal ideas and main forms into which formal ascetic behavior was to be cast in their respective regions. Both men also share the aspect of being creations of their biographers: Anthony of Athanasius; Martin of Sulpicius

Severus. It is Stancliffe's particular virtue to have made this a study not only of Martin himself, but also of the background and "reliability" of his literary creator. She shows how the person of Martin is presented as being little affected by the maelstrom of change in the transitional society of late antique Gaul. She argues that it was his very consistency that made Martin as sort of icon of dependability, a point of reference for those conflicting persons and forces whirling about him. She probes the gap between the historical Martin that lay behind the hagiographical picture of Sulpicius Severus and actual social background in which the 'real' Martin functioned in fifth-century Gaul. Perhaps sometimes too positivistic in her search for rational explanation for literary images (e.g., the phenomenon of miracles), Stancliffe has produced a carefully drawn analysis that will surely become the standard point of departure for future research. (S)

✂ Markus, *TLSuppl* 83 (1984): 42; Babcock, *CHR* 71 (1985): 582-584.

21.44   Van Dam, Raymond. *Leadership and Community in Late Antique Gaul*. Berkeley/Los Angeles: University of California Press, 1985. Pp. xii & 350. B-24; I-10; AAI-3; M-1.

A work that has grown in significance and influence since its initial publication. The focus of Van Dam's analysis is the convergence between the political fragmentation of the Roman empire in Spain and Gaul, and the simultaneous growth in the power and spread of the Christian church and ideology in these same regions. Taking more of a "bottom-up" approach to these problems, permits the author to emphasize the behavior and feelings of ordinary "flesh-and-blood" people and to sense the shifting power networks from the perspective of local communities. This allows him to study the transformation of local aristocracies and the development of local ecclesiastical hierarchies from a novel perspective, and to overcome the divisive division of labor between "church" and "secular" historians who have tended to treat these problems in isolation. He can thereby get the big actors, like Roman emperors and powerful bishops, and their audience, often the poor and the rural, into a single coherent picture. The result is the exhilarating production of a host of new interpretations and problems about the development of Late Antique society in the west, from a re-assessment of what is meant by the labelling of the Bagaudae as "bandits" to the role of accusations of heresy and manichaean adherence in controlling unwanted or marginal persons (in which analysis he pays particular attention to the so-called "Priscillianist heresy" in Spain). Finally, Van Dam offers a novel integrationist interpretation of the function of the cult of the relics of the saints in sixth-century Gaul. The process of the "conversion" of a whole region of the Roman west in the fifth to seventh centuries is seen in an unusual and provocative way. (S)

✂ Benko, *AHR* 91 (1986): 367-368; Harries, *JRS* 76 (1986): 290-292; Mathiesen, *CP* 82 (1987): 371-377.

22
THE ROMAN EMPIRE

More and more students interested in the early church are coming to realize that a wealth of material for understanding this period lies in a general knowledge of the Roman Empire, which was the everyday world of the early Christians. Even though they may have taken steps to guard their meetings from outsiders and may have consciously distanced themselves from various "religious" activities in the day-to-day workings of the society, Christians did not live their lives in isolation from the society around them. Most things, from work and housing, to travel and toilets and bug-infested inns, were shared by Christians with the world around them.

Various chapters in this bibliography include books and articles on the Roman world, particularly when these materials relate directly to understanding early Christian thought and action. In this chapter, we have attempted to collect materials that do not specifically consider the Christian element in the issue under discussion. These works deal more generally with a range of aspects of life in the Roman empire, with which students of the early church must have some acquaintance if they are to place the early Christians in their real context, rather than in some highly idealized world that has too often been used as the backdrop against which early Christians have been understood. Many themes are covered here: religion in its various forms, philosophy, the politics of the empire, the economy of the empire, and Judaism's own position in the Roman world. Each of these areas opens a door to a clearer and more balanced understanding of the Christian movement.

In regard to religion, for example, it is important to understand what the options were during the second and third centuries, as Christians presented their cause to the religiously-interested, even winning many converts to their movement. What made Christianity more appealing than the other religions to those who made a conscious decision to join the church? We can answer that kind of question only after gaining a substantial grasp of the religious character of the age, in all of its diverse aspects.

But in gaining a grasp of the religious character of the age and in explaining something as complex as Christianity's success, we must be careful to maintain a balance. At one extreme, Christianity cannot be made so starkly different from the other options that it has no contacts with the religious world surrounding it. Certain themes, goals, behavior, group assembly, and vocabulary would have been shared by the Christians with segments within the diverse religious society of the day. On the basis of such shared institutions and values, some intelligible dialog about the differences (which certainly did exist) could then have occurred between Christians and those with alternative religious concerns and loyalties. At the other extreme, Christianity is not to be viewed as merely a collection of religious parts from a stock of available religious "building blocks." There need not be parallels in other religions of the Roman world for every feature of Christianity, nor need all the apparent parallels necessarily prove to be revealing or substantive. One might even argue that in cases where there are a number of parallels, the few differences that distinguish the movements may be the more significant features to examine. Also, too much importance can be placed on the "borrowing" of ideas. Almost always, borrowed ideas are modified, and this modification will often be considerably more important than the borrowing itself. Having committed itself to finding parallels and parentage, the "History of Religions" school failed to give adequate weight to the novelty and originality of the Christian movement. Thus the need for balance—Christianity was part of a particular religious world, and the impact of that world on the developing Christian movement must be recognized, but it must be recognized in a way that does not overlook or depreciate the Christian genius and novelty. The Christian movement was different from other religious options— it recognized that itself, as did its opponents and competitors.

Turning from the religious sphere to other matters of life (insofar as such a separation is possible), Christian distinctiveness may have been less dramatic. At least, that is frequently the conclusion that scholars have reached when they have investigated matters such as ethics, family issues, and social relationships, as well as work and housing and social status. While not denying that the Christian message did penetrate into various facets of action and perception, scholars are finding that the lines between the Christian world and the non-Christian were not always starkly drawn. Even putting aside the close parallels between the Christian movement and Judaism (which were substantial and long-lasting), significant parallels can be found between the Christian movement and "pagan" society itself. From older studies, we have learned that the Christian ethical perspective shared much with that of the Stoic. Further, the Christian attitude to slavery was far from revolutionary —Christians may have adopted almost a "status-quo" attitude on the matter; and many Christians seemed to have been at home in the larger intellectual and literary world. Newer studies have emphasized that Christians participated in various areas of life once thought to have been out of bounds to them (e.g. civic office and the military), and they may have shared parts of the larger cultural world (such as art) with the pagan populous.

As well, some understanding of the general economic conditions and social structures of the empire must be gained by the student who wishes to make sense of various features of the early church. For example, the structure of the Roman household or some larger social unit (such as the *collegia*) or the pervasive patron-client relationship may hold a clue to the development of early Christian office. Charity, the status of slaves, and the treatment of widows all are issues of concern within the Christian movement. Such concerns are natural responses by Christians to the economic conditions in which they found themselves. One cannot really understand what Christians were attempting to do unless one understands what is it that needed to be done. Thus, information about famine and food supply, about the welfare system, about wages and debt, all play a role in placing the church historian in the Graeco-Roman world—a world that was perhaps more familiar to early Christians than was even the world of the New Testament—colored as that was by its roots in a peripheral Palestine.

Finally, the political situation, including the imperial administration and judicial procedure, must be understood. Was the empire experiencing political crises, so that suspicion might be cast on any element that did not express its loyalty to the empire in the expected ways? What did it mean to be brought to trial? What did martyrs do to provoke the verdicts and sentences they received? What kind of freedom did an exiled leader have to communicate with the church from which he had been separated? What did it mean to the average citizen of the empire to have a neighbor refuse to participate in the imperial cult? These are questions that require a familiarity with a broader range of literature than merely that stemming from Christian authors.

Roman historians are adding much to our understanding of the world of the early Christians. In this chapter, and in various others within this bibliography, many works by scholars of the Roman Empire are abstracted. Of particular value to users of this bibliography will be the entries abstracted by Brent Shaw, indicated by the mark (S) after the abstract. Shaw is a professor of Classics and Ancient History, whose own work illustrates just how much the scholarship of "secular" historians of the Roman world overlaps with the interests of the church historian.

GENERAL

22.1 ⑤ Baldwin, Barry. "A Bibliographical Survey: The Second Century from Secular Sources 1969-1980." *Second Century* 1 (1981): 173-189.

A brief article, but filled with reference to dozens of major books on various issues related to the Roman empire, from politics to religion, and numerous issues in between. Many of the books and articles in this chapter of our bibliography are discussed by Baldwin, frequently with an evaluation, and some reflection on the place of that work in the context of scholarship. Some of the negative criticisms of Edward Gibbon's classic work are also discussed. A good review of some of the leading characters of the age is provided too.

22.2 ⑱ Wells, Colin. "Further Reading." In *The Roman Empire*. 2d ed. Hammersmith: Fontana, 192. (1984[1]). Pp. 291-332.
Although Wells' book is abstracted later in this chapter [§22.17], it is important to call attention to Wells' highly useful bibliography by a special entry here. The bibliography is detailed and as current as any bibliographical guide we have listed. In addition, brief comments for many of the entries provide insight into the value and place of that work in the context of current scholarship on the Roman world. Further, almost all of the works are in English, covering monographs, journal articles, and essays in collected volumes. Although many of the entries in Wells' bibliography are abstracted in our bibliography (in this chapter and a few others), Wells offers a considerably longer list on a broader range of topics, broken down by subject materials covered in the chapters of the main text, and then by subject subheadings. This now represents one of the finer bibliographical guides to current research on Roman imperial society and politics available to the interested scholar from fields adjacent to, but outside, the specialist circles of professional Roman historians. (S)

22.3 🏛 Shelton, Jo-Ann. *As the Romans Did. A Source Book in Roman Social History*. New York and Oxford: Oxford UP, 1988. Pp. xx + 492. B-11; I-18; CT-4; M-5; B&W-5; T-3.
This is a well organized collection of 425 passages, arranged under fifteen main topics, which are then divided there into sub-topics. The following are covered: the structure of Roman society (including class and patronage); families; marriage; housing and city life; domestic and personal concerns such as meals, illness, and life expectancy; education; occupations; slaves; freedmen; government and politics; the army; the provinces; women; leisure and entertainment; and religion and philosophy. Selections generally have brief introductions and fairly detailed notes. The book includes a 1-page appendix on Roman money and an extremely useful 13-page summary of ancient sources. This is a quick way to get a feel for life in the world of the Roman empire and of matters that were relevant to the early Christians but that were not always addressed in early Christian literature. (S)

22.4 ☛ Alföldy, Géza. *The Social History of Rome.* Translated by David Braund and Frank Pollock. Baltimore: John Hopkins UP, 1988. (1985[1]). Pp. 251. I-4; T-1.

It is mainly the latter half of this work that addresses the period of our bibliography. Alföldy provides a summary of what is known about the social structures of ancient Roman society, dealing with a number of issues of relevance to students of the early church: slavery, client and patron relationships (which gave even the lower class some interest in the stability of the state), the possibility for advancement, the lower "strata" in the cities and the countryside, and various changes that occurred in both the upper and lower strata as the empire experienced crisis and collapse to the barbarians.

22.5 ☛ Boardman, John; Jasper Griffin, and Oswyn Murray, ed. *The Oxford History of the Classical World.* Oxford/New York: Oxford UP, 1986. Pp. x + 882. I-10; B&W-288; C-26; CT-31; M-10.

This detailed survey of the classical world consists of 33 chapters, divided into three sections: "Greece"; "Greece and Rome"; and "Rome." Each chapter is written by an expert in the field (some of whom have done work in the early church: Robin Lane Fox, Peter Brown, Henry Chadwick). Not every topic is covered—the emphasis is on literature and art—though chapters on mythology, philosophy, and religion will be useful for students of the early church, as well as the chapter on Roman Life and Society. Essays in this volume can serve as useful and current introductions to several topics. Useful bibliographies are included, the illustrations are extensive and relevant, and information on the illustrated artifacts is helpful (e.g., size, date, present location, etc.).

22.6 *The Cambridge Ancient History.*

The large-scale standard "encyclopedic" history of the world of antiquity, from early Near Eastern societies to the "fall" of the Roman Empire in the west. The first edition, edited by J.B. Bury, S.A. Cook, and Sir Frank Adcock, covered this span in twelve volumes. Volumes 1-4 covered the Near East, volumes 4-6 the history of the Greek city-states and Macedon; volumes 7-8 the Hellenistic world; and 9-12 the Roman Empire (published between 1925 and 1939). Each volume contains chapters devoted to special subjects written by experts on those fields. These volumes were corrected and revised in various reprints that ran from the 1930s to the 1960s. In the latter decade a completely new edition of the whole work was planned, and is now in progress. Of this second edition, volumes 1-3 (in 7 separate volumes) cover the history of

the early Near East, the Aegean, and the Balkans (1970-1991);
volumes 4-5 cover Persia, and Greece in the sixth and fifth centuries
BCE (1988-1992). In order to hasten the publication process, the
volumes covering Roman history have begun to be issued separately.
Of these, volumes 7.2 and 8 on the rise of Rome, and on the
history of Rome and the Mediterranean to 133 BCE have appeared
(1989). The format of having experts write individual chapters has
been maintained (as well as the provision of accompanying volumes
of illustrative plates). There is a noticeable tendency in the second
edition to balance traditional political history with some social and
economic history. (S)

22.7 ☛ Garnsey, Peter, and Richard Saller. *The Roman Empire: Economy,
Society and Culture*. London: Duckworth, 1987. Pp. viii + 231.
B-21; I-5; M-1.
Two leading historians of the "Cambridge School" offer a synopsis
of the main work done, principally by English-language social
historians, on the basic economic, social and cultural structures of
the society of the Roman Empire at its height. Although giving
broad coverage of all major aspects of the society of the time, the
book concentrates on new and revisionist work done on fundamental
political and social structures through the late 1970s. In political
terms this work stresses the move away from a concern with formal
political institutions (e.g., rational bureaucratic offices) to the
personal power networks established in countervail to them (e.g.,
patron-client relations). In their analysis of the economy the authors
incorporate the criticisms of modernist interpretations of the imperial
economy essayed by Sir Moses Finley, to whom the book is
dedicated, but they also introduce important nuances to his schema
(e.g., on the significance of long-range trade). Finally, in their
study of social hierarchy, much of the new work on the nature of
personal relationships and the types of "family" life typical of Roman
society are investigated. A good guide to the revisionist research of
the period. (S)
✂ Burton, *JRS* 78 (1988): 223-224; Engels, *AHR* 94 (1989): 109-110;
Purcell, *JCS* 86 (1987): 962.

22.8 ☛ Grant, Michael. *History of Rome*. New York: Charles Scribner's
Sons, 1978. Pp. xxi + 537. B-5; CT-7; I-15; B&W-174; M-27; T-6.
This book, of which slightly over half is relevant to our period,
offers a wealth of easy to read material on the Roman Empire. It is
exceptionally well organized and illustrated, and, though it is
somewhat detailed, it will provide the non-expert a handle on the

broad picture of the empire in the time of the early church. In addition, the notes (pp. 475-507) provide a remarkably clear and condensed review of key places, persons, and issues, making it an ideal quick study aid for students. Includes a useful 3-page note on ancient authors and their writings, along with family tree charts of six Roman dynasties.

22.9   Jones. A.H.M. *The Later Roman Empire 284-602: A Social Economic and Administrative Survey*. Norman, OK: University of Oklahoma University Press, 1964. Vol. 1. Pp. 766. T-1. Vol. 2. Pp. 752. I-39; B-13; T-28; M-7.
The culmination of a lifetime's work devoted to the study of the constitutional, administrative, and economic structures of the Roman empire, this great survey is precisely that—a massive work of reference that is firmly anchored in a near-comprehensive reading of the primary sources of the period. Jones was never overly concerned to read, incorporate, or annotate the work of modern scholars, but he had an overriding passion with absorbing every word written by the persons of the time. His survey begins with a general history of the period, and then passes to the core of the work: a detailed survey of the offices of state, the imperial bureaucracy, civil service, the army, and local city administrations. The second volume is devoted mainly to the economy (land, trade, and commerce) and to the cultural institutions of the later empire (mainly those of the Church). Given Jones' mastery of the primary sources, one can almost treat his text as a sort of surrogate "primary document"—a very useful work of reference because of its dense and massive documentation of the primary sources (paragraph by paragraph) in the enormous series of endnotes. Used in this sense, *The Later Roman Empire* will probably remain a "front-line" work of reference for the period. When it comes to interpretation of the evidence, however, one is often best advised to turn to others (e.g., Brown §5.5, Matthews §22.13). (S)
✂ Alexander, *AJP* 87 (1966): 337-350; Greenslade, *JTS* 16 (1965): 220-224; Hammond, *Speculum* 42 (1967-68); Heichelheim, *JRS* 55 (1965): 250-253; Wallace-Hadrill, *EHR* 80 (1965): 785-790; Warmington, *History* 50 (1965): 54-60.

22.10   Koester, Helmut. *History, Culture, and Religion of the Hellenistic Age*. Volume 1 of *Introduction to the New Testament*. Philadelphia: Fortress / Berlin-New York: De Gruyter, 1982. Pp. xxix + 429. G-4; AAI-2; I-10; AI-1; M-7; B&W-15; T-10.
Koester is one of the leading scholars in the field of the New

Testament and of the first couple of centuries of church history. In this work, Koester offers a fairly detailed survey of most of the important issues in the Graeco-Roman world. After a historical survey of the Hellenistic world, the work is broken in thematic sections: "Society and Economics"; "Education, Language, and Literature": "Philosophy and Religion." These are followed by major sections on Judaism and the Roman Empire, with a range of issues addressed, and a historical survey offered. Koester's presentation is useful, and somewhat more free of theological motivations that have marked some of his work on early Christian diversity.

22.11   MacMullen, Ramsay. *Enemies of the Roman Order: Treason, Unrest and Alienation in the Empire.* Cambridge, MA: Harvard UP, 1967. Reprint. New York/London: Routledge, 1993. Pp. x + 370. I-4; B&W-5.
One of the first works systematically to broach the subject of opposition to the Roman order of the emperors. In it MacMullen attempted to trace a growing pattern of resistance extending from within the ruling élite itself (the Republican resistance of recalcitrant senators from Cato and Brutus in the late Republic to the "successors" under the early emperors) to more popular and lower class opposition in the form of urban riots and "barbarian" threats. Bridging these two forms of resistance were ideological types of rebelliousness that are of particular interest to those studying the rise of Christianity: the fractious ideas of pagan philosophers (Stoics, Sceptics, Cynics and their ilk), and the more popular actions of magicians, astrologers, diviners, and prophets. The main narrative accounts are supplemented by appendices on famines (mainly in the cities) and on brigandage. If much of MacMullen's work has now been superseded (on the latter appendices alone) such advances are in no small part due to the fact that he blazed the trail with this fine history of resistance in the empire. It has still not been superseded by any single monograph devoted to the subject. (S)
❧ Brunt, *EHR* 84 (1969): 139-140; Finley, *NYRB* 8.9 (1967): 37-39; Murray, *JRS* 59 (1969): 261-265; Oost, *CP* 63 (1968): 169-170; Rogers, *AJP* 89 (1968): 491-494.

22.12   MacMullen, Ramsay. *Corruption and the Decline of Rome.* New Haven: Yale UP, 1988. Pp. xii + 319. I-3; B-34; FT-1; M-2; T-14.
Originating from a series of lectures delivered at Paris in 1981 at the invitation of the prestigious Collège de France, though bearing the general rubric corruption, MacMullen's work consists of a number of essay-like forays into a subject of central significance—

power. Beginning with a general outline of the current interpretations of the institutions and modes of the working of power in the empire (a most valuable contribution), MacMullen advances to how power actually worked. In this analysis, he traces the great shift in the balance between "private" and "public" interests in the empire wherein the sale of formal public positions, whether informally through patronage networks, or even quite formally (public positions in the bureaucracy and army) directly led to a deterioration in the strength of the state. Whatever one's opinion of the persuasiveness of the central thesis, the wealth of up-to-date scholarship (a trademark of MacMullen's) makes this book a valuable guide to social and political change in the high and later empire. (S)

✃ Barnes, *Classical Views* 34 (1990): 473-475; Colham, *CW* 83 (1989-90): 532-533.

22.13   Matthews, John. *The Roman Empire of Ammianus.* London: Duckworth / Baltimore: Johns Hopkins UP, 1989. Pp. xiii + 608. B-17; I-37.

Although technically centered on the life and work of the late Latin historian Ammianus Marcellinus (about 330 to 391+ CE), this massive book is in fact a wonderful overview of the history and society of the later Roman empire as seen through the life and perceptions of the man whose words are our main record of its events. By placing Ammianus in his social and historical context, Matthews succeeds in imparting a better unitary framework to an understanding of the history of the later empire than that found in most standard historical "textbooks" of the period (compare, e.g., Jones, *The Later Roman Empire* §22.9). Matthews has not only mastered his principal primary source, the writings of Ammianus, but also a mass of current modern scholarship on the society, politics, and economy of the later empire, marvelously compressed into a hundred pages of notes and bibliography set in small type. The book is divided into two halves, the first of which is devoted to the political and military history of the period. The second half, perhaps more interesting to the general reader, is a series of studies devoted to the social and cultural aspects of late imperial society relevant to Ammianus' writings: the emperor's office, the character of government, the practice of warfare, "barbarians" and bandits, the physical environment of town and country, social relations, philosophy and religion, and the disparate cultural milieux of "Greek" and "Roman." Highly recommended as the best current introduction to those aspects of late Antique society that come within its purview. (S)

✃ O'Donnell, *Bryn Mawr Classical Review* 1 (1990): 43-74.

22.14   Rostovtzeff, M. I. *The Social and Economic History of the Roman Empire*. Oxford: Clarendon Press, 1963. (1926[1]). Vol. 1. Pp. 541. B&W-80. Vol. 2. Pp. 306. NI-68; CAI-6; SI-68; T-1; Inscriptions Index-17.

The classic work of the "non-political" aspects of the history of the society of imperial Rome—a magnificent work of both analysis and synthesis penned by the great Russian émigré historian, Mikhail Ivanovich Rostovtzeff, who was compelled to flee his Russian homeland at the time of the Bolshevik Revolution. Although its central theses about the reasons for the decline of the Roman social and political order were heavily colored by his own sad political experiences (and are probably mistaken, as he himself realized), this massive collection of literary, archaeological, epigraphical, numismatic, and other evidence is still a peerless achievement. For any reader seeking a single comprehensive overview of Roman society at its height, Rostovtzeff's work must still represent the critical point of departure. Of particular note is his stunningly effective use of pictorial plates and his accompanying descriptions. This great achievement was matched a decade and a half later by his massive three-volume *Social and Economic History of the Hellenistic World* (1941), which is equally useful for the prospective student. (S)

⤳ Bowersock, *Daedalus* 103 (1973): 15-23; Momigliano, *Cambridge Journal* 7 (1954): 334-346; Reinhold, *Science and Society* 10 (Fall 1946): 361-391; Shaw, *JRS* 82 (1992): 216-228.

22.15   ☛ Starr, Chester G. *The Roman Empire 27 B.C.-A.D. 476. A Study in Survival*. New York/Oxford: Oxford UP, 1982. Pp. xii + 206. I-4; B&W-12; AB-15; T-2; M-2.

Starr attempts to explain why the Empire survived as long as it did. He begins with the emperor, and goes on to deal with the classes and elements of the administration of the empire. Local government and life are then discussed, as are the armed forces. The period focused on (27 CE—211 CE) is considered to be the apex of the early empire. After this, despite the effectiveness of the forces and institutions binding and maintaining the empire for another couple of centuries, change appears more obvious. Starr adopts an analytical approach as opposed to a chronological one. A lucid and informative analysis of this subject. (Sm)

22.16   Wacher, John, ed. *The Roman World*. London and New York: Routledge and Kegan Paul, 1987. Vol. 1. Pp. 478. B&W-120; B-40;

CT-10; T-5; M-78. Vol, 2. Pp. 394. I-23; B&W-107; B-27; T-7; M-33.

This work is composed of approximately two dozen chapter-length entries on major aspects of the social history of the Roman empire at its height, each written by an expert in the field. The main subject areas covered in the first volume are historical surveys, the army and frontiers, cities and towns, and law and government; in the second, rural life and economy, social structure, and religion are discussed. There are good bibliographical guides attached to each section of essays. The collection is edited by a noted Romano-British archaeologist, and the essays, by colleagues of his, are thus heavily skewed in the direction of archaeological evidence and concerns. It is, according to that genre, richly illustrated and lavishly provided with charts and diagrams. It is accordingly strong in those areas which traverse the main interests of the experts involved—for example, the study of Roman villa agriculture (John Percival) and of the Roman army and frontiers (Graham Webster, Valerie Maxfield, Ronald Watson, David Breeze, David Kennedy). It is notably weaker on the subjects of culture and religion that might be more central to the interests of the readers of this guide. (S)

22.17   ☛ Wells, Colin. *The Roman Empire*. 2d ed. London: Fontana, 1992. (1984[1]). Pp. xv + 366. B-42; I-26; AAI-8; B&W-17; CT-1; FT-1; M-9; Greek and Latin Authors-4.

Part of the new Fontana history of the ancient world, Well's compact paperback volume probably represents the best of current general introductions to the history of the empire available to the undergraduate student. Wells begins with the events that marked the political transition from Republic to rule by emperors, but then breaks to discuss the basic source materials. From this point onward, the author alternates between chapters devoted to the recounting of the structure of the events, and interstitial chapters devoted to more general aspects of Roman social, economic, and political life (e.g. chapters on the army and provinces, the economy and society of Italy). In attempting thus to achieve a workable synthesis of political and social history of an enormous Mediterranean empire within the purview of a small paperback volume, Wells has achieved a considerable feat of compression and comprehensibility. Of very great utility, especially in the revised second edition, is the detailed annotated guide to "further reading" (abstracted at §22.2). (S)

✂ Levick, *CR* 35 (1985): 327-328; Starr, *Phoenix* 39 (1985): 187-188.

GOVERNMENT

22.18 🏛 Levick, Barbara. *The Government of the Roman Empire. A Sourcebook.* London and Sydney: Croom Helm, 1985. Pp. 260. AAI-13; B-6; CT-2; T-2; M-8; Geographical Index-11.
A collection of 230 passages or inscriptions, covering topics that range from structure, force, law, finances, communications, transportation, and supply, to the role of the emperor, patronage, assimilation, failings, resistance, and the final crisis of the Roman empire. Levick supplies more extensive notes than are usually to be found in a sourcebook, making it all the more useful to the beginner. Well cross-referenced, but perhaps a different type style should have been used to separate the primary texts from Levick's notes. A useful table of weights, measures, currency, and wealth is included. (S)

22.19 ☛ Millar, Fergus. *The Emperor in the Roman World (31 BC - AD 337).* London: Duckworth, 1977. Pp. xvi + 656. I-14; AAI-7. CT-1.
One of the best entrées to the nature of the government of the Roman empire at its height from Augustus to Constantine. Millar eschews the spectacular aspects of the emperor's role as military commander and religious figurehead to concentrate on his more mundane day-to-day activities. He surveys the entourage of assistants and advisors, friends and slaves, who constituted the administrative infrastructure of the empire. Millar links this survey of personnel to another on the material resources of wealth under the direct control of the emperor and his household. He is then able to place the daily duties of the emperor (correspondence, hearings, and issuance of orders and decisions) in the context of these instruments of imperial power. In the final part of his massive work, Millar analyzes the relationships between the emperor and his subjects: first those at the top—senators and equestrians—followed by the municipal élites in the various towns and cities of the empire, and, last of all, private individuals who approached the emperor for resolution of their problems. Of special interest to students of the early church is Millar's chapter on "Church and Emperor," which includes studies devoted to the subjects of religious toleration, the persecutions, and specific analyses of the Donatist and Arian controversies. Despite some criticisms of its (perhaps) excessive concentration on the civil role of the emperor (see the reviews listed below), this grand overview of how the empire was governed from the top is without peer, and is probably one of the finest general introductions to the subject the student will find in any language. (S)

✂ Bagnall, *CJ* 75 (1979-80): 181-183; Bowersock, *CP* 73 (1978): 346-351; Bradley, *Gnomon* 51 (1979): 258-263; Crook, *CR* 28 (1978): 315-317; Hopkins, *JRS* 68 (1978): 178-186; MacMullen, *TLSuppl* 76 (1977): 418-419; Sumner, *Phoenix* 31 (1977): 277-283.

22.20   Saller, Richard P. *Personal Patronage under the Roman Empire.* Cambridge: Cambridge UP, 1982. Pp. x + 222. B-8; I-6; M-1; T-3.
Probably the fundamental "extra-legal" connection that governed a host of the most significant public powers in the Roman world was the patron-client relationship. Saller begins by investigating the language and ideology of patronage in Roman society, and then advances to study how patronage actually functioned in the distribution of power between the emperor and the free high-status men who served him (principally senators and equestrians who acted as governors and other high-level officials). By both in-depth analytical study of actual Roman cases (the promotion of middle-rank officials, relations between governors and subjects in North Africa) and the use of comparative history (the bureaucracy of pre-modern China) Saller shows how little actual objective merit based on past performance and formal qualifications counted in appointment to positions of power in the Roman state. Rather, the pervasive asymmetrical personal linkages between patrons and clients explain "how such a large empire was governed by so small an administration." This important work should be supplemented by Saller's chapter on "Patronage and friendship in early imperial Rome" in Wallace-Hadrill's *Patronage in Ancient Society* [§23.49]. Saller's work has substantially changed our perceptions about the nature of Roman government, the modes by which it functioned, and, in the manner of Weber, how its administrative "rationality" differs fundamentally from our own (see ch. 2 in §22.7). (S)
✂ Bradley, *CJ* 80 (1985): 357-358; Brunt, *TLSuppl* 81 (1982): 1276; Levick, *Latomus* 42 (1983): 903-905; Sherwin-White, *CR* 33 (1983): 271-273.

22.21   ☛ Weaver, Paul. "Social Mobility in the Early Roman Empire: the Evidence of the Imperial Freedmen and Slaves." *Past & Present* 37 (1967): 3-20. Reprinted in *Studies in Ancient Society*. Edited by M.I. Finley. London: RKP, 1974. Pp. 121-140.
The bureaucracy of the Roman empire was not a genuine formal organization but rather, for the most part, a gigantic extension of the emperor's personal household, the coterie of his slaves and freedmen. In this article Weaver provides an abbreviated summation of his more detailed study (*Familia Caesaris: A Social Study of the Emperor's Freedmen and Slaves*, Cambridge UP, 1972) in which

he not only outlines the function of these "public servants" but studies their internal distinctions, departmental divisions, systems of evaluation and promotion, and relations with society at large. Works such as this one and that of Saller on patronage [§22.20] have substantially altered our understanding of the main mechanisms by which the Roman empire was governed. What is more, the pervasive presence of these élite slaves in the empire, has provoked at least one major re-interpretation of the significance of slavery in the vocabulary of the New Testament and its implications for attitudes towards slavery in the early church (Dale Martin, *Slavery as Salvation: the Metaphor of Slavery in Pauline Christianity*, Yale U.P., 1990). This is a convenient and accessible synopsis of an important but complex book—a brief survey which is likely to dispel misconceived notions (frequently shared by students of the early church) about how the Roman empire was actually governed. (S)

ECONOMIC

22.22   Carson, R.A.G. *Coins of the Roman Empire*. New York: Routledge, 1989. Pp. xvi +367. I-15; B&W-980.
This is a thorough discussion of all aspects of the topic by a former Keeper of Coins and Medals in the British Museum. Topics covered include such things as coin production, mint marks, and forgeries. Of particular importance for students of the early church will be the discussion of the various monetary systems of the empire. The hundreds of illustrations show coins from 31 BCE to 498 CE. These black-and-white photos are produced in fine detail on glossy paper.

22.23   Duncan-Jones, Richard. *The Economy of the Roman Empire. Quantitative Studies*. 2d ed. Cambridge: Cambridge UP, 1977. (1974[1]). Pp. 396. I-18; B-9; T-19.
By putting into publication in one volume a series of previously published studies and new investigations into the quantitative dimensions of the Roman economy, the author provides a good resource on basic economic statistics for ready reference by anyone interested in the subjects covered. These range from the productivity of land (returns and profitability of basic agricultural crops in Italy), to detailed studies and valuable charts and tables on basic known prices for goods and services (for Italy and the richly documented north African provinces of the empire), and what can be known about town and city sizes in the western empire (along with attempts by the imperial government to subsidize population). A valuable set of seventeen appendices include further specific bodies of

evidence (e.g., prices in the city of Rome, the size of large private fortunes, the costs of wine and transportation). A fundamental work of reference on the quantitative dimensions of the economy, and especially good on the systematic presentation of the known evidence. (S)

&< Bradley, *AJP* 96 (1975): 224-229; Frederikson, *JRS* 67 (1977): 199-201; Hopkins, *TLSuppl* 74 (1975): 201; Pleket, *Gnomon* 49 (1977): 55-63; Sherwin-White, *CR* 26 (1976): 244-246;

22.24   Duncan-Jones, Richard. *Structure and Scale in the Roman Economy.* Cambridge, Cambridge UP, 1990. Pp. xvi + 245. B-11; I-12; B&W-29; T-51.

A worthy sequel to his earlier set of quantitative studies on the Roman economy [§22.23], this book contains a similar mix between refurbished journal articles and new studies (eight in this book). They cover subjects basic to any understanding of the Roman world in which Christianity emerged: time and distances in the Mediterranean and their effects on communications; seaborne contacts; and the cohesion of short and long-distance trade. These are followed by a series of studies on demographics (but now see Parkin, *Demography and Roman Society,* 1992) on awareness of age, and on life expectancy. Finally, there are a series of economic studies on land use, distribution of landed property and wealth, and on coinage and taxation. The studies, though sometimes technical and complex, are clearly presented, with a generous use of charts and tables, and so represent a rich and accessible source of basic statistics on Roman imperial society. (S)

22.25   Gallant, Thomas W. *Risk and Survival in Ancient Greece: Reconstructing the Rural Domestic Economy.* Stanford: Stanford UP, 1991. Pp. xvi + 267. B; I; B&W-23; T-18.

Gallant's work represents a high-order synthesis of recent work in economic anthropology and the "new archaeology" of the Mediterranean, and the use of these data to put together a new analysis of the relationship between peasant farming households and the broader environment in which they were placed. As such, Gallant's work is part of a new spectrum of historical work (see Garnsey §22.26 and Sallares §22.27) that is providing students with a much more accurate picture of the ecological and environmental conditions of ancient Mediterranean communities. Although nominally restricted to the ancient environments of Greece, Gallant's analysis is broadly applicable to many other ancient Mediterranean contexts, and so is of considerable interest to students of the early church.

He centers his analysis on the restrictive potentials of a threatening environment which, given the limited technologies of the time, constantly faced households with "crises of subsistence." He considers the "household strategies" (family formation, storage of agricultural crops, the use of friends, kin and other self-help groups) employed to overcome the periodic environmental and economic threats posed to the existence of the family. In pursuit of this end, Gallant usefully includes a great range of relevant ancillary material (e.g. on family and household formation cycles, on the precise growth cycles of crops, on the manpower requirements of the different farming regimes) that is of immense use to anyone wishing to understand the rural environment of Mediterranean antiquity. Generously provided with charts and tables that illustrate the text. (S)

✄ Frost, *Ancient History Bulletin* 6.4 (1992): 187-95.

22.26   Garnsey, Peter. *Famine and Food Supply in the Graeco-Roman World: Responses to Risk and Crisis.* Cambridge: Cambridge UP, 1988. Pp. xix + 303. B-17; I-9; M-2; B&W-10.
This is indeed the first full-length treatment of the subject—a paradox given the fact that every analysis of ancient societies emphasizes the provision of basic foods as central to their economies. Garnsey begins by defining and distinguishing "food crises" from genuine killer "famines" and establishes the relative frequency of the former and the rarity of the latter. He then analyzes responses to both on two levels: the strategies of the rural peasantry (on which see also Gallant §22.25, a former research assistant of Garnsey's) and of large urban centres. The latter aspect is taken up in two large and detailed studies (Parts 3 and 4) devoted, respectively, to Athens and Rome. The book as a whole is marked by clarity of exposition and judicious judgments in an analysis that requires careful assessment of a minutia of fragmented and disparate archaeological and literary evidence. Garnsey is able to establish novel interpretations that have successfully challenged old orthodoxies (e.g., the relatively late dependence of Athens on large-scale grain imports) and is able to offer good insights on the relationship between the management of food supply and politics (e.g., the food riots that periodically rent the city of Rome). (S)

✄ Bradley, *CP* 85 (1990): 238-244; Mattingly, *JRS* 79 (1989): 174-1`75; Rickman, *TLSuppl* (1988): 661; Shaw, *Social History of Medicine* 2 (1989): 205-213.

22.27   Sallares, Robert. *The Ecology of the Ancient Greek World.* Ithaca,

NY: Cornell UP / London: Duckworth, 1991. Pp. x + 588. B-71; I. This enormous volume has been variously castigated as erratic and lacking in point and organization, and praised as a tremendous source of fundamental references to a wide variety of themes and data directly relevant to an understanding of the ecology of the world of Mediterranean antiquity. It is both. The first part of the book parallels the work of Gallant [§22.25] in outlining the fundamental methods needed to study the ancient environment of the Greek world, with the study of population (demography) at its core, including the subjects of age-ranking and, naturally, the problem of the diseases to which these populations were prone. Particularly valuable in itself and as a supplement to Gallant is Sallares' third chapter on the various crops and plants which Greek peasants had at the basis of their agrarian economy. The main difficulty with Sallares' presentation is its sheer prolixity. But there is a veritable mine of valuable information here, both that derived from the primary sources and from a massive reading of the secondary literature (reflected in a sixty-seven page bibliography cast in minute type), that is of considerable use to anyone wishing to consult the book on a particular problematic item concerning how peasants in the ancient Mediterranean lived. If nothing else, therefore, a rather valuable work of reference.

⅜< Frost, *Ancient History Bulletin* 6.4 (1992): 187-195.

MAGIC, ASTROLOGY, AND DEMONOLOGY

22.28 🏛 Betz, Hans Dieter, ed. *The Greek Magical Papyri in Translation (including the Demotic Spells)*. Chicago/London: University of Chicago Press, 1986. Pp. lviii + 339. I; G.

This work, which is an invaluable access to the primary texts on the subject, is prefaced by an introduction to the world of the Greek magical papyri by Betz himself, and to the demotic papyri by Janet Johnson. The core of the book is a generous selection of texts, although some categories important to readers of this guide, such as the ostraka and magical papyri of the Christian period are omitted. The texts are presented in English translation by a stellar cast of modern scholars, including David Aune, Walter Burkert and John O'Neill, with each separate text having its own translator noted. Most of the texts are drawn from Preisendanz's classic collection, the *Papyri Graecae Magicae* (*PGM*) and are keyed to the numbers and lines of that collation. Each text is further provided with extensive annotations which both explain the sometimes frequent appearance of confusing and arcane terms from the world of curses and magical incantations, and also provide the reader with further bibliographic information both on the texts themselves and on the contentious points of interpretation raised by them. An essential work of reference and collection of primary texts for a whole range of popular beliefs critical to a better understanding of the world of the early Church. (S)

✂ Danker, *JBL* 107 (1988): 348-351; Duling, *SC* 7 (1989-1990): 180-182; Faraone, *CW* 80 (1987): 325-326; Gager, *JR* 67 (1987): 80-86;

22.29   🏛 Gager, John G., ed. *Curse Tablets and Binding Spells from the Ancient World.* New York/Oxford: Oxford UP, 1992. Pp. xv + 278. I; G.

This is a collection of primary texts and commentaries edited by John Gager, with contributions by Catherine Cooper, David Frankfurter, Derek Krueger, and Richard Lim. Gager and his colleagues seek to offer a solid introduction the difficult-to-understand, and somewhat recherche, world of "curses" from the Graeco-Roman world. The core of the book, which follows an excellent general introductory survey by Gager, consists of 168 numbered texts, each of which provides the reader with the fundamental primary references to its publication, a translation into English, and a set of explanatory footnotes and endnotes. The texts are arranged in a series of chapters whose headings are self-explanatory, being ones concerning the theatre and circus, sex, love, and marriage, disputes in the law courts, ones concerning matters of business and commerce, and personal vengeance. The magical "curse" texts that do not fit into the categories are then grouped under other headings such as "miscellaneous." Along with the books of Hans Dieter Betz [§22.28] and Georg Luck [§22.30], Gager's work is essential background to the "mentality" of "magic" so necessary to a better understanding of the world in which Christianity emerged. (S)

22.30   🏛 Luck, Georg. *Arcana Mundi: Magic and the Occult in the Greek and Roman Worlds: A Collection of Ancient Texts.* Baltimore, Johns Hopkins UP, 1985. Pp. xv + 395. B-5; I-7; AAI-4.

The current handbook on the subject. Luck offers not only a general introduction to the subject, but also a series of minor introductions to specific aspects of the field: magic, miracles, demonology, divination, astrology, and alchemy. In addition to these general outlines, Luck presents 122 numbered texts in English of important documents, all translated afresh by the author himself. These are subdivided into the headings outlined above. (S)

✂ Bram, *AJP* 109 (1988): 148-152; Robertson, *EMC* 31 (1987): 122-124; Scarborough, *Isis* 77 (1986): 709-710.

22.31   Simon, Bennett. *Mind and Madness in Ancient Greece: the Classical Roots of Modern Psychiatry*. Ithaca/London, Cornell UP, 1978. Pp. 336. index

Simon was professor of psychiatry at the Harvard Medical School at the time he wrote this work (and a practicing psychiatrist and psychoanalyst as well) and was therefore well-trained to undertake an interdisciplinary investigation of ancient Greek "mentality." After surveying the then great debates in psychiatry (from Thomas Szasz and R.D. Laing to Foucault), and the history of scholarship on the Greeks and the "irrational" (Dodds), Simon proposes three theoretical models for comprehending Greek mental life: the poetic model (Homer and the Dramatists), the philosophical model (mainly Plato), and the medical model (mainly Aristotle and the Hippocratic Corpus). He then offers one detailed study of the application of the modern theory and the ancient views: that of hysteria. Simon concludes by debating the social and individual psychological models then prevalent in psychiatry and takes the historical instance of the Greeks as a test case for a way in which these divergent interpretations might be resolved. Fraught with all the problems usually attendant on an outsider's or amateur's intervention, this is nonetheless a competent and thought-provoking work, well worth the investment of time for the professional overview of Greek "mental life" that it gives the reader—and therefore highly relevant to interpreting the mental assumptions of the Hellenistic world, of which the early church was part. (S)
        ✂ Lloyd, *CR* 30 (1980): 318-319.

22.32   ⦿ Brenk, Frederick E. "In the Light of the Moon: Demonology in the Early Imperial Period." *ANRW* II.16.3 (1979): 2068-2145.

An important survey article, with coverage wider than the title would seem to indicate. In fact, Brenk begins with the "early folk tradition" of the prehistoric period, advancing by steps through the evidence for demons in the Homeric poems and in "post-Homeric" literature. The rôle of the demon in Greek philosophical literature marks the end of the initial survey of "western" conceptions of the demonic, after which Brenk "backtracks," as it were, to survey ideas of demonic forces in near eastern societies, amongst the Persians and Jews. The two are then bridged by consideration of Hellenistic Judaism (principally Philo) and the New Testament (mainly on exorcism). Only the final three parts of this large article are specifically Roman and imperial in date (on Plutarch, Lucian, Apuleius, and Apollonius of Tyana). This is a clear exposition of the nature of the primary data on demons, as well as of most of the secondary literature of any note to the date of publication. (S)

22.33   Cumont, Franz *Astrology and Religion among Greeks and Romans.*
        Reprint. New York: Dover, 1960. (1912). Pp. xx + 115. I-5.
        An old and short book, but one that has played a prominent role in
        bringing the subject to the attention of a wide audience. It traces
        astrology from its Chaldean/Babylonian roots to its success in Greece
        and the West. The second half of the book deals with theology,
        mysticism, ethics, and eschatology.

22.34   Dukes, Eugene D. "Magic and Witchcraft in the Writings of the
        Western Church Fathers." PhD Dissertation. Kent State University,
        Ohio, 1972. Pp. 397. [DA, 33A, 1972-1973, 5642]
        A survey of the major patristic writers from the fourth to the eighth
        centuries CE. Introductory chapters discuss the pre-Christian Roman
        background to the practice of the "black arts." Following his review
        of the Christian evidence, the author adds a valuable survey of
        what is known on the subject relevant to the Germanic and Celtic
        cultures encountered by Christian bishops in the Gallic and Spanish
        provinces of the empire. Emphasis is placed on the "normal" role
        of magic in the social context of the ordinary Christian parishioners
        of the period, especially as revealed in the popular sermons that
        bishops addressed to the "rank and file" of their congregations.
        Dukes includes a discussion of the methodological issues involved
        in the evaluation of the reliability of reports in the Church Fathers,
        as well as how their categories of "magic, illusion, witchcraft,
        reason" and "good and evil" differ from ours. (S)

22.35   Smith, Jonathan Z. "Towards Interpreting Demonic Powers in
        Hellenistic and Roman Antiquity." *ANRW* II.16.1 (1978): 425-39.
        In this dense interpretive essay, Smith surveys the main elements
        in "Devil Worship" as his point of departure in which he first
        redefines such demonic activity as a "locative category" of human
        behavior, and then, by the excellent use of diagrammatic presentation,
        offers a critique of the traditional ways (Tylor, Otto, Nilsson, and
        their modern progeny), contending that they have misinterpreted
        the role and meaning of "demons" in ancient societies. Noting the
        heavy propensity of people in such societies to map and define
        their world, he appeals especially to the work of Peter Brown
        [§12.19] as a model of the way in which such "out of place" forces
        can be interpreted by modern-day historians. (S)

PHILOSOPHY

22.36 🏛 Inwood, Brad, and L.P. Gerson. *Hellenistic Philosophy: Intro-ductory Readings*. Indianapolis/Cambridge: Hackett Publishing, 1988. Pp. xii + 266. I-10. G-4.

A selection of 160 numbered passages in English translation on the major Hellenistic philosophies: Epicureanism, Stoicism, and Scepticism. Given the fragmentary nature of sources for the philosophies of the period, and the often out-of-date and misleading translations offered in the only other available readers (e.g., Jason L. Saunder's, *Greek and Roman Philosophy after Aristotle*, 1966, and frequent reprints), the appearance of this set of new translations by two experts in the field marks a watershed in the ability of teachers to instruct Greekless students, and in the ability of general readers to have reliable access to the primary sources. The editors provide a good, brief introduction to the whole field of Hellenistic philosophy, and include a 2-page list of philosophers and sources, and a 5-page index of passages translated. This collection of texts is used to its best effect in combination with A.A. Long's classic survey of Hellenistic philosophy [§22.39]. (S)

22.37 Colish, Marcia L., *The Stoic Tradition from Antiquity to the Early Middle Ages. I. Stoicism in Classical Latin Literature; II. Stoicism in Christian Latin Thought through the Sixth Century.* 2d ed. Leiden, E.J. Brill, 1990. (1985[1]). Vol. 1. Pp. x + 446. B-49; NI-5; SI-3. Vol. 2. Pp. x + 366. B-26; NI-6; SI-2.

This two-volume survey is an indispensable guide to the direct influences of Stoic thought, first on the Roman pagan authors from Cicero and the Satirists to historians, rhetoricians, and the Roman jurisprudents; and, second, on Christian writers in the Latin tradition. Apart from the substantial chapter on Augustine, of most direct interest to readers will be the first chapter in the second volume which deals with the early Latin Fathers, especially Tertullian, Minucius Felix, and Cyprian. Colish prefaces the whole work with a comprehensive survey of Stoicism and its influences. Each chapter in the two volumes is then devoted either to a single author (e.g., Cicero, Augustine) or to a tradition (e.g., Satire, Christian Apology) in which the discrete and general influences of Stoic thinking are traced. References are full, if not lavish (especially the bibliography), so that this work represents perhaps the most useful point of departure for the philosophical tradition that arguably had the greatest impact on the formation of thought in the early Church. (S)

✄ Rist, *JTS* 38 (1987): 186-189.

22.38   Erskine, Andrew. *The Hellenistic Stoa: Political Thought and Action.*
        Ithaca, NY: Cornell UP, 1990. Pp. xi + 233. B-9; I-9.
        Given the simple fact that Stoicism was one of the most pervasive
        philosophies at the time of the Roman Empire, and had great influence
        on Paul's thinking, a clear and thorough analysis of the relationship
        of Stoic thought to social and political action is a great desideratum.
        In this volume Erskine offers an up-to-date synopsis of current
        academic work on the political aspects and implications of Stoic
        philosophy. The study ranges in chronological order, over subjects
        from the ideas of its founder Zeno of Kition on the state, on slavery
        and freedom, and on political participation, to the involvement of
        leading Stoic figures in the Spartan revolution of the mid-third
        century BCE, and the Gracchan revolution at the end of the second.
        Finally, the rôle of Stoic thought in justifying Roman imperialism
        of the late Republic is considered (especially the ideas of Panaitios).
        (S)

22.39   Long, Anthony A. *Hellenistic Philosophy: Stoics, Epicureans,
        Sceptics.* 2d ed. Berkeley/London: University of California Press,
        1986. (1974[1]). Pp. x + 262. B; I; B&W-1
        Without doubt the single best introduction to the subject. The second
        edition of this 1974 classic provides an updated bibliography which
        is one of the better guides to the secondary literature currently
        available. Long devotes the core of his book to the three major
        philosophies of the period: Epicureanism, Scepticism, and Stoicism
        —with the lion's share of the space rightly devoted to the last of
        these. In a valuable penultimate chapter he traces some of the later
        developments of these schools, with special attention given to
        Panaetius, Posidonius, Antiochus, and Cicero. The particular virtues
        of Long's survey are (above all) its simple readability, its clarity
        and simplicity of exposition of what are sometimes arcane and
        recondite subjects, and his even-handed judgment on much disputed
        aspects of philosophical systems that are, after all, known to us
        primarily through collections of highly fragmented texts. When
        used in connection with the Inwood-Gerson reader [§22.36], the
        student is armed just about as well as he or she ever will need be
        for the understanding of the primary pagan élite ideological
        background to the developmental phases of Christianity. (S)
        ᴈ< Kidd, *Philosophical Quarterly* 26 (1976): 169-171; Manning, *Prudentia*
        8 (1976): 56-58; Todd, *Phoenix* 29 (1975): 295-299.

22.40   Rist, John M. ed. *The Stoics.* Berkeley/Los Angeles: University of
        California Press, 1978. Pp. viii + 295. B-5.

A selection of thirteen contributions to the analysis of Stoic philosophy by some of the best of current scholarship. Particularly notable are contributions that emphasize an understanding of the basic elements: Ian Mueller's introduction to "Stoic Logic" and Michael Frede's essay on the "Principles of Stoic Grammar." To select from amongst what remains is an invidious task, but to take as a rule of thumb those that might contribute to a better understanding of the "moral" and "ethical" elements in Stoicism, and that this might have relevance to the early development of Christianity, the following are especially noteworthy: Kerford's chapter on "What does the Wise Man Know?," Margaret Reesor's "Necessity and Fate in Stoic Philosophy," Charlotte Stough's "Stoic Determinism and Moral Responsibility," and I.G. Kidd's "Moral Actions and Rules in Stoic Ethics." All the contributions, however, are of exceptionally high quality and will assist the reader to a better understanding of Stoicism. (S)

22.41   Shaw, Brent D. "The Divine Economy: Stoicism as Ideology." *Latomus* 64 (1985): 16-54.
This study supplements other recent work on Stoicism (e.g. Erskine §22.38) in arguing that Stoicism was the dominant formal system of thought in the "high" period of Antiquity, from the late Hellenistic phase to the early Roman empire. In doing so, Shaw attempts to trace the systematic linkages between the main tenets of Stoic thinking, from Zeno of Kition to Roman "followers" like Epicurus and Seneca, and the social world in which its principal proponent and practitioners lived. The basic argument is that Stoicism, in large part, functioned as an "anchoring ideology" that gave clear direction and interpretation of their world to the political and economic élites of the time. In fulfilling this interpretive function, Stoicism itself evolved in the structure of its ideas from being a radical critique of the world of the Greek city-state of the fourth century BCE to a rather tamer underwriting of the existing social and political order by the time of the early Roman empire.

RELIGION

22.42   🏛 Ferguson, John. *Greek and Roman Religion. A Source Book.* Park Ridge, NJ: Noyes Press, 1980. Pp. ix + 208. I-9; AAI-6.
Ferguson's book is a collection of primary sources, covering a wide spectrum of topics, such as folk religion and afterlife, as well as the mystery religions and ritual in Greek and Roman religion. Through the use of primary sources accompanied by a short introduction and explanation, Ferguson provides an overview of religion

from Homer onward. (W)

22.43   🏛 Grant, Frederick C., ed. *Hellenistic Religions, An Age of Syncretism.*
New York: Liberal Arts Press, 1953. Pp. xxxix + 196.
Based on a text prepared for the Open University. Various aspects
of religion, from the "mainstream" to the esoteric. Included in this
are discussions of "political" religion (local and imperial), temples,
festivals and ritual activity, magic and oracles, healing, and death.
This sourcebook has a detailed introduction, with notes for each
passage to place it in its context. Divided into four sections: Institutional Religion; Criticism of Traditional Religion; Cults (Orphism,
"oriental Cults," Egyptian, Attis and Mithras), with Section Four
dealing with the religious ideas of the philosophers. (W)

22.44   🏛 Grant, Frederick C., ed. *Ancient Roman Religion.* New York:
Liberal Arts Press, 1957. Pp. xxxv + 252.
A collection of primary sources on Roman religion, many of them
quite extensive, and each with introductory notes. The sections on
"Religion under the Empire" and "The Christian Victory and the
Pagan Reaction" are the most relevant, though the latter is very
short. Grant provides a 25-page introduction, in which he discusses
sources of Roman religion, its general character, the early stages,
syncretism (which involved three main elements: mystery religions,
hero gods, and the imperial cult), and later stages, with the growth
of solar monotheism. Each of the seven chapters has a brief
introduction and bibliography.

22.45   Beard, Mary, and John North eds. *Pagan Priests: Religion and
Power in the Ancient World.* Cambridge/Ithaca, NY: Cornell UP /
London: Duckworth, 1990. Pp. xi + 266. I-4; B-5; M-3; T-2; B&W-1.
A series of nine chapters by current authorities in the field, subdivided
into three major topical areas: the Graeco-Roman city-state; "outside"
the city-state (contributions principally on Ptolemaic Egypt and
Babylon); and the Roman empire. Especially significant for the
context of the rise of Christianity are the final three chapters of the
third section, all authored by Richard Gordon. The first of these
traces the relationship between religion and ideology in the shift
from Republic to Empire; the second, entitled "The Veil of Power:
emperors, sacrificers and benefactors," seeks to interpret the significance of the imperial cult in its social context, and the third is a
general consideration of religion in the Roman empire. These studies
successfully break through the barriers that have normally kept
religion, politics and society in separate categories. Whereas there

has been a significant amount of cross-disciplinary study of this type both in Greek religion and in work on the early Church, the subject of "Roman religion" has remained singularly recalcitrant to a more thorough integration of theory and analysis. But Gordon's studies are an unusually successful and insightful deployment of modern anthropological, sociological, and psychological theory in laying bare the "assumed linkages" between representation, belief, ritualistic action, and power. As such, they are probably one of the best introductions to the formal work of state "cult," ritual and belief into which the novel faith of Christianity emerged in the first century of our era. (S)

⅋< Price, *TLSuppl* (1990): 508.

22.46 ☛ Dowden, Ken. *Religion and the Romans.* Classical World Series. London: Bristol Classical Press, 1992. Pp. viii + 102. AB-6; B&W-7; T-3; AAI-5; Index of Key Terms-1.

A short, lively, well-organized, and sometimes tongue-in-cheek introduction to Roman religion and the Roman attitude to other religions. While the book offers a delightful introduction, it goes a step beyond to make one aware just how "Greek" Roman religion was, and even how "Greek" the so-called "oriental" religions were. Dowden also examines Rome's conservatism in light of four qualifying observations: (1) its willingness to admit some foreign religions into Rome itself; (2) its generous attitude to religion in the provinces; (3) the promotion of the cult of the emperor by most emperors, in spite of what they might have said publicly; and (4) the persecution of Christians. With many useful aids and charts, designed particularly as an effective introduction to the field.

22.47 ☛ Ferguson, John. *The Religions of the Roman Empire.* Ithaca, NY: Cornell UP, 1970. Pp. 296. I-19; B&W-87; B-29; CT-3.

A standard work on the subject, taking the year 200 CE as a focal point, thus making the observations highly useful for those studying early Christianity. Almost every topic is covered, from the nature gods, the great mother, the cult of the emperor, and the various minor divine forces to the philosophical perspectives. The ancients' view of Fate (Tyche) is explored, as are the general religious attitudes about death and the "menace" of the future, and the role of shamans (and shams!). Finally, Ferguson considers the general toleration of religious differences in paganism, contrasting that to the Christian inflexibility, and the difficulties that arose from that.

⅋< Fitzmyer, *TS* 52 (1991): 345-347; Hinson, *R&E* 88 (1991): 274; Kent, *AUSS* 29 (1990): 89-91.

22.48 ☛ Finegan, Jack. *Myth & Mystery: An Introduction to the Pagan Religions of the Biblical World.* Grand Rapids: Baker, 1989. Pp. 335. B-18; I-5; T-5; M-6; B&W-9.
A clearly organized introduction dealing with nine religions relevant to the student of the Bible. Five of these are relevant also to the early church: Greek, Roman, Gnostic, Mandaean, and Manichaean. Finegan discusses various aspects of each religion: the history, literature, practice, and world-view. Short passages from the literature of each religion are quoted frequently. The diversity of each is shown; for example, in Gnosticism, the major groups (if there were such clear divisions) and key documents of each group have their own short section. An attempt is made to relate each to the Christian movement. Relevant tables are: "Children of Zeus," with a brief description of their activities; "Equivalences of Greek and Egyptian Deities"; "Twelve Chief Deities in the Roman Pantheon and Their Greek Equivalents."

22.49 ☛ Martin, Luther H. *Hellenistic Religions. An Introduction.* New York/ Oxford: Oxford UP, 1987. Pp. xv + 170. I-6; B-2; T-2.
Martin's work is useful as a different kind of introduction to the variety of religious options in the Mediterranean world. While most introductions provide a connected descriptive narrative, Martin chooses to illustrate and describe Hellenistic religions on a framework of passages from the primary literature. He manages to do this without sacrificing a coherent narrative that covers the major "facts" that students should know, in sections that are often brief. Beyond the level of these particulars, Martin attempts to show that Hellenistic religion was something more than mere syncretism; there was a shared coherent "system" in a world of considerable change. The bibliographies are up to date, with an occasional brief comment.
✄ Ellis, *SWJT* 31 (1988): 58; Tabor, *CRBR* (1991): 275-277.

22.50 Meyer, Ben F., and E.P. Sanders, ed. *Jewish and Christian Self-Definition.* Vol. 3: *Self-Definition in the Greco-Roman World.* Philadelphia: Fortress, 1982. Pp. xx + 295. B-22; NI-10; AAI-21.
The last of three volumes of collected essays on the theme of self-definition in the Graeco-Roman world. The ten chapters are: "Craft Versus Sect: The Problem of Orphics and Pythagoreans" (Burkert); "Are You a Stoic? The Case of Marcus Aurelius" (Rist); "Self-Definition among Epicureans and Cynics" (Malherbe); "Self-Definition in Later Platonism" (Dillon); "Hairesis and Heresy: The Case of the *haireseis iatrikai*" (von Staden); "Sarapis and Isis"

(Tran tam Tinh); "Self-Definition in the Asclepius Cult." (Kee); "Changing Dionysiac Identities" (Henrichs); "The Formation of Authoritative Tradition in the Greek Magical Papyri" (Betz); and "The Imperial Cult: Perspectives and Persistence" (Bowersock).

22.51   Parke, H.W. *Sibyls and Sibylline Prophesy in Classical Antiquity.* Edited by B. McGing. New York/London: Routledge & Kegan Paul, 1992. (1988[1]). Pp. ix + 257. B; I.
An acknowledged expert on oracles and their pronouncements, Parke was working on this, his final book, at the time of his death in 1986. It has been "rescued" by the fine editorial work of one of his students. As with his other works, it is characterized by a thorough coverage of the basic primary source materials, in which Parke attempts to trace the nature and function of one of the most significant, but most poorly known, oracular traditions of antiquity. The first chapter outlines the characteristic features of these oracular pronouncements and the basic ancient source materials relevant to them. The succeeding five studies trace the presence and development of Sibylline oracles in Greece, the specific case of Cumae in southern Italy, in the Classical and Hellenistic periods of Greek history and at Rome. Finally, Parke studies the influence of Sibylline oracles on Christian literature. Of the three appendixes, it is the second on the nature of the "Sibylline Books" themselves, and the third on ecstatic prophesy in the Near East, which are most relevant to students of New Testament and early church history. The corrected paperback edition (1992) has a revised bibliography. (S)
 Potter, *Journal of Roman Archaeology* 3 (1990): 471-483.

RELIGION: "EASTERN" AND MYSTERY RELIGIONS
22.52   Meyer, Marvin W., ed. *The Ancient Mysteries: A Sourcebook.* New York: Harper & Row, 1987. Pp. xii + 256. G-9; B&W-7.
An anthology of ancient texts on the mystery religions, many of which are in new English translations. The mysteries associated with Greece, Egypt, and Syria account for most of the volume. There is one chapter on Mithraism and one on similar elements in Judaism and Christianity. Brief introductions (of about three pages) are provided for each chapter and a paragraph introduction for each selection. A 14-page general introduction provides a good overview of the mysteries. The bibliographies are up to date.

22.53   Burkett, Walter. *Ancient Mystery Cults.* Cambridge, MA: Harvard UP, 1987. Pp. ix + 181. B-13; I-7; B&W-12; Greek Index-3.
Based on the Carl Newell Jackson lectures of 1982, this is a

sympathetic, clear account of the phenomenon of the "mysteries" by a leading scholar in the field. First, Burkett dismisses three stereotypes of the "mysteries": (1) that they were late; (2) that they were "oriental"; or (3) that they were "spiritual" or "religions of salvation." He takes, he says, "a decidedly pagan approach...which abandons the concept of mystery *religions* from the start" for a "comparative phenomenology." Burkert then examines in detail five of the mysteries: Eleusis, Dionysis (Bacchic); Meter; Isis; and Mithras. Of particular interest is Burkert's reflections on the reasons why these failed to survive the collapse of pagan as anything more than curiousities. They were not "self-sufficient sects"—rather, they were "bound to the social system of antiquity." This book provides a clear introduction to the mysteries, and serves as a corrective for an older, but still widely held, view of the mysteries as "religions of salvation"—somewhat like Christianity, to which comparisons have often been made.

22.54   Cumont, Franz V.M. *The Mysteries of Mithra.* Translated by Thomas J. McCormack. New York: Dover Publications, 1956. (1903[1]). Pp. 239. I-9; B&W-50; M-1.
Cumont deals with the origin of Mithraism; its spread in the Roman Empire; Mithra and the imperial power of Rome; doctrine, liturgy, clergy, and devotees of the Mithraic Mysteries; Mithraism and the religions of the Roman Empire; and Mithraic art. A map shows the geographical dissemination of this religion. The downfall of this religion is also considered—a religion which in the early period was a serious rival of Christianity. Now seriously challenged by the work of Gordon [§22.57; 22.58]. (Sm)

22.55   Cumont, Franz V.M.. *Oriental Religions in Roman Paganism.* Introduction by Grant Showerman. New York: Dover, 1956. (1911[1]). Pp. xxiv + 298. I-10.
Cumont considers the success of oriental religions in the West (Rome, Asia Minor, Egypt, Syria, and Persia), the emphasis on astrology and magic, and the transformation of Roman religion under this new influence. He shows considerable sympathy for the vitality of this mixture of Graeco-Roman religion and eastern religions. But modern studies have tended to subvert most of Cumont's principal theses: see, in particular, the work of Richard Gordon [§22.57; 22.58].

22.56   ☛ Godwin, Joscelyn. *Mystery Religions in the Ancient World.* San Francisco: Harper & Row, 1981. B-1; I-4; B&W-158.

This well-illustrated work can be used as an introductory survey of art related to what technically is called the "Mystery" religions. In fact, the running text is a minor part of the book. Most of the text is tied to specific illustrations, of which there are many. In addition, Godwin attempts to show traces of the attitude of the mysteries in Judaism and Christianity, but these sections are far too brief to be helpful or convincing). Besides covering all the standard mystery religions (in individual chapters), he addresses Roman religion, the Imperial cult, and the philosophers, and offers a survey of five general religious perspectives. Primarily of value as a sourcebook on religious art.

22.57   Gordon, Richard L. "Mithraism and Roman Society: Social Factors in the Explanation of Religious Change in the Roman Empire." *Religion* 2 (1972): 92-121.
A milestone article that revolutionized the understanding of the place of Mithraism in Roman society, decisively challenging and largely rejecting the classic models of Franz Cumont [§22.54; 22.55]. Instead of Cumont's "eastern invasion," Gordon proposes a religious system which, apart from some of its vocabulary, was largely to be understood in its development as a peculiarly Roman phenomenon, whose theodicy of earned meritorious salvation was well attuned to its main "catchment" of adherents—professional slaves and freedmen, lower subaltern ranks of the army, lower-level government and municipal bureaucrats. A "must" as a strong antidote to the "orientalism" of Cumont. (S)

22.58   Gordon, Richard L. "Franz Cumont and the Doctrines of Mithraism." In *Mithraic Studies.* Proceedings of the First International Congress of Mithraic Studies. Vol. 1. Edited by J.R. Hinnells. Manchester: Manchester UP, 1975. Pp. 215-248.
Along with his study of the structure and function of the religious cult itself [§22.57], this survey of Franz Cumont's interpretation of Mithraism was responsible for demolishing the modern "Father of Mithraism's" construction of this ancient religious phenomenon. What Gordon demonstrates is that Cumont, under the influence of "eastern-itis," was responsible for establishing a dominant mode of what Mithraism was principally because he was first into the field, and the first systematically to collate all the known evidence. Gordon questions and largely refutes the critical links Cumont hypothesized as the strong eastern connections that are usually used to explain the nature of the cult in the Western Empire, and argues that it is best to abandon the dominant Cumontian drive to explain Mithraism

by "eastern" origins, and instead to seek a sociological explanation of Mithraism in its western imperial context. (S)

22.59   Hinnells, John R., ed. *Mithraic Studies*. Proceedings of the First International Congress of Mithraic Studies. 2 Volumes. Manchester: Manchester UP/Rowman and Littlefield, 1975. Pp. xxx ii + 560. B&W-106; I-17; C-21; AAI-4; MAI-9; Mithraic Sites Index-4; Monuments Index-3.
A sweeping thirty-chapter collection of scholarly works on Mithraism, a serious competitor to Christianity in the early period. Vol. 2 contains most of the relevant articles for this bibliography: "The role of the Roman army in the spread and practice of Mithraism" (Daniels); "The Mithraic cult meal" (Kane); "Mithraism and Gnosticism" (Bianchi); "The idea of judgement of the dead in the ancient Near East (Brandon); "Some thoughts on Isis in relation to Mithras" (Witt); and "Mithras and Christ" (Davidson). With two plenary discussions.

22.60   Hunt, P.N. ed., *Encyclopedia of Classical Mystery Religions*. New York/London: Routledge & Kegan Paul, 1993. Pp. x + 512. I.
A basic reference work including over one thousand entries by noted authorities on the various subjects, such as the Eleusinian, Orphic, Dionysian mysteries of the Hellenistic period, as well as the cults of Isis-Osiris, Cybele-Attis, and Mithra that became major followings in the Roman empire. Each entry is cross-referenced to other appropriate terms and is provided with a brief bibliography that will direct the student to current work on the subject. (S)

22.61   Nash, Ronald H. *Christianity and the Hellenistic World*. Grand Rapids: Zondervan, 1984. Pp. 318. NI-3; SI-4; AB-3.
Nash considers the question of Christianity's dependence on various philosophical and religious systems of the Mediterranean world. Though Nash's motives are clearly apologetic, he does raise a number of points concerning the relationship of Christian beliefs and sacraments to the mystery religions, and he tests Bultmann's Gnostic thesis, the case for pre-Christian Gnosticism, and the influence of the Hermetic writings on Christianity. Also considered are the influences from Stocism and Platonism.

22.62   Nilsson, Martin P. *The Dionysiac Mysteries of the Hellenistic and Roman Age*. Lund, Sweden CWR Gleerup, 1957. Reprint. New York: Arno Press, 1975. Pp. 147. I-3; B&W-37.
While emphasizing primarily the Dionysian cult, Nilsson also brings

to light other mysteries of similar nature, such as the Orphic and Bacchanalian rites. He discusses, as well, the geographical dispersion and versions of the cult (Greek, Roman, Egyptian, and Near East). Two central themes are expressed by Nilsson: (1) the mystery religions were Greek in origin and carried no Eastern influence, and (2) the mysteries contained organized doctrines which concentrated upon the concept of the afterlife and future rewards. The drawback for English readers is that Nilsson provides no translations to the primary sources that he uses. (W)

22.63 ☛ Ulansey, David. *The Origins of the Mithraic Mysteries: Cosmology & Salvation in the Ancient World.* New York/Oxford: Oxford UP, 1989. Pp. xii + 154. B-6; I-8; B&W-45; M-1.
Ulansey contends that Mithraic iconography was an astronomical code. He focuses on, among other things, the tauroctony (or bull slaying) which was a consistent feature of the iconography. His task of deciphering the latter is made all the more difficult by the dearth of literary evidence, in contrast to the iconography, of which there is abundance (see the illustrations in this volume and in Hinnells' second volume §22.59). The work is copiously illustrated, an absolute necessity for a subject of this nature. Of particular usefulness are the charts and maps of astronomical data. (Sm)
☾ Alderink, *CRBR* (1991): 277-280.

22.64 Vermaseren, M.J. *Mithras, the Secret God.* London: Chatto & Windus, 1963. Pp. 200. B-3; I-4; B&W-83.
An attempt to introduce the world of Mithraism, with attention to its history, sanctuaries, pantheon, rituals, liturgy, and art. Vermaseren deals with the success of this religious movement in the Roman world, until a reversal of its fortunes when Emperor Constantine opted for Mithraism's most serious competitor— Christianity.

26.65 Wiens, Devon H. "Mystery Concepts in Primitive Christianity and in its Environment." *ANRW* II.23.2 (1980): 1248-1284. B-6.
Wiens looks at the phenomenon of the similarity between features of early Christianity and the mystery religions, something even the early apologists recognized and tried to explain. After examining the common terminology, Wiens considers the scholarly discussion of the issue, surveying the treatment by the History of Religions school, especially in regard to its contention that a Jewish messianic sect was revolutionized into a new religion by Paul's use of a mystery religion framework. Then he traces the conflict among scholars who took up the History of Religions' perspective and

those who challenged it. Wiens is somewhat sympathetic to the possibility of insights from the History of Religions school, against people such as Nock and Hengel. Various other issues are discussed, including the Christian sacraments, regeneration (new birth), and "dying and rising" divinities.

JUDAISM IN THE ROMAN EMPIRE

22.66   🏛 Linder, Amnon, introduction, translation and commentary, *The Jews in Roman Imperial Legislation*. Detroit: Wayne State UP, 1987. [The Israel Academy of Sciences and Humanities, Jerusalem]. Pp. 436. SI-8; NI-5; AAI-7; Place Names Index-2.

The fundamental collection in translation of all significant Roman imperial legislation in the major law codes relevant to the status of the Jewish populations of the Roman empire. In the first two chapters of this work, Linder introduces the major Roman legal sources, the nature of the compilation and codification, and the main types of legislation relevant to the status of the Jews, along with a synopsis of their general significance. This is followed by two useful tables that list the imperial "laws" by the emperor to which they relate, and then by the reference in the relevant law code in which they are found. The main body of the book contains the texts in translation of 66 numbered items, from the rescript of Antoninus Pius (138-55) on "Permission to Circumcise Sons Born to Jewish Parents," to the law of Justinian, of 8 February 553, on "Permission to Use All Languages in Synagogues." Each entry contains a translation of the text, the original Greek or Latin text (where it exists), a set of detailed explanatory notes on technical terms or problems with the text, and a bibliography of research on each law. The whole is complemented by a series of indexes that guide the researcher to names and items in the laws. Indispensable for the serious researcher. (S)

✄ Horst, *Mnemosyne* 43 (1990): 270-272; Millar, *Gnomon* 62 (1990): 39-42.

22.67   🏛 Whittaker, Molly. *Jews and Christians: Graeco-Roman Views.* Cambridge: Cambridge UP, 1984. Cambridge Commentaries on the Writings of the Jewish and Christian World, 200 B.C.–A.D. 200. Pp. ix + 286. I-12; B-2; CT-4; M-3.

The sixth volume in the Cambridge series of original documents in translation relating to the early Jewish and Christian communities in the Mediterranean, Whittaker's text is divided into three major headings: Judaism, Christianity, and the Pagan Background. Within each section she provides a general background to the translated texts (usually arranged in coherent groupings: e.g., subsections on Moses, Sabbath, Food Laws, Circumcision, Government Attitudes, in the section on "Judaism"). The sets of translated texts in each subsection are accompanied by explanatory notes. All translations were done afresh by the editor. (S)

< R. Grant, *CH* 55 (1986): 508-510; Rowland, *JTS* 37 (1986): 491-492.

22.68   Rabello, Anthony M. "The Legal Condition of the Jews in the Roman Empire." *ANRW* II.13 (1980): 662-762.
A large, and at the level at which it is presented (e.g. an academic article), a near exhaustive description of the principal pieces of legislation of the Roman state with regard to Jews. It can now be supplemented by the work of Amnon Linder who offers the original texts in translation [§22.66]. (S)

22.69   Rajak, Tessa. "Was There a Roman Charter for the Jews?" *Journal of Roman Studies* 74 (1984): 107-23.
Rajak argues, rather decisively, against the traditional view, widespread since the classic work of Juster, that there was a general set of legal protections for Jews in the Roman Empire. While technically correct, in making her case Rajak seems to neglect or ignore many aspects of Jewish ethnic/religious organization, especially amongst communities in the so-called diaspora, that, in effect, gave Jews the possibility of a more systematic appeal to precedent in treatment by Roman generals, governors, and emperors, that was not shared by other ethnic groups in the empire. Still, at the time of publication, this revisionist view provided a much needed corrective to the all-too-ready acceptance of the traditional claim that there existed a "charter" of rights in the strong sense of the word. (S)

23
SOCIETY AND SOCIAL ISSUES

This section covers a variety of topics, a few of which would have their own section in a larger bibliographic work. Some of the "hot" topics in current scholarship on the early church are: the house church, slavery, the economic status of the early Christians, the relationship of these Christians to the larger society in which they lived, and the difference between elite and popular culture and between the urban and rural populations of the time (differences which may have been reflected in the early church also). Further, scholars of the early church are becoming increasingly aware of the importance of the application of insights from sociology and other disciplines for an understanding of the primitive Christian communities. The various themes and new methodological approaches make this an exciting field of research.

One of the debates that is still unresolved is the social status of the early Christians. The earlier view placed them at the lower end of the social and economic hierarchy. Gager is noted for his promotion of this view [§23.11], but many of the more recent works have pointed in the opposite direction, calling attention to the evidence that a number of influential members of the early church probably were of a high social status. The debate is reviewed by Bengt Holmberg (*Sociology and the New Testament: An Appraisal* §23.13). Holmberg and others warn against a transfer of modern categories to ancient societies, for there can be substantial misunderstandings with the use of terms like "class" or "middle class." According to some ways of reckoning, 99.5 percent of the population of ancient Mediterranean society could be designated lower class. But since that large population was itself considerably diverse, other ways of describing the population must be sought. Further, one must be careful not to think that any structure will serve all situations: each city was a different entity, and though there were common urban features, caution must be exercised to do justice to the unique character of each community. Another problem that arises is how to measure the importance or power of the various groups identified. Mere numbers reveals very little about where the power lay.

Of particular importance for understanding the early church is the possibility that those with recognized wealth or status in the society at large may have carried their status over into the Christian community when they converted. This does not mean that the Christian church accepted without question all of the structures of the society around it, though it is probably reasonable to assume that, unless there is evidence to the contrary, Christians continued to function within the Graeco-Roman social structures to which they had been accustomed.

Sometimes this acceptance of the status quo may have worked clearly to the benefit of the early church. The patron-client relationship and the household structure may have solved some problems that the Christians faced. Christians met in the homes of other Christians for their regular communal worship: a wealthy convert may have become "patron" to a "house church" unit largely by providing his or her own home for regular corporate worship. That does not necessarily mean that the owners of the homes where these "house churches" met would, by right, become leaders of the congregation, but the evidence seems to point in that direction for many of the assemblies. Such a prominent role in the church assembly would have been natural for these "patrons." Also, the Christian emphasis on charity, and its willingness to admit into membership individuals in need of assistance, may have quite naturally placed responsibility on the wealthier members. To some extent, the educational level of some of the early leaders suggests that leadership roles went to those of higher social status, though it would be difficult to determine to what degree education was a factor in the selection.

But there is another side of the early church's relationship with the social structures and attitudes of the world surrounding it. Although there were charges and countercharges, with issues often blurred by the language of polemics, Christians did consciously distinguish themselves from the world around themselves. The extent of the distancing, however, is not always clear. With regard to ethical differences, the evidence is somewhat difficult to interpret. For one thing, charges of immorality were standard charges in the polemics of the day, and they may not have accurately reflected the ethical standards of the community being criticized. Furthermore, Christianity was itself varied, and it lacked a central organization in the early period. What we have, then, is the Christians' accusation that Graeco-Roman society was immoral, and that Graeco-Roman society, at least in the second century, responding in kind, by finding Christianity to be morally repulsive. Many of the charges made against the Christians are as shocking to the modern readers as they were to the ancients: cannibalism, incest, orgies, and—to the modern reader, a somewhat puzzling charge of atheism. Some scholars have argued that these accusations were intentionally made to misrepresent and discredit the Christian movement or they were based on misunderstandings of Christian belief and ritual (e.g. the blood and flesh of the Eucharist was mistaken for an act of cannibalism). Numerous Christian apologists of the second century attempted to counter such charges and misunderstandings. It is possible, however, as Stephen Benko has argued and as some apologists themselves admitted, some of these shocking charges could have been true. The apologists sometimes found an adequate scapegoat in one of the Gnostic groups.

Certain scholars have argued that it is difficult to determine the ethical standards maintained by the average member of the early Christian communities. The access we have to the interests and concerns of the early Christians is largely a literary one. Such literature may portray the view of the leadership, or it may portray the ideal rather than the actual, thereby preventing the instructions and exhortations in the early Christian literature from directly revealing to the modern researcher the actual practice of the communities. To some extent, this is the assumption of John Boswell, in *The Kindness of Strangers* [§23.22], though his peculiar way of explaining why the church fathers addressed certain issues is not entirely convincing.

Much of the work relating sociological insights to the study of the early church has focused specifically on the New Testament period. Some of these works are abstracted here because they provide useful information about the church well into the later centuries. As scholars of the early church have discovered, the separation between the New Testament period and the period immediately following it is an arbitrary one, heavily theological, and not recognized by the early Christians until, in the heat of polemics between the "orthodox" and the "heretic," it became a useful tool for creating a particular view of the past. With regard to the sociological questions, no such line is possible. At best, sociologists may wish to differentiate between a rural Galilean original community and an urban Hellenistic missionary group, but even that kind of division may draw the lines too sharply.

GENERAL

23.1   Baker, J. ed. *The Church in Town and Countryside*. Studies in Church History 16. Papers read at the 17th summer meeting and 18th winter meeting of the Ecclesiastical History Society. Oxford: E.H.S. and Blackwell, 1979. Pp. xvi + 486.
       The first five articles are of some importance. R.A. Markus: "Country Bishops in Byzantine Africa"; W. Liebeschuetz: "Problems arising from the Conversion of Syria"; W.H.C. Frend: "Town and Countryside in Early Christianity"; C.E. Stancliffe: "From Town to Country: the Christianisation of the Touraine 370-600"; I.N. Wood: "Merovingian Devotion in Town and Country." The question of the penetration of the Christian movement into the countryside from its urban base is one of the issues that still needs considerable work. This volume helps.

⊱ Briggs, *JEH* 32 (1981): 513-514; Dobson, *EHR* 96 (1981): 897-898; Hinchliff, *JTS* 32 (1981): 308-310; McCaffery, *SJT* 33 (1980): 494-495.

23.2 Brunt, Peter A. "The Roman Mob." *Past & Present* 35 (1966): 3-27. Reprinted in *Studies in Ancient Society*. Edited by M.I. Finley. London: RKP, 1974. Pp. 74-102.

With Brunt's characteristic attention to conclusions that can be derived from the hard evidence, this article represents one of the clearest and most coherent delineations of which persons comprised the "crowd" of common persons in the city of Rome at the end of the Republic, and how they related to the politics of the state. One should not be mislead by the unfortunate title. Brunt does not succumb to any trivial vision of the mass of the citizens as a "mob." Rather he shows how the crowd was involved in the major political episodes of violence in the city of Rome in the last century of the Roman Republic. This article is still fundamental despite the appearance of new work in the last decade, especially that of Wilfried Nippel, that has considerably nuanced our understanding of the nature of "mass behavior" in the city of Rome and its policing. (S)

23.3 Cadoux, C.J. *The Early Church and the World: A History of the Christian Attitude to Pagan Society and the State down to the Time of Constantinus*. Edinburg: T&T Clark, 1955. (1925[1]). Pp. lii + 675. I-53; B-19.

Although published originally in 1925, and not revised, this study remains a gold mine of information respecting general Christian attitudes towards personal conduct as well as to pagan society and the state. Beginning with Christ's teachings with respect to how Christians should deal with outsiders, the state, war, the family, and property, Cadoux covers almost all major ethical issues which affected the early Christians down to Constantinus' time. Much treatment is given to pagan learning and philosophy; state relations; sexuality, marriage, and celibacy; slavery; property; and war. Cadoux gives citations for practically every assertion he makes, providing a highly useful work. (P)

23.4 Carcopino, J. *Daily Life in Ancient Rome: The People and the City at the Height of the Empire*. Translated by E.O. Lorimer. Edited with bibliography and notes by Henry T. Rowell. New Haven and London: Yale UP, 1977. (1940[1]). Pp. 342. I-24; AB-12; M-1.

Although this book appeared over fifty years ago, it still provides a rich and vivid entry into daily life in ancient Rome, covering a wide range of topics, from population, houses, streets, social structure, family, and religion, to education, calendar, occupations, entertainment, and much more. Much work has been done over the last fifty years on some of these themes, seriously dating this book. Nonetheless, the volume will carry the reader quite convincingly into the smells, sights, sounds, and shadows of ancient Rome (largely due to an exceptional English translation). Informative and entertaining reading, though it must be corrected by reference to Dupont's work [§23.9].

23.5   Case, S.J. *The Social Triumph of the Ancient Church.* New York: Harper and Brothers, 1933. Pp. vii + 250; I-12.
From the Rauchenbusch Memorial Lectures of April 18-21, 1933, Case's work, though over fifty years old, is insightful for identifying the kinds of issues that must be examined if Christianity's place in the ancient world is to be understood. He considers the competing philosophical ideas, arguing that Christianity had to move away from its sole emphasis on individual salvation to the broader economic, political, and cultural issues. Attention is given to collegia (still a lively topic), and to the occupations of Christians. Case holds to the view that Christians were from the lower classes, (a view recently challenged), and he speaks of the continued Christian critique of wealth (even after they got it). Questions of social status and marriage are considered, as well as the increasing hostility to Christians as they assumed positions of power in an empire that they had often stood aloof from, sometimes even having sharply criticized Roman law itself.

23.6   Cochrane, Charles N. *Christianity and Classical Culture: A Study of Thought and Action from Augustus to Augustine.* 3d ed. New York: Galaxy Books (OUP), 1957. (1940[1]). Pp. vii + 523. I-7.
Although certainly replaced in parts by specialist studies that have appeared in the decades since its publication, this classic study retains its value because it presents in the scope of a single book the vast range of evidence relevant to the theme. Much under the influence of R.G. Collingwood, Cochrane presented the clash between "paganism" and "Christianity" as a sort of Hegelian dialectic and as a transformation of meta-paradigms, from the antique Graeco-Roman view of nature as a coherent living system (a view of Collingwood's) to a new "anthropology" based on the transcendent and ages-old truth of the logos of Christ. Although rather idealistic in its bent, Cochrane's story is played out as a detailed historical narrative from the early empire to the fifth century, and so retains its great value as a fundamental account of the basic story line of

the conflict between these two worlds. (S)
⊰ MacDonald, *CHR* 48 (1958-59): 494-495.

23.7 ☛ Crook, John A. *Law and Life of Rome, 90 B.C.-A.D. 212*. London, Thames & Hudson / Ithaca: Cornell UP, 1967. Pp. 349. I-11; CT-1. Without doubt, for the non-expert the Roman law is the most difficult, complex, and least accessible of all areas of the corpus of formal texts produced in Roman society. From its first appearance, Crook's book was instantly recognized as a minor classic in this field—a reputation which has only been enhanced over the decades since. It is a marvel not only of compression and comprehensibility, but also of a successful dialog between the ordinary discourses of history and the often more remote and arcane jargon of the Roman lawyers and their modern interpreters. The book concentrates on the main aspects of the civil (as opposed to public or criminal) law that would be of most concern to most "ordinary" citizens of the empire in their daily dealings. Crook moves carefully and logically by first establishing the basic outlines of the law that defined the various status of individuals (the law of "persons") and hence their variable treatment in the law (see Garnsey §22.7 for more detail) and thence to the main judicial institutions of the state. The core of the book is devoted to the areas of the law which, by sheer bulk, were of most interest to the Roman jurists themselves: the law of property, of contract (social obligations) in work, trade, and production. He concludes with a brief piece on the public law status of the person as citizen. If only for the clarity of its exposition and writing, and its sure-footed and careful movement through the veritable minefield of pitfalls that is the discipline of interpreting the Roman law, this is without doubt the best introduction to this most important field for the novice. (S)
⊰ Marshall, *Phoenix* 22 (1968): 274-276; Sherwin-White, *JRS* 59 (1969): 281-282.

23.8 ☛ Davies, J.G. *Daily Life in the Early Church*. Duell, Sloan, and Pearce, 1952. Reprint. New York: Glenwood Press, 1969. Pp. xvi + 268. I-2; B-5; AB-2.
An easy-to-read introduction to some of the practices and concerns of six figures from various social levels in early Christianity (Clement of Alexandria; Paul of Antioch; Victoria of Carthage; Diogenes of Rome, John of Constantinople; and John Cassian of Marseilles). The chapters cover about a 200 year period. It reads like a novel, at times, making it an approachable introductory text. An 11-page appendix on the study of the social history of the church is included.

23.9   Dupont, Florence. *Daily Life in Ancient Rome*. Translated by
       Christopher Woodall. Oxford/New York: Blackwell, 1993. Pp. 314.
       B-8; I-4; B&W-17; T-1.
       Dupont's study of daily life in Rome is worlds apart from its illustrious
       French predecessor, Jerome Carcopino's work of the same name
       [§23.4]. It is not a survey, however well written, of the objects and
       cultural practices of Roman life. Reflecting current trends in the
       writing of history, it is an interpretation of the meaning of the basic
       categories of living in a civilization in many ways alien to our
       own. Even when she is describing traditional subject matter, such
       as the city of Rome and its people and places, it is this sense of
       "otherness" that Dupont seeks to evoke. Moreover, as exemplified
       by sections such as "Time and Action" and "The Roman Body,"
       she introduces a whole new range of topics never covered by the
       traditional surveys. The latter chapter, for example, includes
       subtopics such as "daily body rhythms" and "the kiss." Dupont
       begins with the overwhelmingly male orientation of Roman social
       structure, and moves from that point of departure to explore the
       status of the others—women, slaves, children, foreigners, and the
       moral code of honor that underwrote this peculiar social order. In
       the current Parisian mode, Dupont's prose style (even in translation)
       is rather disconcerting and obtuse, and, even for a survey, its high-
       flown claims are often unsatisfactorily substantiated by the evidence.
       It is, however, a provocative and readable guide to "leading edge"
       re-interpretations of Roman society. (S)

23.10 ☛ Frend, W.H.C. "Town and Countryside in Early Christianity."
       In *The Church in Town and Countryside*. Edited by J. Baker. Oxford:
       E.H.S. and Blackwell, 1979. Pp. 25-42.
       Frend provides a suggestive discussion of the distinction between
       the rural and urban sides of the Christian movement. He reviews
       the history of Israel to find some of the roots for the distinction,
       and he highlights the divisions between city and countryside within
       the Roman world where Christianity was shaped. Frend also con-
       siders the differences in the rural movements of Christianity,
       commenting on the Montanists, Donatists, and the monastic move-
       ment (though perhaps only the early Montanists are "rural" in the
       full sense).

23.11 Gager, John G. *Kingdom and Community: The Social World of
       Early Christianity*. Engelwood Cliffs: Prentice Hall, 1975. Pp. xiii
       + 158. I-10.
       When it first appeared, Gager's slim volume represented a pathbreak-

ing systematic application of modern social theory (Burridge, Geertz, Kuhn, Bellah, Talmon, Berger, Luckmann, Vansina, and others) to a better understanding of the emergence of Christianity as a millenarian movement that gradually "routinized" (Weber) its activities and hierarchies, and succeeded against its competitors. Though his lead was followed by many others (e.g., Malina), Gager's remains the most convincing of these "new" approaches. He traced the gradual formalization of a millenarian cult, its greater formal self-definition and consolidation, its search for legitimation, and, given those characteristics of its growth, the precise ways in which it confronted existing communities within the society of the Roman empire. In his final chapter, Gager attempts to explain the reasons for the success of Christianity, when the social profiles of its believers are compared to those of its main competitors, particularly the worshippers of Isis and Mithras. (S)

⊱< Drewery, *JEH* 27 (1976): 413-14; Kee, *JBL* 95 (1976): 506-508; Quesnell, *CBQ* 38 (1976): 380-382; Stafford, *JAAR* 45 (1977): 236-237; Ward, *Interpretation* 31 (1977): 98-99; Wilson, *JTS* 27 (1976): 207-209;

23.12 Grant, Robert M. *Early Christianity and Society: Seven Studies.* San Francisco: Harper & Row, 1977. Pp. 221. AAI-5; MAI-4; BI-4; SI-6; B-14.

A collection of seven articles, providing sometimes surprising insights into the place of Christians in society. The following issues are addressed: the size of the Christian population, and its middle class origin; the positive Christian attitude to Roman government and hierarchy; the willingness of Christians to pay taxes, the exemptions normally given to priests, and the gaining of such exemption by Christian clergy under Constantine; attitudes to work and to particular occupations; conflicting attitudes to slavery and to private property; provision of charity (from private and government sources); and the transition from house churches to legal possession of pagan temple property.

⊱< Benko, *AHR* 83 (1978): 983; Betz, *HR* 19 (1979): 99-102; Bruce, *EQ* 52 (1980): 120-121; Chesnut, *ATR* 61 (1979): 517-518; Gager, *RSR* 5 (1979): 174-180; Hall, *RS* 15 (1979): 575-577; Hardy, *CH* 47 (1978): 325; Harvey, *ExT* 90 (1979): 83-184; Judge, *Reformed Theological Review* 38 (1979): 55-56; Norris, *JR* 59 (1979): 112-113; Ruether, *CC* 95 (1978): 449-450.

23.13 ◉ Holmberg, Bengt. *Sociology and the New Testament: An Appraisal.* Minneapolis: Fortress, 1990. Pp. viii + 173. B-13; MAI-3.

Although this book focuses on the New Testament, it deals with the major questions and tendencies important to the wider debate.

Holmberg discusses the earlier judgment that the early Christians were from the lower end of the social scale, a view recently promoted by Gager [§23.11]. Holmberg contends that, according to reliable and convincing evidence, Christians frequently came from a higher social level. He also discusses Christianity as a millenarian sect, and offers a detailed analysis of the application of sociology to the study of the New Testament. Various modern authors are discussed: Gager, Theissen, Malherbe, Kee, Malina, Judge, Meeks, and others (many whose primary field is sociology). Holmberg also refers to bibliographic reviews by Harrington and Richter.

᠍✂ *ExT* 102 (1991): 280-281; Bode *BTB* 21 (1991): 169-170.

23.14 Kyrtatas, Dimitris J. *The Social Structure of the Early Christian Communities*. With introduction by Geoffrey de Ste. Croix. London /New York: Verso, 1987. Pp. xiv + 224. MAI-2; NI-7; B-6
Kyrtatas challenges the widely held view that the church drew its converts mainly from the lower classes, arguing that Christian converts came largely from the prosperous and educated circles. This view of Christian origins presents Christianity as a conservative religion, unwilling to challenge the social order. Kyrtatas' Marxist sympathies are clearly evident here, and for that reason alone Kyrtatas offers a provoking view on a central question.

᠍✂ Malina, *BTB* 20 (1990): 128-129; Meeks, *JRS* 78 (1988): 251-252; Wiedemann, *History* 74 (1989): 113-114; Anonymous, *Journal of Psychology and Theology* 18 (1990): 197.

23.15 ☛ MacMullen, Ramsay. *Roman Social Relations, 50 B.C. to A.D. 284*. New Haven/London, Yale UP, 1974. Pp. ix + 212. B-1; I-6; B&W-2.
In this landmark study MacMullen attempted to evoke the main social values that motivated principal social actors in Roman society in the west. He did this by appealing not to the well-documented social codes of the élite, but rather to the behavior, occupations and ideals of the great mass of the population of the Roman empire: the rural peasantry, the landless laborers, petty merchants and traders, service personnel, and craftsmen. He attempts to cumulate their actual work and expressed ideals into a description of the language and symbolism of the class distinctions that rent the Roman world (for a quite different Marxist approach, see Ste. Croix, §23.17). MacMullan provides a mixture of striking anecdotal examples, and of "harder" statistical and numeric assessments, to give the reader an appreciation of the dimensions of the distribution of property and wealth and of social distinction, that were most characteristic

of the different milieux (rural and urban, east and west, rich and poor, and of various ethnic backgrounds) of the empire. There are three valuable appendixes on the ethnic and regional division of the city of Rome, on the vocabulary of "snobbery," and on the fiscal basis of running the city of Rome. As always in MacMullen's works, he offers near-exhaustive annotation to ancient and modern work in his extensive endnotes. (S)

✄ P. Brown, *NYRB* 23.6 (1976): 14-18; Colledge, *CR* 36 (1976): 98-99; Talbert, *JRS* 66 (1976): 236-237.

23.16   Parkin, Tim G. *Demography and Roman Society*. Baltimore/London: Johns Hopkins UP, 1992. Pp. xvi + 225. B-19; I-7; T-12; B&W-10. At long last: a competent and readable introduction to the very difficult subject for ordinary folk of demography, especially if that "science" is to be legitimately applied to ancient populations. Parkin begins by clearly outlining the nature of the evidence available to reconstruct ancient populations (epigraphy, evidence from the Egyptian papyri, legal sources, and skeletal data) and convincingly demonstrates the shortcomings of each. He then proposes a method by which modern sources and studies, especially the details of so-called "life tables," can be usefully exploited in the study of ancient populations. He concludes by investigating various aspects of the demographics of Roman populations, including aging and fertility. This book is a must as a starting point for anyone wishing to study life and death in the Roman world—especially for those who wish to avoid the fatal pitfalls into which most scholars fall who simply assume that they know what can be done with evidence such as ages-at-death on tombstone inscriptions. For such persons Parkin's introduction is a necessary precursor to any easy statement they might want to make about everything from birthing patterns to average life expectancy in this pre-modern world. (S)

23.17   Ste. Croix, Geoffrey E.M. de. *The Class Struggle in the Ancient Greek World from the Archaic Age to the Arab Conquests*. London: Duckworth, 1981. Pp. xi + 732. B-40; I-33. Love it or hate it (as it has indeed been by reviewers of various political stripes) this Marxist interpretation of social relationships in the ancient world is one of the major works of modern historiography on social relationships in the Roman empire. For, despite its title, its contents are devoted mainly to the Roman empire, and hence its considerable relevance to the early Church. It is the single great overview of the entire social world of Antiquity that has been produced since the Second World War, with only Rostovtzeff having

offered anything comparable before that time, though from the
opposite end of the ideological spectrum. Of particular interest is
that Ste. Croix, because of his own personal background in part,
devotes consistent attention to Christianity (e.g., ch. 7.4, "The
attitudes to property of the Graeco-Roman world, of Jesus, and of
the Christian Churches). Ste. Croix is particularly interested in the
Marxian concept of exploitation and the political dimensions by
which surpluses were extracted from the lower classes. He is,
however, very traditional in his insistence on the master/owner-slave
conflict as *the* class conflict that determined the basic structure of
ancient societies. (S)

✄ Badian, *NYRB* 19 (1982): 47-51; Barnes, *Phoenix* 36 (1982): 363-366;
Bradley, *AJP* 103 (1982): 347-350; Brunt, *JRS* 72 (1982): 158-163; Cuff,
Athenaeum 66 (1982): 575-581; Shaw, *Economy and Society* 13 (1983):
208-249.

23.18   Veyne, Paul, ed. *A History of Private Life.* Vol. 1. *From Pagan
        Rome to Byzantium.* Translated by Arthur Goldhammer. Cambridge,
        MA/London: Harvard UP, 1987. Pp. xi + 670. I-10; AB-9; C-16;
        M-1; hundreds of B&W illustrations.

        The intent of this book is to reveal "what it was really like to live,
        work, and die in the ancient world." It is divided into five sections,
        the first three of which are relevant ("The Roman Empire" by Paul
        Veyne; "Late Antiquity" by Peter Brown; and "Private Life and
        Domestic Architecture in Roman Africa" by Yvon Thébert). Some
        of the topics covered are: marriage, slavery, the household, work
        and leisure, pleasures and excesses, tranquilizers, church leadership,
        and monasticism. Of particular interest are Brown's various discus-
        sions of Christian life and morality, with its emphases on abstinence,
        celibacy, and austerity. Extensive and well chosen illustrations.

        ✄ Oosdyke, *Religious Education* 83 (1988): 310-312; Snipes, *CHR* 21
        (1989): 469-70.

23.19   Yavetz, Zwi. *Plebs and Princeps.* Oxford: Clarendon Press, 1969.
        Pp. ix + 170. B-7; I-8.

        Despite its age, this monograph remains (together with the article
        by Brunt [§23.2]) one of the fundamental treatments available on
        the plebeians—that is, the lower class inhabitants of the city of
        Rome in the late Republic and early empire. Yavetz offers discreet
        chapters that analyze the behavior of urban crowds, the nature of
        the political connections between political leaders and the urban
        crowd, the Tribunes in the later Republic, the popularity of Julius
        Caesar, and the institutionalization of the latter trend in the form of
        worship of Caesar (i.e., the emperor) in the early Principate. Full of

attendant social and economic detail on the "lower orders" in the city. (S)

✄ Badian, *Phoenix* 24 (1970): 93-94; Colledge, *CR* 31 (1971): 427-429; Gruen, *AJP* 91 (1970): 487-489.

MARRIAGE AND THE FAMILY

23.20 🏛 Gardner, Jane F., and Thomas Wiedemann. *The Roman Household: A Sourcebook.* London/New York: Routledge, 1991. Pp. xviii + 210. I-8; B-7; B&W-14; AAI-12.

A presentation in English translation of 210 numbered items from literary, legal, epigraphical, and other sources relevant to the subject of family and household in Rome. The major headings include composition and definition of the family, the household as a focus of emotion, the economics of the Roman household, and the more specific subjects of life-cycle, inheritance, and social status criteria such as slavery and manumission, and patronage and friendship. Although it is reasonably reliable on what it does cover (on slavery/ manumission, however, it overlaps with Wiedemann's existing sourcebook on slavery §23.34), there are serious deficits. It contains no house plans, pays no attention to domestic architecture, and includes nothing on marriage, divorce, or other aspects of household or family formation. (S)

23.21 🏛 Hunter, David G., trans. and ed. *Marriage in the Early Church.* Sources of Early Christian Thought. Minneapolis: Fortress, 1992. Pp. viii + 157. B-4.

A collection of eighteen rather extensive passages on the general theme of marriage, from Hermas, Tertullian, Clement of Alexandria, *Acts of Thomas,* Methodius, Lactantius, Chrysostom, Pelagius, Augustine, Paulinus of Nola, Basil of Caesarea, with selections from the imperial legislation. The forty-page introduction traces the subject from the New Testament, into the next centuries, in both orthodox and heretical traditions, illustrating the varied emphases from church support for marriage to more ascetic views. This is a good starting point, as are all the volumes in this series.

23.22 Boswell, John. *The Kindness of Strangers.* New York: Pantheon Books, 1988. Pp. xviii + 488.

The subtitle reveals the content: *The Abandonment of Children in Western Europe from Late Antiquity to the Renaissance.* Only Part I (about 40% of the book) is relevant to our period. After a survey of the "historical" sources dealing with exposure of unwanted children, Boswell turns to the "literary" material (i.e. fiction), where he finds the more revealing clues about social attitudes. Then in Chapter 3, the attitude of the church is considered. Boswell challenges the widespread view that Christians and Jews did not expose their children. Whether Boswell has offered a reasonable interpretation of the material can be argued, but he has at least offered a thorough collection of comments from the fathers on the issue, and of the views in the wider society, with an examination of the bases upon which such actions were justified

⊱ Crossley, *CC* 107 (1990): 402; Ellsberg, *Commonweal* 116 (Sept 8 1989): 474-475. Knox, *NYRB* 36 (June 29, 1989): 9-12.; Thomas, *TLSuppl* (1989): 913-914.

23.23   Dixon, Suzanne. *The Roman Mother*, Norman, OK: University of Oklahoma Press, 1988. Pp. xviii + 286. B&W-10; B-14; I-12; CT-2; AI-7: FT-5; Inscription Index-3.

One of the "new historians" in Roman social history, Dixon's first book centers on one of the most important figures in the context of the Roman family—the mother. She carefully outlines the nature of the basic source materials and gives a general outline of Roman family relations, before proceeding to the place of the mother in the formal framework of the law. She discusses both maternity and official programs and ideologies designed to strengthen it and to encourage fertility. The problem of mother-child relationship (both to sons and daughters) as well as that of "mother substitutes" is considered. One of Dixon's main theses is that it is a mistake to transfer our late 19th and 20th centuries notions of the close emotional mother-child bond, and of mothering, to a society where mothers were expected to be both more distant and more authoritarian. (S)

⊱ Beard, *TLSuppl* (1988): 120; Evans-Gruggs, *CP* 85 (1990): 333-338; Golden, *Classical Views* 34 (1990): 470-473; Phillips, *CJ* 85 (1989-90): 264-266.

23.24   Dixon, Suzanne. *The Roman Family*. Baltimore/London: Johns Hopkins UP, 1992. Pp. xiv + 279. B&W-24; B-23; I-13; CT-2.

A state-of-the art survey of current scholarship on the Roman family, where the new research, especially since the early 1980s onwards, has transformed most of the received views on what constituted the core of family structure, obligation, and sentiment in Roman experience. After reviewing the trends in this new research, Dixon outlines the relationship between family and the law before proceeding to the specific subjects of marriage and family formation, and children. Perhaps best, and most innovative, however, is her final chapter on the life cycle of the family, which attempts to reconstruct the formation, growth, and recession of various family types (élite, freed,

poor) in Roman society. Also impressive are the illustrations which are well chosen and which in themselves form a pictorial text that extends the reader's understanding of the subject. (S)
✄ Shaw, *AHR* 98 (1993): 842.

23.25 Dooley, William Joseph. *Marriage According to St. Ambrose.* The Catholic University of America Studies in Christian Antiquity 11. Washington, DC: Catholic University of America Press, 1948. Pp. xvi + 149. B; I; SI; AAI; MAI.

Part of a rather valuable, and often forgotten, series of monographs published throughout the 1940s, Dooley's study displays the series' merits (good attention to primary sources) and demerits (weak on interpretation). Nevertheless, failing a good modern work on Ambrose on this particular subject (but see the chapter in Brown, *Body and Society* §14.4), Dooley's study is valuable precisely for the former reason. The first two chapters are devoted to Ambrose's conception of marriage and its embedding in a theodicy of salvific purpose. In the chapters that follow, those on marriage and chastity (Ch. 4) and virginity (Ch. 10), have been surpassed by recent work, and there is not much more that those on the institution of marriage, divorce, and separation, and widowhood can add (Chs. 7-9, especially). The remainder of the book is rather valuable: studies on parenting and childhood (Chs. 5-6) and on the ideology of conjugal love as part of marriage (Ch. 3), are especially notable. Again, Dooley's work is not strong on interpretation, but it is a useful guide to what can be found in one of the "Fathers" whose writings were most influential in this respect. (S)

23.26 Goody, Jack. *The Development of the Family and Marriage in Europe.* Cambridge: Cambridge UP 1983. Pp. xii + 308. B-16; I-13; G-1; M-5; T-2.

This study must be read in the context of Goody's other works (especially *Production and Reproduction*, 1976, and, subsequently, *The Oriental, the Ancient and the Primitive*, 1990). His basic argument is that the beginning of the fourth century witnessed a sea-change in the kinship values and connections that marked western Mediterranean and European societies up to that time. Whereas close-kin in-marrying, adoption, the "levirate," and similar practices had been quite acceptable previously, they suddenly became taboo. At the epicenter of these changes, Goody considers that there stood not just the new ideologies of the Christian church, but its vested interest in acquiring vast amounts of property—of substituting itself for the corporate kinship interests of families and descendants in the making of last wills and testaments. In pursuing this interest, the Church gradually strengthened prohibitions against in-marrying, adoption, and other kinship strategies that would have permitted the provision of more family heirs, and simultaneously exalted the value of celibacy and virginity, to much the same end. (S)

ᶾ✕ Shaw & Saller, *Man* 19 (1984): 432-444; Southall, *American Anthropologist* 86 (1984): 724-725; Vann, *Journal of Social History* 19 (1985): 139-142; Zemon Davis, *American Ethnologist* 12 (1985): 149-151.

23.27   Rawson, Beryl, ed. *The Family in Ancient Rome: New Perspectives.* London/Sydney: Croom Helm, 1986. Pp. 279. B-15; SI-4; NI-3.

The first of two major sets of conference papers on new research regarding the nature and structure of the Roman family (for the second see Rawson, §23.28). An especially valuable survey by the editor (Ch. 1) on the then-current state of research on the subject prefaces the whole work; and an appendix (bibliography #1) co-authored with Edyth Binkowski, lists "sources for the study of the Roman family." Broadly speaking, the contributions concentrate on aspects of property and legal power (e.g., John Crook on women's powers to succeed to property, Suzanne Dixon's study of the manipulation of wealth of the women in Cicero's family), and on the status and role of children (e.g., the editor's general contribution on that subject; Keith Bradley's study of "wet-nursing'). (S)

ᶾ✕ Wiedemann, *CR* 37 (1987): 65-67.

23.28   Rawson, Beryl, ed. *Marriage, Divorce, and Children in Ancient Rome.* Oxford: Oxford UP, 1991. Pp. xiv + 252. B-15, I-8; B&W-8; T-13.

The second volume of papers originally read at the Australian National University on new approaches to the analysis of the Roman family (for the first see Rawson §23.27). Published some five years apart, these volumes are as good a measure as any of the rapidity with which the field is developing. Four of the more important contributions that are especially illustrative of this advance, though all are well worth reading, are the editor's first chapter on adult-child relationships, Suzanne Dixon's chapter on the sentimental ideal of the Roman family, Richard Saller's contribution on corporal punishment, authority and obedience in the Roman household, and Andrew Wallace-Hadrill's study of domestic space in the houses and households of Pompeii and Herculaneum. All papers are at the leading edge of what was being done as of the date of the conference in 1988, and so should reward a close reading. (S)

23.29   Rordorf, Willy. "Marriage in the New Testament and in the Early
         Church." *Journal of Ecclesiastical History* 20 (1969): 193-210.
         This remains one of the better surveys of the evidence. In the first
         part of the article Rordorf surveys four major themes: (1) marriage,
         (2) adultery, divorce, and second marriages, (3) attitudes to women,
         and (4) marriage as a sacrament. In each he emphasizes the millennial
         and eschatological context of early views, especially those of Paul.
         In his survey of early patristic literature, Rordorf covers the subject
         of celibacy, and then repeats the same last three subjects as in Part
         One. In addition to a clear review of the primary evidence and
         exceptionally clear-cut statements of his own positions, Rordorf
         tries to relate the development of Christian thinking on these subjects
         as precisely that—a *developmental* process that responds to current
         social contexts and problems. Therefore, he argues, one ought not
         to be trapped by views meant as responses to a society quite different
         from our own. In some senses, however, one feels that Rordorf
         exculpates his sources too much by offering their *Sitz im Leben*
         (e.g., with respect to attitudes to women) as a total excuse for the
         deplorable views expressed in them. (S)

23.30   Shaw, Brent D. "The Family in Late Antiquity: the Experience of
         Augustine" *Past & Present* 115 (1987): 3-51.
         The evidence of Augustine's sermons, letters, and his other more
         theologically oriented writings represent an almost incomparable
         source in Latin reflecting the actual lives, and assumptions underlying
         those lives, of "ordinary persons" living in the later Roman empire
         in the west. Shaw's study employs this material to make some
         initial arguments about the nature of Roman family life, about the
         practices, ideas, and sentiments undergirding relationship between
         husbands and wives, fathers and sons, parents and children; about
         their affective and other ties to more distant relatives; about the
         role of dependants, like slaves and lodgers; and about the way in
         which the family was embedded in the larger structures of neighbor-
         hood, town, and state. The argument focuses on the centrality of
         the so-called nuclear or elementary family (parents and children),
         and its location at the epicenter of a series of concentric circles of
         obligation and ties, giving this peculiar Roman family a definition
         that is different in kind from our nuclear family and elementary
         family life. The significance of Christian ideology to shifts in family
         sentiment and obligation (e.g., marriage, divorce, adultery) are also
         studied.

23.31   Treggiari, Susan. *Roman Marriage: Iusti Coniuges from the Time of Cicero to the Time of Ulpian*. Oxford, Clarendon Press, 1991. Pp. xv + 578. B-20; AAI-2; PI-15; SI-13; CT-3; FT-2.

An enormous work that is bound to become the handbook on this subject for the foreseeable future. In fine detail, Treggiari not only gives thorough and accurate résumés of all important existing scholarship to the late 1980s on the major aspects of marriage (betrothal, ritual of marriage ceremonial, dowry, divorce, and the legal matters pertinent to these) but also gives the reader a near-comprehensive review of the primary source materials relevant to each question. Her sorting out of complex legal matters (for example, the "moral legislation" of the emperor Augustus relevant to marriage, children, and divorce) are exemplary in their clarity and thoroughness. If you want to know any of the basic materials, secondary or primary, relevant to this most important aspect of family formation, this should be your first line of recourse for reference. (S)

23.32   Wicker, Kathleen O'Brien. "First Century Marriage Ethics: A Comparative Study of the Household Codes and Plutarch's Conjugal Precepts." In *No Famine in the Land*. Edited by James W. Flanagan & Anita W. Robinson. Chico, CA: Scholars Press, 1975. Pp. 141-53.

As the title indicates, Wicker takes the so-called "Haustafel" (household codes) literature of the New Testament (especially Ephesians) and compares its code of household conduct with the norms recommended by Plutarch in his small treatise on "Marital Recommendations." Plutarch shaped his recommendations based on traditional élite Greek values: that a marriage should be designed to achieve *sôphrosynê* (control of the passions) and a *symbiôsis* (balance) of two parties in which, however, superior authority naturally rests with the husband. The Household Codes embody many of the same detailed prescriptions found in Plutarch, but differ in the complex analogies they draw between the married couple and God, and Christ and the Church. In addition, they read the significance of procreation and sexuality rather differently (though both stress fidelity, purity, monogamy and restraint). For Plutarch these aspects are subordinate to "love," whereas in the Haustafeln they are seen as one of the principal aims of marriage itself. (S)

23.33   Wiedemann, Thomas. *Adults and Children in the Roman Empire*. New Haven/London, Yale UP, 1989. Pp. xii + 221. B&W-22; B-5; I-7.

A general survey of current knowledge on parent-child relationships in the Roman world, especially its western (Latin) parts. A reasonably up-to-date coverage of existing scholarship, but justly criticized by reviewers for its much weaker presentation of its main theses. (S)

✂ Beard, *TLSuppl* (1990): 71; Countryman *CH* 60 (1991): 85-86; Golden, *Ancient History Bulletin* 4 (1990): 90-94.

SLAVERY AND LABOR

23.34 🏛 Wiedemann, Thomas. *Greek and Roman Slavery*. Rev. ed. Baltimore: Johns Hopkins UP, 1988. (1981[1]). Pp. xviii + 284. B-7; AAI-17; I-9; M-2.

The standard reader on the subject in English (indeed, at the moment, in any language). Literary, legal, epigraphical, archaeological, and other items on slavery in the Graeco-Roman world are presented in English translation, and are arranged in 243 numbered items in the text. The major headings into which these are divided include the slave as a type of property, the problem of debt-bondage, serfdom, manumission, the moral and symbolic value of slaves, sources of slaves, domestic, and rural labor, state slaves, and the problem of treatment and resistance. The final chapter of readings is of particular interest since it treats Stoic and Christian views of slaves and servitude. Well organized, each reading is prefaced by a brief description of the source of the reading and its significance to the subject. (S)

23.35 Geoghegan, Arthur T. *The Attitude Towards Labor in Early Christianity and Ancient Culture*. The Catholic University of America Studies in Christian Antiquity 6. Washington, DC: The Catholic University of America Press, 1945. Pp. xxviii + 250. B; I; AAI; B&W-6.

A little known, and unjustly neglected, study of attitudes towards work in Graeco-Roman and Judaic antiquity. The first part of the book (about one-third of its contents) is devoted to a study of attitudes to work in, respectively, the societies of the Greek city-state, the Roman empire, and among the Jews. The second part (the bulk of the volume) concentrates on a study of attitudes to labor in early Christianity. Beginning with the New Testament (the sayings of Jesus, Apostolic materials), Geoghegan passes to a consideration of texts (principally literary ones) regarding work in the Christian communities, roughly to the end of the fourth century, first in the eastern Mediterranean Chs. 4-5) and then in the West (Ch. 6). Particularly interesting in the latter case are his studies of labor legislation and his collation of the information on the subject to be gained from a reading of Christian epigraphy. Though his analysis is rather dated, Geoghegan's work remains a valuable collation of the sources, and it provides a discussion of them that has not yet been replaced by any single modern work. It is therefore still well worth consulting. (S)

23.36   Finley, Moses I. *Ancient Slavery and Modern Ideology*. New York:
        Viking, 1981; Harmondsworth: Penguin, 1983, Pp. 202. B-10; I-8.
        The major modern interpretation in English of slavery in the Graeco-
        Roman world. It is not restricted to the interplay between the ancient
        phenomenon and modern interpretations, but has a much wider
        focus than its title would seem to indicate. Finley discusses, often
        acerbically, the impact of modern ideological commitment on the
        meaning of ancient slavery. He devotes chapters to the practical
        aspects of the slave system itself in terms of the specific historical
        reasons for its emergence (Ch. 2), and to the supposed "humanity"
        in it—as opposed to the actual elements of dehumanization, repres-
        sion, and punishment that constituted the core of the master-slave
        relationship (Ch. 3). He ends with a chapter devoted to the decline
        of the ancient slave system in which the specific problems of the
        ideological impact of major belief systems, the Stoic and the
        Christian, are critically examined. (S)
        ✂ Badian, *NYRB* 38.16 (22 Oct 1981): 49-53.

23.37   Finley, Moses I. ed. *Classical Slavery*. London: Frank Cass, 1987.
        = *Slavery & Abolition* 8.1 (1987)
        An important collection of specialist studies on various facets of
        Graeco-Roman slavery, which is prefaced by an analytical introduc-
        tion by the editor who takes into account controversies in the subject
        to the mid-1980s. This introduction is followed by an appreciation
        of Sir Moses Finley's own work on these problems by Arnaldo
        Momigliano. The specialist studies include one on the relationship
        between war, piracy, and slaving (Garlan), an important consider-
        ation of the opponents of slavery assumed in Aristotle's defense of
        the institution (Cambiano), one on breeding as a source of slave
        supply (Bradley), one on the relationship between slavery and the
        institution of the family (Saller), and another on the place of the
        servile system in the great transition from slavery to serfdom in the
        later Roman empire (Whittaker). This is a coherent collection of
        high quality papers, almost every one of which makes new and
        fundamental contributions to the understanding of slavery in the
        Graeco-Roman world. (S)

23.38   Hopkins, Keith. *Conquerors and Slaves: Sociological Studies in
        Roman History, 1*, Cambridge, Cambridge UP, 1978. Pp. xiv +
        268. M-1; B&W-4; AB-2; SI-6; B-10; NI-8; T-14.
        Essayed by the leading social historian of Rome in the English-
        speaking world, this collection includes three important studies on
        the impact of slavery on Roman society in Italy. These include

chapters on the growth and maintenance of the slave system, and on the rationality and economics of manumission, based on a detailed study of inscriptions from Delphi. Of particular interest is Hopkins' study of the divinity of the emperors as "a symbol of unity of the Roman empire," especially given the importance of the imperial cult in the persecution of Christians. This final chapter is a valuable supplement to Fishwick's detailed studies of the imperial cult [§20.35], and of Simon Price's scintillating analysis of the same [§20.37]. Hopkins' deliberately works from a strong basis in sociological and anthropological theory, and places emphasis on "counting" and statistics, where this is possible (e.g., in his analysis of the Delphic manumission inscriptions). He is also strong on evocative descriptions that emphasize the meaning and significance of everyday experience (e.g. his description of the rituals of the imperial cult). (S)
℈✕ Miller, *TLSuppl* 77 (1979): 170-171.

23.39 Vogt, Joseph. *Ancient Slavery and the Ideal of Man.* Translated by Thomas Wiedemann. Oxford: Blackwells, 1974. Pp. x + 227. I-9; AB-7.
Joseph Vogt was a man of deeply committed religious ideals, but of somewhat more dubious political background in the late 1930s and early 1940s. After the Second World War, he headed a research institute at the University of Mainz devoted to the detailed investigation of various aspects of ancient slave systems. Almost all of the institute's work is in German, and has not yet been translated into English. This volume, however, is a translation into English of some of the best of Vogt's work. Vogt is a rather meliorist interpreter of the role and significance of slavery in classical societies (hence the need of some antidote, such as the review listed below by Finley). Most of the chapters reflect Vogt's ideological stance on slavery as an "unfortunate price" paid for the great moral and cultural achievements of Graeco-Roman civilization (e.g., his concern with utopianism, liberal arts, the "faithful slave," and the study of slavery by modern humanists). This volume contains an outstanding piece of German positivist scholarship that marked a watershed in our understanding of slave rebellions and wars (the large Ch. 3 at the core of the book). It alone is worth the read. (S)
℈✕ Finley, *TLSuppl* (14 Nov 1975): 1348.

WEALTH, CHARITY, AND PATRONAGE
23.40 Avila, Charles. *Ownership: Early Christian Teaching.* Maryknoll, NY: Orbis, 1983. Pp. xxi + 214. I-6; SI-1.

This volume, the result of a doctorate dissertation rewritten years later for a general audience, was born out of the author's commitment to the cause of the Filipino peasants, whom he helped organize, and parts of his book reflect that concern, such as references to peasant resistance in the ancient world. Avila looks particularly at the works of Clement of Alexandria, Basil the Great, Ambrose, Chrysostom, and Augustine, whose views vary somewhat, but all who find problems with wealth or else specify clear responsibilities that the wealthy have to the poor. Avila considers, too, the Christian efforts to aid the poor. Greek and Latin texts of the passages studied are supplied in a 36-page appendix.

Crook, *JEH* 36 (1985): 138-139; Reed, *Fides et Historia* 17 (1985): 106-109; Stamoolis, *Themelios* 13 (1988): 68-69; TeSelle, *Quarterly Review* 7 (1987): 89-90.

23.41   Countryman, L. William. *The Rich Christian in the Church of the Early Empire: Contradictions and Accommodations.* New York / Toronto: Edwin Mellen, 1980. Pp. ix + 239. B-23.
Countryman (contra Hengel §23.44) thinks that there were only rare instances of early Christian "communism" (e.g. the Jerusalem community). Examining Clement of Alexandria's *Rich Man*, Countryman argues that the dominant Christian attitude towards riches was not extremist, though riches and property were considered *potential* sources of harm, both to individuals and to the church as a whole. Rich laypeople, through almsgiving, were able to provide for many of the needs of the church, but they also were a source of problems. Cyprian's attitude is considered in the final chapter.

Athanassiadi-Fowden, *JTS* 33 (1982): 297-298; Brackett, *CH* 52 (1983): 81; Bray, *EQ* 54 (1982): 245-246; Houlden, *ExT* 93 (1981): 26; Johnson, *CBQ* 44 (1982): 316-317; Osiek, *SC* 3 (1983): 107-109; Pervo, *ATR* 64 (1982): 238-239; Pleket, *VC* 36 (1982): 63-66; Rader, *JAAR* 50 (1982): 310; Walsh, *TS* 43 (1982): 143-145; Ziesler, *SJT* 35 (1982): 383-384.

23.42   González, Justo L. *Faith & Wealth: A History of Early Christian Ideas on the Origin, Significance, and Use of Money.* San Francisco: Harper & Row, 1990. Pp. xvi + 240. I-6.
The first 90 pages deal with the Mediterranean (Jewish, Greek, and Roman) attitudes, providing a useful review of the Roman economy throughout the first three centuries (agriculture, industry, trade, and taxation) and the first-century Christian position on these matters. The almost uniform early Christian position on matters of usury, private property, and wealth is discussed in detail, covering almost all Christian writing on the topic, with special chapters on the Cappadocians, Ambrose, Jerome, Chrysostom, and Augustine, and

on the impact of the new Constantinian order, especially as reflected in the Donatists and monasticism.

⊰ Finn, *CBQ* 54 (1992): 348-350; Green, *CRBR* (1991): 300-303; Houlden, *ExT* 101 (1990): 377-378; Johnson, *TS* 51 (1990): 517-518; Johnson, *TT* 47 (1990): 324-325; LeMasters, *CC* 107 (1990): 941-942; Liggett, *Encounter* 51 (1990): 410-412.

23.43 Hands, Arthur Robinson. *Charities and Social Aid in Greece and Rome*. London: Thames & Hudson, 1968. Pp. 222. SI-6; NI-6.
Arguably still the best handbook on a most important subject concerning the rise of Christianity in the Mediterranean. Important not only for the scholarship in its own right, but also because it makes the basic theses of one of the pathbreaking works on the subject, Bolkestein's *Wohltätigkeit und Armenpflege* (1939), available to an English readership. Following the basic lineaments of Bolkestein's arguments, Hands shows how the "poor" were defined quite differently by the city-states and empires of antiquity (Ch. 5, "The Poor"), and how that peculiar view then worked out in terms of who did and did not deserve public and private assistance (Ch. 6, "Pity for the Destitute"; Ch. 7, "The Provision of Basic Commodities"). All this provides a valuable background to a better understanding of how revolutionary Christian views were when faced with the basic problem of poverty. Especially valuable is the collection of 81 numbered documents in translation (pp. 175-209) on basic aspects of private and public charity in the Graeco-Roman world. (S)

⊰ Duncan-Jones, *JRS* 59 (1969): 287-289; Errington, *JHS* 90 (1970): 254-255.

23.44 Hengel, Martin. *Property and Riches in the Early Church: Aspects of a Social History of Early Christianity*. Translated by John Bowden. London, SCM / Philadelphia, Fortress, 1974. Pp. viii + 96. B-4.
Now combined with Hengel's *Acts and the History of Earliest Christianity* under in one volume with the title *Earliest Christianity*. Hengel begins his investigation with the "fixed" attitudes of the fourth-century, post-Constantinian Church Fathers, and then goes backwards in time to discover the roots of this Christian view by contrasting it with Greek and Roman ideals. This is followed by an investigation of the attitudes to wealth in the Tanakh and in Rabbinic Judaism, and thence to the centrality of Jesus' message and its interpretation in the Pauline writings. Hengel's basic thesis is that although there did not emerge a truly distinctive Christian view on the subject (most of what emerged later was under the heavy influence of "pagan" philosophical teachings), "primitive Christianity" did

contain a "radical critique of riches." This critique, however, does not offer a secure basis for a modern morality. Hengel's bibliography is a valuable guide to what (little) good modern scholarship existed on the subject up to the time he composed the original (1973). (S)

✂ Gager, *Interpretation* 30 (1976): 426+; Horsley, *JAAR* 44 (1976): 568-569; Mealand, *Theology* 78 (1975): 655-656.

23.45   Maloney, Robert P. "The Teaching of the Fathers on Usury: An Historical Study on the Development of Christian Thinking." *Vigiliae Christianae* 27 (1973): 241-265.

Referring to John T. Noonan's 1957 study (*The Scholastic Analysis of Usury*), which covered later medieval developments, Maloney notes that there has been no systematic modern study of the early Christian teaching on usury (other, that is, than Ignaz Seipel's early 1907 work, *Die Wirtschaftlichen Lehren der Kirchenväter*). He notes that, except for the oblique allusions in Matthew 25.27 and Luke 19.23, there really is nothing on the subject in the New Testament, and therefore the early Church Fathers, from Clement of Alexandria and Tertullian to Ambrose and Augustine, had to base their teachings on Old Testament prohibitions and on extrapolations of the practice's incompatibility with "Christian love." From the beginning, the Fathers developed these two sources into a systematic sanction with regard to usury (sometimes linking it to a general protection that was owed to "the poor"). Despite the secular legality of "lending for a profit," they unreservedly condemned such practices as gravely sinful in nature. (S)

23.46   Mullin, Redmond. *The Wealth of Christians*. Exeter: Paternoster, 1983. Pp. 256. I-6; B-8.

Only the first 67 pages are relevant to this bibliography. Mullin provides an introductory survey of the attitudes to wealth, poverty, and charity in the Graeco-Roman and Jewish worlds, trying to find roots for Christian attitudes, and noting where Christians seem to provide something new. The short chapter on the early church emphasizes the important role of charity for the early Christians (reasons, methods of distribution, fundraising), and points to dangers that arose in the alliance between church and state. A brief comment is made to defend the treatment of wealth by Clement of Alexander. Little attention is given to the secondary literature.

✂ Elliott, *Theology* 87 (1984): 395-397; Hartropp, *Churchman* 99 (1985): 82-83; Hibma, *Reformed Review* 39 (1985): 80-81; Huelin, *ExT* 96 (1984): 63; Knox, *Reformed Theological Review* 43 (1984): 85-86.

23.47   Osiek, Carolyn. *Rich and Poor in the Shepherd of Hermas. An Exegetical-Social Investigation.* CBQ Monograph Series 15; Washington, DC: Catholic Biblical Association of America, 1983. Pp. xi + 184. bibliography, indexes of passages cited and of persons.
Setting the text of the *Shepherd of Hermas* in the context of existing scholarship, Osiek prefaces the main part of her study with a review of the Old and New Testament texts relevant to the subject of poverty and wealth. Following upon her treatment of the poverty-wealth in the *Shepherd* generally, she concentrates detailed exegesis on *Mandate* 8:10 and the Second *Similitude*. The study is then closed with an attempt to place the text of the *Shepherd* in its second century context in urban Rome. She sees the author as coming from a Lukan/James tradition wherein the poor and humble are "those preferred and protected by God," but that the actual social make-up of the Christian community at Rome to whom the author directed his treatises maintained traditional values that were recalcitrant to such a hypervalution of poverty and the poor—a problem he tried to bridge by appealing to both rich and poor as necessary constituents of a strong Christian community. (S)
⊰ Countryman, *SC* 5 (1985-86): 180-181; Davies, *CBQ* 47 (1985): 363-364; Mayer, *Currents* 12 (1985): 121.

23.48   Ste. Croix, G.E.M. de. "Early Christian Attitudes to Property and Slavery." In *Church Society and Politics*. Papers read at the thirteenth summer meeting and the fourteenth winter meeting of the Ecclesiastical Society. Edited by D. Baker. Oxford: Basil Blackwell, 1975. Pp. 1-38.
This article reproduces, often word-for-word, some of the important parts of Ste. Croix massive work on the subject [§23.17] published after some unexpected delays, it seems, some six years later. The material in the article concentrates on the *Christian* attitudes.

23.49   Wallace-Hadrill, Andrew, ed. *Patronage in Ancient Society.* London / New York: Routledge, 1989. Pp. 255. I-5; AAI-3.
An understanding of the patron-client relationship may be particularly useful for gaining some insight into the structure of the early Christian communities, and into its methods and successes in its efforts at conversion. This volume provides eleven essays on the topic of patronage, from a variety of disciplines. While all contributions are useful for gaining an understanding of this fundamental social relationship, the following are particularly helpful for students of the early church: "Personal patronage" (Braund); "Patronage and the rural poor" (Garnsey and Woolf); "Bandits, elites and rural

order" (Hopwood); "Client-patron relationship...in Juvenal" (Cloud); and "Patronage: relation and system" (Johnson and Dandeker). Each chapter has a fairly detailed bibliography.

24
THEOLOGY

The third edition of *The Shorter Oxford English Dictionary on Historical Principles* defines theology as follows: it is "the study or science which treats of God, His nature and attributes, and His relations with man and the universe; 'the science of things divine'; divinity." In addition, it describes theology as "a particular theological system or theory." In effect, then, there are really two related but differing meanings of the term: one relatively narrow, the other quite broad. According to the first meaning, theology is that discipline which deals specifically with the nature of God and his relationship to the universe. According to the second, it is practically anything that deals with transcendent matters or those mundane matters that relate in some way to the transcendent. A work that discusses the doctrine of the Trinity is theology in the first sense of the word; studies that are concerned with such diverse fields as christology, soteriology, pneumatology, angelology, demonology, eschatology, and the nature of humankind from a religious standpoint are theology in the second sense. While a few of the books and articles listed below are theological in the narrow, first sense of theology, most are such in the broad, second meaning of that word. Although christological studies could rightly be included in this chapter, they appear separately in chapter eight which is devoted to that subject alone. The abundance of works on early Christian concepts of the person and work of Christ makes this necessary.

From the first century on, it became impossible for Christian writers to separate theology in either sense of the word from philosophy despite the Apostle Paul's condemnation of philosophy as "vain" and Tertullian's stern denunciation of it. The book of Acts describes Paul himself as quoting Stoic philosophers with approval (Acts 17:28), and Tertullian's works are filled—evidently largely unconsciously—with Stoic ideas. Those ideas are obviously present in his Trinitarian terminology—terminology now part and parcel of orthodox Christian doctrine. For example, when Tertullian wrote of God's substance (*substantia*), he borrowed the Stoic idea that everything that exists is material in some sense or other. It would be wrong to assume, however, that Stoicism was the sole philosophy that played a role in influencing early Christian theology. Although Stoicism was important, in the long run Platonism and Neo-Platonism had even greater impact on the development of Christian doctrine.

It is not surprising that these various schools of Hellenistic philosophy had such an effect on Christian thought. Shortly after the death of Jesus, his followers founded congregations beyond Palestine which soon began to welcome Gentiles into their membership. Those Gentiles brought a number of their traditions and ideas into the church with them, and the church began to adopt many Hellenistic concepts rather unconsciously. It would be wrong to assume that Gentile Christians alone were responsible for this process, however. The Judaism out of which Christianity grew was itself already heavily influenced by Hellenistic thought and, in particular, by Platonism. This fact is clearly demonstrated by the influence that that philosophy had on Philo of Alexandria. Through him it was passed on to second-century Christian apologists such as Justin Martyr and later church fathers.

It is therefore quite understandable that church fathers from the second-century apologists on came to use Hellenistic philosophical concepts and terms to defend and to explain Christianity in an essentially non-Jewish world. So as years went by, Christian doctrine became increasingly Hellenistic and less Jewish in nature. Yet this gradual change was probably inevitable: to thrive, Christianity had to come to grips with issues raised by the philosophers and philosophically minded Christians. Yet despite the introduction of Stoic, Platonic, and other philosophical concepts into Christian theology, the theology maintained most of its basic Jewish nature. Thus it would be wrong to emphasize too strongly the Hellenistic philosophical element in Christian theology, though it was not without influence.

That the earliest Christians were primarily Jewish in outlook and belief has always been recognized by everyone except Marcion and the early Gnostics. What has not been generally understood, though, is that those Christians often held theological concepts which were quite different from those developed by later Gentile Christianity. Important studies produced since the Second World War demonstrate this clearly. As Jean Daniélou [§24.11; 24.12] and others have shown, early Christian christology was rooted to a great extent in Jewish angelology. Accordingly, the Archangel Michael was sometimes held to be the pre-existent Christ as, for instance, in the Shepherd of Hermas.

Many early Jewish beliefs such as the one just mentioned above disappeared from main-line Gentile Christianity, and that Gentile Christianity went on to develop in a very different direction. Yet Christian theology remained primarily Jewish despite what amounted to a heavy Greek philosophical overlay. All this is clearly outlined in the many studies of the evolution of Christian theology from the time of Christ to the European middle ages.

While certain fields of early Christian theology have been well plowed, as is shown below, it must be recognized that others have not been. Although there are numerous studies devoted to the doctrine of the Trinity, the person of Christ, and the nature of humankind, there are far fewer on the Holy Spirit, eschatology, angelology, and ecclesiology. These latter fields have simply not been of as great concern to the scholarly world as the former. Yet the studies on such topics are generally of excellent quality.

From a scholarly standpoint, the devil and the angelic forces of darkness have received short shrift indeed. Satan has never been very popular, and twentieth-century men and women often tend to deny his existence. Thus it is not surprising that so few recent studies have been produced in an area that has always been of great interest to large numbers of Christians. Fortunately, however, J.B. Russell [§24.32] gives us some insights into early Christian beliefs about the devil, demons, and the problem of evil.

Finally, although Christianity is pre-eminently a historical religion, there are few works which relate to the historical-theological beliefs of the early Church. L.G. Patterson's *God and History in Early Christianity* [§24.30] is about the only major study of this subject in English. (P)

24.1 🏛 Greenslade, S.L. trans. and ed. *Early Latin Theology: Selections from Tertullian, Cyprian, Ambrose and Jerome.* Library of Christian Classics 5. Philadelphia: Westminster, 1956. Pp. 415. I-8; BI-5; AAI-3.

This volume of the Library of Christian Classics is composed of certain essays and letters of the four Latin Fathers named in the title plus brief introductions to them and their works. The works included are Tertullian's *The Prescription against the Heretics, On Idolatry,* and *De Pudicitia;* Cyprian's *The Unity of the Catholic Church, The Problem of the Lapsed,* and *The Baptismal Controversy;* eight letters by Ambrose; and six by Jerome. Although representing only a limited selection of these Fathers' writings, the essays and letters in question provide a great deal of information regarding the issues which they and the church of their day faced. The select bibliography is useful. (P)

24.2 🏛 Wiles, Maurice and Mark Santer, eds. *Documents in Early Christian Thought.* Cambridge: Cambridge UP, 1975. Pp. x + 268.
The documents are arranged topically. "Introductory material and annotation have been kept to a minimum." The subjects covered are God, the Trinity, Christ, the Holy Spirit, sin and grace, tradition and scripture, the church, the sacraments, Christian living, the church

and society, and the final goal. Strangely, the earliest works which appear are those of Irenaeus and Tertullian. Thus the writings of both the Apostolic Fathers and the apologists have been ignored. So, too, have those of any heretics. Despite these weaknesses, the documents included are useful: they give a clear picture of the development of orthodoxy from the second through the fifth centuries. (P)

24.3   Bethune-Baker, J.F. *An Introduction to the Early History of Christian Doctrine to the Time of the Council of Chalcedon.* London: Methuen, 1958. (1903[1]). Pp. xxvi + 458. I-8
Published originally in 1903, this work is quite dated. Yet it is useful as a fairly complete basic guide to the development of early Christian doctrine. Written from an Anglican point of view, it emphasizes a tradition of Catholic orthodoxy. It relates the teachings of the early, post-apostolic church to certain modern teachings, particularly those surrounding baptism and the Eucharist. Among its strong points are an appendix of additional notes and a section entitled "Addenda 1948." The addenda are a list of "recent studies" to 1948 on the subjects discussed in certain chapters. (P)

24.4   Berchman, Robert M. *From Philo to Origen: Middle Platonism in Transition.* Brown Judaic Studies 69. Chico, CA: Scholars Press, 1984. Pp. 359. I-7; B-14.
This is a difficult book for the non-specialist, both because of the nature of the subjects studied and the author's rather difficult style. Nonetheless, it is a useful source for obtaining well-documented overviews of the thinking of the philosopher-theologians from Philo to Origen. It is divided into three parts. In Part One, Berchman deals with the "Theoretic or Physics" of Philo, Clement of Alexandria, Albinus, Moderatus, Nichomachus, Numenius, and Origen. Part Two covers the epistemology, dialectical logic, and dialectical rhetoric of the same persons. Part Three is a demonstration of Middle Platonic Theoretic and epistemology as illustrated in Origen's *Periarchon* (*De Principiis*). Origen is treated more as a philosopher than a theologian. (P)
✂ Drewery, *ExT* 98 (1986): 90; Gallagher, *JAAR* 54 (1986): 764-765; Meredith, *JTS* 37 (1986): 557-559.

24.5   Bigg, Charles. *The Christian Platonists of Alexandria.* Oxford: Clarendon Press, 1886. Pp. xxvii + 304.
Based on eight Bampton lectures delivered in 1886, this book remains valuable despite its age. It includes a variety of topics on Alexandrian

Christian thinking, all of which are listed in a detailed Synopsis of Contents. Chapter VII is of special interest; it deals with reformed paganism, particularly with trinitarian and unitarian Platonism. *The Christian Platonists* therefore continues to serve as an important examination of the relationship between Christianity and Platonism. Caution must be exercised in its use, however, because subsequent scholarship has thrown more light on some of the topics that Bigg discusses. Except for footnotes, this volume lacks critical apparatus. (P)

24.6 Blumenthal, H.J. and R.A. Markus, eds. *Neoplatonism and Early Christian Thought. Essays in honour of A.H. Armstrong.* London: Variorum Reprints, 1981. Pp. 256. I-6.

This Collection is divided into four sections: "Platonism and Christianity Before Plotinus"; "Plotinus and His Contemporaries"; "St. Augustine and his Neoplatonic Background"; and "Later Neoplatonism and the Christian Tradition." The relevant chapters are: "Plutarch, Platonism and Christianity" (Whittaker); "Stoic Logic in the *Contra Celsum*" (Rist); "Soma-Sema Formula" (de Vogel); "Marius Victorinus" (Clark); "Neoplatonism in St. Augustine's *De Civitate Dei*" (Russell); "Augustine on the Measurement of Time" (O'Daly); "Augustine's Theory of Personality" (Crouse); "Hellenism and Christianity in St. Basil's Address *Ad Adulescentes*" (Fortin); "Augustine and Gregory the Great on Visions and Prophecies" (Markus); and three chapters on Plotinus and Gnosticism (O'Brien; Hadot; and Igal).

୫< Louth, *JTS* 33 (1982): 577-578; Meredith, *Sobornost* 4 (1982): 225-226.

24.7 Burgess, Stanley M. *The Spirit and the Church: Antiquity.* Peabody, MA: Hendrickson, 1984. Pp. x + 216. B-7. I-10.

Burgess gives a clear analysis of early "orthodox" beliefs concerning the Holy Spirit from Clement of Rome through the Latin theologians of the fourth and fifth centuries. He also includes a section on Gnostic religion, Marcionism, dynamic and modalistic Monarchianism, and Montanism. He uses an account of the passion of Perpetua and Felicitas to represent "a developing trend to recognize the legitimate exercise of the charismata in a class of believers...who lived beyond the expectations considered normal for the ordinary believer." In the second section, he covers the period from Nicaea to Augustine—a time of greater doctrinal definition. (P)

୫< Applegate, *JRPR* 13 (1990): 142-155; Bundy, *Pneuma* 7 (1985): 81-82; Menzies, *Paraclete* 22 (May-Sept 1988): 30-31.

24.8   Burkill, T.A. *The Evolution of Christian Thought.* Ithaca/London: Cornell UP, 1971. Pp. xii + 505. I-16; B-2.

The first three sections of this book trace the history of "ancient Catholicism" from the Apostolic Fathers through the medieval schism of the eastern and western churches. The next four sections deal with medieval, Reformation, and post-reformation development. Particularly useful to the history of the early church are Burkill's surveys of Arianism, Nestorianism, the Monophysites and Monothelites, Iconoclasticism, Pelagianism, Monasticism, and the emergence of the Papacy. (P)

24.9   Chadwick, Henry. *Early Christian Thought and the Classical Tradition: Studies in Justin, Clement, and Origen.* Oxford: Clarendon Press, 1966. Pp. 174. I-4.

A collection of four chapters stemming from the Hewett Lectures of 1962 by one of the leading scholars in the field. In "The Vindication of Christianity," Chadwick deals with Justin's apologetic attempts to relate Christianity to pagan culture; in "The Liberal Puritan," with moral attitudes of Clement of Alexandria and his depth of genuine attachment to Christianity. In the last two chapters ("The Illiberal Humanist" and "The Perennial Humanist"), Chadwick deals with Origen. The question of Origen's orthodoxy is treated with considerable sympathy. The work contains much of use, though it is not as focused on the topic of its title as some of the reviewers wished. (P)

✂ J.G. Davies, *ExT* 78 (1966): 59-60; R.M. Grant, *USQR* 22 (1967): 378-381; Hinson, *R&E* 63 (1966): 488-489; Musurillo, *TS* 27 (11966): 680-681; R.A. Norris, *JR* 47 (1967): 156-157; Richardson, *CH* 36 (1967): 85-86; Stewart, *JTS* 18 (1967): 224-227.

24.10   ☛ Daley, Brian E. *The Hope of the Early Church: A Handbook of Patristic Eschatology.* Cambridge: Cambridge UP, 1991. Pp. xiv + 300. B-21; I-23.

As the subtitle indicates, this is simply a handbook of early Christian eschatology. Hence it makes no pretense of being a major study of "last things" as seen by the first Christians. Its strengths are that it provides a broad overview of patristic eschatology from primitive Semitic Christianity to the sixth century. It also includes a most useful bibliography of works in a variety of languages which, unfortunately, demonstrates how little has been done by English-speaking scholars in the area of patristic studies. Although Daley is to be commended for what he has done, further studies of early Christian eschatological musings and teachings are needed. (P)

≫ Baukham, *Theology* 95 (1992): 142-143; Gould, *JEH* 43 (1992): 141; R.M. Grant, *JR* 73 (1993): 86; Marmorstein, *AUSS* 30 (1992): 244-245; McWilliam, *TS* 53 (1992): 746-748.

24.11   Daniélou, Jean. *A History of Early Christian Doctrine*. Volume One. Translated and edited by John A. Baker. London: Dartman, Longman, and Todd / Philadelphia: Westminster, 1964. Pp. xvi + 446. I-8; B-12; AAI-14.

This is an expanded edition of *Théologie du Judés-Christianisme*. Daniélou's study explores the literary history of Jewish Christianity, heterodox Jewish Christianity, Jewish Christian exegesis, plus Jewish-Christian views of the Trinity and angelology (angel christology), the son of God, apocalyptic, redemption, the Church, baptism and the Eucharist, organization of the Christian community, holiness, and millenarianism. Important aspects to this work are examinations of early Christian writings, such as the Shepherd of Hermas, which demonstrate that the pre-existent Christ was sometimes regarded as an angel or the Archangel Michael. This is a key work in the history of early Christian doctrine. (P)

24.12   Daniélou, Jean. *A History of Early Christian Doctrine Before the Council of Nicaea*. Volume Three. *The Origins of Latin Christianity*. Translated by David Smith and John Austin Baker. Edited and with a Postscript by John A. Baker. London: Dartman, Longman & Todd / Philadelphia: Westminster, 1977. Pp. xvi + 511. I-7; B-9; AAI-18.

This is the last in Daniélou's massive treatment of Christian theology before Nicaea. The volume is divided into four sections: Latin Judeo-Christianity; Christianity and Latin Culture; The Latin Fathers and the Bible; and Latin Theology. To some extent, it is largely a volume on Tertullian, the outstanding Latin theologian of that age. A 9-page defence of Daniélou's work and summary of the third volume is provided by Baker. Baker lists four main concerns: Christian institutions (with some special pleading); order and simplicity in theology; openness to secular thought; and moralism. (P)

24.13   Froom, Le Roy Edwin. *The Prophetic Faith of our Fathers*. Vol. 1. Washington, DC: Review and Herald, 1950. Pp. 1006. B-35; B&W-51. T-9.

One of Froom's purposes in writing this work was to demonstrate the "main-line" roots of Seventh-Day Adventism. Thus the reader must be aware of Froom's particular prejudices. Nonetheless, *The*

Prophetic Faith of our Fathers gives a useful and generally accurate historical synopsis of Jewish and Christian exegesis regarding such matters as the coming—and second coming—of the messiah, eschatology, and millenarianism from pre-Christian times to the high Middle Ages. Much of it relates to early Christian prophetic speculation and shows the continuing impact of Jewish thought on such speculation. Special attention is given to interpretations of Daniel and Revelation. The bibliography is particularly useful. (P)

24.14 ☛ González, Justo L. *A History of Christian Thought.* Volume I. *From the Beginnings to the Council of Chalcedon.* Nashville: Abingdon, 1987. (1970¹). Pp. 400. I-12; B-4.
In this work, González rejects the approach to church history taken by such men as Vincent of Lérins, Adolph von Harnack, and Anders Nygren. Rather, he has produced a history based on the doctrine of the Incarnation. Written originally in Spanish, *A History of Christian Thought* was expanded and improved when translated into English. Since González wrote it for students who have little knowledge of church history or doctrine, it is a good study for "beginners." Doctrinal developments and controversies are given a standard treatment with unadorned explanations, a factor which is more a strength than a weakness for those not immersed in theology. (P)
✄ Johnson, *JAAR* 41 (1973): 144-148; Mackenzie, *CH* 40 (1971): 207.

24.15 ☛ González, Justo L. *A History of Christian Thought.* Volume II. *From Augustine to the Eve of the Reformation.* Nashville: Abingdon, 1987. (1971¹). Pp.361. I-20; B-3.
The material found in this volume covers the entire period of medieval history. Thus only the first 100 pages of it are relevant to the time period covered by this bibliography. Nevertheless, it is useful to the student of the early church. Chapter 2 discusses western theology after Augustine, while Chapter 3 recounts the story of eastern theology between the Fourth and Sixth Ecumenical Councils. These chapters are brief but solid summaries of an era less well studied than that prior to 381 CE. Unfortunately, the bibliography is overly short. (P)
✄ Collins, *WTJ* 35 (1973): 335-338; Mackenzie, *CH* 41 (1972): 404.

24.16 ☛ Hall, Stuart G. *Doctrine and Practice in the Early Church.* Grand Rapids: Eerdmans, 1991. Pp. x + 262. I-12; B-4.
This is a clear introduction to the main theological issues of the first five centuries. Hall explains the various conflicts and debates, outlines the issues, and identifies the key characters. The work is

detailed enough to be of value to the scholar, yet it is not beyond the scope of the beginning student, for Hall regularly explains terms, issues, and people, with brief comments in parentheses. Further, reference to literature is coded to selections in two important collections of sources (*A New Eusebius* §3.23 and *Creeds, Councils and Controversies* §3.24). A solid and usefully organized book.
⊰ Bray, *EQ* 65 (1993): 87-88; Volz, *CH* 61 (1992): 439.

24.17 Hanson, R.C.P. "The Doctrine of the Trinity Achieved in 381." *Scottish Journal of Theology* 36 (1983): 41-57.
While standard histories of the Arian Controversy have been little more than the biased "propaganda," Hanson contends that what happened at Constantinople in 381 CE was appropriate. While he is critical of the pro-Nicenes (particularly Athanasius), he asserts that pre-fourth century Christian concepts of the nature of God were tainted by pagan philosophy. He argues, also, that since Arius and those who followed him were rooted in that older tradition, their positions were unsatisfactory as well. What was taught by the Cappadocians at Constantinople with respect to Christ and the Holy Spirit was therefore a doctrinally positive development. (P)

24.18 Heron, A.I.C. *The Holy Spirit: The Holy Spirit in the Bible, the History of Christian Thought, and Recent Theology.* Philadelphia: Westminster, 1983. Pp. xi + 212. BI-2; AAI-3; I-7.
A short but excellent study of Christian pnuematology from its Old Testament origins through to the present, with pages 63–98 dealing specifically with the post-apostolic early church. In those pages, Heron gives brief overviews of the pneumatological teachings of Irenaeus, Tertullian, Origen, Cyril of Jerusalem, Athanasius, the Cappadocian Fathers, and Augustine. For those wanting an introduction of the subject of the Holy Spirit this is a good book; it gives a balanced view of the debate over whether the Spirit is a force or a person. The notes and the bibliography are both quite useful. (P)
⊰ Culpepper, *Faith and Mission* 2 (1984): 102-103; Dodd, *CTJ* 19 (1982): 100-103; Hunter, *Pneuma* 7 (1985): 165-166; McKim, *Reformed Review* 39 (1986): 137; Tinsley, *Theology* 87 (1984): 302-303.

24.19 Jaeger, Werner. *Early Christianity and the Greek Paideia.* London/ Oxford/New York: Oxford UP, 1961. Pp. 154. I-10.
Given originally as the Carl Newell Jackson Lectures for 1960, this book is simply a sketch of the impact of Greek thought on Christianity. It is a short, somewhat unsatisfactory but useful synopsis of the

Greek element in Christian ideas from the book of Acts through to
the Cappadocian Fathers. Although Jaeger rightly shows that
Christianity was not just an "oriental religion," he sometimes fails
to give adequate attention to the Hebraic, biblical thought of certain
early Christian theologians, in particular Origen. He also overlooks
a number of secondary works that were available to him when he
lectured and wrote. (P)
✀ Furnish, *Perkins Journal* 15 (1962): 36-37; F.C. Grant, *ATR* 44 (1962):
229-230; Schoedel, *CH* 31 (1962): 240-241.

24.20   Kelly, J.N.D. *Early Christian Doctrines.* 5th ed. London: Adam
and Charles Black, 1977. (1960[1]). Pp. 511. I-11.
Early Christian Doctrines remains one of the most important works
in the field, in part because the fifth edition is a thoroughly updated
revision. Developed as a chronological history, it covers virtually
all philosophical and theological issues that were important to the
early church. Part I discusses the background to doctrinal development, tradition, and scripture, and the scriptures themselves. Part II
describes and evaluates pre-Nicene theology. Part III examines issues
from Nicaea to Chalcedon, and Part IV is an epilogue on "The
Christian Hope." While Kelly makes his intellectual position clear—
he regards the development of orthodox doctrine positively— he is
outstandingly fair. His writing style is particularly clear. (P)
✀ Garrett, *R&E* 57 (1960): 85-86; Hope, *PSB* 53 (1960): 83; Wolf, *ATR*
42 (1960): 373-374.

24.21   Lohse, Bernard. *A Short History of Christian Doctrine.* Translated
by Ernest Stoeffler. Philadelphia: Fortress Press, 1980. Pp. xii +
304; I-29; B-7; CT-14.
Lohse's work is an attempt to demonstrate the importance of dogma
against scholars such as Harnack who have argued for a non-dogmatic
Christianity. He asserts that dogmatic pronouncements began during
Christ's ministry and became multiplied and more complex as time
went by. Usually, when new pronouncements were made, they
indicated that something was of vital import to the church. The
subjects covered in the body of this volume are dogma and the
history of dogma, the Trinity, christology, sin and grace, word and
sacrament, and justification. The last two chapters deal with
contemporary dogmatic problems. (P)

24.22   Louth, Andrew. *The Origins of the Christian Mystical Tradition.
From Plato to Denys.* Oxford: Clarendon Press, 1981. Pp. xvii+
215; I-5; AB-6.

Early Christian mysticism was influenced decisively by the Platonic concept of the soul's relation to God. Thus Louth reviews Platonic ideas from Plato to Plotinus with emphasis on Philo. He then discusses the mystic tradition in the Fathers and shows how the mystic and dogmatic traditions relate. He describes how Origen, Athanasius, Gregory of Nyssa, early Montanism, and Dionysius the Areopagite were characteristic of eastern Christian mysticism while Augustine was representative of mysticism in the west. Chapter IX does not fit the book's theme: it deals with "Platonic Mysticism and St. John of the Cross." Although short, the bibliography is useful, being broken down in relation to chapters. (P)

✂ Bouyer, *Sobornost* 4 (1982): 70-74; Cant, *ExT* 92 (1981): 318-319; Countryman, *SC* 3 (1983): 246-248; Elder, *ATR* 64 (1982): 243-245; Hardy, *Speculum* 57 (1982): 635-637; Largo, *JAAR* 50 (1982): 640-641; Lienhard, *TS* 43 (1982): 353-355; Macleod, *JTS* 33 (1982): 275-278; Monti, *CH* 52 (1983): 353; Rorem, *JR* 64 (1984): 247-249; Strousma, *Numen* 29 (1982): 278-282; Williams, *JEH* 33 (1982): 613-615; Anonymous, *Downside Review* 99 (1981): 230-233.

24.23 McGiffert, Arthur C. *A History of Christian Thought.* Vol. I. *Early and Eastern: From Jesus to John of Damascus.* New York/ London: Scribner's, 1932. Pp. xi + 352. I-8; B-12.

This book is rather out-of-date from the standpoint of more recent scholarship, but it is a generally useful survey of early Christian thought in the Eastern Roman Empire. It gives more detailed discussions of heretical movements and orthodox church fathers than do many works of similar nature. The chapter on heretics demonstrates the stress that Irenaeus placed on scripture, tradition, and episcopal succession as buttresses against heresy. The struggle with Montanism is seen as having strengthened the authority of the church. Except for those particularly interested in eastern Christianity as such, other books on early Christian thought are superior. (P)

24.24 McGiffert, Arthur C. *A History of Christian Thought.* Vol. II. *The West From Tertullian to Erasmus.* New York/ London: Scribner's, 1933. Pp. xii + 420. I-8; B-16.

This book is also somewhat out of date, and much of it does not relate to the early church. Nonetheless, the first six chapters are useful. They deal with Tertullian, Cyprian, Arnobius, Jerome, Augustine, Pelagius, the Semi-Pelagians, and Gregory the Great. The attention shown to Augustine is properly extensive. That given to Pelagius and the Semi-Pelagians gives a clear picture of their thinking and their controversy with Augustine. For a background study to later western developments in church history, Volume II remains valuable. (P)

24.25   Meijering, E.P. *Orthodoxy and Platonism in Athanasius: Synthesis or Antithesis?* Leiden: Brill, 1968. Pp. iii + 201. B-2; NI-3.
This work is a three-part analysis of Athanasius' use of Platonic thought. In Part I Meijering evaluates the major works of Athanasius and discusses the character of his apologetic treatises and the *Orations contra Arianos.* In Part II he examines the relationship between orthodoxy and Platonism as seen by Athanasius. In Part III he looks at "the reappearance of some of Athanasius' questions in the thought of some modern Protestant theologians." He concludes that Athanasius was not unjustified in expressing his faith in Platonic language. While a fine study for the scholar, Meijering's use of long, untranslated passages of Greek makes it difficult for the ordinary reader. (P)
≫< Armstrong, *JTS* 21 (1970): 189-190; Holland, *SJT* 24 (1971): 485-487.

24.26   Nock, Arthur D. *Early Gentile Christianity and Its Hellenistic Background.* New York/Evanston/London: Harper & Row/ Harper Torchbooks, 1964. Pp. xxi + 155. B-4.
Nock gives a short résumé of the Hellenistic world view and religions which served as the intellectual and social context for the development of Christianity as a "missionary religion." He shows how conversion to Christianity differed from conversion to other cults. Christian concepts are compared both to Hellenistic ones and to the actual practice of Christianity itself. Some attention is given to discussing Christianity's relationship with the various Hellenistic philosophical movements. After a brief note on the resurrection, Nock evaluates the relationship of the mystery religions to the Christian sacraments during the period from the second century into the fourth. (P)
≫< Reumann, *JBL* 83 (1964): 424-426.

24.27   Norris, Richard A. *God and World in Early Christian Theology.* New York: Seabury, 1965. Pp. x +177. B-5.
By focusing on how early Christian writers tried to maintain fidelity to the Bible while remaining in harmony with the philosophical outlook which they held in common with their pagan contemporaries, Norris illustrates the significance of primitive Christian doctrine to modern theology. He discusses Greek and Hellenistic cosmology, Justin and Platonism, Irenaeus, and the Gnostic Problem, Tertullian's Latin perspective, Origen's new Christian Platonism, and the overall achievement of the Christian church. The value of this book is that

it deals clearly with problems of early Christian thinking. The bibliography is helpful, particularly for non-specialists. (P)

❧ Bromiley, *CT* 10 (1966): 37; Floyd, *Downside Review* 85 (1967): 350-351; R.M. Grant, *JR* 46 (1966): 66-67.

24.28 O'Meara, Dominic, ed. *Neoplatonism and Christian Thought.* Albany: State University of New York Press, 1982. Pp. xviii + 297. I-5

Only the first two parts of this book relate to the early church. Part I is a series of articles on patristic thought which discuss "the Platonic and Christian Ulysses," "Origen's doctrine of the Trinity and some later Neoplatonic theories," "a Neoplatonic commentary on the Christian Trinity: Marius Victorinus," and "the Neoplatonism of St. Augustine." Part II includes four essays on later Neoplatonic views of "divine creation and the eternity," one on two Neoplatonic Christian commentators of Aristotle, one on links between the Pseudo-Dionysius and Proclus, and "the problem of general concepts in Neoplatonic and Byzantine thought." Although all these essays are for specialists, they demonstrate the major impact of Neoplatonic on early post-apostolic Christianity. (P)

❧ Kenney, *JAAR* 54 (1986): 185-186; Sharples, *RS* 20 (1984): 705-708; Zeyl, *CSR* 12 (1983): 365-366.

24.29 Osborn, Eric. *The Beginning of Christian Philosophy.* Cambridge: Cambridge UP, 1982. Pp. xiv + 321. B-16; I-3; BI-2; AAI-10 MAI-2.

Using the tools of analytical philosophy, Osborn elucidates specific questions which were central to the thinking of Justin, Irenaeus, Tertullian, and Clement of Alexandria. These questions relate to God, man, and his freedom, the world and its maker, history and continuity, and "the word made flesh." Osborn argues that the second century was the most innovative period in the history of the early church, a period which should not be read in terms of the fourth century. Organized in a fashion which makes it easy to study, this is a most informative work. (P)

❧ Downing, *Theology* 85 (1982): 292-293; Hanson, *ExT* 93 (1982): 185-186; Hinson, *R&E* 79 (1982): 705-706; Hoffmann, *PBR* 2 (1983): 125-128; Olsen, *TS* 43 (1982): 552-553; Sibley, *JAAR* 51 (1983): 518-519; Stead, *RS* 18 (1982): 513-515; Whittaker, *SC* 4 (1984): 60-62; Williams, *JEH* 35 (1984): 145-147; Williams, *JR* 64 (1984): 379-380; Wright, *SJT* 36 (1983): 418-420.

24.30 Patterson, L.G. *God and History in Early Christian Thought.* New York: Seabury, 1967. Pp. ix + 181. B-15.

Designed as a companion to R.A. Norris's *God and the World in Early Christianity,* this volume is largely a review of fairly recent studies of Patristic writers. Patterson points out that the term history was not used in the New Testament despite the "historical nature" of Judaism and Christianity. He discusses the period from Justin Martyr to Origen, deals at length with Tertullian and Origen, and evaluates Eusebius as a historian. Finally, he analyses the "Crisis of the Christian Empire" from Augustine to Gregory the Great. From the standpoint of those interested in the relationship of history to Christianity, this is a very useful work. (P)

24.31   Pelikan, Jaroslav. *Development of Christian Doctrine: Some Historical Perspectives.* New Haven and London: Yale UP, 1969. Pp. xiii + 149. I-3.
        Given originally as the St. Thomas More lectures at Yale in 1965, this small volume discusses the problem of doctrinal development in Christianity largely from the perspectives of Newman and Dewart. It focuses on historical study and, in particular, on "the task of Patristic research." In Part Two, Pelikan deals with a number of questions relating to the development of the doctrine of original sin, Mariology, and the Filioque doctrine; and it is here that he takes a careful look at various Patristic sources. He holds that "one must refine dogma by history." (P)
        ✂ Musurillo, *TS* 30 (1969): 500-501; Norwood, *CT* 13 (May 13, 1969): 15-16; Wiles, *JTS* 21 (1970): 255-257.

24.32   Russell, J.B., and Jeffery Burton. *Satan: The Early Christian Tradition.* Ithaca: Cornell UP, 1981. Pp. 258. I-6; B&W-13; B-11; AB-12.
        Russell studies the problem of evil, Satan, and the demons in early Christian thinking. In this volume, he shows that the early church did not deal adequately with evil from a rational standpoint. Yet Gnostics, Apologists, Irenaeus, Tertullian, Clement of Alexandria, Origen, and Augustine did discuss the devil, demons, and the nature of evil. Russell reviews their thinking and shows how Augustine's concept of evil has been the major one influencing western Christian thought since the fifth century. Finally, Russell attempts to deal philosophically with evil in the context of the Christian doctrine of the benevolence of God. He holds that both God and the devil exist. (P)
        ✂ Boswell, *Speculum* 60 (1985): 458-461; Davis, *TT* 39 (1982): 366-367; Ferguson, *CH* 52 (1983): 202-203; Hinson, *R&E* 79 (1982): 540-541; Kelly, *JR* 67 (1987): 518-528; Pelikan, *Commentary* 83 (1987): 63-66;

Peters, *AHR* 87 (1982): 1043-1044; Smalley, *JEH* 33 (1982): 447-448; Smith, *JAAR* 55 (1987): 410-411.

24.33   Swete, Henry B. *The Holy Spirit in the Ancient Church.* London: Macmillan, 1912. Pp. viii + 429. BI-1; SI-3; AAI-2; Greek and Latin Index-3.

Although Swete regards his work as a history rather than a theological study, he gives a detailed account of Christian pneumatological doctrine from sub-apostolic times to that of Gregory the Great in the west and John of Damascus in the east. He holds that the ecclesiastical development of doctrine was Spirit guided. Thus, developed orthodox theology is based on an ongoing revelation of truth. Nonetheless, Swete gives due attention to the pneumatology of various heresies—Montanism, Monarchianism, and Arianism— plus the differences between Antiochene and Alexandrian teachings about the Holy Spirit. There are two additional "notes" on the *Didache* and the *Odes of Solomon.* (P)

24.34   ☞ Urban, Linwood. *A Short History of Christian Thought.* New York/Oxford: Oxford UP, 1986. Pp. xv + 319. I-13; B-14.

Although this is a general history of Christian thought, Chapters II, III, IV, and V contain much information on doctrinal developments and heresies within the early church. The topics covered therein are the Trinity, the Incarnation, the Atonement, and the Fall and Original Sin. Of them, the chapter dealing with the Fall and Original Sin is particularly instructive. In it, Urban gives a detailed account of how early Christians regarded the origin and nature of sin. Explanations of all doctrines are given in the light of modern theology. Extremely well written and easy to understand, this book contains an excellent bibliography. (P)

✂ Heft, *TS* 48 (1987): 585-586; Hinson, *R&E* 83 (1986): 651-652; Maanschreck, *CH* 56 (1987): 144-145; Nutt, *Interpretation* 41 (1987): 106; Patterson, *ATR* 69 (1987): 191-193; TeSelle, *CRBR* 1 (1988): 339-340.

24.35   ☞ Wiles, Maurice. *The Christian Fathers.* 2d ed. London: SCM, 1977. (1966[1]). Pp. 190. B-2; I-2.

Wiles provides a summary of the beliefs of the early Christian writers down to 451 CE, covering the following topics: Image of God; Divine Christ; Incarnation; Sin and Salvation; Sacraments; Church; and Ethics. Wiles is better known for more controversial works, in which the Fathers are handled with less sympathy (*The Making of Christian Doctrine* [§8.21] and *The Remaking of Christian Doctrine*), and he reviews some of his own work in the preface.

With the 5-page biographical guide to the Fathers, this work offers a clear introductory sketch of patristic theology and its theologians, with frequent probing questions.

✂ Wright, *Churchman,* 80 (1966): 144-145.

25
WOMEN

In the last two decades an examination of women's roles in history has exploded in the field of biblical and early Christian studies as it has in most other areas of the humanities and social sciences. For the first time, adequate attention is being to be paid to those roles. From a scholarly standpoint that is all to the good: it is important that we obtain a more holistic view of what really took place in times past, and we must never forget that women, though comprising half the population, never had anything like half the voice in public affairs and in literary production.

As far as the early Christian, post-apostolic church is concerned, it is still true, however, that our knowledge of the roles of women in early Christian times is still inadequate. As feminist scholars often emphasize, the data from which studies can be drawn are very limited. Most of the documents that we have were written by men and reflect male biases. Furthermore, the genre of most accounts written in the Roman world does not contribute to our knowledge of women. The majority of authors wrote from within what is commonly called the "great man" tradition of historical interpretation. So when men did discuss women in writing, they focused on exceptional individuals in the same way that they did when writing about men. And since men commonly exercised more authority both within the church and in the larger Roman world, there simply were far more prominent men than there were women. The perspectives of social history, which have become so significant since the Second World War, did not exist in that world. Thus many of the questions which are asked about women, children, and even about men today would have been meaningless to persons living during the first centuries of the Christian era. Because of a paucity of information, caused in large part by the worldview of those living in Roman times, our knowledge of the roles of women in the early church will probably always remain incomplete, and many questions about those roles will remain unanswerable.

Nonetheless, many of the works which have been produced in recent years do give us a clearer picture of women in early Christianity. From these works, it seems that there was a marked devolution in the status of women in the Christian community after the apostolic age. The New Testament is surprisingly positive towards them, taken in the context of the times and the cultures in which it was written. Even considering the subordinationist passages in the Pauline writings at such places as 1 Corinthians 11:2-16; 14:33,34; and 1 Timothy 2:9-15, women fare rather well. Besides the important roles that they play in the gospel accounts, the Apostle Paul, who is often regarded as a "male chauvinist" by radical feminists, penned the famous egalitarian passage at Galatians 3:28 and may even have recognized a woman as an apostle at Romans 16:7. But as Jean Daniélou demonstrates in his *The Ministry of Women in the Early Church* [§25.17] the New Testament attitude toward women was gradually replaced by one which was far more negative. Tertullian's works show that in the West at least, they came to be seen as more easily tempted by the devil and therefore less spiritual than men.

The reason for this change in attitude may be explained in part by the growing routinization of church governance under a male hierarchy. But what seems far more important is the fact that churchmen fell more completely under the influence of popular attitudes towards women which were current in the larger Roman world. That world emphasized the importance of woman as wife and child bearer. Hence she could not be regarded as man's equal in the political and social fields. She therefore came to be seen more fully as subordinate to him. In consequence, those passages of Scripture which stressed her subordination were quoted ever more frequently in the writings of the Fathers, and Eve's seduction by the serpent in Eden was often used to demonstrate female weakness to temptation.

Since maleness was regarded as superior to femaleness in a spiritual sense, a significant body of Christians gradually developed the concept of the "male woman"—the idea that virtue was a male characteristic to be emulated by truly spiritual women. Out of this concept, perhaps along with a desire to gain both greater fleshly and spiritual freedom, arose an emphasis on the value of female virginity (along with that of male virginity or at least chastity). Yet this did not come about without some opposition, as David Hunter shows in his article "Resistance to the Virginal Ideal in Late Fourth Century Rome: The Case of Jovinian" [§14.9]. Furthermore, there is a real question as to whether, by pursuing a life of celibacy, early Christian women did become more independent. The evidence on that score is incomplete and rather mixed.

Another problem that the study of women in early Christianity faces is the fact that the subject has become so thoroughly politicized in our day. It is therefore uncertain just how much accurate information one can get from studies on either side of the "woman's issue." Certainly much of what has been written by feminist scholars in recent years has served to redress the balance against attitudes expressed about women in the past. But perhaps it is important to note the cautions and reservations of Susanne Heine [§25.25] who holds that some feminist scholars, even prominent ones such as Elaine Pagels [§14.16- 14.17], have been driven too far by theories not adequately substantiated by the evidence. While bibliographers as such should probably take no stand on this debate, it is important that the student be made aware of it.

A final point needs to be stressed here about how to approach the topic of women in early Christianity. Remember that second through seventh century Christians did not live in a vacuum; they were members of the larger Roman world. As such, they were greatly affected by the laws, morals, and mores of that world. Thus students should familiarize themselves with the general roles and legal status of women under Roman rule. Consequently, they may well wish to begin study of early Christian women by the examination of outstanding works such as Jane Gardner's *Women in Roman Law and Society* [§25.22]. (P)

25.1   🏛 Brock, Sebastian P., and Susan Ashbrook Harvey. Translators and introducers. *Holy Women of the Syrian Orient.* The Transformation of the Classical Heritage 13. Berkeley/Los Angeles: University of California Press, 1987. Pp. xii + 197. NI-3; B&W-1; AB-11; M-1.

This book, which is a fresh translation into English from the Syriac originals of the hagiographic accounts of the lives of Syrian female saints, is prefaced by a general introduction to the subject. The accounts include those of Mary, the niece of Qidun (Ch. 1); Pelagia of Antioch (Ch. 2); a selection of Persian martyrs, that includes Martha, Tarbo, the Martyrs of Kirkuk, the History of Karka d-Beth Slokh, Thekla and companions, and Anahid (Ch. 3); the women martyrs of Najran (Ch. 4); examples from the "Lives of the Eastern Saints" by John of Ephesus (Ch. 5); Anastasia (Ch. 6); Febronia (Ch. 7); and Shirin (Ch. 8). Ranging from personal eyewitness accounts to more fantastically elaborated romances, the stories concerning these holy women are presented to redress the imbalance in the attention previously given to male saints from this same region. The accounts are distributed over the period between the fourth and seventh centuries CE. The introduction by the editors is a clear and coherent entrée to what might otherwise be a difficult and remote subject. (S)

✂ Ward, *New Blackfriars* 69 (1988): 403-404; Wickham, *JTS* 40 (1989): 353.

25.2 🏛 Clark, Elizabeth A., ed. *Women in the Early Church.* Wilmington, Delaware: Michael Glazier, 1983. Message of the Fathers of the Church 13. Pp. 260. B-2.

With a short eleven-page introduction, and a collection of passages largely from leading orthodox men in early Christianity. The passages are grouped in five thematic chapters, dealing with the following issues: (1) creation, fall, and marriage; (2) Apocryphal Acts and Martyrdom; (3) asceticism; (4) women in the wider world; and (5) women as models and mentors. Brief comments place the passages in context, thus aiding the beginning student.

✂ Cunningham, *TS* 45 (1984): 771-772; Dekar, *Theodolite* 7 (1986): 43-44; DeLeeuw, *JES* 23 (1986): 128-130; Holmes, *Fides et Historia* 17 (1984): 108-109; Wilson-Kastner, *CSR* 14 (1985): 97-98; Yanney, *CCR* 5 (1984): 126-127.

25.3 🏛 Clark, Elizabeth A. *The Life of Melania the Younger.* Studies in Women and Religion 14. New York: Edwin Mellen, 1984. Pp. ii + 299. B-32; I-7.

Clark's translation is based on an examination of Greek and Latin manuscripts and a careful evaluation of the information surrounding this fifth-century ascetic woman. The translation and commentary are most interesting. The *Life* shows how important the renunciation of sexuality and severe asceticism were becoming to Roman Christian women. It tells much about Christian liturgy, piety, and theological disputes, as well as about many other aspects of life during that period. Although Melania is presented as committedly "orthodox," Clark says orthodoxy during the period was hard to determine. (P)

✂ Callam, *TS* 47 (1986): 190-191; H. Chadwick, *JEH* 38 (1987): 488-489; Frankforter, *CH* 55 (1986): 87-88.

25.4 🏛 Kraemer, Ross S., ed. *Maenads, Martyrs, Matrons, Monastics: A Sourcebook on Women's Religions in the Greco-Roman World.* Philadelphia: Fortress, 1988. Pp. xxix + 429. C-8; B&W-52; NI-4; Divine Names Index-3.

In this very useful collection of primary sources on the participation of women in various aspects of religious cult and practice in the ancient world, Kraemer offers 135 numbered passages that are largely taken from existing English translations (e.g. Loeb texts, the Ante-Nicene Fathers series). Although her purview is cast over "pagan" (i.e. Greek and Roman) cults, Judaism, and Christianity, the texts are grouped neither chronologically nor according to one of those large religious persuasions, but rather according to broad thematic categories (e.g. "Rituals and Festivals," the actual activities

of the women themselves, participation of women in religious offices
and conversion). The work is only as good as the original source
translations, but its utility is considerably enhanced by the inclusion
in one collection of extracts from the Mishnah, magical papyri,
curse tablets, papyrological sources, and inscriptions. (S)

25.5 🏛 LaPorte, Jean. *The Role of Women in Early Christianity*. Studies
in Women and Religion 7. New York/Toronto: Edwin Mellen, 1982.
Pp. 189. BI-2; NI-3; MAI-1; Names of Women Index-1.
In this survey of the original Greek and Latin sources LaPorte
covers five major areas: women in martyrdom, women in conjugal
life, women in contemplative life, women in the ministry, and
women as symbol. In each of these chapters, LaPorte offers a brief
resumé by way of preface and then gives the substance of each of
the sources in translation (again, along with brief contextual remarks).
Neither a sourcebook as such, nor a synthetic monograph, LaPorte's
brief book falls somewhere between the two and yet manages to
offer a rather good synoptic view of the whole subject, as well as a
convenient survey of the primary sources. (S)
✂ Bonner, *JEH* 36 (1985): 139-140; Clark, *RSR* 9 (1983): 381; D'Angelo,
SC 5 (1985-1986): 55-57; Kilmartin, *TS* 44 (1983): 714-715; Marshall-
Green, *R&E* 85 (1988): 581.

25.6 Aspegren, Kerstin. *The Male Woman: A Feminine Ideal in the
Early Church*. Edited by René Kieffer. Acta Universitatis
Upsaliensis, Uppsala Women's Studies, A: Women in Religion 4.
Uppsala: Uppsala UP, 1990. Pp. 189. B.
An adumbrated and fragmentary manuscript left to us by the
premature death of Aspegren. What the finished work would have
looked like would have been something of a treat, but what is left
(which is well edited by René Kieffer and includes an appendix on
Methodius of Olympus by Ragnar Holte, Aspegren's supervisor) is
well worth the read. After defining what she means by gender
(femaleness and manliness) and "equivalence" and "equality" of
treatment, Aspegren advances to chapters that treat the ideologies
of Plato and Aristotle on women. In the next chapter, on Stoicism,
she demonstrates the fundamental ideological shift that the Stoics
forged, subordinating both household and society to the primacy of
the relationship of the married couple. The succeeding chapters on
women's real position in Hellenistic society and on the ideas of
Philo are less successful. The core of her thesis, centered on the
figure of Thekla (ch. 7) and on the female-male transition (how
"good" women had to be interpreted as "becoming manly"), centered

on Perpetua (ch. 8), are well done. This is as convincing a demonstration as any of the power of a dominant ideology of "manliness" and how it was assumed even by independent women. (S)

25.7   Bavel, T.J. van. "Augustine's View on Women." *Augustiniana* 39 (1989): 5-53.

In a thorough review of all the significant texts, presented both in the original and in translation, van Bavel deals with the subject of the natural inferiority of women, the subordination of women within marriage, the inscription of good women as "virile," and the new egalitarian requirements of Christian moral behavior within marriage imposed on both men and women. Van Bavel's interpretation is frankly favorable to Augustine, as an attempt to see him as a man of his times and, in the view of this reviewer, perhaps too sympathetic an interpreter of the effects of Augustine's statements (excusing them via their theological import). Nonetheless, the layout of the original texts is scrupulous, the translations frank and accurate, and the presentation of the evidence such that any reader could fairly make up his or her own mind, whatever van Bavel's own views. (S)

25.8   Buckley, Jorunn Jacobsen. *Female Fault and Filfillment in Gnosticism.* Chapel Hill: University of North Carolina Press, 1986. Pp. xv + 180. I-6.

Buckley's work is a careful, scholarly examination of six Gnostic documents made to determine how they deal with the issue of the feminine both in female deities and women. Discussed largely in relation to their roles in the Genesis creation accounts, mythologies surrounding females are broken down into three models: the female as the lower or middle element in a three-part schema, the female as a stage to be overcome (the male being the goal), and the female split into a higher and lower image of herself. Buckley makes no attempt to classify Gnostic females according to simplifying formulas, however, but treats them individually, in their own contexts. Significant in her study is her emphasis on the importance of rituals within Gnosticism. She asserts that much can be learned from those rituals to help understand their soteriological systems in relation to women. (P)

⊰ Aune, *History of Religions* 27 (1987): 224; Good, *CRBR* 1 (1988): 299-301; Good, *JR* 68 (1988): 330-331; McGuire, *JTS* 40 (1989): 234-238; Williams, *JAAR* 56 (1988): 767-770.

25.9   Burrus, Virginia. *Chastity as Autonomy: Women in the Stories of the Apocryphal Acts.* Studies in Women and Religion 23. Lewiston, NY/Queenston, ON: Edwin Mellen, 1987. Pp. 136. I.

Beginning with a historical review of the scholarship regarding the principal influences on the composition of the Apocryphal Acts (primarily literary ones stemming from the Hellenistic "Romantic Novel" and from the world of oral folklore), Burrus passes on to a structural analysis of the content of the Acts themselves (mainly under the influence of Propp) with attention to their peculiar focus on female main characters. It is the latter aspect of the Acts, along with ethnographic parallels, that allows Burrus to argue for a female authorship of the documents ("authorship" taken here in a broad sense). Finally, in her "socio-historical interpretation" she concludes by showing how the Acts reflect tensions in which women were caught up in high imperial society: their seclusion in the house, the demands made on them to marry and obey, the restriction on their social and economic activities, and how the stories use chastity as a sort of ideological leverage by which women could assert some autonomy over their lives as against the overpowering repression of the social norms of the time. (S)

✂ Pervo, *CBQ* 51 (1989): 364-365; Pervo, *CRBR* 1 (1989): 300-301; Smith, *Ethics* 99 (1989): 692.

25.10   Cameron, Averil, and Amélie Kuhrt. *Images of Women in Antiquity.* London-Canberra: Croom Helm, 1983. Pp. xi + 323. B-17; NI-3; B&W-17; SI-2; T-13.

One of the first attempts in English to collate the work of new feminist scholars on the field. The first two sections of the book include papers on perceptions and power relationships, the third covers women at home, the fourth and fifth sections provide materials on biology and birth, a sixth section contains information on women's economic roles, and the seventh, and perhaps the most relevant, deals with religion and cult. Subject areas covered, beyond Graeco-Roman societies, are those of the ancient Near East (Egypt, Assyria, Nuzi, and the Hittites) as well as those of Byzantium (Judith Herrin) and the Celtic world (Wendy Davis). Many of the contributions have now been supplanted by more recent and comprehensive research (e.g., the excellent chapter by Susan Ashbrook Harvey on women in early Syrian Christianity is now replaced by her book [§17.11]). Of continuing interest are the chapters by Susan Walker on housing and domestic architecture, on infanticide by Sarah Pomeroy, and on wealth by Riet van Bremen. (S)

✂ Mortley, *Journal of Religious History* 13 (1985): 306.

25.11   Cantarella, E. *Pandora's Daughters. The Role of Women in Greek and Roman Antiquity.* Translated by Maureen B. Fant. Foreword by Mary K. Lefkowitz. Baltimore/London: John Hopkins UP, 1987. Pp. xv + 229. I-9.

Set in a broad historical context, *Pandora's Daughters* is the first history of women in ancient Greece and Rome to be written from a legal perspective. Cantarella shows how literary, anecdotal, and juridical sources can and cannot be used to determine what Greek and Roman men thought about women and how they treated them. She deals with Plato and Aristotle's attitudes towards women, the role of women in classical literature, homosexuality, and love in Greece and with the hypothesis of matriarchy, the periods of the Roman kings and Republic, the Empire, and Byzantine times. Although not specifically concerned with women in the early Church, it gives the broader historical, cultural, and legal context in which they lived. To be used with caution. (P)

✄ Gold, *CW* 82 (1988-89): 454-455; Jones, *AncPhil* 8 (1988): 138-141; King, *JHS* 108 (1988): 248; Pomeroy, *AHR* 93 (1988): 674-675; Schuller, *Gnomen* 60 (1988): 445-447.

25.12   Castelli, Elisabeth. "Virginity and Its Meaning for Women's Sexuality in Early Christianity." *Journal of Feminist Studies in Religion* 2 (1982): 61-88.

Beginning with the thesis that recent feminist scholarship has attempted to explain the reasons for the attraction of ascetic forms of Christianity to women, Castelli essays both a survey of the problem and an answer. She begins with the problems posed by the sources, almost all of them being male-authored accounts, and then she outlines the difficulties imposed on modern interpreters who want to ask about the female experience of asceticism and virginity. She closely ties the rise in the cult of asceticism and virginity in the fourth century to the Church's political ascendancy and to the concurrent lapse in the ideal of the martyr/saint. She then reviews the ideology of virginity and the concurrent rhetorical disparagement of earthly marriage. She emphasizes how little can be known of the practical effects or experiences of this ideology as felt by women themselves. Castelli concludes that the ideology of virginity was no less domesticating and circumscribing of women's sexuality than was the ideology of marriage—that this ideology simply theologized existing oppressive patriarchal ideologies of a woman's sexuality, and therefore called upon her "to participate in a profound self-abnegation, self-denial, even self-destruction." (S)

25.13   Clark, Elizabeth A. *Jerome, Chrysostom, and Friends: Essays and Translations.* New York: Edwin Mellen, 1979. Pp. + 254. I-6.

By reviewing and translating some of the works of John Chrysostom and Jerome, Clark attempts to analyze the attitudes of these two major early church figures with respect to women and sexuality. As she states, an examination of the sources shows the ambivalence of Chrysostom to women despite his personal warmth to his friend, supporter, and confidant, the deaconess Olympias. In addition, Clark also discusses Chrysostom's condemnation of the idea that celibates of both sexes should live in communities together or become involved in "spiritual marriages." As a whole, the book illustrates the thesis that there was an elevation of status for celibate women within patristic Christianity, but not for married ones. The oft repeated theory that early Christianity exalted women's status in general is not borne out by the evidence. (P)

⨞ Bromiley, *TSF Bulletin* 5 (1982): 22; Quitslund, *Horizons* 14 (1987): 150-152; Rexine, *Orthodox Thought and Life* 4 (1987): 56-58; Winslow, *ATR* 64 (1982): 239-242; Anonymous, *CCR* 9 (1988): 90-91.

25.14   Clark, Elizabeth A. "Ascetic Renunciation and Feminine Advancement: A Paradox of Late Ancient Christianity." *Anglican Theological Review* 63 (1981): 240-257.

Upper-class women in late antiquity who practiced ascetic renunciation followed much the same path as ascetic men. Although certain limitations were placed on such women, particularly if they lived with parents or husbands, they were far freer than were ordinary married women who continued to co-habit with their husbands. The Church, or better stated, a life of renunciation in the Church, offered these women personal liberty to express themselves publicly and to maintain control over their power, wealth, and piety. Clark asserts that they would have been hidden to history had they followed the traditional domestic pattern. (P)

25.15   Clark, Elizabeth A. *Ascetic Piety and Women's Faith: Essays on Late Ancient Christianity.* Studies in Women and Religion 20. Lewiston, NY: Edwin Mellen, 1986. Pp. xv + 425.

This volume is a series of essays presented by Clark and, in one case, by Clark and Diane Hatch, to various audiences. Thus they vary in style. They are thematically consistent, however, and do give a picture of Christian female piety in late Roman times. They demonstrate that by becoming ascetics, women were no longer the familial "cement" that they had been in earlier times. Therefore, they were changing the nature of society. Yet this change did not come easily, and some proponents of the celibate life, such as Jerome and Augustine, came under sharp attack as "heretics" by certain Christian writers. (P)

✂ Hunter, *TS* 49 (1988): 380-381; Warren, *Mystics Quarterly* 16 (1990): 52-53; Yound, *JTS* 39 (1988): 668.

25.16 Cooper, Kate. "Insinuations of Womanly Influence: An Aspect of the Christianization of the Roman Aristocracy." *Journal of Roman Studies* 82 (1992): 150-64

Cooper's article is another in the trend to direct searching questions at the assumption, common at least since Harnack, that women were the vanguard of the Christianization of the empire, especially of its élite ranks (see, e.g., Salzman §25.43). Rather than question the actual numbers involved or the numeric trends, Cooper is more concerned to analyze the literary tropes of influential women in the Christianization process. She points out how these literary sources, whatever else they might say, have little or no reference to actual women or the real-life experiences of women of the time. Rather, they were part of a "Roman male discourse about female power [that] served more often than not as a rhetorical strategy within competition for power among males themselves." Statements about women and their influence were used either to shore up a man's honor or to shame him, to bring him into disrespect and so to derogate from his power. Detailed analysis of some of Augustine's letters (especially *Letter*, 262, regarding the matron Ecdicia) is offered in support. (S)

25.17 Daniélou, Jean. *The Ministry of Women in the Early Church.* Translated by Glyn Simon. 2d ed. Leighton Buzzard, Beds: Faith Press, 1974. Pp. 31.

A short but useful examination of the various roles played by women in the early church, particularly in apostolic times. Although nothing is said about women's roles during the ministry of Jesus, much attention is given to them in connection with Paul's evangelism and the churches which he founded. While Daniélou argues that women could not teach in Christian congregations, he shows that they held specific ministries as evangelists and prophets. He also discusses the importance of widows in the church and indicates how later writers, in particular Tertullian, attempted to downplay the importance of women in the apostolic church because of male chauvinism. (P)

25.18 Davies, John G. "Deacons, Deaconesses and the Minor Orders in the Patristic Period." *Journal of Ecclesiastical History* 14 (1963): 1-15.

The title of this article is somewhat misleading. Only the first section of five and a third pages of it is devoted to the subject of women deacons or deaconesses. The remainder of the article deals with the rise of minor male orders. The first section is important, however, as a survey of Romans 16:1 and 1 Timothy 3:2, the only New Testament passages which may relate directly to an order or proto-order of deaconesses. That section also discusses Pliny's letter to Trajan, which mentions "two slave girls called ministers," who may have been deaconesses, and the Syriac Didascalia, which defines the duties of deaconesses precisely. (P)

25.19   Davies, Steven L. *The Revolt of the Widows. The Social World of the Apocryphal Acts.* Carbondale, IL: Southern Illinois UP, 1980. Pp. x + 139. I-5; B-4.

A study of the five major apocryphal Acts, along with the Acts of Xanthippe and Polyxena. Davies thinks that the Acts were authored by and intended for a body of women in the church who emphasized sexual abstinence. These Acts reflect a period slightly earlier than the time of their composition (late 2nd/early 3rd centuries), during which the leadership in the church was shifting from the charismatic to the more structured (and patriarchal).

    ⊰< Clark, *CH* 51 (1982): 335-336; Pervo, *SC* 2 (1982): 47-49; Osiek, *CBQ* 44 (1982): 318-319; Phillips, *Horizons* 9 (1982): 353-354; Wiens, *JBL* 101 (1982): 470-471.

25.20   Fiorenza, Elizabeth Schüssler. *In Memory of Her: A Feminist Reconstruction of Christian Origins.* New York: Crossroads, 1983. Pp. xxv + 351. BI-5.

Taking as her cue as the notice of the anonymous woman of Mark 14:9, Fiorenza essayed a three-pronged attack on the "patriarchalist" theology that has provided the orthodox interpretation of the history of the Jesus movement and the Christian church to the west. In part one, entitled "Seeing-Naming-Reconstituting," Fiorenza lays the theoretical foundations for the work proper by surveying various feminist theoretical approaches to re-doing biblical (and especially New Testament) criticism, and by proposing her own "hermeneutics of suspicion." Rather meliorist in her interpretation of the positions and power of women within the original "Jesus movement" (Chs. 4-5), she forcefully analyzes the deliberate re-reading and forgetting of this reality beginning with Pauline ideology (Ch. 6). No doubt correctly, she sees the embedding of the early missionary movements

and ecclesiastical structure of the early church in the household
and family as producing a patriarchal ideology, most clearly manifest
in the so-called household codes, that quite deliberately dis-
empowered women (Chs. 7-8). Fiorenza's work is very strong and
convincing in its negative critique of the formation of this "patriarchal
ideology," but much less persuasive (to this excerptor, at least) in
its claims to be able to reconstruct a prior alternative world of
women behind this malignant veil of power. Manifesting all the
exhilaration of a work that was, and is, revolutionary in intent, it
also shares the faults of any rebellious rhetoric (e.g., a frequent
leaping to unwarranted conclusions). Any deliberate reconstruction
of the past that is designedly so committed risks merely mapping
its own constructions. The dangers were already signalled in her
appeal to Alex Haley's *Roots* as a model of reconstructing the past,
a model which, alas, has turned out to be an utterly fictitious fraud.
(S)

%< Babcock, *SC* 4 (1984): 177-184; Barton, *Theology* 88 (1985): 134-137;
Grant, *JR* 65 (1985): 83-88; Harrison, *Horizons* 11 (1984): 150-153; Hughes,
ATR 69 (1987): 287-299; King, *RS* 20 (1984): 699-702; Koening, *Horizons*
11 (1984): 144-146; Kraemer, *JBL* 104 (1985): 722-725; Kraemer, *RSR* 11
(1985): 6-9; Mercadante, *TSF Bulletin* 8 (1985): 28-30; Murphy-O'Connor,
Revue biblique 91 (1984): 287-294; O'Connor, *CC* 100 (1983): 1114-1117;
Padgett, *EQ* 58 (1986): 121-132; Perkins, *Horizons* 11 (1984): 142-144;
Ruether, *Horizons* 11 (1984): 146-150; Schneiders, *USQR* 39 (1984): 236-
240; Scroggs, *CTSR* 75 (1985): 27-30; West, *RSR* 11 (1985): 1-4; [response
by Fiorenza, *Horizons* 11 (1984): 154-157; *Anima* 10 (1984): 109-112].

25.21   Forrester Church, F. "Sex and Salvation in Tertullian." *Harvard
Theological Review* 68 (1975): 83-101.
Beginning with the classic text from *De cultu feminarum* about
women being "the gateway of the Devil," Forrester Church essays
a strikingly iconoclastic exegesis of the theme of women in Tertullian.
Despite overwhelming evidence to the contrary, Forrester Church
claims that Tertullian's text has been misinterpreted as a species of
misogynism, that Tertullian does not identify women wholly with
flesh, and does not classify "flesh" as so inferior to spirit as to
denigrate women as such—so that Tertullian "believed women and
men to be equally capable" of spiritual liberation. This conclusion
seems dubious, and the argument that precedes even more so. But
if the researcher wishes to read a strained effort to present Tertullian
in a somewhat more favorable light in respect to women and
sexuality, then this is as good an attempt as any. (S)

25.22   ☛ Gardner, Jane F. *Women in Roman Law and Society.* London/

Sydney: Croom Helm, 1986. Bloomington, IN: Indiana UP, 1991. Pp. 281. B-10; I-5.

This has become the standard work on the subject and, given the quality of the work, it is likely to remain so for some time. Gardner, who has a fine command of the intricacies of the Roman law, rarely sets a foot awry in a complicated field strewn with minefields of misinterpretation and potential technical misunderstandings. In short, Gardner has provided everyone with the best that anyone could ask for: a good and dependable guide to the basics of the classical Roman law on the subject. She begins with the inferior status of women in the law (guardianship) before advancing to the specific subject of marriage, divorce, dowry, sexual offenses, children, and property (inheritance). She then deals with women of different status groups (slaves and freedwomen) and the law of women at work, before her closing and eminently sensible remarks on the so-called emancipation of women in Roman society. Highly recommended as an entrée to a most difficult subject. (S)

⊱< Cherry, *CR* 37 (1987): 263-265; Dixon, *Phoenix* 43 (1989): 84-88; Rawson, *EMC* 33 (1989): 89-93; Saller, *CP* 83 (1988): 263-264.

25.23 ☞ Gryson, Roger. *The Ministry of Women in the Early Church.* Translated by Jean Laporte and Mary Louise Hall. Collegeville, MN: Liturgical Press, 1976. Pp. xvii + 156. B-4.

A general survey of the role of women in the early church, this study covers the period from the first through the sixth century. Although Chapter 1 is devoted to women in the New Testament, the bulk of the material is taken from church fathers, legal sources from the fourth to the sixth centuries (plus the legislation of Justinian), and both Greek and Latin theological works from the post-Nicene era. While Gryson argues that women assumed an important role and enjoyed a place of choice in the Christian community, he holds that there is no evidence that they exercised leadership roles in the community. This work is a useful introductory survey. (P)

25.24 Harvey, Susan Ashbrook. "Women in Early Syrian Christianity." In *Images of Women in Antiquity.* Edited by Averil Cameron and Kuprt Amelie. Detroit: Wayne State UP, 1983. Pg. 288-298.

Harvey holds that the Syriac speaking world of early Christian times was particularly receptive and sensitive toward "feminine aspects of the divine." She conjectures that this was because of the role of the feminine in ancient near-Eastern religion. She argues that Wisdom (*Hokhma*) and Shekinah speculation in Judaism played a part, as did emphasis on the feminine role of the Holy Spirit.

Asceticism eventually colored the development of Christianity in the Syrian Orient, and the popularity of celibacy became general. Over time, Graeco-Roman attitudes, which were less sympathetic to women, came to dominate. (P)

25.25   Heine, Susanne. *Women and Early Christianity. Are the Feminist Scholars Right?* Translated by John Bowden. London: SCM, 1987. Pp. vi + 182. NI-3; BI-3.

Heine's study is an attempt to show that the claims of feminist scholars with respect to early Christianity are largely misguided and should be transcended. After examining data from the first centuries of Christian history, she argues that it is difficult to get a full overview of early Christian attitudes towards women. She holds that many of the theses of feminist scholars are too positive toward Jesus and too negative toward Paul. In addition, she is highly suspicious of certain feminist interpretations of Gnosticism, criticizing Elaine Pagels and others for instances of poor scholarship. Heine's work is not, however, a traditional defense of male authority; it is an attempt to reconcile men and women "to preserve their humanity and life together." This is an important book. (P)

❧ Alsford, *Themelios* 14 (1988): 23-26; Bloesch, *CT* 34 (Oct 8, 1990): 747-6; Clark, *Modern Theology* 4 (1988): 288-289; Gench, *Interpretation* 44 (1990): 101-102; Morley, *Theology* 91 (1988): 361-362; Pentz, *Reformed Journal* 38 (1988): 26-28; Rodd, *ExT* 99 (1987): 66-68; Witherington, *CRBR* 1 (1988): 205-207.

25.26   Hickey, Anne Ewing. *Women of the Roman Aristocracy as Christian Monastics.* Studies in Religion 1. Ann Arbor: UMI Research Press, 1987. Pp. vii + 151. B-4; I-3; T-1.

Hickey attempts to explain why so many women in the late fourth and fifth centuries in Roman society chose the ascetic life. She asks, "Is the female embrace of ascetic spirituality simply an internalization of patriarchal dichotomies which dissociate woman from the source of her authenticity?" Through a social science approach she attempts to demonstrate that the role of women, and particularly that of Roman matrons, was a socially ambiguous one which was exacerbated by the collision of pagan and Christian ideals in Roman senatorial households. This is an important book: Besides dealing with the primary question she raises, Hickey gives an excellent résumé of recent studies which deal with ascetic women in Roman society during the early stages of the Christian monastic movement. (P)

25.27   King, Karen L., ed. *Images of the Feminine in Gnosticism.* Studies
        in Antiquity and Christianity. Philadelphia: Fortress, 1988. Pp. xxi
        + 455. B-22; I-9.
        This volume contains 31 essays and responses on gender imagery
        in Gnosticism plus a plenary address by Elaine Pagels. The papers
        in question were originally delivered at a conference sponsored by
        the Society of Biblical Literature in November 1985, where a number
        of issues respecting Gnostic sources were raised. These included
        questions involving Gnostic attitudes towards women, the relation-
        ship of gendered images in myth and metaphor to the real lives of
        women and men, and how much can really be ascertained about
        Gnostic attitudes in view of the scarcity of reliable Gnostic data.
        This is a book for scholars. (P)
        ᖚ< Collins, *CBQ* 53 (1991): 524-525; Epp, *JBL* 110 (1991): 561-562;
        Hall, *JEH* 41 (1990): 515-516; Henrich, *Currents* 17 (1990): 305-306;
        Marshall-Green, *R&E* 87 (1990): 148-149; Tuckett, *ExT* 101 (1990): 216.

25.28   Klawiter, Frederick C. "The Role of Martyrdom and Persecution in
        Developing the Priestly Authority of Women in Early Christianity:
        a Case Study of Montanism," *Church History* 49 (1980) 251-61
        Based on the surviving source materials regarding the proliferation
        of the so-called Montanist movement in Asia Minor (mainly from
        Labriolle's classic studies), Klawiter argues that women "were
        permitted to rise to ministerial status through their role as confessor-
        martyrs," and the fact that God/Christ spoke directly through the
        female prophetesses Priscilla and Maximilla. He argues that the
        visions of Perpetua and Saturus in the early third century *Passion
        of Perpetua and Felicitas* clearly demonstrate the belief in such
        powers being achieved by "confessors," including women—and
        further, that the basic difference between orthodox Catholic views
        on the subject and those of the Montanists was that the former only
        accepted bestowal of authority by baptism of the Spirit for those on
        the way to actual martyrdom, whereas the latter accepted the suffering
        of imprisonment as sufficient credentials for the achievement of
        such spiritual authority. (S)

25.29   ◉ Kraemer, Ross S. "Women in the Religions of the Greco-Roman
        World." *Religious Studies Review* 9 (1983): 127-139.
        An excellent bibliographical article which summarized studies of
        women in the ancient Graeco-Roman world up to 1983. It notes
        that there has been a significant increase in such studies since the
        1960s. Roughly two folio pages are devoted to early Christianity,
        while lesser space is given to discussions of the study of women in

Judaism and other religions. Although in need of update, the article and the list of sources at the end of it are extremely useful. They may serve as the best place to begin the study of women in early Christianity. (P)

25.30   Kraemer, Ross Shepard, *Her Share of the Blessings: Women's Religions Among Pagans, Jews, and Christians in the Greco-Roman World*. Oxford/New York: Oxford UP, 1992. Pp. xi + 275. B-20; I-7.

As one of the first synoptic analyses of women's religion in the Graeco-Roman world, with a strong emphasis on Jewish and Christian women, Kraemer's is a valuable overview of the enormous spate of feminist research in this field over the last decade and a half. Her main theoretical framework is a straight-line application of Mary Douglas' "grid-group" theory. This complex theory, however, does not obscure the value of this survey, because Kraemer's method is to concentrate less on the theory and more on the actual practice of what women did. Hence she discusses participation in ritual (e.g., in Bacchic cult cells, and the religious rituals of Roman citizen women), but not to the exclusion of analysis of typical problems, for example, of the special role usually attributed to women in conversion, in ecstatic experiences such a prophesy, and in so-called heretical movements. In all of this, Kraemer does not just survey existing views, but rather offers skeptical criticisms of them. A useful list of "Ancient Sources and Translations" is appended. (S)

25.31   MacHaffie, Barbara J. *Her Story: Women in Christian Tradition*. Philadelphia: Fortress Press, 1986. Pp. xi + 183. I-3; BI-3.

Although this book deals with post-apostolic, early Christianity in only one chapter out of ten, it deserves to be included in this bibliography simply because of its prominence. It is, admittedly, a somewhat tongue-in-cheek attempt to redress the supposed super-abundance of works written about "his story" or the accounts of great men in the Christian tradition by detailing those of Christian women throughout the ages. Unfortunately, it makes too many bold assertions with little neutral data or concrete data of any kind for that matter. Because of its bias, it frequently ignores serious interpretive problems. (P)

25.32   MacMullen, Ramsay. "Women in Public in the Roman Empire." *Historia* 29 (1980): 208-218. Reprinted in MacMullen, *Changes in the Roman Empire: Essays in the Ordinary*. Princeton: Princeton

UP, 1990. Pp. 162-168.

This article, along with his parallel one on the economic and political presence of women ("Women's Power in the Principate," *Klio* [1986]), is a typical MacMullenish production in that it is a well written and thoroughly researched piece that combines original insights with a synopsis of current secondary research. MacMullen outlines the problem of the deportment of women in public, especially in terms of dress, where the practice of "veiling" or covering the head is of particular interest to New Testament scholars. His approach to the subject is marked by acuity of vision, a refusal to accept traditional opinions where they are not underwritten by the evidence, and by a clear-sighted attempt to define the terms of what is meant (e.g., by "veiling") so that the student will emerge from a reading with a firm knowledge of the parameters of the problem based on a sharp reading of primary sources. Highly recommended. (S)

25.33   McNamara, Jo Ann. "Wives and Widows in Early Christian Thought." *International Journal of Women's Studies* 2 (1979): 575-592.

Somewhat wider in scope than its title might indicate, the aim of McNamara's study is to "assess the effect of Christian principles on the changing positions of women in the family during the first three centuries after Christ." She argues that although Christian ideology and practice did owe something both to Judaic norms and the current realities in Roman society, it nevertheless had at its center a quite different core derived from the teachings of Jesus and Paul. Thus Christian ideology emphasized a concern with marriage as a means to control the body and to produce children in a way that was almost blind to all the other social implications of marriage and sexuality. In another way, however, Christian ideology did potentially permit greater freedom since it reduced the subordination of women to their husbands alone. Once freed of them by their spouse's death, they achieved much greater latitude of action as widows than was previously possible. (S)

25.34   McNamara, Jo Ann. *A New Song: Celibate Women in the First Three Christian Centuries.* New York: Institute for Research in History and Haworth Press, 1983. Pp 154. B-6; I-2.

In this avowedly feminist work, McNamara argues that the tradition of communitarian female celibacy began before St. Anthony's famous flight to the desert: he placed his orphaned sister in a house of consecrated women before that flight. MacNamara also holds that celibacy was a means of escaping both the procreative role of wife and mother and the common stigma of having a body looked upon as regularly "polluted" by menstruation. Starting with women in the New Testament, McNamara moves through what is an idealized account of early Christian womanhood to the martyrdom of Perpetua. (P)

✂ Lamirande, *AHR* 89 (1984): 1316-1317.

25.35   Miles, Margaret R. *Carnal Knowing: Female Nakedness and Religious Meaning in the Christian West.* Boston, Beacon Press. Reprint. New York: Vintage Books, 1991. Pp. xxv + 254. B-12; I-12; B&W-31.

The principal focus of this investigation, well encapsulated in its title, is to analyze the linkages between one type of body, the female, and its display, to the ideological images of women in mainstream western theology. In Part One of her text, Miles considers two contexts in Christian religious practice in which the nude body was evaluated—in the rite of baptism and in the corporeal "virility" ascribed to female ascetics and martyrs. In the latter half of her book, Miles then links these practices to the imagery and interpretation of female nakedness, in the primal Genesis texts regarding Adam and Eve, to the subsequent interpretation of this myth from Tertullian and Augustine to Luther. She appends to this studies of the female body as an iconographic figure mainly using medieval pictorial representations and on the exploitation of the female body in Christian rhetoric as a "grotesque." The problem of gender and religious meaning is then examined in the light of various alternatives for reclaiming the female body proposed by recent feminist theory. (S)

✂ Ellsberg, *Commonweal* 117 (1990): 666-668; Keshgegian, *ATR* 73 (1991): 345-347; McNamara, *Women's Review of Books* 8 (1990): 21-22; Nelson, *CC* 107 (1990): 711-712; Quitslund, *CC* 40 (1990-91): 560-562.

25.36   Mortley, Raoul. *Womanhood. The Feminine in Ancient Hellenism, Gnosticism, Christianity, and Islam.* Sidney: Delacroix, 1981. Pp. x + 119. I-1.

Mortley's rather small book covers a broad variety of topics with sophistication. These include Plutarch, Philo, and the cult of Isis; androgynous motifs, hermaphrodites, and the sex of the gods, earliest Christianity and Gnosticism, later Christianity, woman in Islam, and "the portrait of woman." Of particular importance are Mortley's discussions of androgynous concepts in paganism, Judaism, and Christianity, and his analysis of the Paul's thinking as expressed at Galatians 3:28. This volume serves as an excellent introductory study. (The latter chapters are not relevant.) (P)

25.37   Plumpe, Joseph C. *Mater Ecclesia: An Inquiry into the Concept of the Church as Mother in Early Christianity*. Catholic University of America Studies in Christian Antiquity 5. Washington, DC: Catholic University of America Press, 1943. Pp. xxi + 149. B-4; I-10; AAI-6; MAI-3; B&W-4.

The ideology of the Church not as the somewhat masculine "body of Christ" but rather as the "mother" (*mater*) of all believers, is one that came to have increasing prominence as the Church achieved a real prestige and power that came to dwarf even those of the state itself. In fact, there seems to be a rather close correlation between these two developments. In this old, but still valuable, study, Plumpe attempted to trace the roots of this conception—somewhat interestingly, in the light of studies of the last decade or so (e.g. Elaine Pagels)—to core Gnostic conceptions that became prominent in Alexandrian Christian circles. He then examines its earliest appearances in the west, in Irenaeus' account of the martyrs of Lyons, in Tertullian, and thence in Cyprian. The one weak point in Plumpe's otherwise strong study of the original source materials is his concern with origins and derivations of the conception, and hence the (unjustified?) disappointment that his study stops short of what was the most significant period of development and deployment of the ideology. Useful, even so. (S)

25.38   ☛ Pomeroy, Sarah B. *Goddesses, Whores, Wives, and Slaves: Women in Classical Antiquity*. New York: Schocken, 1975. Pp. xiii + 265. B-9; I-6.

A landmark study. It was the first modern synopsis and analysis on this scale in any language. As such it opened up the possibilities for research on women in antiquity that has flourished in the decades since its publication. Of particular interest here are the last chapters on "Women of the Roman Lower Classes" and "The Role of Women in the Religion of the Romans" because of their direct relevance to the rise of Christianity. Because it was such a novel production, it has, alas, become "dated" in almost every respect. A revised version is in preparation, and will, no doubt, become the same sort of "standard work" as the original. In the meantime, it is still useful as a quick entrée to the field, though it must now be supplemented by more specific research done since the time of its publication. (S)

☞< Badian, *NYRB* 22 (1975): 28-31; Fantham, *Phoenix* 30 (1976): 80-84; Lacey, *Prudentia* 8 (1976): 51-56; Lloyd-Jones, *TLSuppl* 74 (1975): 1074-1075.

25.39   Rader, R. *Breaking Boundaries. Male/Female Friendship in Early Christian Communities.* New York: Paulist, 1983.
Rader's thesis is that while the roles of women improved during late Roman times, particularly from that of Constantine, there had been a traditional attitude within the Graeco-Roman world which held that *friendship,* as such, between members of the opposite sexes was impossible. However, as time went by, such friendships did develop within the context of Christianity. Significantly, Rader attributes the increase of these friendships to the rise of celibacy and celibate communities within the church. Her work contains particularly useful chapters on "Normative Greco-Roman and Judaic Male/ Female Relationship," "Early Christian Themes: Unity and Reconciliation," "Martyrdom," "Syneisaktism: Spiritual Marriage," "Celibacy and the Monastic Life," and "Celibacy and the Friendship Ideal." (P)
⊱< Hunter, *RSR* 9 (1983): 381; Kraemer, *JES* 23 (1986): 127-128; Ramsey, *Worship* 58 (1984): 475-476.

25.40   Ruether, Rosemary Radford, ed. *Religion and Sexism: Images of Woman in the Jewish and Christian Traditions.* New York: Simon and Schuster, 1974. Pp. 357.
Several chapters in this staunchly feminist volume are relevant to early Christian studies. These include Phyllis Bird's "Images of Women in the Old Testament," Bernard Prusak's "Women: Seductive Siren and Source of Sin," Constance Parvey's "The Theology and Leadership of Women in the New Testament," "Misogynism and Virginal Feminism in the Fathers of the Church," and "Images of Women in the Talmud." As the foreface indicates (p.9), "the essays in this volume have been written to fill a growing need for a more exact idea of the role of religion, specifically the Judeo-Christian tradition, in shaping cultural images that have degraded and suppressed women."

25.41   Ruether, Rosemary Radford. *Mary—The Feminine Face of the Church.* Philadelphia: Westminster, 1977.
This rather simple volume was written as an attempt to give "a glimpse of the truly feminine face of the church." It begins with short overviews of goddess worship in pre-Israelite and contemporary non-Israelite societies, then moves to an equally short discussion of the feminine in Israelite religion. Following that, it deals briefly with the way in which Mary has been viewed in the context of the New Testament, historic Catholicism, historic Protestantism, and the contemporary world of Christianity. Although written by a noted

feminist scholar, it is more a study guide to emphasize feminist values within Christian churches than a scholarly work. Nonetheless, it serves a useful purpose in giving a reasonably accurate overview of how Mary has been understood throughout Christian history. With an 18-page appendix ("For the Leaders of Study Groups") by Donald M. Stein. (P)

✂ Maryland, *Theology* 83 (1980): 312-313; O'Connor, *Horizons* 5 (1978): 94-96; Thieme, *ATR* 63 (1981): 212-214.

25.42   Salisbury, Joyce E. *Church Fathers, Independent Virgins*. New York/London: Verso, 1991. Pp. vii + 168. B-9; I-11.

Although the principal focus of her monograph is the study of the lives of seven ascetic women of eastern Christianity contained in a tenth-century manuscript from the Escorial, Salisbury's book is in fact a more general survey of the problem of female virginity/ continence and its interpretation and containment by the early Fathers of the Church. Her main interpretive line is that virginity and a life of celibacy as voluntarily assumed by women could be instruments of self empowerment, specifically in terms of freedom from social expectations (Ch. 4), freedom of thought (Ch. 5), freedom of movement (Ch. 6) and freedom from the constraints of gender identification (Ch. 7). In the midst of investigating these specific claims, Salisbury provides a brief, clear and coherent introduction to the general subject of sexuality and virginity in the early church. Her chapter on "Augustine's Sexual Revolution" (Ch. 3) is outstanding. (S)

25.43   Salzman, Michele Renee. "Aristocratic Women: Conductors of Christianity in the Fourth Century." *Helios* 16 (1989): 207-220.

Harnack's classic position on gender and conversion held that Christianity was particularly attractive to women, and that, especially amongst the upper classes, women converted at significantly higher rates than men. Salzman questions this truism, which has developed into a virtual dogma, especially since Peter Brown's article [§4.4] on the "Christianization" of the Roman aristocracy, in which women were presented as the vanguard of this process. Salzman bases her study not on striking individual cases taken from the literary sources, but rather on a mass of data provided by prosopographical entries, principally from *The Prosopography of the Later Roman Empire*, from which she has extracted 319 cases of senatorial men and women from the period 282-423 CE whose religious affiliations are known. Statistical sorting of these data would seem to show that women did not, on the whole, convert to Christianity earlier than men, or involve themselves in mixed marriages that would have encouraged them to function as converters within the context of the family. (S)

25.44   Thurston, Bonnie Bowman. *The Widows: A Woman's Ministry in the Early Church.* Minneapolis: Fortress, 1989. Pp. 141.
A brief survey of the literature relevant to the question of the status of the "widows" in the early church. The first half deals with the New Testament; the second half is broken into the period of the Apostolic Fathers (called the Apostolic Period), Tertullian, the Third Century, and The Widow as Altar, with two brief excursuses: "Extra-church Sources on Women in Early Christianity" and "Ascetic Tendencies in Early Christianity." Thurston argues that an order of widows existed as part of the clergy in the first three centuries, but lost its position to the growing order of deaconess in a new context of a Christian empire. The core of the "widows" survived, however, in the monastic movement.
⊰ Barton, *ExT* 101 (1990): 313; Bradshaw, *SC* 7 (1989-90): 241; Crawford, *Interpretation* 44 (1990): 428-429; Davies, *CBQ* 53 (1991): 347-348; Heaney-Hunter, *TS* 51 (1990): 368-369; Hinson, *R&E* 87 (1990): 498-499; Mollenkott, *CC* 107 (1990): 313-314; Pervo, *ATR* 73 (1991): 332-333.

25.45   Tucker, Ruth A., and W.L. Liefeld. *Daughters of the Church. Women and Ministry from New Testament Times to the Present.* Grand Rapids: Zondervan, 1987. Pp. 552. I-8; B&W-68; BI-4; B-30.
This volume is a general history of women in church history, written neither from a traditionalist or a feminist perspective. Chapter 3 ("The Rise of the Church and the Downfall of Rome: Martyrs and Sex Objects") is the only section which deals specifically with the post-apostolic Christian church. Basically, it gives a series of short, thumbnail biographies of Christian women from the second through the fifth centuries. Although the information given lacks depth, it may be useful to students who know little about the period. (P)
⊰ Bridges, *R&E* 85 (1988): 724-726; Clendenin, *JETS* 31 (1988): 331-333; Snyder, *Daughters of Sarah* 15 (1989): 24-25; Watson, *Ashland TJ* 21 (1989): 64.

25.46   Warner, Marina *Alone of all Her Sex: The Myth and the Cult of the Virgin Mary.* New York: Alfred A. Knopf, Inc., 1976. Pp. xxviii + 400 & XX. Contains a list of "Illustrations," IX-XIII.
Although much of Marina Warner's account of Mariology deals with later church history, she discusses Mary in the Gospels, in the Apocrypha, and as seen by early Christianity. Warner deals specifically with the subjects of the virgin birth, Mary as the second Eve,

and Mary in the context of early Christian virgins and Martyrs. Not a chronological history as such, *Alone of All Her Sex* is useful in understanding a particular strand of Christian piety. It gives a detailed evaluation of that strand historically, mythologically, and artistically. It is embellished with illustrations. For those interested in the Marian tradition, it is extremely valuable. (P)

⊱< Falk, *RSR* 4 (1978): 81-85; Harris, *SJT* 39 (1986): 282-284; Nelson, *Religion* 7 (1977): 206-225; Pearce, *Churchman* 99 (1985): 271-272; Pfaff, *CH* 46 (1977): 234-236; Saliba, *TS* 38 (1977): 375-377; Tremmel, *Iliff Review* 34 (1977): 55-57.

25.47   Witherington, Ben., III. *Women in the Earliest Churches.* SNTSM 59. Cambridge: Cambridge UP, 1988. Pp. 300. B-14; T-2.
Although Witherington deals mainly with the New Testament period, he sets the basis for understanding the status of women in the next several centuries. He claims that women were treated better by first-century Christian males than by those in later centuries. While he asserts that early Christianity preserved patriarchy, it granted to women active roles and a status nearly equal to that of men within the church. Yet despite such liberal attitudes, the Christian community soon adopted a position which subordinated women, especially in marriage. Consequently, celibacy became a means of escaping the governance of a husband and the trials of childbearing. Virgin females were also exalted spiritually for having become "men" through virtue. (P)

⊱< Davies, *CBQ* 52 (1990): 368-369; Flora, *Ashland Theological Journal* 22 (1990): 99-101; Osiek, *JBL* 109 (1990): 359-360.

25.48   Yarbrough, Anne. "Christianization in the Fourth Century: The Example of Roman Women. *Church History* 45 (1976): 149-165.
A survey article principally devoted to an investigation of Peter Brown's claims about the nature of the Christianization of the élite households of the late Roman aristocracy. While agreeing with Brown's contentions about the critical rôle of the conversion of élite families, and the rôle of women in that process, Yarbrough disputes the precise effect of this on the process of Christianization, (of both the élite and of Roman fourth-century society in general). Specifically, Yarbrough claims that the extreme externally directed asceticism of these women (from a few élite families, principally documented in Jerome's letters) was not of the "inner-worldly" type (drawing on Weber's distinctions) that could produce genuine religious change on a large-scale and a congruence between belief and society. Rather, this inner-directed asceticism was self-

destructive and explains why Jerome's vision of a society of such Christian households was "doomed to failure." What these female ascetics did accomplish was the "negative" achievement of draining this strand of Christianity to the margins, thus permitting a "syncretic working out of pagan and Christian cultures." (S)

26
WORSHIP AND THE LITURGY

In the fall of 1992, as the bibliography was coming to a conclusion, I found "hot off the press" Paul Bradshaw's book *The Search for the Origins of Christian Worship* (London: SPCK, 1992). No book that I had examined during my work on the bibliography reflected so well what we had hoped our bibliography might itself do. In this book, Bradshaw, with clarity and precision, dealt with the liturgy in all its features, and he offered a thorough and insightful survey of the various positions towards the liturgy taken over this century—sometimes with an almost blow-by-blow account of the scholarly exchanges in the debate. Further, he sensed that there were key methodological problems in the way that scholars approached these topics, and he set down, in condensed but clear form, ten working principles to guide further discussion.

If there were books like Bradshaw's on the variety of topics that we have dealt with in this bibliography—books with possible titles like "The Search for the Origins of Christian Hierarchy," or "The Search for the Origins of Christian Creeds," or "The Search for the Origins of the Christian Canon"—we would not need our bibliography. Almost every work that we have listed in the section on "Worship and the Liturgy" is referred to in Bradshaw's book, and in most cases, extensively discussed. The discussion that follows here relies much on Bradshaw's work.

His book is particularly important because of the apparent need to reconsider, and to frequently qualify or completely discard, much of the older work on the liturgy that still shapes the discussion. Although the nature of scholarship in any field involves some revision or rejection of past opinion, more often than not scholars are building on solid foundations, and their own work carries a great debt to the scholarship of the past. In some fields, the older scholarship had reached such a level of insight and balance, the modern scholar is left to do little more than tidy up the edges, perhaps by reference to some new minor textual variant, or to some more significant discovery (such as the Nag Hammadi material) that may have impact tangentially on a topic, which otherwise remains unchanged in conclusions reached about it decades ago. The work on the Ignatian letters by J.B. Lightfoot [§3.46] is one example of that kind of seminal investigation, it seems to me.

Bradshaw, who is Professor of Liturgy at the University of Notre Dame, Indiana, does not think that any seminal work exists in the field of early Christian liturgy. The fault for this state of affairs is not that the liturgy has been neglected by scholars of the early church, or that no massive investigations have been done. Bradshaw is prepared to call Gregory Dix's *The Shape of the Liturgy* [§26.35] magisterial. The problem is that the attempts to establish the origins of Christian liturgy are built so fully on past judgments regarding early Jewish liturgy that any weakness in the scholarship on Jewish liturgy will also make scholarly conclusions about Christian liturgy suspect. And weakness is what Bradshaw (and now many Jewish scholars themselves) find in past scholarship on Jewish liturgy. Too many assumptions about the uniformity of early practice have been made: the rabbinic texts have been treated as a seamless whole, in spite of having over a 400-year period of editing, and of the revolution in Jewish thinking caused by the destruction of the temple. In regard to the latter, if there were substantial changes in Jewish liturgical practice stemming from the fall of Jerusalem (say, for example, if Rabbinic Judaism attempted in some way to incorporate temple practice into daily religious life), those kinds of changes would probably have had little impact on Christian liturgical practice, since Judaism and Christianity had already gone their own way by that point. That is not to deny the continuing influence of Judaism on Christianity, but much of what may seem like Jewish influence could be more directly the influence of Jewish Scriptures, which continued to inform Christianity after the break from Judaism.

What is perhaps most surprising about the present debate, as Bradshaw—quite unconsciously perhaps—has portrayed it, is that the History of Religions' contribution to our knowledge of the origins of Christian liturgy is apparently now judged by many to be so minimal that it need not even be mentioned. Bradshaw simply does not refer to that background at all. Thus the qualifications that Bradshaw calls for in regard to the Jewish contribution to the shape of the Christian liturgy is not intended to take us back to the days when, for example, Christian baptism and the Eucharist were seen to be rather wholesale borrowings from the pagan world about them. In Bradshaw's book, there is no listing in the index for Mithraism or the Mysteries. Even the celebration of Christmas on December 25, the very day of the popular pagan feast of the winter solstice and the day of the celebration (since 274 CE) of the birthday of the invincible sun, is judged not to have significant pagan roots! The day is fixed, rather, by Christian reflection on the *death* of Jesus and calculations from that date, a theory that goes back almost a hundred years to Louis Duchesne's 1903 work, *Christian Worship: Its Origin and Evolution* [§26.6] translated from his 1899 French *Origines du culte chrétien*.

The following section of the bibliography is divided into several subtopics and is arranged by alphabetical order within these divisions. In some ways, each topic deserves a chapter in itself, and some users of this bibliography will recognize immediately their need for more detailed references. Bradshaw's works are a good place to begin [§26.1; 26.4].

GENERAL

26.1 ⒷBradshaw, Paul F. *A Bibliography of Recent Liturgical Studies.* Runxcorn, England: Alcuin, 1989. Pp. 38.

This handy bibliography, arranged in sub-sections, lists the most influential English language books and articles on the subject of liturgy published from 1979 to 1989. For many of the entries, Bradshaw indicates the nature of the work, whether introductory, scholarly, a standard work, or an edition of texts, and whether the work contains an extensive bibliography. The entries are not otherwise annotated. Together with T.J. Tiller's bibliography of works from 1960 to 1974 (*A Modern Liturgical Bibliography*), this provides a fairly thorough overview of recent research in English, but one must be aware that this does not hint at the very important and extensive amount of work carried on in French, Italian, and German. The last page provides the addresses of 14 periodicals relevant to the study of liturgy. (F)

26.2 ⒷThompson, Bard. *A Bibliography of Christian Worship.* ATLA Bibliography Series 25. Metuchen, NJ/London: ATLA and Scarecrow Press, 1989. Pp. xlii + 789. AI-42; Church Bodies Index-4.

Although this bibliography is not annotated, it is comprehensive, and should therefore be consulted in serious work. Of primary interest are the sections on other bibliographies, dictionaries, and encyclopedias, and periodicals. Also, there is a 54-page section on the early church, and there are subsections on the early church in most of the other sections: see specifically the sections on sacramental theology, the Eucharist, baptism and confirmation, ordination, penance, death and burial, the Daily Office, readings for the year, church architecture, and music.

✄ Becker, *Hymn* 42 (April 1991): 44-46; Boonstra, *CTJ* 26 (1991): 234-235.

26.3 ⒷVismans, Thomas A., and Lucas Brinkhoff. *Critical Bibliography of Liturgical Literature.* Translated by Raymond W. Fitzpatrick and Clifford Howells. Nijmegen: Bestelcentrale der V.S.K.B. Publ., 1961. Pp. 79. AI-4.

Divided into six chapters, with brief but useful comments. The main focus is on the Roman Rite, though chapters cover general literature, history of the liturgy, liturgical books of the Roman rite, the liturgical year, the place of divine worship and vestments, and rites of the non-Roman liturgies. Many entries are of foreign language works, as is to be expected in a work not originally directed to an English audience. Somewhat dated, but still useful, especially for the non-English material.

26.4 ◉ Bradshaw, Paul F. *The Search for the Origins of Christian Worship: Sources and Methods for the Study of Early Liturgy.* London: SPCK, 1992. Pp. xii + 217. T-3; MAI-7; SI-5.

As described in detail in the introduction to this chapter, Bradshaw's work is the place to start an investigation in the field of worship and the liturgy. After explaining the recent revisions in the understanding of the development of the Jewish liturgy, upon which our understanding of the Christian liturgy has been built over the past decades, Bradshaw discusses worship in the New Testament, the problematic ancient church orders, other major liturgical sources, a full variety of liturgical topics (the Eucharist, baptism, Sabbath, Easter, etc.), and offers ten principles for interpreting early liturgical evidence. Bradshaw thinks that the early period was more multiform in practice, and he turns many accepted conclusions on their heads, or calls attention to recent scholarship that does.

⊰< Houlden, *Theology* 96 (1993): 76-77.

26.5 Davies, J.G., ed. *The New Westminster Dictionary of Liturgy and Worship.* Philadelphia: Westminster, 1986. Published in Great Britain by SCM under the title *A New Dictionary of Liturgy and Worship.* Based on *The Westminster Dictionary of Worship*, 1979. (1972^1). Pp. xvi + 544. B&W-57.

This is a standard one-volume reference work on the broad topic of liturgy, with entries written by scores of experts from a variety of traditions. Although it is designed to cover the whole history of Christianity, many of the articles relate to the early church. The bibliographies are brief, but up-to-date. On average, entries are 1 to 2 pages long, though some entries are much longer (22 pages on baptism, for example). Those who have access to *The Encyclopedia of Early Christianity* [§2.15] will find that volume more focused and just as complete for information on the early church's treatment of these issues.

⊰< Crehan, *JTS* 24 (1973): 625; Hinson, *R&E* 70 (1973): 258-259; Jones, *JTS* 40 (1989): 358-359; Keifer, *Worship* 47 (1973): 181-183; Porter, *ATR* 56 (1974): 248-249; Willis, *JEH* 24 (1973): 285-286.

26.6   Duchesne, L. *Christian Worship: Its Origin and Evolution. A Study of the Latin Liturgy up to the Time of Charlemagne.* 4th ed. Translated by M.L. McClure. London, SPCK, 1912. Pp. xx + 595. I-17.
Bradshaw says that this book was a standard for much of the twentieth century. It covers all the topics, with extensive material on the Eucharist, festivals, baptism, ordination, liturgical vestments, and numerous other related issues. Duchesne is criticized by Bradshaw for assuming a primitive uniformity of form, with local diversity and variety being later developments, and for taking evidence from one area and making it a basis for wider claims. Nevertheless, Duchesne's work is filled with original ideas and suggestive insights, such as his dating for the birth of Jesus.

26.7   Hoffman, Lawrence A. *Beyond the Text: A Holistic Approach to Liturgy.* Bloomington/Indianapolis: Indiana UP, 1987. Pp. vii + 213. I-7.
Unlike most of the books on liturgy listed in this section, the aim of this book is not to provide the earliest form of this or that liturgical text or to compare various rites. Rather, Hoffman argues for a new attitude toward the study of the liturgy, which is to have as its goal the description of what it is people are about in liturgical activity. He draws heavily from the social sciences, and his illustrations are clear enough to make the point even when the theory is not completely grasped. Although most of his illustrations come from Jewish sources, the approach he proposes is of equal relevance for the study of the Christian liturgy. The introduction offers a solid summary of his concerns. (F)

26.8   Jones, Cheslyn, Geoffrey Wainwright, Edward Yarnold, and Paul Bradshaw, eds. *The Study of Liturgy.* 2d ed. London: SPCK, 1992. (1978[1]). Pp. xxviii + 601. NI-5; SI-6; B&W-8.
This is an update of what has served as a standard text on the study of Christian liturgy since its original publication in 1978, drawing together the work of over two dozen authors from five different traditions. The focus of the book is on the historical development of liturgy, treated in Part II, where five main elements are examined: initiation, Eucharist, ordination, the divine office, the calendar, and various other items, under the rubric of "setting." Bibliographies accompany each chapter. (F)

26.9   Kavanagh, Aidan. "Liturgical and Credal Studies." In *A Century of Church History: The Legacy of Philip Schaff.* Edited by Henry W. Bowden. Carbondale and Edwardsville, IL: Southern Illinois UP,

1988. Pp. 216-244.

Although this article deals mainly with the critical discussion of liturgy and ritual since the Reformation and touches only briefly on liturgy in the early church, it is useful in providing some sense of the issues that dominate the present study of the liturgy, with which even historical studies of early Christian liturgy must engage to some extent.

26.10   Ratcliff, E.C. *Liturgical Studies.* Edited by A.H. Couratin and D.H. Tripp. London: SPCK, 1976. Pp. vi + 250. SI-4; PI-3.

This volume consists of a collection of 15 articles (11 of which are relevant). Section I, "The Early History of the Eucharist Liturgy," consists of chapters on the Sanctus and the Pattern of the Early Anaphora; the Eucharistic Institution Narrative of Justin Martyr's *First Apology*; the Anaphoras of Addai and Mari and the anaphora described in the Liturgical Homilies of Narsai, and two chapters on the Roman *Canon Missae.* Section II, "The Early History of the Baptismal Liturgy," consists of chapters on Justin Martyr and Confirmation; the Relation of Confirmation to Baptism; and the Old Syrian Baptismal Tradition. Section III, "The Liturgy of Ordination," contains two relevant articles: Questions concerning the Appointment of a Bishop, and the Rite of Inthronization of Bishops and Archbishops. With a 10-page bibliography of Radcliff's works and a note on Ratcliff as Liturgist.

26.11   ☛ Volz, Carl A. *Faith and Practice in the Early Church.* Minneapolis: Augsburg, 1983. Pp. 223.

This book could have been placed in a number of different chapters, for it covers a wide range of issues, with a heavy emphasis on theology, structures of authority, and social issues. About 20% of the volume does focus on the themes of this chapter, offering brief summaries on worship, baptism, the Eucharist, devotional practices, and music. Some attention is also given to church buildings, penance, a range of theological issues, scripture, creeds, councils, the bishop of Rome, wealth, marriage, and family. In all, a good introduction to the forces that help account for the particular developments that have occurred in Christian belief and practice.

✀ Klawiter, *W&W* 6 (1986): 240-243; Weinrich, *CTQ* 49 (1985): 223-224.

BAPTISM AND INITIATION

26.12   🏛 Whitaker, E.C. *Documents of the Baptismal Liturgy.* London: SPCK, 1970. Pp. xxii + 256.

This is a collection of ancient sources on the rite of baptism. It is arranged chronologically for the ante-Nicene evidence, and then largely geographically for the last ten sections. Each text has a brief note, usually indicating the critical edition of the text being cited. A 10-page introductory essay deals largely with the novel features of the Syrian rite, especially the absence of anointing with oil, and Whitaker considers what that might indicate about confirmation in the Syrian church, and about the larger question of the origin of that rite. With a two-page glossary.

26.13   Aland, Kurt. *Did the Early Christian Church Baptize Infants?* Translated and with an introduction by G.R. Beasley-Murray. London: SCM, 1963. Pp. 120. BI-1; AAI-2; MAI-1.

This book is largely a response to Jeremias' *Infant Baptism in the First Four Centuries* [§26.14], published three years earlier. Aland finds no evidence for the practice of infant baptism before the end of the second century. He thinks the celibacy demanded by the Marcionite church and by some of the Gnostics would have limited the number of children born to Christians. Further, most members of the early church were converted as adults, so the question of infant baptism is pushed to the side, and even many of the adult converts postponed their baptism. As well, the church generally viewed children as sinless; this would have provided no pressing reason for infant baptism. Only as more children were born to Christian parents and as the church distanced itself from extreme ascetic tendencies did the matter need to be addressed, and as emphasis was placed on "original sin," the church had to become more sympathetic to infant baptism.

>< Barnard, *CQR* 164 (1963): 512-514; R.M. Grant, *CH* 32 (1963): 473-474; R.P.C. Hanson, *JTS* 15 (1964): 149-151; Reumann, *JBL* 83 (1964): 212-214.

26.14   Jeremias, J. *Infant Baptism in the First Four Centuries.* Translated by David Cairns. Philadelphia: Westminster, 1960. Pp. 112. B-4; BI-2; AAI-2; MAI-3; SI-1; B&W-5.

Jeremias argues that the church regularly baptised infants from the beginning, and he appeals to several kinds of evidence. One, Jewish proselyte baptism included children; two, Christian baptism may have been seen as a parallel to Jewish circumcision, thus involving children; three, the story of Jesus blessing the children could have served as encouragement for infant baptism. Then Jeremias reviews the inscriptional and literary evidence to the end of the third century. But Jeremias admits a crisis in infant baptism in the fourth century, where parents postponed the baptism of their children. This would allow their children to be baptized after they had "sown their wild oats," which baptism would then blot out. Jeremias provides an 8-page list of the early evidence for infant baptism. This book should be read along with Aland's response above [§26.13], and Jeremias' reply, *The Origins of Infant Baptism* (London: SCM, 1963). ✂ M. Barth, *Interpretation* 16 (1962): 207-210; H. Chadwick, *ExT* 72 (1961): 231; Henkey, *CBQ* 23 (1961): 507-508; Hughes, *Churchman* 75 (1961): 124-125; Hunt, *SWJT* 4 (1961): 123-125; Meister, *TT* 19 (1962): 295-296; Perkin, *SJT* 14 (1961): 441-444; Richardson, *USQR* 17 (1962): 257-261.

26.15 ⊛ Kretschmar, Georg. "Recent Research on Christian Initiation." *Studia Liturgica* 12 (1977): 87-106.

This brief, but detailed, article addresses the question of whether or not there was a normative pattern for initiation in the Church Fathers, and if so, what it was. In a short space, the reader is introduced to the major theories, primary sources, and secondary literature involved in the investigation. It is all the more valuable since it summarizes a largely non-English body of literature. (F)

26.16 Lampe, G.W.H. *The Seal of the Spirit. A Study in the Doctrine and Confirmation in the New Testament and the Fathers.* London/New York/Toronto: Longmans, Green, 1951. Pp. xv + 340. I-8; BI-4; B-6.

The latter 70% of this volume deals with the patristic period. It is a response to Dix's contention that the early church had a *pre*-baptismal anointing, equivalent to Jewish circumcision. Lampe argues that the spirit was received through the water alone in baptism; all other features are later additions—in particular, the post-baptismal anointing, which was to become standard. ✂ Greenslade, *JEH* 3 (1952): 104-106; Fulton, *ExT* 63 (1952): 168-169; Oulton, *JTS* 3 (1952): 251-254; H.E.W. Turner, *CQR* 153 (1952): 232-237.

26.17 Lewis, Jack P. "Baptismal Practices of the Second and Third Century Church." *Restoration Quarterly* 26 (1983): 1-17.

Lewis admits "a major indebtedness" for the material in his study to Benoit's *Le Bapteme Chrétien au Second Siècle*. Baptism is shown to be important in the early period, and was associated in some ways with the forgiveness of sins, being required before one could receive the Eucharist. The procedure for baptism was not uniform, but some period of instruction was required. For the most part, immersion (usually three times) was expected, though there was some flexibility, depending on circumstances. Brief discussions on the formula of baptism and the validity of baptism by heretics are provided. Lewis then engages in the debate between Jeremias

[§26.14] and Aland [§26.13], concluding that "the case for infant baptism remains short of demonstration for the second century," though he sees some interesting cases that may suggest infant baptism.

26.18 Riley, Hugh M. *Christian Initiation. A Comparative Study of the Baptismal Liturgy in the Mystagogical Writings of Cyril of Jerusalem, John Chrysostom, Theodore of Mopsuestia and Ambrose of Milan.* CUA Studies in Christian Antiquity 17. Washington, DC: Catholic University of America, 1974. Pp. xxxiii + 481. I-16; AAI-5; MAI-2; BI-5; B-9; T-39.

A detailed study on the subject of Christian initiation, with attention to some of the primary players in the debates. Riley provides extensive charts showing the opinions or practice of Cyril, Chrysostom, Theodore, and Ambrose on almost every conceivable aspect of initiation, from renunciation and profession, to anointing and baptism, post-baptismal ceremonies, and "mystagogical interpretation." This makes it a good resource volume for the study of the topic.

✂ Austin, *ATR* 58 (1976): 502-503; *JEH* 26: 396-397; Guzie, *Parabola* 1 (1976): 111-112; Maloy, *JAAR* 45 (1977): 93-94; Winkler, *Worship* 52 (1978): 162-164.

EUCHARIST AND EUCHARISTIC PRAYER

26.19 🏛 Jasper, R.C.D., and G.J. Cuming. *Prayers of the Eucharist: Early and Reformed.* Texts Translated and Edited with Commentary. 3d ed. Collegeville, MN: Liturgical Press, 1992. Pp. ix + 314.

This handy sourcebook, written by two of the leading liturgiologists, brings together the most important prayer texts for the study of the Eucharist from the New Testament to modern prayer books. Along with many new English translations of ancient sources, the authors provide introductions and selected bibliographies for each of the texts. (F)

26.20 Bouley, Allan. *From Freedom to Formula: The Evolution of the Eucharistic Prayer from Oral Improvisation to Written Texts.* Studies in Christian Antiquity 21. Washington: Catholic University of America, 1981. Pp. xvii + 302.

The last three (of five) chapters are most relevant. These chapters, covering prayer in the first three centuries, provide an extensive and complete collection of important eucharistic texts, and a careful analysis of each. Hippolytus is the main witness. The Spanish and Gallican liturgy is also considered. Bouley makes a distinction between "oral" and "written" prayer, and this part of his work is criticized by Cuming in the *JTS* review mentioned below.

⊱⊰ Cuming, *JTS* 34 (1983): 281-283; Cutrone, *TS* 43 (1982): 546-547; Fink, *Worship* 56 (1982): 271-272; Wegman, *VC* 40 (1986): 192-193.

26.21 ⊙ Cuming, Geoffrey. "The Early Eucharistic Liturgies in Recent Scholarship." In *The Sacrifice of Praise*. Edited by Bryan Spinks. Roma: C.L.V., 1981. Pp. 65-69.

A very concise summary of the main avenues of research and the views current on the various patristic sources for eucharistic liturgies up to the late 1970s. (F)

26.22 ⊙ Dugmore, C.W. "The Study of the Origins of the Eucharist: Retrospect and Revaluation." *Studies in Church History* II. Papers read at the second winter and summer meetings of the Ecclesiastical Historical Society. Edited by G.J. Cuming. London: Nelson, 1985. Pp. 1-18.

This is a clear and concise review of the major theories and writers on the question of the origin of the Eucharist, and almost as important (though not indicated in the title), to the origins of the Christian celebration of Easter, and to a lesser extent, to the celebration of Sunday. Various authors are considered: Chwolson, Billerbeck, Jeremias, Oesterley, Dix, Cullmann, Rordorf, Jungmann, and others. Dugmore emphasizes the various meals that played a role in Jesus' ministry. Although he reaches no firm conclusion himself, Dugmore's analysis of the weaknesses of the various positions is clear and useful in providing a grasp of the debate.

26.23 ⊙ Jasper, Ronald. *The Search for an Apostolic Liturgy: A Brief Survey of the Work of British Scholars on the Origins of the Eucharistic Liturgy*. London: Alcuin, 1963. Pp. 30.

Jasper surveys the most significant contributions by British scholars in the nineteenth and twentieth centuries to uncover the origin of the eucharistic liturgy. He leads the reader past the earlier scholars who assumed an "original liturgy," showing what a true "quest for the Holy Grail" this was, through the work of Gregory Dix, by whose time the model was reversed: an early *diverse* practice was increasingly standardized in the fourth century. (F)

26.24 Jungmann, Josef A. *The Mass of the Roman Rite*. Translated by Francis A. Brunner. 2d ed. Notre Dame: University of Notre Dame Press. 1959. (1950^1). Pp. xiv + 567. I-13.

This classic study of the development of the Eucharist was written during the war and published originally in German in 1949. It was released in English in two volumes the following year. This second edition was revised and condensed somewhat to form one volume. The first part of the book is an historical survey of the Mass through the centuries, with eleven chapters focusing on the early church. Although parts three and four follow the order of the Mass, the roots of each portion of the Mass in the patristic period are examined. With the help of a fairly extensive index, the scholar wishing to study a particular area should find the entire study, and not just the historical survey, helpful. Jungmann discusses developments in music, vestments, and architecture as well. (Ph)

26.25   Jungmann, Josef A. *The Mass: An Historical, Theological, and Pastoral Survey.* Translated by Julian Ferandes. Edited by Mary Ellen Evans. Collegeville: Liturgical Press, 1976. Pp. xv + 312. I-11; SI-2; Latin Index-1; Greek and Hebrew Index-2.
This book, published after the death of its author, is an impressive survey of the history and theology of the Eucharist. Although not specifically a study of the early church, five of the eight chapters of the historical survey focus on the early church, and the patristic sources are discussed extensively in the section on the theology of the Eucharist. For a discussion of early liturgy, it is best to consult Dix [§26.35]. (Ph)

26.26   Jungmann, Josef A. *The Place of Christ in Liturgical Prayer.* Forword by Balthasar Fischer. London: Geoffrey Chapman / Collegeville, Liturgical Press, 1989. (1965[1]). Pp. xx + 300. I-21.
Originally written in German in 1925, with a second German edition in 1962, shortly after which an English translation became available. This study of the character and function of Christ as seen in prayers taken from the Eucharistic liturgies of the early church is an interesting complement to Jungmann's other work on the Eucharist. In the first part he examines the place of Christ in a variety of different liturgies, while in the second he sketches an historical survey of the idea of Christ in early Christian prayer. By concentrating on prayer "to" and prayer "through" Christ, he thinks that it is possible to see the impact on liturgical prayer of the church's struggle, particularly in the West, against Arianism. (Ph)

26.27   Kretschmar, Georg. "Early Christian Liturgy in the Light of Contemporary Historical Research." *Studia Liturgica* 16 (1986-1987): 31-53.
This is a difficult article, but packed with information summarizing the research into the history of the Eucharistic prayer in the era of

the church Fathers. Beginning with the earliest certain order of the Eucharist in which prayer texts occur (the early third-century *Apostolic Tradition* of Hippolytus), Kretschmar attempts to probe into the earlier period. He examines the sources behind the *Apostolic Tradition*, the possibility of recovering ancient forms from later liturgies, the Jewish roots of Christian liturgy, and the idea of the Eucharist as sacrifice. (F)

26.28 Lietzmann, Hans. *Mass and Lord's Supper. A Study in the History of the Liturgy.* Translated by Dorothea H.G. Reeve. Introduction by Robert Douglas Richardson. Leiden: E.J. Brill, 1979. Pp. xxvi + 753. I-5.

This volume has two advantages. It makes available in translation Lietzmann's *Messe und Herrenmahl* (Berlin, 1926), and it provides Richardson's own extensive dialog with Lietzmann's thesis. Lietzmann believed eucharistic practice had two roots: a continuation of the frequent meals Jesus had had with his disciples, and a cultic sacrificial meal related to the Passover. The latter was originated by Paul. Richardson grants to the Gospel of Mark a more original version of eucharistic understanding.

✂ Cuming, *JTS* 31 (1980): 606-608; Hardy, *JEH* 32 (1981): 377-378; Shepherd, *CH* 50 (1981): 465-466.

26.29 Rordorf, Willy, et al. *The Eucharist of the Early Christians.* Translated by M.J. O'Connell. New York: Pueblo, 1978. Pp. ix + 224. B-5.

A collection of ten articles on the topic of the Eucharist. Each author studies a particular document or person: *The Didache* (W. Rordorf); Clement of Rome (G. Blond); Ignatius (R. Johanny); Justin (M. Jourjon); Irenaeus (A. Hamman); Clement of Alexandria (A. Méhat); Tertullian (V. Saxer); Cyprian (R. Johanny); Origen (P. Jacquemont); and the *Didascalia* and *Constitutiones Apostolorum* (M. Metzger).

26.30 Spinks, Bryan. *The Sanctus in the Eucharistic Prayer.* Cambridge: Cambridge UP, 1991. Pp. xiii + 260. B-20; MAI-3; Index to Prayers and Rites-3.

This book is a scholarly examination of the origins of the sanctus (the prayer based on Isaiah 6:3). First, Spinks examines the earliest sources (the Hebrew Bible, Jewish worship, early Christian writings); then he considers the use of the Santus in various regional rites of the church (East Syrian and Syro-Byzantine on the one hand and Egyptian and western eucharistic prayers on the other). After

establishing his theory of the origin of the sanctus, he traces its development from the seventh century to the present. (F)
ℨ< Bradshaw, *JR* 73 (1993): 88-89.

26.31 ◉ Talley, T.J. "The Eucharistic Prayer of the Ancient Church According to Recent Research: Results and Reflections." *Studia Liturgica* 11 (1976): 138-158.
A useful and detailed survey of the debate regarding the development of Eucharistic prayer, with special attention to its relationship to the Jewish "Grace after Meals." (F)

LITURGY AND PRAYER
26.32 🏛 McKinnon, James W. ed. *Music in Early Christian Literature.* Cambridge Readings in the Literature of Music. Cambridge: Cambridge UP, 1987. Pp. xi + 180. B-6; Musical and Liturgical Terms Index-3.
This volume contains translations of 398 Greek, Latin, and Syriac passages dealing with hymns and music generally; some of the entries are hymns themselves. Each selection has brief introductory notes. The chapters are largely divided by geography and chronology and include material up to 450 CE. It is intended to be "inclusive" rather than "representative" in some (but not all) areas, and it can serve as a tool for the serious researcher. Also addressed are the topics of liturgical chant, musical imagery, and Christian attitudes towards pagan music.
ℨ< Richardson, *R&E* 86 (1989): 660-661; Ferguson, *RQ* 31 (1989): 120-121; Jeffery, *Worship* 63 (1989): 185-188.

26.33 Ⓑ Dorneich, Monica. *The Lord's Prayer: A Bibliography.* Freiburg im Breisgau: Herder, 1982. Pp. 240.
Although with German introductions and indexes, and with a heavy emphasis of German literature, this is still a useful guide to the literature in English of the Lord's Prayer. The bibliography is divided into two main parts: various entries in the first part, which deals with books and articles written since 1945, are relevant to this bibliography. Not annotated.

26.34 Bradshaw, Paul F. *Daily Prayer in the Early Church. A Study of the Origin and Early Development of the Divine Office.* London: Alcuin Club/SPCK, 1981 / New York: Oxford, 1982. Pp. x + 191. B-3; I-2; AAI-11.
Bradshaw fills the need for a modern, informed work on the topic. After discussing the first-century evidence, he examines daily prayer

in the second and third centuries, which was largely private prayer by individuals. In Chs. 4 and 5 he examines the East: Ch. 4: the change after the conversion of Constantine, when some elements of daily prayer became public (morning and evening prayer and the cathedral office); and Ch. 5: the monastic influence (concept of "continuous prayer" and the use of the Psalter). In Chs. 6 and 7, he explores the development of cathedral and monastic office in the West, and the influences from monasticism on the divine office. The adoption of specific times for prayer was intended, it seems, to emphasize continual communion with God.

✂ Bradshaw, replying to Winkler, *Worship* 56 (1982): 264-266; DeLeeuw, *JES* 19 (1982): 594-595; Harris, *St. Mark's Review* 110 (June 1982) 40-43; Jasper, *ExT* 93 (1982): 158; Loath, *Religion* 12 (1982): 184-185; Rusch, *CH* 52 (1983): 351; Winkler, *Worship* 56 (1982): 27-35; Winkler's reply to Bradshaw, *Worship* 56 (1982): 266-267.

26.35   Dix, Gregory. *The Shape of the Liturgy*. London: Arthur and Charles Black, 1945. Reprint. New York: Seabury, 1982. Pp. xxi + 777; I-11; T-1.

About two-thirds of this work is relevant for our period. According to Bradshaw, after Dix's work "it became axiomatic...to look for Jewish antecedents" for the Christian liturgy. Dix believed that the "shape" (i.e. things "done") of the liturgy had a primitive archetype or "shape," but there was variety in the actual words. The structure of synagogue worship played an important role in the shape of Christian liturgy, Dix argued. He further attempted to show how the liturgy changed. This is a massive work, filled with comment on the Eucharist, agape, Lord's Prayer, kiss of peace, the divine office, the Christian calendar, vestments, and a host of other topics related to the liturgy, including a useful 6-page "present state of the question"—from a 1943 perspective (pp. 209-214).

26.36   Fisher, Eugene J., ed. *The Jewish Roots of Christian Liturgy*. Mahwah, NJ: Paulist, 1990. Pp. 222. B-3.

A collection of essays published during the 1970s and 1980s in the *Service International de Documentation Judeo-Chretienne*, a Roman Catholic journal devoted to Jewish-Christian relations. The contributions are grouped under four headings, the latter not important to this bibliography. The sections contain the following articles (with shortened titles): (1) in Jewish Origins and Christian Liturgy: "Jewish Roots" (Cavaletti); "Beginnings of Christian Liturgy" (Burnes); "Rabbinic Concept of Shekinah and Matthew 18:20 (Sievers); in (2) Liturgy and Life Cycles: "Jewish Liturgy of Marriage" (Finkel);

"Jewish and Christian Marriage" (Nocent); "Jewish Concept of Death" (Laras); "Liturgy in Face of Death" (Di Sante); "He Slept with His Fathers" (Jung); in (3) Sabbath and Sunday: "Sabbath and Sunday" (Fisher); "Jewish Sabbath" (Kahn); "Christian Sunday" (Nocent); "Tensions Between Sabbath and Sunday" (Flusser); and "Sabbath: Call to Justice and Freedom" (Dupuy). The book is stronger on the theological and devotional aspects than on the historical, but provides a useful introduction to Jewish influences. (F)

ᢞ Hoffman, *CC* 41 (1991): 264-267; Williamson, *Mid-Stream* 30 (1991): 177-179.

26.37 Hahn, Ferdinand. *The Worship of the Early Church.* Philadelphia: Fortress, 1973.

Hahn argues that elements of Jewish practice in Christian ritual (such as fasting and Sabbath observance) were not originally part of the church's practice. Original Christianity represented a more profound break with Judaism. This book is generally praised by Bradshaw.

ᢞ Aune, *CBQ* 36 (1974): 109-110; Cox, *R&E* 71 (1974): 253-254; Furnish, *Perkins Journal* 27 (1974): 61-62.

26.38 Jungmann, J.A. *The Early Liturgy to the Time of Gregory the Great.* Translated by Francis A. Brunner. Notre Dame: University of Notre Dame Press, 1959. Pp. x + 314. I-6.

According to Bradshaw, this volume is "largely out of date," yet it was the "classic" work which Bradshaw sought to replace when he set out to write his own book. This work is divided chronologically into five sections and 23 chapters. Topics covered include the Eucharist, baptism Sunday and Easter, the Apostles' Creed, daily devotions, veneration of martyrs, geographically varied liturgies, and the Roman liturgy just before Gregory the Great, and there is a brief comment on sources in the introduction. Of particular interest are Chapters 11 and 12, in which Jungmann addressed the question of pagan influence on Christian practice. He denies its significance, but allows for some possible, but heavily qualified, influence in the fourth century.

ᢞ Cope, *CQR* 162 (1961): 126-127; Lamb, *SJT* 13 (1960): 333-334.

26.39 Rordorf, Willy. "The Lord's Prayer in the Light of its Liturgical Use in the Early Church." *Studia Liturgica* 14 (1980-1981): 1-19.

Although Rordorf here applies patristic evidence to the service of New Testament interpretation, insisting that clues as to the original meaning of the Lord's Prayer may come from a consideration of the liturgical use made of it in the early church, this article is an excellent treatment of liturgical practice in the patristic period. Rordorf concludes that the Lord's Prayer, the Kiss of Peace, and the Eucharist formed a liturgical unity. (F)

26.40   Taft, Robert. *The Liturgy of the Hours in East and West: The Origins of the Divine Office and its Meaning for Today.* Collegeville, Liturgical Press, 1986. Pp. xvii + 421. B-17; AAl-8; SI-17; Index to Liturgical Pieces-3.

The only major historical treatment in this century of the development of the Divine Office, this work is of particular importance in redressing the deficiency of the study of Eastern and Gallic offices. Part I forms the backbone of the study (more than half of the book), detailing the formation of the Daily Office from Jewish prayer practice to the cathedral and monastic offices of the fourth century. Parts II and III survey the developments in Eastern and Western Christianity respectively, and Part IV concludes with a theological summary. (F)

✗ Aune, *Currents* 15 (1988): 216-217; Bradshaw, *Orientalia christiana periodica* 52 (1986): 473-475; Bradshaw, *Worship* 60 (1986): 544-546; Guiver, *JTS* 38 (1987): 602-605; Henderson, *TS* 48 (1987): 398; Menard, *CH* 56 (1987): 383-384.

26.41   Vokes, F.E. "The Lord's Prayer in the First Three Centuries." In *Studia Patristica* X. Edited by F.L. Cross. Berlin: Akademie-Verlag, 1970. Pp. 253-260.

Vokes argues that, though the Lord's Prayer goes back to Jesus, it was not part of the formal prayers of early Christians. Basing his argument somewhat on what is thought to be known about Jewish prayers, he concludes that the frequency of prayer and the specific wording (as opposed to the general content) was not fixed. There is little evidence within the New Testament itself or in the second-century literature for the use of the Lord's Prayer, and its form does not seem to have influenced the early Christian prayers that have been preserved. But by the middle of the third century, a number of theologians (Tertullian, Cyprian, and Origen) are writing treatises on prayer, giving special attention to this prayer.

PENANCE

26.42   Fitzgerald, Allan. *Conversion Through Penance in the Italian Church of the Fourth and Fifth Centuries: New Approaches to the Experience of Conversion from Sin.* Studies in the Bible and Early Christianity 15. Lewiston/Queenston/Lampeter: Edwin Mellen, 1988. Pp. 565.

B-20; I-10.
The early church, especially in response to apostasy stemming from the persecutions, struggled with the issue of the reconcilation of sinners back into the church. Baptism had played a primary role in dealing with sin; the question became whether there was another mechanism for dealing with post-baptismal sin. Fitzgerald deals with this question in the context of the church in Italy in the two centuries immediately after the conversion of Constantine. He shows how an emphasis on God's mercy was used against the various rigorous positions. The story of "Peter and the Rooster" was repeatedly used to illustrate God's mercy to the sinner.
⨝ Walker, *PRS* 18 (1991): 103-106; Eno, *CHR* 76 (1989): 102-103.

26.43   Poschmann, Bernhard. *Penance and the Anointing of the Sick.* Translated by Francis Courtney. New York: Herder and Herder, 1964. Pp. xi + 257.
Originally published in German in 1951, Poschmann work is, according to Karl Rahner, despite its flaws "the best comprehensive presentation of the whole of the history of penance." Approximately 130 pages are devoted to penance and the anointing of the sick in the early church. Several chapters, including one on the early church, are summaries of much fuller treatments published in three volumes on the history of penance. Although an important work and an asset to anyone working in this area, the usefulness of the book is hampered by the lack of an index. Each section is preceded by a bibliography, which is, of course, dated and heavily weighted with foreign language publications. (Ph)

26.44   Rahner, Karl. *Penance in the Early Church.* Volume 15 of *Theological Investigations.* Translated by Lionel Swain. New York: Crossroad. 1982. Pp. xii + 451. B-13; I-5.
This is a collection of eight articles, seven of which are revised versions of articles written by Rahner from 1936 to 1955. The articles were written independent of one another and beyond the introductory chapter, which offers a short survey of the history of penance and the scholarship dealing with it, there is no effort to sketch in a comprehensive way the development of penance in the first centuries. Instead, each article focuses on the theology of a particular person such as Tertullian or Origen. (Ph)

26.45   Watkins, Oscar D. *A History of Penance: being a Study of the Authorities.* Vol. 1. *The Whole Church to A.D. 450.* Burt Franklin Research and Source Works 16. New York: Burt Franklin, 1961.

Originally published in 1920. Pp. xxix + 496. Extensive table of
contents.
Although old, this work offers a detailed review of the evidence of
church discipline up to 450 CE. Sections are clearly divided, focused
on a particular individual, document, or geographical area. Then,
in the last thirty pages of the 500-page Volume One, there is an
extensive summary by topic of the materials. Here Walkins deals
with variations in practice, the procedure of penance, the ministry
of penance, and expressions of absolution.

PILGRIMAGE
26.46 🏛 Wilkinson, J.D. *Egeria's Travels in the Holy Land.* Rev. ed.
Warminster: Aris and Philips, 1981. (1971[1]). Pp. xv + 320. B-4;
BI-3; B&W-23; CT-1; I-4; M-10; NI-4; Places and Monuments
Index-6.
This is an account of a pilgrim who travelled in the East in the late
300s, leaving a detailed narrative not only of the trip but of church
life and practice. About 120 pages of Wilkinson's work consist of
a new translation of *Egeria's Travels,* and various extracts from
other ancient authors on the subject. There are, in addition, 20
pages of notes on these texts, and an extensive introduction of 88
pages, in which are discussed critical questions of text, date, and
author, along with an account of the increasing importance of the
"Holy Land" for Christians, and the development of the idea of
holy places and pilgrimages. Also, the Jerusalem church is described
in detail, with an emphasis on its buildings and liturgy. With 11
brief appendices.

26.47 Hunt, E.D. *Holy Land Pilgrimage in the Later Roman Empire A.D.
312-460.* Oxford: Clarendon Press, 1982. Pp. x + 264; I-8; B-13;
M-1.
Hunt discusses the transformation of local centers of devotion in
and around Jerusalem into centres of pilgrimage. Although travel
by Christians to Jerusalem occurred before the conversion of Constantine, it is with that conversion and with the dedication of Helena,
the emperor's mother, that Jerusalem became a significant center,
filled with identifiable holy sites specifically related to Jesus. Hunt
compares the differences between eastern and western views, noting
that most pilgrims came from the west. Also discussed are Egeria
and Eudocia, the monastic influence in Palestine, and the attempt
by Julian to de-Christianize the city. Primary attention is given to
the period of Theodosius I and his sons.
⊱Cameron, *AHR* 89 (1984): 106; Frend, *JTS* 34 (1983): 302-304; Meyer,

JEH 35 (1984): 165; Rexine, *GOTR* 29 (1984): 419-420

SAINTS

26.48   Attwater, Donald. *The Penguin Dictionary of Saints.* 2d ed. Revised and updated by Catherine Rachel John. London: Penguin, 1983 (1965[1]). Pp. 352. B-2; G-8.

This volume is intended to be a "quick reference to the lives and legends" of notable saints. Entries are usually brief, but longer than those found in the more comprehensive listing of saints in the volume listed immediately below. Bibliographical references are extremely rare; (Farmer's dictionary [§26.51] should be consulted for bibliographic information). Both this volume and Farmer's will give suitable introductory information about the important early saints. In a brief introduction, Attwater discusses terminology, martyrs, confessors, canonization, the history of research on the subject, and the limits of the information available (e.g. we know almost nothing about many of the saints). Includes a 12-page list of feasts and a 2-page list of emblems.

26.49   *The Book of Saints: A Dictionary of Servants of God canonized by the Catholic Church.* Compiled by the Benedictine monks of St. Augustine's Abbey, Ramsgate. 6th ed. London: A & C Black, 1989. (1921[1]). Pp. xvi + 606. B&W-134; B-3.

This is a major revision of the earlier editions, primarily because the revision of the calendar by the Vatican in 1969 removed many of the popular saints of the Middle Ages, and shifted the emphasis somewhat away from its previous European and Italian focus. This work is far more comprehensive than the other dictionaries listed in this section, but the notes are often very brief: on average five or six lines, and frequently fewer. Basic information is given: religious order; status (martyr, confessor, virgin); feast day; and year of death. With a 2-page list of patron saints and an 8-page index of emblems. (Sm)

26.50   Brown, Peter. *The Cult of the Saints. Its Rise and Function in Latin Christianity.* Chicago: University of Chicago Press, 1981. Pp. xv + 187; I-9.

Originally delivered as the Haskell Lectures of 1978, Brown discusses the shift in religious perspective that separates the classical world from the medieval. Brown looks at the Latin west. Particularly with regard to death do we see this shift. Whereas death was once terrifying, in Christian circles relics and graves of holy persons became positive *loci* for divine benefit. Brown sees fundamental differences between the Christian cult and similar ideas in paganism. Under the control of the bishops, the cult of the saints expanded even into the countryside, and in part is responsible for the Christianization of these areas. Brown admits that his focus is on the view of the "highly articulate," rather than on other existing, but less accessible, views (such as that of the sick, the poor, or pilgrims), whose lives were affected by the saints in profound, and perhaps quite different, ways.

< Darling, *CH* 52 (1983): 203-204; Henry, *TT* 39 (1982): 365-366; Hinson, *R&E* 78 (1981): 601-602; Kopecek, *SC* 2 (1982): 55-57; McCulloh, *Speculum* 58 (1983): 152-154; Norris, *ATR* 64 (1982): 403-405; Santer, *Theology* 84 (1981): 465-466; Scholz, *AHR* 86 (1981): 1080-1081; Walker, *RS* 20 (1984): 324-325.

26.51   Farmer, David Hugh. *The Oxford Dictionary of Saints.* 2d ed. Oxford: Clarendon, 1978. Pp. xxiv + 440. G-7; Feast Calendar-5.

The focus is clearly English, and there is a comprehensive listing of English saints, and saints with notable cult in England. As well, the major saints of Ireland, Scotland, and Wales are listed, along with those saints that are important to the church in general. Byzantine saints, though, are usually omitted. Thus this volume is of limited use to the student of the early church, though there are half-page articles on people such as Ignatius and Polycarp and a page on Perpetua and Felicitas. Also of interest is a 13-page discussion of the veneration of saints, again from an English perspective. It does have the fullest entries of the dictionaries listed here, and serviceable bibliographies for each entry, unlike the other dictionaries.

< Bent, *Ecumenical Review* 40 (1988): 113-114.

SABBATH, SUNDAY, AND EASTER

26.52   🏛 Strand, K.A. *The Early Christian Sabbath. Selected Essays and a Source Collection.* Worthington, OH: Ann Arbor Publishers, 1979. Pp. 80.

In two parts, the first contains 4 articles by Strand (3 originally published): Sabbath Fast; Sabbath in Coptic Sources; Tertullian and the Sabbath; and Sabbath, Sunday, and Easter. The second part contains English translations of patristic thought on the Sabbath fast and on the Quartodeciman controversy.

26.53   Bacchiocchi, Samuele. *Anti-Judaism and the Origin of Sunday.* Rome: Pontifical Gregorian UP 1975. Pp. 141.

Bacchiocchi, a Seventh-Day Adventist, argues that the church did not change from Sabbath to Sunday worship until after its first one hundred years. He points to the Messianic significance of the Sabbath and to references to the Sabbath in the New Testament writings (not all of which are negative: e.g. "Sabbath rest" in Hebrews). Christians dropped the Sabbath in order to disassociate themselves clearly from the Jews, who had come to experience hostility in the empire as a result of their various unsuccessful revolts. Sunday worship was not intended initially as a commemoration of the day of the resurrection; that was part of a larger theological construct.

26.54 Bacchiocchi, Samuele. *From Sabbath to Sunday: A Historical Investigation of the Rise of Sunday Observance in Early Christianity.* Rome: Pontifical Gregorian U.P., 1977. Pp. 372.
In this revised version of his doctoral dissertation at the Pontifical Gregorian University, Bacchiocchi tries to explain the change from Sabbath to Sunday that occurred in early Christian worship. His central thesis is that the Sabbath continued to play its traditional role even in the Gentile Christian communities until the Roman church, under pagan influence, adopted Sunday as a way to escape from anti-Jewish hostility. Also see his work titled *An Examination of the Biblical and Patristic Texts of the First Four Centuries to Ascertain the Time and Causes of the Origin of Sunday as the Lord's Day* (1975), and the work listed immediately below. An important critique of this work is provided by Strand [§26.52].
✃ Bandstra, *CTJ* 14 (1979): 213-221; Beckwith, *Churchman* 94 (1980): 81-82; Borchert, *R&E* 78 (1981): 111-112; Ciferni, *Worship* 53 (1979); 160-162; Hughes, *JETS* 22 (1980): 256-257; Jasper, *JEH* 30 (1979): 475-476; Louth, *JTS* 31 (1980): 206; McKenna, *BTB* 9 (1979): 94-96; Stott, *EQ* 51 (1979): 184-185; Strand, *AUSS* 17 (1979): 85-104.

26.55 Bauckham, R.J. "Sabbath and Sunday in the Post-Apostolic Church." In *From Sabbath to Lord's Day: A Biblical, Historical and Theological Investigation.* Edited by D.A. Carson. Grand Rapids: Zondervan, 1982. Pp. 251-298.
Bauckham reviews the evidence for Sabbath observance among Christians after the first century. Although Sunday had become the Christian day of worship, many Christians, even *Gentile* Christians, apparently kept the Sabbath. This was part of a general, and long lasting, grass-roots judaizing trend, which was opposed by the leaders. If leaders refer to the Sabbath positively, it is in a meta-phorical sense. Bauckham engages in a debate with Bacchiocchi [§26.53; 26.54] over the origin of the Sunday tradition in Christianity. He then deals with later writers, into the fourth century, and concludes with a discussion of the Sunday rest, and the various regulations

about this, with an imperial law as early as 321 CE.

26.56   Beckwith, Roger T., and Wilfred Stott. *This is the Day. The Biblical Doctrine of the Christian Sunday in its Jewish and Early Church Setting*. London: Marshall, Morgan & Scott, 1978. Pp. x + 181. I-3; AAI-2; BI-4; PI-2; B-4.

Stott's section (the larger part of the book) deals with the church fathers. More in line with the traditional understanding of Sunday observance (which views the Christian Sunday as standing in basic continuity with the Jewish Sabbath, and thus replacing it), Stott's position is challenged now in a number of recent works. Stott defends his position by attempting to show a difference in attitude in regard to the Sabbath for Hellenistic and "Semitic Judaism." He contends that the criticism of the Sabbath by Paul and the Fathers is not specifically criticism of the Sabbath but of abuses of the Sabbath. This work is explicitly put forward as an attempt to encourage the practice of a Sabbath-like Sunday for the modern church.

&< Hughes, *JETS* 22 (1980): 254-256; Jasper, *JEH* 30 (1979): 475-476; Levack, *SJT* 32 (1979): 280-281.

26.57   Dugmore, C.W. "Lord's Day and Easter." In *Neotestamentica et Patristica*. Supplements to *NovT* VI. Leiden: E.J. Brill, 1962. Pp. 272-281.

Dugmore challenges scholars such as McArthur and Cullmann, who have argued that Sunday was the key day of Christian worship and Eucharist from the very beginning. He contends that the first clear evidence of Sunday worship comes in the mid-second century (Justin). He tries to account for the earlier use of the phrase "the Lord's Day," suggesting that it refers specifically to Easter rather than to Sunday, and his whole argument stands or falls on his success here. Also discussed is the role of Easter, and attention is drawn to the opinions of Jeremias and Dix. Although Sunday was in use by Christians by the mid-second century in some areas, Dugmore argues that the Sabbath "did not disappear as a day of Christian worship until the late fourth or early fifth century."

26.58   Hall, S.G. "The Origins of Easter." *Studia Patristia* 15.1 (1984): 554-567.

This is a dense and tightly argued piece, dealing with the Quartodeciman controversy. Hall reviews the two sides in the debate: Holl, Richard, and Huber, who contend that the Romans did not celebrate Easter until the time of Victor; and Duchesne, Mohrmann, and Cantalamessa, who argue that the Romans did celebrate Easter, but were simply non-Quartodecimans. Hall's responses are thought-provoking. He contends that the Quartodeciman option was more dominant, even in Rome, and he argues that much of the "Easter Controversy" could have taken place as *internal conflicts within* a diverse Quartodeciman camp. His analysis of the problems of the Quartodeciman position are detailed and suggestive. Finally he comments on the anti-Marcionite and anti-Gnostic character of *annual* Easter celebration.

26.59   Rordorf, Willy. *Sunday. The History of the Day of Rest and Worship in the Earliest Centuries of the Christian Church.* Translated by A.A.K. Graham. London: SCM, 1968. Pp. xvi + 336; AI-6; AAI-4; BI-2; NTI-5; SI-1; PI-8; B-4.

This is considered the classic investigation of the topic. Rordorf examines the Jewish background to Constantine, when the first Sunday legislation was brought in. Rordorf considers such related matters as the "seven-day week" (the planetary week of the Romans) and the various names for Sunday, in addition to the primary question of the origins of the Christian observance of Sunday. Rordorf does not find the roots of Sunday observance in the Jewish Sabbath, and he argues that the idea of the day of rest for Christians was late, as was the appeal to the Sabbath in connection to the role of Sunday for Christians. Sunday observance stemmed from the meals that the resurrected Jesus had with his disciples, and became immediately the widespread Gentile pattern, though a renewed interest in the Sabbath took place in the fourth and fifth centuries. This work is fully informed regarding the scholarship on the subject; the notes and references are extensive.

⊰⊱ See Strand entry below [§26.60]; Dunkly, *JAAR* 38 (1970): 109-110; Green, *Churchman* 83 (1969): 48-49; W. Robinson, *CT* 13 (1969): 26-27; Wickham, *JTS* 20 (1969): 297-299.

26.60   ◉ Strand, Kenneth A. "From Sabbath to Sunday in the Early Christian Church: A Review of Some Recent Literature. Part I: Willy Rordorf's Reconstruction." *Andrews University Seminary Studies* 16 (1978): 333-342; and "Part II: Samuele Bacchiocchi's Reconstruction." 17 (1979): 85-104.

Strand provides a solid review of the two major works on the Sabbath, finding both weak at crucial points and both useful at other points. In particular, Bacchiocchi's work on the New Testament material, on the early use of the pagan seven-day week, and on early Mithraism in Rome are commended, though the significant role for Rome in the spread of Sunday worship is shown to be weak. Rordorf's work on the later period is found to be useful, especially regarding Sunday as a day of *rest* in the Constantinian period, and regarding the various names for that day.

MODERN AUTHOR INDEX

GENERAL INDEX

Boldface section numbers indicate locations in the bibliography dedicated specifically to the index entry. It is best to start there.

A

Abgar §21.32; 21.34
Abortion §14.3; 14.8
Absolution §26.45
Abstinence (see "Celibacy")
Acmonia §21.8
Acts of Martyrs (Acta Martyrum) §3.28; 3.46; 10.9; 20.2; 20.3; 20.4; 25.2
Acts of Paul §18.17
Acts of Thomas §4.26; 23.21
Adam §14.6; 14.16; 14.17; 19.31; 25.35
Addai §21.34; 26.10
Adoption §23.26
Adultery §23.29; 23.30
Adults §23.33
Adversus Judaeos §16.8; 16.9; 16.14; 16.18; 16.25; 16.29; 16.31; 16.33; 16.37
Aegean §18.19; 22.6
Aelius Aristides §12.20; 12.38
Africa (also see "North Africa") §5.19; 11.5; 12.1; 23.1; 23.18
Afterlife (also see "Death") §16.17; 22.42
Agape §26.35
Age of Anxiety §12.25
Aging §23.16
Agriculture §22.16; 22.23; 22.25; 22.27; 23.42
Akiba §19.37
Albinus §24.4
Alchemy §22.30
Alexander of Alexandria §8.2

Alexander of Abonu-teichus §12.7; 12.20
Alexandria §4.3; 5.19; 9.38; 16.34; 17.19; 21.1; 21.8; 21.13; 21.16
Alexandrian Christianity §4.1; 17.8; 21.10; 24.5; 24.33; 25.37
Alexandrian School §3.22; 7.10; 7.14; 19.6; 19.13; 19.14; 19.33; 19.38
Allegorical Exegesis §3.57; 16.18; 19.6; 19.7; 19.13; 19.15; 19.18; 19.20; 19.25; 19.26; 19.28; 19.30; 19.31; 19.33; 19.35; 19.41
Alpha And Omega §6.10; 6.14
Altar of Victory §12.22
Amalasuntha §4.3
Ambrose §3.3; 3.20; 3.44; 5.15; 10.2; 10.18; 13.12; 14.2; 14.4; 14.9; 14.11; 19.31; 19.32; 23.25; 23.40; 23.42; 23.45; 24.1; 26.18
Ambrosiaster §14.10
Ammianus Marcellinus §22.13
Amphilochius of Iconium §7.2; 7.10
Amusements §5.22
Anahid §25.1
Anaphora §26.10
Anast §17.9
Anastasia §25.1
Anastasius §17.9
Anastos §3.39
Anatolia (also see "Asia

T

Tacitus §4.2; 12.6; 12.7; 20.6

Talmud §16.13; 25.40

Targum §16.5

Tatian §4.12; 12.8

Taxes §22.24; 23.12; 23.42

Teachings of Silvanus §15.8

Technology §2.17

Temples §5.1; 6.20; 12.39; 23.12

Terracotta Artifacts §6.11

Tertullian §3.3; 3.7; 3.19; 3.22;
    3.59–3.61; 4.2; 4.9; 4.18;
    4.27; 7.2; 8.1; 9.2; 9.13;
    9.23; 9.33; 10.2; 10.4; 10.15;
    10.18; 12.8; 14.2; 14.4; 14.6;
    14.7; 14.10; 14.20; 16.9;
    19.2; 19.4; 19.6; 19.19;
    19.22; 19.39; 20.20; 21.5;
    22.37; 23.21; 23.45; 24.1;
    24.2; 24.12; 24.18; 24.24;
    24.27; 24.29; 24.30; 24.32;
    25.17; 25.35; 25.44; 26.29;
    26.41; 26.52

Text-types §4.28; 7.29; 7.30

Textiles §6.4

Textual Criticism §1.33; 7.18;
    7.28–7.36

Textus Receptus §7.35

Thaïs §17.6

Theatre (also see
    "Entertainment") §22.29

Theban Legion §20.15

Thekla §14.5; 25.1; 25.6;

Theodora §11.34; 17.11

Theodore of Mopsuestia §3.20;
    7.1; 8.1; 8.18; 19.1; 19.14;
    26.18

Theodoret of Cyrrus §3.20; 5.8;
    14.2; 19.29

Theodoric §11.20

Theodosian Code §11.17; 16.29

Theodosius I **§11.17-11.18**;

26.47

Theodosius II §11.17

Theognostus §8.4

Theological Diversity (see
    "Regional Christianity" and
    "Heresy"

Theology §1.31; 3.40; 21.42;
    chapter 24

Theophilus §4.12; 4.13; 8.7;
    12.12

Thesaurus Linguae Graecae
    (TLG) §2.15

Thomas Tradition (also see
    "Gospel of Thomas") §15.4;
    15.21; 18.19; 21.34

Toledo §11.31

Tome of Leo §13.4

Torture (also see "Punishment")
    §20.32

Tosefta §16.5

Touraine §12.1; 23.1

Towns (see "Cities")

Tractate Marsanes §15.7

Trade (also see "Economy" §2.4;
    2.6; 22.7; 22.9; 22.24; 23.42

Tradition §4.12; 18.25; 18.32;
    21.1; 24.2; 24.20; 24.23

Trajan §10.2; 12.7; 20.14

Trajectory §18.27

Tranquilizers §23.18

Transportation §22.18; 22.23

Tree of Life §6.8

Trimorphic Protennoia §15.14;
    15.21

Trinitarian Issues (also see
    "Christological Issues")
    §3.22; 3.55; 3.56; 3.61; 4.14;
    4.18; 4.24; 8.2; 8.3; 8.16;
    8.20; 8.21; 13.12; 13.13;
    13.16; 24.2; 24.11; 24.21;
    24.28; 24.34

"Triumph of Barbarism and
    Religion" §11.21

ABOUT THE AUTHOR
AND CONTRIBUTORS

Thomas A. Robinson PhD (McMaster), Associate Professor of Religious Studies at the University of Lethbridge, is author of *Greek Verb Endings: A Reverse Index; The Bauer Thesis Examined: The Geography of Heresy in the Early Christian Church;* and *Mastering Greek Vocabulary*; co-author (with Steve Mason) of *An Early Christian Reader;* and is the co-editor of two collections of essays.

Brent D. Shaw PhD (Cambridge), Professor of History at the University of Lethbridge, has taught at the University of Birmingham, England and was the Magie Professor of Greek and Roman History at Princeton University (1989-1990). He is a contributor to the revised *Cambridge Ancient History* and to *Civilization of the Ancient Mediterranean,* and has published in such journals as *Classical Philology, Past & Present, Latomus, Journal of Roman Studies,* and *Journal of Jewish Studies.* He also co-edited the selected papers of Sir Moses Finley, *Economy and Society in Ancient Greece.*

M. James Penton PhD (Iowa), Professor Emeritus of the University of Lethbridge, has taught in the field of early church history in the Department of History. He has also taught at the University of Puerto Rico, Northern Michigan University, the University of Iowa, the University of Wisconsin-Whitewater, and the University of Calgary.

Terence L. Donaldson ThD (Wycliffe College / University of Toronto), Professor of New Testament and Biblical Languages at the College of Emmanuel & St. Chad and an Associate Member of the Department of Religious Studies at the University of Saskatchewan. He is author of *Jesus on the Mountain: A Study in Matthean Theology,* and has published in such journals as *Catholic Biblical Quarterly, Journal of Biblical Literature, Journal for the Study of Judaism,* and *Journal for the Study of the New Testament.*

Michael P. DeRoche PhD (McMaster) teaches in the Religious Studies Department of the University of Calgary, and has taught at the University of Lethbridge and McMaster University. He has published in *Vetus Testamentum, Journal of Biblical Literature, Catholic Biblical Quarterly,* and *Journal for the Study of the Old Testament.*